What Do We Deserve?

What Do We Deserve?

A READER ON JUSTICE AND DESERT

Louis P. Pojman
Owen McLeod
Editors

New York • Oxford
OXFORD UNIVERSITY PRESS
1999

Oxford University Press

Oxford New York
Athens Auckland Bangkok Bogotá Buenos Aires Calcutta
Cape Town Chennai Dar es Salaam Delhi Florence Hong Kong Istanbul
Karachi Kuala Lumpur Madrid Melbourne Mexico City Mumbai
Nairobi Paris São Paulo Singapore Taipei Tokyo Toronto Warsaw

and associated companies in
Berlin Ibadan

Published by Oxford University Press, Inc.
198 Madison Avenue, New York, New York 10016
http://www.oup-usa.org

Library of Congress Cataloging-in-Publication Data

Pojman, Louis P.
    What do we deserve? : a reader on justice and desert / Louis P.
Pojman, Owen McLeod.
        p.   cm.
    Includes bibliographical references and index.
    ISBN 0-19-512217-8 (cloth).—ISBN 0-19-512218-6
(pbk.)
    1. Merit (Ethics) I. McLeod, Owen. II. Title.
BJ1500.M47P65 1998   97-46362
170—DC21   CIP

9 8 7 6 5 4 3 2 1
Printed in the United States of America
on acid-free paper

Dedicated to our parents

Mary Adelia and Mac McLeod
Louis A. and Helen Pojman

CONTENTS

PREFACE   ix

I. Historical Interpretations of Desert / 1
Introduction: Louis P. Pojman

1. Plato: Justice as Harmony in the Soul and State / 10
2. Aristotle: Justice as Equality According to Merit / 15
3. Thomas Hobbes: Merit as Market Value / 20
4. Adam Smith: Of Merit and Demerit / 23
5. Immanuel Kant: Moral Worth as Alone Deserving Happiness / 31
6. John Stuart Mill: Justice, Desert and Utility / 42
7. Henry Sidgwick: Justice as Desert / 47
8. W. D. Ross: What Things Are Good? / 56

II. Contemporary Interpretations of Desert / 61
Introduction: Owen McLeod

A. The Concept of Desert / 70
9. Joel Feinberg: Justice and Personal Desert / 70
10. John Kleinig: The Concept of Desert / 84
11. David Miller: Deserts / 93
12. Julian Lamont: The Concept of Desert in Distributive Justice / 101

B. Desert and Responsibility / 114
13. Galen Strawson: The Impossibility of Moral Responsibility / 114
14. Harry Frankfurt: Freedom of the Will and the Concept of a Person / 125
15. David Miller: Desert and Determinism / 135
16. Fred Feldman: Desert: Reconsideration of Some Received Wisdom / 140

C. The Rawlsian Debate / 149
17. Herbert Spiegelberg: An Argument for Equality from Compensatory Desert / 149
18. John Rawls: A Theory of Justice / 157
19. Robert Nozick: Anarchy, State, and Utopia / 165
20. Michael Sandel: Liberalism and the Limits of Justice / 177
21. Owen McLeod: Desert and Institutions / 186
22. Samuel Scheffler: Responsibility, Reactive Attitudes, and Liberalism in Philosophy and Politics / 196

D. The Role and Significance of Desert / 210

23. Michael A. Slote: Desert, Consent and Justice / 210
24. Norman Daniels: Merit and Meritocracy / 224
25. Robert Goodin: Negating Positive Desert Claims / 234
26. Robert Young: Egalitarianism and the Modest Significance of Desert / 245
27. Fred Feldman: Adjusting Utility for Justice: A Consequentialist
    Reply to the Objection from Justice / 259
28. Owen McLeod: Desert and Wages / 271
29. Louis P. Pojman: Does Equality Trump Desert? / 283
30. Shelly Kagan: Equality and Desert / 298

BIBLIOGRAPHY   315

PREFACE

Every little action deserves a reaction.
  Bob Marley, "Satisfy My Soul"

In 1965 Brian Barry predicted that desert would disappear from the moral scene. For a while, it looked as if his prediction would come true. In 1971 John Rawls argued that the concept of desert has no place within the theory of justice. Earlier that same year, John Kleinig had already acknowledged that "the notion of desert seems . . . to have been consigned to the philosophical scrap heap."

It appears that philosophers have been rummaging around in the scrap heap lately. In the past two decades, there has been a steady revival of philosophical interest in desert. It is not surprising that this should happen. The concept of desert has a venerable tradition in the history of philosophical ethics. More important, perhaps, is the fact that desert is pervasive in commonsense morality. And, as the epigraph suggests, commonsense morality's position is that desert itself is pervasive.

It is astonishing, then, that up till now no anthology has been dedicated to the concept of desert. This volume remedies that conspicuous lack. It contains thirty selections from the classical and contemporary literature on desert. It is divided into two main parts: Part I, Historical Interpretations, and Part II, Contemporary Interpretations. Part II is divided into four sections: A. The Concept of Desert, B. Desert and Responsibility, C. The Rawlsian Debate, and D. The Role and Significance of Desert. Abstracts precede each reading, and a bibliography appears at the end of the work. We have tried to produce a balanced book, offering the best representative articles of both prodesert and antidesert positions that we could find.

Our own interests in desert developed independently. Owen McLeod wrote a doctoral dissertation on desert at the University of Massachusetts, Amherst, in 1995 and taught a seminar on the subject at Yale that same year. Meanwhile, Louis Pojman was thinking and writing about desert at the University of Mississippi and, more recently, at the United States Military Academy. Each was entertaining the possibility of an anthology on desert. A third philosopher, Shelly Kagan, brought the two of us together. This book is the result. Our sincere hope is that it will foster an even wider debate over the nature and significance of the concept of desert in moral and political philosophy, as well as in ordinary life.

We have received encouragement and helpful advice from many people. We are especially grateful to Fred Feldman, Shelly Kagan, Wallace Matson, Larry Temkin, and several anonymous reviewers for Oxford University Press. Special thanks are due also to our editor, Robert Miller, to his assistant, Liam Dalzell, and to Karen Shapiro of Oxford University Press, for their enthusiastic support and exemplary professionalism.

Owen McLeod, Yale University
Louis Pojman, United States Military Academy
April 1, 1998

What Do We Deserve?

PART I
HISTORICAL INTERPRETATIONS OF DESERT

DESERT: AN HISTORICAL INTRODUCTION

The Homeric king does not gain his position on the grounds of strength and fighting ability. He belongs to a royal house, and inherits wealth, derived from the favored treatment given to his ancestors, which provides full armor, a chariot, and leisure. Thus equipped, he and his fellow *agathoi* [nobles], who are similarly endowed, form the most efficient force for attack and defence which Homeric society possesses. Should they be successful, their followers have every reason to commend them as *agathoi* and their way of life as *arete* [virtuous]; should they fail, their followers have every reason to regard this failure, voluntary or not, as *aischron* [shameful]. A failure . . . in the Homeric world must result either in slavery or annihilation. Success is so imperative that only results have any value; intentions are unimportant.

(A. W. H. Adkins, *Merit and Responsibility: A Study of Greek Values*, 1960, p. 35)

An impartial spectator can never feel approval in contemplating the uninterrupted prosperity of a being graced by no touch of a pure and good will, and consequently a good will seems to constitute the indispensable condition of our very worthiness to be happy.

(Immanuel Kant, *Groundwork of the Metaphysics of Morals*, 1781; trans. H. J. Paton)

It seems to be one of the fixed points of our considered judgments that no one deserves his place in the distribution of native endowments, any more than one deserves one's initial starting place in society. The assertion that a man deserves the superior character that enables him to make the effort to cultivate his abilities is equally problematic; for his character depends in large part upon fortunate family and social circumstances for which he can claim no credit.

Even the willingness to make an *effort*, to try, and so to be deserving in the ordinary sense is itself dependent in practice upon happy family and social circumstances.

(John Rawls, *A Theory of Justice*, 1971)

The Classical and Contemporary Attitudes on Desert

In these three quotations we see three different attitudes toward desert and merit, representing three different periods of social and political philosophy. In the first quotation, characterizing ancient Greek Homeric society (900–800 B.C.) and reflected in Homer's *Iliad*, we encounter an attitude that judges value in terms of success, particularly military success, or failure. One is *agathos*, that is, good or noble, because of one's class together with the results of one's action. "To be *agathos* one must be brave, skillful, and successful in war and in peace; and one must possess the wealth and (in peace) the leisure which are at once the necessary conditions for the development of these skills and the natural reward of their successful employment."[1] Whether or not one had good or bad intentions, whether or not one was responsible for the success or failure is irrelevant. We want to know only whether your track record (or, in some cases, your family's track record) indicates prospects for success or failure. We may call this a *strict meritocracy*. One of its corollaries is the idea of strict liability. Regardless of your intentions, if you did a heinous deed, you are guilty. This is reflected in Sophocles' *Oedipus The King*, in which the City of Thebes is cursed with plague and drought for the deeds of a wise and righteous King Oedipus. Oedipus has brought pollution to the city by unwittingly committing parricide in self-defense and marrying Jocasta, who turns out to be his mother. Reward and punishment are tied to the objective features and consequences of the deed, not to the inner workings of the heart. Although by the time of Sophocles the Homeric values inherent in the play had ceased to be dominant, a sense of the potency of these features is present. Though the Athenians recognized personal responsibility and intentions, they were still haunted by the thought of strict liability, of fate as a valid basis for praise and blame. Note in this regard the Athenian judgment of the eight generals at the Battle of Arginusae (403 B.C.), who, though they won the war and did everything reasonably to be expected to protect the lives of their men, still incurred unacceptable losses (four thousand men and twenty-five ships). They were condemned to death for what was most likely beyond their control.

It wasn't always your actual deed that counted, but who you were. The *agathoi* were seen to be intrinsically more meritorious than everyone else, good by pedigree. An instance in which this custom is in conflict with actual outcomes is narrated in the twenty-third book of the *Illiad*. The Achaians held a horse race in which Achilles was to award two prizes. First prize went to the actual winner. Antilochus, son of Nestor, came in second, but Achilles decided to give second prize to Eumelius because he was of a nobler rank, even though he had come in last. Antiloches complained, saying, in effect, "If it is preordained that some other criterion than merit is to count for the award, why should we have a race at all?" Achilles was moved by this logic and gave the prize to Antilochus, offering Eumelius a treasure of his own. Merit there is—two kinds—one related to class and the other to achievement. But one looks in vain for anything like moral desert.

In the second quotation, from Immanuel Kant's (1724–1804) *Groundwork*, we see that intention has replaced outcome as the decisive criterion of worth. For Kant, moral goodness is the paramount value, and the conscientious will the essence of moral goodness. Conscientiousness is "a jewel that shines in its own light." Success and failure, those values lauded in a strict meritocracy, are now said to be of no moral importance, for one can not be held responsible for what one has no control over. This view represents a thick concept of moral desert, which in turn assumes a thick concept of personal responsibility for one's actions, which in turn presupposes a deep notion of free will. Accordingly, if we do not have free will, we are not morally responsible for our actions and, hence, would not deserve rewards and punishment. We may call this a *desert-based system*, where natural or preinstitutional desert defines our moral worth. It presupposes a common human nature and a natural moral law that transcends cultural diversity, by which all people should be assessed. It is our intentions that count, how well we live within the light we have, our natural light. We can find versions of this theory in Socrates, who held that virtue is knowledge, so that virtue and happiness are correlative. "No evil can come to the good man" (*Apology* 40C), and no one would do evil voluntarily, for wisdom teaches us that it is the good that is good for us. Not only did the virtuous *deserve* to be happy; a lawlike universe ensured that they *got* what they deserved. The Stoics carried on this legacy, but perhaps it first becomes prominent within a whole culture in the Hebrew Bible (Old Testament), where motive, the good will, becomes tantamount to goodness itself: "Man looks on the outward appearance, but God looks on the heart" (I Sam. 16:7), and in the New Testament: "If readiness to give is present, it is acceptable according to what a man has, not according to what he has not" (II Cor. 8:12).

Happiness is the reward of moral goodness, unhappiness the reward of moral badness. Again, in the Hebrew Bible we read that the righteous person "is like a tree planted by streams of water that yields its fruit in its season, and its leaf does not wither. In all that he does, he prospers." The wicked are doomed, "like chaff which the wind drives away" (Psalms 1). Similarly, we read in Obadiah 1:15, "As you have done, it shall be done to you, your deeds shall return on your own head." This may be called the reciprocal Golden Rule: As you do, you shall be done by. In the New Testament we read that "he who sows sparingly will also reap sparingly, and he who sows bountifully will also reap bountifully" (II Cor. 9:6). In the Gospel of Matthew Jesus tells the Parable of the Talents, in which a Master, about to depart on a journey, gives five talents to one servant, two to another, and one to a third and instructs them to improve on these endowments. The servant with five talents proceeds to use his talents to make five more talents, the servant with two talents uses his talents to make two more, but the single-talent servant hides his talent, fearing that he might lose it. Upon the master's return, the servants are called to give an account of their stewardship and are rewarded and punished in proportion to what they have done with the talents. The master praised and rewarded the two servants who doubled their talents for their fidelity. He punished the man who hid his talent in the ground, accusing him of wasting a precious gift (Matt. 25:14–30). The parable is instructive in providing a paradigm of desert. We are stewards of our talents and will be judged by an Infallible Impartial Judge on the basis of what we do with them. Those who use their talents wisely and industriously deserve to be rewarded, while those who neglect their talents deserve reprobation.

The Parable doesn't elaborate on exactly which criterion (merit or desert) is the proper basis for reward. Results don't tell the whole story. One could imagine the five-talent servant investing his money but having bad luck and the one-talent servant finding a talent along the road and so doubling his output. But this is only a parable and should not be expected to yield a definitive distribution scheme. Nevertheless, the overall thrust of the Old and the New Testaments inclines toward identifying *effort* as the decisive criterion of merit, what I have called the paradigm notion of desert. "If readiness is there, it is acceptable"—a sentiment similar to Kant's later thesis that the good will is the only intrinsically good thing, "a jewel that shines in its own light." Moral effort is a necessary condition for judgment, and may properly be so since we are responsible for our deeds. We have free will.

And because we are responsible beings and because a Cosmic Justice reigns, we may rest assured that judgment is certain. Justice will be done. Paul writes, "[God] will render to every man according to his works: to those who by patience in well-doing seek for glory and honor and immortality, he will give eternal life; but for those who are factious and do not obey the truth, but obey wickedness, there will be wrath and fury" (Rom 2:6–8) and, again, "Whatsoever a man sows, that shall he also reap" (Gal. 6:7).

The same idea is present in the Hindu and Buddhist doctrine of *karma*. Cosmic justice ineluctably rules the world, so we will inevitably get what we deserve, being reincarnated in a form appropriate to our deeds in this life. The doctrine of heaven and hell in Christianity set forth this idea in an even more vivid fashion: The vicious deserve their eternal punishment and the virtuous (or at least the faithful) eternal bliss. According to Dante's *Inferno*, there are several different levels of hell, so that one's punishment for sin is to spend eternity with people exactly like one's self.

Leibniz put the matter thus:

> Thus it is that the pains of the damned continue, even when they no longer serve to turn them away from evil, and that likewise the rewards of the blessed continue, even when they no longer serve for strengthening them in good. One may say nevertheless that the damned ever bring upon themselves new pains through new sins, and that the blessed ever bring upon themselves new joys by new progress in goodness: for both are founded on the ***principle of the fitness of things***, which has seen to it that affairs were so ordered that the evil action must bring upon itself chastisement.[2]

The scales of cosmic justice will be balanced.

And even as God ruled the world through the adherence to an objective moral order, giving each what he or she deserved, so the State's duty was to attempt to do the same on earth. Justice was, in the words of ancient Greek poet Simonides (see reading 1), rendering each person his or her due (*suum cuique tribuere*). As the ancient Roman jurist Ulpian interprets the idea:

> Justice is a constant and perpetual will to give every man his due. The principles of law are these: to live virtuously, not to harm others, to give his due to everyone. Jurisprudence is the knowledge of divine and human things, the science of the just and the unjust. Law is the art of goodness and justice. By virtue of this [lawyers] may be called priests, for we cherish justice and profess knowledge or goodness and equity, separating right from wrong and legal from illegal. [3]

The classic idea of *justice as desert* underlies our concept of punishment as retribution, "an eye for an eye, a tooth for a tooth, a life for a life." The sociologist Emil Durkheim once noted, "There is no society where the rule does not exist that the punishment must be proportioned to the offense."[4] It also holds place in at least a core sense of property acquisition. We observe this fittingness in the Lockean notion of property rights. In fact, Desert and Natural Rights, as opposed to institutional rights, are closely related to each other. Desert is typically based on what we have done (or what has been done to us), whereas basic or natural rights signify claims we make. I have a natural right to life (or, more accurately, a right not to be killed), but we would not say that I deserve not to be killed (though we might say I didn't deserve to be killed when someone murders me or the State executes me by mistake). A Lockean notion of property rights seems to be closer to a desert claim than to a standard entitlement. I have a natural right to my own body (which I own but do not deserve—nor do I not deserve it—the concept simply isn't relevant here), but I extend my property right to natural objects by mixing my labor with them. By tilling the soil, planting crops, cutting down a tree, and making a chair, I come to own the land, the fallen tree, the chair. I have added value to the external object, so I own it. This process resembles a desert claim more than a typical natural right claim.

Karl Marx seems to hold a theory of desert based on labor derived from Locke's theory via Adam Smith. His Labor Theory of Value holds that the carpenter who creates the chair, investing ten hours of labor in the process, creates ten units of value and so deserves all ten units of remuneration. If the carpenter works for an entrepreneur, the entrepreneur can deduct for the tools, investment, and minimal profit but must not steal what is the carpenter's lot. The carpenter deserves the value of his product minus the overhead. Marx, of course, believed that the means of production ought to be made into common property, but, at least in his *Critique of the Gotha Program*, he attacks Lasallian socialists' uncritical notion of ownership, in which "the instruments of labor are common property and the proceeds of labor belong undiminished with equal right to all members of society." Marx notes the socialist ideal of distributing goods equally but rhetorically asks, "To those who do not work as well? What remains then of the 'undiminished proceeds of labor'? Only to those members of society who work? What remains then of the 'equal right'? Of all members of society?"[5] Rejecting equal distribution of goods, Marx argues that the first phase of the communist society will adhere to the labor theory of value. The worker will receive in accordance with his production, "with an equal performance of labor, and hence an equal share in the social consumption fund, one will in fact receive more than another, one will be richer than another, and so on." Only in the "higher phase of communist society, after the enslaving subordination of the individual to the division, and therewith also the antithesis between mental and physical labor, has vanished," in the more abundant society, will society "inscribe on its banners: from each according to his ability, to each according to his need." Until that time, the formula for justice must be from each according to his ability, to each according to his contribution.

So Locke and Marx both hold to a theory of natural property rights that is desert based.

In our third quotation at the head of this essay, from Rawls, a contemporary skepticism about free will and responsibility has replaced both meritocracy and desert-based systems. A liberal system of values, influenced by the social sciences, which tend to explain our actions in terms of heredity and, especially, environment, holds that we don't deserve our talents or even our conscientiousness. Our talents and abilities are the products of the Natural Lottery (heredity, family, and environment). We don't deserve our talents, including the talent to be moral or make an effort to learn and work. So, the argument proceeds, we don't deserve what our talents produce. "Even the willingness to make an *effort*, to try, and so to be deserving in the ordinary sense, is itself dependent in practice upon happy family and social circumstances." Moral and intellectual excellence and superior ability to perform important tasks are, from a moral point of view, arbitrary and must not be used as bases for differential distribution of primary goods, especially economic goods, social status, and the bases of self-respect. These goods become ours, not because we deserve them, but because we have a right to them. They are our entitlements. The notions of merit, which characterizes Greek culture, and natural or *preinstitutional* desert, which characterizes desert-based systems like Kant's, evaporate. Justice now is defined in terms of what reasonable people would agree to in a hypothetical contractual position, such as Rawls's veil of ignorance. Justice, as the tendency toward equal distribution of primary goods, replaces the classical notion of justice (from the Greek Simonides to Kant) as giving each person what he or she deserves. Desert is transformed into *institutional* arrangements, entitlements, and sanctions, which create expectations of rewards and punishments. The net result is that the idea of *justice as desert*, a thesis held for centuries as constitutive of sound moral and political theory, is in our day rejected out of hand by the dominant political philosophy. Desert, once enjoying the endorsement of philosophers and kings, in word, if not in deed, now suffers as a pariah in an age cynical about individual responsibility.

As Sam Scheffler has argued (see reading 22), most contemporary political philosophy, especially liberal political philosophy, the dominant contemporary form, has renounced or greatly undermined the notion of desert.[6] I think it has also under emphasized the notion of merit. Besides Rawlsian liberals, Utilitarians, like J. J. C. Smart, tend to emphasize maximizing utility, not desert or the responsibility on which desert depends. Recall Smart's famous retort, "The notion of the responsibility [for an outcome] is a piece of metaphysical nonsense."[7] Libertarians like Nozick, who trust in market forces and invisible hands to bring about utility, ignore these concepts. Communitarians and Socialists largely reject desert and merit as reflecting an overly individualistic view of social reality. To quote Brian Barry, these concepts flourish in a society "where people are regarded as rational independent atoms held together in a society by a 'social contract' from which all must benefit. Each person's worth (desert) can be precisely ascertained."[8]

Time and space prohibit an extensive discussion of the causes of the present skepticism over desert and merit, but it is in part due to the attenuation of religious explanations of the world. Most contemporary political philosophers doubt that cosmic justice rules the universe or that an ultimate judgment will produce a Kantian outcome where the people are happy in proportion to their deserts. This skepticism regarding the validity of desert is partly attributable to the explanatory power of the social sciences, which offer social and psychological causes for our behavior that tend to diminish responsibility. Related to this factor is the appeal of philosophical determinism, which undermines the idea of responsibility, and hence of desert, altogether (see the readings in Part II, B). Another factor is the sheer impracticality of distributing goods according to desert. As Sidgwick notes in reading 7 and as Rawls, Young, and others note in Part II, which focuses on contemporary views, even if we admit desert as an ideal, it is exceedingly difficult, and in some cases impossible, to measure how much people deserve various goods. All of these claims can and will be challenged in our readings, but I must leave the discussion there, merely observing that we have come full circle from the Homeric Greeks, who also did without a notion of desert. Their culture was one that lacked a concept of desert; they were predesert, while our political culture tends to be postdesert.

Here we might pause to note the difference between the two related notions *desert* and *merit*, which I have been discussing, and which are often used as synonyms. "Merit" is a broader notion, corresponding to the Greek work *axia* and referring to any quality or value that is the basis for differential behavior, such as praise, rewards, and income (and the negative *demerit* refers to the basis for negative attributions). Grades are an example of a merit-based distribution scheme. We grade students on objective qualities, not on the student's needs, pedigrees, or even deserts. Merit refers to external factors, such as results. "Desert," on the other hand, at least in central historical uses, is connected with the internal, the voluntary, with what we intend, with the strength of our effort. The Good Samaritan deserved gratitude from the assaulted Jew whom he helped, not simply because he succeeded in helping him but because he intended to help him. His goodness would have deserved reward even if he hadn't succeeded. More will be said in the articles about various desert-bases (e.g., there is *compensatory desert*, which doesn't fit this pattern), but I suggest this as at least one significant difference. I discuss this further in my article at the end of this anthology.

Let me turn to our readings.

We begin with two selections from Plato's *Republic* (Books I and IV). In the first, Polemarchus quotes the Greek poet Simonides to the effect that justice is "rendering to each his due." Socrates drives Polemarchus into a corner, but the significance of the dialogue is that (1) this is the first place we find the formula that will be used as a definition of justice for millennia and (2) it becomes an abbreviated version of Plato's own theory. Exactly what the phrase means is another question. What is one's due? The metaphor suggests property—giving back what another already owns, what I have borrowed, found, or promised, what one has a title to or is entitled to. Jesus' statement, "Render unto Caesar the things that are Caesar's and to God the things that are God's" (Luke 20:25) reflects this interpretation. But what about *unowned* goods? Others have interpreted the formula more widely as having to do with what is appropriate or fitting, so that, for instance, we respect the laws of the country we are visiting, even though we don't believe in those laws ourselves. The Kantian interpretation narrows the notion of "rendering to each his due" to what one morally deserves. By itself, "render to each his or her due" seems a formal definition, which lacks content. It is substantive theories of justice that fill in the missing content—whether it be essential worth based on some feature of human beings (e.g., our rationality or possessing the image of God), our capacity to carry out various social functions, contracts we have entered into, or our moral character.

Plato goes on, in the second part of this reading, to identify justice with a hierarchical harmony in the soul and the community at large in which each entity does what it is best at doing. His definition of justice, an elaboration of the one given by Polemarchus, is "the having and doing of one's own and what belongs to oneself."

Aristotle (384–322 B.C.), in our second reading, defines formal justice in terms of equality: Treat equals equally and unequals unequally. Injustice, it follows, is treating equals unequally and unequals equally. Like Simonides' definition in Plato's dialogue, this is a purely formal definition, for by itself the formula doesn't tell us what the criterion of assessment is. Aristotle offered the notion of *merit* (Greek *axia*) but allowed that what was deemed meritorious could differ from society to society—for an aristocratic society, excellence of mind; for a plutocratic society, wealth; for a democratic society, equal resources; and so forth. The significance of Aristotle's thought is that he uses the ambiguous Greek word *isos* (which means both "fair" and "equal") to define jsutice, so that an adventitious connection occurred between these two different concepts, justice being seen as a kind of equality, as a kind of egalitarianism. If this is correct, then an accident of the Greek language may account for some egalitarian tendencies in the history of political philosophy. But Aristotle was no egalitarian himself and thought that a hierarchical meritocracy was the best social arrangement.

The significance of Thomas Hobbes (1588–1679) is that he reduces desert or merit to one's power to influence others, especially the power to procure market value (how society rates one under different contingencies). Hobbes distinguishes this kind of merit or worth from one's *worthiness*, one's inherent merit, one's innate capacities. How does social justice work? Social justice, rendering one's due, is simply doing what you have contracted or promised to do for another, for, unless there is an enforceable contract, no such thing as justice arises.

In our fourth selection, from Adam Smith's *Theory of Moral Sentiments*, we encounter the hypothesis that the sense of merit or desert is a judgment arising from the feelings of gratitude and resentment. When we are intentionally harmed, we resent it and want to punish the guilty. When we are intentionally benefited, we want to reciprocate and reward our benefactor. We proceed to project our feeling onto other people and universalize the judgments that those who benefit others should be rewarded in proportion to their good deeds and those who harm others should be punished in proportion to their bad deeds.

We turn to Kant's theory of desert with its normative notion of being weighed on the scales of deontological morality. In Kant we find a paradoxical tension between the inherent merit or dignity of a human being as a member of the kingdom of ends (never treat a human being as a means only but always withal as an end in himself) and the differential value that is earned by one's moral integrity, the degree of one's commitment to duty. With regard to our inherent worth, we are all equal, but with regard to our moral worth, we are unequal. In fact, people can actually annihilate their inherent worth through immoral acts. Although it is a contradiction to act morally in order to gain a reward, one can hope to be worthy of the deepest reward, happiness, by being moral. Justice, according to Kant, consists in being happy or unhappy in exact proportion to one's moral character.

John Stuart Mill (1806–1873), the most important utilitarian of the nineteenth century, saw desert as the heart of justice and justice as the handmaiden of utility. In Section V of his *Utilitarianism* he characterizes justice as the moral principle that requires us to give to each what he or she deserves. "We should treat all equally well . . . who have deserved equally well of us, and . . . society should treat all equally well who have deserved equally well of it. . . . This is the highest abstract standard of social and distributive justice." Here Mill seems to be a rule utilitarian, holding that abiding by the rule of justice as desert will in the long run result in the highest aggregate utility.

We come to Henry Sidgwick's (1838–1900) *The Methods of Ethics*, a neglected classic in moral and social philosophy. Sidgwick, developing ideas found in Adam Smith, characterizes desert as based on primordial feelings of gratitude and its opposite, resentment. "Good desert" (rewarding) is gratitude universalized, and "ill desert" (punishment) is resentment universalized. These primitive instincts (gratitude and resentment) are so basic that any philosophy that ignores them is doomed to be defeated as ignoring a fundamental posit of human nature (even of animal nature). This selection is important for its discussion of determinism. Sidgwick points out more perspicuously than anyone before him, even Kant, that if determinism is true, responsibility vanishes and with it our notion of desert. If reason compels us to accept determinism as true, all would not be lost, for we would then have to become utilitarians, rewarding on the basis of expected consequences, rather than on the basis of effort or contribution. Sidgwick also points out the impossibility of a fine-grained analysis of individual deservingness, so the concept, especially Good desert, is useful within a "very limited range."

We conclude our historical readings with a selection from W. D. Ross (1877–1971). Ross is the one ethical intuitionist in these readings, though his conclusion regarding desert is similar to Kant's, namely, that it is self-evident that the good deserve to be happy and the bad unhappy in direct proportion to their degree of virtue and vice. Ross offers the following thought experiment: Imagine two worlds with equal populations and equal amounts of happiness. In World A the virtuous are all happy and the vicious all miserable, while in World B the virtuous are miserable and the vicious happy. Would you not agree, Ross asks, that World A is the better world? Isn't it obvious that there is natural or preinstitutional desert based on moral character?

Although there is great variety of opinion as to what constitutes desert, the formula "to each his or her due" was held by almost every philosopher examined in this historical section. Plato and Aristotle gave that formula a meritocratic criterion, in terms of the more excellent types of human beings, but others gave it a distinctly moral criterion (Aquinas, Smith, Kant, Mill, Sidgwick, and Ross). All held that desert was in the nature of things (*physis*), not merely conventional (*nomos*). Hobbes alone gave it a purely transactional, contractual interpretation, devoid of preinstitutional content. Now, in the late twentieth century, in the era of postdesert, Hobbes's position on desert is close to the dominant one in political philosophy. All desert is institutional. The question is, Is this really true?

Notes

1. A. W. H. Adkins, *Merit and Responsibility: A Study in Greek Ethics* (University of Chicago, 1960), p. 32f. A reviewer states that the three quotations present answers to different questions. My point is that they reveal different overall assessments of the values of desert and merit. Homeric society valued merit over desert and equality, Kant valued desert over merit and equality, and Rawls and modern Liberalism tend to value equality over desert and merit.
2. G. W. Leibniz, *Theodicy* (trans. E. M. Huggard), 1698.
3. Ulpian in the *Digest* of the Roman book of law *Corpus Juris*, ca. 200 B.C.
4. Emil Durkheim, *The Rules of Sociological Method* (Oxford University Press, 1952).
5. Karl Marx, *Critique of the Gotha Program*, published in *Karl Marx: Selected Writings*, ed. D. McLellan (Oxford University Press, 1977), pp. 566f.
6. Sam Scheffler, "Responsibility, Reactive Attitudes, and Liberalism in Philosophy and Politics," *Philosophy and Public Affairs* 21 (Fall 1992).
7. J. J. C. Smart, "An Outline of a System of Utilitarian Ethics," in J. J. C. Smart and Bernard Williams, eds., *Utilitarianism: For and Against* (Cambridge University Press, 1973), p. 54.
8. Brian Barry, *Political Arguments* (London: Routledge & Kegan Paul, 1965), p. 112f.

1. Justice as Harmony in the Soul and State

PLATO

Plato (427–347 B.C.) is recognized as preeminent among the first Greek philosophers, whose writings indeed virtually define the scope of philosophy. Name a philosophical issue: Be it in metaphysics, epistemology, aesthetics, ethics, or political philosophy, one can generally learn from what Plato had to say about it. Alfred North Whitehead said that the whole of European philosophy "consists of a series of footnotes to Plato." He was born into an Athenian aristocratic family at the end of the Periclean Golden Age of Greek democracy. He was Socrates' disciple, and the source of many of his ideas was Socrates, who, however, wrote nothing. He was the founder of the Academy in Athens, the ancestor to the first university, Aristotle's teacher, and an adviser to rulers. Among his important works are *Apology, Phaedo, Gorgias, Meno,* and the *Republic,* from which the present selection is taken.

Most of Plato's dialogues are presented in the form of conversations between Socrates (470–399 B.C.) and others, sometimes Sophists or disciples, such as Plato's brothers, Adeimantus and Glaucon. To what degree the thoughts set forth are actually those of Socrates or are more or less original with Plato is controversial.

Plato's theory identifies justice with wholeness in the State and the soul. When that which is excellent (Greek *aristoi* whence derives the English "aristocrat") reigns and the other classes (in the State) or faculties (in the soul) are properly ruled by it, we have a state of justice, a state constitutive of happiness. In the State the workers must be obedient to the Auxiliaries, and these to the Guardians. In the soul, the baser parts (those having to do with the passions, the stomach and the genitals) must be subservient to the spirited part, which in turn must be subservient to the reasoning faculty. When each part plays its proper role, does and receives its due, we have justice. In Book I Plato discusses Polemarchus's definition that justice consists in rendering to each his due. Plato shows that this definition is fraught with difficulties, but later in Book IV he defines *justice* in a manner similar to this—as "the having and doing of one's own and what belongs to oneself." This idea of giving to each his or her due will become the formal definition of justice with the Romans and throughout the Middle Ages, lasting even to modern times. As far as I can determine, this is the first recorded instance of its use. With this principle as foundational, Plato builds a meritocratic political theory. Since people are different and have different talents, justice requires that they play different roles in a hierarchical chain of command. He believed that men and women should have equal opportunity to achieve the highest status in society, to become Guardians. To this end he advocated the abolition of the family, the source of unjust privilege. A necessary condition of justice as social harmony is for a philosopher, a wise person, to become king.

Book I

We enter the dialogue between Cephalus, an elderly businessman, and Socrates. Cephalus's son, Polemarchus, is listening and soon enters the conversation:

CEPHALUS: Let me tell you, Socrates, that when a man begins to realize that he is going to die, he is filled with apprehensions and concern about matters that before did not occur to him. The tales that are told of the world below and how the men who have done wrong here must pay the penalty there, though he may have laughed them down hitherto, then begin to torture his soul with the doubt that there may be some truth in them. And apart from that the man himself either from the weakness of old age or possibly as being now nearer to the things beyond has a somewhat clearer view of them. Be that as it may, he is filled with doubt, surmises, and alarms and begins to reckon up and consider whether he has ever wronged anyone. Now he to whom the ledger of his life shows an account of many evil deeds starts up even from his dreams like a child again and again in affright and his days are haunted by anticipations of worse to come. But on him who is conscious of no wrong that he has done a sweet hope ever attends and a goodly, to be nurse of his old age, as Pindar too says. For a beautiful saying it is, Socrates, of the poet that when a man lives out his days in *justice* and piety, "sweet companion with him, to cheer his heart and nurse his old age, accompanies hope, who chiefly rules the changeful mind of mortals." That is a fine saying and an admirable sentiment. It is for this, then, that I affirm that the possession of wealth is of most value, not it may be to every man but to the good man. Not to cheat any man even unintentionally or play him false, not remaining in debt to a god for some sacrifice or to a man for money, so to depart in fear to that other world—to this result the possession of property contributes not a little. It has also many other uses. But, setting one thing against another, I would lay it down, Socrates, that for a man of sense this is the chief service of wealth.

SOCRATES: An admirable sentiment, Cephalus. But speaking of this very thing, *justice*, are we to affirm thus without qualification that it is truth telling and paying back what one has received from anyone, or may these very actions sometimes be just and sometimes unjust? I mean, for example, as everyone I presume would admit, if one took over weapons from a friend who was in his right mind and then the lender should go mad and demand them back, that we ought not to return them in that case and that he who did so return them would not be acting justly—nor yet would he who chose to speak nothing but the truth to one who was in that state.

C: You are right.

S: Then this is not the definition of justice—to tell the truth and return what one has received. (Polemarchus joins the conversation)   But it is, Socrates, said Polemarchus breaking in, if indeed we are to put any faith in Simonides.

S: Tell me, then, you the inheritor of the argument, what it is that you affirm that Simonides says and rightly says about justice.

P: That it is just, he replied, *to render to each his due.* In saying this I think he speaks well.

S: I must admit, that it is not easy to disbelieve Simonides. For he is a wise and inspired man. But just what he may mean by this you, Polemarchus, doubtless know, but I do not. Obviously he does not mean what we were just speaking of, this return of a deposit to anyone whatsoever even if he asks it back when not in his right mind. And yet what the man deposited is due to him in a sense, is it not?

P: Yes.

S: But it ought not to be returned to him at all if he is not in his right mind—(P)True.

S: It is then something other than this that Simonides must, as it seems, mean by the saying that it is just to render back what is due.

P: Something else in very deed, for he believes that friends owe it to friends to do them some good and no evil.

S: I see. You mean that he does not render what is due or owing who returns a deposit of gold if this return and the acceptance prove harmful and the returner and the recipient are friends. Isn't that what you say Simonides means?

P: Quite so.

S: But how about this—should one not render to enemies what is their due?

P: By all means, what is due and owing to them, and there is due and owing from an enemy to an enemy what also is proper for him, some evil.

S: It was a riddling definition of justice, then, that Simonides gave after the manner of poets, for

Reprinted from *The Dialogues of Plato,* trans. Benjamin Jowett; 3^d ed. (London: Macmillan, 1896).

while his meaning, it seems, was that justice is rendering to each what befits him, the name that he gave to this was "the due."

P: What else do you suppose? . . .

S: May I ask whether by friends you mean those who seem to a man to be worthy or those who really are so, even if they do not seem, and similarly of enemies?

P: It is likely, that men will love those whom they suppose to be good and dislike those whom they deem bad.

S: Do not men make mistakes in this matter so that many seem good to them who are not and the reverse? (P)—Yes.

S: For those, then, who thus err the good are their enemies and the bad their friends? (P) Certainly.

S: But all the same it is then just for them to benefit the bad and injure the good?

P: It would seem so.

S: But again, the good are just and incapable of injustice.

P: True.

S: On your reasoning then it is just to wrong those who do no injustice.

P: Nay, nay, Socrates, the reasoning can't be right.

S: Then, it is just to harm the unjust and benefit the just.

P: That seems a better conclusion than the other.

S: It will work out, then, for many, Polemarchus, who have misjudged men that it is just to harm their friends, for they have got bad ones, and to benefit their enemies, for they are good. And so we shall find ourselves saying the very opposite of what we affirmed Simonides to mean.

P: Most certainly, it does work out so. But let us change our ground, for it looks as if we were wrong in the notion we took up about the friend and the enemy. . . . That the man who both seems and is good is the friend, but that he who seems but is not really so seems but is not really the friend. And there will be the same assumption about the enemy.

S: Then on this view it appears the friend will be the good man and the bad the enemy.

P: Yes.

S: So you would have us qualify our former notion of the just man by an addition. We then said it was just to do good to a friend and evil to an enemy, but now we are to add that it is just to benefit the friend if he is good and harm the enemy if he is bad?

P: By all means, that, I think, would be the right way to put it.

S: Is it then, the part of a good man to harm anybody whatsoever?

P: Certainly it is. A man ought to harm those who are both bad and his enemies.

S: When horses are harmed does it make them better or worse?

P: Worse.

S: And men, my dear fellow, must we not say that when they are harmed it is in respect of the distinctive excellence or virtue of man that they become worse?

P: Assuredly.

S: And is not justice the specific virtue of man?

P: That too must be granted.

S: Then it must also be admitted, my friend, that men who are harmed become more unjust.

S: By justice then do the just make men unjust, or in sum do the good by virtue make men bad?

P: Nay, it is impossible.

S: It is not, I take it, the function of heat to chill but of its opposite—[Yes.]—Nor of dryness to moisten but of its opposite.

P: Assuredly.

S: Nor yet of the good to harm but of its opposite.

P: So it appears.

S: But the just man is good?

P: Certainly.

S: It is not then the function of the just man, Polemarchus, to harm either friend or anyone else, but of his opposite, the unjust.

P: I think you are altogether right, Socrates.

S: If, then, anyone affirms that it is just to render to each his due and he means by this that injury and harm is what is due to his enemies from the just man and benefits to his friends, he was no truly wise man who said it. For what he meant was not true. For it has been made clear to us that in no case is it just to harm anyone.

P: I concede it.

We turn to Book IV, where Socrates advocates the ideas of a division and specialization of labor (those specially adept at each function should specialize in it alone). He then defines justice as minding one's business or "the having and doing of one's own and what belongs to oneself." Socrates (S) is speaking with Plato's brother, Glaucon (G).

S: Listen then and learn if there is anything in what I say. For what we laid down in the beginning as a universal requirement when we were founding our city, this I think, or some form of this, is justice. And what we did lay down, and often said, if you recall, was that each one man must perform one social service in the state for which his nature was best adapted. (G)—Yes.

S: And again, that to do one's own business and not to be a busybody is justice is a saying that we have heard from many and have very often repeated ourselves.

G: We have.

S: This, then, my friend, if taken in a certain sense appears to be justice, this principle of doing one's own business. Do you know whence I infer this?

G: No, but tell me.

S: I think that this is the remaining virtue in the state after our consideration of soberness, courage, and intelligence, a quality which made it possible for them all to grow up in the body politic and which when they have sprung up preserves them as long as it is present. And I hardly need to remind you that we said that justice would be the residue after we had found the other three.

G: That is an unavoidable conclusion.

S: But moreover, if we were required to decide what it is whose indwelling presence will contribute most to making our city good, it would be a difficult decision whether it was the unanimity of rulers and ruled or the conservation in the minds of the soldiers of the convictions produced by law as to what things are or are not to be feared, or the watchful intelligence that resides in the guardians, or whether this is the chief cause of its goodness, the principle embodied in child, woman, slave, free, artisan, ruler, and ruled, that each performed his one task as one man and was not a versatile busybody.

G: Hard to decide indeed.

S: A thing, then, that in its contribution to the excellence of a state vies with and rivals its wisdom, its soberness, its bravery, is this principle of everyone in it doing his own task. (G) —Yes.

S: And is not *justice* the name you would have to give to the principle that rivals these as conducting to the virtue of a state?

G: By all means. . . .

S: Will not this be the chief aim of their decisions, that no one shall have what belongs to others or be deprived of his own?

G: Nothing else but this.

S: On the assumption that this is just? (G)—Yes.

S: From this point of view too, then, the having and doing of one's own and what belongs to oneself would admittedly be justice.

G: That is so.

S: Consider now whether you agree with me. A carpenter undertaking to do the work of a cobbler

or a cobbler of a carpenter or their interchange of one another's tools or honors or even the attempt of the same man to do both—the confounding of all other functions would not, think you, greatly injure a state, would it?

G: Not much.

S: But when, I fancy, one who is by nature an artisan or some kind of money-maker tempted and incited by wealth or command of votes or bodily strength or some similar advantage tries to enter into the class of the soldiers or one of the soldiers into the class of counselors and guardians, for which he is not fitted, and these interchange their tools and their honors or when the same man undertakes all these functions at once, then, I take it, you too believe that this kind of substitution and meddlesomeness is the ruin of a state.

G: By all means.

S: The interference with one another's business, then, of three existent classes, and the substitution of the one for the other, is the greatest injury to a state and would most rightly be designated as the thing which chiefly works it harm.

G: Precisely so.

S: And the thing that works the greatest harm to one's own state, will you not pronounce to be injustice? (G)—Yes.

S: This, then, is injustice. Again, let us put it in this way. The proper functioning of the money-makers, the helpers, and the guardians, each doing his own work in the state, being the reverse of that just described, would be justice and would render the city just.

G: I think the case is thus and no otherwise.

S: Let us not yet affirm it quite fixedly, but if this form, when applied to the individual man, is accepted there also as a definition of *justice*, we will then concede the point—for what else will there be to say? But if not, then we will look for something else. But now let us work out the inquiry in which we supposed that, if we found some larger thing that contained justice and viewed it there, we should more easily discover its nature in the individual man. And we agreed that this larger thing is the city, and so we constructed the best city in our power, well knowing that in the good city it would of course be found. What, then, we thought we saw there we must refer back to the individual and, if it is confirmed, all will be well. . . . Then a just man too will not differ at all from a just city in respect of the very form of justice, but will be like it.

G: Yes, like.

S: But now the city was thought to be just because three natural kinds [the workers, Auxiliaries, and Guardians] existing in it performed each its own function, and again it was sober, brave, and wise because of certain other affections and habits of these three kinds.

G: True.

S: Then, my friend, we shall thus expect the individual also to have these same forms in his soul, and by reason of identical affections of these with those in the city to receive properly the same appellations. . . .

S: Must not this be a kind of civil war of these three principles, their meddlesomeness and interference with one another's functions, and the revolt of one part against the whole of the soul that it may hold therein a rule which does not belong to it, since its nature is such that it befits it to serve as a slave to the ruling principle? Something of this sort, I fancy, is what we shall say, and that the confusion of these principles and their straying from their proper course is injustice and licentiousness and cowardice and brutish ignorance and, in general, all turpitude.

G: Precisely this.

S: Then, to act unjustly and be unjust and in turn to act justly—the meaning of all these terms becomes at once plain and clear, since injustice and justice are so.

G: How so?

S: Because, these are in the soul what the healthful and the diseaseful are in the body; there is no difference.

G: In what respect?

S: Healthful things surely engender health and diseaseful disease. (G)—Yes.

S: Then does not doing just acts engender justice and unjust injustice?

G: Of necessity.

S: But to produce health is to establish the ele-ments in a body in the natural relation of dominating and being dominated by one another, while to cause disease is to bring it about that one rules or is ruled by the other contrary to nature.

G: Yes, that is so.

S: And is it not likewise the production of justice in the soul to establish its principles in the natural relation of controlling and being controlled by one another, while injustice is to cause the one to rule or be ruled by the other contrary to nature?

G: Exactly so.

S: Virtue, then, as it seems, would be a kind of health and beauty and good condition of the soul, and vice would be disease, ugliness, and weakness. (G)—It is so.

S: Then is it not also true that beautiful and honorable pursuits tend to the winning of virtue and the ugly to vice?

G: Of necessity.

S: And now at last, it seems, it remains for us to consider whether it is profitable to do justice and practice honorable pursuits and be just, whether one is known to be such or not, or whether injustice profits, and to be unjust, if only a man escape punishment and is not bettered by chastisement.

G: Nay, Socrates, I think that from this point on our inquiry becomes an absurdity—if, while life is admittedly intolerable with a ruined constitution of body even though accompanied by all the food and drink and wealth and power in the world, we are yet to be asked to suppose that, when the very nature and constitution of that whereby we live is disordered and corrupted, life is going to be worth living, if a man can only do as he pleases, and pleases to do anything save that which will rid him of evil and injustice and make him possessed of justice and virtue—now that the two have been shown to be as we have described them.

2. Justice as Equality According to Merit

ARISTOTLE

Aristotle (384–322 B.C.) was born in Stagira in Macedon, the son of a physician. He was a student of Plato at the Academy in Athens and the tutor of Alexander the Great. Aristotle saw ethics as the branch of political philosophy concerned with a good life. It is thus a practical, rather than a purely theoretical, science. In the selections from *Nicomachean Ethics* and *Politics*, Aristotle defines justice as a kind of equality. He identifies two kinds: (1) that which consists in observance of the law, which characterizes the law-abiding person; and (2) that which characterizes the person who takes only what is due him. This *just* is the fair, in Greek *isos*, which also means "equal." This play on words led to the formula that "justice is equality," but Aristotle did not mean what the phrase would mean to an egalitarian—an equal distribution of resources or welfare to each person. On the contrary, he thought people merited different quantities of different goods.

The principle of equality—treat equals equally and unequals unequally—requires that each person be rendered benefits and burdens according to how he has contributed to the whole. If all have contributed equally, all will receive equally. If some have contributed more, they will receive more in proportion to their contribution. Aristotle's notion of justice is not numerical (or arithmetical), not Bentham's "each to count as one and no one to count for more than one," but "proportional," each counting according to his contribution to the whole. Rather than level or erase distinctions between people, it brings them into the distributive scheme.

Aristotle's formula is one of *formal* equality, which enjoins giving equals equal shares and unequals unequal shares, but it does not specify the criterion by which the distribution is to be made. The theory may be represented as an equality of ratios. Let A and B be two individuals, X and Y be degrees of some value-producing property P, and Q be some good. Then:

$$\frac{\text{A has X degree of P}}{\text{B has Y degree of P}} = \frac{\text{A should have X degree of Q}}{\text{B should have Y degree of Q}}$$

A's having P to degree X is to B's having P to degree Y as A's deserving or meriting Q to degree X is to B's deserving or meriting Q to degree Y. For example, if A has twice B's widget-making ability (P), A should receive twice the reward (Q) appropriate to degree Y. The Greek word for "desert" or "merit," *axia*, means "one's worth or value." The term has its origin in economic relations—one's "price." Referring to scales in the market, *axios* means "weighing as much." The metaphor "the scales of justice" is derived from the scales of the market.

This second type of Justice is further divided into two subtypes: *distributive* and *corrective* or rectificatory. The former is "manifested in distribution of honor or money or the other things that fall to be divided among those who have a share in the constitution . . . , and [the latter] is that which plays a rectifying part in transactions between man and man."

Our first selection is from Book V of the *Nicomachean Ethics*, where the principle of equality is set forth. Our second selection is from the *Politics*, where Aristotle discusses the relationship between equality and merit.

From *Nichomachean Ethics*, Book V

But at all events what we are investigating is the justice which is *part* of virtue; for there is a justice of this kind, as we maintain. Similarly, it is with injustice in the particular sense that we are concerned.

That there is such a thing is indicated by the fact that while the man who exhibits in action the other forms of wickedness acts wrongly indeed, but not graspingly (*e.g.* the man who throws away his shield through cowardice or speaks harshly through bad temper or fails to help a friend with money through meanness), when a man acts graspingly he often exhibits none of these vices—no, nor all together, but certainly wickedness of some kind (for we blame him) and injustice. There is, then, another kind of injustice which is a part of injustice in the wide sense, and a use of the word "unjust" which answers to a part of what is unjust in the wide sense of "contrary to the law." Again, if one man commits adultery for the sake of gain and makes money by it, while another does so at the bidding of appetite though he loses money and is penalized for it, the latter would be held to be self-indulgent rather than grasping, but the former is unjust, but not self-indulgent; evidently, therefore, he is unjust by reason of his making gain by his act. Again, all other unjust acts are ascribed invariably to some particular kind of wickedness, for example adultery to self-indulgence, the desertion of a comrade in battle to cowardice, physical violence to anger; but if a man makes gain, his action is ascribed to no form of wickedness but injus-

tice. Evidently, therefore, there is apart from injustice in the wide sense another, "particular," injustice which shares the name and nature of the first, because its definition falls within the same genus; for the significance of both consists in a relation to one's neighbor, but the one is concerned with honour or money or safety—or that which includes all these, if we had a single name for it—and its motive is the pleasure that arises from gain; while the other is concerned with all the objects with which the good man is concerned.

It is clear, then, that there is more than one kind of justice, and that there is one which is distinct from virtue entire; we must try to grasp its genus and differentia.

The unjust has been divided into the unlawful and the unfair, and the just into the lawful and the fair. To the unlawful answers the aforementioned sense of injustice. But since the unfair and the unlawful are not the same, but are different as a part is from its whole (for all that is unfair is unlawful, but not all that is unlawful is unfair), the unjust and injustice in the sense of the unfair are not the same as but different from the former kind, as part from whole; for injustice in this sense is a part of injustice in the wide sense, and similarly justice in the one sense of justice in the other. Therefore we must speak also about particular justice and particular injustice, and similarly about the just and the unjust. The justice, then, which answers to the whole of virtue, and the corresponding injustice, one being the exercise of virtue as a whole, and the other that of vice as a whole, towards one's neighbour, we may leave on

---

Reprinted from *Nicomachean Ethics*, trans. W. D. Ross (1925), by permission of Oxford University Press and from *Politics*, trans. Benjamin Jowett (1896).

one side. And how the meanings of "just" and "unjust" which answer to these are to be distinguished is evident; for practically the majority of the acts commanded by the law are those which are prescribed from the point of view of virtue taken as a whole; for the law bids us practise every virtue and forbids us to practise any vice. And the things that tend to produce virtue taken as a whole are those of the acts prescribed by the law which have been prescribed with a view to education for the common good. But with regard to the education of the individual as such, which makes him without qualification a good man, we must determine later whether this is the function of the political art or of another; for perhaps it is not the same to be a good man and a good citizen of any state taken at random.

Of particular justice and that which is just in the corresponding sense, (A) one kind is that which is manifested in distributions of honour or money or the other things that fall to be divided among those who have a share in the constitution (for in these it is possible for one man to have a share either unequal or equal to that of another), and (B) one is that which plays a rectifying part in transactions between man and man. Of this there are two divisions; of transactions (1) some are voluntary and (2) others involuntary—voluntary such transactions as sale, purchase, loan for consumption, pledging, loan for use, depositing, letting (they are called voluntary because the origin of these transactions is voluntary), while of the involuntary (a) some are clandestine, such as theft, adultery, poisoning, procuring, enticement of slaves, assassination, false witness, and (b) others are violent, such as assault, imprisonment, murder, robbery with violence, mutilation, abuse, insult.

We have shown that both the unjust man and the unjust act are unfair (*anison*) or unequal (*anisou*); now it is clear that there is also a mean between two unequals, namely, that which is equal (*ison*); for in any kind of action in which there is a more and a less there is also what is equal. If, then, the unjust is unequal, the just is equal, as all men believe even apart from argument. And since the equal is the mean, the just will be a mean

as well. Now equality implies at least two things. the just, then, must be both intermediate and equal and relative (i.e. for certain persons). And *qua* intermediate it must be between certain things (which are respectively greater and less); *qua* equal, it involves *two* things; *qua* just, it is for certain people. The just, therefore, involves at least four terms; for the persons for whom it is in fact just are two, and the things in which it is manifested, the objects distributed, are two. And the same equality will exist between the persons and between the things concerned; for as the latter—the things concerned—are related, so are the former; if they are not equal, they will not have what is equal, but this is the origin of quarrels and complaints—when either equals have and are awarded unequal shares, or unequals equal shares.

This is plain from the fact that awards should be "according to desert" (*axian*). For all men agree that what is just in distribution must be according to desert in some sense, thought they do not all specify the same sort of desert, but democrats identify it with the status of freeman, supporters of oligarchy with wealth (or with noble birth), and supporters of aristocracy with excellence (*aretai* = virtue).

Justice is therefore a sort of proportion; for proportion is not a property of numerical quantity only, but of quantity in general, proportion being equality of ratios, and involves at least four terms. . . . the ratio between one pair is the same as that between the other pair; for there is a similar distinction between the persons and between things. As the term A, then, is to B, so will C be to D, and therefore, alternatively, as A is to C, B will be to D. Therefore also the whole is in the same ratio to the whole, and this coupling the distribution effects and, if the terms are so combined, effects justly. The conjunction, then, of the terms A with C and of B with D is what is just in distribution, and the species of the just is intermediate, and the unjust is what violates the proportion; for the proportional is intermediate, and the just is proportional.[1] (Mathematicians call this kind of proportion geometrical; for it is in geometrical proportion that it follows that the whole is to the whole as either part is to the corresponding part.) This proportion is not continuous; for we cannot get a single term standing for a person and a thing.

This, then, is what the just is—the proportional; the unjust is what violates the proportion. Hence one term becomes too great, the other too small, as indeed happens in practice; for the man who acts unjustly has too much, and the man who is unjustly treated too little, of what is good. In the case of evil the reverse is true; for the lesser evil is reckoned a good in comparison with the greater evil, since the lesser evil is rather to be chosen than the greater, and what is worthy of choice is good, and what is worthier of choice a greater good.

From *Politics*, Book III

Let us begin by considering the common definitions of oligarchy and democracy, and what is justice oligarchical and democractical. For all men cling to justice of some kind, but their conceptions are imperfect and they do not express the whole idea. For example, justice is thought by them to be, and is, equality, not, however, for all, but only for equals. And inequality is thought to be, and is, justice; neither is this for all, but only for unequals. When the persons are omitted, then men judge erroneously. The reason is that they are passing judgment on themselves, and most people are bad judges in their own case. And whereas justice implies a relation to persons as well as to things, and a just distribution, as I have already said in the Ethics, embraces alike persons and things, they acknowledge the equality of the things, but dispute about the merit of the persons, chiefly for the reason which I have just given,—because they are bad judges in their own affairs; and secondly, because both the parties to the argument are speaking of a limited and partial justice, but imagine themselves to be speaking of absolute justice. For those who are unequal in one respect, for example wealth, consider themselves to be unequal in all; and any who are equal in one

respect, for example freedom, consider themselves to be equal in all. But they leave out the capital point. For if men met and associated out of regard to wealth only, their share in the state would be proportioned to their property, and the oligarchical doctrine would then seem to carry the day. It would not be just that he who paid one mina should have the same share of a hundred minae, whether of the principal or of the profits, as he who paid the remaining ninety-nine. But a state exists for the sake of a good life, and not for the sake of life only: if life only were the object, slaves and brute-animals might form a state, but they cannot, for they have no share in happiness or in a life of free choice. Nor does a state exist for the sake of alliance and security from injustice, nor yet for the sake of exchange and mutual intercourse; for then the Tyrrhenians and the Carthaginians, and all who have commercial treaties with one another, would be the citizens of one state. True, they have agreements about imports, and engagements that they will do no wrong to one another, and written articles of alliance. But there are no magistracies common to the contracting parties who will enforce their engagements; different states have each their own magistracies. Nor does one state take care that the citizens of the other are such as they ought to be, nor see that those who come under the terms of the treaty do no wrong or wickedness at all, but only that they do no injustice to one another. Whereas, those who care for good government take into consideration [the larger question of] virtue and vice in states. Whence it may be further inferred that virtue must be the serious care of a state which truly deserves the name: for [without this ethical end] the community becomes a mere alliance which differs only in place from alliances of which the members live apart; and law is only a convention, 'a surety to one another of justice,' as the sophist Lycophron says, and has no real power to make the citizens good and just.

In all sciences and arts the end is a good, and the greatest good and in the highest degree a good in the most authoritative of all—this is the political science of which the good is justice, in other words, the common interest. All men think justice to be a sort of equality; and to a certain extent they agree with what we have said in our philosophical works about ethics. For they say that what is just is just *for* someone and that it should be equal for equals. But there still remains a question: equality or inequality of what? Here is a difficulty which calls for political speculation. For very likely some persons will say that offices of state ought to be unequally distributed according to superior excellence, in whatever respect, of the citizen, although there is no other difference between him and the rest of the community; for those who differ in any one respect have different rights and claims. But, surely, if this is true, the complexion or height of a man, or any other advantage, will be a reason for his obtaining a greater share of political rights. The error here lies upon the surface, and may be illustrated from the other arts and sciences. When a number of flute-players are equal in their art, there is no reason why those of them who are better born should have better flutes given to them; for they will not play any better on the flute, and the superior instrument should be reserved for him who is the superior artist. If what I am saying is still obscure, it will be made clearer as we proceed. For if there were a superior flute-player who was far inferior in birth and beauty, although either of these may be a greater good than the art of flute-playing and may excel flute-playing in a greater ratio than he excels the others in his art, still he ought to have the best flutes given to him, unless the advantages of wealth and birth contribute to excellence in flute-playing, which

they do not. Moreover, upon this principle any good may be compared with any other. For if a given height may be measured against wealth and against freedom, height in general may be so measured. Thus if A excels in height more than B in excellence, even if excellence in general excels height still more, all goods will be comparable; for if a certain amount is better than some other, it is clear that some other will be equal. But since no such comparison can be made, it is evident that there is good reason why in politics men do not ground their claim to office on every sort of inequality. For if some be slow, and others swift, that is no reason why the one should have little and the others much; it is in gymnastic contests that such excellence is rewarded. Whereas the rival claims of candidates for office can only be based on the possession of elements which enter into the composition of a state. And therefore the well-born, or free-born, or rich, may with good reason claim office; for holders of offices must be freemen and tax-payers: a state can be no more composed entirely of poor men than entirely of slaves. But if wealth and freedom are necessary elements, justice and valour are equally so; for without the former qualities a state cannot exist at all, without the latter not well.

NOTE

1. In other words, as Person A is to thing C, so Person B will be to thing D. If A is twice as worthy as B and C and D are amounts of a common good whose distribution should be according to worth, A should receive twice as much of that good as B. So C would be twice as much as D.

3. Merit as Market Value

THOMAS HOBBES

Thomas Hobbes (1588–1679), arguably the greatest English political philosopher, gave classic expression to the idea that morality and politics arise out of a social contract. He was born in Westbury, England, the son of an eccentric vicar. On the day of his birth (April 5) the Spanish Armada, the greatest naval fleet the world had seen up to that time, was spotted off the coast of southern England. The chronicler John Aubrey reports that Hobbes's mother, only seven months pregnant, startled by the news, went into labor and delivered him. Hobbes wrote of this experience, "Unbeknownst to my mother at that time she gave birth to twins, myself and fear. And fear has been my constant companion throughout life." Hobbes's lifetime was filled with the dangers of war—the Spanish Armada, the religious wars in Europe, the civil war in England. His political philosophy may be read as a proposed remedy for the fear and insecurity of people desperately in need of peace and tranquility.

Hobbes is known today primarily for his masterpiece of political theory, *Leviathan* (1651), a book written during the English civil wars (1642–1652), sometimes referred to as "The Great Rebellion," which pitted the forces of monarchy (the royalists) under Charles I against those of Parliament under Oliver Cromwell. Hobbes's work was intended to support the royalists, as he believed that the monarchy was the best guarantee for orderly and stable government. Yet the royalists misconstrued his interpretation as supporting the rebels, no doubt because Hobbes rejected the usual grounds for the monarchy, the divine right of kings. For this reason, and because the book conveyed a materialist view of human nature, thought to be dangerous to religion, it was suppressed or violently attacked throughout Hobbes's lifetime.

What are the doctrines that his contemporaries found so controversial? First of all, Hobbes breaks from the medieval notion that the State is a natural organism, based on natural devotion and interdependence. He develops a moral and political theory based not on natural affection but on psychological egoism. Hobbes argues that people always act from self-interest, to obtain gratification and to avoid harm. However, if we lived in a "state of nature"—without government—life would be "solitary, poor, nasty, brutish and short," for everyone would have reason to fear everyone else. There would be no security of life or possessions, and cooperative endeavors would be impossible. Prudent persons in that condition would find it in the interest of every individual to contract with everyone else to set up a Sovereign, that is, a government authorized to employ force to keep the peace in accordance with rules of conduct that our reason tells us to be necessary for communal life: the "Laws of Nature." In effect, then, human beings must live either in dreadful anarchy or as subjects of the great Leviathan, awesome and powerful, inspiring fear but offering protection from violence and harm.

In our short selection "Of Power, Worth, Dignity, Honour, and Worthiness" we encounter Hobbes's theory that human beings, as egoists, are ever seeking power and that all our values can be reduced to kinds of powers. A person's merit or **worth** is one's market value, one of his powers. Hobbes distinguishes **worth** from **worthiness**, the inherent qualities of the person. He goes on to place merit within the context of a contract. No one has merit outside of an institutional arrangement where rules are set forth, so that those who meet the conditions merit the prizes or rewards.

Chapter 10. Of Power, Worth, Dignity, Honour, and Worthiness

The power of a man, (to take it universally) is his present means, to obtain some future apparent good; and is either original or instrumental.

Natural power, is the eminence of the faculties of body, or mind: as extraordinary strength, form, prudence, arts, eloquence, liberality, nobility. Instrumental are those powers, which acquired by these, or by fortune, are means and instruments to acquire more: as riches, reputation, friends, and the secret working of God, which men call good luck. For the nature of power, is in this point, like to fame, increasing as it proceeds; or like the motion of heavy bodies, which the further they go, make still the more haste.

The greatest of human powers, is that which is compounded of the powers of most men, united by consent, in one person, natural, or civil, that has the use of all their powers depending on his will; such as is the power of a commonwealth: or depending on the wills of each particular; such as is the power of a faction or of divers factions leagued. Therefore to have servants, is power; to have friends, is power: for they are strengths united.

Also riches joined with liberality, is power; because it procureth friends, and servants: without liberality, not so; because in this case they defend not; but expose men to envy, as a prey.

Reputation of power, is power; because it draweth with it the adherence of those that need protection.

So is reputation of love of a man's country, (called popularity) for the same reason.

Also, what quality soever maketh a man beloved, or feared of many; or the reputation of such quality, is power; because it is a means to have the assistance, and service of many.

Good success is power; because it maketh reputation of wisdom, or good fortune; which makes men either fear him, or rely on him.

Affability of men already in power, is increase of power; because it gaineth love.

Reputation of prudence in the conduct of peace or war, is power; because to prudent men, we commit the government of ourselves, more willingly than to others.

Nobility is power, not in all places, but only in those commonwealths, where it has privileges: for in such privileges consists their power.

Eloquence is power, because it is seeming prudence.

Form is power; because being a promise of good, it recommendeth men to the favour of women and strangers.

The sciences, are small power; because not eminent; and therefore, not acknowledged in any man; nor are at all, but in a few, and in them, but of a few things. For science is of that nature, as none can understand it to be, but such as in a good measure have attained it.

Arts of public use, as fortification, making of engines, and other instruments of war; because they confer to defence, and victory, are power: and though the true mother of them, be science, namely the mathematics; yet, because they are brought into the light, by the hand of the artificer, they be esteemed (the midwife passing with the vulgar for the mother) as his issue.

The value, or WORTH of a man, is as of all other things, his price; that is to say, so much as would be given for the use of his power: and therefore is not absolute; but a thing dependent on the need and judgment of another. An able conductor of soldiers, is of great price in time of war present, or imminent; but in peace not so. A learned and uncorrupt judge, is much worth in time of peace; but not so much in war. And as in other things, so in men, not the seller, but the buyer determines the price. For let a man (as most men do) rate themselves at the highest value they can; yet their true value is no more than it is esteemed by others.

The manifestation of the value we set on one another, is that which is commonly called honoring, and dishonoring. To value a man at a high rate, is to honour him; at a low rate, is to dishonor him. But high, and low, in this case, is to be understood by comparison to the rate that each man setteth on himself.

The public worth of a man, which is the value set on him by the commonwealth, is that which men commonly call DIGNITY. And this value of him by the commonwealth, is understood, by offices of command, judicature, public employment; or by names and titles, introduced for distinction of such value.

To pray to another, for aid of any kind, is to HONOUR; because a sign we have an opinion he has power to help; and the more difficult the aid is, the more is the honour.

To obey, is to honour, because no man obeys them, whom they think have no power to help, or hurt them. And consequently to disobey, is to dishonour.

To give great gifts to a man, is to honour him; because it is buying of protection, and acknowledging of power. To give little gifts, is to dishonor; because it is but alms, and signifies an opinion of the need of small helps.

Worthiness is a thing different from the worth or value of a man, and also from his merit or desert, and consists in a particular power or ability for that whereof he is said to be worthy; which particular ability is usually named fitness or aptitude.

For he is worthiest to be a commander, to be a judge, or to have any other charge, that is best fitted with the qualities required to the well discharging of it; and worthiest of riches, that has the qualities most requisite for the well using of them: any of which qualities being absent, one may nevertheless be a worthy man, and valuable for something else. Again, a man may be worthy of riches, office, and employment that nevertheless can plead no right to have it before another, and therefore cannot be said to merit or deserve it. For merit presupposes a right, and that the thing deserved is due by promise . . .

Of Merit

He that performs first in the case of a Contract, is said to **Merit** that which he is to receive by the performance of the other; and he has it as his **Due**. Also when a Prize is propounded to many, which is to be given to him only that wins; or money is thrown among many, to be enjoyed by them that catch it; though this be a free gift; yet so to win or to catch is to **Merit**, and to have it as **Due**. For the Right is transferred in the offering of the Prize, and in throwing down the money; though it be not determined to whom, but by the event of the contention. But there is between these two sorts of **Merit** this difference, that in Contract, I **Merit** by virtue of my own power, and the Contractors need; but in this case of Free gift, I am to Merit only by the kindness of the Giver. In Contract, I Merit at the Contractors hand that he should depart with his right; In this case of Gift, I Merit not that the giver should part with his right; but that when he has parted with it, it should be mine, rather than another's. And this I think to be the meaning of that distinction of the Schools between *meritum congrui* [merit based on conformity] and *meritum condigni* [merit based on worthiness]. For God Almighty having promised Paradise to those men, hoodwinked with carnal desires, that can walk through this world according to the precepts and limits prescribed by him, they say he that shall so walk shall merit Paradise *ex congruo* [by conforming]. But because no man can demand a right to it, by his own righteousness or any other power in himself, but by the free grace of God only, they say no man can merit Paradise *ex condigno* [by being worthy]. This, I say, I think is the meaning of that distinction; but because disputers do not agree upon the signification of their own terms of art longer than it serves their turn, I will not affirm anything of their meaning; only this I say: when a gift is given indefinitely, as a prize to be contended for, he that wins merits and may claim the prize as due.

4. Of Merit and Demerit

ADAM SMITH

Adam Smith (1723–90), the famous Scottish economist and author of *The Wealth of Nations*, was educated at Glasgow and Oxford universities. He was Professor of Logic at the University of Glasgow. A friend of David Hume, he shared many of Hume's views on economics and ethics, particularly the belief that morality arises not from reason but from sympathy, when "we enter into the situations of other men and share with them in the passions which those situations excite in us." A corollary of his moral sentiment theory is the thesis that merit (or good desert) and demerit (or ill desert) arise from the sentiments of gratitude and resentment. When others act in ways intended to benefit us or others, we feel either direct or vicarious gratitude and want to reciprocate or see the benefactor rewarded. When others act in ways intended to harm us or others, we feel resentment and want the malefactors punished. This idea that reward and punishment are the sentiments of gratitude and resentment universalized is often credited to Henry Sidgwick, but Smith deserves the credit.

Section I
Of the Sense of Merit and Demerit

Introduction

There is another set of qualities ascribed to the actions and conduct of mankind, distinct from their propriety or impropriety, their decency or ungracefulness, and which are the objects of a distinct species of approbation and disapprobation. These are Merit and Demerit, the qualities of deserving reward, and of deserving punishment.

It has already been observed, that the sentiment or affection of the heart, from which any action proceeds, and upon which its whole virtue or vice depends, may be considered under two different aspects, or in two different relations: first, in relation to the cause or object which excites it; and, secondly, in relation to the end which it proposes, or to the effect which it tends to produce: that upon the suitableness or unsuitableness, upon the proportion or disproportion, which the affection seems to bear to the cause or object which excites it, depends the propriety or impropriety, the decency or ungracefulness of the consequent action; and that upon the beneficial or hurtful effects which the affection proposes or tends to produce, depends the merit or demerit, the good or ill desert of the action to which it gives occasion. Wherein consists our sense of the propriety or impropriety of actions, has been explained in the former part of this discourse. We come now to consider, wherein consists that of their good or ill desert.

Reprinted from *The Theory of the Moral Sentiments* (1759). I have used the L. A. Selby-Bigge edition of *British Moralists* (Clarendon Press, 1897), which contains a note by the editor.

Chap. I

That whatever appears to be the proper object of gratitude, appears to deserve reward; and that, in the same manner, whatever appears to be the proper object of resentment, appears to deserve punishment

To us, therefore, that action must appear to deserve reward, which appears to be the proper and approved object of that sentiment, which most immediately and directly prompts us to reward, or to do good to another. And in the same manner, that action must appear to deserve punishment, which appears to be the proper and approved object of that sentiment which most immediately and directly prompts us to punish, or to inflict evil upon another.

The sentiment which most immediately and directly prompts us to reward, is gratitude; that which most immediately and directly prompts us to punish, is resentment.

To us, therefore, that action must appear to deserve reward, which appears to be the proper and approved object of gratitude; as, on the other hand, that action must appear to deserve punishment, which appears to be the proper and approved object of resentment.

To reward, is to recompense, to remunerate, to return good for good received. To punish, too, is to recompense, to remunerate, though in a different manner; it is to return evil for evil that has been done.

There are some other passions, besides gratitude and resentment, which interest us in the happiness or misery of others; but there are none which so directly excite us to be the instruments of either. The love and esteem which grow upon acquaintance and habitual approbation, necessarily lead us to be pleased with the good fortune of the man who is the object of such agreeable emotions, and consequently, to be willing to lend a hand to promote it. Our love, however, is fully satisfied, though his good fortune should be brought about without our assistance. All that this passion desires is to see him happy, without regarding who was the author of his prosperity. But gratitude is not to be satisfied in this manner. If the person to whom we owe many obligations, is made happy without our assistance, though it pleases our love, it does not content our gratitude. Till we have recompensed him, till we ourselves have been instrumental in promoting his happiness, we feel ourselves still loaded with that debt which his past services have laid upon us.

The hatred and dislike, in the same manner, which grow upon habitual disapprobation, would often lead us to take a malicious pleasure in the misfortune of the man whose conduct and character excite so painful a passion. But though dislike and hatred harden us against all sympathy, and sometimes dispose us even to rejoice at the distress of another, yet, if there is no resentment in the case, if neither we nor our friends have received any great personal provocation, these passions would not naturally lead us to wish to be instrumental in bringing it about. Though we could fear no punishment in consequence of our having had some hand in it, we would rather that it should happen by other means. To one under the dominion of violent hatred it would be agreeable, perhaps, to hear, that the person whom he abhorred and detested was killed by some accident. But if he had the least spark of justice, which, though this passion is not very favourable to virtue, he might still have, it would hurt him excessively to have been himself, even without design, the occasion of this misfortune. Much more would the very thought of voluntarily contributing to it shock him beyond all measure. He would reject with horror even the imagination of so execrable a design; and if he could imagine himself capable of such an enormity, he would begin to regard himself in the same odious light in which he had considered the person who was the object of his dislike. But it is quite otherwise with resentment: if the person who had done us some great injury, who had murdered our father or our brother, for example, should soon afterwards die of a fever, or even be brought to the scaffold upon account of some other crime, though it might sooth our hatred, it would not fully gratify our resentment. Resentment would prompt us to desire, not only that he should be punished, but that he should be punished by our means, and upon account of that particular injury which he had done to us. Resentment cannot be fully gratified, unless the offender is not only made to grieve in his turn, but to grieve for that particular wrong which we have suffered from him. He must be made to repent and be sorry for this very action, that others, through fear of the like punishment, may be terrified from being guilty of the like offence. The natural gratification of this passion tends, of its own accord, to produce all the political ends of punishment; the correction of the criminal, and the example to the public.

Gratitude and resentment, therefore, are the sentiments which most immediately and directly prompt to reward and to punish. To us, therefore, he must appear to deserve reward, who appears to be the proper and approved object of gratitude; and he to deserve punishment, who appears to be that of resentment.

Chap. II

Of the proper objects of gratitude and resentment

To be the proper and approved object either of gratitude or resentment, can mean nothing but to be the object of that gratitude, and of that resentment, which naturally seems proper, and is approved of.

But these, as well as all the other passions of human nature, seem proper and are approved of, when the heart of every impartial spectator entirely sympathizes with them, when every indifferent by-stander entirely enters into, and goes along with them.

He, therefore, appears to deserve reward, who, to some person or persons, is the natural object of a gratitude which every human heart is disposed to beat time to, and thereby applaud: and he, on the other hand, appears to deserve punishment, who in the same manner is to some person or persons the natural object of a resentment which the breast of every reasonable man is ready to adopt and sympathize with. To us, surely, that action must appear to deserve reward, which every body who knows of it would wish to reward, and therefore delights to see rewarded: and that action must as surely appear to deserve punishment, which every body who hears of it is angry with, and upon that account rejoices to see punished.

1. As we sympathize with the joy of our companions when in prosperity, so we join with them in the complacency and satisfaction with which they naturally regard whatever is the cause of their good fortune. We enter into the love and affection which they conceive for it, and begin to love it too. We should be sorry for their sakes if it was destroyed, or even if it was placed at too great a distance from them, and out of the reach of their care and protection, though they should lose nothing by its absence except the pleasure of seeing it. If it is man who has thus been the fortunate instrument of the happiness of his brethren, this is still more peculiarly the case. When we see one man assisted, protected, relieved by another, our sympathy with the joy of the person who receives the benefit serves only to animate our fellow-feeling with his gratitude towards him who bestows it. When we look upon the person who is the cause of his pleasure with the eyes with which we imagine he must look upon him, his benefactor seems to stand before us in the most engaging and amiable light. We readily therefore sympathize with the grateful affection which he conceives for a person to whom he has been so much obliged; and consequently applaud the returns which he is disposed to make for the good offices conferred upon him. As we entirely enter into the affection from which these returns proceed, they necessarily seem every way proper and suitable to their object.

2. In the same manner, as we sympathize with the sorrow of our fellow-creature whenever we see his distress, so we likewise enter into his abhorrence and aversion for whatever has given occasion to it. Our heart, as it adopts and beats time to his grief, so is it likewise

animated with that spirit by which he endeavours to drive away or destroy the cause of it. The indolent and passive fellow-feeling, by which we accompany him in his sufferings, readily gives way to that more vigorous and active sentiment by which we go along with him in the effort he makes, either to repel them, or to gratify his aversion to what has given occasion to them. This is still more peculiarly the case, when it is man who has caused them. When we see one man oppressed or injured by another, the sympathy which we feel with the distress of the sufferer seems to serve only to animate our fellow-feeling with his resentment against the offender. We are rejoiced to see him attack his adversary in his turn, and are eager and ready to assist him whenever he exerts himself for defence, or even for vengeance within a certain degree. If the injured should perish in the quarrel, we not only sympathize with the real resentment of his friends and relations, but with the imaginary resentment which in fancy we lend to the dead, who is no longer capable of feeling that or any other human sentiment. But as we put ourselves in his situation, as we enter, as it were, into his body, and in our imaginations, in some measure, animate anew the deformed and mangled carcass of the slain, when we bring home in this manner his case to our own bosoms, we feel upon this, as upon many other occasions, an emotion which the person principally concerned is incapable of feeling, and which yet we feel by an illusive sympathy with him. The sympathetic tears which we shed for that immense and irretrievable loss, which in our fancy he appears to have sustained, seem to be but a small part of the duty which we owe him. The injury which he has suffered demands, we think, a principal part of our attention. We feel that resentment which we imagine he ought to feel, and which he would feel, if in his cold and lifeless body there remained any consciousness of what passes upon earth. His blood, we think, calls aloud for vengeance. The very ashes of the dead seem to be disturbed at the thought that his injuries are to pass unrevenged. The horrors which are supposed to haunt the bed of the murderer, the

ghosts which, superstition imagines, rise from their graves to demand vengeance upon those who brought them to an untimely end, all take their origin from this natural sympathy with the imaginary resentment of the slain. And with regard, at least, to this most dreadful of all crimes, Nature, antecedent to all reflections upon the utility of punishment, has in this manner stamped upon the human heart, in the strongest and most indelible characters, an immediate and instinctive approbation of the sacred and necessary law of retaliation.

Chap. III

That where there is no approbation of the conduct of the person who confers the benefit, there is little sympathy with the gratitude of him who receives it: and that, on the contrary, where there is no disapprobation of the motives of the person who does the mischief, there is no sort of sympathy with the resentment of him who suffers it

It is to be observed, however, that, how beneficial soever on the one hand, or how hurtful soever on the other, the actions or intentions of the person who acts may have been to the person who is, if I may say so, acted upon, yet if in the one case there appears to have been no propriety in the motives of the agent, if we cannot enter into the affections which influenced his conduct, we have little sympathy with the gratitude of the person who receives the benefit: or if, in the other case, there appears to have been no impropriety in the motives of the agent, if, on the contrary, the affections which influenced his conduct are such as we must necessarily enter into, we can have no sort of sympathy with the resentment of the person who suffers. Little gratitude seems due in the one case, and all sort of resentment seems unjust in the other. The one action seems to merit little reward, the other to deserve no punishment.

1. First, I say, That wherever we cannot sympathize with the affections of the agent,

wherever there seems to be no propriety in the motives which influenced his conduct, we are less disposed to enter into the gratitude of the person who received the benefit of his actions. A very small return seems due to that foolish and profuse generosity which confers the greatest benefits from the most trivial motives, and gives an estate to a man merely because his name and sirname happen to be the same with those of the giver. Such services do not seem to demand any proportionable recompense. Our contempt for the folly of the agent hinders us from thoroughly entering into the gratitude of the person to whom the good office has been done. His benefactor seems unworthy of it. As when we place ourselves in the situation of the person obliged, we feel that we could conceive no great reverence for such a benefactor, we easily absolve him from a great deal of that submissive veneration and esteem which we should think due to a more respectable character; and provided he always treats his weak friend with kindness and humanity, we are willing to excuse him from many attentions and regards which we should demand to a worthier patron. Those Princes, who have heaped, with the greatest profusion, wealth, power, and honours, upon their favourites, have seldom excited that degree of attachment to their persons which has often been experienced by those who were more frugal of their favours. The well-natured, but injudicious prodigality of James the First of Great Britain seems to have attached nobody to his person; and that Prince, notwithstanding his social and harmless disposition, appears to have lived and died without a friend. The whole gentry and nobility of England exposed their lives and fortunes in the cause of his more frugal and distinguishing son, notwithstanding the coldness and distant severity of his ordinary deportment.

2. Secondly, I say, That wherever the conduct of the agent appears to have been entirely directed by motives and affections which we thoroughly enter into and approve of, we can have no sort of sympathy with the resentment of the sufferer, how great soever the mischief which may have been done to

him. When two people quarrel, if we take part with, and entirely adopt the resentment of one of them, it is impossible that we should enter into that of the other. Our sympathy with the person whose motives we go along with, and whom therefore we look upon as in the right, cannot but harden us against all fellow-feeling with the other, whom we necessarily regard as in the wrong. Whatever this last, therefore, may have suffered, while it is no more than what we ourselves should have wished him to suffer, while it is no more than what our own sympathetic indignation would have prompted us to inflict upon him, it cannot either displease or provoke us. When an inhuman murderer is brought to the scaffold, though we have some compassion for his misery, we can have no sort of fellow-feeling with his resentment, if he should be so absurd as to express any against either his prosecutor or his judge. The natural tendency of their just indignation against so vile a criminal is indeed the most fatal and ruinous to him. But it is impossible that we should be displeased with the tendency of a sentiment, which, when we bring the case home to ourselves, we feel that we cannot avoid adopting.

Chap. IV

Recapitulation of the foregoing chapters

1. We do not, therefore, thoroughly and heartily sympathize with the gratitude of one man towards another, merely because this other has been the cause of his good fortune, unless he has been the cause of it from motives which we entirely go along with. Our heart must adopt the principles of the agent, and go along with all the affections which influenced his conduct, before it can entirely sympathize with, and beat time to, the gratitude of the person who has been benefited by his actions. If in the conduct of the benefactor there appears to have been no propriety, how beneficial soever its effects, it does not seem to demand, or necessarily to require, any proportionable recompense.

But when to the beneficent tendency of the

action is joined the propriety of the affection from which it proceeds, when we entirely sympathize and go along with the motives of the agent, the love which we conceive for him upon his own account, enhances and enlivens our fellow-feeling with the gratitude of those who owe their prosperity to his good conduct. His actions seem then to demand, and, if I may say so, to call aloud for a proportionable recompense. We then entirely enter into that gratitude which prompts to bestow it. The benefactor seems then to be the proper object of reward, when we thus entirely sympathize with, and approve of, that sentiment which prompts to reward him. When we approve of, and go along with, the affection from which the action proceeds, we must necessarily approve of the action, and regard the person towards whom it is directed, as its proper and suitable object.

2. In the same manner, we cannot at all sympathize with the resentment of one man against another, merely because this other has been the cause of his misfortune, unless he has been the cause of it from motives which we cannot enter into. Before we can adopt the resentment of the sufferer, we must disapprove of the motives of the agent, and feel that our heart renounces all sympathy with the affections which influenced his conduct. If there appears to have been no impropriety in these, how fatal soever the tendency of the action which proceeds from them to those against whom it is directed, it does not seem to deserve any punishment, or to be the proper object of any resentment.

But when to the hurtfulness of the action is joined the impropriety of the affection from whence it proceeds, when our heart rejects with abhorrence all fellow-feeling with the motives of the agent, we then heartily and entirely sympathize with the resentment of the sufferer. Such actions seem then to deserve, and, if I may say so, to call aloud for, a proportionable punishment; and we entirely enter into, and thereby approve of, that resentment which prompts to inflict it. The offender necessarily seems then to be the proper object of punishment, when we thus entirely sympathize with, and thereby

approve of, that sentiment which prompts to punish. In this case too, when we approve, and go along with, the affection from which the action proceeds, we must necessarily approve of the action, and regard the person against whom it is directed, as its proper and suitable object.

Chap. V

The analysis of the sense of Merit and Demerit

1. As our sense, therefore, of the propriety of conduct arises from what I shall call a direct sympathy with the affections and motives of the person who acts, so our sense of its merit arises from what I shall call an indirect sympathy with the gratitude of the person who is, if I may say so, acted upon.

As we cannot indeed enter thoroughly into the gratitude of the person who receives the benefit, unless we beforehand approve of the motives of the benefactor, so, upon this account, the sense of merit seems to be a compounded sentiment, and to be made up of two distinct emotions; a direct sympathy with the sentiments of the agent, and an indirect sympathy with the gratitude of those who receive the benefit of his actions.

We may, upon many different occasions, plainly distinguish those two different emotions combining and uniting together in our sense of the good desert of a particular character or action. When we read in history concerning actions of proper and beneficent greatness of mind, how eagerly do we enter into such designs? How much are we animated by that highspirited generosity which directs them? How keen are we for their success? How grieved at their disappointment? In imagination we become the very person whose actions are represented to us: we transport ourselves in fancy to the scenes of those distant and forgotten adventures, and imagine ourselves acting the part of a Scipio or a

Camillus, a Timoleon or an Aristides.* So far our sentiments are founded upon the direct sympathy with the person who acts. Nor is the indirect sympathy with those who receive the benefit of such actions less sensibly felt. Whenever we place ourselves in the situation of these last, with what warm and affectionate fellow-feeling do we enter into their gratitude towards those who served them so essentially? We embrace, as it were, their benefactor along with them. Our heart readily sympathizes with the highest transports of their grateful affection. No honours, no rewards, we think, can be too great for them to bestow upon him. When they make this proper return for his services, we heartily applaud and go along with them; but are shocked beyond all measure, if by their conduct they appear to have little sense of the obligations conferred upon them. Our whole sense, in short, of the merit and good desert of such actions, of the propriety and fitness of recompensing them, and making the person who performed them rejoice in his turn, arises from the sympathetic emotions of gratitude and love, with which, when we bring home to our own breast the situation of those principally concerned, we feel ourselves naturally transported towards the man who could act with such proper and noble beneficence.

2. In the same manner as our sense of the impropriety of conduct arises from a want of sympathy, or from a direct antipathy to the affections and motives of the agent, so our sense of its demerit arises from what I shall here too call an indirect sympathy with the resentment of the sufferer.

As we cannot indeed enter into the resentment of the sufferer, unless our heart beforehand disapproves the motives of the agent, and renounces all fellow-feeling with them; so upon this account the sense of demerit, as well as that of merit, seems to be a compounded sentiment, and to be made up of two distinct emotions; a direct antipathy to the sentiments of the agent, and an indirect sympathy with the resentment of the sufferer.

We may here too, upon many different occasions, plainly distinguish those two different emotions combining and uniting together in our sense of the ill desert of a particular character or action. When we read in history concerning the perfidy and cruelty of a Borgia or a Nero, our heart rises up against the detestable sentiments which influenced their conduct, and renounces with horror and abomination all fellow-feeling with such execrable motives. So far our sentiments are founded upon the direct antipathy to the affections of the agent: and the indirect sympathy with the resentment of the sufferers is still more sensibly felt. When we bring home to ourselves the situation of the persons whom those scourges of mankind insulted, murdered, or betrayed, what indignation do we not feel against such insolent and inhuman oppressors of the earth? Our sympathy with the unavoidable distress of the innocent sufferers is not more real nor more lively, than our fellow-feeling with their just and natural resentment. The former sentiment only heightens the latter, and the idea of their distress serves only to inflame and blow up our animosity against those who occasioned it. When we think of the anguish of the sufferers, we take part with them more earnestly against their oppressors; we enter with more

---

*Smith thinks of all four as men of great military prowess and patriotism whose services were not properly appreciated. Publius Cornelius Scipio Africanus led the Romans to victory against Hannibal in the Second Punic War. He later retired from public life embittered by attacks on his family. Marcus Furius Camillus delivered Rome from invasion by the Gauls and is called by Livy the 'second founder' of the city. Tradition has it that after an earlier military success he was accused of having unfairly distributed the booty and so he went into voluntary exile. Timoleon of Corinth overthrew the despotic rule of his brother and then, many years later, was sent by the Corinthians to liberate Sicily from tyrants and invaders. Between these two exploits he lived in retirement because his mother and his kinsmen blamed him for having allowed his brother to be put to death. Aristides 'the Just' was an Athenian statesman and general who took a leading part in the defeat of the Persian invaders of Greece at the battles of Salamis and Plataea. He was ostracized for a time owing to political rivalry with Themistocles.

eagerness into all their schemes of vengeance, and feel ourselves every moment wreaking, in imagination, upon such violators of the laws of society, that punishment which our sympathetic indignation tells us is due to their crimes. Our sense of the horror and dreadful atrocity of such conduct, the delight which we take in hearing that it was properly punished, the indignation which we feel when it escapes this due retaliation, our whole sense and feeling, in short, of its ill desert, of the propriety and fitness of inflicting evil upon the person who is guilty of it, and of making him grieve in his turn, arises from the sympathetic indignation which naturally boils up in the breast of the spectator, whenever he thoroughly brings home to himself the case of the sufferer.[1]

NOTE

1. To ascribe in this manner our natural sense of the ill desert of human actions to a sympathy with the resentment of the sufferer, may seem, to the greater part of people, to be a degradation of that sentiment. Resentment is commonly regarded as so odious a passion, that they will be apt to think it impossible that so laudable a principle, as the sense of the ill desert of vice, should in any respect be founded upon it. They will be more willing, perhaps, to admit that our sense of the merit of good actions is founded upon a sympathy with the gratitude of the persons who receive the benefit of them; because gratitude, as well as all the other benevolent passions, is regarded as an amiable principle, which can take nothing from the worth of whatever is founded upon it. Gratitude and resentment, however, are in every respect, it is evident, counterparts to one another; and if our sense of merit arises from a sympathy with the one, our sense of demerit can scarce miss to proceed from a fellow-feeling with the other.

5. Moral Worth as Alone Deserving Happiness

IMMANUEL KANT

Immanuel Kant (1724–1804), who was born in a deeply pietistic Lutheran family in Konigsberg, Germany, lived in that town his entire life. At sixteen he entered the University of Konigsberg, where he studied under the tutelage of Martin Knutzen and read works of Leibniz. After graduation he worked as a tutor; in 1755 he was offered an unsalaried lectureship at his alma mater, receiving his fees directly from his students. He served in this capacity until 1770, when he was promoted to the Chair of Logic and Metaphysics. For the next ten years he worked on his magnum opus, *Critique of Pure Reason* (1781). In 1783 he wrote a shorter *Prolegomena to Any Future Metaphysic* "for the benefit of teachers," and in 1785 he wrote his first major work in ethics, *Foundation for the Metaphysic of Morals*. A successor to that work, *Critique of Practical Reason*, appeared in 1788, and in 1793 he published his theory of rational religion, *Religion within the Limits of Reason Alone*.

Kant was an outstanding lecturer and excellent conversationalist who was known for his generosity and friendliness. He lived a quiet, duty-bound, methodical life, so regular that citizens were said to have set their clocks by his walks. He would leave his home at precisely 4:30 in the afternoon and walk up and down the street on which he lived exactly eight times.

In his own lifetime Kant was recognized as one of the premier philosophers in the Western tradition. Although he made major contributions to virtually every philosophical topic, he is best known for his deontological theory of ethics, which is centered in the idea of the categorical imperative.

Kant's Ethical Theory

In Kant's classic work *Foundation for the Metaphysic of Morals*, written in1785, he outlines his ethical system. Kant is concerned to reject those ethical theories, such as the Theory of Moral Sentiments set forth by the Scottish moralists Francis Hutcheson (1694), Adam Smith (1723–1790), and David Hume (1711–1776), in which morality is contingent and hypothetical. The Moral Sentiment view is contingent in that it is based on human nature and, in particular, on our feelings or sentiments. Had we been created differently, we would have a different nature and, hence, different moral duties. Morality, on this view, consists of hypothetical imperatives in that they depend on our desires for their realization. For example, we should obey the law because we want a peaceful, orderly society. We should seek peace because it is necessary for personal happiness. The naturalistic ethicists were typically utilitarians who sought to maximize human happiness.

Kant rejects this naturalistic, utilitarian account of ethics. Ethics is not *contingent* but *absolute*, and its duties or imperatives are not *hypothetical* but *categorical* (nonconditional). Ethics is based not on feeling but on reason. It is because we are rational beings that we are valuable and capable of discovering moral laws binding on all persons at all times. As such, our moral duties are dependent not on feelings but on reason. They are unconditional, universally valid, and necessary, regardless of the possible consequences or opposition to our inclinations.

Kant's first formulation of his *categorical imperative* is "Act only on that maxim whereby thou canst at the same time will that it would become a universal law." This imperative is given as the criterion (or second-order principle) by which to judge all other principles. If we could consistently will that everyone would do some type of action, then there is an application of the categorical imperative enjoining that type of action. If we cannot consistently will that everyone would do some type of action, then that type of action is morally wrong. Kant argues, for example, that we cannot consistently will that everyone make lying promises, for the very institution of promising entails or depends on general adherence to keeping the promise or an intention to do so.

Kant sets forth a retributive theory of desert in terms of rewards and punishments. "Just so reward follows a good deed not in order to encourage to further good deeds, but because of the deed itself. . . . The ground for doing a good action should not lie in the reward but the action should be rewarded because it is good."[1] Human actions derive worth, not from their benefits, but from their fulfilment of the moral law. We ought to do our duty without regard to reward, but those who act from such respect for duty, are worthy of esteem. "The less inner worth a man has, the less esteem does he deserve."[2] The more inner worth a man has, the more esteem he deserves. But one who merely does one's duty is simply neutral regarding merit. He has no merit nor demerit. He should be neither praised nor blamed. Merit is the fulfilment of duty beyond what can be required by the law. Demerit is the failure to do even one's minimal duty. Only those who are moral heroes merit reward. But merit may also refer to the quality of one's will in overcoming one's weak character, temptation, or obstacles to doing one's duty. The greater the obstacles one must overcome to do one's duty, the more meritorious one's actions.

We begin with the classic section from Kant's *Foundation for the Metaphysic of Morals* on the good will as the only absolutely good thing, where he sets forth an argument for the thesis that commitment to moral duty alone deserves the rewards of happiness. After two short selections from *Introduction to the Metaphysics of Morals* on the relationship of morality to happiness, we turn to a selection from *Critique of Pure Reason*, where Kant elaborates on the nature of being deserving of happiness. Finally, we read the classic passage on retributivism from *The Science of Right*.

On the Good Will

Nothing can possibly be conceived in the world, or even out of it, which can be called good, without qualification, except a good will. Intelligence, wit, judgement, and the other talents of the mind, however they may be named, or courage, resolution, perseverance, as qualities of temperament, are undoubtedly good and desirable in many respects; but these gifts of nature may also become extremely bad and mischievous if the

Reprinted from *Foundations for the Metaphysic of Morals*, trans. T. K. Abbott will which is to make use of them, and which, therefore, constitutes what is called character, is not good. It is the same with the gifts of fortune. Power, riches, honour, even health, and the general well-being and contentment with one's condition which is called happiness, inspire pride, and often presumption, if there is not a good will to correct the influence of these on the mind, and with this also to rectify the whole principle of acting and adapt it to its end. The sight of a being who is not adorned with a single feature of a pure and good will, enjoying unbroken prosperity, can never give pleasure to an impartial rational spectator. Thus a good will appears to constitute the indispensable condition even of being worthy of happiness.

There are even some qualities which are of service to this good will itself and may facilitate its action, yet which have no intrinsic unconditional value, but always presuppose a good will, and this qualifies the esteem that we justly have for them and does not permit us to regard them as absolutely good. Moderation in the affections and passions, self-control, and calm deliberation are not only good in many respects, but even seem to constitute part of the intrinsic worth of the person; but they are far from deserving to be called good without qualification, although they have been so unconditionally praised by the ancients. For without the principles of a good will, they may become extremely bad, and the coolness of a villain not only makes him far more dangerous, but also directly makes him more abominable in our eyes than he would have been without it.

A good will is good not because of what it performs or effects, not by its aptness for the attainment of some proposed end, but simply by virtue of the volition; that is, it is good in itself, and considered by itself is to be esteemed much higher than all that can be brought about by it in favor of any inclination, nay even of the sum total of all inclinations. Even if it should happen that, owing to special disfavor of fortune, or the stingy provision of a step-motherly nature, this will should wholly lack power to accomplish its purpose, if with its greatest efforts it should

yet achieve nothing, and there should remain only the good will (not, to be sure, a mere wish, but the summoning of all means in our power), then, like a jewel, it would still shine by its own light, as a thing which has its whole value in itself. Its usefulness or fruitfulness can neither add nor take away anything from this value. It would be, as it were, only the setting to enable us to handle it the more conveniently in common commerce, or to attract to it the attention of those who are not yet connoisseurs, but not to recommend it to true connoisseurs, or to determine its value.

There is, however, something so strange in this idea of the absolute value of the mere will, in which no account is taken of its utility, that notwithstanding the thorough assent of even common reason to the idea, yet a suspicion must arise that it may perhaps really be the product of mere high-flown fancy, and that we may have misunderstood the purpose of nature in assigning reason as the governor of our will. Therefore we will examine this idea from this point of view.

In the physical constitution of an organized being, that is, a being adapted suitably to the purposes of life, we assume it as a fundamental principle that no organ for any purpose will be found but what is also the fittest and best adapted for that purpose. Now in a being which has reason and a will, if the proper object of nature were its conservation, its welfare, in a word, its happiness, then nature would have hit upon a very bad arrangement in selecting the reason of the creature to carry out this purpose. For all the actions which the creature has to perform with a view to this purpose, and the whole rule of its conduct, would be far more surely prescribed to it by instinct, and that end would have been attained thereby much more certainly than it ever can be by reason. Should reason have been communicated to this favored creature over and above, it must only have served it to contemplate the happy constitution of its nature, to admire it, to congratulate itself thereon, and to feel thankful for it to the beneficent cause, but not that it should subject its desires to that weak and delusive guidance and meddle bunglingly with the purpose of nature. In a word, nature would have taken care that reason should not break forth into practical exercise, nor have the presumption, with its weak insight, to think out for itself the plan of happiness, and of the means of attaining it. Nature would not only have taken on herself the choice of the ends, but also of the means, and with wise foresight would have entrusted both to instinct.

And, in fact, we find that the more a cultivated reason applies itself with deliberate purpose to the enjoyment of life and happiness, so much the more does the man fail of true satisfaction. And from this circumstance there arises in many, if they are candid enough to confess it, a certain degree of misology, that is, hatred of reason, especially in the case of those who are most experienced in the use of it, because after calculating all the advantages they derive, I do not say from the invention of all the arts of common luxury, but even from the sciences (which seem to them to be after all only a luxury of the understanding), they find that they have, in fact, only brought more trouble on their shoulders, rather than gained in happiness; and they end by envying, rather than despising, the more common stamp of men who keep closer to the guidance of mere instinct and do not allow their reason much influence on their conduct. And this we must admit, that the judgement of those who would very much lower the lofty eulogies of the advantages which reason gives us in regard to the happiness and satisfaction of life, or who would even reduce them below zero, is by no means morose or ungrateful to the goodness with which the world is governed, but that there lies at the root of these judgements the idea that our existence has a different and far nobler end, for which, and not for happiness, reason is properly intended, and which must, therefore, be regarded as the supreme condition to which the private ends of man must, for the most part, be postponed.

For as reason is not competent to guide the will with certainty in regard to its objects and the satisfaction of all our wants (which it to some extent even multiplies), this being an end to which an implanted instinct would have

led with much greater certainty; and since, nevertheless, reason is imparted to us as a practical faculty, i.e., as one which is to have influence on the will, therefore, admitting that nature generally in the distribution of her capacities has adapted the means to the end, its true destination must be to produce a will, not merely good as a means to something else, but good in itself, for which reason was absolutely necessary.

This will then, though not indeed the sole and complete good, must be the supreme good and the condition of every other, even of the desire of happiness. Under these circumstances, there is nothing inconsistent with the wisdom of nature in the fact that the cultivation of the reason, which is requisite for the first and unconditional purpose [moral duty], does in many ways interfere, at least in this life, with the attainment of the second, which is always conditional, namely, happiness. Nay, it may even reduce it to nothing, without nature thereby failing of her purpose. For reason recognizes the establishment of a good will as its highest practical destination, and in attaining this purpose is capable only of a satisfaction of its own proper kind, namely that from the attainment of an end, which end again is determined by reason only, notwithstanding that this may involve many a disappointment to the ends of inclination.

We have then to develop the notion of a will which deserves to be highly esteemed for itself and is good without a view to anything further, a notion which exists already in the sound natural understanding, requiring rather to be cleared up than to be taught, and which in estimating the value of our actions always takes the first place and constitutes the condition of all the rest. In order to do this, we will take the notion of duty, which includes that of a good will, although implying certain subjective restrictions and hindrances. These, however, far from concealing it, or rendering it unrecognizable, rather bring it out by contrast and make it shine forth so much the brighter.

I omit here all actions which are already recognized as inconsistent with duty, although they may be useful for this or that purpose, for with these the question whether they are done from duty cannot arise at all, since they even conflict with it. I also set aside those actions which really conform to duty, but to which men have no direct inclination, performing them because they are impelled thereto by some other inclination. For in this case we can readily distinguish whether the action which agrees with duty is done from duty, or from a selfish view. It is much harder to make this distinction when the action accords with duty and the subject has besides a direct inclination to it. For example, it is always a matter of duty that a dealer should not over charge an inexperienced purchaser; and wherever there is much commerce the prudent tradesman does not overcharge, but keeps a fixed price for everyone, so that a child buys of him as well as any other. Men are thus honestly served; but this is not enough to make us believe that the tradesman has so acted from duty and from principles of honesty: his own advantage required it; it is out of the question in this case to suppose that he might besides have a direct inclination in favor of the buyers, so that, as it were, from love he should give no advantage to one over another. Accordingly the action was done neither from duty nor from direct inclination, but merely with a selfish view.

On the other hand, it is a duty to maintain one's life; and, in addition, everyone has also a direct inclination to do so. But on this account the often anxious care which most men take for it has no intrinsic worth, and their maxim has no moral import. They preserve their life as duty requires, no doubt, but not because duty requires. On the other hand, if adversity and hopeless sorrow have completely taken away the relish for life; if the unfortunate one, strong in mind, indignant at his fate rather than desponding or dejected, wishes for death, and yet preserves his life without loving it—not from inclination or fear, but from duty—then his maxim has a moral worth. . . .

To duty every other motive must give place, because duty is the condition of a will good in itself, whose worth transcends everything.

➤ We noted Kant's first formulation of the categorical imperative in the Introduction to this section. He offers a second formulation: "So act as to treat humanity, whether in your own person or in that of any other, in every case as an end and never as merely a means only." Each person by virtue of his or her reason has dignity and profound worth, which entails that he or she must never be exploited or manipulated or merely used as a means to our idea of what is for the general good. However, according to Kant, although rational beings have this intrinsic worth, this dignity beyond price, this worth and dignity can be diminished, even obliterated, by immoral action. He writes:

Lying is the throwing away and, as it were, the obliteration of one's dignity as a human being. A man who does not himself believe what he says to another (even if it be only a person existing in idea) has even less worth than if he were a mere thing; for because of the things's property of being useful, the other person can make some use of it, since it is a thing real and given. But to communicate one's thoughts to someone by words which (intentionally) contain the opposite of what one thinks is an end directly contrary to the natural purposiveness of his capacity to communicate his thoughts. In so doing, he renounces his personality and, as a liar, manifests himself as a mere deceptive appearance of a man, not as a true man. Veracity in one's statements is called honesty, and when these statements are at the same time promises, sincerity . . . Lying. . . . , as intentional untruth in general, does not need to be harmful to others in order to be declared blameworthy, for then it would be a violation of the rights of others. Its cause may be mere levity or even good nature; indeed, even a really good end may be intended by lying. Yet to lie even for these reasons is through its mere form a crime of man against his own person and a baseness which must make a man contemptible in his own eyes. (Kant, *Introduction to the Metaphysic of Morals* [1785], trans. W. Hastie [Edinburgh, 1887]).

Kant's theory seems to be the following. Human beings, qua rational beings, have intrinsic worth, **merit** (German, *verdienst*; Latin, *meritarum*), so they should never be treated as means only and not as ends in themselves. But they can obliterate that worth by immoral acts, thus undermining their essential dignity. When they act immorally, they deserve to be punished, deserve to be unhappy. Here is another passage to consider:

When any one does, in conformity with duty, more than he can be compelled to do by the law, it is said to be **meritorious** (meritum). What is done only in exact conformity with the law, is what is due. And when less is done than can be demanded to be done by the law, the result is moral demerit (demeritum) or culpability.

The juridical effect or consequence of a culpable act of demerit is punishment; that of a meritorious act is reward, assuming that this reward was promised in the law and that it formed the motive of the action. The coincidence or exact conformity of conduct to what is due has no juridical effect.

Benevolent remuneration has no place in juridical relations. The good or bad consequences arising from the performance of an obligated action—as also the consequences arising from failing to perform a meritorious action—cannot be imputed to the agent. The good consequences of a meritorious action—as also the bad consequences of a wrongful action—may be imputed to the agent.

The degree of the imputability of actions is to be reckoned according to the magnitude of the hindrances or obstacles which it has been necessary for them to overcome. The greater the natural hindrances in the sphere of sense, and the less the moral hindrance of duty, so much the more is a good deed imputed as meritorious. This may be seen by considering such examples as rescuing a man who is an entire stranger from great distress, and at very considerable sacrifice.

Conversely, the less the natural hindrance, and the greater the hindrance on the ground of duty, so much the more is a transgression imputable as culpable.

Hence the state of mind of the agent or doer of a deed makes a difference in imputing its consequences, according as he did it in passion or performed it with coolness and deliberation. (ibid)]

Of the Ideal of the Summum Bonum as a Determining Ground of the Ultimate End of Pure Reason

Reason conducted us, in its speculative use, through the field of experience and, as it can never find complete satisfaction in that sphere, from thence to speculative ideas—which, however, in the end brought us back again to experience, and thus fulfilled the purpose of reason, in a manner which, though useful, was not at all in accordance with our expectations. It now remains for us to consider whether pure reason can be employed in a practical sphere, and whether it will here conduct us to those ideas which attain the highest ends of pure reason, as we have just stated them. We shall thus ascertain whether, from the point of view of its practical interest, reason may not be able to supply us with that which, on the speculative side, it wholly denies us.

The whole interest of reason, speculative as well as practical, is centered in the three following questions:

1. WHAT CAN I KNOW?
2. WHAT OUGHT I TO DO?
3. WHAT MAY I HOPE?

The first question is purely speculative. We have, as I flatter myself, exhausted all the replies of which it is susceptible, and have at last found the reply with which reason must content itself, and with which it ought to be content, so long as it pays no regard to the practical. But from the two great ends to the attainment of which all these efforts of pure reason were in fact directed, we remain just as far removed as if we had consulted our

---

Reprinted from the *Critique of Pure Reason*, trans. J. M. D. Meiklejohn (New York: Colonial Press, 1900).

ease and declined the task at the outset. So far, then, as knowledge is concerned, thus much, at least, is established, that, in regard to those two problems, it lies beyond our reach.

The second question is purely practical. As such it may indeed fall within the province of pure reason, but still it is not transcendental, but moral, and consequently cannot in itself form the subject of our criticism.

The third question: If I act as I ought to do, what may I then hope?—is at once practical and theoretical. The practical forms a clue to the answer of the theoretical, and—in its highest form—speculative question. For all hoping has happiness for its object and stands in precisely the same relation to the practical and the law of morality as knowing to the theoretical cognition of things and the law of nature. The former arrives finally at the conclusion that something is (which determines the ultimate end), because something ought to take place; the latter, that something is (which operates as the highest cause), because something does take place.

Happiness is the satisfaction of all our desires: *extensively*, in regard to their multiplicity; *intensively*, in regard to their degree; and *protensively*, in regard to their duration. The practical law based on the motive of *happiness* I term a pragmatical law (or prudential rule); but that law, assuming such to exist, which has no other motive than the *worthiness of being happy*, I term a moral or ethical law. The first tells us what we have to do, if we wish to become possessed of happiness; the second dictates how we ought to act, in order to deserve happiness. The first is based upon empirical principles; for it is only by experience that I can learn either what inclinations exist which desire satisfaction, or what are the natural means of satisfying them. The second takes no account of our desires or the means of satisfying them, and regards only the freedom of a rational being, and the necessary conditions under which alone this freedom can harmonize with the distribution of happiness according to principles. This second law may therefore rest upon mere ideas of pure reason, and may be cognized a priori.

I assume that there are pure moral laws which determine, entirely a priori (without regard to empirical motives, that is, to happiness), the conduct of a rational being, or in other words, to use which it makes of its freedom, and that these laws are absolutely imperative (not merely hypothetically, on the supposition of other empirical ends), and therefore in all respects necessary. I am warranted in assuming this, not only by the arguments of the most enlightened moralists, but by the moral judgement of every man who will make the attempt to form a distinct conception of such a law.

Pure reason, then, contains, not indeed in its speculative, but in its practical, or, more strictly, its moral use, principles of the possibility of experience, of such actions, namely, as, in accordance with ethical precepts, might be met with in the history of man. For since reason commands that such actions should take place, it must be possible for them to take place; and hence a particular kind of systematic unity—the moral—must be possible. We have found, it is true, that the systematic unity of nature could not be established according to speculative principles of reason, because, while reason possesses a causal power in relation to freedom, it has none in relation to the whole sphere of nature; and, while moral principles of reason can produce free actions, they cannot produce natural laws. It is, then, in its practical, but especially in its moral use, that the principles of pure reason possess objective reality.

I call the world a *moral world*, in so far as it may be in accordance with all the ethical laws—which, by virtue of the freedom of reasonable beings, it can be, and according to the necessary laws of morality it ought to be. But this world must be conceived only as an intelligible world, inasmuch as abstraction is therein made of all conditions (ends), and even of all impediments to morality (the weakness or depravity of human nature). So far, then, it is a mere idea—though still a practical idea—which may have, and ought to have, an influence on the world of sense, so as to bring it as far as possible into conformity with itself. The idea of a moral world has, therefore, objective reality, not as referring to an object of intelligible intuition—for of such an object we can form no conception whatever—but to the world of sense—conceived, however, as an object of pure reason in its practical use—and to a corpus mysticum of rational beings in it, in so far as the free will of the individual is placed, under and by virtue of moral laws, in complete systematic unity both with itself and with the freedom of all others.

That is the answer to the first of the two questions of pure reason which relate to its practical interest: *Do that which will render you unworthy of happiness*. The second question is this: If I conduct myself so as not to be unworthy of happiness, may I hope thereby to obtain happiness? In order to arrive at the solution of this question, we must inquire whether the principles of pure reason, which prescribe a priori the law, necessarily also connect this hope with it.

I say, then, that just as the moral principles are necessary according to reason in its practical use, so it is equally necessary according to reason in its theoretical use to assume that every one has ground to hope for happiness in the measure in which he has made himself worthy of it in his conduct, and that therefore the system of morality is inseparably (though only in the idea of pure reason) connected with that of happiness.

Now in an intelligible, that is, in the moral world, in the conception of which we make abstraction of all the impediments to morality (sensuous desires), such a system of happiness, connected with and proportioned to morality, may be conceived as necessary, because freedom of volition—partly incited and partly restrained by moral laws—would be itself the cause of general happiness; and thus rational beings, under the guidance of such principles, would be themselves the authors both of their own enduring welfare and that of others. But such a system of self-rewarding morality is only an idea, the carrying out of which depends upon the condition that every one acts as he ought; in other words, that all actions of reasonable beings be such as they would be if they sprung from a

Supreme Will, comprehending in, or under, itself all particular wills. But since the moral law is binding on each individual in the use of his freedom of volition, even if others should not act in conformity with this law, neither the nature of things, nor the causality of actions and their relation to morality, determine how the consequences of these actions will be related to happiness; and the necessary connection of the hope of happiness with the unceasing endeavor to become worthy of happiness, cannot be cognized by reason, if we take nature alone for our guide.

This connection can be hoped for only on the assumption that the cause of nature is a supreme reason, which governs according to moral laws. I term the idea of an intelligence in which the morally most perfect will, united with supreme blessedness, is the cause of all happiness in the world, so far as happiness stands in strict relation to morality (as the worthiness of being happy), the *Ideal of the Supreme Good*. It is only in the ideal of the supreme original good, that pure reason can find the ground of the practically necessary connection of both elements of the highest derivative good, and accordingly of an intelligible, that is, moral world. Now since we are necessitated by reason to conceive ourselves as belonging to such a world, while the senses present to us nothing but a world of phenomena, we must assume the former as a consequence of our conduct in the world of sense (since the world of sense gives us no hint of it), and therefore as future in relation to us. Thus God and a future life are two hypotheses which, according to the principles of pure reason, are inseparable from the obligation which this reason imposes upon us.

Morality per se constitutes a system. But we can form no system of happiness, except in so far as it is dispensed in strict proportion to morality. But this is only possible in the intelligible world, under a wise author and ruler. Such a ruler, together with life in such a world, which we must look upon as future, reason finds itself compelled to assume; or it must regard the moral laws as idle dreams, since the necessary consequence which this same reason connects with them must, without this hypothesis, fall to the ground. Hence also the moral laws are universally regarded as commands, which they could not be did they not connect a priori adequate consequences with their dictates, and thus carry with them promises and threats. But this, again, they could not do, did they not reside in a necessary being, as the Supreme Good, which alone can render such a teleological unity possible.

Leibniz termed the world, when viewed in relation to the rational beings which it contains, and the moral relations in which they stand to each other, under the government of the Supreme Good, the *kingdom of Grace*, and distinguished it from the *kingdom of Nature*, in which these rational beings live, under moral laws, indeed, but expect no other consequences from their actions than such as follow according to the course of nature in the world of sense. To view ourselves, therefore, as in the kingdom of grace, in which all happiness awaits us, except in so far as we ourselves limit our participation in it by actions which render us unworthy of happiness, is a practically necessary idea of reason.

Practical laws, in so far as they are subjective grounds of actions, that is, subjective principles, are termed maxims. The judgements of morality according to in its purity and ultimate results are framed according to ideas; the observance of its laws, according to maxims. The whole course of our life must be subject to moral maxims; but this is impossible, unless with the moral law, which is a mere idea, reason connects an efficient cause which ordains to all conduct which is in conformity with the moral law an issue either in this or in another life, which is in exact conformity with our highest aims. Thus, without a God and without a world, invisible to us now, but hoped for, the glorious ideas of morality are, indeed, objects of approbation and of admiration, but cannot be the springs of purpose and action. For they do not satisfy all the aims which are natural to every rational being, and which are determined a priori by pure reason itself, and necessary.

Happiness alone is, in the view of reason, far from being the complete good. Reason does not approve of it (however much inclination may desire it), except as united with desert. On the other hand, morality alone, and with it, mere desert, is likewise far from being the complete good. To make it complete, he who conducts himself in a manner not unworthy of happiness, must be able to hope for the possession of happiness. . . .

Happiness, therefore, in exact proportion with the morality of rational beings (whereby they are made worthy of happiness), constitutes alone the supreme good of a world into which we absolutely must transport ourselves according to the commands of pure but practical reason. This world is, it is true, only an intelligible world; for of such a systematic unity of ends as it requires, the world of sense gives us no hint. Its reality can be based on nothing else but the hypothesis of a supreme original good. In it independent reason, equipped with all the sufficiency of a supreme cause, founds, maintains, and fulfils the universal order of things, with the most perfect teleological harmony, however much this order may be hidden from us in the world of sense.

➤ Next we see how Kant's theory applies to the concept of punishment.

The Right to Punish

The right to punish is the right that the sovereign has the supreme power to inflict pain on a subject on account of his having committed a crime. It follows that the sovereign of the state cannot himself be punished; we can only remove ourselves from his jurisdiction. A transgression of the public law which makes him who commits it unfit to be a citizen constitutes a crime, either simply as a private crime, or as a public crime. Private crimes are brought before a civil court; public crimes before a criminal court. Embezzle-

Reprinted from Kant, *The Science of Right* (1790), trans. W. Hastie (Edinburgh, 1893).

ment or misappropriation of money or goods entrusted in trade, and fraud in buying and selling, if done before the eyes of the party who suffers, are private crimes. On the other hand, counterfeiting money or forging bills of exchange, theft, robbery, and similar acts, are public crimes, because through them the commonwealth and not just a single individual is thereby endangered. These crimes may be divided into those of base character and those of a violent character.

Judicial punishment is to be distinguished from natural punishment. In natural punishment, vice punishes itself, and does not come before the legislator. Judicial punishment can never be used merely as a means for promoting some other good either for the criminal himself or for civil society, but instead must in all cases be imposed on him only on the grounds that he has committed a crime. For one man ought never be used as a means subservient to the purposes of someone else, nor be mixed up with the subjects real right. His innate personality [i.e., his right as a person] protects him against such manipulation, even though he may indeed be condemned to lose his civil personality. He must first be found to be deserving of punishment before any consideration is given to the utility of this punishment for himself or for his fellow citizens. The penal law is a categorical imperative, and woe to him who creeps through the serpent-windings of utilitarianism to discover some advantage to be gained by releasing the criminal from punishment or by reducing the amount of it—in keeping with the Pharisaic maxim: "It is better that one man should die than that the whole people should perish." For if justice and righteousness perish, human life would no longer have any value in the world. If this is so, what should one think of the proposal to permit a criminal who has been condemned to death to remain alive, if, after consenting to allow dangerous experiments to be performed on him, he would be allowed to survive if he came through them? It is argued that physicians might thereby obtain new information that benefits the community. Any court of justice would repudiate such a proposal with scorn if it were made by

a medical college, for justice ceases to be justice if it can be bartered away for any consideration, no matter how noble.

What kind and degree of punishment does public justice adopt as its principle and standard? None other than the principle of equality which is exemplified by the pointer on the scales of justice, which is made to incline no more to one side than the other. Accordingly, any undeserved evil that you inflict on someone else among the people is one that you do to yourself. If you vilify him, you vilify yourself; if you steal from him, you steal from yourself; if you kill him, you kill yourself. Only the Law of retribution (*jus talionis*) can determine precisely the kind and degree of punishment; it must be well understood, however, that this judgment must be made in the court of justice and not in one's private judgment. All other standards are wavering and unreliable, and, because extraneous considerations are mixed with them, they cannot be compatible with the principle of pure and strict legal justice.

It may appear, however, that the difference in social status would not allow for the retributive principle of rendering like for like. However, even though these class distinctions may not make it possible to apply this principle to the letter, it can still always remain applicable in its effects if regard is had to the special sensibilities of the higher classes. Thus, for example, the imposition of a fine for slander may have no direct proportion to the injustice of the original injury, for someone who is wealthy can easily afford to make insults whenever he wishes. Yet the attack committed on the aggrieved party may have its equivalent in pain inflicted upon the pride of the aggressor, especially if he is condemned by the judgment of the Law, and might be required not only to make a public apology to the offended person, but also at the same time to kiss his hand, even though he be socially inferior. Similarly, if a man of a higher class has violently attacked an innocent citizen who is socially inferior to him, he may be condemned, not only to apologize, but to undergo solitary and painful confinement, because by this means, in addition to the discomfort suffered, the pride of the offender will be painfully affected, and thus humiliation will compensate for the offenses as like for like.

But how then should we understand the statement: "If you steal from another, you steal from yourself"? In this way, that whoever steals anything makes the property of all insecure. He therefore robs himself (in accordance with the Law of retribution) of the security of any possible ownership. He has nothing and can also acquire nothing, but he still wants to live, and this is not possible unless others support and sustain him. But, because the state will not support him gratis, he must let the state have his labor at any kind of work it may wish to use him for convict labor, and so he becomes a slave, either for a certain period of time or indefinitely, as the case may be.

If, however, he has committed a murder, he must die. In this case, there is no substitute that will satisfy the requirements of legal justice. There is no sameness of kind between death and remaining alive even under the most miserable conditions, and consequently there is also no equality between the crime and the retribution unless the criminal is judicially condemned and put to death. But the death of the criminal must be kept entirely free of any maltreatment that would make an abomination of the humanity residing in the person suffering it.

Even if a civil society resolved to dissolve itself by common agreement of all its members—which might be supposed in the case of a people inhabiting an island resolving to separate and scatter themselves throughout the world—the last murderer remaining in prison must first be executed, so that everyone will duly receive what his actions are worth and so that bloodguiltiness will not remain upon the people; for otherwise they might all be regarded as participators in the murder as a public violation of justice.

The equalization of punishment with crime is therefore only possible by cognition of the judge extending even to the penalty of death, according to the right of retribution. . . .

Anyone who is a murderer—i.e., has committed a murder, commanded one, or taken part in one—must suffer death. That is what justice as the Idea of the judicial authority wills in accordance with universal laws that are grounded a priori.

NOTES

1. Kant, *Lectures on Ethics*, trans. Lewis Infield (London: Methuen, 1930), p. 56.
2. Ibid., p. 49.

6. Justice, Desert and Utility

JOHN STUART MILL

John Stuart Mill (1806–1873), one of the most important British philosophers of the nineteenth century, was born in London and educated by his father, James Mill, a first-rate philosopher in his own right, learning Greek at the age of three and Latin at the age of eight. By the time he was fourteen, he had received a thorough classic education at home. He began work as a clerk for the East India Company at the age of seventeen and eventually became a director of the company. Influenced by the work of Jeremy Bentham (1748–1832), Mill embraced utilitarianism and ardently worked for social reform. When he was twenty-five, Mill became close friends with Harriet Taylor, a married woman, which relationship, though reportedly Platonic, caused a scandal. After her husband died, they were married in 1851. She exercised an enormous influence on his philosophical work, especially on his social political thought, which Mill acknowledged as a joint venture.

Mill was a prolific writer. His *System of Logic* (1848) is one of the most original works on inductive logic ever written. His *On Liberty* (1859) is recognized as a classic work in political philosophy, and his *Utilitarianism* (1861), from which the present selection is taken, is recognized as the classic work in nineteenth-century utilitarianism.

The problem Mill addresses in this selection is that of the relationship between justice and utility. No greater objection to utilitarianism has ever been launched than the criticism that it violates the principle of justice. Mill argues that, far from being opposed to justice, justice is really a handmaiden of utility. He characterizes justice as the moral principle that commands us to give to everyone his or her due, what a person deserves: "we should treat all equally well . . . who have deserved equally well of us, and . . . society should treat all equally well who have deserved equally well of it. . . . This is the highest abstract standard of social and distributive justice." But, Mill argues, this principle itself rests on a deeper principle, that of Utility, from which justice as desert is derived.

IN ALL ages of speculation, one of the strongest obstacles to the reception of the doctrine that Utility or Happiness is the criterion of right and wrong, has been drawn from the idea of justice. The powerful sentiment, and apparently clear perception, which that word recalls with a rapidity and certainty resembling an instinct, have seemed to the majority of thinkers to point to an inherent quality in things; to show that the just must have an existence in Nature as something absolute, generically distinct form every variety of the Expedient, and, in idea, opposed to it, though (as is commonly acknowledged) never, in the long run, disjoined from it in fact.

To throw light upon this question, it is necessary to attempt to ascertain what is the distinguishing character of justice, or of injus-

Reprinted from *Utilitarianism*, published in 1863.

tice: what is the quality, or whether there is any quality, attributed in common to all modes of conduct designated as unjust (for justice, like many other moral attributes, is best defined by its opposite), and distinguishing them from such modes of conduct as are disapproved, but without having that particular epithet of disapprobation applied to them. If in everything which men are accustomed to characterize as just or unjust, some one common attribute or collection of attributes is always present, we may judge whether this particular attribute or combination of attributes would be capable of gathering round it a sentiment of that peculiar character and intensity by virtue of the general laws of our emotional constitution, or whether the sentiment is inexplicable, and requires to be regarded as a special provision of Nature. . . .

To find the common attributes of a variety of objects, it is necessary to begin by surveying the objects themselves in the concrete. Let us therefore advert successively to the various modes of action, and arrangements of human affairs, which are classed, by universal or widely spread opinion, as Just or as Unjust. The things well known to excite the sentiments associated with those names are of a very multifarious character. I shall pass them rapidly in review, without studying any particular arrangement.

In the first place, it is mostly considered unjust to deprive any one of his personal liberty, his property, or any other thing which belongs to him by law. Here, therefore, is one instance of the application of the terms just and unjust in a perfectly definite sense, namely, that it is just to respect, unjust to violate, the legal rights of any one. But this judgment admits of several exceptions, arising from the other forms in which the notions of justice and injustice present themselves. For example, the person who suffers the deprivation may (as the phrase is) have forfeited the rights which he is so deprived of: a case to which we shall return presently.

But also, Secondly; the legal rights of which he is deprived, may be rights which ought not to have belonged to him; in other words, the law which confers on him these rights, may be a bad law. When it is so, or when (which is the same thing for our purpose) it is supposed to be so, opinions will differ as to the justice or injustice of infringing it. Some maintain that no law, however bad, ought to be disobeyed by an individual citizen; that his opposition to it, if shown at all, should only be shown in endeavoring to get it altered by competent authority. This opinion (which condemns many of the most illustrious benefactors of mankind, and would often protect pernicious institutions against the only weapons which, in the state of things existing at the time, have any chance of succeeding against them) is defended, by those who hold it, on grounds of expediency; principally on that of the importance, to the common interest of mankind, of maintaining inviolate the sentiment of submission to law. Other persons, again, hold the directly contrary opinion, that any law, judged to be bad, may blamelessly be disobeyed, even though it be not judged to be unjust, but only inexpedient; while others would confine the licence of disobedience to the case of unjust laws: but again, some say, that all laws which are inexpedient are unjust; since every law imposes some restriction on the natural liberty of mankind, which restriction is an injustice, unless legitimated by tending to their good. Among these diversities of opinion, it seems to be universally admitted that there may be unjust laws, and that law, consequently, is not the ultimate criterion of justice, but may give to one person a benefit, or impose on another an evil, which justice condemns. When, however, a law is thought to be unjust, it seems always to be regarded as being so in the same way in which a breach of law is unjust, namely, by infringing somebody's right; which, as it cannot in this case be a legal right, receives a different appellation, and is called a moral right. We may say, therefore, that a second case of injustice consists in taking or withholding from any person that to which he has a moral right.

Thirdly, it is universally considered just that each person should obtain that (whether good or evil) which he deserves; and unjust that he should obtain a good, or be made to undergo an evil, which he does not deserve. This is, perhaps, the clearest and most emphatic form in which the idea of justice is conceived by the general mind. As it involves the notion of desert, the question arises, what constitutes desert? Speaking in a general way, a person is understood to deserve good if he does right, evil if he does wrong; and in a more particular sense, to deserve good from those to whom he does or has done good, and evil from those to whom he does or has done evil. The precept of returning good for evil has never been regarded as a case of the fulfilment of justice, but as one in which the claims of justice are waived, in obedience to other considerations. . . .

➤ Mill discusses the etymological origins of the notion of justice and argues that it can be properly seen as a part of utility. He develops this last point in what follows.

Is, then, the difference between the Just and the Expedient a merely imaginary distinction? Have mankind been under a delusion in thinking that justice is a more sacred thing than policy, and that the latter ought only to be listened to after the former has been satisfied? By no means. The exposition we have given of the nature and origin of the sentiment, recognizes a real distinction; and no one of those who profess the most sublime contempt for the consequences of actions as an element in their morality, attaches more importance to the distinction than I do.

While I dispute the pretensions of any theory which sets up an imaginary standard of justice not grounded on utility, I account the justice which is grounded on utility to be the chief part, and incomparably the most sacred and binding part, of all morality. Justice is a name for certain classes of moral rules, which concern the essentials of human well-being more nearly, and are therefore of more absolute obligation, than any other rules for the guidance of life; and the notion which we have found to be of the essence of the idea of justice, that of a right residing in an individual implies and testifies to this more binding obligation.

The moral rules which forbid mankind to hurt one another (in which we must never forget to include wrongful interference with each other's freedom) are more vital to human well-being than any maxims, however important, which only point out the best mode of managing some department of human affairs. They have also the peculiarity, that they are the main element in determining the whole of the social feelings of mankind. It is their observance which alone preserves peace among human beings: if obedience to them were not the rule, and disobedience the exception, every one would see in every one else an enemy, against whom he must be perpetually guarding himself. What is hardly less important, these are the precepts which mankind have the strongest and the most direct inducements for impressing upon one another. By merely giving to each other prudential instruction or exhortation, they may gain, or think they gain, nothing: in inculcating on each other the duty of positive beneficence they have an unmistakable interest, but far less in degree: a person may possibly not need the benefits of others; but he always needs that they should not do him hurt. Thus the moralities which protect every individual from being harmed by others, either directly or by being hindered in his freedom of pursuing his own good, are at once those which he himself has most at heart, and those which he has the strongest interest in publishing and enforcing by word and deed. It is by a person's observance of these that his fitness to exist as one of the fellowship of human beings is tested and decided; for on that depends his being a nuisance or not to those with whom his is in contact.

Now it is these moralities primarily which compose the obligations of justice. The most marked cases of injustice, and those which give the tone to the feeling of repugnance which characterizes the sentiment, are acts of wrongful aggression, or wrongful exercise of power over some one; the next are those which consist in wrongfully withholding from him something which is his due; in both cases, inflicting on him a positive hurt, either in the form of direct suffering, or of the privation of some good which he had reasonable ground, either of a physical or of a social kind, for counting upon.

The same powerful motives which command the observance of these primary moralities, enjoin the punishment of those who violate them; and as the impulses of self-defence, of defence of others, and of vengeance, are all called forth against such persons, retribution, or evil for evil, becomes closely connected with the sentiment of justice, and is universally included in the idea. Good for good is also one of the dictates of justice; and this, though its social utility is evident, and though it carries with it a natural human feeling, has not at first sight that obvious connection with hurt or injury, which, existing in the most elementary cases of just and unjust, is the source of the characteristic intensity of the sentiment. But the connection, though less obvious, is not less real.

He who accepts benefits, and denies a return of them when needed, inflicts a real hurt, by disappointing one of the most natural and reasonable of expectations, and one which he must at least tacitly have encouraged, otherwise the benefits would seldom have been conferred. The important rank, among human evils and wrongs, of the disappointment of expectation, is shown in the fact that it constitutes the principle criminality of two such highly immoral acts as a breach of friendship and a breach of promise. Few hurts which human beings can sustain are greater, and none wound more, than when that on which they habitually and with full assurance relied, fails them in the hour of need; and few wrongs are greater than this mere withholding of good; none excite more resentment, either in the person suffering, or in a sympathising spectator. The principle, therefore, of giving to each what they deserve, that is, good for good as well as evil for evil, is not only included within the idea of justice as we have defined it, but is a proper object of that intensity of sentiment, which places the just, in human estimation, above the simply Expedient.

Most of the maxims of justice current in the world, and commonly appealed to in its transactions, are simply instrumental to carrying into effect the principles of justice which we have now spoken of. That a person is only responsible for what he has done voluntarily, or could voluntarily have avoided; that it is unjust to condemn any person unheard; that the punishment ought to be proportioned to the offence, and the like, are maxims intended to prevent the just principle of evil for evil from being perverted to the infliction of evil without that justification. The greater part of these common maxims have come into use from the practice of courts of justice, which have been naturally led to a more complete recognition and elaboration than was likely to suggest itself to others, of the rules necessary to enable them to fulfil their double function, of inflicting punishment when due, and of awarding to each person his right.

That first of judicial virtues, impartiality, is an obligation of justice, partly for the reason last mentioned; as being a necessary condition of the fulfilment of the other obligations of justice. But this is not the only source of the exalted rank, among human obligations, of those maxims of equality and impartiality, which, both in popular estimation and in that of the most enlightened, are included among the precepts of justice. In one point of view, they may be considered as corollaries from the principles already laid down. If it is a duty to do to each according to his deserts, returning good for good as well as repressing evil by evil, it necessarily follows that we should treat all equally well (when no higher duty forbids) who have deserved equally well of us, and that society should treat all equally well who have deserved equally well of it, that is, who have deserved equally well absolutely. This is the highest abstract standard of social and distributive justice; towards which all institutions, and the efforts of all virtuous citizens, should be made in the utmost possible degree to converge.

But this great moral duty rests upon a still deeper foundation, being a direct emanation from the first principle of morals, and not a mere logical corollary from secondary or derivative doctrines. It is involved in the very meaning of Utility, or the Greatest Happiness Principle. That principle is a mere form of words without rational signification, unless one person's happiness, supposed equal in degree (with the proper allowance made for kind), is counted for exactly as much as another's. Those conditions being supplied, Bentham's dictum, "everybody to count for one, nobody for more than one," might be written under the principle of utility as an explanatory commentary. The equal claim of everybody to happiness in the estimation of the moralist and the legislator, involves an equal claim to all the means of happiness, except in so far as the inevitable conditions of human life, and the general interest, in which that of every individual is included, set limits to the maxim; and those limits ought to be strictly construed. As every other maxim of justice, so this, is by no means applied or held applicable universally; on the contrary, as I have already remarked, it bends to every person's ideas of social expediency. But in whatever case it is deemed applicable at all, it is held to be the dictate of justice. All persons are deemed to have a *right* to equality of treatment, except when some recognized social expediency requires the reverse. And hence all social inequalities which have ceased to be considered expedient, assume the character not of simple inexpediency, but of injustice, and appear so tyrannical, that people are apt to wonder how they ever could have been tolerated; forgetful that they themselves perhaps tolerate other inequalities under an equally mistaken notion; of expediency, the correction of which would make that which they approve seem quite as monstrous as what they have at last learnt to condemn.

The entire history of social improvement has been a series of transitions, by which one custom or institution after another, from being a supposed primary necessity of social existence, has passed into the rank of a universally stigmatized injustice and tyranny. So it has been with the distinctions of slaves and freemen, nobles and serfs, patricians and plebeians; and so it will be, and in part already is, with the aristocracies of color, race, and sex.

It appears from what has been said, that justice is a name for certain moral requirements, which, regarded collectively, stand higher in the scale of social utility, and are therefore of more paramount obligation, than any others; though particular cases may occur in which some other social duty is so important, as to overrule any one of the general maxims of justice. Thus, to save a life, it may not only be allowable, but a duty, to steal, or take by force, the necessary food or medicine, or to kidnap, and compel to officiate, the only qualified medical practitioner. In such cases, as we do not call anything justice which is not a virtue, we usually say, not that justice must give way to some other moral principle, but that what is just in ordinary cases is, by reason of that other principle, not just in the particular case. By this useful accommodation of language, the character of indefeasibility attributed to justice is kept up, and we are saved from the necessity of maintaining that there can be laudable injustice.

The considerations which have now been adduced resolve, I conceive, the only real difficulty in the utilitarian theory of morals. It has always been evident that all cases of justice are also cases of expediency: the difference is in the peculiar sentiment which attaches to the former, as contradistinguished from the latter. If this characteristic sentiment has been sufficiently accounted for; if there is no necessity to assume for it any peculiarity of origin; if it is simply the natural feeling of resentment, moralised by being made coextensive with the demands of social good; and if this feeling not only does but ought to exist in all the classes of cases to which the idea of justice corresponds; that idea no longer presents itself as a stumbling-block to the utilitarian ethics.

Justice remains the appropriate name for certain social utilities which are vastly more important, and therefore more absolute and imperative, than any others are as a class (though not more so than others may be in particular cases); and which, therefore, ought to be, as well as naturally are, guarded by a sentiment not only different in degree, but also in kind; distinguished from the milder feeling which attaches to the mere idea of promoting human pleasure or convenience, at once by the more definite nature of its commands, and by the sterner character of its sanctions.

7. Justice as Desert

HENRY SIDGWICK

Henry Sidgwick (1838–1900), a British moral philosopher, developed a complex and sophisticated account of utilitarianism. He was educated at Cambridge University, where he received an appointment. However, in 1869 he resigned his appointment because of religious doubts. In 1883 he was reinstated as the University's first secular professor of philosophy. His greatest work is *Methods of Ethics*, in which he outlines three methods of ethical thinking: intuitionism, individual hedonism (egoism), and universal hedonism (utilitarianism), which he attempts to reconcile into a comprehensive system.

In the selection before us, Sidgwick analyzes the concept of justice, first examining it as Law. He rejects this as an adequate definition of justice, since some laws are unjust and we apply the concept to situations where no laws exist. Next he examines the claim that "Justice is Equality," a claim he reduces to "impartiality in the observance or enforcement of general rules allotting good and evil to individuals." But this only gives us a formal criterion—bad laws can be impartially enforced (e.g., slavery for unpopular minorities). Next, Sidgwick proposes the idea that justice consists in freedom, in allowing people to do what they want, so long as they don't infringe on the rights of others. But this individualist notion, important though it be, seems too negative and does not give us a firm basis for social construction. What is needed is a deeper ideal. Here he proposes the ideal of *gratitude*, "the natural impulse to requite benefits" (along with its opposite, *resentment*, as the impulse to requite harms), as the primitive foundation upon which a theory of justice as desert may be founded, one balanced by freedom, but, complimenting freedom, as creating obligations between members of society. Nevertheless, Sidgwick avers, this ideal suffers severe problems in institutional application.

We have seen that in delineating the outline of duty, as intuitively recognized, we have to attempt to give to common terms a definite and precise meaning. This process of definition always requires some reflection and care, and is sometimes one of considerable difficulty. But there is no case where the difficulty is greater, or the result more disputed, than when we try to define Justice.

Perhaps the first point that strikes us when we reflect upon our notion of Justice is its connection with Law. There is no doubt that just conduct is to a great extent determined by Law, and in certain applications the two terms seem interchangeable. Thus we speak indifferently of 'Law Courts' and 'Courts of Justice,' and when a private citizen demands Justice, or his just rights, he commonly means to demand that law should be carried into effect. Still, reflection shows that we do not mean by Justice merely conformity to Law. For, first, we do not always call the violators

Reprinted from Henry Sidgwick, *The Methods of Ethics*, 7th ed. (London: Macmillan, 1907).

of law unjust, but only of some Laws: not, for example, duellists or gamblers. And secondly, we often judge that Law as it exists does not completely realize Justice; our notion of Justice furnishes a standard with which we compare actual laws, and pronounce them just or unjust. And, thirdly, there is a part of just conduct which lies outside the sphere of Law as it ought to be; for example we think that a father may be just or unjust to his children in matters where the law leaves (and ought to leave) him free. . . .

➤ Sidgwick next examines the notion that Justice is Equality, which he argues is true but incomplete, for all equality comes to in this regard is impartial treatment, leaving out exactly what must be the content of law or justice. After this, he discusses the idea that justice has to do with avoiding "running counter to natural and normal expectations," which, again, he finds partly valid, but incomplete, for moral progress may require to frustrate some natural expectations. We join him in his discussion of freedom as a definition of justice.

There is, however, one mode of systemizing these Rights and bringing them under one principle, which has been maintained by influential thinkers; and which, though now perhaps somewhat antiquated, is still sufficiently current to deserve careful examination. It has been held that Freedom from interference is really the whole of what human beings, originally and apart from contracts, can be strictly said to *owe* each other: at any rate, that the protection of this Freedom (including enforcement of Free Contract) is the sole proper aim of Law, i.e., of those rules of mutual behavior which are maintained by penalties inflicted under the authority of Government. All natural Rights, on this view, may be summed up in the Right of Freedom; so that the complete and universal establishment of this Right would be the complete realization of Justice,—the Equality at which Justice is thought to aim being interpreted as Equality of Freedom.

Now when I contemplate this as an abstract formula, though I cannot say that it is

self-evident to me as the true fundamental principle of Ideal Law, I admit that it commends itself much to my mind; and I might perhaps persuade myself that it is owing to the defect of my faculty of moral (or jural) intuition that I fail to see its self-evidence. But when I endeavour to bring it into closer relation to the actual circumstances of human society, it soon comes to wear a different aspect.

In the first place, it seems obviously needful to limit the extent of its application. For it involves the negative principle that no one should be coerced for his own good alone; but no one would gravely argue that this ought to be applied to the case of children, or of idiots, or insane persons. But if so, can we know *a priori* that it ought to be applied to all sane adults? since the above-mentioned exceptions are commonly justified on the ground that children, etc., will manifestly be better off if they are forced to do and abstain as others think best for them; and it is, at least, not intuitively certain that the same argument does not apply to the majority of mankind in the present state of their intellectual progress. Indeed, it is often conceded by the advocates of this principle that it does not hold even in respect of adults in a low state of civilisation. But if so, what criterion can be given for its application, except that it must be applied wherever human beings are sufficiently intelligent to provide for themselves better than others would provide for them? and thus the principle would present itself not as absolute, but merely a subordinate application of the wider principle of aiming at the general happiness or well-being of mankind.

But, again, the term Freedom is ambiguous. If we interpret it strictly, as meaning Freedom of Action alone, the principle seems to allow any amount of mutual annoyance except constraint. But obviously no one would be satisfied with such Freedom as this. If, however, we include in the idea absence of pain and annoyance inflicted by others, it becomes at once evident that we cannot prohibit all such annoyances without restraining freedom of action to a degree that would be intolerable; since there is scarcely any gratification of a man's natural impulses which may not cause some annoyance to others. Hence in distinguishing the mutual annoyances that ought to be allowed from those that must be prohibited we seem forced to balance the evils of constraint against pain and loss of a different kind: while if we admit the Utilitarian criterion so far, it is difficult to maintain that annoyance to individuals is never to be permitted in order to attain any positive good result, but only to prevent more serious annoyance.

Thirdly, in order to render a social construction possible on this basis, we must assume that the right to Freedom includes the right to limit one's freedom by contract; and that such contracts, if they are really voluntary and not obtained by fraud or force, and if they do not violate the freedom of others, are to be enforced by legal penalties. But I cannot see that enforcement of Contracts is strictly included in the notion of realising Freedom; for a man seems to be most completely free when no one of his volitions is allowed to have any effect in causing the *external* coercion of any other. If, again, this right of limiting Freedom is itself unlimited, a man might thus freely contract himself out of freedom into slavery, so that the principle of freedom would turn out suicidal; and yet to deduce from this principle a limited right of limiting freedom by contract seems clearly impossible.

But if it be difficult to define freedom as an ideal to be realised in the merely personal relations of human beings, the difficulty is increased when we consider the relation of men to the material means of life and happiness.

For it is commonly thought that the individual's right to Freedom includes the right of appropriating material things. But, if Freedom be understood strictly, I do not see that it implies more than his right to non-interference while actually using such things as can only be used by one person at once: the right to prevent others from using at any future time anything that an individual has once seized seems an interference with the free action of others beyond what is needed to secure the freedom, strictly speaking, of the ap-

propriator. It may perhaps be said that a man, in appropriating a particular thing, does not interfere with the freedom of others, because the rest of the world is still open to them. But others may want just what he has appropriated: and they may not be able to find anything so good at all, or at least without much labour and search; for many of the instruments and materials of comfortable living are limited in quantity. This argument applies especially to property in land: and it is to be observed that, in this case, there is a further difficulty in determining how much a man is to be allowed to appropriate by 'first occupation.' If it be said that a man is to be understood to occupy what he is able to use, the answer is obvious that the use of land by any individual may vary almost indefinitely in extent, while diminishing proportionally in intensity. For instance, it would surely be a paradoxical deduction from the principle of Freedom to maintain that an individual had a right to exclude others from pasturing sheep on any part of the land over which his hunting expeditions could extend. But if so can it be clear that a shepherd has such a right against one who wishes to till the land, or that one who is using the surface has a right to exclude a would-be miner? I do not see how the deduction is to be made out. Again, it may be disputed whether the right of Property, as thus derived, is to include the right of controlling the disposal of one's possessions after death. For this to most persons seems naturally bound up with ownership: yet it is paradoxical to say that we interfere with a man's freedom of action by anything that we may do after his death to what he owned during his life: and jurists have often treated this right as purely conventional and not therefore included in 'natural law.'

Other difficulties might be raised: but we need not pursue them, for if Freedom be taken simply to mean that one man's actions are to be as little as possible restrained by others, it is obviously more fully realised without appropriation. And if it be said that it includes, beside this, facility and security in the gratification of desires, and that it is Freedom in this sense that we think should be equally distributed, and that this cannot be realised without appropriation; then it may be replied, that in a society where nearly all material things are already appropriated, this kind of Freedom is not and cannot be equally distributed. A man born into such a society, without inheritance, is not only far less free than those who possess property, but he is less free than if there had been no appropriation. It may be said that, having freedom of contract, he will give his services in exchange for the means of satisfying his wants; and that this exchange must necessarily give him more than he could have got if he had been placed in the world by himself; that, in fact, any human society always renders the part of the earth that it inhabits more capable of affording gratification of desires to each and all of its later-born members than it would otherwise be. But however true this may be as a general rule, it is obviously not so in all cases: as men are sometimes unable to sell their services at all, and often can only obtain in exchange for them an insufficient subsistence. And, even granting it to be true, it does not prove that society, by appropriation, has not interfered with the natural freedom of its poorer members: but only that it compensates them for such interference, and that the compensation is adequate: and it must be evident that if compensation in the form of material commodities can be justly given for an encroachment on Freedom, the realisation of Freedom cannot be the one ultimate end of distributive Justice.

It seems, then, that though Freedom is an object of keen and general desire, and an important source of happiness, both in itself and indirectly from the satisfaction of natural impulses which it allows, the attempt to make it the fundamental notion of theoretical Jurisprudence is attended with insuperable difficulties: and that even the Natural Rights which it claims to cover cannot be brought under it except in a very forced and arbitrary manner. But further, even if this were otherwise, an equal distribution of Freedom does not seem to exhaust our notion of Justice. Ideal Justice, as we commonly conceive it, seems to demand that not only Freedom but

all other benefits and burdens should be distributed, if not equally, at any rate justly,— Justice in distribution being regarded as not identical with Equality, but merely exclusive of arbitrary inequality.

How, then shall we find the principle of this highest and most comprehensive ideal?

We shall be led to it, I think, by referring again to one of the grounds of obligation to render services, which was noticed in the last chapter: the claim of Gratitude. It there appeared that we have not only a natural impulse to requite benefits, but also a conviction that such requital is a duty, and its omission blameworthy, to some extent at least; though we find it difficult to define the extent. Now it seems that when we, so to say, *universalise* this impulse and conviction, we get the element in the common view of Justice, which we are now trying to define. For if we take the proposition 'that good done to any individual ought to be requited by him,' and leave out the relation to the individual in either term of the proposition, we seem to have an equally strong conviction of the truth of the more general statement 'that good deeds ought to be requited.'[1] And if we take into consideration all the different kinds and degrees of services, upon the mutual exchange of which society is based, we get the proposition 'that men ought to be rewarded in proportion to their deserts.' And this would be commonly held to be the true and simple principle of distribution in any case where there are no claims arising from Contract or Custom to modify its operation.

For example, it would be admitted that— if there has been no previous arrangement— the profits of any work or enterprise should be divided among those who have contributed to its success in proportion to the worth of their services. And it may be observed, that some thinkers maintain the proposition discussed in the previous section—that Law ought to aim at securing the greatest possible Freedom for each individual—not as absolute and axiomatic, but as derivative from the principle that Desert ought to be requited; on the ground that the best way of providing for the requital of Desert is to leave men as free as possible to exert themselves for the satisfaction of their own desires, and so to win each his own requital. And this seems to be really the principle upon which the Right of Property is rested, when it is justified by the proposition that 'every one has an exclusive right to the produce of his labour.' For on reflection it is seen that no labour really 'produces' any material thing, but only adds to its value: and we do not think that a man can acquire a right to a material thing belonging to another, by spending his labour on it—even if he does so in the *bona fide* belief that it is his own property—but only to adequate *compensation* for his labour; this, therefore, is what the proposition just quoted must mean. The principle is, indeed, sometimes stretched to explain the original right of property in materials, as being in a sense 'produced' (*i.e.* found) by their first discoverer; but here again, reflection shows that Common Sense does not grant this (as a *moral* right) absolutely, but only in so far as it appears to be not more than adequate compensation for the discoverer's trouble. For example, we should not consider that the first finder of a large uninhabited region had a moral right to appropriate the whole of it. Hence this justification of the right of property refers us ultimately to the principle 'that every man ought to receive adequate requital for his labour.' So, again, when we speak of the world as justly governed by God, we seem to mean that, if we could know the whole of human existence, we should find that happiness is distributed among men according to their deserts. And Divine Justice is thought to be a pattern which Human Justice is to imitate as far as the conditions of human society allow.

This kind of Justice, as has been said, seems like Gratitude universalised: and the same principle applied to punishment may similarly be regarded as Resentment universalised; though the parallel is incomplete, if we are considering the present state of our moral conceptions. History shows us a time in which it was thought not only as natural, but as clearly right and incumbent on a man, to requite injuries as to repay benefits: but as moral reflection developed in Europe this notion was repudiated, so that Plato taught that it could never be right really to harm any one, however he may have harmed us. And this is the accepted doctrine in Christian societies, as regards requital by individuals of personal wrongs. But in its universalised form the old conviction still lingers in the popular view of Criminal Justice: it seems still to be widely held that Justice requires pain to be inflicted on a man who has done wrong, even if no benefit result either to him or to others from the pain. Personally, I am so far from holding this view that I have an instinctive and strong moral aversion to it: and I hesitate to attribute it to Common Sense, since I think that it is gradually passing away from the moral consciousness of educated persons in the most advanced communities: but I think it is still perhaps the more ordinary view.

This, then, is one element of what Aristotle calls Corrective Justice, which is embodied in criminal law. It must not be confounded with the principle of Reparation, on which legal awards of damages are based. We have already noticed this as a simple deduction from the maxim of general Benevolence, which forbids us to do harm to our fellow-creatures: for if we have harmed them, we can yet approximately obey the maxim by giving compensation for the harm. Though here the question arises whether we are bound to make reparation for harm that has been quite blamelessly caused: and it is not easy to answer it decisively. On the whole, I think we should condemn a man who did not offer some reparation for any serious injury caused by him to another—even if quite involuntarily caused, and without negligence: but perhaps we regard this rather as a duty of Benevolence—arising out of the general sympathy that each ought to have for others, intensified by this special occasion—than as a duty of strict Justice. If, however, we limit the requirement of Reparation, under the head of strict Justice, to cases in which the mischief repaired is due to acts or omissions in some degree culpable, a difficulty arises from the divergence between the moral view of culpability, and that which social security requires. Of this I will speak presently. In any case there is now no danger of confusion or collision between the principle of Reparative and that of Retributive Justice, as the one is manifestly concerned with the claims of the injured party, and the other with the deserts of the wrongdoer: though in the actual administration of Law the obligation of paying compensation for wrong may sometimes be treated as a sufficient punishment for the wrongdoer.

When, however, we turn again to the other branch of Retributive Justice, which is concerned with the reward of services, we find another notion, which I will call Fitness, often blended indistinguishably with the notion of Desert, and so needing to be carefully separated from it; and when the distinction has been made, we see that the two are liable to come into collision. I do not feel sure that the principle of 'distribution according to Fitness' is found, strictly speaking, in the analysis of the ordinary notion of Justice: but it certainly enters into our common conception of the ideal or perfectly rational order of society, as regards the distribution both of instruments and functions, and (to some extent at least) of other sources of happiness. We certainly think it reasonable that instruments should be given to those who can use them best, and functions allotted to those who are most competent to perform them: but these may not be those who have rendered most services in the past. And again, we think it reasonable that particular material means of enjoyment should fall to the lot of those who are susceptible of the respective kinds of pleasure; as no one would think of allotting pictures to a blind man, or rare wines to one who had no taste: hence we should probably think it fitting that artists should have larger shares than mechanics in the social distribution of wealth, though they may be by no means more deserving. Thus the notions of Desert and Fitness appear at least occasionally conflicting; but perhaps, as I have suggested, Fitness should rather be regarded as a utilitarian principle of distribution, inevitably limiting the realisation of what is abstractly just, than as a part of the interpretation of Justice proper: and it is with the latter that we are at present concerned. At any

rate it is the Requital of Desert that constitutes the chief element of Ideal Justice, in so far as this imports something more than mere Equality and Impartiality. Let us then examine more closely wherein Desert consists; and we will begin with Good Desert or Merit, as being of the most fundamental and permanent importance; for we may hope that crime and its punishment will decrease and gradually disappear as the world improves, but the right or best distribution of the means of wellbeing is an object that we must always be striving to realise.

And first, the question which we had to consider in defining Gratitude again recurs: whether, namely, we are to apportion the reward to the effort made, or to the results attained. For it may be said that the actual utility of any service must depend much upon favourable circumstances and fortunate accidents, not due to any desert of the agent: or again, may be due to powers and skills which were connate, or have been developed by favourable conditions of life, or by good education, and why should we reward him for these? (for the last-mentioned we ought rather to reward those who have educated him). And certainly it is only in so far as *moral* excellences are exhibited in human achievements that they are commonly thought to be such as God will reward. But by drawing this line we do not yet get rid of the difficulty. For it may still be said that good actions are due entirely, or to a great extent, to good dispositions and habits, and that these are partly inherited and partly due to the care of parents and teachers; so that in rewarding these we are rewarding the results of natural and accidental advantages, and it is unreasonable to distinguish these from others, such as skill and knowledge, and to say that it is even ideally just to reward the one and not the other. Shall we say, then, that the reward should be proportionate to the amount of voluntary effort for a good end? But Determinists will say that even this is ultimately the effect of causes extraneous to the man's self. On the Determinist view, then, it would seem to be ideally just (if anything is so) that all men should enjoy equal amounts of happiness: for there seems to be no justice in making *A* happier than *B*, merely because circumstances beyond his own control have first made him better. But why should we not, instead of 'all men,' say 'all sentient beings'? for why should men have more happiness than any other animal? But thus the pursuit of ideal justice seems to conduct us to such a precipice of paradox that Common Sense is likely to abandon it. At any rate the ordinary idea of Desert has thus altogether vanished. And thus we seem to be led to the conclusion which I anticipated in Book i. chap. v.: that in this one department of our moral consciousness the idea of Free Will seems involved in a peculiar way in the moral ideas of Common Sense, since if it is eliminated the important notions of Desert or Merit and Justice require material modification. At the same time, the difference between Determinist and Libertarian Justice can hardly have any practical effect. For in any case it does not seem possible to separate in practice that part of a man's achievement which is due strictly to his free choice from that part which is due to the original gift of nature and to favouring circumstances: so that we must necessarily leave to providence the realisation of what we conceive as the theoretical ideal of Justice, and content ourselves with trying to reward voluntary actions in proportion to the worth of the services intentionally rendered by them.

If, then, we take as the principle of ideal justice, so far as this can be practically aimed at in human society, the requital of voluntary services in proportion to their worth, it remains to consider on what principle or principles the comparative worth of different services is to be rationally estimated. There is no doubt that we commonly assume such an estimate to be possible; for we continually speak of the 'fair' or 'proper' price of any kind of services as something generally known, and condemn the demand for more than this as extortionate. It may be said that the notion of Fairness or Equity which we ordinarily apply in such judgments is to be distinguished from that of Justice; Equity being in fact often contrasted with strict Justice, and conceived as capable of coming into collision with it. And this is partly true: but I think the wider and

no less usual sense of the term Justice, in which it includes Equity or Fairness, is the only one that can be conveniently adopted in an ethical treatise: for in any case where Equity comes into conflict with strict justice, its dictates are held to be in a higher sense just, and what ought to be ultimately carried into effect in the case considered—though not, perhaps, by the administrators of law. I treat Equity, therefore, as a species of Justice; though noting that the former term is more ordinarily used in cases where the definiteness attainable is recognized as somewhat less than in ordinary cases of rightful claims arising out of law or contract. On what principle, then, can we determine the "fair" or "equitable" price of services? When we examine the common judgments of practical persons in which this judgment occurs, we find, I think, that the 'fair' in such cases is ascertained by a reference to analogy and custom, and that any service is considered to be 'fairly worth' what is usually given for services of the kind. Hence this element of the notion of Justice may seem, after all, to resolve itself into that discussed [earlier]: and in some states of society it certainly appears that payment to be given for services is as completely fixed by usage as any other customary duty, so that it would be a clear disappointment of normal expectation to deviate from this usage. But probably no one in a modern civilised community would maintain in its full breadth this identification of the Just with the Usual price of services: and so far as the judgments of practical persons may seem to imply this, I think it must be admitted that they are superficial or merely inadvertent, and ignore the established mode of determining the market prices of commodities by free competition of producers and traders. For where such competition operates the market value rises and falls, and is different at different places and times; so that no properly instructed person can expect any fixity in it, or complain of injustice merely on account of the variations in it.

Can we then say that 'market value' (as determined by free competition) corresponds to our notion of what is ideally just?

This is a question of much interest, because this is obviously the mode of determining the remuneration of services that would be universal in a society constructed on the principle previously discussed, of securing the greatest possible Freedom to all members of the community. It should be observed that this, which we may call the Individualistic Ideal, is the type to which modern civilised communities have, until lately, been tending to approximate: and it is therefore very important to know whether it is one which completely satisfies the demands of morality; and whether Freedom, if not an absolute end or First Principle of abstract Justice, is still to be sought as the best means to the realisation of a just social order by the general requital of Desert.

At first sight it seems plausible to urge that the 'market value' represents the estimate set upon anything by mankind generally, and therefore gives us exactly that 'common sense' judgment respecting value which we are now trying to find. But on examination it seems likely that the majority of men are not properly qualified to decide on the value of many important kinds of services, from imperfect knowledge of their nature and effects; so that, as far as these are concerned, the true judgment will not be represented in the market-place. Even in the case of things which a man is generally able to estimate, it may be manifest in a particular case that he is ignorant of the real utility of what he exchanges; and in this case the 'free' contract hardly seems to be fair: though if the ignorance was not caused by the other party to the exchange, Common Sense is hardly prepared to condemn the latter as unjust for taking advantage of it. For instance, if a man has discovered by a legitimate use of geological knowledge and skill that there is probably a valuable mine on land owned by a stranger, reasonable persons would not blame him for concealing his discovery until he had bought the mine at its market value: yet it could not be said that the seller got what it was really worth. In fact Common Sense is rather perplexed on this point: and the *rationale* of the conclusion at which it arrives, must, I conceive, be sought in economic considerations, which take us

quite beyond the analysis of the common notion of Justice.

Again, there are social services recognised as highly important which generally speaking have no price in any market, on account of the indirectness and uncertainty of their practical utility: as, for instance, scientific discoveries. The extent to which any given discovery will aid industrial invention is so uncertain, that even if the secret of it could be conveniently kept, it would not usually be profitable to buy it.

But even if we confine our attention to products and services generally marketable, and to bargains thoroughly understood on both sides, there are still serious difficulties in the way of identifying the notions of 'free' and 'fair' exchange. Thus, where an individual, or combination of individuals, has the monopoly of a certain kind of services, the market-price of the aggregate of such services can under certain conditions be increased by diminishing their total amount; but it would seem absurd to say that the social Desert of those rendering the services is thereby increased, and a plain man has grave doubts whether the price thus attained is fair. Still less is it thought fair to take advantage of the transient monopoly produced by emergency: thus, if I saw Crœsus drowning and no one near, it would not be held fair in me to refuse to save him except at the price of half his wealth. But if so, can it be fair for any class of persons to gain competitively by the unfavorable economic situation of another class with which they deal? And if we admit that it would be unfair, where are we to draw the line? For any increase of the numbers of a class renders its situation for bargaining less favourable: since the market price of different services depends partly upon the ease or difficulty of procuring them—as Political Economists say, 'on the relation between the supply of services and the demand for them'—and it does not seem that any individual's social Desert can properly be lessened merely by the increased number or willingness of others rendering the same services. Nor, indeed, does it seem that it can be decreased by his own willingness, for it is strange to reward a man less because he is zealous and eager in the performance of his function; yet in bargaining the less willing always has the advantage. And, finally, it hardly appears that the social worth of a man's service is necessarily increased by the fact that his service is rendered to those who can pay lavishly; but his reward is certainly likely to be greater from this cause.

Such considerations as these have led some political thinkers to hold that Justice requires a mode of distributing payment for services, entirely different from that at present effected by free competition: and that all labourers ought to be paid according to the intrinsic value of their labour as estimated by enlightened and competent judges. If the Socialistic Ideal—as we may perhaps call it—could be realised without counter-balancing evils, it would certainly seem to give a nearer approximation to what we conceive as Divine Justice than the present state of society affords. But this supposes that we have found the rational method of determining value: which, however, is still to seek. Shall we say that these judges are to take the value of a service as proportionate to the amount of happiness produced by it? If so, the calculation is, of course, exposed to all the difficulties of the hedonistic method discussed in Book ii.: but supposing these can be overcome, it is still hard to say how we are to compare the value of different services that must necessarily be combined to produce happy life. For example, how shall we compare the respective values of necessaries and luxuries? for we may be more sensible of the enjoyment derived from the latter, but we could not have this at all without the former. And, again, when different kinds of labour co-operate in the same production, how are we to estimate their relative values? for even if all mere unskilled labour may be brought to a common standard, this seems almost impossible in the case of different kinds of skill. For how shall we compare the labour of design with that of achievement? or the supervision of the whole with the execution of details? or the labour of actually producing with that of educating producers? or the service of the *savant* who discovers a new principle, with that of the inventor who applies it?

I do not see how these questions, or the difficulties noticed in the preceding paragraph, can be met by any analysis of our common notion of Justice. To deal with such points at all satisfactorily we have, I conceive, to adopt quite a different line of reasoning: we have to ask, not what services of a certain kind are intrinsically worth, but what reward can procure them and whether the rest of society gain by the services more than the equivalent reward. We have, in short, to give up as impracticable the construction of an ideally just social order, in which all services are rewarded in exact proportion to their intrinsic value. And, for similar reasons, we seem forced to conclude more generally, that it is impossible to obtain clear premises for a reasoned method of determining exactly different amounts of Good Desert. Indeed, perhaps, Common Sense scarcely holds such a method to be possible: for though it considers Ideal Justice to consist in rewarding Desert, it regards as Utopian any general attempt to realise this ideal in the social distribution of the means of happiness. In the actual state of society it is only within a very limited range that any endeavour is made to reward Good Desert. Parents attempt this to some extent in dealing with their children, and the State in rewarding remarkable public services rendered by statesmen, soldiers, etc.: but reflection on these cases will show how very rough and imperfect are the standards used in deciding the amount due. And ordinarily the only kind of Justice which we try to realise is that which consists in the fulfilment of contracts and definite expectations; leaving the general fairness of Distribution by Bargaining to take care of itself.

NOTE

1. If the view given in the text be sound, it illustrates very strikingly the difference between natural instincts and moral intuitions. For the impulse to requite a service is, on its emotional side, quite different from that which prompts us to claim the fruits of our labour, or "a fair day's wages for a fair day's work." Still, our apprehension of the *duty* of Gratitude seems capable of being subsumed under the more general intuition 'that *desert* ought to be requited.'

8. What Things Are Good?

W. D. ROSS

William David Ross (1877–1971) was a philosopher as well as the Provost of Oriel College, Oxford University. He was an outstanding scholar of Plato and Aristotle, making important contributions in interpreting and translating their works. His most notable work, however, was in ethics, in particular his book *The Right and the Good* (1930), from which the present selection is taken. Ross was an ethical intuitionist who thought that moral principles were self-evident upon reflection. We intuitively know, for example, that it is morally right to keep promises and to show gratitude for benefits rendered. He developed the idea of *prima facie rightness* as opposed to *absolute rightness*. In many situations, more than one objectively valid moral principle may be applicable, so reflective intuition is necessary to adjudicating the competing claims. Each competing principle gives us a *prima facie duty*, but the one that wins out is our *actual duty*.

In the selection before us, Ross argues that four things are intrinsically good. Knowledge is the fourth one, which does not concern us here. The first two are pleasure and virtue. But he thinks it is intuitively obvious that we must organize the first two values in a way so that it is the virtuous that receive appropriate pleasure. This is the third value: the apportionment of pleasure and pain to the virtuous and the vicious, respectively.

Our next step is to inquire what kinds of thing are intrinsically good. (I) The first thing for which I would claim that it is intrinsically good is virtuous disposition and action, i.e. action, or disposition to act, from any one of certain motives, of which at all events the most notable are the desire to do one's duty, the desire to bring into being something that is good, and the desire to give pleasure or save pain to others. It seems clear that we regard all such actions and dispositions as having value in themselves apart from any consequence. And if any one is inclined to doubt this and to think that, say, pleasure alone is intrinsically good, it seems to me enough to ask the question whether, of two states of the universe holding equal amounts of pleasure, we should really think no better of one in which the actions and dispositions of all the persons in it were thoroughly virtuous than of one in which they were highly vicious. To this there can be only one answer. Most hedonists would shrink from giving the plainly false answer which their theory requires, and would take refuge in saying that the question rests on a false abstraction. Since virtue, as they conceive it, is a disposition to do just the acts which will produce most pleasure, a universe full of virtuous persons would be bound, they might say, to contain more pleasure than a universe full of vicious persons. To this two answers may be made. (*a*) Much pleasure,

Reprinted from *The Right and the Good* (Oxford University Press, 1930).

and much pain, do not spring from virtuous or vicious actions at all but from the operation of natural laws. Thus even if a universe filled with virtuous persons were bound to contain more of the pleasure and less of the pain that springs from human action than a universe filled with vicious persons would, that inequality of pleasantness might easily be supposed to be precisely counteracted by, for instance, a much greater incidence of disease. The two states of affairs would then, on balance, be equally pleasant; would they be equally good? And (*b*) even if we could not imagine any circumstances in which two states of the universe equal in pleasantness but unequal in virtue could exist, the supposition is a legitimate one, since it is only intended to bring before us in a vivid way what is really self-evident, that virtue is good apart from its consequences.

(2) It seems at first sight equally clear that pleasure is good in itself. Some will perhaps be helped to realize this if they make the corresponding supposition to that we have just made; if they suppose two states of the universe including equal amounts of virtue but the one including also widespread and intense pleasure and the other widespread and intense pain. Here too it might be objected that the supposition is an impossible one, since virtue always tends to promote general pleasure, and vice to promote general misery. But this objection may be answered just as we have answered the corresponding objection above.

Apart from this, however, there are two ways in which even the most austere moralists and the most anti-hedonistic philosophers are apt to betray the conviction that pleasure is good in itself. (*a*) One is the attitude which they, like all other normal human beings, take towards kindness and towards cruelty. If the desire to give pleasure to others is approved, and the desire to inflict pain on others condemned, this seems to imply the conviction that pleasure is good and pain bad. Some may think, no doubt, that the mere thought that a certain state of affairs would be *painful* for another person is enough to account for our conviction that the desire to produce it is bad. But I am inclined to think that there is in-

volved the further thought that a state of affairs in virtue of being painful is *prima facie* (i.e. where other considerations do not enter into the case) one that a rational spectator would not approve, i.e. is *bad*; and that similarly our attitude towards kindness involves the thought that pleasure is good. (*b*) The other is the insistence, which we find in the most austere moralists as in other people, on the conception of merit. If virtue deserves to be rewarded by happiness (whether or not vice also deserves to be rewarded by unhappiness), this seems at first sight to imply that happiness and unhappiness are not in themselves things indifferent, but are good and bad respectively.

Kant's view on this question is not as clear as might be wished. He points out that the Latin *bonum* covers two notions, distinguished in German as *das Gute* (the good) and *das Wohl* (well-being, i. e. pleasure or happiness); and he speaks of 'good' as being properly applied only to actions, i.e. he treats 'good' as equivalent to 'morally good', and by implication denies that pleasure (even deserved pleasure) is good. It might seem then that when he speaks of the union of virtue with the happiness it deserves as the *bonum consummatum* he is not thinking of deserved happiness as good but only as *das Wohl*, a source of satisfaction to the person who has it. But if this exhausted his meaning, he would have no right to speak of virtue, as he repeatedly does, as *das oberste Gut*; he should call it simply *das Gute*, and happiness *das Wohl*. Further, he describes the union of virtue with happiness not merely as 'the object of the desires of rational finite beings', but adds that it approves itself 'even in the judgement of an impartial reason' as 'the whole and perfect good', rather than virtue alone. And he adds that 'happiness, while it is pleasant to the possessor of it, is not of itself absolutely and in all respects good, but always presupposes morally right behaviour as its condition'; which implies that *when* that condition is fulfilled, happiness *is* good. All this seems to point to the conclusion that in the end he had to recognize that while virtue alone is morally good, deserved happiness also is not merely a source of satisfaction to its possessor, but objectively good.

But reflection on the conception of merit does not support the view that pleasure is always good in itself and pain always bad in itself. For while this conception implies the conviction that pleasure when deserved is good, and pain when undeserved bad, it also suggests strongly that pleasure when undeserved is bad and pain when deserved good.

There is also another set of facts which casts doubt on the view that pleasure is always good and pain always bad. We have a decided conviction that there are bad pleasures and (though this is less obvious) that there are good pains. We think that the pleasure taken either by the agent or by a spectator in, for instance, a lustful or cruel action is bad; and we think it a good thing that people should be pained rather than pleased by contemplating vice or misery.

Thus the view that pleasure is always good and pain always bad, while it seems to be strongly supported by some of our convictions, seems to be equally strongly opposed by others. The difficulty can, I think, be removed by ceasing to speak simply of pleasure and pain as good or bad, and by asking more carefully what it is that we mean. Consideration of the question is aided if we adopt the view (tentatively adopted already) that what is good or bad is always something properly expressed by a that-clause, i.e. an objective, or as I should prefer to call it, a *fact*. If we look at the matter thus, I think we can agree that the fact that a sentient being is in a state of pleasure is always in itself good, and the fact that a sentient being is in a state of pain always in itself bad, when this fact is not an element in a more complex fact having some other characteristic relevant to goodness or badness. And where considerations of desert or of moral good or evil do not enter, i. e. in the case of animals, the fact that a sentient being is feeling pleasure or pain is the whole fact (or the fact sufficiently described to enable us to judge of its goodness or badness), and we need not hesitate to say that the pleasure of animals is always good, and the pain of animals always bad, in itself and apart

from its consequences. But when a moral being is feeling a pleasure or pain that is deserved or undeserved, or a pleasure or pain that implies a good or a bad disposition, the total fact is quite inadequately described if we say 'a sentient being is feeling pleasure, or pain'. The total fact may be that 'a sentient and moral being is feeling a pleasure that is undeserved, or that is the realization of a vicious disposition', and though the fact included in this, that 'a sentient being is feeling pleasure' would be good if it stood alone, that creates only a presumption that the total fact is good, and a presumption that is outweighed by the other element in the total fact.

Pleasure seems, indeed, to have a property analogous to that which we have previously recognized under the name of conditional or *prima facie* rightness. An act of promise-keeping has the property, not necessarily of being right but of being something that is right if the act has no other morally significant characteristic (such as that of causing much pain to another person). And similarly a state of pleasure has the property, not necessarily of being good, but of being something that is good if the state has no other characteristic that prevents it from being good. The two characteristics that may interfere with its being good are (*a*) that of being contrary to desert, and (*b*) that of being a state which is the realization of a bad disposition. Thus the pleasures of which we can say without doubt that they are good are (i) the pleasures of non-moral beings (animals), (ii) the pleasures of moral beings that are deserved and are either realizations of good moral dispositions or realizations of neutral capacities (such as the pleasures of the senses).

In so far as the goodness or badness of a particular pleasure depends on its being the realization of a virtuous or vicious disposition, this has been allowed for by our recognition of virtue as a thing good in itself. But the mere recognition of virtue as a thing good in itself, and of pleasure as a thing *prima facie* good in itself, does not do justice to the conception of merit. If we compare two imaginary states of the universe, alike in the total amounts of virtue and vice and of pleasure and pain present in the two, but in one of which the virtuous were all happy and the vicious miserable, while in the other the virtuous were miserable and the vicious happy, very few people would hesitate to say that the first was a much better state of the universe than the second. It would seem then that, besides virtue and pleasure, we must recognize (3), as a third independent good, the apportionment of pleasure and pain to the virtuous and the vicious respectively. And it is on the recognition of this as a separate good that the recognition of the duty of justice, in distinction from fidelity to promises on the one hand and from beneficence on the other, rests. . . .

PART II
CONTEMPORARY INTERPRETATIONS OF DESERT

Hard workers deserve success. Wrongdoers deserve punishment. Victims of negligence deserve compensation. The best-qualified applicant deserves the job. Good students deserve good grades. The virtuous deserve happiness.

Many people would accept these platitudes without thinking twice. But a philosopher should not. As David Lewis put it, "It is the profession of philosophers to question platitudes that others accept without thinking twice."[1] The philosopher should question why (if at all) hard workers deserve success, or why (if at all) the best-qualified applicant deserves the job, and so on.

More likely than not, the answers to those general questions will depend on the answers to even more general questions about desert—questions about its nature, and about its relationships to other philosophically interesting concepts.

In this Introduction, I ask a few of those general questions about desert and sketch some of the answers that they have received (or could receive). My aim is not to provide a summary of all the articles that follow—though I will mention many of their ideas, and refer to them in the footnotes. Rather, my aim is to supply readers with the rudiments of a framework for thinking philosophically about desert, as well as for organizing at least some of the ideas in the essays that follow.

Five Questions about Desert

There are many questions that a philosopher might ask about desert. I shall focus on five of them. These five are not the only philosophically important questions about desert, but they are among them.

1. What sort of thing is desert? Imagine drawing up a list of the sorts of things that exist. The list might mention physical objects, properties, events, sets, and perhaps more (or perhaps less). A preliminary question one might ask about desert, then, is this: What sort of thing is it? How does it fit into our "ontological scheme"?

The contemporary literature is agreed that desert is a property.[2] More specifically, it is a "triadic" property, or three-place relation: it binds three sorts of thing: (a) a subject, (b) a thing deserved by the subject, and (c) a basis in virtue of which the subject deserves it. If so, then all desert-claims, fully spelled out, will have the following form: 'A deserves x in virtue of y', where A is the subject of desert, x what A deserves, and y the basis of A's desert of x.[3]

2. What sorts of things can be deserving? Suppose desert is a three-place relation. Then an obvious question presents itself: What sorts of thing can *be* deserving?

The most uncontroversial bearers of desert are people. People are thought to deserve, or be capable of deserving, many things: punishment, reward, apologies, compensation, admiration, contempt, wages, grades, prizes, and so on. But is desert limited to people? Can nonpersons be deserving, too?

A conservative view is that *only* people can be deserving and that any attribution of desert to nonpersons is either incoherent, false, or translatable into some claim of "personal" desert, or perhaps into a claim that does not mention desert at all. So, for example, suppose someone says, "The dog deserves a treat." On the conservative view, this claim could be incoherent, since dogs (it is claimed) neither deserve nor fail to deserve anything. The concept of desert does not apply to them. Or it could be coherent but false: The dog does not deserve a treat, since dogs cannot literally deserve anything. Or it could be coherent and even true, provided that it is translatable into some other claim, e.g., "You deserve the satisfaction of giving your dog a treat," or "Giving the dog a treat will reinforce its good behavior."

The conservative thesis, though it seems extreme, has at least one plausible consideration in its favor: It can appear analytic. For it is plausible that a person *just is* the sort of thing that can deserve good or ill.

A liberal view is that just about anything can be literally deserving: persons, animals, natural objects, artifacts, and so on. This view is supported by ordinary language. For in addition to making desert-claims about people, we also say that the pet deserves our love, the Olympic Peninsula our respect, the proposal our support, the nation our loyalty, the painting our admiration. It is possible, of course, that some of these claims are translatable into claims that would be consistent with the conservative view. But it is not obvious that this is so, and the burden of proof (and of translation!) is on the conservatives.

A moderate view is that not only persons but also the "higher animals" can be deserving. For example, on this view it might be literally true that blue whales deserve to be saved from slaughter. But the "lower" animals, such as rats and clams, cannot literally deserve anything, nor can inanimate objects, whether natural or human-made.

The moderate view appears unstable. For why is it that "higher" animals are thought deserving? Is it because they are alive? If so, then the view must expand to include all living things. But why draw the line even at living things? Surely dead *people* deserve various things, e.g., that their legal wills be executed, that their remains be respected, and so on. Perhaps dead animals can also be deserving. For example, it may be that the corpse of an animal from an extinct or nearly extinct species deserves to be preserved in a museum. If so, this would not be due to the fact that the animal was once alive, or every dead animal would deserve a place in a museum! Rather, it may be due to the animal's *rarity*. But inanimate objects, natural or human-made, can be rare as well—in which case there is pressure on the moderate view to expand into a much more liberal view.

There is pressure in the other direction, as well. For it might be that various animals are thought to be deserving, not because they are alive or rare, but because of the relevant properties they share with people. If so, then economy would be gained by simply admitting that the higher animals are people, that possession of those qualities is sufficient for personhood. In that case, the moderate position collapses into the conservative view that only people can be deserving.

3. What are the bases of desert? Recall that desert-claims have the form 'A deserves x in virtue of y', where y is the basis of A's desert, or the grounds in virtue of which A deserves x. This raises a third question: What are the bases of desert?[4]

Philosophers are agreed that desert requires a basis. There is also agreement that this basis of a thing's desert must in some important sense be a fact *about that thing*.[5] So, for example, the fact that 3 is a prime number, or that a particular star is two billion years old, is not a basis for your deserving anything. In order for a fact to be a basis of your desert, it must be a fact about you, e.g., that you have worked hard, innocently suffered, are a person, and so on.

So, desert must have a basis, and the basis of a thing's desert must be a fact about that thing. Is there anything more that can be said?

Many writers on desert have assumed that a necessary condition on something's being a desert base is that the deserving subject is *responsible* for it.[6] A standard version of this condition can be stated more precisely:

> DR   A deserves x in virtue of y only if A is responsible for y.

This assumption plays a central role in contemporary discussions about desert. Some have used it to argue that we never deserve anything and that desert is therefore a useless concept in ethical theory. This argument usually proceeds as follows.[7] All of the actions we perform and attributes we possess—in short, all would-be bases for desert—are determined by factors for which we are not responsible, such as our genetic makeup, early training, and environment. This premise is combined with DR, for the conclusion that no one ever deserves anything. And if no one ever deserves anything, then the concept of desert is of no use to ethical theorists.

There are other, less dramatic uses of DR. A good example can be found in the literature on desert of wages.[8] Much of this literature centers around the question: Does the wage a worker deserves depend on the effort exerted or on actual productivity (regardless of effort)? Sometimes the following answer is proposed: Wages are deserved either for effort or productivity; people are responsible only for their efforts, not for the success or productivity of those efforts; DR is true; thus, it is the worker's effort, not productivity, that determines the deserved wage.

In spite of DR's wide acceptance, it has not gone unchallenged.[9] To some, it seems obvious that we can be deserving in virtue of things for which we are not responsible. Consider a person who innocently suffers a brutal mugging. The victim is not responsible for the attack. Yet in virtue of it, the victim deserves compensation. Or consider the case of a person who innocently suffers a painful and fatal disease. She is not responsible for contracting it, yet she deserves medical care and sympathy. Or consider the simple fact that you are a person. No one is responsible for this, yet in virtue of being a person you deserve a modicum of respect. These and other cases suggest that if there is a connection between desert and responsibility, it is not captured by DR.

Another attempt to specify the desert bases does so by linking them with the grounds of certain *emotions* or *attitudes*.[10] A version of this view can be brought out as follows.[11] There is a class of attitudes that we take up toward people in virtue of various qualities they possess or actions they perform. Those attitudes include admiration, gratitude, disgust, resentment, and so on. These have been called the "appraising attitudes."

And the idea here is that the bases for appraising attitudes are, or at least coincide with, the bases for desert. Put another way:

DAA   y is a desert base if and only if y is the basis of an appraising attitude.

If correct, DAA would provide a useful principle for determining desert bases. For example, it is sometimes held that need is a basis for desert (say, of medical care). Yet need does not seem to be the basis of any appraising attitude. We do not respect or resent people, admire or detest them, because of their needs. Thus, if DAA is true, then need is not a basis for desert.

On the other hand, it seems clear that exerting effort (for example) is a basis for admiring a person. If DAA is true, it follows that effort is a basis for desert.

However, there is a problem with DAA. To see it, consider the distinction between something's actually *being* admired, resented, and so forth, on the one hand, and that thing's being *appropriately* admired, resented, and so forth, on the other. For example, many admired Hitler even though it would have been appropriate to detest him. And many resented Martin Luther King Jr., even though it would have been appropriate to admire him.

This allows us to ask: Is DAA the thesis that y is a basis for desert if and only if y *happens* to be the object of an appraising attitude? Or is it instead the view that y is a basis for desert if and only if y is an *appropriate* basis for an appraising attitude? If the former, then DAA reduces to an implausible form of conventionalism about desert bases; if the latter, then DAA is in danger of being vacuous. For what else could make y an "appropriate" basis for an appraising attitude, except for the fact that those who have y *deserve* to be the object of that attitude?[12]

Yet another way of attempting to determine the bases for desert proceeds in two stages.[13] First, draw up a list of all the sorts of treatment that can be deserved: prizes, rewards, punishments, grades, compensation, and so on. Second, for each form of treatment, attempt to specify the basis or bases for which it is deserved.

There are two potential problems with this approach. First, just as it is difficult to draw up a catalogue of bases for desert, it seems just as difficult to draw up a list of forms of deservable treatment. Second, this way of proceeding has a tendency to reinforce the assumption that for every sort of deservable treatment, there is a desert base or set of desert bases unique to it. This assumption may be correct, but there is another possibility.[14] According to it, there is a single set of desert bases, and possession of any or all of them can influence the extent to which one deserves any given form of deservable treatment. If this latter view of the relationship between desert bases and deserved treatment is correct, then attempting to match deserved treatments to their bases might not be the best way to determine the bases of desert.

Yet another method for determining desert bases follows directly from "institutional" theories of desert.[15] On that sort of theory, the bases for desert are determined by the rules or purposes of social institutions. If a theory of this sort is correct, then discovering the bases for desert will be as easy (or difficult) as discovering the rules or purposes of social institutions.

Still other possibilities remain, but there is no space to discuss them. Suffice it to say that the third question (What are the bases for desert?) is one of the deepest and most pressing for any theorist of desert.

4. How do desert bases work? Suppose we have arrived at a complete catalogue of desert bases. How do these bases work? How do they ground desert?

A plausible way to answer this question is based on a distinction borrowed from ethical theory. This is the distinction between *prima facie moral rightness* and *all-things-considered* or *all-in moral rightness.* To see this distinction, imagine that you have made a promise to a friend. In virtue of this, it would now be morally right for you to help your friend. However, the rightness of your act is prima facie at best. It might not be all-in morally right for you to help your friend. Your promise might, for example, have been to help your friend by murdering his enemy! In that case, you probably have an all-in obligation to *break* your promise. Still, the fact that you promised does count in favor of the rightness of the action. It just so happens that, in this case, the prima facie rightness that the act would inherit in virtue of being a promise-keeping is outweighed by the prima facie wrongness of murder. In any case, the all-in rightness or wrongness of an action is determined by all the aspects in virtue of which the action would be prima facie right, when weighed against all the aspects in virtue of which it would be prima facie wrong.[16]

The suggestion is that desert works in a similar way. There is a difference between *prima facie desert* and *all-in desert.* Possession of any given desert base makes one prima facie deserving, but it might not make one all-in deserving. For example, you might have exerted intense effort toward achieving some end. If, as is usually held, effort is a basis for deserving success, then you prima facie deserve success in virtue of your efforts. However, you might not be all-in deserving of success. Perhaps this is because your efforts were directed at an evil end—say, bombing a public building full of innocent people. In such a case, the prima facie desert of success that you gained in virtue of having exerted effort is outweighed by the prima facie desert of failure and punishment that you gained in virtue of plotting such an evil act.

In any case, it seems plausible to suppose that there is a distinction between prima facie and all-in desert and that the question of whether A all-in deserves x is determined by all the bases in virtue of which A prima facie deserves x, as weighed against all the bases in virtue of which A prima facie deserves to not get x. If the former outweigh the latter, then A all-in deserves x. Otherwise A all-in deserves to not get x. This seems to be how desert bases work.

An interesting question is whether desert bases "weigh" the same in every situation or not. (I suspect that they do not.) Another interesting question is how, if at all, we manage to do the weighing. Unfortunately, all we can do here is raise these questions.

5. What relationships does desert bear to other concepts of philosophical interest? This is a large question, since desert is thought to bear interesting relations to a variety of such concepts. Let me focus on a few of what seem to be the most important.

> (a) *Justice.* A venerable view is that justice has something to do with desert. An extreme version of this view has it that justice obtains *only* to the extent that things get exactly what they deserve. At the other extreme is the view, common among many contemporary theorists of justice, that desert has nothing at all to do with justice.[17] A moderate view is that getting what's deserved is a part, though not the whole, of justice. The moderate view admits of many variations, depending on how much emphasis is placed on desert. Some argue that desert is "half" of justice; the other half is, say, being treated in accordance with one's consent.[18] Others want to claim that desert plays, or ought to play, only an insignificant role in answering questions of justice.[19]

> (b) *Moral obligation.* Considerations of desert seem relevant to what one morally ought to do.[20] For example, suppose that you are grading exams. You want to do what's right by your students. Therefore, you try to determine what grade each student *deserves.* This is not to deny that factors other than desert might also be

relevant to the question of what grade you ought to assign. The point is that what a student deserves has some (perhaps large) effect on the moral status of assigning a particular grade. If, for example, the student deserves a C, then that is a weighty moral reason for giving the student a C.

This point can be put by saying that if A deserves (either prima facie or all-in) to receive x from B, then B has a prima facie moral obligation to see to it that A gets x.[21] This is distinct from the false claim that, in such a case, B has an all-in obligation to see to it that A gets x. For it could be that factors having nothing to do with A's desert outweigh the prima facie moral obligation that it creates. For example, even if the student deserves a C, it could be that assigning this grade will wreck the student's chances of getting into any medical school. Combine this with the fact that the exam was extremely difficult, that no one did any better, and so forth, and a case could be made for saying that although the student deserves a C, it would be morally wrong to give her less than (say) a B.

> (c) *Intrinsic value.* Compare two people, A and B. A has experienced a lot of good fortune in his life. So far, everything has gone his way. B's life, in contrast, has been full of bad fortune. So far, everything has turned out badly for her. Now suppose that some good fortune will fall into either A's life or B's. Intuitively, it would be *better* for it to fall into B's. This intuition is not based on the fact that B would therefore get some enjoyment; after all, A might get the same amount of enjoyment if the good fortune were to fall into *his* life. Rather, it seems to be based on the thought that in virtue B's being *more deserving* of this good fortune than A, B's getting it would be *intrinsically better* than A's getting it.

Consider another example. A has behaved badly, whereas B has been virtuous. Suppose that some ill fortune will fall into either A's life or B's. Intuitively, it would be better (or not as bad) for it to fall into A's. This intuition is not based on the fact that A would suffer. After all, B would suffer just as much if the ill fortune were to fall into her life. Rather, the intuition seems to be based on the thought that in virtue of A's being *more deserving* of ill fortune than B, A's suffering it would not be as *intrinsically bad* as B's. Indeed, it might be that because of A's many horrible deeds, his suffering this ill fortune would be *intrinsically good.*

These examples suggest that desert and intrinsic value are connected as follows.[22] If x is intrinsically good, then deserving x enhances the intrinsic goodness of getting it. Likewise, if x is intrinsically bad, then deserving x mitigates the intrinsic badness of suffering it, perhaps even up to the point of making it intrinsically good. (Notice that neither connection is to be confused with the obviously false claim that the amount of pleasure or pain a person *feels* is proportional to that person's desert!)

> (d) *Equality.* Equality is thought to be important to justice. So is desert. This raises questions about desert's relationship to equality.

One view is that desert and equality are bound to conflict. People have different deserts, it is said, and to treat them accordingly would result in various kinds and degrees of inequality.[23] The opposite view is that desert and equality cannot conflict, since what we deserve *is* equality (of treatment, welfare, or whatever).[24]

For argument's sake, suppose that desert and equality can conflict. In those cases where they do, which is more important? Does desert trump equality, or does equality always outweigh desert?

At one extreme is the view that in every case of conflict, equality outweighs desert.[25] A possible argument for this view is that it is more difficult to determine what's deserved than what constitutes equality; thus, as a matter of policy, we should always err on the side of equality.[26]

At the other extreme, it is held that desert trumps equality. This view seems supported by comparing the imagined fortunes of a sinner with those of a saint.[27] The sinner enjoys the same amount of happiness as the saint; there is equality in this respect. But the sinner is getting much more happiness than he deserves, while the saint is getting much less. If equality trumps desert, then there is nothing morally objectionable about this situation. Yet the situation surely is morally objectionable, precisely in virtue of its equality. It would be better in this and all other cases for people to get what they deserve, even if this leads to inequalities.

Between these extremes is the view that in some cases desert outweighs equality, and in other cases it does not. Perhaps the argument will be that in cases where deserts are difficult to determine and equality is easy to achieve, then equality outweighs desert, but in cases where deserts are clear and comparatively easy to meet, desert outweighs equality.[28]

> (e) *Merit.* The words "desert" and "merit" are often used interchangeably. But it is possible that the concepts of desert and merit are distinct from each other.

One view is that merit is a quite specific kind of desert: A merits x if and only if x is a position, and A would perform excellently in x.[29] This might be the notion that "meritocrats" have in mind when they urge that positions be assigned on the basis of merit only. In any event, on this view every case of merit is a case of desert, but not every case of desert is a case of merit.

The opposite view is that desert is a species of merit.[30] On this conception, merit is based on any quality that is an appropriate basis for distributing benefits (or burdens, in the case of demerit), whereas desert is based on a subset of those properties. The reason for this is that, on the view under consideration, desert is based (primarily) on voluntary action, whereas merit can be based on attributes or actions that are obtained or performed non-voluntarily. For example, it is possible to *merit* a prize in a beauty contest in virtue of one's naturally good looks. But the prize is not *deserved* in virtue of those good looks, since one is not responsible for having them. On this view, every case of desert is a case of merit, but not every case of merit is a case of desert.

> (f) *Entitlement.* To be entitled to something is to have a legitimate claim or right to it. But there is more than one kind of right. Some rights–e.g., legal rights—are merely conventional. We have them only if the relevant conventions exist. But other rights, some say, are not dependent on conventions. These are the so-called "natural rights." Examples of purported natural rights include the right to life, to property, and to the pursuit of one's own happiness. If there are any such rights, then we have them irrespective of what conventional rights (if any) exist.

Does desert bear any interesting connection to the concept of natural right?[31] A possible view is that if there are any natural rights, then they are based on what we (naturally) deserve. For example, we have a natural right to life because we deserve to live. That said, perhaps the relationship between natural rights and desert is just the opposite. Perhaps we deserve property, for example, at least when we have worked for it, because we have a natural right to what we have worked for. On this conception, natural rights ground desert. Yet a third view is that to deserve something just is to have a natural right to it. One does not ground the other: They are one and the same. A fourth (but inelegant) possibility is that some deserts are grounded in natural rights, while other natural rights are grounded in desert.

Of course, not everyone believes in natural rights. But everyone believes in conventional rights or entitlements. They are a fact of life. So what relationship, if any, does desert bear to the concept of merely conventional entitlement?

Rather than mention a variety of possible answers to this question, let me focus on just one.[32] According to it, being entitled to something—having a conventional right to it—is a basis for deserving it. For example, suppose that you are legally entitled to a share of your family's fortune. In virtue of this, you prima facie deserve that share. Or suppose that an athlete is entitled by the rules of the game to a medal. Because of this, the athlete prima facie deserves the medal.

In each case, the desert is prima facie, and not necessarily all-in, since there are other factors that might outweigh the entitlement-based desert. If, for example, you murder your parents in order to get your share of the family fortune, then your entitlement-based desert of that share could be outweighed by the punishment you deserve in virtue of the viciousness of your act.

Why should anyone accept that entitlement is a basis for desert? Here is one suggestion. Theorists of desert divide over the question of whether desert is "institutional" or "preinstitutional." Institutionalists maintain that desert is explicable entirely in terms of the rules or purposes of social institutions. On a crude version of this view, to deserve something just is to be conventionally entitled to it. Preinstitutionalists, in contrast, claim that desert is entirely preinstitutional: It is not grounded in or explicable in terms of the rules or purposes of social institutions and in fact provides a higher standard against which those rules or purposes can be morally evaluated.

This disagreement between institutionalists and preinstitutionalists is profound, but the thesis that conventional entitlement is a basis for desert suggests a possible compromise. The compromise is to admit that at least some desert is institutional—that is, desert that is based in conventional entitlements—while allowing that other deserts— for example, those based on being a person, or hard work, or morally good behavior— are not purely institutional. If this compromise is accepted, then it may be possible to enjoy the advantages of institutional and preinstitutional theories of desert, while avoiding their inadequacies.

Conclusion

I hope it is clear by now that even the most casual philosophical reflection on desert raises deep, difficult, and intriguing questions. The papers that follow contain some of the best, most recent attempts to answer them (and many others). There is no doubt that not all the answers are satisfactory, and that even more questions about desert have yet to be raised. Perhaps this collection will prompt more and even better work.

Notes

1. *Convention* (Harvard University Press, 1969), page 1.
2. See Chapters 9–12.
3. John Kleinig's threefold division (Chapter 10) of desert-claims into "raw," "institutional," and "specific" appears to imply that desert is sometimes a three-place relation, and sometimes not. But this is merely an appearance. Kleinig's division amounts to noting that *what* one deserves— the x in 'A deserves x in virtue of y'—can be more or less complex.
4. Chapter 9 is perhaps the most sustained attempt to answer this question. Also relevant are Chapters 11, 12, 16, 21, and 28.
5. For both points, see Chapter 9.
6. For discussion and references, see Chapters 15 and 16.

7. Chapters 13–16 are relevant here. See also Chapters 12, 18, 19, and 22.
8. For more discussion, see Chapter 12.
9. For example, in Chapters 15 and 16.
10. Early examples of this type of view can be found in Chapters 4 and 7. Modern versions appear in Chapters 9 and 11.
11. This view can be found in Chapter 11.
12. This objection is not decisive. The proponent of DAA could argue that it is appropriate to bear a particular appraising attitude towards those who have y, not because this is what they deserve but rather because (say) an impartial, benevolent spectator would bear that attitude toward those who have y. (This appears to be Adam Smith's view; see Chapter 4.) Whether this is a *plausible* view is a separate question.
13. This is the method pursued in Chapter 9.
14. This view is defended in Chapter 28.
15. See Chapter 21 for a discussion of institutional theories of desert. Also relevant is Chapter 22.
16. The classic statement of a theory of prima facie duties is W. D. Ross's *The Right and The Good* (Oxford University Press, 1930).
17. See Chapter 22 for documentation of this trend, as well as an interesting attempt to diagnose it.
18. This is the view defended in Chapter 23.
19. See Chapters 25 and 26.
20. For an attempt to accommodate this point within a consequentialist framework—something that others have thought impossible—see Chapter 27.
21. Chapter 9 makes this point.
22. For a more rigorous attempt to state (some of) desert's connections to intrinsic value, see Chapter 27.
23. Chapter 26 begins with this point.
24. This view, or something like it, can be found in Chapter 17.
25. Chapter 25 argues that *need* always outweighs desert.
26. See Chapter 26 for discussion of this argument.
27. For an elaborate and extended employment of this type of argument, see Chapter 30. Also relevant is Chapter 29.
28. I suspect that one reason why views diverge so starkly on the question of desert's relationship to equality is that parties to the debate do not sufficiently distinguish questions of *value* from questions of *obligation*. For it could be that desert is "more valuable" than equality and in that sense "trumps" it. But from this it does not follow that, in cases of conflict, it must be obligatory to treat in accordance with desert rather than to treat equally.
29. See Chapter 24 for a similar but importantly different conception of merit.
30. This view is defended in Chapter 30.
31. For brief discussion of this question, see Chapter 9.
32. This view is defended in Chapter 21.

A. THE CONCEPT OF DESERT

9. Justice and Personal Desert

JOEL FEINBERG

Joel Feinberg is Professor Emeritus of Philosophy at the University of Arizona, Tucson. He has published scores of articles and several books in ethics, political theory, and philosophy of law, including the three-volume *The Moral Limits of the Criminal Law* (1984–1986). Feinberg is a pioneer in the study of desert.

Feinberg's aim in this seminal paper is to "analyze" the concept of desert—first, by cataloguing the sorts of treatment that people can deserve, and second, by stating the basis or bases on which each such treatment can be deserved. A central feature of Feinberg's influential analysis is that for each type of deservable treatment, there is a desert base or set of desert bases unique to it.

Feinberg advances several other claims, including the following. (i) Desert is a "natural" moral notion; it is conceptually and morally prior to social institutions and can be used to evaluate them. Feinberg is thus an early advocate of a "preinstitutional" conception of desert. (ii) Desert requires a "base"—that is, an action performed or characteristic possessed by the person *in virtue of which* he or she is deserving. (iii) "Responsive attitudes," such as gratitude or disgust, are the primary things that people deserve; other modes of treatment, such as punishment, are deserved only insofar as they are expressions of those attitudes.

What is it to deserve something? This guileless question can hardly fail to trouble the reflective person who ponders it. Yet until its peculiar perplexities are resolved, a full understanding of the nature of justice is impossible, for surely the concepts of justice and desert are closely connected. This essay has as its ulterior purpose the illumination of that connection; its direct aim is analysis of the concept of personal desert.

The phrase "personal desert" is no pleonasm. Many kinds of things other than persons are commonly said to be deserving. Art objects deserve admiration; problems deserve careful consideration; bills of legislation deserve to be passed. Although such statements are not wholly unrelated to questions about justice, they are less central than statements about the deserts of persons and will not be considered here. Nor shall we consider statements construing natural events as deserts, such as "The villain crushed in the landslide got what he deserved." Persons are in this manner often held to deserve things

Reprinted from *Nomos* VI: *Justice*, eds. C. J. Friedrich and John W. Chapman (NY: Atherton, 1963), pp. 63–97.

other than treatment at the hands of their fellows; but this eassay will be concerned only with personal desert of other-personal bestowals.

On those rare occasions when personal-desert statements are discussed by philosophers, they are often held to stand in some close logical connection to rules, or they are explicated in terms of rights and obligations; and when philosophers themselves make judgments about personal deserts, the deserved modes of treatment they have in mind are almost invariably punishment and rewards. The following schematic analysis will suggest, on the contrary, that desert is a "natural" moral notion (that is, one which is not logically tied to institutions, practices, and rules); that it represents only a part, and not necessarily the most important part, of the domain of justice; and that reward and punishment are only two among the several irreducibly distinct modes of treatment persons are said to deserve. The first section of the essay deals with some generic aspects of desert, particularly its relations to rules and to the rule-connected concept of qualification and the relation between desert statements and reasons. Then, since further analysis of personal desert depends on what mode of treatment is said to be deserved, the second section examines some of the generic modes of deserved treatment. The final section discusses the relation between desert and social utility as well as some of the unfortunate consequences of treating personal desert as a kind of "moral entitlement."

I

Desert Propriety

To say that a person deserves something is to say that there is a certain sort of propriety in his having it. But this is also true of the statements that he is eligible for, qualified for, or entitled to something, that he has a claim on it or a right to it, or simply that he ought to have it. Our first task, then, is to characterize the particular kind of propriety

distinctive of desert. This may be most effectively done by contrasting it with other forms of propriety.

Consider first what it means to be "eligible" for something. According to *Webster's*, a person is eligible when he is "fitted or qualified to be chosen," when he is "legally or morally suitable." Eligibility is a kind of minimal qualification, a state of not being disqualified. We discover whether a person is eligible for some office or employment, prize, or reward by determining whether he satisfies certain eligibility conditions as specified by a rule or regulation. For example, to be eligible for varsity athletics, one needs a medical certificate, better than a C average, and at least sophomore standing; to be eligible for the presidency of the United States, one must be thirty-five or older and a "natural-born" citizen.

Eligibility is one kind of qualification: satisfaction of some important preliminary necessary condition. Another kind of qualification, equally rule-connected, is satisfaction of a sufficient condition for, say, an office or prize. So, for example, in this sense a man qualifies for the presidency of the United States by winning a majority of the electoral votes, or for first place in the hundred-yard dash by crossing the finish line before his competitors. Anyone who qualifies in this strong sense can claim the office or the prize as his *right*; according to the rules he is entitled to it.

I think it clear that qualification in neither of these senses is the same as desert. There are millions of persons eligible to be president who do not deserve to be, and it is often plausible and always intelligible to say that the man in fact elected president did not deserve to be. To deserve something, one must be qualified in still a third sense: one must satisfy certain conditions of worthiness which are written down in no legal or official regulation. Thus to be "truly qualified" for the presidency, a person must be intelligent, honest, and fair-minded; he must have a program which is really good for the country and the tact and guile to make it effective. Any candidate who satisfies these and similar conditions to a degree greater than his rivals deserves to be president. But these conditions are not requirements specified by some rule in the sense of authoritative, public, sanctioned regulation, or in the sense of "canon," or in the sense of "rule of procedure." At best they are the conditions "required" by the private standards or principles of a sensitive voter.

In respect to modes of treatment which persons can deserve, then, we can distinguish three kinds of conditions. There are those whose satisfaction confers eligibility ("eligibility conditions"), those whose satisfaction confers entitlement ("qualification conditions"), and those conditions not specified in any regulatory or procedural rules whose satisfaction confers worthiness or desert ("desert bases").

Desert Bases

If a person is deserving of some sort of treatment, he must, necessarily, be so *in virtue of* some possessed characteristic or prior activity. It is because no one can deserve anything unless there is some basis or ostensible occasion for the desert that judgments of desert carry with them a commitment to the giving of reasons. One cannot say, for example, that Jones deserves gratitude although he has done "nothing in particular." If a person says that Jones deserves gratitude, then he must be prepared to answer the question "For what?" Of course, he may not know the basis of Jones's desert, but if he denies that there is any basis, then he has forfeited his right to use the terminology of desert. He can still say that we *ought* to treat Jones well for "no reason in particular" or simply "for the sake of being nice," but it is absurd to say that Jones *deserves* good treatment for no reason in particular. Desert without a basis is simply not desert.

Not any old basis will do, however. A characteristic of mine cannot be a basis for a desert of yours unless it somehow reveals or reflects some characteristic of yours. In general, the facts which constitute the basis of a subject's desert must be facts about that subject. If a student deserves a high grade in a course, for example, his desert must be in virtue of some fact about *him*—his earlier performances, say, or his present abilities. Perhaps his teacher *ought* to give him a high grade because it will break his neurotic mother's heart if he does not; but this fact, though it can be a reason for the teacher's action, cannot be the basis of the student's desert.

There are two ways in which a judgment of desert can be infelicitous. On the one hand, it can either lack a basis altogether or else have a logically inappropriate one; on the other hand, it may simply be false or incorrect. To put the point another way, either the judgment may lack an appropriate "basal reason," or the basal reason may not be a justifying reason. The claim that a person deserves to be beaten up "just for the hell of it" lacks any basal reason; in fact, a basis is explicitly denied. The claim that a mother's mental health is the basis of a student's desert puts forth a logically inappropriate basal reason. Both of these claims egregiously misuse the word "deserve." Not only do they lack good reasons (justifying ones), but they lack the right kind of reason and are as offensive to sense as to morals. On the other hand, the frequent contention that ability per se is a desert basis for reward commits neither of these mistakes; it cites the right kind of reason for desert, namely, a fact about the person. In my opinion, however, it is not a good reason, although this is admittedly a notoriously controversial question involving the conflict of rival value systems, a question not easily settled.

A logically inappropriate basis for a person's deserving some mode of treatment may, of course, be a relevant and even a conclusive reason in support of the judgment that he ought to be given that mode of treatment. "Ought" judgments sometimes have a certain finality about them; we say that *S* ought to get *X* "all things considered" or "in the final judgment." On the other hand, they often have a quite different force. When we have not had time to survey all the relevant reasons, when we are unable to strike a balance, or simply when we are generalizing about classes of cases, we are likely to use the word "ought" in a *ceteris paribus* or *pro tanto* sense. We say that *S* ought to get *X* "other things being equal" or insofar as some one kind of reason among many has bearing on the situation. That a subject deserves *X* entails that he ought to get *X* in the *pro tanto* sense of "ought," but not in the "all things considered" or "on balance" sense. This is simply another way of saying that a person's desert of *X* is always a reason for giving *X* to him, but not always a conclusive reason, that considerations irrelevant to his desert can have overriding cogency in establishing how he ought to be treated on balance.

We have yet to give a complete account of the requisite character of desert bases. It is necessary that a person's desert have a basis and that the basis consist in some fact about himself, but neither of these conditions is sufficient. They do not, for example, exclude need as a desert basis for reward or ignorance as a desert basis for punishment. Both seem inappropriate, and yet they are, after all, facts about the deserving subject. It is impossible, however, to list the necessary and sufficient conditions for personal desert in the abstract, for the bases of desert vary with the mode of deserved treatment. Here we have had to content ourselves with pointing out a few important generic properties of desert which do not vary from context to context.

II

A philosophical analysis of the concept of desert can go no further without paying separate attention to each of the major kinds of treatment which persons can be said to deserve. For if we consider the schema "*S* deserves *X* in virtue of *F*," where *S* is a person, *X* a mode of treatment, and *F* some fact about *S*, it is clear that the values of *F* (the various desert bases) are determined in part by the nature of the various *X*'s in question. What makes a man deserving of a high grade in a mathematics course, for instance, is not identical to that which makes him deserving of unemployment compensation.

What are the various kinds of treatment that persons deserve from other persons? They are varied, but they have at least one thing in common: they are generally "affective" in character, that is, favored or disfavored, pursued or avoided, pleasant or unpleasant. The deserved object must be something generally regarded with favor or disfavor even if, in some particular case, it is regarded with indifference by a person said to deserve it. If we were all perfect stoics, if no event were ever more or less pleasing to us than any other, then there would be no use for the concept of desert.

The varieties of deserved treatment are many, and they are heterogeneous to a degree not usually appreciated. For the sake of convenience and with no claim to taxonomic precision or completeness, I have divided them into five major classes and then grouped these under two generic headings. The five classes are as follows:

1. Awards of prizes
2. Assignments of grades
3. Rewards and punishments
4. Praise, blame, and other informal responses
5. Reparation, liability, and other modes of compensation

I have not included positions of honor and economic benefits on this basic list because they are usually subsumed under one or another or some combination of the other headings. The problem of subsuming offices and honorable positions I have reserved for the end of this section, and a brief discussion of economic benefits is attached as an appendix to this essay.

The two generic headings are (1) forms of treatment that define contexts in which desert is a "polar" concept and (2) those that do not. In respect to polar desert, one can be said to deserve good or to deserve ill—reward or punishment, praise or blame, and so on. Polar desert is central to what has traditionally been called the concept of retributive justice. Nonpolar desert, on the other hand, has a different sort of symmetry. When it is a prize, an honorable office, or a grade that is in question, we divide persons not into those who deserve good and those who deserve ill, but rather into those who deserve and those who do not. Nonpolar desert is central to what philosophers have traditionally called the concept of distributive justice. Let us consider nonpolar contexts first and begin with the awarding of prizes.

Prizes

When prizes are awarded to the victors in individual and group games, races, and tournaments, in essay, cooking, or corn-husking contests, in spelling bees, and the like, they consist either of independently valuable objects or of medals, distinctions, or titles. In any case, they are taken to be tangible expressions of admiration, of "recognition" of talent, as means of honoring the victor. Only one competitor wins (barring ties); the others must lose or there can be no "distinction" attached to winning the prize. If everyone qualifies for the prize, then no one has won it, for the aim of the competition is to separate the best from the others.

Although the concept of desert seems at home in this context, there appears to be no use for the concept of ill desert, or at any rate ill desert and no desert come to the same thing. Either a contestant deserves the prize or he does not; there is no further alternative of deserving ill, no analogue of punishment. Moreover, since desert is here distinguished from mere worthiness, there are no degrees of desert. If the prize rightly went to Green, we can say that Jones came closer to deserving it than Smith, but not that he deserved it more than Smith, for neither deserved it.

Among the various rules which govern games, tournaments, and contests are those which specify the basis of the competition (throwing the javelin, baking a cake, writing an essay) and the conditions to be satisfied by the winner. The latter, which may be called "victory conditions," represent the form taken by qualifying conditions in competitive contexts. They vary from those which allow the victor to be determined with mathematical precision (as in broad-jumping, spelling bees, and races) to those that leave wide scope for interpretation and judgment, as in essay contests or cake-baking competitions. The basis of the competition is always some sort of skill or other esteemed trait. If it were not, then, like lotteries and raffles, the activity might still be a kind of game, but not a competitive one.

The general distinction between desert bases and qualifying conditions applies clearly to competiive situations. The desert basis is always preeminent possession of the skill singled out as a basis of competition, whereas the qualifying condition is satisfaction of the victory condition specified by the rules. The distinction is often obscured, however, by our tendency in competitive situations to use the word "desert" in two ways— not only in its customary sense of "worthiness" but also for "qualification." Even when this happens, though, our important distinction is reintroduced in new language: deserving a prize is distinguished from deserving to win a prize. In a contest of skill in which the winner can be determined by exact measurement, such as a high-jumping contest, there can be no question of who deserves the prize (qualification). It is deserved by the contestant who has demonstrably satisfied the condition of victory, in this case by jumping in the prescribed way the highest distance off the ground. There might still be controversy, however, over who deserved to win. To be sure, the victor deserved the prize, but who deserved to be victor? Perhaps the man who truly deserved to win did not in fact win because he pulled up lame, or tore his shoe, or suffered some other unforeseeable stroke of bad luck. In a contest of skill the man who deserves to win is the man who is most skilled, but (because of luck) he is not in every case the man who does win.

In a contest of skill whose rules specify a condition of victory which cannot be determined with precision but which is at least in part a matter of judgment, such as a beauty pageant or an essay contest, there can be controversy both over who deserves the prize (that is, who satisfied the imprecise victory conditions) and who deserved to win (that is, who is the most worthy or skilled at the basis of competition). If the prize is awarded to a person who does not deserve it (that is, did not qualify for it), then it is either because the judge is venal or because he erred in applying the victory criteria to the facts. Moreover, there are several possible grounds for maintaining that the person who deserves the prize is not the person who deserved to win it. The latter may have had bad luck or an off day, or the victory conditions written into the rules might themselves have been ill chosen, not truly gauging excellence at the skill which is the ostensible basis for the competition.

In a game of chance, finally, such as a lottery or a game of roulette, controversy can arise only over who deserves the prize, and even here it would turn only on relatively trivial matters of fact, for the satisfaction of the victory conditions specified by the rules of such games is usually determinable with precision. In a game of chance one cannot speak of who "really deserved to win"—that is, who has the most skill at that sort of thing—for, *ex hypothesi*, no skill is involved. Here we would all gain in clarity if we resolved to use only the legalistic language of qualification and entitlement and not speak of desert at all.

Grades

The nonpolar concept of desert finds application not only in formalized competitive situations but also in contexts calling for assessment of skill or quality generally. Following J. O. Urmson, I shall call such contexts "grading situations." The point of grading, unlike that of awarding prizes, is not to express any particular attitude toward its object, but simply to make as accurate as possible an appraisal of the degree to which it possesses some skill or quality. The desert basis of a grade is the actual possession to the appropriate degree of the quality assessed.

There are various formal procedures for grading qualities, each involving its own criteria or qualifying conditions for each grade. In the case of most human qualities which we try to grade by formal criteria (of course, there are many which we could not hope to grade that way), and especially skills and abilities, the formal grading procedure takes the form

of a test. Performance on the test then establishes qualification, in the sense of entitlement for some grade, in a manner dictated by rules.

It is not essential to a grading situation that the concept of desert have a positive-negative symmetry, and for that reason I have characterized the concept when applied in such contexts as "nonpolar"; but, of course, a relatively crude system of grading can utilize a polar concept of desert. If we are concerned to divide our apples into only two groups, those which are edible and those which are not, for example, we can speak of all the apples in the unsorted pile as deserving either the good or the bad grade. Most grading situations, however, involve a much greater range of alternatives. Some systems for grading students, for example, allow the use of each of the first one hundred positive integers as grading labels. Here there is a whole continuum of deserts; in other situations there are triads or quintets of marks deserved, and rarely are there only two possibilities—"high" or "low," "good" or "bad," "passing" or "failing."

Grading human beings, however, is still more complicated than this. Human interests themselves have an essential polarity: desires are either satisfied or to some extent frustrated, ambitions fulfilled or to some degree disappointed. And since persons are concerned with how they and their fellows are graded, they tend by their interests to convert grading systems into systems of reward and punishment. Whatever grade an ambitious student gets, he takes it as a reassuring compliment or a slap on the wrist, for relative to his ambition it is usually something welcome or unwelcome. What especially complicates discussions of human grading is that the grades are used by the graders themselves or by others for ulterior purposes—filling positions, granting licenses and privileges, and so on—and that these further purposes are well known to those who are to be graded. But to avoid confusion we should remember that a grade as such is simply a way of ranking something—an apple or a man—in respect to some quality or skill, an appraisal which may be put to some future use or may simply be put on the record for no other purpose than to register the truth.

Rewards and Punishments

We come now to contexts in which the concept of desert is essentially and necessarily polar. These are situations such that, if there is any desert at all, it must be either a good or a bad desert. The word "prize," which fits only a nonpolar concept of desert, has no antonym; neither do the grading expressions "73" or "B minus." But the responses which persons are said to deserve in polar contexts come in neat contrasting pairs—reward and punishment, compensation and liability, charge and credit, praise and blame—one word in each pair standing for a mode of response presumably either pleasant or unwelcome. The similarity here to the nonpolar contexts of competition and grading is only partial and contingent. Failure to win a prize or a grade of C minus might be unpleasant and unwelcome, but unpleasantness is not in the same way an essential part of their *raisons d'être*; suffering is an accidental and unintended consequence of competitions and gradings, not what those undertakings are for. The point of a competition is to single out a winner, not to penalize the losers; the point of a grade is to accurately appraise achievement, not (simply) to please or hurt. It is an essential and intended element of punishment, however, that the victim be made to suffer, and of liability that he be made to pay; these are not mere regrettable derivatives of the undertakings, but rather their *termini ad quem*.

Henry Sidgwick shrewdly observed that reward is "gratitude universalized" and that punishment is "resentment universalized." There is little doubt that the services and deprivations which we call "rewards" and "punishments" are conventional means of expressing gratitude and resentment, for these attitudes are prototypically those involved in the "urge to reward" and the "urge to punish." Consider typical occasions for the expression of these "urges." A whole town is endangered by a plague, and one heroically diligent scientist working against long odds perfects a serum which saves the day. Is not the feeling which prompts the normal urge to reward this man precisely gratitude and the need to give it expression? And when vigi-

lantes and lynch mobs organize to punish a murderer, are not they propelled by their resentment of what has been done? Of course, it is not up to me to feel grateful for a benefit done one stranger by another; and, according to *Webster*'s, resentment too is largely confined to responses to personal injury and affront. That is why Sidgwick defined punishment and reward as resentment and gratitude "universalized." Originating in private feelings and reactions, they become social devices for sharing imaginatively in the resentment and gratitude of all victims and beneficiaries.

Important as Sidgwick's insight is, however, it is not the whole truth about the "expressive functions" of reward and punishment. Gratitude and resentment are the most noticeable, probably the most common, and almost certainly the original attitudes expressed by reward and punishment, but they are no longer the only ones. In fact, they are probably not even necessary. If an entire community, for example, adopted the cold-blooded Kantian attitude toward punishment, approving of it only because it vindicates the moral law and eschewing altogether any personal resentment toward criminals, the result would no doubt still be recognizable as punishment, although in no sense could it be said to "express" public resentment. And the father who rewards his small son with a quarter for bringing home a good report card is hardly expressing his gratitude; after all, *he* is not the beneficiary of some service.

Rewards are, then, as Sidgwick realized, conventionally recognized means of expressing gratitude for services rendered. But they are also, as Sidgwick did not realize, means of expressing recognition, appreciation, or approval of merit or excellence. Similarly, punishment is a standard vehicle for the expression of resentment of injury received and also (but perhaps much less commonly) for the expression of recognition and disapproval of evil. The word "recognition" deserves a brief comment. When the father paid his son a quarter, he acknowledged his son's achievement without necessarily feeling joy, gratitude, or any other emotion. His reward was tangible and public evidence of his acknowledgment; it testified to his recognition. Note that "testimonial dinners" are so called because they manifest the public recognition of the achievmenets of the recipient; they "testify" to his virtues. On some theories, at least, punishment, *mutatis mutandis*, does the same sort of thing.

The responsive attitudes typically expressed by reward and punishment—gratitude, appreciation, approval, "recognition," resentment, disapproval, condemnation—and indeed all the attitudes and responses expressed by deserved modes of treatment have an important characteristic in common. It is essential to all that they have a kind of phenomenological target, that they be felt in virtue of something. All of these states of mind or attitudes contain as introspectible elements their own ostensible occasions. To resent someone, for example, is not merely to dislike him, but to have a negative feeling toward him in virtue of something he has done, and what follows the "in virtue of" is as much a part of the feeling as is its unfriendly or aggressive character.

These attitudes are not mere automatic responses to stimuli, but self-conscious responses to desert bases, not mere "reactions to," but "requitals for." If a person asks "What for?" in reply to a declaration that the speaker resents him (or is grateful to him), he does not mean "For what purpose?" These feelings are not the sorts of things that can have purposes. Rather, he means "In return for what injury [or service]?" So interpreted, the question is always pertinent. These attitudes, then, have ostensible desert logically built in to them. We do not use such words as "resent" and "grateful" unless there is an ostensible desert basis of the logically appropriate sort for our feeling. We can be fond of a person for no apparent reason, but we cannot be grateful "for nothing at all"; we can feel hostility for no apparent reason, but we cannot resent someone for "no reason at all." Bradley, in a famous line, wrote that punishment without desert is not punishment. This seems to me to be wrong; but it is clear, I think, that resentment without an ostensible desert basis is not resentment. The point that emerges is that the attitudes in question are

all felt as deserved; they cannot be freely or gratuitously bestowed or deliberately entertained "in the public interest" or "for utilitarian reasons" without any further basis. And the impossibility is not merely psychological. We can, after all, artificially induce baseless anger. But if we could do the same with resentment, it would not be resentment. We would have to call it something else.

Legal punishment and official rewards are tied up in rules and regulations, offices and functions, duties and prerogatives; they are formalized and institutionalized to an extent not even suggested by a mere concern with the attitudes they typically express. Punishment, after all, consists of such treatment as forcible seizure of property, incarceration, and whipping—never the mere feeling of resentment; and reward is the tangible expression of gratitude or recognition—never its mere harboring. Moreover, punishment is a prerogative reserved for those with the requisite authority and then only under certain strict conditions specified by law or, in the cases of families and private organizations, by what might be called "house rules." Reward and punishment, then, like other modes of deserved treatment, have qualifying conditions as well as desert bases, and these are specified by rules and regulations and confer rights and duties.

Probably because private rewards, unlike "private punishments," are harmless and even benign in their social consequences, governments rarely administer programs of reward on a large scale. Most government grants are either utilitarian inducements and subsidies or compensations. Rewards are, however, given by a large variety of private individuals and groups for a large variety of (basal) reasons, so there is no easy way of generalizing about their qualifying conditions. These are usually determined by criteria of excellence reflecting the values of the conferring groups or, when they are directly analogous to punishments, are reserved for acts of daring or self-sacrificing heroism. A person can be entitled to a reward he does not deserve, or deserving of a reward he has not qualified for. An informer who, from the basest motives, betrays his brother is entitled to the advertised reward, but he surely does not deserve it. The wife who sacrifices all to nurse her hopelessly invalid husband through endless tortuous years until death deserves a reward, but unless she qualifies under some set of institutional rules, she may not be entitled to one; she may not even be eligible for one.

It is much easier to generalize about punishment, or at least legal punishment. Its universal qualifying condition is expressible in two words, namely, "legal guilt." What legal guilt is itself is a far more complex matter, defined by thick and ponderous rule books. It is consequent on conviction after a fair trial according to due process, which in turn is defined by an elaborate code of procedural rules.

Of all those modes of official treatment for which a person might qualify under some institutional rules, only punishment seems resistant to the language of rights; for unless we are philosophers in the idealist tradition, we do not as a rule say of a criminal who is "qualified" for punishment that he is entitled to it or that he has a claim or a right to it. It is tempting, if only in the interest of symmetry and conceptual tidiness, to hold that a convicted criminal has a perfect legal right to his punishment, whether he wants it or not, in quite the same sense as that in which a person who qualifies for an advertised reward has a right to it, whether he wants it or not. Perhaps the difference is simply this: a renounced right ceases, sooner or later, to be a right, and the criminal's "right" to be punished is well-nigh certain to be renounced.

Praise and Blame

When we come to informal responses which have the nature of requitals but are not tied to institutional rules, the distinction between desert bases and qualifying conditions collapses. It takes no special authority to praise or blame, and anyone can admire or deplore. These modes of treatment are not restricted to such special officials as judges, referees, instructors, and welfare administrators, operating under public rules specifying invariant conditions. Consequently, praise and blame,

admiration and contempt, applause and jeering, and so on, though manifestly responses persons are sometimes worthy of, are never treatments people are qualified for. Just as the winners in lotteries are entitled to their prizes but cannot be said to deserve them, so persons sometimes deserve praise or blame but are never entitled to them.

Compensation, Reparation, and Liability

Still another mode of treatment which persons are often said to deserve is compensation for loss or injury. We say that persons deserve compensation for harm wrongly inflicted by others, in which case it is called "redress of injury," "amends," or "reparation" and functions not only to repair the damage but also to "restore the moral equilibrium," as would an apology or expression of remorse. Reparation "sets things straight" or "gives satisfaction." But not all injuries are tortiously inflicted. Some are the results of risks voluntarily incurred in the service of others, some are unavoidable accidents, and others are the inevitably iniquitous consequences of the specialization of labor in a technologically complex society. I shall reserve the term "reparation" for redress of injury and speak of "compensation" for losses which are no one's fault.

Desert of reparation for wrongful injury is, I believe, a polar concept, despite the grammatical awkwardness in speaking of its other "pole." If reparation is to be received by a victim, it would seem that it must be given by a wrongdoer; and it seems to follow that, if one person deserves to take, another deserves to give. But, of course, we do not talk that way. We no more say of a tortfeasor that he deserves to make reparation than we say of a warden that he deserves to punish. What we do say is that the wrongdoer deserves to be held liable for the harm he has caused; he deserves to be forced to compensate his innocent (or relatively innocent) victim. The other pole of deserved reparation is deserved liability.

Compensation for harm which is no assignable person's fault is, however, a different matter. The unemployed may deserve compensation for their loss, but it is not necessarily true that there is someone who deserves to be held liable for it. Workers in especially unpleasant, onerous, or hazardous jobs may deserve compensatory bonuses, but we would probably not express this claim by saying that their employers or any other assignable individuals deserve to have liablity imposed on them. In short, where compensation is not the redressing of injury and, hence, where it lacks the character of the mandatory repayment of a debt, desert is nonpolar. Either the suffering innocent deserve aid and succor or they do not, and that is the end of the matter. When the moral equilibrium is not unbalanced, there is no compensatory analogue of deserved punishment.

When a person suffers a loss, it may be the fault of another person or it may be no one's fault; and, as we have seen, the nature of desert differs in the two cases. There is, however, a third possibility: the loss or injury may be his own fault. In that case, though he may well be entitled to help, we should be loath to say that he deserved it; for we do not as a rule compensate people for their folly or indolence, and even when we do, it is not because we think they deserve it. Herein lies the difference between helping a person out of a jam simply through charitable beneficence and giving him aid he deserves.

If reward is the tangible expression of one or more of a small range of such appropriate attitudes as gratitude, recognition, or approval, what can proffered help be said to express? Again, I think that our answer depends on whether it is reparation of injury by a culpable party or simply compensation for unforeseeable bad luck that we are talking about. Reparation can express sympathy, benevolence, and concern, but, in addition, it is always the acknowledgment of a past wrong, a "repayment of a debt," and hence, like an apology, the redressing of the moral balance or the restoring of the *status quo ante culpum*. In the case of mere compensation, it is none of these extra things. In either case, however, the proffered help implies the recognition of

a loss for which the victim himself cannot be held wholly to blame. Thus compensation, though it is often a conventional expression of sympathy, can never express mere pity. There is nothing pitiable about a person who deserves help.

As in the case of all the other modes of treatment here discussed, so too in respect to compensation and reparation there can be desert without qualification, and vice versa. A man may be technically entitled to unemployment compensation, for example, because his situation satisfies the qualifying condition of a badly drawn rule, when in fact he does not "really" deserve it; on the other hand, deserving victims of economic blight may have "exhausted their benefits" under the law and thus fail to qualify.

Offices and Positions of Honor

I have listed what seem to be the major headings, the *summa genera*, under which the various treatments persons deserve can be grouped. This is an important start in classifying the types of deserved treatment generally, but it raises some nasty problems of subsumption. Under which heading, for example, should we subsume those high offices and positions of honor and responsibility which Sidgwick called "functions and instruments?" Are presidencies, chairmanships, generalships, professorships, papacies, and the like prizes awarded to winners in rule-governed competitions? Sidgwick thought it natural to so regard them, especially when (in his elegant words) they "are interesting and delightful in themselves, or such as are normally and properly attended with dignity and spendor of life, fame, material comfort, and freedom from sordid cares." Other writers, of whom A. C. Ewing is perhaps the most prominent, find it more natural to regard positions of honor as rewards, means by which gratitude or at least recognition of past achievement, service, or contribution is expressed.

Still others prefer to downgrade these aspects of honorable offices and regard them instead as positions of trust and responsibility to be filled in accordance with the criteria of present ability and future promise (what Sidgwick called "fitness" for the job and rather inaccurately characterized as a utilitarian consideration), rather than desert in either of its more familiar senses. "We certainly think it reasonable," Sidgwick admitted, "that instruments should be given to those who can use them best, and functions allotted to those who are most competent to perform them: but these may not be those who have rendered most services in the past. . . . Thus the notions of desert and fitness appear at least occasionally conflicting. . . ." Fitness and desert, however, are not quite so opposed as Sidgwick maintained. Consider the situation in which officials make careful appraisals of the relevant abilities and potentialities of each candidate for a job, that is, assign a grade to the fitness of each, and then use that grade as a desert basis. There is surely no logical oddness in the statement: "In virtue of his special fitness, Jones deserves the job." And if the position is a competitive one, a prize to be awarded to the winner, then fitness very likely is the basis of the competition, to be demonstrated by performance on some test, and *a fortiori* is at home with, rather than in conflict with, desert. Sidgwick saw the distinction between regarding a "function" as a reward (for past services) and as a prize (for present fitness), but he misconstrued it as a distinction between fitness and desert by preempting the concept of desert for rewards and therefore considering only past service as a desert basis.

How we select our criteria of desert, then, for such modes of treatment as selection or appointment to coveted positions depends on how we conceive those positions—whether we regard them as prizes, rewards, or compensations, to mention three possibilities. To make the matter even more complicated, many positions of honor are properly subsumable under two or more of our major rubrics at once. Consider, for example, a C. P. Snow-like contest between two leading candidates for the mastership of a Cambridge college. Candidate *A* is, on the whole, more fit for the function (considered simply as a function). He is a better administrator, a tireless worker, a clever money-raiser, and has a cooler head. In view of this superior fitness, his partisans claim that he deserves the position, conceiving it as a sort of prize. Candidate *B* is a rather older man, past his peak in all respects, but on the basis of his previous scholarly achievement much more distinguished than *A* and also better liked. His partisans argue that his distinction deserves recognition and that only the mastership would be a suitable reward. One man deserves the job when it is conceived as a prize, the other deserves it in its aspect as a reward. The conflict is not desert against advantage, justice against utility, but desert against desert.

The problem can be even more complicated. Partisans of candidate *A*, though admitting that candidate *B*'s scholarly achievements deserve recognition, might counter that candidate *A* has worked much harder for the well-being of the college and especially has won gifts and endowments for it, making possible increases in salary for each fellow; hence his past services deserve gratitude, of which the mastership would be a suitable expression. One candidate deserves reward as an expression of recognition, the other deserves reward as an expression of gratitude. And it can get still worse. *B* through bad luck, had been passed over twenty years earlier, though everyone presently agrees that he deserved the job then more than did his rival. Some of his supporters argue that only his election now can redress that injury, that he deserves reparation. But partisans of *A* point out that *A* has injured his health and suffered private pecuniary losses in his efforts to bring more contributions to the college and that therefore he deserves the compensation represented by the mastership. And so it goes—desert of prize against desert of reward, gratitude against recognition, compensation against reparation.

This familiar story should be sufficient to lay to rest the philosophical myths that desert is a single factor to be weighed against other ("utilitarian") considerations in ethical decisionmaking and that it represents uniquely the claim of justice. It is high time that this simplistic account, an offspring of another period's quarrels between intuitionists and teleologists, retributionists and utilitarians, is rejected once and for all. The claims of justice are hardly exhausted in the vacuous principle that everyone ought, *ceteris paribus*, to get what he deserves. Suppose that we decide that, "all things considered," candidate *A* deserves the mastership (assuming that *that* make sense), and then we discover that candidate *B* is *entitled* to the mastership (it was formally promised to him twenty years earlier; or a long-forgotten rule makes mandatory the selection of an entomologist for every other mastership, and he is the only entomologist in the college). Surely, we would not describe this conflict of reasons as a conflict between justice and utility. Rather, it is a conflict between desert and entitlement, between one claim of justice and another. Moreover, it seems plainly false that in *every* such ethical conflict desert has the stronger claim, that persons *always* ought, on balance, to get what they deserve.

Finally, suppose that, as they are trying to choose between *A*'s desert and *B*'s entitlement, the fellows receive a telegram from a Texas oil tycoon offering to make a gift of one million dollars to the college with no (further) strings attached, but only if they elect *A*. Now, at last, *there* is a genuine utilitarian consideration to be thrown into the balance with like considerations of profit and gain.

III

Having presented this analysis of the concept of desert, I shall conclude by briefly indicating three kinds of errors it might forestall.

Naïve Utilitarianism

A utilitarian, I suppose, is anyone who is greatly impressed by the social utility of good things and in one way or another reduces the goodness to, or identifies it with, the utility. There is no doubt that the modes of treatment discussed in this essay have considerable social utility. The awarding of prizes directly promotes cultivation of the skills which constitute bases of competition and indirectly stimulates such socially valuable conditions

as physical fitness, keenness, and competitive ardor. Assigning grades of various sorts to persons increases predictability, order, and control, permitting efficient allocation of men and resources. Hope of reward creates incentive to do worthy deeds, and the threat of punishment deters wrongdoing. Awards of reparation ease private resentments and promote domestic tranquility. Compensation distributes losses and handicaps more broadly and induces workers to take disagreeable but necessary jobs. So far, so good: utilitarianism has its points. It is in error only when it misconstrues the relevance of social utility.

First of all, utility is not a desert basis for any deserved mode of treatment. It follows from our analysis of desert statements that to say "*S* deserves *X* because giving it to him would be in the public interest" is simply to misuse the word "deserves." Secondly, utilitarian qualifying conditions, though not conceptually absurd, would in most cases be self-defeating. A utilitarian grading criterion, for example, could not very well do the job of a good grading criterion, namely, to allow as accurate as possible an appraisal of some skill or quality. If we are concerned to appraise a student's knowledge of mathematics, a "math exam" would surely be more useful for the purpose than a direct appeal to "utility." A utilitarianism which interprets utility as either a universal desert basis or a universal qualifying condition, then, is more than naïve; it is either absurd or self-defeating.

What is the relevance of social utility to "modes of deserved treatment"? Let us start from the beginning and work up to it. Men, or at least "reasonable men," naturally entertain certain responsive attitudes toward various actions, qualities, and achievements. They recognize and admire; they assess objectively; they are grateful and appreciative, resentful and disapproving; they feel remorse, sympathy, and concern. No part of this account, so far, has anything to do with utility. Now each of these responsive attitudes has its own appropriate kind of target. We do not "naturally" feel grateful for what we take to be injury or remorse for someone else's behavior; these are logically incongruous targets. But even when the object of the attitude is logically appropriate, it may still lack a certain kind of propriety. Glee, for example, is an inappropriate response to another's suffering, and, if some humanitarian philosophers are right, no kind of *Schadenfreude* is ever a fitting response to another's ill fortune. I am not sure how, if at all, these judgments of moral appropriateness are to be verified; but I suspect that they resemble certain aesthetic judgments—for example, that crimson and orange are clashing colors—more than they resemble judicial pronouncements—for example, that a certain person is to be punished for a crime or that a certain runner is to be awarded the prize for the hundred-yard dash.

If this is so, then the kind of propriety characteristic of personal desert is not only to be contrasted, as it was above, with qualification under a rule or regulation; it is also to be likened to, or even identified with, a kind of "fittingness" between one person's actions or qualities and another person's responsive attitudes. This view suggests in turn that responsive attitudes are the basic things persons deserve and that "modes of treatment" are deserved only in a derivative way, insofar perhaps as they are the natural or conventional means of expressing the morally fitting attitudes. Thus punishment, for example, might be deserved by the criminal only because it is the customary way of expressing the resentment or reprobation he "has coming."

So long as we stay on the level of responsive attitudes, there is still no place for utilitarian considerations. For example, that some person has done us a favor is a reason for his deserving our gratitude whether or not there is any utility in it. Gratitude is a "fitting" response to service. But now we come to the question of giving vent to our feelings, translating our appraisals into grades, impressing our recognition on deserving persons, and so on. We could simply do these things directly, with no further rigmarole, as we do when we praise and blame, for example, or we could harbor our attitudes unexpressed; but, instead, we often establish imposing institutions, formulate elaborate regulations, appoint referees and appraisers, judges and administrators, and

require that persons prove their deserts by qualifying for them in trials and tests and competitions.

Here, at last, is where utilitarian considerations enter in, and they have a double role. They give a reason (in addition to natural inclination) for expressing and acknowledging our attitudes and appraisals in public and conventional ways. We could, after all, merely harbor our resentments of the wrongdoer, but doing that would neither unload our aggressions nor deter crime; we could simply feel sympathy toward the unemployed, but doing that would not prevent food riots. Secondly, in requiring people to satisfy qualifying conditions specified by public regulations and administered by impartial officials, we have a system which, in respect to many kinds of activity, is probably the most reliable guide to the deserts themselves. We could allow all the responsive attitudes free expression (like praise and blame) without requiring their objects to qualify publicly; but, by and large, that would be a hit-or-miss approach. Desert is not always readily manifest, and when it is not, the "deserved modes of treatment" would be like shots in the dark. Qualifying conditions specified by the rules of competitions, tests, trials, and the like, then, are often necessary to minimize injustice. And though this is not strictly a "utilitarian consideration," it yields one immediately: we are all better off—happier, more secure—for living in a society where threat of injustice is minimized.

Inflated Desert Theory

If utilitarian theories are apt to misconstrue the relevance of utility, antiutilitarian theories are apt to inflate the role of desert. One of the aims of the various institutional practices we have considered is to guarantee that persons get what they deserve with a minimum of injustice. But to make this the paramount consideration in each single case and so try to give prizes, grades, rewards, and the like to those who deserve them instead of those who qualify for them (when these are different) would be to abrogate the controlling rules, overload officials with dangerous discretion to be used as they see fit, and thus, in the long run, given human fallibility, generate more injustice than is avoided. It may not be just (in some cosmic sense) for a prize to go to the second fastest runner rather than to his unlucky superior who pulled up lame. But giving judges discretion to award prizes to competitors whom they regard as most deserving even when they do not qualify under the rules would cause bitter resentment and bickering (utilitarian considerations) and lead to inevitable injustices. Desert is always an important consideration in deciding how we are to treat persons, especially when we are not constrained by rules or where rules give us some discretion; but it is not the only consideration and is rarely a sufficient one.

Desert as Moral Entitlement

The final kind of mistake precluded by this analysis tends to be committed by philosophers who hold a parajuridical conception of morality. These philosophers take legal institutions as their models, consciously or not, in explicating puzzling moral concepts and then obscure the distinction between the moral and the legal (or institutional) by interpreting the former as an eccentric species of the latter. In the case at hand, the distinction between entitlement and desert is obscured by making desert a peculiar *kind* of entitlement, instead of a notion in essential contrast with entitlement. Desert confers rights, says this theory, but not the ordinary kind of right of the sort winners of competitions and claimants of rewards have, for example, but rather "moral rights," assigned by special "moral rules," which in turn are implicitly treated as regulations of a special "moral institution." There are, of course, a variety of legitimate uses of the expression "moral right," but this is almost certainly not one of them. The defeated presidential candidate who deserved to win, for instance, is not by that token entitled to the office, nor does he have any right to it. These rights are conferred by votes, not by deserts. And I fail to see how matters are clarified by qualifying the alleged entitlement as "moral." The defeated candidate has no right to the office, moral or otherwise, unless of course "moral right" is simply another, eccentric way of referring to his deserts. "Deserve," "fitting," and "appropriate," on the one hand, and "right," "entitlement," and "rule," on the other, are terms from altogether different parts of our ethical vocabularies; they are related in such a way that there is no paradox in saying of a person that he deserves (it would be fitting for him to have) certain modes of treatment which, nevertheless, he cannot claim as his due.

This analysis has attempted to show in just what sense the moral notion of desert is prior to a system of public bestowals (one of the aims of the latter is to give people what they deserve) and in what sense it is not (bestowals can often be most justly conferred if the system is governed rather strictly by qualifying rules). We have also seen the variety of conflicts which are possible between desert and desert and between desert and entitlement. These conflicts within the category of justice are as subtle and difficult as any others in ethics, and it is doubtful that general principles can be formulated to dictate *a priori* the preferred manner of their resolution in every case. But if desert and entitlement are not distinct in nature, the question of their relation cannot be difficult or complicated; for then there could be only "real," or "higher," entitlement (desert) and "lower," or "inferior," entitlement (qualification), and in cases of conflict the higher would always take precedence over the lower. This is what comes of efforts to compare the incomparable by positing a special cosmic institution in which the one has a subordinate and the other a superior place, of attempts to unify contrasting ethical and institutional concepts by locating them at opposite ends of a common scale. It is important to emphasize, then, in concluding, that desert is a *moral* concept in the sense that it is logically prior to and independent of public institutions and their rules, not in the sense that it is an instrument of an ethereal "moral" counterpart of our public institutions.

10. The Concept of Desert

JOHN KLEINIG

John Kleinig is Professor at John Jay College of Criminal Justice. His books include *Punishment and Desert* (1974), *Paternalism* (1984), and *Ethical Issues in Psychosurgery* (1985).

Kleinig attempts to answer three crucial questions about desert: (i) What sorts of things can be deserving? Kleinig is prepared to accept that not only persons but also nonpersons (e.g., works of art, natural objects) can be literally deserving. (ii) What sorts of treatment can be deserved? Kleinig's view is that "anything which is pleasant or unpleasant can be said to be deserved (by people, that is)." (iii) What constraints are there on possible bases for desert? Kleinig defends the view that desert is "never simply forward-looking." That is, the basis of desert at any given time is necessarily rooted in an action performed, or attribute acquired, prior to that time. Kleinig's paper is noteworthy also for its threefold division of desert-claims into "raw," "institutionalized," and "specific" and for the distinction it draws between desert and entitlement.

It seems to be very often the case that the claims of justice and fairness can be fulfilled only if people are given their deserts, whether good or ill. Yet the notion of desert seems by and large to have been consigned to the philosophical scrap heap. No doubt this has something to do with the unpopularity of intuitionism, with which it is usually associated, and the present popularity of consequentialism or utilitarianism, with which it is usually contrasted. In Sect. I of this paper three types of desert claims will be distinguished. Sects. II–IV will be devoted to a consideration of some of the constitutive elements of such desert claims, Sect. V to the force of making desert claims, and Sect. VI to some of the relations between the various types of desert claims distinguished in Sect. I.

I

We may distinguish three general *types* of desert claims:

(a) *Raw desert claims*, which have the (at least implicit) general form: "*X* deserves *A* in virtue of *B*." Raw desert claims are not dependent on any legal or quasi-legal system of rules and therefore the responsibility for their fulfillment does not devolve upon any particular person or authority. Take the following examples.

(i) Peters deserves to get good weather for his holidays. He's planned everything so carefully.

(ii) Smith deserves a break-through. He's been working at that problem for years now.

Reprinted from the *American Philosophical Quarterly* 8:1 (January 1971), by permission.

(iii) Martin deserves to be punished. He lied to Jackson and Burns about ringing up yesterday.

Although we may be prepared to say quite specifically that Peters deserves "good weather" and Smith deserves a "breakthrough," there is no one whom we would hold responsible if they did not get it. In Martin's case (assuming that he is an adult and that lying as such does not constitute a legal or quasi-legal offense), if he is punished, then he probably has no grounds for complaint, but if he is not, then no one in particular is to blame for this. Raw desert claims are to be contrasted with:

(b) *Institutionalized desert claims*, which have the (at least implicit) general form: "X deserves A of Y in virtue of B." The deserved treatment in these cases presupposes a context of legal or quasi-legal rules—as in the following cases:

(i) Nolan deserved the prize for his efforts. His painting was by far the best.
(ii) Mckenzie deserves to go to jail for robbing that old lady.
(iii) Menzies deserved to be honored for his contribution to Commonwealth relations.

In each of these cases a claim is implicitly made on some particular authority: the competition sponsors or judges, the law, and the monarchy respectively. Sometimes only the context will tell us whether or not a desert claim is institutionalized. Claims such as "X deserves compensation" and "X deserves punishment" need to be specified more fully before we can tell what type they are. There is a third type of desert claim, which I call:

(c) *Specific desert claims*. These are usually, but not necessarily, of the same general form as institutionalized desert claims, but they concern not so much *what* is deserved as *how much* is deserved; e.g.:

(i) Nolan deserved every bit of the $500 he got for the First Prize.

(ii) McKenzie deserved about 5 years jail for his offense.
(iii) Menzies deserved at least a K.C.M.G.

Discussion of (c) will be held over until Sect. VI.

II

I want to go on now to consider, in order, that which is said to be deserving (X), that which is deserved (A), and the grounds of desert (B).

The Deserving (X)

In his *Review of the Principal Question in Morals*, Richard Price informs us that

> The epithets, *right* and *wrong*, are, with strict propriety, applied only to actions; but *good* and *ill* desert belong rather to the *agent*. It is the *agent* alone, that is capable of happiness or misery; and, therefore, it is he alone that can properly be said to *deserve* these.

By insisting that desert applies "with strict propriety" or "properly" only to agents, Price implicitly recognizes the fact that we do not always speak as though this were the case. For we commonly make statements like "Nolan's painting deserved the First Prize" or "Alexander's manuscript deserves publication." These, Price would say, are only elliptical ways of saying "Nolan deserved the First Prize for his painting" or "Alexander deserves to have his manuscript published." Now it might be possible to rephrase all such desert claims in this way, but even if it is, Price fails to distinguish cases where the grounds for desert relate primarily to qualities possessed by the agent, and cases where they relate primarily to that which the agent has produced (a painting, a manuscript, etc.). Price does not appear to see this point.

However, we may think that he was not far wrong. For in the examples we have given, nonhuman objects which could be said to deserve a particular kind of treatment or consideration did not do so apart from their being artefacts or products of some intentional agent or agency. But this will not quite do. We can quite properly speak of the Niagara Falls being deservedly famous or of the Western Australian coastline deserving to be as well known as that of the East. Here there is no presumption that these sights are human artefacts. Of course the fact that they are not artefacts limits the sorts of things that they can deserve—praise and fame are about all.

One implication which the foregoing has for our analysis of desert claims is that it indicates that desert is not a specifically moral notion. Although desert claims often—perhaps usually—have moral overtones there does not seem to be any necessity that they should. We would be more correct in saying that desert belongs within the general field of evaluation than that it is tied to moral contexts.

which is capable of giving us "happiness or misery" (Price), or, to put it more generally, anything which is pleasant or unpleasant. Deserved treatment is not something toward which we remain indifferent. We are glad when our arguments are given serious consideration, and upset if they are just passed off. To have a manuscript accepted for publication is an achievement, to have it rejected a disappointment. We enjoy being rewarded and dislike being punished.

In the case of institutionalized desert claims, that which is deserved (A), is characteristically treatment which comes as the intended result of some agent or agency—honors, prizes, success, compensation, reward, and punishment (in so far as they are institutionally based). But this does not necessarily hold for raw desert claims; e.g., "Peters deserves to get good weather for his holidays" and "Smith deserves a break-through."

III

The Deserved (A)

Contrary to much philosophical opinion, reward and punishment are not the only proper objects of desert. True, some of the things which people can be said to deserve, such as prizes and honors, are, in so far as they are deserved, reducible to rewards. But other things which people can deserve are not subsumable under the twofold classification of reward and punishment. We might say of someone who has suffered through another's negligence, that he deserved some sort of compensation. Or we might speak of people deserving praise and blame (and these cannot always be subsumed under the categories of reward and punishment).

I do not want to suggest that these categories of things which may be said to be deserved (rewards, punishments, praise, blame, compensation) are necessarily exhaustive. Anything which is pleasant or unpleasant can be said to be deserved (by people, that is). It is logically possible to deserve anything

IV

The Grounds of Desert (B)

When we say "X deserves A" we are implicitly committed to holding reasons for X's desert. It is logically absurd for X to deserve A for no reason in particular, or for no reason at all. However, not any sort of reasons are appropriate to the making of desert claims. Desert can be ascribed to something or someone only on the basis of characteristics possessed or things done by that thing or person. That is, desert is never simply forward-looking. This was recognized by the classical retributivists and has understandably been responsible for the traditional conflict of so-called retributive and utilitarian justifications of punishment.

If a manuscript is said to deserve publication, this is said not on the basis of the impact which it is likely to make or some future benefits which it will bring, but on the basis of the quality of its contents. If a student deserves to pass an examination, he does so, not because this will encourage him or get him a scholarship, but in virtue of his performance (and his performance is not necessarily limited to the examination itself, for a student may have failed the examination, yet deserve to have passed). If a person deserves compensation for some loss, then he does so not because things will be very difficult for him if he does not get some, but because his loss has been sustained through someone else's mismanagement, negligence, or deception, etc. When a person deserves to be punished, he does so, not because it will reform him or deter others, but because he has done something morally wrong. A person may deserve to be punished even though carrying it out would have disastrous effects on him and/or society. The disastrous consequences could be reasons for not punishing him, but not for his not deserving to be punished.

We need, however, to note that desert claims can be made only on the basis of characteristics possessed or things done by the *subject* of the claim. Sir Robert Menzies did not deserve a knighthood because Dame Pattie happened to be a very active social worker, or because it would have fulfilled her greatest ambition for him. For these were not things done by Sir Robert himself, and although they could conceivably have been reasons for conferring a knighthood on him, they could not conceivably be reasons for his deserving a knighthood.

I want now to digress briefly to consider some aspects of Duncan-Jones' attempt to give an act-utilitarian analysis of desert claims. We might argue, he suggests, that

> When we say a man is responsible, and has certain deserts, the whole meaning of our statement can be resolved into two clauses: (1) he has done a good or bad action, or a right or wrong action; (2) it is useful to apply certain sanctions to him—useful, that is, in the way of influencing his habits and other people's.

Nevertheless, although these two clauses "convey the whole of our meaning when we ascribe responsibility or desert, they are not the whole of what we have in mind." For we "tend to feel repugnance towards bad actions and those who do them, and to have friendly and warm feelings towards those who do good actions." Thus,

> our spontaneous feelings back up the policy which, on utilitarian grounds, ought to be adopted. But suppose in exceptional cases, it were established that penalties for the bad and rewards for the virtuous would do more harm than good, our sentiments would not be correspondingly apportioned: we should still wish the good to prosper and the bad to suffer. In consequence, we come to feel that there is a sort of intrinsic tie between the moral value of a man's character or conduct and the way in which he ought to be treated.

But this account obliterates the distinction which I have been hinting at, between deserved treatment and needed treatment. A person may very well deserve treatment of a certain sort without needing it, and may need it without deserving it. A rich man may well deserve compensation for some financial loss occasioned to him as a result of another's negligence, yet most probably he will not need it. In fact, the person on whom the burden of compensation falls may need it far more than the rich man. On the other hand, a child who has come from a tough background may need all the encouragement and help it can get from its teacher yet such encouragement and help can hardly be said to be deserved, even if it brings forth good results.

Furthermore, Duncan-Jones suggests that when we ascribe desert, we have in mind more than utilitarian considerations. We are also expressing our repugnance, though this does not form part of what we mean by "deserve." It is true that desert claims can be used as vehicles of sheer animus, especially in such phrases as "It serves you right," and that this is detachable from the meaning of "desert." On these occasions desert claims are not being used to ascribe desert but to express malice; or, as Duncan-Jones would put it, they express the fulfillment of our wish that the bad should suffer. However, desert does not involve a *wish* that the bad should suffer, even though I think we might agree with Strawson that there is a feeling of re-sentiment or indignation toward a person who has done a wrong act which is conceptually related to our judgment of his responsibility for that act, and cannot be detached from it. But resentment and moral indignation are not to be confused with feelings of ill-will, and the *wish* that the bad should suffer.

Leaving aside cases in which inanimate objects can be said to be deserving, I want to consider in more detail the precise nature of the things done or characteristics possessed for which X or X's producer can be held responsible, and which support or justify the claim that X deserves A. For it is at this point that an important confusion has crept into many philosophical discussions of desert.

Brian Barry has maintained that the grounds for desert claims can be of two different sorts, and on the strength of this he has argued that there are two senses of *desert*. He contrasts two sentences:

(1) "Anyone who climbs that rock deserves £50 and I hereby offer it"; and
(2) "Since £50 has been offered for climbing the rock and I have climbed it, I deserve it."

In the first sentence *desert* "might be taken to prescribe specific amounts of differentials," whereas in the second *desert* is used in a "subsidiary sense," and it is claimed only that "given the prize is so much, so-and-so deserves it more than anyone else in that he fulfills the conditions laid down better than anyone else." Barry considers that (1) is more appropriate to wage determination and punishment, whereas (2) is more at home when used "in connection with the contest procedure." In such cases, "the prize may have been set up not to reward desert but to stimulate productions of suitable kinds; nevertheless, it generates a sense of desert in the subsidiary sense."

This second sense of "desert," I would maintain, is not a genuine sense of "desert" at all. Instead, what Barry has given us is an analysis of "entitlement" and "liability," and desert is not a kind of entitlement or liability. Desert, unlike entitlement and liability, is not created by satisfying the conditions laid down in a system of legal or quasi-legal rules, even if some things can be deserved only because of a pre-existing system of legal or quasi-legal rules. These latter cases would correspond with what I have called institutionalized desert claims. To say that a person deserves a higher wage than he is getting is not to say he is entitled to it. This, I guess, is one of the reasons for having unions and arbitration courts: to endeavor to secure wages commensurate with employees' deserts. The person who is entitled to the prize for winning a competition of skill is not necessarily the person who deserves it. His win may be a fluke, or the result of moves that are shrewd though permissible (within the rules of the game). It is only to confuse the issue to speak of people having a moral right or entitlement to treatment of a particular kind. Of course we do, as Feinberg properly points out, speak of "moral rights," but we do this in connection with what we consider to be basic human rights, and not in connection with the parochial claims involved in ascribing desert. Our moral right to freedom from interference is not something which we are said to *deserve*.

Now there are of course occasions when what a person deserves is conferred by a system of rules; e.g., the painting that deserves to win may actually win. Nevertheless, though entitlement and desert may coincide in such cases, the grounds of the entitlement are not precisely the same as the grounds of desert. In this particular case, the grounds for entitlement include the decision of the judges that this particular painting be given First Prize, and this is provided for in the conditions according to which the competition is conducted, namely, "The judges' decision shall be final." The judges could have chosen an inferior painting, and then *that* would have been entitled to the prize: though the decision may well have caused an uproar. The grounds of desert are found primarily in the quality of the painting, and perhaps secondarily in the circumstances surrounding its production; e.g., the age of the artist, whether he was in some way handicapped, etc. In other words, the desert relates to what could be very loosely called the "skill" or "ability" displayed in the painting. If we take the case of payment for labor, a person deserves what he gets by virtue of such things as his industry, efficiency, etc. But he is entitled to what he gets solely by virtue of an agreement or contract between his employer and himself. He may get sacked because he is lazy, inefficient, etc.; i.e., because he does not deserve what he is getting. But until he gets sacked, he is entitled to the pay even though he does not deserve it. The distinction between entitlement and desert enables us to distinguish the situation where the employer cheats the employee from that in which he exploits him.

Barry's confusion of desert with entitlement arises mainly from his failure to distinguish properly between institutionalized and raw desert claims. He correctly recognizes that some desert claims arise independently of any legal or quasi-legal rules and that others arise only because of an already existing system of legal or quasi-legal rules. His mistake lies in thinking that the difference necessitates two different senses of desert, whereas I have suggested that the difference lies rather in the fact that institutionalized desert claims at least implicitly prescribe a dispenser of deserts. In so far as the two senses are different, this is because desert has been confused with entitlement.

We can now state more clearly the type of grounds (*B*) by virtue of which *X* is said to deserve *A*. These must be such as *evaluate* (at least implicitly) the characteristics possessed or things done by *X*. This can be seen if we look again at the sorts of considerations which we actually adduce in making desert claims. For example, relevant to saying that a person deserves a promotion will be such things as his initiative, efficiency, and industry (all of which involve here, at least, an evaluation). Or, if we look at the sorts of considerations which will be relevant to saying that Woods deserves to fail his exams, we shall point to such things as laziness, poor performance, and cheating.

It is at this point, I think, that many of the problems surrounding the notion of desert arise. Desert claims rely on evaluation of char-

acteristics possessed or things done by their subjects (if the description of such characteristics or things done is not implicitly evaluative). On what basis are such evaluations made? This is obviously too big a question to go into here. Not only am I doubtful whether it can be given any general answer, but to attempt to give it one is irrelevant to my purposes in this paper. What I think can be pointed out, however, is that on the analysis I have given, the concept of desert is relatively (though certainly not absolutely) neutral as between various ethical and value theories. Certainly, an intuitionist could make use of the concept, but so equally might a consequentialist, provided of course that the latter was willing to modify or complicate his theory. For example, it does not seem impossible to argue that the evaluations on which desert claims are based should be made on utilitarian grounds, even though desert claims do not themselves have the same forward-looking character. This way of fitting desert claims into general utilitarian theory must not be identified with rule-utilitarianism, which, as I have suggested, can give at most an analysis of entitlement and liability; nevertheless, it would involve a modification to utilitarianism similar to that involved in rule-utilitarianism.

V

The Force of Desert Claims

So far I have suggested that it is appropriate and correct to say of a certain subject, *X* that it deserves *A*, where *A* is a form of pleasant or unpleasant treatment, when *X* possesses characteristics or has done something, *B*, which constitute a positive or negative evaluation of *X*. Naturally the criteria of evaluation will differ with different kinds of subjects. Those for saying that a natural rock formation is deservedly famous are not going to be the same as for saying that McKenzie was deservedly punished.

But what is the force of the remark: "*X* deserves *A*" or "*X* was deservedly *A*ed"? What role do desert claims play in our language? I have already indicated that in saying that *X* deserves *A* we are *evaluating* or *appraising* *X*. As well, I noted that desert claims are sometimes used as expressions of vindictiveness, as in: "It served you right." Some writers have regarded desert claims as paradigm expressions of vengefulness. But if our analysis so far has been in the right direction, we should be able to see that this is not so, and that the use of desert claims as expressions of vindictive feeling is to prevert them from their central role. Apart from anything else desert claims can be properly made in too many different contexts to be susceptible to this sort of analysis (this is the danger of restricting one's examples to those of punishment), and unless we hold a rather crude emotivist theory, the fact that they are based on evaluations renders this interpretation even more implausible.

In saying that *X* deserves *A* we can be claiming any of the following things, depending on the context:

"*X* ought to get or suffer *A*";

"It would be a good thing to give *X* (for *X* to suffer) *A*";

"If *X* gets or suffers *A* he has no grounds for complaint."

I do not want to suggest that these formulations are equivalent, and that "*X* deserves *A*" is always interchangeable with any one of these statements. "*X* deserves *A*" is just one formulation of "*X* ought to get or suffer *A*," etc.—such that the grounds of the claim are *in virtue of* characteristics or acts of *X* rather than *in order to* produce certain consequences. The latter may also constitute legitimate grounds for ought claims. Sometimes situations arise in which we say "*X* deserves *A* although *X* ought not to get or suffer *A*." For example, if jailing a man for theft would (because of prison conditions) endanger his life, then, provided that other possible means of punishment were also open to objections, we could argue that he ought not to be punished, even though he deserved it. We would probably ask that his sentence be suspended. Similarly, were the punishment of a convicted

spy likely to trigger off a nuclear war, then we would have a ground for saying that he ought not to be punished. But this would in no way eliminate the fact that he deserved to be punished.

This I think forces us to distinguish, with Feinberg, two types of ought judgments, first, those in which we say that *X* ought to get *A* "all things considered," "in the final judgment," or "on balance"—and secondly, those in which we say that *X* ought to get *A* "*pro tanto*" or "other things being equal." "*X* deserves *A*" he considers, entails an ought judgment of the latter kind:

> A person's desert of *X* is always a reason for giving *X* to him, but not always a conclusive reason. . . . Considerations irrelevant to his desert can have overriding cogency in establishing how he ought to be treated on balance.

VI

To conclude this paper I want to make a few comments on the relation of specific desert claims to raw and institutionalized desert claims.

In each of the examples I gave an institutional framework was pre-supposed. Prize-giving, knighthoods, and imprisonment are social institutions. However, it is not necessary for specific desert claims to presuppose an institutional framework, even though they usually do. The statement, "Peters deserves to get good weather (but not a trip around the world) for his holidays" can be construed as a specific desert claim, yet no institution which can supply such treatment needs be presupposed.

Consideration of the possibility of making and justifying specific desert claims raises a problem of considerable magnitude, namely that of the commensurability of values. Only quantities, and not qualities, can be measured, it is argued, and so it is impossible to talk intelligibly of a person deserving so much of a particular kind of treatment, be it imprisonment, hard cash, or public title. I think it has to be admitted that on the surface this is a strong objection and that the onus rests on the person who wants to make such claims to justify them. On the other hand, I don't think it is a necessarily insuperable problem, partly because it presupposes a distinction between fact and value which is not uncontroversial.

However, it's not my intention to get embroiled in this dispute. What I want to do, rather, is to criticize one way of avoiding the problem which I have just mentioned. It is sometimes claimed that although desert considerations are relevant to whether or not a person ought to receive reward, punishment, compensation, praise, or blame, etc., nevertheless, the *amount* which he receives must be determined by other, maybe consequentialist considerations. Bosanquet, in *The Philosophical Theory of the State*, puts forward a view something like this. While maintaining that punishment is the wrongdoer's "right, of which he must not be defrauded," he also insists that the state "cannot estimate either pain or moral guilt. . . . The graduation of punishments must be almost entirely determined by experience of their operation as deterrents."

This view has a number of unwelcome consequences. For one thing, it is artificially stipulative and restrictive, since it necessitates our discarding a number of significant locutions relating to the severity of punishment. Except, I think, in a secondary legal sense, it is open to us to speak of penalties as just or unjust only if we can also determine whether or not they are deserved. If we succumb to the view that the determination of specific deserts is either impossible or unnecessary, then we remove from ourselves the possibility of criticizing penalties inflicted on wrongdoers from the point of view of their justice or, rather, injustice. This is a high price to pay. Bosanquet's view would also rule out the possibility of our speaking of some people deserving greater penalties or heavier punishments than others.

Second, if other, say utilitarian, considerations are used to determine how much pun-

ishment a person ought to suffer, then the possibility is left open that a person will suffer appreciably more or less punishment than he deserves—witness the case of exemplary punishments. Such punishments are unjust. To obviate this objection, Bosanquet would need to show either that utilitarian considerations would never lead to a person's suffering more punishment than he deserved, or, alternatively, why utilitarian considerations cannot override desert in the determination of whether or not a person ought to suffer punishment, whereas they can in the determination of how severe a punishment a person ought to suffer. Neither of these possibilities seems to have much to commend it.

It would seem, then, that if the claims of justice are to be fulfilled, then not only the question whether or not a person ought to get rewarded, punished, compensated, etc., but also the question how much he ought to get, must be settled by reference to desert considerations and this of course necessitates facing up to the problems involved in measuring and relating values.

There is just one final point I want to make to avoid a possible confusion. There is some ambiguity in the examples I have given as to what, exactly, is said to be determined by desert. Take the example: "Nolan deserved every bit of the $500 he got for the First Prize." We can distinguish (somewhat artificially) the following four elements in it:

First, there is the *pleasant treatment* which is involved in awarding Nolan the $500 as First Prize. Pleasant treatment, as we have seen, is a proper object of desert.
Second, since the statement presupposes an institutional context, it is quite appropriate to speak of the deserved treatment as a *prize*.
Third, a specific *amount* of money and a specific *grade* of prize are said to be deserved, and there is no linguistic impropriety in this.

These three elements correspond to the distinctive features of raw, institutionalized, and specific desert claims. But there is a fourth element which can be discerned, and which might be thought to constitute a legitimate desert, namely that Nolan deserved to get five hundred *dollars* as First Prize, rather than, say, a cup, an overseas trip, or a scholarship. It seems to me that the determination of what *sort* of deserved treatment to give a person is, within certain limits, settable on other, perhaps consequentialist, grounds. For example, in an Art Competition a money prize might act as a greater incentive than possible alternatives.

Much more can, and I guess at some stage must, be said about desert claims. But perhaps it is some advance to see that desert is not the mysterious notion that it is sometimes supposed to be, that it is neither an exclusive possession of the intuitionist nor an intolerable thorn in the side of a consequentialist, and that the problems confronting the justification of desert claims are for the most part simply the problems faced by any kind of evaluation.

11. Deserts

DAVID MILLER

David Miller is Professor of Politics at Nuffield College, Oxford. He is the author of many articles and books, including *Social Justice* (1976) and *Market, State, and Community* (1989).

What are the bases for desert? Miller proposes an answer: "The range of possible desert bases coincides with the range of possible bases for appraising attitudes." This view can be brought out as follows. There are some attitudes, such as anxiety and joy, that do not seem to require a specific object. One can be anxious or joyful, but at nothing in particular. Other attitudes are not like that. They do require an object. These attitudes include admiration, gratitude, disgust, resentment, and so on. Miller calls these the "appraising attitudes." Miller's view seems to be that the appropriate bases of appraising attitudes are, or at least "coincide" with, the bases for desert.

This view, if correct, provides Miller with a way to determine what is a desert base and what is not. So, for example, some have held that need is a basis for desert. Yet, Miller argues, need is not an appropriate basis of admiration of resentment or, indeed, any appraising attitude. It is not appropriate to admire or resent on the basis of a person's needs. Thus, need is not a basis for desert. Miller offers a similar argument against regarding entitlement as a desert base.

1. Desert, Entitlement, and Need

. . . [W]e had occasion to discuss the view, held by J. S. Mill and others, that the concepts of justice and rights are co-extensive; that every claim of justice can be presented as a claim of individual rights. This view we rejected, as based upon a fallacious chain of argument, but not before observing how easily the two concepts came to be identified. The ordinary use of the concept of a right is not precise, and indeed the great majority of assertions concerning justice can be re-expressed in terms of that concept without manifest verbal impropriety. The reasons for imposing a more rigorous use in this area are philosophical in character, not linguistic. They have to do with the distinctive character of rights-claims, with the values which are being appealed to when such claims are made. Desert- and need-claims, we shall see, have an entirely different moral standing. The contrast is lost if we allow casual everyday speech to blind us to the distinctions in question.

The concept of desert has a tendency to expand in the same way as the concept of a right, with similar results. In its widest, loosest sense, 'A deserves X' means 'It is fitting for A to have X' or 'X is due to A'. If we recall our abstract definition of justice as *suum*

Reprinted from *Social Justice* (Oxford University Press, 1976), by permission.

cuique, we can see how, in this widest sense, desert encompasses the whole of justice. Justice means 'to each his due'; desert refers to what it is fitting for each person to have. Hence, as Hospers put it, 'justice is getting what one deserves; what could be simpler?'

Taking 'desert' in this widest sense, we can find cases in which claims of rights and need are expressed, perfectly naturally, in the language of desert. Consider the following statements.

(1a) Since £50 has been offered for climbing the rock and I have climbed it, I deserve it.[1]
(1b) The man who breasts the tape first deserves first prize.
(2a) Old-age pensioners deserve to be exempted from prescription charges.
(2b) The hungriest child deserves the last piece of cake.

On reflection it seems clear that (1a) and (1b) are really claims of rights. On the verbal level, 'deserves' can in each case be replaced by 'is entitled to'; but, more importantly, if we ask in each case for the ground upon which the person concerned should be allocated the benefit, we find typical right-creating circumstances. In (1a) we have an extended *promise* made by the person who offered the £50, hence a right in whoever fulfils the qualifying conditions.[2] In (1b) we have a set of *publicly established rules*, i.e. the rules of the race, and the man who qualifies under these rules has a right to the prize. Analogously, statements (2a) and (2b) are really claims of need. If prescription charges are to be imposed, pensioners should have special exemption because their need for medicine is especially great, both absolutely and in relation to their slender resources. The cake is due to the hungriest child because he needs it more than any of the others. As with statements (1a) and (1b), the verbal form (the use of the concept of desert) conceals the real grounds on which the claim is made.

But, it may be said, this argument rests on a false assumption. You claim that in these cases 'desert' is used in a loose sense, and the statements are really statements of a different type; but why should not people's rights and needs serve as a *basis* for their deserts? Why cannot you have genuine desert claims which are grounded on claims of rights or need? More than one writer has seen nothing odd in taking need as a basis of desert.

The full answer to this must wait upon the detailed analysis of the concept of desert in the following section, but by way of a preliminary this may be said: desert is a matter of fitting forms of treatment to the specific qualities and actions of individuals, and in particular good desert (i.e. deserving benefit as opposed to punishment) is a matter of fitting desired forms of treatment to qualities and actions which are generally held in high regard. If we compare the notion of rights, and consider our analysis of the types of right-creating situations, we shall see that they make no reference to the particular qualities of the individuals concerned. For instance, someone makes me a promise, and I thereby acquire a right; this happens irrespective of what I am or do. Or I qualify for a benefit under a rule; here, of course, there may or may not be a qualifying condition, but even if there is it may be one (such as 'being an adult') which segregates people without reference to their own peculiar qualities or actions.

The cases considered earlier ((1a) and (1b)) are somewhat more complicated, for in order to gain the entitlement the people concerned had to perform specific actions, probably requiring unusual personal qualities. For this reason questions both of desert and of entitlement are involved, though the questions remain separate. To become entitled to the £50, I had simply to climb to the top of the rock, nothing more nor less. To decide whether I deserved that sum, we should have to investigate several other matters, such as the difficulty of the climb (perhaps the person who made the offer had overlooked a simple route) and my own capacities as a climber. Similarly, in the case of the race, the man who is entitled to the prize—the first man to reach the tape—may not be the man who deserves to win it, as Feinberg points out. 'Perhaps the man who truly deserved to win did not in fact win because he pulled up lame, or tore his shoe, or suffered some other unforeseeable stroke of bad luck.'

In short, then, the reason for keeping rights and deserts distinct, and refusing to consider rights as a *basis* for desert lies in the contrast between a principle which attaches benefits to persons without essential reference to personal qualities (but *with* reference to earlier transactions, etc.) and a principle which is exclusively concerned with apportioning advantages to personal characteristics.

The principle of need is also concerned with apportioning advantages to the particular characteristics of each person. Every man should be given advantages according to the extent and nature of his needs. Yet need is inappropriate as a basis of desert; being needy cannot make us deserving. To explain this, we should look at the second point I made about desert: 'good desert is a matter of fitting desired forms of treatment to qualities and actions which are generally held in high regard'. What disqualifies needs from being taken as grounds for desert is, first, that (for most needs) everyone has them until they are satisfied, and, second, that no one wishes to have them, or admires others for having them. The point can be reinforced by considering contexts in which needs might be looked upon as valued possessions. It is, for instance, sometimes claimed that our personal needs for love and affection from others are valuable, and that those who lack these needs are deprived—'people who need people are the luckiest people in the world', in the words of a popular song. If this is so, having such personal needs is a possible basis for desert— one might at least deserve praise or congratulation for being needy in this way. If this still sounds odd, it is probably because the great majority are 'people who need people', hence there is nothing outstanding or exceptional in having the needs we have been considering.

Needs are not unique in being generally inappropriate as a basis of desert. The same is true of beliefs, or preferences, or interests; we cannot claim that people deserve benefits because of what they believe, and again the reason is that there is nothing in the actual holding of a belief (as opposed to the process of arriving at it) which we can appropriately admire.

I shall have more to say about 'need' later, but I hope that I have said enough at this point to justify my claim that rights, deserts, and needs must be kept separate, and that the central sense of 'desert' must be distinguished from its wider use, as featured in statements (1a)–(2b).

2. The Concept of Desert

I shall confine my remarks in this and the following sections to desert of benefits, or 'good desert' as it is sometimes called, and make no more than passing reference to deserved harm, whose main sub-categories are deserved blame and punishment. I think that this is not only excusable in a discussion of social justice but positively advantageous, in so far as those who have treated deserved benefit and harm together have often arrived at a distorted understanding of the former due to excessive concentration on the problems raised by the latter. When we consider what it is to deserve punishment, we quickly discover that desert here carries a moral sense—men are held to deserve punishment for moral wrongs they have committed. By analogy, good desert is given a moral sense as well, and the problem becomes one of apportioning external advantages to the moral virtues of individuals. Yet few desert judgements made in practical contexts have this character. When we argue about whether a particular employee deserves a higher wage than he is now earning, we mention his skill, his responsibilities, the effort he puts into his work, but not his moral character. It is plain that the kind of desert which is relevant to social justice is rarely *moral* desert.[3]

It is in fact most important to keep in mind the range and variety of judgements which we make using the concept of desert, even if the extended uses discussed in the last section are excluded. Restrictive theories about the features of men's conduct which *must* serve as a basis for their deserts can often be exploded by taking examples from an area which had not been considered by the proponent of the theory. This variety shows itself in at least two ways. There is (1) the contrast between desert judgements which are broad and unspecific, and those which are more specific *either* because they state with some precision what is deserved *or* because they state from whom it is deserved. Thus compare 'Jones deserves to succeed' with 'Jones deserves at least £4,000 a year' or 'Jones deserves a salary increase from his employer'. There is also (2) the range of generic modes of treatment which may be deserved: rewards, honours, prizes, offices, income, praise, recognition, etc. The diversity here is important, because the reasons which can be given for saying that a person deserves one of these modes of treatment may be specific to that mode. The reasons for which one deserves a prize are rarely of the same kind as the reasons for which one deserves a reward.

In all these cases, however, there must be *a* reason for deserving. Whenever we make a claim of the form 'A deserves X', whatever X is, we must be prepared to indicate the feature of A, or A's conduct, in virtue of which he deserves X. If I say 'Smith deserves to win the mile', it is proper for someone else to ask 'Why does he deserve to?' and I must be able to reply (for example) 'He has trained harder than anyone else.' The reason must be a descriptive statement about the person or his conduct. I shall call such a statement the desert basis.

To understand the relationship between a desert basis and a judgement of desert, it is helpful to switch our attention away from desert proper for a moment and look at certain attitudes which one person may hold towards another: attitudes such as admiration, approval, and gratitude, for which I shall use the generic term 'appraising attitudes'. It is plain that, like judgements of desert, these appraising attitudes demand a basis, which consists of features of the person (or his conduct) towards whom the attitude is held. If I admire someone, I must admire him *for* some-

thing (for his intelligence, or for his skill at playing the violin).

Several points are worth making about these attitudes. First, it is contingent that we have them at all. In other words, it is not hard to imagine a world in which men never took up attitudes such as admiration towards one another. Second, we do not generally have a point or purpose in holding them. If someone acts in a way which causes us to feel gratitude, we feel it because this is the response that his behaviour evokes. We may *express* our gratitude for various different reasons: to give our benefactor satisfaction, or to encourage him to benefit us in the future, for instance. But the purpose of expressing an attitude is obviously quite different from the attitude itself. Third, there is a close but complex relationship between these appraising attitudes and the concept of desert. This relationship has several aspects.

(1) If we did not adopt these attitudes towards one another, we would not and could not use the concept of desert. If the behaviour of others did not arouse our admiration and approval we could not say that they deserved honours, prizes, and the rest. The words would have no meaning for us.

(2) The range of possible desert bases coincides with the range of possible bases for appraising attitudes. I have already made use of this claim when I argued that, except in special cases, a person could not deserve on the basis of his need, because we do not admire, etc., people for their needs. The same point shows what is wrong with such a judgement as 'Jones deserves a pay increase because it would further the public interest if he had one'. We cannot admire or approve of someone on the basis of a relationship between his income and the public interest. We can only admire Jones for what Jones is or does.

(3) The existence of appraising attitudes makes intelligible the connection between a desert judgement and its basis. Consider again the connection between 'Smith deserves to win the mile' and 'Smith has trained harder than anyone else'. We would accept this fact about Smith as a reason for his desert because

on the whole we admire the kind of determination and effort which goes into a course of training. Now it is not actually necessary for me, the maker of the judgement, to have this attitude of admiration myself. I may, for instance, so thoroughly disapprove of athletics that I cannot regard the time and effort that goes into training as in any way admirable or worth while. Still, I live in a community in which most people would take up the relevant appraising attitude towards hard athletic training, and hence I can give Smith's training as a reason for his desert. (In a similar way, someone lacking any aesthetic sense can call objects beautiful and point out the features in virtue of which they are beautiful according to general opinion, even though he himself lacks the appropriate aesthetic response to those features.)

Although we have done something to limit the range of possible desert bases by exploring their connection with appraising attitudes, it does not seem that at this stage we can limit it any more narrowly. Men may take up favourable appraisng attitudes towards many different features of people's character and conduct, and nothing by way of conceptual analysis can show us which of these attitudes they *ought* to take up. But now a query must be raised about the adequacy of relating desert judgements solely to the desert basis, as this has been defined. Consider again the judgement 'Jones deserves at least £4,000 a year'. Does not this depend on the existence of a rule establishing how much people of a certain capacity are to be paid? Are we not tacitly invoking such a rule when we make the judgement, the rule therefore being as much the grounds of our judgement as the desert basis (facts about Jones)?

It appears to me that if we look closely at the statement in question, we can distinguish three claims that are made by its use. There is first of all a favourable general appraisal of Jones, expressed in the claim that he deserves a reasonable income. Second, Jones's deserts (of income) are compared with those of other wage earners. Third, this comparison is expressed in numerical terms by the claim that £4,000 a year or more would adequately represent Jones's position on the scale of wage earners. It is plain that the third of these claims is conventional, in that the accuracy of the figure of £4,000 depends upon the wage levels enjoyed by other wage earners. Had Jones been working in 1965 instead of 1975, his deserts might have been accurately expressed by saying that he deserved at least £2,000 a year. Yet it would be odd to say that even the third claim depended on a rule; it would be better to say that it depended upon established practice—the current set of wage rates. And neither of the first two claims depends on anything of this kind. They can be derived directly from knowledge of the characteristics of Jones and other wage earners which are taken as a basis for their desert. Finally, it is the first and particularly the second claim which are really the basic desert judgements here. We could make a judgement of the second type (comparing Jones's deserts with those of other wage earners) without being able to make a judgement of the third type (stating how much income Jones deserved)—for example, if we were ignorant of current wage rates. But we could not make the third judgement without being able to make the second.

The point must be driven home, because an account of desert which construes desert judgements as derivative from rules fundamentally misconceives that concept, and makes desert into a kind of entitlement. To qualify for a benefit under a rule may well be to have a right to that benefit, but it is not to deserve it. If Brown is a Grade C official, and Grade C officials are awarded £3,000 a year, then Brown has a right to £3,000, but he does not thereby deserve it. To show that he deserves the income in question, we should have to refer to features of his job and the efforts and capacities which he puts into it; in short, to the qualities of Brown and his conduct (though with implied reference to the analogous qualities of other wage earners). Because desert is independent of rules, it forms part of prosthetic, not conservative, justice. It is a principle which can serve to modify an existing distribution of rights, for the people who have these rights may not be the people who deserve to have them, according to some criterion of desert. We may then demand that the established rules and practices be changed in order that the deserving shall come to have rights, and the undeserving to lose them. For this reason Feinberg describes desert as a 'natural' moral notion, one that is prior to institutions, rules, etc., and a standard by which such institutions and rules may be judged.

The case in which these arguments may look least plausible is that of games and competitions, and the desert of prizes which results once such practices are established. For not only is it impossible to deserve first prize until a first prize has been established, but the desert basis itself (e.g. Smith's hard training in the athletic case) seems to be dependent upon the competitive institution. How could a period of training form a ground for deserving a prize unless there was to be a race *for* which the training was undertaken? If a man spends long hours running around the country, but with no race in prospect, he could not deserve anything on that basis.

Yet on closer scrutiny, it seems that although the existence of an athletic competition allows the runners' deserts to be manifested, it does not create those deserts. The basis of desert is still certain qualities which the runner possesses, such as effort and determination, and towards which we hold favourable appraising attitudes. Indeed, were we not to hold such attitudes, it is inconceivable that we should set up competitions and award prizes for athletic achievements. Here again the desert is prior to institutions and practices. Further, when such competitions are established we try to ensure that they measure accurately the qualities which we admire, and which we wish to form the basis of victory. Piaget discovered that children of about twelve would accept or reject proposed changes in the rules of the game of marbles according to whether they favoured skill in shooting, or on the other hand gave too much weight to luck.

Desert, then, denotes a relationship between an individual and his conduct, and modes of treatment which are liked or disliked. When we make a judgement of desert, we are judging the appropriateness of this particular individual, with his qualities and past behaviour, receiving a given benefit or harm—an appropriateness which is made intelligible by considering the appraising attitudes that we may take up towards the person. Having seen this, we can understand what is wrong with utilitarian attempts to reinterpret the concept as part of a consequentialist moral framework. It is not clear to me exactly how a utilitarian analysis of desert judgements might proceed, but the main possibilities seem to be as follows (corresponding to the distinction between act- and rule-utilitarianism):

(1) A deserves X = Some or all of the consequences of giving X to A would be good (i.e. would contribute to the general happiness).

(2) A deserves X = A qualifies for X under a rule whose adoption would be good (i.e. would contribute to the general happiness).

The first possibility, then, is that desert judgements should be analysed in straightforward consequentialist fashion. When we say that Jones deserves £4,000 a year, we mean that it will be useful to give him that amount, presumably because of the encouragement it will offer to himself and others to perform the valuable work he is now undertaking. Rewards and other deserved benefits are here seen as direct incentives to the production of future good. It should be apparent, in the light of the foregoing, why this fails to capture the meaning of 'desert' as that concept is properly understood. Desert judgements are justified on the basis of *past* and *present* facts about individuals, never on the basis of states of affairs to be created in the future. Desert is a 'backward-looking' concept, if we regard the present as the limit of the past; utility is a forward-looking principle. Furthermore, although the awarding of deserved benefits undoubtedly serves as an incentive to people to perform the actions or to acquire the skills which make up the basis of desert, it is unlikely that the boundaries of *this* practice will coincide with those of a practice deliberately aimed at maximizing future good. A reward can only act as an incentive if it is capable of modifying the conduct of those to whom it is given, and this generates cases in which our judgements of desert will not correspond to the proposed utilitarian principle. Suppose that a certain community wants to increase its birth rate and so institutes a system of child benefits, giving parents special allowances or privileges for each child they have. These could be understood either as straightforward incentives to have children, or as rewards for the performance of socially valuable actions. The difference will emerge if we imagine within the community a religious sect whose sexual practices are strictly governed by their religious beliefs, with the result that the family size of a sect member is unaffected by the introduction of the system of benefits. If the benefits are pure incentives, they will not be given to parents who also belong to the sect—the saving can be put to better use by increasing the benefits of non-members. If they are rewards, however, the sect members must be given what they deserve, for they have performed the required socially valuable actions.

The rule-utilitarian analysis ((2) above) may appear at first sight to avoid these difficulties, and to give a better account of the concept of desert. For on this theory the direct justification of a desert judgement is a description of the person who forms its subject which shows that he falls under a certain rule, and so the 'backward-looking' logic of desert is preserved. Consequences are only considered at a different point, when a justification for the rule itself is required. However, the example of the child allowances may again be pressed into service to show that the consistent rule-utilitarian will choose to adopt different rules from the person who wishes to reward desert. A rule which awards equal benefits to all parents with a given number of children is less efficient than a rule which restricts the allowances to those outside the sect but gives slightly higher sums. Provided the

latter rule can be applied (i.e. provided it is possible to distinguish the members of the sect from everyone else) the utilitarian is bound to adopt it. So again we find a divergence between child allowances given as deserved rewards and child allowances given as incentives to population growth.

No doubt a utilitarian will be able to think of further arguments to show that the first rule should be adopted in preference to the second, if he wishes to show that a sophisticated utilitarianism can reproduce the outlines of the concept of desert. I want, however, to leave this debate (which has been thoroughly worked over in the opposite case of deserved punishment) to consider a more radical utilitarian position. This would abandon the attempt to make utilitarianism fit around the existing concept of desert, on the grounds that the existing concept is logically untenable. The reason is that determinism is true, and determinism is incompatible with judgements of desert as they are usually understood. The concept should either be abandoned entirely, or used in a new sense which is openly utilitarian. As Sidgwick put it:

> The only tenable Determinist interpretation of Desert is, in my opinion, the Utilitarian: according to which, when a man is said to deserve reward for any services to society, the meaning is that it is expedient to reward him, in order that he and others may be induced to render similar services by the expectation of similar rewards.

NOTES

1. Taken from B. Barry, *Political Argument*, p. 112.
2. Barry says that this example exemplifies a subsidiary sense of desert. J. Kleinig in 'The Concept of Desert', *American Philosophical Quarterly*, viii (1971), argues that entitlement, not desert, is involved. In agreeing with Kleinig, I hope that I have taken account of what is true in Barry's position.
3. Though at the same time judgements of desert are always moral judgements. Desert is moral when based upon qualities or actions of the indi-

vidual which have moral value in themselves—courage, honesty, etc. It is non-moral when based on morally neutral qualities—intelligence, ability, etc. Yet 'Jones deserves a high mark for his ability' is as much a moral judgement as 'Brown deserves a medal for his courage', in the sense that each entails a weak 'moral-ought' judgement: 'Jones ought, prima facie, to get a high mark'; 'Brown ought, prima facie, to get a medal'. Desert judgements are low-level moral judgements, only indirectly related to the universal imperatives which have been considered by some recent writers to be the central cases of moral judgements. In this respect they resemble such claims as 'His behaviour was rude', 'She is always honest', etc.

12. The Concept of Desert in Distributive Justice

JULIAN LAMONT

Julian Lamont is a Postdoctoral Research Fellow at the Queensland University of Technology and is completing a book on Income Justice. He is currently vice president of the International Economics and Philosophy Society.

Philosophers divide on the question of what degree of responsibility or "voluntariness" desert requires. Lamont suggests that this and other desert-related debates proceed on the mistaken assumption that desert requires the same degree of responsibility in every case. Lamont argues that different forms of treatment require different levels of responsibility and that this is to be explained by the nature of desert: It is not an "internally defined" concept. Rather, deserts are determined by "external goals and values," which themselves require different degrees of responsibility. Lamont concludes that debates about desert, and desert of wages in particular, should focus not on desert itself but rather on the appropriateness of the external goals and values that people and institutions have established.

Samuel Scheffler has recently argued[1] that desert plays an important part in people's commonsense attitudes to public policy. In the philosophical literature as well there have been many important and enduring arguments over what desert requires in terms of distributive justice.[2] While it is these debates which are the motivation behind this paper, my aims here are mainly conceptual, not normative. One aim is to show that desert requires external values and goals to make it determinate—that the criteria for its application are not entirely 'internally determined' by the concept itself. I shall argue against a presumption underlying many of these debates, that the disputes about desert can be resolved by appeals to and by analysis of desert itself. In particular, I shall focus on debates over what is the 'correct' degree of voluntariness

for the application of desert-claims, and over what is the 'correct' desert-basis for the distribution of economic benefits like jobs and income. In many of these debates, writers have believed that they have understood the true moral and/or conceptual nature of desert, and they have summarily used this supposed understanding to assert or reject certain desert-claims, commonly with little in the way of supporting argument. I shall argue that this is a mistake, and using this form of argument entails a crucial misunderstanding of part of the conceptual and moral nature of desert. Furthermore, I shall argue that, once the nature of desert *is* understood, it will be seen that it probably cannot provide sufficient support for such summary assertions or rejections of desert-claims. Recognizing this will provide us with a better idea of what *ac-*

Reprinted from *The Philosophical Quarterly* 44:174 (1994), by permission.

tually divides the various positions. A related goal of this paper is *to relocate the debates* over what role, if any, desert should play in distributive justice.

Desert can usefully be thought of as a three-place relation[3] of the form 'A deserves X in virtue of f' (the *desert-basis*). Unless specifically stated otherwise, f will be a quality possessed by a person, including qualities like 'having performed action a'.

I

The delineation of what does or does not count as a basis for desert-claims has been one of the most fecund areas for philosophical analysis and debate on the concept of desert. There are two types of reasons for asserting that a person does not deserve a certain benefit: first, the merely factual reason that the particular quality which constitutes the desert-basis is not possessed by that person; second, that the quality which the person possesses is not a legitimate desert-basis. Everyday denials of desert-claims are most often of the first type. Because of their analytic concerns, the most common denials made by political philosophers are of the second type, and it is this type which is of interest here.

Unfortunately, when a writer denies a particular desert-claim it is often unclear exactly what the structure of the denial is. To see the problem, take these denials of desert from arguments over job distribution:

> And since they do not deserve their abilities they do not in any strong sense deserve to be admitted because of their abilities
>
> *(Wasserstrom p. 167).*

> Does the most skilful player deserve to win an athletic competition? It seems a natural enough thing to say. . . . [But] when we think of the most skilful as the most deserving, it may be because we think of them as having worked hardest . . . [and] sometimes that assumption is not true
>
> *(Rachels pp. 156f.).*

> Suppose that the abilities and traits that qualify a person for high reward jobs are pri-

marily the result of natural and social contingencies over which he has little control. . . . . Then it seems one's qualification for meritocratic job placement are largely the result of happy or unhappy accident, and one has done little to *deserve* them
>
> *(Daniels p. 222).*

Now this type of denial is not unique to arguments over job distribution. It is also common in debates about the just distribution of income and wealth.[4] The arguments are variations on the form 'f is not a legitimate basis for deserving X, because there are many things which contribute to A's having the quality f over which A has little control'. People who use this reasoning usually have in mind one of the following two versions of the argument.

When it is asserted that 'f is not a legitimate basis for deserving X' (or something of this nature) this is sometimes because the writer believes that f is conceptually illegitimate. For instance, it is often believed that analysis of the concept of desert yields the claim that if there are many things which contribute to A's having the quality f over which A has little control, then A cannot deserve X. Now there are differences of opinion about how little control constitutes too little. Opinion ranges from anything less than complete voluntary control to no control at all. What is important for our purposes, though, is that whatever point (or range) on the spectrum these writers choose, they each believe that their position is supported by a conceptual analysis of desert itself. Writers using the other version of the argument, that the desert-basis f is *morally* illegitimate, usually have a similar belief. They believe that a correct understanding of the moral nature of desert will support their claims.[5]

Neither of these views is correct. The concept of desert is not a purely *internally* defined concept: i.e., examination of the concept itself will not yield the appropriate desert-basis for the particular case being considered. As will become clear when we examine some of the different arguments, external goals and values—goals and values which *cannot* be found by an examination of the concept of desert itself—will normally enter into people's determination of what they consider a legitimate desert-basis.

For example, each of the writers quoted above believes that desert (in the particular case examined by each) requires a degree of voluntariness that has not been met. Those writers who hold that people do not deserve their jobs, and also those who hold that people do not deserve income or wealth because of their productivity or effort, etc., normally share a common belief. They believe that desert requires a higher degree of voluntariness than do those who believe that jobs or incomes are commonly deserved. For ease of reference, let us call these writers the HV (higher voluntariness) group, and let us call those writers who believe that desert has a lower minimum requirement (and who hence more commonly believe that jobs and income are deserved) the LV (lower voluntariness) group (although this is convenient, it should be noted that it is slightly artificial, as the writers' views tend to fall along a spectrum).

So how do those who tend to fall into the LV group support their claims? One of their arguments has been that even if the higher requirement is true, many people actually satisfy this requirement (or with a better institutional framework would satisfy it), and hence are deserving. The merits of this argument are peripheral to our concerns here. But another commonly employed argument is the legitimacy argument mentioned a moment ago, this time used to support the opposite conclusion. Those who sympathize with the LV view argue that the degree of voluntariness appealed to in the denials of desert-claims is not required by the concept of desert. We can see how this argument can be made by looking at everyday examples of desert-claims. David Miller gives (p. 97) the following examples: the most skilful shot deserving to win at marbles, or the ablest candidate deserving the scholarship. Innumerable examples support the LV writers' case. One need only turn to any form of mass media, or listen to people's conversation: the nurses deserve a pay rise; Dennis Connor de-

served a second chance at the America's Cup; the dead fighter-pilot deserved a medal; surgeons do not deserve their huge incomes; Steffi Graf deserved to win a Grand Slam; Joe Bloggs' wife deserved to be treated better.

Now these examples do not presuppose that the people concerned must have a high degree of voluntary control over the qualities used as desert-bases. What people normally must do to support such desert-claims is, first, identify the quality which they are taking to be the desert-basis, and then establish that the person actually possesses that quality.

For instance, the desert-bases to support the above claims might be: the nurses, because their work has become relatively more difficult in recent times; Dennis Connor, because he had exhibited the level of yachting ability which made it quite plausible to believe that he could win back the Cup; the fighter-pilot, because his heroic actions saved three other pilots; the surgeons, because their pay is held up only by artificial labour-supply restrictions; Steffi Graf, because she was clearly of the same standard as past Grand Slam winners; Joe Bloggs' wife, because she had sacrificed so much in support of her husband. Now all these desert-claims weaken the argument of HV theorists. The claims support the view that desert itself does not require a high degree of voluntariness. If it did, then most of the everyday desert-claims would be rendered false. As LV theorists note, while people making these everyday claims must be committed to the belief that the desert-bases were not acquired unfairly, they need not be committed to the strong voluntariness requirements suggested by HV theorists. However, LV theorists have usually wanted to use these examples and arguments to do more than just make their point about voluntariness.

LV theorists have usually wanted to go on to assert that HV denials of the desert-claims exhibit a mistaken interpretation of the conceptual and/or moral nature of desert; and, moreover, that their own desert-claims are correct—for example, that people do deserve jobs because of their abilities, or that people do deserve income or wealth on the grounds of their productivity or efforts, etc. But their appeal to desert in this way fails to establish their counter-claims for just the same reason as we noted with respect to the HV claims. We can see, then, one of the reasons why arguments over the role of desert in distributive justice have been so protracted and unfruitful. Each group has thought that its claims alone are justified by the true conceptual or moral nature of desert. My suggestion is that this type of justification is not possible. The concept of desert, including the core moral component of that concept, is not rich enough to yield such determinate judgements.

When people make desert-claims they are not simply telling us what desert itself requires. They unwittingly introduce external values, and make their desert-judgements in the light of those values. The reason why so many writers have been able to affirm so confidently such a diverse and conflicting set of desert-claims in debates over distributive justice is not because the true conceptual and moral core of desert is so complex and difficult to discern. It is because the true conceptual and moral core of desert allows the introduction of external values and goals. It is the diversity and conflicting nature of these values which explains the diversity and conflicting nature of desert-claims. This is why differences of opinion over what should constitute the desert-basis are not going to be solved by examination of desert itself. The differences do not lie at that level, but rather at the level of values. Unfortunately, it is probably easier to argue about desert itself than it is about values. That is why appealing to desert has been so attractive in the past. Writers of very different persuasions (even those who wish to reject desert-claims completely) believed that examining desert itself would yield the conclusion they desired, a relatively easy victory, really, and that those who thought otherwise simply did not understand desert correctly. Unfortunately, none of them can secure the desired conclusion so easily.

It should be noted that many writers simply make their claims that quality f is the right (or wrong) desert-basis without ever setting out the structure of their arguments, so it is often difficult to assess what are the grounds for their claims. One could assume that these writers have a correct understanding of the concept of desert, and that they believe others share this understanding, and hence see no need to go into more detail. It is not clear, though, why such an assumption would be warranted. Almost none of the writers has specified any set of external values and asserted that it is the correctness of *these* values which supports the relevant desert-claims, and/or which makes other desert-claims morally illegitimate. Given this, there is good reason to believe that their arguments are not of the correct structure, and that they do believe that a proper understanding of desert justifies their positions (in that it will yield both the appropriate voluntariness requirements and the morally correct desert-basis).

An implication of the position being argued for here is that we can now understand why it is not necessary to use the same desert-basis and the same requirement of voluntariness across claims. At some level of understanding, this has been obvious to those debating everyday cases, if not to many writers on distributive justice (at least while writing on that topic). In fact, it has rarely been clear that an implication of the arguments of many writers on desert in distributive justice is this requirement of consistency across different areas. The main reason why it has not been recognized is probably because most have not been primarily interested in giving an analysis of desert as such. Rather, they have been concerned with making substantive points about distributive justice. They have often simply made their desert-claim or denial, and then either moved on to another topic or explored the implications of their claims *for distributive justice*. They have rarely explored the implications of their arguments for desert-claims outside that area.

For instance, HV theorists never go through all the everyday desert-claims which would be made false by their position. They have failed either to provide an argument for why the claims are false, or to explain why their claims do not lead to this implication. The problem for these theorists is that, if desert does itself yield the morally correct desert-basis, and does itself yield the requisite degree of voluntariness, then it is not clear how they can consistently explain the enormous diversity of desert-bases which are regularly used. It seems very difficult *from their theoretical standing* to claim that desert itself requires degree *X* of voluntariness in one distributive justice debate, but a different one in another debate (or in another area outside distributive justice). It is theoretically difficult for them to argue that, say, academic excellence is the correct desert-basis for distributing fellowships, but not income. If the notion of desert being used across the different situations *is* the same, and if desert itself yields the morally and conceptually correct desert-basis, then there seems to be no way for them to explain the use of different voluntariness-requirements and different desert-bases across claims. The alternative course, and one sometimes taken, is to say that the notion of desert is different across the different situations. But this fractures the notion of desert, for no good reason except to save an implausible theory. Within the theory being proposed here it is relatively easy to explain this phenomenon—the notion of desert is the same across the situations, but the desert-basis in each area is determined by the relative values and goals in that area and is not part of the notion of desert itself.

It is even quite possible to propose different desert-bases within one area. Many of the examples mentioned earlier can be used to illustrate the point. But let us take the practice of assessing students. This practice normally has behind it some purpose, or at least some defining value, which plays an essential role in the setting of the desert-basis. For instance, sometimes it is to indicate a person's demonstrated potential in a particular occupation or in higher education. In such cases, students who are clearly above or below the threshold for a B grading do not deserve that grade, no matter how little or how hard they have tried. Sometimes the purpose is simply to indicate to the students (and perhaps their parents)

their objective mastery of the subject (and this type of grading can be very different from the previous one). Sometimes the grade, especially in younger classes, is to indicate to the students their level of effort in the subject. Sometimes the desert-basis is decided by other persons or institutions, sometimes by the teachers themselves. What is important to notice is that *the desert-basis is determined by other values or purposes*, rather than by something internal to the notion of desert itself.

One objection to the position being argued for here is that it may be thought that desert is being conflated with the distinct, though related, notion of entitlement. While confusion of these two notions has been a common stumbling-block in discussions of desert, no such confusion is present here. To see this, take the case of student assessment again. Suppose the purpose of the grading is to indicate the student's mastery of the subject, but it has been decided to tie grades directly to particular scores. Then students will be entitled to those grades which correspond to the scores they obtain, even though those may not be the ones they deserve.

It is consistent with the position being argued for here that desert is sometimes logically prior to, and independent of, existing public institutions and rules. In fact, it can sometimes be used as a criterion for judging them. Confusion of the two concepts of desert and entitlement often leads one to the contrary position. Although a person may simultaneously deserve and be entitled to something, it is none the less common for one of these to be so without the other. For instance, the defeated presidential candidate who deserved to win is not, by that token, entitled to the office. Conversely, it does not follow automatically that the successful candidate, who is entitled to the office, deserved to win. It is important to keep in mind that the claims associated with the two concepts are distinct (and may even compete). The type of considerations illustrated by the case of student grades is repeated across the spectrum of desert-claims. For instance, I suggest the reason why most people would not say a runner deserved to win the women's Olympic 100 metres if she could only run the distance in 25 seconds, no matter how hard she had been training, is because there is a defining value different from effort which influences the choice of desert-basis here. The value is that of *excellence in sprinting*. This is the value, external to the notion of desert, which is normally taken as defining the desert-basis in sprints. Of course in other contexts there are other defining values. For example, sometimes the value is one's performance relative to one's own past performances; that is the purpose behind handicaps in golf or aggregate point athletic competitions. There it does not matter how objectively good a person is. Desert is based on relative improvement.

Although the most common mistake made in analysing the concept of desert has been to think that its criteria for application are entirely determined internally, this mistake is not universal—John Rawls is an exception. He asserts that desert is entirely *externally* defined by preexisting *institutions or practices*. This is incorrect too, but, as with any mistake that Rawls has made, there have been numerous writers who have pointed it out.

The positive thesis of this paper is that *assessment of desert is usually made in the light of other goals and values* (though not necessarily in the light of pre-existing institutions or practices) *which are separate from desert itself*. Desert is a partly externally defined concept, in the sense that people's goals and values enter into setting the desert-bases. Once this is realized, it should not be surprising, given that people have different value systems, that they use different and sometimes conflicting desert-bases. Although there is likely to be a reasonable amount of consensus in any given society about the relative importance of different values (including the value of the quality of will displayed, which is the motivating value behind the voluntariness requirements), there is also likely to be enough disagreement to generate heated debates. The important point to see is that these debates are not about desert itself, but about external values—consideration of desert itself is best left to the side in trying to resolve these debates.

In a full-blown analysis of desert, the reasons why the debates in the past have been mistaken could be explored further. No doubt one of the reasons is that one of the defining characteristics of desert (and something which *does* come from examination of the concept itself) is that it does require some minimum degree of voluntariness. For instance, Brian Barry notes (p. 108) that 'a person's having been able to have done otherwise is a *necessary condition* of ascribing desert'. These requirements help distinguish desert from entitlement. As David Miller correctly notes (p. 97), someone who accidentally apprehends a wanted criminal does not thereby deserve a reward, even though possibly entitled to one. It seems clear that, for a quality to count as a ground for desert, the person concerned must, in some sense, be able 'to take credit for' that ground.[6] But the unpacking of this notion of 'taking credit for' and the exact form of the minimum requirements is beyond the scope of this paper. What is important for our purposes here is to understand that while examination of desert itself will yield these minimum requirements, further examination of the notion will *not* solve most of the important disputes about the role of desert in distributive justice.

II

If resorting to conceptual and/or moral claims about desert itself is the *incorrect* way of arguing about desert-claims, then it is important to see how to object to particular desert-bases *without* doing this. To see how it is possible, take the following case involving the award of a fellowship.

The fellowship's terms include that it is to be awarded to the person who has attained the greatest mastery of computer science subjects. Suppose that there is one student, call her A, who clearly has greater mastery than anyone in the university. Another student, call him B, is also vying for the fellowship. The notable feature of B is that he has worked very hard to achieve his high academic level, harder in fact than *A*. But there is no doubt that *B* is not a scholar of the same standard as *A*. Now in such a situation there is nothing about the concept of desert which rules out the possibility of asserting that *A* deserves the fellowship, even though she may have worked less hard than *B*. This is because the university has set up the fellowship *for the person who has attained the greatest mastery of computer science*. *A* is that person, and hence can deserve the fellowship.

In spite of appearances this is a quite complex example, and it can be used to illustrate some salient features of different debates over desert. Let us assume, for the sake of argument, that *A* is naturally brighter than *B*. Now appealing to some feature of desert itself will not make it possible to use this fact to assert that *A* does not deserve the fellowship. But though this line of attack fails there is a sentiment expressed in it which many have thought has moral force and should be able to be captured. The crucial question is whether the moral force comes from desert itself or whether it comes from a value external to desert that some (or many) people hold. My suggestion is that it is the latter. Recognition of the tendency by many (or some) to relate desert, in particular circumstances, to the effort a person displays should not push one to deny that it is within the conceptual and moral limits set by the concept of desert to claim that *A* deserves the fellowship. If the fellowship is for the person who has the best mastery of computer science, and *A* is that person, then there is nothing *within* the concept of desert preventing the claim that *A* deserves the fellowship. If there is to be an objection, then it is not to be levelled at this line of reasoning. Moreover, if one wants to assert that the claim that *A* deserves the fellowship is morally mistaken, then one cannot do so by appeal to some moral feature about desert.

It may be objected that there is a confusion of entitlement with desert in this case. Perhaps it is thought that being the person who has attained the greatest mastery of computer science can only *entitle* *A* to the fellowship rather than make her deserve it. I think this is

a mistake. This can be brought out by constructing an example in which *A* has still attained the greatest mastery but is not entitled to the fellowship. Let us introduce another candidate, *C*, who is less competent than *A*. Keeping the rest of the story the same, add only this: it has been decreed by the fellowship committee that the final general examination of the final year in computer science will be used as the criterion to ascertain who has best mastered the subject. Now suppose *A* is sick on the day of the examination and consequently does not perform well, and *C* tops the examination. Here we have a case in which *A* is not entitled to the fellowship even though she remains the person with the greatest mastery of computer science. *C* is entitled to the fellowship, even though he does not deserve it. It is still within the moral and conceptual limits set by the concept of desert itself to claim that *A* is the student who deserved it but did not get it. Of course, this claim may turn out to be morally wrong, all things considered, though this judgement cannot be made by examining the concept of desert alone. There has been no confusion of entitlement and desert.

The presidential example, used earlier to illustrate the distinction between desert and entitlement, can also be used, with some embellishment, to illustrate this point. People may assert that candidate *A* deserved to win. She deserved to win because she, of all the candidates, had the best interests of the people at heart and had demonstrated the greatest competence and knowledge of how to implement the policies to promote those interests. Candidate *B* also had the best interests of the people at heart, and worked harder than *A*, but lacked *A*'s expertise. Candidate *C* won the election and hence is entitled to be president.

If there has been no confusion of entitlement and desert in the fellowship case, then the question remains whether there is any room for objecting to the claim that *A* deserves the fellowship. One way of doing this is to make a distinction between deserving to win the fellowship, as it is constituted, and deserving more money. There is a certain benefit to be distributed, and in such situations it is always legitimate to ask who deserves it (and the answer to such a question may provide a reason to change the institutional arrangements). It is then consistent to claim that A deserves to win the fellowship, so constituted, but that B is more deserving of the extra money. So there will be two competing desert-claims in a single case, each with its own desert-base.

The fellowship case illustrates that a further distinction is possible, apart from that between entitlement and desert. Often it is the case that the institutions which set up entitlement rules also, to varying degrees, specify what *the institution* takes as the dominant desert-basis (which, in line with the argument of this paper, will reflect the institution's value-ranking). The entitlement rules are usually designed so that entitlement will follow closely the prescriptions of the desert-basis (though, as we have seen, they can clearly come apart). So sometimes we can identify an *institutional desert-basis*. Of course, institutions are not always all that clear themselves on what they take as the desert-basis. Also, the 'institutions' are sometimes not clearly defined entities (for instance, where the 'institution' is some tradition or social custom). Nevertheless, institutional desert-bases sometimes carry practical weight when one is deciding what to do. But it is important to see that the fact that an institution chose a particular desert-basis does not preclude objections that that desert-basis is not the right or best one. The institution chose one—it may be wrong. Furthermore, it can be seen that the claim that some particular person is entitled to a benefit does not preclude somebody from plausibly arguing that that person does not deserve it, even though possessing the quality which is the institutionally recognized desert-basis.

Once this is recognized, it may be best to make the structure of these objections explicit. In the fellowship case described, the desert-basis and the entitlement rules have been chosen by the university, so here there is a clear institutional desert-basis. But this still does not prevent someone from objecting

that student A does not deserve the fellowship. If my earlier argument is correct, this objection cannot be made on the grounds that a conceptual and moral analysis of the notion of desert makes it illegitimate to claim that A deserves the fellowship, because her mastery of computer science is not something over which she had full voluntary control. However, we can understand a different but legitimate sort of objection, against the way the fellowship was set up. A may deserve the fellowship *on the desert-basis chosen by the university*—one could call this (after Kleinig) 'institutional deserving'. However, it may be argued that the wrong desert-basis was chosen, and that the fellowship should never have been set up in the way it was; that it was misguided; that A is not the type of person who deserves fellowships from the university; that we should value more the effort displayed by the candidates rather than their objective academic achievement; and that the fellowship should have been founded in such a way as to reflect that valuation. It could thus be properly claimed that A does not deserve the fellowship because her qualities are not those the university should use as the basis for fellowships.

In section I we saw that desert is *not* an internally defined concept, and that assessment of desert is not usually made independently of other goals and values. We saw that failure to realize this has led to protracted and misguided arguments. It has also led to the presupposition of an analysis of desert in debates over distributive justice which could not make sense of most everyday desert claims. In the present section we have seen how there are a number of possible ways to object to particular desert-bases *without* resorting to conceptual and/or moral claims about desert itself. We have seen that, when someone objects that a person does not deserve some particular benefit, we can understand that as *an objection to the relative valuation expressed by the particular choice of desert-basis or to the scope which the desert-claims are given*. We now have the conceptual framework necessary to explore this analysis of desert further in the context of some recurring debates about distributive justice.

III

Among those who think that desert should play some role in determining income distribution, one of the long-standing debates has been between those who think 'effort' should be the desert-basis and those who think 'productivity' should be. Now I do not presume to be able to solve here the hoary argument between these antagonists. However, the above analysis does allow us to understand, criticize and advance the argument between them.

Both groups of theorists have wrongly thought that desert itself will provide them with the conclusions they desire. 'Effort theorists' have often argued that people do not deserve economic benefits on the basis of their productivity, because their productivity is not something sufficiently under voluntary control; and furthermore, that people can deserve economic benefits only on the basis of effort, because effort is the only factor over which they have enough control. As we have seen, morally laudable though the goals of this argument are, they cannot be established via this argument. But the everyday counter-examples which the 'productivity theorists' may use to show that desert does not presuppose such a high degree of voluntariness cannot be used to help support their position either. Desert, by itself, implies that some minimum degree of voluntariness must be met. It implies neither that the degree of voluntariness presupposed by the productivity theorists' desert-basis is correct, nor that their desert-basis is the morally legitimate one.

Both factions, then, often appeal to examples outside the direct debate at hand (e.g., state of nature examples). The examples normally yield contrary principles. For instance, certain state of nature examples seem to yield the principle that people deserve the value of the products they have made, while other examples yield the principle that equal effort deserves equal reward. Most people find that

each of the principles is plausible (within the context of the specific examples). The reason for this, I suggest, is that *each* of the examples appeals to an area or situation where there is a much greater consensus of values than there is in the broader context which the writer was originally addressing. What each of the theories in fact does is focus on a situation in which the consensus mirrors the result to be argued for in the original area under consideration. Once this is realized, the conclusions reached by people considering the examples can be seen, despite appearances, not to be contrary. They can be explained by the thesis being proposed here.

People have a plurality of values. One of those values is the quality of will a person displays. Another is the realization of artistic beauty in the world; another, happiness; another, physical excellence; and so on. In different situations, the realization of some of these values will be viewed as relatively more important than in others. If you believe that the concept of desert itself yields the unique requirements which need to be met for a desert-claim to be morally and conceptually legitimate, then you will find puzzling the different desert-judgements that you and others make in the different state of nature examples. It will seem that the judgements are inconsistent because they appear to give different weights to different factors, instead of flowing from one unique set of requirements. But the judgements are not inconsistent. Apart from certain minimum voluntariness requirements, and the priority it gives to the past and present over the future, desert gives no unique set of conceptual and moral requirements. It takes its requirements from external values. The relative importance of these varies for (most) people depending on what type of situation or area they are considering. The examples, then, should not force people to adopt the view of one antagonist or the other in some debate about distributive justice. It should not make them believe that they must adopt one or the other in order to be consistent in their judgements about desert. The examples should force people to give up the view that desert itself has one set of requirements. With that view gone, one can go about the serious business of working out what is the relative importance of different values in the different debates.

The above discussion does not resolve the dispute over what the desert-basis *should* be. However, it helps explain how the dispute cannot be resolved by the means which have been previously employed, and also points to what is the appropriate arena in which to conduct the debate, i.e., arguments about relative values.[7] It follows that it would further help to clarify and advance the debate if the external values which underlie the different desert-claims were made explicit. Let me briefly try to do this, in order to show how they help to determine the desert-claims within each theory.

For both effort and productivity desert-theories, the primary defining value or goal is a good standard of living; collectively it could be called 'the social product.' It is only through activity directed towards raising the social product that people, *under these theories*, come to deserve income. Other theories could have different defining values or goals (for instance, that people could come to deserve income through activity directed towards raising religious consciousness, through morally laudable acts, etc.), but effort and productivity theories share a common value. What is important to notice about this value is that it does not evolve from an internal consideration of the concept of desert. Nothing about the concept itself says *it is only through activities directed towards this goal* that one can come to deserve income—there is nothing in terms of the concept of desert preventing the judgement that income is deserved instead for other activities. This is important to keep in mind, because the theories, although having the same primary value, differ in the relative importance they place on it, and also in their secondary values; and *none* of these differences can be traced to desert itself.

The secondary defining value or goal for the productivity theory could be characterized as the value of giving people their marginal product (in this particular case, the secondary values are distributive while the primary value is aggregative). It has as its motivation the desire that people receive benefits in proportion to the value of the goods and services they have provided to society. Income, therefore, is given to people in proportion to how much they raise others' living standards.

The effort theory has a different secondary defining value for desert-claims: the value of rewarding people for the *effort* they exert in contributing towards the social product. It is not the social product *per se*, but rather *the effort in producing the social product* that is valued more. The more effort people exert in contributing towards raising the social product, the more they deserve.

When there is a choice, between a system that results in higher living standards but does not reward people in proportion to their effort, and a system which rewards people proportionately, the effort theorists would prefer the latter. This is not because they have no interest in living standards. It is not a matter of indifference to them where people's efforts are directed. For instance, under their system people who direct their effort towards what are considered to be socially unproductive goals will not thereby deserve economic benefits (of course, it is quite possible for yet another group of desert-theorists to value another type of effort most highly). Effort theorists prefer the effort-based system to the productivity-based one because they believe there is more value in effort being rewarded proportionately than there is in rewarding contribution proportionately. It is just this type of dispute about relative valuations which provides the proper arena for arguments about the role of desert in distributive justice.

Although the introduction of external values and goals is crucial for desert-claims, it is important to understand that this does not turn the notion of desert into a consequentialist one. It is true that if my analysis is correct then desert does have, in some sense, a greater affinity with consequentialism than has been thought in the past. It allows external values a role to play in the determination of desert-claims. But this fact alone does not make desert into a consequentialist notion. To see the distinction, it is best to begin with past criticism of philosophers' attempts (particularly by utilitarians) to 're-interpret' desert into a consequentialist notion.

Joel Feinberg notes: 'It follows from our analysis of desert statements that to say "*S* deserves *X* because giving it to him would be in the public interest" is simply to misuse the word "deserves"' (*Doing and Deserving* p. 81). Feinberg is correct that this type of construal of the word 'deserves' is mistaken. This utilitarian proposal is *not* an interpretation of desert at all. However, agreement with this point of Feinberg's does not damage the contention of this paper, that desert admits of external values and purposes.

To see this, take a case where the affinity is greatest between desert and a form of utilitarianism. Suppose two persons, David and Jenny, value happiness extremely highly. Suppose David adopts as his distribution principle some form of utilitarianism, e.g., 'Distribute income in such a way that, over the long run, happiness will be maximized'. Suppose Jenny believes there are moral reasons to adopt a non-utilitarian distribution principle which uses desert as its distribution criterion. Given her value system, she may adopt as her desert-basis 'contribution to happiness', so that under her principle people might gain, say, economic benefits in proportion to their contribution to the society's happiness. Now a system operating under such a principle would certainly have similarities to one operating under a utilitarian principle (many non-utilitarian systems do)—giving benefits to people on the basis of their contribution to society's happiness is likely to encourage people to contribute to society's happiness. But the justification for the distribution of benefits is fundamentally different. Under the desert principle the justification is that the person has contributed to society's happiness. Under the utilitarian principle the justification for the benefit is that it will maximize happiness. So even here, where what is valued in both cases is happiness, the justifications (and some, if not all, of the payments) are different.

What marks out Jenny's desert-based system is having other values apart from happiness. Nevertheless, it is also true that her valuation of happiness plays a crucial role in her determination of the morally correct desert-basis. The same is true for other proposed desert-bases for economic distribution. The basis which one believes is justified will partly depend on relative valuations external to desert. So desert will allow in some values, when the desert-basis is being set, which are similar to those which utilitarians embrace. Although Feinberg correctly points out *one way* in which desert cannot admit values such as happiness or social utility, this does not exclude admitting these values in other ways which respect the concept of desert. As we have seen, there are *legitimate* ways in which these values can enter in setting the desert-basis.

David Miller also seems to miss the possible legitimate ways that social utility could be linked to desert:

> It is probably true that the most convincing reasons which can be given for taking contribution, rather than effort, as a basis for reward are utilitarian in character. By rewarding people according to the value of their different contributions, we encourage them to develop the skills and abilities which produce a superior contribution, and this result is socially useful. But to use such utilitarian arguments to establish a principle of desert seems to me inconsistent
>
> (*Social Justice* p. 103).

Miller is also correct that utilitarian considerations cannot be taken into account, in the manner he cites, when setting the desert-basis. However, as we have seen, it need not always be illegitimate to take utility and/or social product considerations into account when setting the desert-basis—it will depend on how it is done.

Consider, for instance, the two income desert-bases discussed a moment ago—contribution to the social product and effort in contributing to the social product—and a third, 'compensation' for the burdens (or dis-utility) people incur in contributing to the social product. For all three of these desert-bases, people need to value increases in the social product in order to adopt them as desert-bases, *and this valuing will not come from an internal analysis of desert.* It is because society values the social product that people can deserve benefits by contributing to it. So the social product can enter in this manner into the setting of the desert-basis. As we have seen, the role of these external values is in no way a peculiar feature of these particular desert-bases. It is present in most ascriptions of desert, and it is this point that eludes writers such as Feinberg and Miller in their discussions of what roles the social product or utility can play in the setting of desert-bases.

It should be noted that there is an alternative way in which desert can be linked to external values and particularly to utilitarianism. This, however, has already been explored by a number of writers in the past with respect to a particular system of justification of retributive principles of punishment. Under this system, particular punishments are justified on the grounds of desert, but the practice as a whole is justified because it maximizes happiness in the long run. This is *not* the form of the desert-claims made in my example above. It is, of course, possible for a utilitarian to adopt some system of payments, mirroring the desert-based system described, in the belief that such a system will maximize happiness—utilitarians are always free to suggest that an apparently conflicting system is the one which maximizes happiness. But the payments will still be justified in different ways. Under the desert-based system it is *because* people have contributed to society's happiness that they deserve X. The fact that giving them X may also have the effect of maximizing happiness in the long run does not enter into the justification.

It may be objected, though, that the admission of external values violates the essentially 'backward-looking' nature of desert mentioned earlier. As David Miller has said

(p. 93), 'Desert judgements are justified on the basis of *past* and *present* facts about individuals, never on the basis of states of affairs to be created in the future. Desert is a "backward-looking" concept, if we regard the present as the limit of the past; utility is a forward-looking principle.' Now Miller's suggested division of concepts into 'forward-looking' and 'backward-looking' is not as clear-cut as it may appear. When one is considering what system of payments will coincide with giving people what they deserve, one is engaged in an activity that seems to be rather closely akin to an activity which is *forward-looking* (or perhaps, in some sense, timeless). But his main point still holds—there are certain ways in which desert cannot admit consideration of states of affairs to be created in the future. From the above discussion it should be possible to see that the proposal here does not violate this quality of desert. To reiterate, the proposal is *not* that people 'deserve' X because giving it to them will promote external value V. It is that people value V and it is because they value V that they believe people deserve X for 'realizing', 'instantiating', 'contributing to' or 'trying to promote' V. Of course, the domain of V ranges across an extensive and heterogeneous set of values, from 'effort in promoting world understanding' to 'speed of foot'. One of the purposes of this paper has been to show that this diversity of values enters in a direct way in arguments about what is the proper desert-basis.

There have been numerous debates about what role, if any, desert should play in various decisions about distributive justice, and about what is the morally right desert-basis. It should be clear from the arguments of this paper that what is required to advance these debates are decisions about what is more valuable, and supporting argument for those decisions. This *type* of decision is *not* unfamiliar, as the above analysis and consideration of examples has shown. As it turns out, we make this type of decision, perhaps unknowingly, every day when we make desert-judgements, be they when we are commenting on who deserved to win the race, or on what grade a student deserves, or on who deserves a salary rise. The purpose of the above discussion has been to make the nature of the choice conceptually clearer.

University of Wollongong

NOTES

1. In *Philosophy and Public Affairs* 1992 (full bibliographic references at end).
2. For analyses of desert which provide a useful background to the issues discussed in this paper see Feinberg, Kleinig, Sterba, Sadurski, Sher 1987, Young.
3. See Feinberg pp. 58–61; Miller pp. 117–8; Galston p. 170.
4. Writers who have made the type of claims I have in mind include Ryan; Rawls *TJ* pp. 311–12; Nagel *PPA* 1973; Dick; Wasserstrom; Zaitchik; Daniels; Rachels; Weinberg pp. 21–3; Sadurski pp. 116–38; Milne.
5. The most sophisticated version of this type of argument is given by Sher, *Desert* ch. 5.
6. A related topic is that of moral luck: see Nagel 1982, Williams, Richards, Adler. There is some merit in Richards' explanation of some of the paradoxical features of desert pointed out by Nagel. However, his argument for the claim that all true desert is luckless rests on an untenable thesis that all desert is based on character (see Adler).
7. The question of where the dispute between these two positions lies has rarely been addressed directly or adequately. One of the earliest attempts was by Michael A. Slote. Unfortunately, Slote only proceeds to give examples of how the same disagreement arises in non-political contexts (where it is also difficult to resolve) and he does not analyse either the nature or the source of the disagreement. George Sher (*Desert* pp. 102–4) has made the best attempt that I know of, but he still looks to desert itself rather than to external values.

References

Adler, J.E. 1987: 'Luckless Desert is Different Desert', *Mind* 96, pp. 247–9.

Barry, B. 1965: *Political Argument* (London: Routledge & Kegan Paul).

Christman, J. 1988: 'Entrepreneurs, Profits, and Deserving Market Shares', *Social Philosophy and Policy* 6, pp. 1–16.

Cummiskey, D. 1987: 'Desert and Entitlement: a Rawlsian Consequentialist Account', *Analysis* 47, pp. 15–19.

Daniels, N. 1978: 'Merit and Meritocracy', *Philosophy and Public Affairs* 7, pp. 206–23.

Dick, J.C. 1975: 'How to Justify a Distribution of Earnings', *Philosophy and Public Affairs* 4, pp. 248–72.

Feinberg, J. 1970: *Doing and Deserving* (Princeton UP).

Galston, W. 1980: *Justice and the Human Good* (Univ. of Chicago Press).

Gaus, G.F. 1990: *Value and Justification* (Cambridge UP).

Holmgren, M. 1986: 'Justifying Desert-claims', *Journal of Value Inquiry* 20, pp. 265–78.

Kleinig, J. 1971: 'The Concept of Desert', *American Philosophical Quarterly* 8, pp. 71–8.

Miller, D. 1976: *Social Justice* (Oxford UP).

Milne, H. 1986: 'Desert, Effort and Equality', *Journal of Applied Philosophy* 3, pp. 235–43.

Nagel, T. 1973: 'Equal Treatment and Compensatory Discrimination', *Philosophy and Public Affairs* 2, pp. 348–63.

——1982: 'Moral Luck', in G. Watson (ed.), *Free Will* (Oxford UP), pp. 174–96.

Rachels, J. 1978: 'What People Deserve', in J. Arthur and W. Shaw (eds), *Justice and Economic Distribution* (Engelwood Cliffs: Prentice-Hall), pp. 150–63.

Rawls, J. 1955: 'Two Concepts of Rules', *Philosophical Review* 64, pp. 3–32.

——1972: *A Theory of Justice* (Oxford UP).

Richards, N. 1986: 'Luck and Desert', *Mind* 95, pp. 198–209.

Ryan, J.A. 1942: *Distributive Justice* (New York: Macmillan, 3rd edn).

Sadurski, W. 1985: *Giving Desert its Due* (Dordrecht: Reidel).

Scheffler, S. 1992: 'Responsibility, Reactive Attitudes, and Liberalism in Philosophy and Politics', *Philosophy and Public Affairs* 21, pp. 299–323.

Sher, G. 1979: 'Effort, Ability and Personal Desert', *Philosophy and Public Affairs* 8, pp. 361–76.

——1987: *Desert* (Princeton UP).

Sidgwick, H. 1907: *The Methods of Ethics* (London: Macmillan).

Slote, M.A. 1973: 'Desert, Consent and Justice', *Philosophy and Public Affairs* 2, pp. 323–47.

Sterba, J. 1976: 'Justice and the Concept of Desert', *The Personalist* 57, pp. 188–97.

Sverdlik, S. 1983: 'The Nature of Desert,' *Southern Journal of Philosophy* 21, pp. 585–94.

Waller, B. 1987: 'Just and Nonjust Deserts', *Southern Journal of Philosophy* 25, pp. 229–38.

Wasserstrom, R. 1976: 'The University and the Case for Preferential Treatment', *American Philosophical Quarterly* 13, pp. 165–70.

Weinberg, L.T. 1979: 'An Answer to the "Liberal"

Objection to Special Admissions', *Educational Theory* 29, pp. 21–3.

Williams, B.A.O. 1981: 'Moral Luck', in *Moral Luck* (Cambridge UP), pp. 20–39.

Young, R. 1992: 'Egalitarianism and Personal Desert', *Ethics* 102, pp. 319–41.

Zaitchik, A. 1977: 'On Deserving to Deserve', *Philosophy and Public Affairs* 6, pp. 370–88.

B. DESERT AND RESPONSIBILITY

13. The Impossibility of Moral Responsibility

GALEN STRAWSON

Galen Strawson teaches philosophy at Jesus College, Oxford University, and is the author of several works in metaphysics, including *Freedom and Belief* (1986). In this article Strawson develops in several forms what he calls the "Basic Argument," which holds that, in order for us to be ultimately morally responsible for our actions, we must, in some significant sense, be the cause of ourselves (the *causa sui*). But since no one can be the cause of himself or herself, no one is ultimately morally responsible for one's actions. Since desert claims, rewards, and punishments (for example, the kind of punishment and reward attached to hell and heaven) seem to require responsibility for actions, it would follow that no one deserves rewards and punishments. Strawson points out that the argument resists the compatibilist's claim that free will and determinism are compatible, since the compatibilist cannot avoid the crucial premise about self-causation (*causa sui*). Nor does the libertarian defense get around the problem, since all that the incompatibilist libertarian can show is that indeterminism may be true. But indeterminism only gives us randomness, not purposeful action, let alone self-causation. So it seems that the Basic Argument survives criticism. Moral responsibility is impossible, and no one deserves rewards and punishments.

Strawson admits that, while this creates severe problems for ethics, it doesn't eliminate it. We need to rethink our moral categories to take into consideration the Basic Argument.

I

There is an argument, which I will call the Basic Argument, which appears to prove that

we cannot be truly or ultimately morally responsible for our actions. According to the Basic Argument, it makes no difference whether determinism is true or false. We can-

Reprinted from *Philosophical Studies* 75 (1994), by permission.

not be truly or ultimately morally responsible for our actions in either case.

The Basic Argument has various expressions in the literature of free will, and its central idea can be quickly conveyed. (1) Nothing can be *causa sui*—nothing can be the cause of itself. (2) In order to be truly morally responsible for one's actions one would have to be *causa sui*, at least in certain crucial mental respects. (3) Therefore nothing can be truly morally responsible.

In this paper I want to reconsider the Basic Argument, in the hope that anyone who thinks that we can be truly or ultimately morally responsible for our actions will be prepared to say exactly what is wrong with it. I think that the point that it has to make is obvious, and that it has been underrated in recent discussion of free will—perhaps because it admits of no answer. I suspect that it is obvious in such a way that insisting on it too much is likely to make it seem less obvious than it is, given the innate contrasuggestibility of human beings in general and philosophers in particular. But I am not worried about making it seem less obvious than it is so long as it gets adequate attention. As far as its validity is concerned, it can look after itself.

A more cumbersome statement of the Basic Argument goes as follows.

(1) Interested in free action, we are particularly interested in actions that are performed for a reason (as opposed to 'reflex' actions or mindlessly habitual actions).

(2) When one acts for a reason, what one does is a function of how one is, mentally speaking. (It is also a function of one's height, one's strength, one's place and time, and so on. But the mental factors are crucial when moral responsibility is in question.)

(3) So if one is to be truly responsible for how one acts, one must be truly responsible for how one is, mentally speaking—at least in certain respects.

(4) But to be truly responsible for how one is, mentally speaking, in certain respects, one must have brought it about that one is the way one is, mentally speaking, in certain respects. And it is not merely that one must have caused oneself to be the way one is,

mentally speaking. One must have consciously and explicitly chosen to be the way one is, mentally speaking, in certain respects, and one must have succeeded in bringing it about that one is that way.

(5) But one cannot really be said to choose, in a conscious, reasoned, fashion, to be the way one is mentally speaking, in any respect at all, unless one already exists, mentally speaking, already equipped with some principles of choice, 'P1'—preferences, values, pro-attitudes, ideals—in the light of which one chooses how to be.

(6) But then to be truly responsible, on account of having chosen to be the way one is, mentally speaking, in certain respects, one must be truly responsible for one's having the principles of choice P1 in the light of which one chose how to be.

(7) But for this to be so one must have chosen P1, in a reasoned, conscious, intentional fashion.

(8) But for this, i.e. (7), to be so one must already have had some principles of choice P2, in the light of which one chose P1.

(9) And so on. Here we are setting out on a regress that we cannot stop. True self-determination is impossible because it requires the actual completion of an infinite series of choices of principles of choice.

(10) So true moral responsibility is impossible, because it requires true self-determination, as noted in (3).

This may seem contrived, but essentially the same argument can be given in a more natural form. (1) it is undeniable that one is the way one is, initially, as a result of heredity and early experience, and it is undeniable that these are things for which one cannot be held to be in any way responsible (morally or otherwise). (2) One cannot at any later stage of life hope to accede to true moral responsibility for the way one is by trying to change the way one already is as a result of heredity and previous experience. For (3) both the particular way in which one is moved to try to change oneself, and the degree of one's success in one's attempt at change, will be determined by how one already is as a result of heredity and previous experience. And (4) any further changes that one can bring about only after one has brought about certain initial changes will in turn be determined, via the initial changes, by heredity and previous experience. (5) This may not be the whole story, for it may be that some changes in the way one is are traceable not to heredity and experience but to the influence of indeterministic or random factors. But it is absurd to suppose that indeterministic or random factors, for which one is ex hypothesi in no way responsible, can in themselves contribute in any way to one's being truly morally responsible for how one is.

The claim, then, is not that people cannot change the way they are. They can, in certain respects (which tend to be exaggerated by North Americans and underestimated, perhaps, by Europeans). The claim is only that people cannot be supposed to change themselves in such a way as to be or become truly or ultimately morally responsible for the way they are, and hence for their actions.

II

I have encountered two main reactions to the Basic Argument. On the one hand it convinces almost all the students with whom I have discussed the topic of free will and moral responsibility.[1] On the other hand it often tends to be dismissed, in contemporary discussion of free will and moral responsibility, as wrong, or irrelevant, or fatuous, or too rapid, or an expression of metaphysical megalomania.

I think that the Basic Argument is certainly valid in showing that we cannot be morally responsible in the way that many suppose. And I think that it is the natural light, not fear, that has convinced the students I have taught that this is so. That is why it seems worthwhile to restate the argument in a slightly different—simpler and looser—version, and to ask again what is wrong with it.

Some may say that there is nothing wrong with it, but that it is not very interesting, and not very central to the free will debate. I doubt whether any non-philosopher or beginner in

philosophy would agree with this view. If one wants to think about free will and moral responsibility, consideration of some verion of the Basic Argument is an overwhelmingly natural place to start. It certainly has to be considered at some point in a full discussion of free will and moral responsibility, even if the point it has to make is obvious. Belief in the kind of absolute moral responsibility that it shows to be impossible has for a long time been central to the Western religious, moral, and cultural tradition, even if it is now slightly on the wane (a disputable view). It is a matter of historical fact that concern about moral responsibility has been the main motor—indeed the *ratio essendi*—of discussion of the issue of free will. The only way in which one might hope to show (1) that the Basic Argument was not central to the free will debate would be to show (2) that the issue of moral responsibility was not central to the free will debate. There are, obviously, ways of taking the word 'free' in which (2) can be maintained. But (2) is clearly false none the less.

In saying that the notion of moral responsibility criticized by the Basic Argument is central to the Western tradition, I am not suggesting that it is some artificial and local Judaeo-Christian-Kantian construct that is found nowhere else in the history of the peoples of the world, although even if it were that would hardly diminish its interest and importance for us. It is natural to suppose that Aristotle also subscribed to it,[2] and it is significant that anthropologists have suggested that most human societies can be classified either as 'guilt cultures' or as 'shame cultures'. It is true that neither of these two fundamental moral emotions necessarily presupposes a conception of oneself as truly morally responsible for what one has done. But the fact that both are widespread does at least suggest that a conception of moral responsibility similar to our own is a natural part of the human moral-conceptual repertoire.

In fact the notion of moral responsibility connects more tightly with the notion of guilt than with the notion of shame. In many cultures shame can attach to one because of what some member of one's family—or government—has done, and not because of anything one has done oneself; and in such cases the feeling of shame need not (although it may) involve some obscure, irrational feeling that one is somehow responsible for the behaviour of one's family or government. The case of guilt is less clear. There is no doubt that people can feel guilty (or can believe that they feel guilty) about things for which they are not responsible, let alone morally responsible. But it is much less obvious that they can do this without any sense or belief that they are in fact responsible.

III

Such complications are typical of moral psychology, and they show that it is important to try to be precise about what sort of responsibility is under discussion. What sort of 'true' moral responsibility is being said to be both impossible and widely believed in?

An old story is very helpful in clarifying this question. This is the story of heaven and hell. As I understand it, true moral responsibility is responsibility of such a kind that, if we have it, then it *makes sense*, at least, to suppose that it could be just to punish some of us with (eternal) torment in hell and reward others with (eternal) bliss in heaven. The stress on the words 'makes sense' is important, for one certainly does not have to believe in any version of the story of heaven and hell in order to understand the notion of true moral responsibility that it is being used to illustrate. Nor does one have to believe in any version of the story of heaven and hell in order to believe in the existence of true moral responsibility. On the contrary: many atheists have believed in the existence of true moral responsibility. The story of heaven and hell is useful simply because it illustrates, in a peculiarly vivid way, the *kind* of absolute or ultimate accountability or responsibility that many have supposed themselves to have, and that many do still suppose themselves to have. It very clearly expresses its scope and force.

But one does not have to refer to religious faith in order to describe the sorts of every-

day situations that are perhaps primarily influential in giving rise to our belief in true responsibility. Suppose you set off for a shop on the evening of a national holiday, intending to buy a cake with your last ten pound note. On the steps of the shop someone is shaking an Oxfam tin. You stop, and it seems completely clear to you that it is entirely up to you what you do next. That is, it seems to you that you are truly, radically free to choose, in such a way that you will be ultimately morally responsible for whatever you do choose. Even if you believe that determinism is true, and that you will in five minutes time be able to look back and say that what you did was determined, this does not seem to undermine your sense of the absoluteness and inescapability of your freedom, and of your moral responsibility for your choice. The same seems to be true even if you accept the validity of the Basic Argument stated in section I, which concludes that one cannot be in any way ultimately responsible for the way one is and decides. In both cases, it remains true that as one stands there, one's freedom and true moral responsibility seem obvious and absolute to one.

Large and small, morally significant or morally neutral, such situations of choice occur regularly in human life. I think they lie at the heart of the experience of freedom and moral responsibility. They are the fundamental source of our inability to give up belief in true or ultimate moral responsibility. There are further questions to be asked about why human beings experience these situations of choice as they do. It is an interesting question whether any cognitively sophisticated, rational, self-conscious agent must experience situations of choice in this way. But they are the experiential rock on which the belief in true moral responsibility is founded.

IV

I will restate the Basic Argument. First, though, I will give some examples of people who have accepted that some sort of true or ultimate responsibility for the way one is is a necessary condition of true or ultimate moral responsibility for the way one acts, and who, certain that they are truly morally responsible for the way they act, have believed the condition to be fulfilled.

E.H. Carr held that "normal adult human beings are morally responsible for their own personality". Jean-Paul Sartre talked of "the choice that each man makes of his personality", and held that "man is responsible for what he is". In a later interview he judged that his earlier assertions about freedom were incautious; but he still held that "in the end one is always responsible for what is made of one" in some absolute sense. Kant described the position very clearly when he claimed that "man *himself* must make or have made himself into whatever, in a moral sense, whether good or evil, he is to become. Either condition must be an effect of his free choice; for otherwise he could not be held responsible for it and could therefore be *morally* neither good nor evil." Since he was committed to belief in radical moral responsibility, Kant held that such self-creation does indeed take place, and wrote accordingly of "man's character, which he himself creates" and of "knowledge of oneself as a person who . . . is his own originator" John Patten, the current British Minister for Education, a Catholic apparently preoccupied by the idea of sin, has claimed that "it is . . . self-evident that as we grow up each individual chooses whether to be good or bad." It seems clear enough that he sees such choice as sufficient to give us true moral responsibility of the heaven-and-hell variety.[3]

The rest of us are not usually so reflective, but it seems that we do tend, in some vague and unexamined fashion, to think of ourselves as responsible for—answerable for—how we are. The point is quite a delicate one, for we do not ordinarily suppose that we have gone through some sort of active process of self-determination at some particular past time. Nevertheless it seems accurate to say that we do unreflectively experience ourselves, in many respects, rather as we might experience ourselves if we did believe that we had engaged in some such activity of self-determination.

Sometimes a part of one's character—a desire or tendency—may strike one as foreign or alien. But it can do this only against a background of character traits that are not experienced as foreign, but are rather 'identified' with (it is a necessary truth that it is only relative to such a background that a character trait can stand out as alien). Some feel tormented by impulses that they experience as alien, but in many a sense of general identification with their character predominates, and this identification seems to carry within itself an implicit sense that one is, generally, somehow in control of and answerable for how one is (even, perhaps, for aspects of one's character that one does not like). Here, then, I suggest that we find, semi-dormant in common thought, an implicit recognition of the idea that true moral responsibility for what one does somehow involves responsibility for how one is. Ordinary thought is ready to move this way under pressure.

There is, however, another powerful tendency in ordinary thought to think that one can be truly morally responsible even if one's character is ultimately wholly non-self-determined—simply because one is fully self-consciously aware of oneself as an agent facing choices. I will return to this point later on.

V

Let me now restate the Basic Argument in very loose—as it were conversational—terms. New forms of words allow for new forms of objection, but they may be helpful none the less.

(1) You do what you do, in any situation in which you find yourself, because of the way you are.

So

(2) To be truly morally responsible for what you do you must be truly responsible for the

way you are—at least in certain crucial mental respects.

Or:

(1) What you intentionally do, given the circumstances in which you (believe you) find yourself, flows necessarily from how you are.

Hence

(2) You have to get to have some responsibility for how you are in order to get to have some responsibility for what you intentionally do, given the circumstances in which you (believe you) find yourself.

Comment. Once again the qualification about 'certain mental respects' is one I will take for granted. Obviously one is not responsible for one's sex, one's basic body pattern, one's height, and so on. But if one were not responsible for anything about oneself, how one could be responsible for what one did, given the truth of (1)? This is the fundamental question, and it seems clear that if one is going to be responsible for any aspect of oneself, it had better be some aspect of one's mental nature.

I take it that (1) is incontrovertible, and that it is (2) that must be resisted. For if (1) and (2) are conceded the case seems lost, because the full argument runs as follows:

(1) You do what you do because of the way you are.

So

(2) To be truly morally responsible for what you do you must be truly responsible for the way are—at least in certain crucial mental respects.

But

(3) You cannot be truly responsible for the way you are, so you cannot be truly responsible for what you do.

Why can't you be truly responsible for the way you are? Because

(4) To be truly responsible for the way you are, you must have intentionally brought it about that you are the way you are, and this is impossible.

Why is it impossible? Well, suppose it is not. Suppose that

(5) You have somehow intentionally brought it about that you are the way you now are, and that you have brought this about in such a way that you can now be said to be truly responsible for being the way you are now.

For this to be true

(6) You must already have had a certain nature N in the light of which you intentionally brought it about that you are as you now are.

But then

(7) For it to be true you and you alone are truly responsible for how you now are, you must be truly responsible for having had the nature N in the light of which you intentionally brought it about that you are the way you now are.

So

(8) You must have intentionally brought it about that you had that nature N, in which case you must have existed already with a prior nature in the light of which you intentionally brought it about that you had the nature N in the light of which you intentionally brought it about that you are the way you now are . . .

Here one is setting off on the regress. Nothing can be *causa sui* in the required way. Even if such causal 'aseity' is allowed to belong unintelligibly to God, it cannot be plausibly be supposed to be possessed by ordinary finite human beings. "The *causa sui* is

the best self-contradiction that has been conceived so far", as Nietzsche remarked in 1886:

> it is a sort of rape and perversion of logic.
> But the extravagant ride of man has man-
> aged to entangle itself profoundly and fright-
> fully with just this nonsense. The desire for
> "freedom of the will" in the superlative
> metaphysical sense, which still holds sway,
> unfortunately, in the minds of the half-edu-
> cated; the desire to bear the entire and ulti-
> mate responsibility for one's actions one-
> self, and to absolve God, the world,
> ancestors, chance, and society involves
> nothing less than to be precisely this *causa
> sui* and, with more than Baron Münch-
> hausen's audacity, to pull oneself up into
> existence by the hair, out of the swamps of
> nothingness . . .
>   *(Beyond Good and Evil, §21).*

The rephrased argument is essentially exactly the same as before, although the first
two steps are now more simply stated. It may
seem pointless to repeat it, but the questions
remain. Can the Basic Argument simply be
dismissed? It is really of no importance in the
discussion of free will and moral responsibility? (No and No) Shouldn't any serious defense of free will and moral responsibility
thoroughly acknowledge the respect in which
the Basic Argument is valid before going on
to try to give its own positive account of the
nature of free will and moral responsibility?
Doesn't the argument go to the heart of things
if the heart of the free will debate is a concern about whether we can be truly morally
responsible in the absolute way that we ordinarily suppose? (Yes and Yes)

We are what we are, and we cannot be
thought to have made ourselves *in such a way*
that we can be held to be free in our actions
in such a way that we can be held to be
morally responsible for our actions *in such a
way* that any punishment or reward for our
actions is ultimately just or fair. Punishments
and rewards may seem deeply appropriate or
intrinsically 'fitting' to us in spite of this argument, and many of the various institutions
of punishment and reward in human society
appear to be practically indispensable in both

their legal and non-legal forms. But if one
takes the notion of justice that is central to
our intellectual and cultural tradition seriously, then the evident consequence of the
Basic Argument is that there is a fundamental sense in which no punishment or reward
is ever ultimately just. It is exactly as just to
punish or reward people for their actions as it
is to punish or reward them for the (natural)
colour of their hair or the (natural) shape of
their faces. The point seems obvious, and yet
it contradicts a fundamental part of our natural self-conception, and there are elements
in human thought that move very deeply
against it. When it comes to questions of responsibility, we tend to feel that we are somehow responsible for the way we are. Even
more importantly, perhaps, we tend to feel
that our explicit self-conscious awareness of
ourselves as agents who are able to deliberate
about what to do, in situations of choice, suffices to constitute us as morally responsible
free agents in the strongest sense, whatever
the conclusion of the Basic Argument.

VI

I have suggested that it is step (2) of the restated Basic Argument that must be rejected,
and of course it can be rejected, because the
phrases 'truly responsible' and 'truly morally
responsible' can be defined in many ways. I
will briefly consider three sorts of response to
the Basic Argument, and I will concentrate
on their more simple expressions, in the belief that truth in philosophy, especially in areas of philosophy like the present one, is almost never very complicated.

(I) The first is *compatibilist*. Compatibilists believe that one can be a free and
morally responsible agent even if determinism is true. Roughly, they claim, with many
variations of detail, that one may correctly be
said to be truly responsible for what one does,
when one acts, just so long as one is not
caused to act by any of a certain set of constraints (kleptomaniac impulses, obsessional
neuroses, desires that are experienced as alien,
post-hypnotic commands, threats, instances

of *force majeure*, and so on). Clearly, this sort of compatibilist responsibility does not require that one should be truly responsible for how one is in any way at all, and so step (2) of the Basic Argument comes out as false. One can have compatibilist responsibility even if the way one is is totally determined by factors entirely outside one's control.

It is for this reason, however, that compatibilist responsibility famously fails to amount to any sort of true *moral* responsibility, given the natural, strong understanding of the notion of true moral responsibility (characterized above by reference to the story of heaven and hell). One does what one does entirely because of the way one is, and one is in no way ultimately responsible for the way one is. So how can one be justly punished for anything one does? Compatibilists have given increasingly refined accounts of the circumstances in which punishment may be said to be appropriate or intrinsically fitting. But they can do nothing against this basic objection.

Many compatibilists have never supposed otherwise. They are happy to admit the point. They observe that the notions of true moral responsibility and justice that are employed in the objection cannot possibly have application to anything real, and suggest that the objection is therefore not worth considering. In response, proponents of the Basic Argument agree that the notions of true moral responsibility and justice in question cannot have application to anything real; but they make no apologics for considering them. They consider them because they are central to ordinary thought about moral responsibility and justice. So far as most people are concerned, they are the subject, if the subject is moral responsibility and justice.

(II) The second response is *libertarian*. Incompatibilists believe that freedom and moral responsibility are incompatible with determinism, and some of them are libertarians, who believe that that we are free and morally responsible agents, and that determinism is therefore false. In an ingenious statement of the incompatibilist-libertarian case, Robert Kane argues that agents in an undetermined world can have free will, for they can "have

the power to make choices for which they have ultimate responsibility". That is, they can "have the power to make choices which can only and finally be explained in terms of their own wills (i.e. character, motives, and efforts of will)". Roughly, Kane sees this power as grounded in the possible occurrence, in agents, of efforts of will that have two main features: first, they are partly indeterministic in their nature, and hence indeterminate in their outcome; second, they occur in cases in which agents are trying to make a difficult choice between the options that their characters dispose them to consider. (The paradigm cases will be cases in which they face a conflict between moral duty and non-moral desire.)

But the old objection to libertarianism recurs. How can this indeterminism help with *moral* responsibility? Granted that the truth of determinism rules out true moral responsibility, how can the falsity of determinism help? How can the occurrence of partly random or indeterministic events contribute in any way to one's being truly morally responsible either for one's actions or for one's character? If my efforts of will shape my character in an admirable way, and in so doing are partly indeterministic in nature, while also being shaped (as Kane grants) by my already existing character, why am I not merely lucky?

The general objection applies equally whether determinism is true or false, and can be restated as follows. We are born with a great many genetically determined predispositions for which we are not responsible. We are subject to many early influences for which we are not responsible. These decisively shape our characters, our motives, the general bent and strength of our capacity to make efforts of will. We may later engage in conscious and intentional shaping procedures—call them S-procedures—designed to affect and change our characters, motivational structure, and wills. Suppose we do. The question is then why we engage in the particular S-procedures that we do engage in, and why we engage in them in the particular way that we do. The general answer is that we engage in the particular S-procedures that we do engage in, given the circumstances in which we find ourselves, because of certain features of the way we already are. (Indeterministic factors may also play a part in what happens, but these will not help to make us responsible for what we do.) And these features of the way we already are—call them character features, or C-features—are either wholly the products of genetic or environmental influences, deterministic or random, for which we are not responsible, or are at least partly the result of earlier S-procedures, which are in turn either wholly the product of C-features for which we are not responsible, or are at least partly the product of still earlier S-procedures, which are in turn either the products of C-features for which we are not responsible, or the product of such C-features together with still earlier S-procedures—and so on. In the end, we reach the first S-procedure, and this will have been engaged in, and engaged in the particular way in which it was engaged in, as a result of genetic or environmental factors, deterministic or random, for which we were not responsible.

Moving away from the possible role of indeterministic factors in character or personality formation, we can consider their possible role in particular instances of deliberation and decision. Here too it seems clear that indeterministic factors cannot, in influencing what happens, contribute to true moral responsibility in any way. In the end, whatever we do, we do it either as a result of random influences for which we are not responsible, or as a result of non-random influences for which we are not responsible, or as a result of influences for which we are proximally responsible but not ultimately responsible. The point seems obvious. Nothing can be ultimately *causa sui* in any respect at all. Even if God can be, we can't be.

Kane says little about moral responsibility in his paper, but his position seems to be that true moral responsibility is possible if indeterminism is true. It is possible because in cases of "moral, prudential and practical struggle we . . . are truly 'making ourselves' in such a way that we are ultimately respon-

sible for the outcome". This 'making of ourselves' means that "we can be ultimately responsible for our present motives and character by virtue of past choices which helped to form them and for which we were ultimately responsible" (op. cit., p. 252). It is for this reason that we can be ultimately responsible and morally responsible not only in cases of struggle in which we are 'making ourselves', but also for choices and actions which do not involve struggle, flowing unopposed from our character and motives.

In claiming that we can be ultimately responsible for our present motives and character, Kane appears to *accept* step (2) of the Basic Argument. He appears to accept that we have to 'make ourselves', and so be ultimately responsible for ourselves, in order to be morally responsible for what we do. The problem with this suggestion is the old one. In Kane's view, a person's 'ultimate responsibility' for the outcome of an effort of will depends essentially on the partly indeterministic nature of the outcome. This is because it is only the element of indeterminism that prevents prior character and motives from fully explaining the outcome of the effort of will (op. cit, p. 236). But how can this indeterminism help with moral responsibility? How can the fact that my effort of will is indeterministic in such a way that its outcome is indeterminate make me truly responsible for it, or even help to make me truly responsible for it? How can it help in any way at all with moral responsibility? How can it make punishment—or reward—ultimately just?

There is a further, familiar problem with the view that moral responsibility depends on indeterminism. If one accepts the view, one will have to grant that it is impossible to know whether any human being is ever morally responsible. For moral responsibility now depends on the falsity of determinism, and determinism is unfalsifiable. There is no more reason to think that determinism is false than that it is true, in spite of the impression sometimes given by scientists and popularizers of science.

(III) The third option begins by accepting that one cannot be held to be ultimately responsible for one's character or personality or motivational structure. It accepts that this is so whether determinism is true or false. It then directly challenges step (2) of the Basic Argument. It appeals to a certain picture of the self in order to argue that one can be truly free and morally responsible in spite of the fact that one cannot be held to be ultimately responsible for one's character or personality or motivational structure. This picture has some support in the 'phenomenology' of human choice—we sometimes experience our choices and decisions as if the picture were an accurate one. But it is easy to show that it cannot be accurate in such a way that we can be said to be truly or ultimately morally responsible for our choices or actions.

It can be set out as follows. One is free and truly morally responsible because one's self is, in a crucial sense, independent of one's character or personality or motivational structure—one's CPM, for short. Suppose one is in a situation which one experiences as a difficult choice between A, doing one's duty, and B, following one's non-moral desires. Given one's CPM, one responds in a certain way. One's desires and beliefs develop and interact and constitute reasons for both A and B. One's CPM makes one tend towards A or B. So far the problem is the same as ever: whatever one does, one will do what one does because of the way one's CPM is, and since one neither is nor can be ultimately responsible for the way one's CPM is, one cannot be ultimately responsible for what one does.

Enter one's self, S. S is imagined to be in some way independent of one's CPM. S (i.e. one) considers the deliverances of one's CPM and decides in the light of them, but it—S— incorporates a power of decision that is independent of one's CPM in such a way that one can after all count as truly and ultimately morally responsible in one's decisions and actions, even though one is not ultimately responsible for one's CPM. Step (2) of the Basic Argument is false because of the existence of S.

The trouble with the picture is obvious. S (i.e. one) decides on the basis of the deliverances of one's CPM. But whatever S decides, it decides as it does because of the way it is (or else because partly or wholly because of the occurrence in the decision process of indeterministic factors for which it—i.e. one— cannot be responsible, and which cannot plausibly be thought to contribute to one's true moral responsibility). And this returns us to where we started. To be a source of true or ultimate responsibility, S must be responsible for being the way it is. But this is impossible, for the reasons given in the Basic Argument.

The story of S and CPM adds another layer to the description of the human decision process, but it cannot change the fact that human beings cannot be ultimately self-determining in such a way as to be ultimately morally responsible for how they are, and thus for how they decide and act. The story is crudely presented, but it should suffice to make clear that no move of this sort can solve the problem.

'Character is destiny', as Novalis is often reported as saying. The remark is inaccurate, because external circumstances are part of destiny, but the point is well taken when it comes to the question of moral responsibility. Nothing can be *causa sui*, and in order to be truly morally responsible for one's actions one would have to be *causa sui*, at least in certain crucial mental respects. One cannot institute oneself in such a way that one can take over true or assume moral responsibility for how one is in such a way that one can indeed be truly morally responsible for what one does. This fact is not changed by the fact that we may be unable not to think of ourselves as truly morally responsible in ordinary circumstances. Nor is it changed by the fact that it may be a very good thing that we have this inability—so that we might wish to take steps to preserve it, if it looked to be in danger of fading. As already remarked, many human beings are unable to resist the idea that it is their capacity for fully explicit self-conscious deliberation, in a situation of choice, that suffices to constitute them as truly morally responsible agents in the strongest possible sense. The Basic Argument shows that this is a mistake. However self-consciously aware we are, as we deliberate and reason, every act and operation of our mind happens as it does as a result of features for which we are ultimately in no way responsible. But the conviction that self-conscious awareness of one's situation can be a sufficient foundation of strong free will is very powerful. It runs deeper than rational argument, and it survives untouched, in the everyday conduct of life, even after the validity of the Basic Argument has been admitted.

VII

There is nothing new in the somewhat incantatory argument of this paper. It restates certain points that may be in need of restatement. "Everything has been said before", said André Gide, echoing La Bruyère, "but since nobody listens we have to keep going back and beginning all over again." This is an exaggeration, but it may not be a gross exaggeration, so far as general observations about the human condition are concerned.

The present claim, in any case, is simply this: time would be saved, and a great deal of readily available clarity would be introduced into the discussion of the nature of moral responsibility, if the simple point that is established by the Basic Argument were more generally acknowledged and clearly stated. Nietzsche thought that thoroughgoing acknowledgement of the point was long overdue, and his belief that there might be moral advantages in such an acknowledgment may deserve further consideration.

NOTES

1. Two have rejected it in fifteen years. Both had religious commitments, and argued, on general and radical sceptical grounds, that we can know almost nothing, and cannot therefore know that true moral responsibility is not possible in some way that we do not understand.
2. Cf. *Nichomachean Ethics* III. 5.
3. Carr in *What Is History?*, p. 89; Sartre in *Being and Nothingness, Existentialism and Humanism*, p. 29, and in the *New Left Review* 1969 (quoted in Wiggins, 1975); Kant in *Religion within the Limits of Reason Alone*, p. 40, *The Critique of Practical Reason*, p. 101 (Ak. V. 98), and in *Opus Postumum*, p. 213; Patten in *The Spectator*, January 1992.

   These quotations raise many questions which I will not consider. It is often hard, for example, to be sure what Sartre is saying. But the occurrence of the quoted phrases is significant on any plausible interpretation of his views. As for Kant, it may be thought to be odd that he says what he does, in so far as he grounds the possibility of our freedom in our possession of an unknowable, non-temporal noumenal nature. It is, however, plausible to suppose that he thinks that radical or ultimate self-determination must take place even in the noumenal realm, in some unintelligibly non-temporal manner, if there is to be true moral responsibility.

14. Freedom of the Will and the Concept of a Person

HARRY FRANKFURT

Harry Frankfurt (b. 1929) is Professor of Philosophy at Princeton University. He has also been a professor of philosophy at Yale University. He has made important contributions to the study of free will and to Descartes scholarship. With regard to the free-will/determinism debate, Frankfurt is a compatibilist, holding that no contradiction exists between an act's being determined and the agent's being held responsible for it. But whereas most compatibilists (e.g., Walter Stace) defend their position by a hypothetical interpretation of the formula "S is free in case S *could have done otherwise,"* Frankfurt offers a theory of the will in order to account for our notion of freedom. What distinguishes humans from other animals is our ability to deliberate and choose courses of actions. The strategy goes like this: Both animals and humans have straightforward or *first-order desires*—for example, desires to eat, to be comfortable, to sleep—but whereas animals act directly on their wants, humans can weigh them and accept or reject them. For example, Jill may have the *first-order* desire to smoke a cigarette, but she may also want to be healthy. She compares the two desires and forms a *second-order* desire, say, to refrain from smoking based on her desire to remain healthy. But since it is possible that she may have the *second-order* desire to refrain from smoking without wanting to act on it, there is one more step in the process. She must make her desire her will, her *volition,* and be committed to act on the desire not to smoke. The person must *identify* himself with the *second-order* desire and thereby make it a *second-order* volition. As Frankfurt writes elsewhere, "to the extent that a person identifies himself with the springs of his actions, he takes a responsibility for those actions and acquires moral responsibility for them."

What philosophers have lately come to accept as analysis of the concept of a person is not actually analysis of *that* concept at all. Strawson, whose usage represents the current standard, identifies the concept of a person as "the concept of a type of entity such that *both* predicates ascribing states of consciousness *and* predicates ascribing corporeal characteristics . . . are equally applicable to a single individual of that single type."[1] But there are many entities besides persons that have both mental and physical properties. As it happens—though it seems extraordinary that this should be so—there is no common English word for the type of entity Strawson has in mind, a type that includes not only human be-

Reprinted from *Journal of Philosophy* 68:1 (January 1971), by permission of the author and the *Journal of Philosophy*. Some notes have been deleted and others renumbered.

ings but animals of various lesser species as well. Still, this hardly justifies the misappropriation of a valuable philosophical term.

Whether the members of some animal species are persons is surely not to be settled merely by determining whether it is correct to apply to them, in addition to predicates ascribing corporeal characteristics, predicates that ascribe states of consciousness. It does violence to our language to endorse the application of the term 'person' to those numerous creatures which do have both psychological and material properties but which are manifestly not persons in any normal sense of the word. This misuse of language is doubtless innocent of any theoretical error. But although the offense is "merely verbal," it does significant harm. For it gratuitously diminishes our philosophical vocabulary, and it increases the likelihood that we will overlook the important area of inquiry with which the term 'person' is most naturally associated. It might have been expected that no problem would be of more central and persistent concern to philosophers than that of understanding what we ourselves essentially are. Yet this problem is so generally neglected that it has been possible to make off with its very name almost without being noticed and, evidently, without evoking any widespread feeling of loss.

There is a sense in which the word 'person' is merely the singular form of 'people' and in which both terms connote no more than membership in a certain biological species. In those senses of the word which are of greater philosophical interest, however, the criteria for being a person do not serve primarily to distinguish the members of our own species from the members of other species. Rather, they are designed to capture those attributes which are the subject of our most humane concern with ourselves and the source of what we regard as most important and most problematical in our lives. Now these attributes would be of equal significance to us even if they were not in fact peculiar and common to the members of our own species. What interests us most in the human condition would not interest us less if it were also a feature of the condition of other creatures as well.

Our concept of ourselves as persons is not to be understood, therefore, as a concept of attributes that are necessarily species-specific. It is conceptually possible that members of novel or even of familiar nonhuman species should be persons; and it is also conceptually possible that some members of the human species are not persons. We do in fact assume, on the other hand, that no member of another species is a person. Accordingly, there is a presumption that what is essential to persons is a set of characteristics that we generally suppose—whether rightly or wrongly—to be uniquely human.

It is my view that one essential difference between persons and other creatures is to be found in the structure of a person's will. Human beings are not alone in having desires and motives, or in making choices. They share these things with the members of certain other species, some of whom even appear to engage in deliberation and to make decisions based upon prior thought. It seems to be peculiarly characteristic of humans, however, that they are able to form what I shall call "second-order desires" or "desires of the second order."

Besides wanting and choosing and being moved *to do* this or that, men may also want to have (or not to have) certain desires and motives. They are capable of wanting to be different, in their preferences and purposes, from what they are. Many animals appear to have the capacity for what I shall call "first-order desires" or "desires of the first order," which are simply desires to do or not to do one thing or another. No animal other than man, however, appears to have the capacity for reflective self-evaluation that is manifested in the formation of second-order desires.

I

The concept designated by the verb 'to want' is extraordinarily elusive. A statement of the form "*A* wants to *X*"—taken by itself, apart from a context that serves to amplify or to specify its meaning—conveys remarkably little information. Such a statement may be consistent, for example, with each of the following statements: (a) the prospect of doing X elicits no sensation or introspectible emotional response in A; (b) A is unaware that he wants to X; (c) A believes that he does not want to X; (d) A wants to refrain from X-ing; (e) A wants to Y and believes that it is impossible for him both to Y and to X; (f) A does not "really" want to X; (g) A would rather die than X; and so on. It is therefore hardly sufficient to formulate the distinction between first-order and second-order desires, as I have done, by suggesting merely that someone has a first-order desire when he wants to do or not to do such-and-such, and that he has a second-order desire when he wants to have or not to have a certain desire of the first order.

As I shall understand them, statements of the form "A wants to X" cover a rather broad range of possibilities. They may be true even when statements like (a) through (g) are true: when A is unaware of any feelings concerning X-ing, when he is unaware that he wants to X, when he deceives himself about what he wants and believes falsely that he does not want to X, when he also has other desires that conflict with his desire to X, or when he is ambivalent. The desires in question may be conscious or unconscious, they need not be univocal, and A may be mistaken about them. There is a further source of uncertainty with regard to statements that identify someone's desires, however, and here it is important for my purposes to be less permissive.

Consider first those statements of the form "A wants to X" which identify first-order desires—that is, statements in which the term 'to X' refers to an action. A statement of this kind does not, by itself, indicate the relative strength of A's desire to X. It does not make it clear whether this desire is at all likely to play a decisive role in what A actually does or tries to do. For it may correctly be said that A wants to X even when his desire to X is only one among his desires and when it is far from being paramount among them. Thus, it may be true that A wants to X when he strongly prefers to do something else instead; and it may be true that he wants to X despite

the fact that, when he acts, it is not the desire to X that motivates him to do what he does. On the other hand, someone who states that A wants to X may mean to convey that it is this desire that is motivating or moving A to do what he is actually doing or that A will in fact be moved by this desire (unless he changes his mind) when he acts.

It is only when it is used in the second of these ways that, given the special usage of 'will' that I propose to adopt, the statement identifies A's will. To identify an agent's will is either to identify the desire (or desires) by which he is motivated in some action he performs or to identify the desire (or desires) by which he will or would be motivated when or if he acts. An agent's will, then, is identical with one or more of his first-order desires. But the notion of the will, as I am employing it, is not coextensive with the notion of first-order desires. It is not the notion of something that merely inclines an agent in some degree to act in a certain way. Rather, it is the notion of an *effective* desire—one that moves (or will or would move) a person all the way to action. Thus the notion of the will is not coextensive with the notion of what an agent intends to do. For even though someone may have a settled intention to do X, he may nonetheless do something else instead of doing X because, despite his intention, his desire to do X proves to be weaker or less effective than some conflicting desire.

Now consider those statements of the form "A wants to X" which identify second-order desires—that is, statements in which the term 'to X' refers to a desire of the first order. There are also two kinds of situation in which it may be true that A wants to want to X. In the first place, it might be true of A that he wants to have a desire to X despite the fact that he has a univocal desire, altogether free of conflict and ambivalence, to refrain from X-ing. Someone might want to have a certain desire, in other words, but univocally want that desire to be unsatisfied.

Suppose that a physician engaged in psychotherapy with narcotics addicts believes that his ability to help his patients would be enhanced if he understood better what it is like for them to desire the drug to which they are addicted. Suppose that he is led in this way to want to have a desire for the drug. If it is a genuine desire that he wants, then what he wants is not merely to feel the sensations that addicts characteristically feel when they are gripped by their desires for the drug. What the physician wants, insofar as he wants to have a desire, is to be inclined or moved to some extent to take the drug.

It is entirely possible, however, that, although he wants to be moved by a desire to take the drug, he does not want this desire to be effective. He may not want it to move him all the way to action. He need not be interested in finding out what it is like to take the drug. And insofar as he now wants only to *want* to take it, and not to *take* it, there is nothing in what he now wants that would be satisfied by the drug itself. He may now have, in fact, an altogether univocal desire *not* to take the drug; and he may prudently arrange to make it impossible for him to satisfy the desire he would have if his desire to want the drug should in time be satisfied.

It would thus be incorrect to infer, from the fact that the physician now wants to desire to take the drug, that he already does desire to take it. His second-order desire to be moved to take the drug does not entail that he has a first-order desire to take it. If the drug were now to be administered to him, this might satisfy no desire that is implicit in his desire to want to take it. While he wants to want to take the drug, he may have *no* desire to take it; it may be that *all* he wants is to taste the desire for it. That is, his desire to have a certain desire that he does not have may not be a desire that his will should be at all different than it is.

Someone who wants only in this truncated way to want to X stands at the margin of preciosity, and the fact that he wants to want to X is not pertinent to the identification of his will. There is, however, a second kind of situation that may be described by 'A wants to want to X'; and when the statement is used to describe a situation of this second kind, then it does pertain to what A wants his will to be. In such cases the statement means that A

wants the desire to X to be the desire that moves him effectively to act. It is not merely that he wants the desire to X to be among the desires by which, to one degree or another, he is moved or inclined to act. He wants this desire to be effective—that is, to provide the motive in what he actually does. Now when the statement that A wants to want to X is used in this way, it does entail that A already has a desire to X. It could not be true both that A wants the desire to X to move him into action and that he does not want to X. It is only if he does want to X that he can coherently want the desire to X not merely to be one of his desires but, more decisively, to be his will.

Suppose a man wants to be motivated in what he does by the desire to concentrate on his work. It is necessarily true, if this supposition is correct, that he already wants to concentrate on his work. This desire is now among his desires. But the question of whether or not his second-order desire is fulfilled does not turn merely on whether the desire he wants is one of his desires. It turns on whether this desire is, as he wants it to be, his effective desire or will. If, when the chips are down, it is his desire to concentrate on his work that moves him to do what he does, then what he wants at that time is indeed (in the relevant sense) what he wants to want. If it is some other desire that actually moves him when he acts, on the other hand, then what he wants at that time is not (in the relevant sense) what he wants to want. This will be so despite the fact that the desire to concentrate on his work continues to be among his desires.

II

Someone has a desire of the second order either when he wants simply to have a certain desire or when he wants a certain desire to be his will. In situations of the latter kind, I shall call his second-order desires "second-order volitions" or "volitions of the second order." Now it is having second-order volitions, and not having second-order desires generally, that I regard as essential to being a person. It is logically possible, however unlikely, that there should be an agent with second-order desires but with no volitions of the second order. Such a creature, in my view, would not be a person. I shall use the term 'wanton' to refer to agents who have first-order desires but who are not persons because, whether or not they have desires of the second order, they have no second-order volitions.

The essential characteristic of a wanton is that he does not care about his will. His desires move him to do certain things, without its being true of him either that he wants to be moved by those desires or that he prefers to be moved by other desires. The class of wantons includes all nonhuman animals that have desires and all very young children. Perhaps it also includes some adult human beings as well. In any case, adult humans may be more or less wanton; they may act wantonly, in response to first-order desires concerning which they have no volitions of the second order, more or less frequently.

The fact that a wanton has no second-order volitions does not mean that each of his first-order desires is translated heedlessly and at once into action. He may have no opportunity to act in accordance with some of his desires. Moreover, the translation of his desires into action may be delayed or precluded either by conflicting desires of the first order or by the intervention of deliberation. For a wanton may possess and employ rational faculties of a high order. Nothing in the concept of a wanton implies that he cannot reason or that he cannot deliberate concerning how to do what he wants to do. What distinguishes the rational wanton from other rational agents is that he is not concerned with the desirability of his desires themselves. He ignores the question of what his will is to be. Not only does he pursue whatever course of action he is most strongly inclined to pursue, but he does not care which of his inclinations is the strongest.

Thus a rational creature, who reflects upon the suitability to his desires of one course of action or another, may nonetheless be a wanton. In maintaining that the essence of being a person lies not in reason but in will, I am far from suggesting that a creature without reason may be a person. For it is only in virtue of his rational capacities that a person is capable of becoming critically aware of his own will and of forming volitions of the second order. The structure of a person's will presupposes, accordingly, that he is a rational being.

The distinction between a person and a wanton may be illustrated by the difference between two narcotics addicts. Let us suppose that the physiological condition accounting for the addiction is the same in both men, and that both succumb inevitably to their periodic desires for the drug to which they are addicted. One of the addicts hates his addiction and always struggles desperately, although to no avail, against its thrust. He tries everything that he thinks might enable him to overcome his desires for the drug. But these desires are too powerful for him to withstand, and invariably, in the end, they conquer him. He is an unwilling addict, helplessly violated by his own desires.

The unwilling addict has conflicting first-order desires: he wants to take the drug, and he also wants to refrain from taking it. In addition to these first-order desires, however, he has a volition of the second order. He is not neutral with regard to the conflict between his desire to take the drug and his desire to refrain from taking it. It is the latter desire, and not the former, that he wants to constitute his will; it is the latter desire, rather than the former, that he wants to be effective and to provide the purpose that he will seek to realize in what he actually does.

The other addict is a wanton. His actions reflect the economy of his first-order desires, without his being concerned whether the desires that move him to act are desires by which he wants to be moved to act. If he encounters problems in obtaining the drug or in administering it to himself, his responses to his urges to take it may involve deliberation. But it never occurs to him to consider whether he wants the relations among his desires to result in his having the will he has. The wanton addict may be an animal, and thus incapable of being concerned about his will. In any event he is, in respect of his wanton lack of concern, no different from an animal.

The second of these addicts may suffer a first-order conflict similar to the first-order conflict suffered by the first. Whether he is human or not, the wanton may (perhaps due to conditioning) both want to take the drug and want to refrain from taking it. Unlike the unwilling addict, however, he does not prefer that one of his conflicting desires should be paramount over the other; he does not prefer that one first-order desire rather than the other should constitute his will. It would be misleading to say that he is neutral as to the conflict between his desires, since this would suggest that he regards them as equally acceptable. Since he has no identity apart from his first-order desires, it is true neither that he prefers one to the others nor that he prefers not to take sides.

It makes a difference to the unwilling addict, who is a person, which of his conflicting first-order desires wins out. Both desires are his, to be sure; and whether he finally takes the drug or finally succeeds in refraining from taking it, he acts to satisfy what is in a literal sense his own desire. In either case he does something he himself wants to do, and he does it not because of some external influence whose aim happens to coincide with his own but because of his desire to do it. The unwilling addict identifies himself, however, through the formation of a second-order volition, with one rather than with the other of his conflicting first-order desires. He makes one of them more truly his own and, in so doing, he withdraws himself from the other. It is in virtue of this identification and withdrawal, accomplished through the formation of a second-order volition, that the unwilling addict may meaningfully make the analytically puzzling statements that the force moving him to take the drug is a force other than his own, and that it is not of his own free will but rather against his will that this force moves him to take it.

The wanton addict cannot or does not care which of his conflicting first-order desires wins out. His lack of concern is not due to his inability to find a convincing basis for preference. It is due either to his lack of the capacity for reflection or to his mindless indifference to the enterprise of evaluating his own desires and motives. There is only one issue in the struggle to which his first-order conflict may lead: whether the one or the other of his conflicting desires is the stronger. Since he is moved by both desires, he will not be altogether satisfied by what he does no matter which of them is effective. But it makes no difference to *him* whether his craving or his aversion gets the upper hand. He has no stake in the conflict between them and so, unlike the unwilling addict, he can neither win nor lose the struggle in which he is engaged. When a *person* acts, the desire by which he is moved is either the will he wants or a will he wants to be without. When a *wanton* acts, it is neither.

III

There is a very close relationship between the capacity for forming second-order volitions and another capacity that is essential to persons—one that has often been considered a distinguishing mark of the human condition. It is only because a person has volitions of the second order that he is capable both of enjoying and of lacking freedom of the will. The concept of a person is not only, then, the concept of a type of entity that has both first-order desires and volitions of the second order. It can also be construed as the concept of a type of entity for whom the freedom of its will may be a problem. This concept excludes all wantons, both infrahumans and human, since they fail to satisfy an essential condition for the enjoyment of freedom of the will. And it excludes those suprahuman beings, if any, whose wills are necessarily free.

Just what kind of freedom is the freedom of the will? This question calls for an identification of the special area of human experience to which the concept of freedom of the will, as distinct from the concepts of other sorts of freedom, is particularly germane. In dealing with it, my aim will be primarily to locate the problem with which a person is most immediately concerned when he is concerned with the freedom of his will.

According to one familiar philosophical tradition, being free is fundamentally a matter of doing what one wants to do. Now the notion of an agent who does what he wants to do is by no means an altogether clear one: both the doing and the wanting, and the appropriate relation between them as well, require elucidation. But although its focus needs to be sharpened and its formulation refined, I believe that this notion does capture at least part of what is implicit in the idea of an agent who *acts* freely. It misses entirely, however, the peculiar content of the quite different idea of an agent whose *will* is free.

We do not suppose that animals enjoy freedom of the will, although we recognize that an animal may be free to run in whatever direction it wants. Thus, having the freedom to do what one wants to do is not a sufficient condition of having a free will. It is not a necessary condition either. For to deprive someone of his freedom of action is not necessarily to undermine the freedom of his will. When an agent is aware that there are certain things he is not free to do, this doubtless affects his desires and limits the range of choices he can make. But suppose that someone, without being aware of it, has in fact lost or been deprived of his freedom of action. Even though he is no longer free to do what he wants to do, his will may remain as free as it was before. Despite the fact that he is not free to translate his desires into actions or to act according to the determinations of his will, he may still form those desires and make those determinations as freely as if his freedom of action had not been impaired.

When we ask whether a person's will is free we are not asking whether he is in a position to translate his first-order desires into actions. That is the question of whether he is free to do as he pleases. The question of the freedom of his will does not concern the relation between what he does and what he wants to do. Rather, it concerns his desires themselves. But what question about them is it?

It seems to me both natural and useful to construe the question of whether a person's will is free in close analogy to the question of whether an agent enjoys freedom of action. Now freedom of action is (roughly, at least) the freedom to do what one wants to do. Analogously, then, the statement that a person enjoys freedom of the will means (also roughly) that he is free to want what he wants to want. More precisely, it means that he is free to will what he wants to will, or to have the will he wants. Just as the question about the freedom of an agent's action has to do with whether it is the action he wants to perform, so the question about the freedom of his will has to do with whether it is the will he wants to have.

It is in securing the conformity of his will and his second-order volitions, then, that a person exercises freedom of the will. And it is in the discrepancy between his will and his second-order volitions, or in his awareness that their coincidence is not his own doing but only a happy chance, that a person who does not have this freedom feels its lack. The unwilling addict's will is not free. This is shown by the fact that it is not the will he wants. It is also true, though in a different way, that the will of the wanton addict is not free. The wanton addict neither has the will he wants nor has a will that differs from the will he wants. Since he has no volitions of the second order, the freedom of his will cannot be a problem for him. He lacks it, so to speak, by default.

People are generally far more complicated than my sketchy account of the structure of a person's will may suggest. There is as much opportunity for ambivalence, conflict, and self-deception with regard to desires of the second order, for example, as there is with regard to first-order desires. If there is an unresolved conflict among someone's second-order desires, then he is in danger of having no second-order volition; for unless this conflict is resolved, he has no preference concerning which of his first-order desires is to be his will. This condition, if it is so severe that it prevents him from identifying himself in a sufficiently decisive way with *any* of his conflicting first-order desires, destroys him as a person. For it either tends to paralyze his will and to keep him from acting at all, or it tends to remove him from his will so that his will operates without his participation. In both cases he becomes, like the unwilling addict though in a different way, a helpless bystander to the forces that move him.

Another complexity is that a person may have, especially if his second-order desires are in conflict, desires and volitions of a higher order than the second. There is no theoretical limit to the length of the series of desires of higher and higher orders; nothing except common sense and, perhaps, a saving fatigue prevents an individual from obsessively refusing to identify himself with any of his desires until he forms a desire of the next higher order. The tendency to generate such a series of acts of forming desires, which would be a case of humanization run wild, also leads toward the destruction of a person.

It is possible, however, to terminate such a series of acts without cutting it off arbitrarily. When a person identifies himself *decisively* with one of his first-order desires, this commitment "resounds" throughout the potentially endless array of higher orders. Consider a person who, without reservation or conflict, wants to be motivated by the desire to concentrate on his work. The fact that his second-order volition to be moved by this desire is a decisive one means that there is no room for questions concerning the pertinence of desires or volitions of higher orders. Suppose the person is asked whether he wants to want to want to concentrate on his work. He can properly insist that this question concerning a third-order desire does not arise. It would be a mistake to claim that, because he has not considered whether he wants the second-order volition he has formed, he is indifferent to the question of whether it is with this volition or with some other that he wants his will to accord. The decisiveness of the commitment he has made means that he has decided that no further question about his second-order volition, at any higher order, remains to be asked. It is relatively unimportant whether we explain this by saying that this commitment implicitly generates an endless series of confirming desires of higher orders, or by saying that the commitment is tantamount to a dissolution of the pointedness of

all questions concerning higher orders of desire.

Examples such as the one concerning the unwilling addict may suggest that volitions of the second order, or of higher orders, must be formed deliberately and that a person characteristically struggles to ensure that they are satisfied. But the conformity of a person's will to his higher-order volitions may be far more thoughtless and spontaneous than this. Some people are naturally moved by kindness when they want to be kind, and by nastiness when they want to be nasty, without any explicit forethought and without any need for energetic self-control. Others are moved by nastiness when they want to be kind and by kindness when they intend to be nasty, equally without forethought and without active resistance to these violations of their higher-order desires. The enjoyment of freedom comes easily to some. Others must struggle to achieve it.

IV

My theory concerning the freedom of the will accounts easily for our disinclination to allow that this freedom is enjoyed by the members of any species inferior to our own. It also satisfies another condition that must be met by any such theory, by making it apparent why the freedom of the will should be regarded as desirable. The enjoyment of a free will means the satisfaction of certain desires—desires of the second or of higher orders—whereas its absence means their frustration. The satisfactions at stake are those which accrue to a person of whom it may be said that his will is his own. The corresponding frustrations are those suffered by a person of whom it may be said that he is estranged from himself, or that he finds himself a helpless or a passive bystander to the forces that move him.

A person who is free to do what he wants to do may yet not be in a position to have the will he wants. Suppose, however, that he enjoys both freedom of action and freedom of the will. Then he is not only free to do what he wants to do; he is also free to want what he wants to want. It seems to me that he has, in that case, all the freedom it is possible to desire or to conceive. There are other good things in life, and he may not possess some of them. But there is nothing in the way of freedom that he lacks.

It is far from clear that certain other theories of the freedom of the will meet these elementary but essential conditions: that it be understandable why we desire this freedom and why we refuse to ascribe it to animals. Consider, for example, Roderick Chisholm's quaint version of the doctrine that human freedom entails an absence of causal determination.[2] Whenever a person performs a free action, according to Chisholm, it's a miracle. The motion of a person's hand, when the person moves it, is the outcome of a series of physical causes; but some event in this series, "and presumably one of those that took place within the brain, was caused by the agent and not by any other events" (18). A free agent has, therefore, "a prerogative which some would attribute only to God: each of us, when we act, is a prime mover unmoved" (23).

This account fails to provide any basis for doubting that animals of subhuman species enjoy the freedom it defines. Chisholm says nothing that makes it seem less likely that a rabbit performs a miracle when it moves its leg than that a man does so when he moves his hand. But why, in any case, should anyone *care* whether he can interrupt the natural order of causes in the way Chisholm describes? Chisholm offers no reason for believing that there is a discernible difference between the experience of a man who miraculously initiates a series of causes when he moves his hand and a man who moves his hand without any such breach of the normal causal sequence. There appears to be no concrete basis for preferring to be involved in the one state of affairs rather than in the other.

It is generally supposed that, in addition to satisfying the two conditions I have mentioned, a satisfactory theory of the freedom of the will necessarily provides an analysis of one of the conditions of moral responsibility. The most common recent approach to the problem of understanding the freedom of the

will has been, indeed, to inquire what is entailed by the assumption that someone is morally responsible for what he has done. In my view, however, the relation between moral responsibility and the freedom of the will has been very widely misunderstood. It is not true that a person is morally responsible for what he has done only if his will was free when he did it. He may be morally responsible for having done it even though his will was not free at all.

A person's will is free only if he is free to have the will he wants. This means that, with regard to any of his first-order desires, he is free either to make that desire his will or to make some other first-order desire his will instead. Whatever his will, then, the will of the person whose will is free could have been otherwise; he could have done otherwise than to constitute his will as he did. It is a vexed question just how 'he could have done otherwise' is to be understood in contexts such as this one. But although this question is important to the theory of freedom, it has no bearing on the theory of moral responsibility. For the assumption that a person is morally responsible for what he has done does not entail that the person was in a position to have whatever will he wanted.

This assumption *does* entail that the person did what he did freely, or that he did it of his own free will. It is a mistake, however, to believe that someone acts freely only when he is free to do whatever he wants or that he acts of his own free will only if his will is free. Suppose that a person has done what he wanted to do, that he did it because he wanted to do it, and that the will by which he was moved when he did it was his will because it was the will he wanted. Then he did it freely and of his own free will. Even supposing that he could have done otherwise, he would not have done otherwise; and even supposing that he could have had a different will, he would not have wanted his will to differ from what it was. Moreover, since the will that moved him when he acted was his will because he wanted it to be, he cannot claim that his will was forced upon him or that he was a passive bystander to its constitution. Under these conditions, it is quite irrelevant to the evaluation of his moral responsibility to inquire whether the alternatives that he opted against were actually available to him.

In illustration, consider a third kind of addict. Suppose that his addiction has the same physiological basis and the same irresistible thrust as the addictions of the unwilling and wanton addicts, but that he is altogether delighted with his condition. He is a willing addict, who would not have things any other way. If the grip of his addiction should somehow weaken, he would do whatever he could to reinstate it; if his desire for the drug should begin to fade, he would take steps to renew its intensity.

The willing addict's will is not free, for his desire to take the drug will be effective regardless of whether or not he wants this desire to constitute his will. But when he takes the drug, he takes it freely and of his own free will. I am inclined to understand his situation as involving the overdetermination of his first-order desire to take the drug. This desire is his effective desire because he is physiologically addicted. But it is his effective desire also because he wants it to be. His will is outside his control, but, by his second-order desire that his desire for the drug should be effective, he has made this will his own. Given that it is therefore not only because of his addiction that his desire for the drug is effective, he may be morally responsible for taking the drug.

My conception of the freedom of the will appears to be neutral with regard to the problem of determinism. It seems conceivable that it should be causally determined that a person is free to want what he wants to want. If this is conceivable, then it might be causally determined that a person enjoys a free will. There is no more than an innocuous appearance of paradox in the proposition that it is determined, ineluctably and by forces beyond their control, that certain people have free wills and that others do not. There is no incoherence in the proposition that some agency other than a person's own is responsible (even *morally* responsible) for the fact that he enjoys or fails to enjoy freedom of the will. It is possible that a person should be morally responsible for what he does of his own free will and that some other person should also be morally responsible for his having done it.

On the other hand, it seems conceivable that it should come about by chance that a person is free to have the will he wants. If this is conceivable, then it might be a matter of chance that certain people enjoy freedom of the will and that certain others do not. Perhaps it is also conceivable, as a number of philosophers believe, for states of affairs to come about in a way other than by chance or as the outcome of a sequence of natural causes. If it is indeed conceivable for the relevant states of affairs to come about in some third way, then it is also possible that a person should in that third way come to enjoy the freedom of the will.

NOTES

1. P. F. Strawson, *Individuals* (London: Methuen, 1959), pp. 101–102. Ayer's usage of 'person' is similar: "it is characteristic of persons in this sense that besides having various physical properties . . . they are also credited with various forms of consciousness" [A. J. Ayer, *The Concept of a Person* (New York: St. Martin's, 1963), p. 82]. What concerns Strawson and Ayer is the problem of understanding the relation between mind and body, rather than the quite different problem of understanding what it is to be a creature that not only has a mind and a body but is also a person.
2. "Freedom and Action," in K. Lehrer, ed., *Freedom and Determinism* (New York: Random House, 1966), pp. 11–44.

15. Desert and Determinism

DAVID MILLER

For biographical information on Miller, see Chapter 11.

Miller investigates the argument that determinism undermines desert. That argument, according to Miller, has two premises: (1) A person can deserve something only on the basis of some voluntary action or voluntarily acquired attribute; (2) Determinism, according to which nothing ever happens without being caused to do so, is true. If these premises are correct, it is supposed to follow that no one ever deserves anything.

Miller claims that each premise is open to attack. People are often held to be deserving in virtue of actions and attributes for which they are not, or at least not wholly and ultimately, responsible. And determinism does not obviously rule out the possibility of voluntary actions; it does so only if voluntary actions must be uncaused, and this is an open question. Moreover, it has not been proven that all our actions are causally determined in the way that determinism implies. Besides, accepting determinism would involve a radical transformation in the way that we regard other people.

Determinism and Desert

The argument that determinism undermines the concept of desert is best understood when set out as two separate steps:

1. A man can only deserve treatment (benefit or harm) on the basis of his own voluntary action, or of characteristics he has voluntarily acquired.
2. Determinism shows that no action is voluntary in the sense required by the concept of desert.

Thus desert is first linked to voluntary, or freely chosen, action, and then determinism is shown to exclude freedom in the strong sense which desert seems to demand. Conversely, the argument can be halted at either stage. A few have denied the linking of desert to voluntary action. Many more have argued that determinism allows the requisite freedom of choice, or more strongly that only determinism allows it. I cannot hope to say anything original on the second topic, though I shall explain my position later. As for the first topic, there is something to be gained by approaching it in terms of deserved benefit, and not, as usually happens, in terms of deserved punishment.

One of the few who have denied that personal merit depends upon the voluntary acts of the person concerned is Hume. Hume argued that there were many qualities a man might possess which were useful or agreeable to himself or to others. Because men possessed the capacity to enter sympathetically into one another's feelings, they looked favourably upon such qualities and regarded their possession as meritorious. The list of

Reprinted from *Social Justice* (Oxford University Press, 1976), by permission.

qualities which constituted merit included natural abilities such as wit and good looks, as well as the moral virtues, benevolence, courage, and the rest. Hume discussed the view that a sharp distinction should be made between the moral virtues and other good qualities on the grounds that the moral virtues alone were voluntarily acquired, and that therefore only they should be regarded as carrying merit; but he rejected this position, pointing out that virtues such as courage 'depend little or not at all on our choice'. In fact, he argued, the distinction between virtues and other abilities has been invented by moralists who have observed that the former class alone can be implanted and encouraged by the social mechanisms of praise, blame, reward, and punishment. But ordinary men, who do not have any such social purpose in view when they judge merit and demerit, ignore the distinction, and praise natural abilities as readily as moral qualities.

Hume's opinion accords well with the analysis of desert set out in the last section. If we consider the attitudes of admiration, approval, etc., it is plain that we do not adopt them only towards qualities believed to be voluntarily acquired. When we admire the superlative skill of a musician, we do not ask about the conduct which led to its acquisition before granting our admiration. The attitude is held directly towards the quality as it now exists, and the question 'voluntarily acquired or not?' is simply not considered. If the close relation between appraising attitudes and desert is admitted, it seems inconceivable that such judgements as 'Green (the musician) deserves recognition' should not be made on the same basis: on the basis of the skill alone, without reference to the manner of its acquisition. And this is indeed our practice. When we say that the prettiest girl deserves to win the beauty contest, the most skilful shot deserves to win at marbles, the ablest candidate deserves the scholarship, we look no further than the present qualities of the individuals concerned. We do not inquire into their past histories. If we were to undertake such an inquiry, we should be forced to conclude that the qualities forming the basis of desert were,

to a greater or lesser extent, involuntary. Physical beauty is almost wholly inherited, skill at marbles rather less so. Intellectual capacity is partly inborn, partly formed by education, which itself is a mixture of the voluntary and the involuntary.

If we turn to cases in which an action, rather than a quality, forms the basis of desert[1] we arrive at a similar conclusion. It is true that we cannot deserve benefits for actions which are involuntary or unintentional. If I apprehend a wanted man by accident (e.g. the floor collapses and I fall on top of him) I do not deserve a reward, though I may be entitled to one. Yet if we consider actions which do constitute a basis for desert, two points stand out:

1. Even if the action is wholly voluntary, it may require personal qualities which are not— e.g. I am able to save a drowning man because of my (inherited) physical strength.
2. Actions which are not fully voluntary may still deserve rewards and other benefits—e.g. I am blackmailed into hunting down a dangerous criminal.

It seems, then, that ordinary judgement does not support the view that a man's deserts depend upon his voluntary actions alone. But it would be wrong to think that ordinary judgement is wholly consistent on the issue. One can detect some inclination to relate desert to the quality of will which a man displays, rather than to other characteristics which affect his actions but which are outside his control. If, for instance, we go back to the case of the scholarship cited above, someone might well adopt the following attitude: it is right that the scholarship be awarded to A, the most able candidate, yet he is really less deserving than B, who has only slightly less ability but who has a much poorer academic background. B has struggled to achieve his present standard, whereas A has always been helped by superior teaching, etc. There is no doubt that this argument carries weight. Or again, consider the case of the drowning man. Suppose that two men jump in to save him, and that one manages to reach him while the other, who has tried just as hard but is physically weak, fails and has to turn back. We would say that the first man deserves more gratitude (and reward, perhaps) than the second, yet the second deserves *some* thanks for having tried to help. He could not actually do good to the drowning man because of his physical incapacity, but his intentions were as laudable as those of the man who actually brought off the rescue.

Some people would want to go further here, and say that desert *should depend entirely upon what is within a man's control,* that is on his efforts and the choices he makes. If the drowning man knew that his two would-be rescuers had tried equally hard to save him, he should recognize that they deserved equal gratitude and reward. Although ordinary judgement does not yet accept this view, it might be said that we can detect an historical trend towards its adoption. Primitive moral thinking does not distinguish between the voluntary and non-voluntary parts of conduct, and it has taken many generations to reach the developed conception of personal responsibility which we now have. We have simply failed to follow out the full implications of this conception in our use of the concept of desert. Again, it may be said, a distinction must be drawn between moral judgements and natural responses. The man who is saved from drowning naturally feels more warmly towards the swimmer who has actually rescued him. The *moral* judgement of the two men's deserts must ignore this emotional response and consider only what each intended and tried to do.

Such an argument looks most persuasive when good and ill desert are considered together. Indeed, it has usually been advanced with reference to deserved blame and punishment, and extended by analogy to deserved praise, reward, etc. The linking of ill desert to a man's voluntary actions is well-established. We do not blame people for physical defects which they did not bring upon themselves, nor do we punish people for what they could not have helped doing. We would regard it as immoral if a law were enacted which only some people were physically able to keep (for example, a law demanding that every citizen should run five miles each day). In other words, to deserve blame or punishment a man must have committed a wrong act which he could have avoided committing. Why, then, should we not restrict deserved praise, etc., to those actions which a man has voluntarily performed, or those qualities which he has voluntarily acquired?

We have seen that ordinary judgement does not support this conclusion (though neither does it clearly repudiate it). We praise the highly intelligent and the skilful, despite the fact that we do not blame the stupid and the clumsy. But the view we are now considering would wish to impose a greater consistency on our thinking, by bringing our judgements of deserved benefit into line with our judgements of deserved harm. Against this, it may be said that there is a real moral difference between the two kinds of desert. Inflicting harm upon a person is an evil in itself, hence it can only be justified by a stringent type of desert. (Many, of course, would say that even this is not sufficient justification; we shall not consider such a view here). A man only deserves harm when he 'brings it upon himself' by a voluntary action. But since conferring benefit is generally speaking a good, we can afford to be less stringent in our judgements of desert. Certainly, it would be extremely difficult to separate the voluntary from the non-voluntary aspects of character formation, and so to tell which of a man's qualities were proper grounds for desert. Perhaps the revised principle for ascribing good desert would be impossible to use in practice.

Returning, then, to the principle that a man can only deserve treatment (benefit or harm) on the basis of his own voluntary actions, or of characteristics he has voluntarily acquired, our assessment must be as follows. So far as deserved benefit goes, ordinary thinking gives us no clear guide as to whether the principle is to be accepted. In some of our judgements we base desert entirely upon voluntary action, in others we do not. Further, the philosophical arguments in favour of the principle are not decisive. The verdict must be: not proven.

Now for someone who rejects this principle, determinism creates no difficulties for the concept of desert, or at least for good desert. This was Hume's position, believing as he did both in determinism and in a concept of personal merit which made no reference to voluntariness. It is perhaps the most comfortable position to take on the issue. Yet because I feel that the arguments for the principle have *some* weight, I want to look very briefly at the further question whether someone who accepts the principle is forced to choose between determinism and desert; whether a concept of desert based on voluntary action is incompatible with the thesis of determinism.

Let us take determinism to be the thesis that every event has a causally sufficient set of antecedents. Why should this be thought to raise difficulties for our concept of voluntary action? A direct problem occurs only if a voluntary action has to be in some way uncaused; that is to say, if the series of happenings within the agent which lead up to it must include at least one for which there is no causally sufficient set of antecedents. Holders of this position have spoken of a 'contra-causal type of freedom' being required.[2] Their opponents argue that a voluntary action is simply one whose causal antecedents are of a particular kind. According to this view, when we describe an action as voluntary, we are not ruling out causal explanation in general, we are simply excluding certain *kinds* of causal antecedents—such circumstances as physical coercion, threats, fits of madness, etc.[3] Obviously, if this latter view is correct, there is no incompatibility between determinism and our concept of voluntary action.

At first sight it seems that the 'compatibility' view must be correct. Take a simple example: A makes a suggestion to B, who considers it, and then acts upon it. B's action is voluntary, but can be causally explained by reference to A's suggestion and B's mental make-up; there is no incompatibility here. However, to be certain that B's action really was voluntary, we should have to be sure that his present character and mental dispositions were not produced by factors of an inadmis-

sible type—for example, that he had not been rendered susceptible to suggestions of a certain type through brain-washing. Our concept of voluntary action excludes cases where the disposition to act has been induced by constraining factors. To take a practical example, lawyers have been able to secure acquittals (from 'ordinary men' in the jury box) by exhibiting their clients' behaviour as the inevitable outcome of circumstances beyond their control—home backgrounds, early experiences, etc.

This throws the relationship between determinism and voluntary action into a new light. For determinism may be taken to have the consequence that every action can ultimately be shown to result from causes which are commonly held to exclude freedom. This would not follow directly from the determinist thesis, but from the observation that as we gain in knowledge of the immediate and more distant causes of human action, we find that more of these actions have to be shifted from the voluntary to the non-voluntary category, since they turn out to be consequences of one or other of the varieties of constraint. Determinism, however, entails that there are no breaks in the chain of causation which leads up to any action, and therefore that there is no inherent reason why our knowledge of the causal antecedents of action should not be increased indefinitely. It is therefore possible, given sufficient knowledge, that the number of actions believed to be voluntary will eventually shrink to zero, every action being interpreted as the outcome of constraining causes such as coercion or indoctrination.

Even if we accept this, however, it is still a moot point whether our concept of voluntary action should be abandoned as a result of a belief in determinism. For we cannot yet explain most human actions in the way that the determinist promises us we shall—i.e. in such a way that their non-voluntary character is apparent. Until we can, there seems no alternative but to go on using the traditional concepts. We may also follow Strawson[4] in pointing out how our ordinary dealings with people are infused with attitudes which depend upon contrasting voluntary and non-voluntary actions—attitudes such as resentment, gratitude, and forgiveness. To treat people at all times as the objects of circumstances rather than as free agents would, if it were possible at all, mean a transformation of human relationships. Since we normally only regard people in this way when we believe that they are incapable of sustaining ordinary interpersonal relations—say as a result of mental derangement—Strawson implies that the transformation would necessarily be a loss. He asks how it could possibly be *rational* to make this change as a result of an abstract belief in the consequences of determinism.

To summarize, the argument that determinism undermines the concept of desert is open to attack at both its stages. The claim that a man can only deserve benefits (in particular) on the basis of voluntary actions or qualities cannot be convincingly vindicated; and neither can the claim that determinism destroys the distinction between the voluntary and the non-voluntary. People are willing to believe both that a man deserves rewards and other benefits for the actions he performs, and that these actions can be explained in causal terms. If, therefore, we find that the concept of desert has become less popular in recent years, we cannot, in the case of good desert especially, explain this change by reference to a growing belief in determinism. An explanation of a different kind must be sought.

NOTES

1. Hume believed that actions only possessed merit in so far as they were taken as signs of persistent qualities belonging to the agent: 'If any *action* be either virtuous or vicious, it is only as a sign of some quality or character. It must depend upon durable principles of the mind, which extend over the whole conduct, and enter into the personal character.' *A Treatise of Human Nature,* vol. ii, p. 272. But in this belief he was surely mistaken. If a cowardly man performs a courageous deed or an unjust man acts fairly, we regard these actions as meritorious even if we are fully aware that they are exceptional and correspond to no persistent character trait. Indeed, in the former case at least, we may even regard the merit of the action as increased by its atypical character, because for a cowardly man to perform a courageous act requires both courage and unusual self-mastery.
2. See C. A. Campbell, 'Is "Freewill" a Pseudo-problem?' *Mind,* 1x (1951).
3. See especially A. G. N. Flew, 'Divine Omnipotence and Human Freedom' in A. Flew and A. MacIntyre (eds.), *New Essays in Philosophical Theology* (London, 1955); A. J. Ayer, 'Freedom and Necessity' in *Philosophical Essays* (London, 1954); P. Nowell-Smith, *Ethics* (Harmondsworth, 1954), ch. 20.
4. P. F. Strawson, 'Freedom and Resentment', *Proceedings of the British Academy,* xlviii (1962).

16. Desert: Reconsideration of Some Received Wisdom

FRED FELDMAN

Fred Feldman is Professor of Philosophy at the University of Massachusetts at Amherst. He is the author of *Introductory Ethics* (Prentice-Hall, 1978), *Doing the Best We Can* (Reidel, 1986), and *Confrontations with the Reaper* (Oxford, 1992), as well as recent articles on ethics in *Mind, The Philosophical Review, Philosophy and Phenomenological Research,* and *Ethics.*

A collection of his essays in moral philosophy, Utilitarianism, Hedonism and Desert, was published in 1997 by Cambridge University Press. He is currently at work on a book on hedonism.

In this article the author considers two bits of received wisdom about desert. The first links desert to time: If you deserve in virtue of some fact, then that fact must be in the past. The second links desert to responsibility: If you deserve in virtue of some fact, then you must bear responsibility for that fact. After showing that many philosophers endorse these doctrines, he tries to show that each bit of received wisdom is false. He also speculates about the popularity of the views.

According to an ancient and plausible view, the *justice* of an arrangement is the extent to which receipt of goods and evils corresponds to desert in that arrangement. John Hospers apparently had precisely this in mind when he said that "justice is getting what one deserves. What could be simpler?" (1961, p. 433). Mill said that ". . . it is universally considered just that each person should obtain that (whether good or evil) which he *deserves* . . ." (1957, p. 55). Others have rejected this view as too simplistic (Feinberg 1963, p. 90, Sher 1987, p. 49, Slote 1973, p. 333, etc.) but have nevertheless maintained that there is an important conceptual link between justice and desert. Since justice is important, so is desert.

1. Desert Requires A Base

It is natural to suppose that whenever a person deserves something, there is some answer to the question "Why does he deserve this?". For example, suppose a certain man deserves ten years in the penitentiary. There must be some explanation for this fact. Perhaps it is that he has been found guilty of a serious crime, and the most appropriate or fitting penalty would be ten years. Suppose another person deserves

Reprinted from *Mind* 104:413 (January 1995), by permission of Oxford University Press.

a reward. Perhaps she deserves it because she risked her life to save a drowning child. Whether we speak of desert in connection with prizes or grades, rewards or punishments, praise or blame, reparation or liability, it seems necessary that if a person deserves something, there is some "desert base"[1]: some fact to which we can appeal in order to explain this person's desert of this good or evil.

In his recent book on desert, Wojciech Sadurski affirms two general theses about desert and desert bases. Neither thesis is new. Each has been affirmed countless times by writers on desert. I think it is fair to say that they are part of the received wisdom about desert. Yet it also seems to me that each of these theses is false.

In this paper I first state the two doctrines about desert and say a few words about their popularity. I then explain why I think that each is false. I conclude with some speculations about the popularity of these views. I seek an explanation for the fact that they have been so widely believed.

2. A Thesis About Desert And Responsibility

The first thesis links the concept of desert to the concept of responsibility. Sadurski states the thesis in this passage:

> When we are pronouncing judgments of desert we are inevitably making judgments about persons whom we hold responsible for their actions. It makes no sense to attribute desert, positive or negative, to persons for actions or facts over which they have no control. In particular, as people have no control over their natural assets . . . it would be unjust to consider those assets *per se* as relevant to any considerations of desert.
>
> *(Sadurski 1985, p. 117)*

Sadurski's point seems to be that a person cannot deserve anything in virtue of an action or fact unless she is responsible for that action or fact.

James Rachels affirms the same thesis. He puts it this way:

> The concept of desert serves to signify the ways of treating people that are appropriate responses to them, *given that* they are responsible for those actions or states of affairs. That is the role played by desert in our moral vocabulary.
>
> *(Rachels 1978, p. 157)*

Similar remarks could be culled from the writings of many other philosophers[2]. It is part of the received wisdom about desert. Roughly, the idea is this:

DR: If *S* deserves *x* in virtue of the fact that *S* did or suffered *y*, then *S* is responsible for doing or suffering *y*.

There are very many positive instances of DR. Consider a typical case in which someone deserves punishment. Suppose a thug attacks a figure-skater. As a result of the attack, the figure-skater is unable to compete in the national championships. It would be quite natural for us to think that the thug deserves punishment in virtue of the fact that he attacked the figure-skater. But we would all retract this claim about desert if we learned that the thug bore no responsibility for the attack. Suppose, for example, that he had been hypnotized at the time, or that he had been coerced, or that he suffered from some mental impairment that made it impossible for him to control his actions. In any of these cases, the thug would not have been responsible for his action. If we thought he was not responsible for the attack, we would no longer think he deserved punishment for having done it. (Of course, under some of these imagined circumstances, we might continue to think it would be a good idea to lock him up. However, in such cases we would want him locked up for *treatment* or to put him out of circulation, not because he deserves *punishment.*)

The example involving the figure-skater concerns desert, according to the law, of punishment. But not all cases focus narrowly on desert of punishment. Consider desert of grades. Suppose a student submits an excellent paper. You think she deserves an A, and you think she deserves it in virtue of the fact that she wrote a paper that contains clear, accurate, and well-reasoned discussion of interesting arguments. Now you learn that the student did not write the paper; she paid a friend to write it for her. The student is not responsible for the content of the paper. Accordingly, you change your mind about her deserts. You no longer think she deserves an A. This is connected with the fact that you no longer think she is responsible for the clear and interesting arguments contained in the paper. According to DR, it is always this way: if a person deserves something in virtue of some fact, then that person must be responsible for that fact.

3. A Thesis About Desert And Time

Sadurski states a second thesis about desert. According to this thesis, desert base and desert necessarily stand in a certain temporal relation. Specifically, desert base must always precede desert. Sadurski puts it this way: ". . . desert considerations are always past oriented. When talking about desert, we are evaluating certain actions which have already happened. That is why it is a confusion to base desert upon utilitarian grounds . . ." (1985, p. 117).

Again, the doctrine is part of the received wisdom about desert. Many philosophers have affirmed the same view. Rachels (1978, p. 154) expresses an extreme version of the principle when he says: ". . . the basis of all desert is a person's own *past* actions". According to this version of the thesis, desert bases are always actions, and they always precede the fact of desert. Joel Feinberg defends a somewhat weaker version: "If a person is deserving of some sort of treatment he must, necessarily, be so *in virtue of* some characteristic or *prior* activity" (1963, p. 72). Apparently, Feinberg would say that where a desert base involves activity, that activity must precede the fact of desert. John Kleinig endorses a similar view.[3] He says "Desert can be ascribed to something or someone only on the basis of characteristics possessed or things done by that thing or person. That is, desert is never simply forward-looking" (Kleinig 1971, p. 73).

In his article on "Rectificatory Justice" John Cottingham says this:

> The essentially backward-looking nature of justice-as-rectification seems hard to deny. Verbs like "to rectify" and "to correct" share with many other verbs (including "to punish", "to blame", "to thank", "to regret", "to renounce"), what we might call an inherently "retrospective" logic: we cannot understand such verbs without grasping that their use involves an intrinsic and automatic reference back to some past event or state of affairs.
>
> *(Cottingham 1992, p. 662)*

Cottingham seems to be saying that an injustice can be rectified only *after the fact*. We cannot rectify an injustice prior to its occurrence. He apparently means to claim that this is an essential feature of the "logic" of justice as rectification. If this is in fact what Cottingham means to say, then his view is quite similar to Sadurski's view about desert and time. Where compensatory justice is involved, Cottingham presumably would say that a person is deserving of compensation only if he or she has already suffered some loss.

The second bit of received wisdom is this:

DT: If at t S deserves x in virtue of the fact that S did or suffered something at t', then t' cannot be later than t.

Many relatively clear-cut cases of desert conform to DT. Consider, for example, cases in which someone deserves some *prize*. In his discussion of prizes, Feinberg says that the prize ". . . is deserved by the contestant who has demonstrably satisfied the condition of victory . . ." (1963, p. 77). This may seem right. Certainly it would seem strange to say that one of the contestants already deserves the prize *before* the contest, in virtue of the fact that he will *later* perform so well. In such cases, desert arises only after the desert base has taken place.

Desert of *rewards and punishments* seems similarly rooted in the past. In the typical case, a person deserves a reward in virtue of the fact that he has performed some meritorious service, such as saving a life, or preventing an injury. Similarly, when a person deserves punishment, we naturally think it is because he has done some wrong. In the legal context, most of us would be outraged by the suggestion that someone deserves punishment today for the crimes that he will commit tomorrow (see Feinberg 1963, pp. 80–5).

The desert associated with *compensation and reparation* seems firmly rooted in the past, too. Commentators have pointed out that it hardly makes sense to say that someone already deserves "reparations" for the injuries he will suffer later. How can we "repair" that which is not already broken? If the point of such activities is "to restore the moral equilibrium" then it is no wonder that the desert base must precede the desert. One cannot "restore" an equilibrium that has not yet been upset. Equally, there is a puzzle about the notion that a person might already deserve compensation for work that she will perform tomorrow. (Of course, it might be generous or helpful or nice to pay someone in advance; and in some cases a worker might deserve the money before the work. But in these cases the desert base would most naturally be taken to be need, or prior injury, or some past injustice. The mere fact that I will work tomorrow seems not to justify the claim that I already deserve my paycheck.)

In some cases we say that someone deserves good fortune simply because he has suffered so much bad fortune. Again, bad luck in the past provides a basis for saying that I deserve better luck in the future.

In all these cases, and in many more like them, the desert base either precedes or is simultaneous with the fact of desert. In none of these cases is the desert base entirely in the future. Thus, the examples are consistent with DT.

4. The Refutation Of DR

In spite of the fact that it seems to be part of the received wisdom about desert, DR is clearly false. There are countless perfectly ordinary cases in which we deserve things in

virtue of facts for which we bear no responsibility. A familiar sort of case involves compensation for injury. Suppose, for example, that a fast food restaurant is careless with its hamburgers. Many customers become ill with food poisoning. Those customers deserve several things: an apology; some compensation for their illness; a refund of the money they spent on the bad hamburgers. The customers deserve these things in virtue of the fact that they are innocent victims of the restaurant's carelessness. Yet in any typical case the customers bear no responsibility for the fact that they were poisoned.

Consider again the case of the figure-skater and the thug (mentioned above in §2). The example was used to illustrate the fact that sometimes a person (the thug) deserves something (punishment) in virtue of something for which he was responsible (the attack). Yet the very same example also illustrates the fact that sometimes a person deserves something in virtue of something for which she bears no responsibility. For the figure-skater deserves an apology and some compensation in virtue of the fact that she was viciously attacked. Yet she bears no responsibility for the attack.[4]

Perhaps it will seem that I must have gotten the principle wrong. The counterexamples are so obvious that it may seem that no one could seriously believe DR. Perhaps the intended principle is really this:

DR′: If *S* deserves *x* in virtue of the fact that *S* did or suffered *y,* then *somebody* is responsible for the fact that *S* did or suffered *y*.[5]

In the hamburger case cited above, the innocent diners are not responsible for getting poisoned, and that's why the example refutes DR. However, the staff of the fast food restaurant *are* responsible for selling the spoiled hamburgers. Thus, the example does not run counter to DR′. A corresponding point holds in the case of the figure-skater and the thug. The skater is not responsible for the attack, but the thug is. Perhaps DR′ is a better formulation of the received wisdom in question.

I think DR′ is also false. I think that there are familiar cases in which no one is responsible for a certain misfortune, and yet the person who suffers that misfortune deserves something in virtue of the fact that he has suffered. Consider, for example, a case in which a young child becomes ill with a painful disease. Suppose the child suffers for a while with this disease, and eventually dies. The parents are overwhelmed with grief. Surely no one bears any responsibility for their misfortune, and yet the grieving parents might deserve various things in virtue of enduring it. At the very minimum, they deserve some expression of sympathy from their friends and neighbours.

Many moral philosophers have endorsed the principle that each of us, merely in virtue of being a person, deserves a certain minimal amount of respect. If we do deserve anything in virtue of being persons, then we have further evidence for the independence of responsibility and desert. It is pretty clear that I am not responsible for the fact that I am a person. Although my parents may bear some responsibility for the fact that I exist, it is not clear that either they or anyone else is responsible for the fact that I am a person. If no one is responsible for this fact, and yet I deserve some respect in virtue of being a person, then desert is further severed from responsibility.

Let us now turn to the evaluation of DT.

5. The Refutation Of DT

We naturally say that if a person has been short-changed in the past, then she deserves some extra benefit now. Our talk of desert in such a case seems linked to the idea of "balance" or "fairness" or "appropriateness" in the allocation of good and evil. If this is so, then one wonders why it is not equally natural to say that if a person *will be* short-changed in the future, then she *already* deserves some extra benefit now. Future mis-allocations are surely as bad as past ones; present re-allocations surely serve to bring about balance and fairness just as much as future ones would; if desert in such cases is fundamentally a matter of achieving balance and fairness in allocations of good and evil, then it is hard to see how there can be any justification for insisting

that harms be suffered before compensatory benefits are distributed. Why wait? Why not say that those who will be harmed later already deserve their compensation today? What justifies the alleged temporal asymmetry of desert and its base?

Imagine a graph showing the good and bad fortunes that befall a person, S, throughout his life. Suppose the graph looks like this:

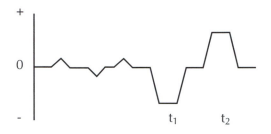

Suppose that the dip at t_1 represents a serious misfortune that S then suffers, and the rise at t_2 represents a compensating bit of good fortune that S enjoys at t_2. Since the size of the rise at t_2 is equal to the size of dip at t_1, we may want to say that the t_2 rise compensates for the t_1 fall. S may complain that his life is pretty boring (only two dips; only three rises—and these pretty small) but (given obvious assumptions) it's hard to see how he can complain about unfairness. His misfortunes seem to have been compensated.

I have not told you the direction of time in the example. I did not say that t_1 is earlier than t_2. One wonders why it should matter which way time is flowing. If S suffers a misfortune at t_1, and enjoys a bit of good fortune at t_2, then, from the "extra-temporal perspective", the goods and bads of S's life pretty nearly balance out. Thus, there is a question about the relevance of temporal priority in DT.

I am convinced that DT is not true. Furthermore I think that there are familiar examples that show that it is not true. One fairly clear example concerns the sometimes extraordinary benefits that are given to children who have contracted fatal diseases. Organizations such as the Make-a-Wish Foundation provide very generous benefits (such as visits to Disneyland) for such children. It seems to me that the rationale for such benefits is clear:

since the children are quite innocent, and are going to suffer terrible harms, they deserve extraordinary benefits. Since it will be impossible to provide these benefits to the children after they suffer the harms, the Make-a-Wish Foundation gives them the benefits in advance.

A second example concerns soldiers who volunteer for suicidal missions. In some contexts these soldiers are thought to be deserving of great honours. Celebrations may be held; they may be given medals or promotions. Then they go off to perform the actions in virtue of which they deserve to be so treated. Again, the desert base is rooted in the future, not the past.

If one wished to defend DT, one could of course try to force these examples into the requisite temporal shape. Thus, one could admit that the sick children deserve the benefits they receive from the Make-a-Wish Foundation, but could deny that they deserve these benefits in virtue of the harms they will later suffer. Rather, it could be insisted, such children are deserving in virtue of the fact that they *have contracted fatal diseases,* or the fact that they *have already suffered.* These are facts about the past, and are thus consistent with DT.[6]

In the case of the soldiers, one could say that they deserve their medals in virtue of the fact that they *volunteered (or were chosen) for their suicidal missions.* Again, it could be claimed that the desert base is "properly" in the past.

I reject these desperate manoeuvres. It seems clear to me that the sick children do deserve special consideration, not only because they have already suffered, but also in virtue of the fact that they are going to suffer. Perhaps this can be made more plausible by appeal to a thought-experiment. Suppose there are two sick children in the hospital. Suppose each has a painful disease. The first has suffered for several months, and has been quite miserable. Yet the doctors are perfectly certain that she will soon become well, and in a short time will be fully recovered with no lingering effects. The second has also suffered for several months, and has also been miserable. In his case, however, the prognosis is different. The doctors are perfectly certain that he will

soon die. There is no cure for his fatal affliction. In this situation, the Make-a-Wish Foundation offers a special treat for exactly one sick child. Imagine that this is an all-expense-paid trip to Disneyland. The Foundation stipulates that the treat is to be given to the most deserving child in the hospital.

It seems clear to me that, in the absence of any unusual and so far unstated factors, the child with the fatal disease would be the more deserving, precisely because he is going to suffer the greater misfortune. Though his past sufferings are no greater than the other child's, he is destined to suffer worse misfortunes in the future. This explains the fact that he is the more deserving of the two.

6. Why DR Has Been Believed

It is hard to understand why so many philosophers have accepted DR. I have never seen an argument for it. My suspicion is that some may have accepted it simply as a result of failure to consider a sufficiently wide variety of examples. Perhaps these philosophers focused exclusively on a narrow range of cases involving desert of things like punishment and reward; perhaps in all these cases the one who deserves is also responsible for the desert base; perhaps these philosophers assumed without further reflection that all cases would be like these few. And yet, if we consider the class of cases involving desert of sympathy, condolence, and compensation for innocent suffering, we immediately see that there can be desert without responsibility.

Another possible explanation is that advocates of DR focused exclusively on cases in which the deserving person deserves in virtue of some action he or she performed. In such cases, the person is typically responsible for the action. Again, hasty generalization might be the culprit.

7. Why DT Has Been Believed

DT seems rather more natural and plausible. Counterexamples are less common. But the counterexamples are fairly obvious. What accounts for the attractiveness of this principle?

For a time I thought that the plausibility of DT should be explained by appeal to a certain confusion. I thought that another principle was true, and that this other principle was easily confused with DT. I am no longer convinced by this explanation. Nevertheless, it may be useful to discuss it.

According to a popular view, ordinary facts about the past are entirely "settled": from the perspective of the present, there is nothing we can do to prevent them, or "undo" them. Thus, if I have already suffered an injury, the fact that I have suffered this injury is settled; it is an unalterable fact.

Determinists may hold that all facts about the future are already settled. This is a controversial position. A more moderate view is that at least some facts about the future are in this sense settled. Thus, for example, consider the fact that the sun will rise tomorrow, and the fact that the seasons will change at approximately their appointed times, and the fact that each of us will eventually die. It is reasonable to suppose that facts such as these are settled— though in some cases the precise dates are not yet settled. They are like facts about the past, since there is nothing we can do to prevent them. No matter what possible course of action we take, these things will happen.

However, certain other facts about the future seem still unsettled. Suppose a certain mugger is contemplating a mugging, and has not yet made up his mind whether he will mug me or whether he will mug another innocent victim. If this mugger's reflections have genuine point—if his choice of victim is really still "up to him"—then it is not yet settled that I will be injured by him in a mugging.

It might be thought that there is an important connection between desert and this sort of settledness. Specifically, it might be thought that this is true:

DS: If at t S deserves x in virtue of the fact that S did or suffered something at t', then the fact that S did or suffered that thing at t' is already settled at t.

Inspection will reveal, I think, that every example so far mentioned in connection with DT in fact conforms to DS. When the desert base is in the past it is already settled. All such cases conform to DS. Cases in which the desert base is in the future conflict with DT, but they may seem to conform to DS, since in all the cases so far discussed the desert base is settled at the time of desert. Consider, for example, the case involving the Make-a-Wish Foundation. I wanted to say that the child with the fatal disease deserved special treatment in virtue of the fact that he will later suffer a great misfortune. The example refuted DT. However, the example does not refute DS, since the child's suffering was described as inevitable, or settled, even though still in the future. DS (unlike DT) permits the child to be deserving in virtue of this future, but settled fact.

The account I formerly accepted goes like this: it is possible that the appeal of DT derives largely from its confusion with DS. DS is true; it's easy to confuse DS with DT. Perhaps some philosophers have confused DT with DS, and have for this reason erroneously thought that DT is true.

I am no longer quite so happy with this explanation, since I no longer think that DS is true. I think there are cases in which, at a certain time, someone deserves something in virtue of a certain fact but that fact is *not* settled at the time of desert. Consider this example: a customs inspector may realize that he is about to invade the privacy of a traveller. The traveller has done nothing wrong, and yet his bags are going to be searched. The inspector says "I'm sorry sir, but you will have to open all these bags, and allow us to search through them". The inspector is apologizing for something that is about to happen. It is reasonable to suppose that the innocent traveller deserves the apology even before his privacy has been invaded.

The crucial fact about this example is that, at the time of the apology, the customs inspector may recognize that he is under no *compulsion* to inspect the bags; he may recognize that it is still fully in his power to refrain from inspecting them. Thus, while it is a fact that he is going to inspect the bags, it is not yet a settled fact. It is something that he is going to do, but freely. The example thus shows that DS is false. Therefore, we cannot explain the plausibility of DT by saying that it has been mistaken for DS, which is the truth in these matters. In order to make use of this line of explanation, we must suppose that philosophers have made *two* mistakes. First, they mistakenly supposed that DS is true. Second, they confused DT with DS.[7]

So we are left with our question: why have so many philosophers accepted DT?

Perhaps a different confusion explains this mistake. A fundamental constraint on our system of criminal justice is that no one shall be punished for a crime he has not yet committed. In some cases, our commitment to this constraint is almost fanatical. Even when we know that a certain person will commit a crime, we maintain that he is legally innocent until he commits the crime, and is proven guilty. The police insist that their hands are tied—the man does not deserve to be punished until he has actually done what we all know he intends to do.

There are of course lots of good reasons for insisting upon this policy. One is epistemic. Even when we have quite good evidence, we rarely know precisely what the future will bring. There is always (or almost always) the chance that the person will not commit the crime. Thus, it is safer to adopt the general policy of always waiting to see what the future brings. If he commits the crime, we can immediately step in and set the wheels of justice grinding. If he does not commit the crime, we will have avoided a terrible injustice.

There is a second important factor in such cases. Consider a typical case in which it seems quite likely that a certain person will commit some crime. We think he will deserve the legally mandated punishment only if he will be responsible for the crime; and we think he will be responsible for the crime only if he will commit it "freely"; and we think that if he will commit it "freely", then it cannot yet be quite certain that he will commit it. There must still be some possibility that he will decide not to commit it. So we insist upon a legal system that prohibits punishment-in-advance.

There is yet a third reason to avoid laws that permit punishment-in-advance. Suppose the law permitted punishment-in-advance. Surely there would be safeguards. Advance punishment would be permitted only in cases in which it is perfectly certain that the suspect is going to commit the crime. (That is, it is certain that he will commit the crime *unless the law steps in and prevents his doing so.*) But if we have such sure-fire knowledge that the suspect is going to commit the crime, it would make even better sense to step in and prevent that criminal behavior. However, if we lock the pre-criminal up, or otherwise prevent his crime, he will not commit the crime. In this case, he cannot possibly deserve punishment for committing it. Antecedent punishment, in such a case, would be deprived of its desert base. Thus, in order to be sure that those who are punished really deserve their punishment, we insist upon a system that permits punishment only after the crime has been committed.

There is a fourth reason. Suppose a person appears at the police station and offers to pay a fine for speeding. She says that she is going to speed later in the day, and wants to pay the fine in advance so as to avoid red tape and inconvenience. The police officer does not accept her check, and does not agree that she deserves the fine. Rather, he takes steps to ensure that she does not speed. To accept the money and agree that she deserves the fine would be to acknowledge that she is going to speed, and in effect to grant her permission to do so, and this the officer cannot do.

For all these reasons, and perhaps for others as well, we are whole-heartedly committed to a judicial system that prohibits punishment-in-advance. Part of this commitment involves the principle that no judge or jury may determine that a certain person deserves punishment under the law at a time in virtue of the fact that he will later commit a certain crime. For the commission of a crime to serve as a desert base for punishment in a court of law, the crime must already have been committed.

I suppose it is possible that some philosophers may have confused this legal principle about desert of punishment with the much more general principle DT. It should be obvious that the truth of the legal principle (if it is true) implies nothing about the truth of DT.

8. Concluding Remarks

It is widely assumed that desert is intimately linked to responsibility and time. Principles DR and DT express elements of the received wisdom about this alleged linkage. Yet it is clear upon reflection that neither principle is true. A person may deserve sympathy or even compensation for injuries received though neither he nor anyone else is responsible for those injuries. A person may deserve benefits for harms received even though she has not yet suffered those harms. If there is any connection between desert and responsibility, it is far more complex than the connections indicated by DR and DR′; if there is any connection between desert and time, it is far more complex than the connections indicated by DT and DS.

NOTES

1. I believe that Feinberg (1963) introduced the term.
2. In a widely cited passage Rawls (1971, p. 104) discusses the notion that people with "greater natural endowments" deserve the superior character that those assets make possible. Rawls says that the view is "surely incorrect". He explains his position by pointing out that such a person's ". . . character depends in large part upon fortunate family and social circumstances for which he can claim no credit". Rawls's view seems to be that no one deserves his character because no one is responsible for ("can claim credit for") something upon which his character depends. This is at least quite similar to DR.
3. Brian Barry seems to commit himself to the same doctrine. He says, "Desert looks to the past—or at most to the present—whereas incentive and deterrence are forward looking notions . . ." (Barry 1965, p. 111). David Miller apparently means to defend precisely the same principle: "Desert judgements are justified on the basis of *past* and *present* facts about individuals, never on the basis of states of affairs to be created in the future. Desert is a

'backward-looking' concept . . ." (Miller 1976, p. 93).
4. Klenig, Sher and others have endorsed the view that we can deserve such things as compensation and apology in virtue of harms innocently suffered. These philosophers have at least implicitly recognised that DR is false. Kleinig (1971, p. 74) explicitly rejects it.
5. Sadurski hints at this idea when he says "To say 'I didn't deserve such a tragedy to happen to me' would make sense only under the condition that someone can properly be held responsible for what actually happened" (1985, p. 118).
6. One could insist that the children actually do not deserve any benefits; the Make-a Wish Foundation gives them the benefits simply out of kindness and sympathy. I find this suggestion deeply implausible—perhaps even offensive.
7. An interesting feature of the example involving the customs inspector is this: although the later invasion of the traveller's privacy is not *settled* at the time of desert, the inspector *knows for certain* that it is going to occur. This may suggest that the relevant fact is neither *being in the past* nor *being settled,* but is rather *being known for certain.* In other words:

DK: If at t S deserves x in virtue of the fact that S did or suffered something at t', then the fact that S did or suffered that thing at t' is already *known for certain* at t.

I am convinced that DK is false. I may deserve the prize for best essay in virtue of the fact that my essay was the best of those submitted. However, it may be that no one knows that my essay was the best of those submitted. I didn't read the other submissions; the judges were careless or inept—they didn't recognise that mine was best. If DK has any appeal, I suspect that it is due to a confusion of the fact that S deserves x with the fact that someone would be justified in claiming that S deserves x.

References

Barry, Brian 1965: *Political Argument.* London & New York: Routledge & Kegan Paul.

Cottingham, John 1992: "Justice; Rectificatory", in Lawrence Becker, ed., *Encyclopedia of Ethics.* New York & London: Garland Publishing Co.

Feinberg, Joel 1963: "Justice and Personal Desert", in C. J. Friedrich and J. W. Chapman, eds., *Nomos VI: Justice.* New York: Atherton Press.

Hospers, John 1961: *Human Conduct.* New York: Harcourt, Brace & World, Inc.

Kleinig, John 1971: "The Concept of Desert". *American Philosophical Quarterly* 8, pp. 71–8.

Mill, J. S. 1957: *Utilitarianism.* Indianapolis: Liberal Arts Press.

Miller, David 1976: *Social Justice.* Oxford: The Clarendon Press.

New, Christopher 1992; "Time and Punishment". *Analysis* 52, pp. 35–40.

Rachels, James 1978: "What People Deserve", in *Justice and Economic Distribution*, ed. John Arthur and William H. Shaw Englewood Cliffs: Prentice-Hall.

Rawls, John 1971: *A Theory of Justice.* Cambridge: Harvard University Press.

Rescher, Nicholas 1966: *Distributive Justice.* Indianapolis: Bobbs-Merrill.

Sadurski, Wojciech 1985: *Giving Desert Its Due: Social Justice and Legal Theory.* Dordrecht: D. Reidel Publishing Co.

Sher, George 1987: *Desert.* Princeton: Princeton University Press.

Sidgwick, Henry 1962: *The Methods of Ethics.* London: Macmillan & Co.

Slote, Michael 1973: "Desert, Consent, and Justice". *Philosophy and Public Affairs* 2, pp: 323–47.

Smilansky, Saul 1994: The Time to Punish". *Analysis* 54, pp. 50–3.

C. THE RAWLSIAN DEBATE

17. An Argument for Equality from Compensatory Desert

HERBERT SPIEGELBERG

Herbert Spiegelberg taught philosophy for many years at Lawrence College in New York. He was a leading representative of the Phenomenological School of Philosophy, best known for his two-volume work *The Phenomenological Movement: A Historical Introduction* (The Hague: Martinus Nijhoff, 1960). In this article, written at the beginning of the Second World War, when German National Socialism had denounced democracy and its commitment to human equality, Spiegelberg attempts to defend the thesis that all humans are equal. Against the Nietzscheans who assert that "Equality of all men is the biggest lie ever told," Spiegelberg argues that it is a deep truth. The idea of equality, he argues, was first manifested in the " 'Christian dynamite' of the idea of human equality before God," and its "final outcome is modern secular democracy."

What is significant about Spiegelberg's argument is that, rather than see equality and desert as opposites, he links them in a way that makes desert the basis for equality. His argument may be called "The Argument for Equality from Compensatory Desert," since his main thesis is that all undeserved discriminations call for redress. By *discrimination*

Reprinted from "A Defense of Human Equality," *Philosophical Review* 52:2 (1944).

he means all inequalities of privilege or handicap. By *undeserved* he means lacking moral justification. By *redress* he means any measure that "restores the unsettled balance." Arguing that all inequalities of birth are undeserved discriminations, he concludes that they should be redressed and that, consequently, we ought to build an egalitarian democratic society wherein everyone has equal dignity.

Spiegelberg goes on to set this theory within the framework of a prospering commonwealth so that it rules out downscaling of the better-off and leads to a notion of stewardship wherein the better off see their advantages as creating special responsibilities in helping the less well off.

This article is important both for its argument for human equality and for the influence it had on John Rawls's Theory of Justice (see next reading); Rawls begins his section on Equality with a reference to Spiegelberg's argument.

In society all are equal. No society can be founded upon anything but the concept of equality, never upon that of freedom. It is equality that I want to find in society; freedom that is the moral freedom to subordinate myself, I bring along anyway. The society which I enter is therefore bound to tell me: You shall be equal with all the rest of us. All it can add is: We wish you would also be free; that is, we wish you to renounce your privileges with full conviction, by free and intelligent assent.

(J. W. Goethe, "Maximen und Reflexionen", *Werke*, 1887)

. . . [S]ince Plato and Aristotle, justice and equality, if not actually identified, have always been thought to be intimately related. Yet, according to the traditional conception, justice demands only that an equal share be assigned to equals, and not equal to unequals. So this kind of justice can never justify equal treatment of unequal human beings, once inequality-in-fact has been admitted.

The Argument from the "Moral Chance" of Inequality

There is, however, a deeper sense of justice in which it does require equality not only of equals but of unequals as well.

The argument for the demand of universal equality based on this conception which I am going to suggest rests on the following two premises: (1) *undeserved discriminations call for redress* [and] (2) *all inequalities of birth constitute undeserved discriminations.* I shall conclude that (3) *all inequalities of birth call for redress.* Such redress implies, at least in principle, the cancellation of all inequalities of birth by equalization. In this sense, then, it follows that (4) *equality is a fundamental ethical demand.*

(1) In the first premise the term "discrimination" means any kind of unequal lot by way of privilege or handicap ; "undeserved" indicates the lack of legitimating support by a moral title such as moral desert; "redress" stands for any measure which restores the unsettled balance.

The premise that undeserved discriminations call for redress thus implies that only morally deserved inequalities justify unequal lots: without such special justification all persons, whether equal or unequal, ought to have equal shares.

I submit that the first premise thus interpreted contains a truth which is at least as self-evident as any other ethical insight. In order to make this truth fully apparent one might in addition refer to the severe moral disequilibrium which the violation of the demand for redress entails. This disequilibrium is, moreover, apt to rouse in a person with a clearly developed sense of justice and fairness a feeling of outrage. A further confirmation may be found in the sphere of Law. Here the lack of a title for a particular benefit serves, under specified conditions, as the basis of an action for restitution because of "unjust enrichment". A legal institution of this type is, as a rule, not unconnected with ethical truths. In the case under discussion it may well be claimed that the ethical demand for redress of undeserved discriminations forms the ultimate basis for the legal regulation.

(2) It will require much more to establish my second premise to the effect that all inequalities of birth constitute undeserved discriminations. All I can do at this place is to point out certain aspects of the fundamental status of man which may help to make this assertion more evident.

Among our inequalities some are *initial* inequalities or inequalities of birth. Others arise only during the course of our lives. It is next to impossible to determine how many of the second inequalities are morally deserved. Most of them are certainly on a level very different from that of the inequalities of birth. But even they are based on the conditions, equal or unequal, implied by our birth. The first step toward determining the ethical significance of our inequalities is therefore to appraise the inequalities of birth.

There is a sense in which none of our unequal characteristics, whether actual or potential, is part and parcel of our innermost selves. We find ourselves "born into" very different stations of life, into extremely varied social environments and groups, into most diverse families, nations, states, denominations, classes, majorities or minorities. Moreover, we awake to the consciousness of our selfhood to discover ourselves already irrevocably assigned to the "roles" of being male or female, white or colored, native or foreign, strong or weak in physical and mental constitution. We are in these respects from the very beginning equipped with very unequal "gifts", both in body and mind. We thus distinguish clearly between ourselves, who are born into such different stations, and the physical and mental equipment into which we are born, which is, as it were, allotted to us.

But it is not only this natal endowment which we thus distinguish from ourselves, who are "born into" it. The inequality of these endowments is likewise an initial fate into which we find ourselves born. Inequality, too,

is therefore something extraneous to our innermost selves.

It is this fundamental human plight of being born into our initial stations and their inequalities which is sometimes rather vaguely referred to by the phrases "chance of birth" or "accident of birth". To be sure, these expressions are nowadays used very loosely and thoughtlessly. Generally they are applied only to the more peripheral circumstances of a man's life. I maintain that these phrases are the expression of a fundamental aspect of human existence.

For it is chance in a specific and very definite sense which is ultimately responsible for all we initially are and have. Prior to any conscious action or choice of our own we find ourselves already born into our stations and into their inequalities. They are, as it were, thrown upon us, certainly without any consciousness of our having deserved them. Nor is there any objective evidence that they depend upon any moral desert. This lack of a moral title and primarily of any moral desert for our initial shares I am going to call here "moral chance". I maintain that in this moral sense it is merely chance which discriminates between us, which grants or denies one individual a set of brilliant "gifts", mental and physical health and vigor, or the heritage of a great family tradition, and which makes him a member of this or that vaunted community and withholds this privilege from other "less fortunate" fellow beings.

Ethics offers no brief for any such discriminations of moral chance. It allows for no inherited desert. In its court everyone is given an equal start. And for each one the initial score is zero. This equality of our initial score is the basic ethical equality among all human beings. It follows that all initial inequalities in the form of privileges and handicaps are ethically unwarranted.

The fact that all our inequalities of birth are thus without a moral title establishes at the same time a secondary ethical equality: In the fate of being blindly subject to the unequal chances of our unequal births we are all equals.

The ethical equality of our initial scores

and the ensuing equality in the moral chance of our factual inequality do not, however, imply that our innermost selves are completely equal. To be sure, there may be good reasons for believing in such an ultimate equality. But even if these reasons should be inconclusive and if, consequently, our innermost selves should be unequal, we should remain equal in the fate of being equally born to the same ethical start and to the position of equally lacking a moral title to whatever inequalities of birth there may be among us. The only essential similarity between these selves refers to the fact that they are all *human* selves, equipped with the fundamental characteristics of human nature, and primarily with reflective selfconsciousness.[1]

Such reflections are by no means unfamiliar to the man in the street. Whenever he tries to do full justice to others, he finds, for instance, that "After all, it is not the poor devil's fault that he 'happens to be' illegitimate. You cannot hold him responsible for having a poor constitution. You cannot blame him for having been born stupid." Or, in evaluating the merits of a man, the average person is likely to argue that "After all, he just 'happened to have' a fine 'start', a marvelous physique and a brilliant mind, and you cannot credit him for that personally. But look at what he made of that start." It seems, then, that in daily life we distinguish very well between the chance equipment of a person and his personal merits or demerits, and that we discount the former when we try to judge him fairly.

(3) The next step follows directly from the preceding premises: If it is mere chance in the moral sense here defined which underlies our initial factual inequalities, these are in an ultimate sense void of moral justification. Our unequal shares constitute an "unjust enrichment" (or an unjustified deprivation), *i.e.*, undeserved discriminations. "Corrective justice" demands redress for inequalities which are supported by nothing but the "chance of birth" in accordance with the equality of our initial ethical score of zero.

(4) But does such redress necessarily call for the establishment of absolute equality? Certainly not in *all* cases of unjustified dis-

crimination. Such discrimination may require nothing beyond the restoration of the status quo. Or it may demand some kind of an amend for irreparable damage.

Furthermore, it should be clear that inequalities which do not represent initial advantages or disadvantages but merely varieties on an equal level are in no way subject to cancellation. The postulate of equality does not require dull uniformity. Only inequalities that involve privileges or handicaps call for anything like redress.

In the case of most of our natal inequalities, however, the principle of redress does require, if not a total redistribution, at least some kind of equalization of fates, much according to the same principles which in the case of a public calamity demand an equalization and compensation for abnormal individual losses. High inheritance taxes, far-reaching social-security measures, are some of the more obvious means to promote such equalization. And, even more important, the postulate of equality calls for the greatest possible prevention of initial inequalities by equal social and medical hygiene and protection. Moreover, in as far as the science of genetics provides us with reliable knowledge about human heredity, it suggests a eugenic policy which prevents the birth of hopelessly handicapped individuals.

On the other hand, the demand for equality does not require that, regardless of the consequences, every privilege or handicap be discarded and equality be made retroactive, as fanatical levellers would have it. That this is not the case can best be seen by considering that equalization constitutes by no means an unambiguous program. It can be achieved by a variety of procedures none of which, judged alone by the standards of the desired equality, would seem preferable. Thus one way of establishing equality would be by achieving *equality in kind,* another by securing only *equivalent* shares. Equality in kind may in turn be realized by three different methods:

1. by the transfer of an excessive share from the overprivileged to the underprivileged party. Such a procedure would obvi-

ously be feasible only in the case of material goods; it would be out of the question in the case of mental advantages.

2. by an increase in the assets of the underprivileged party up to the level of the overprivileged without depriving the latter of his present benefits. In the case of the mentally handicapped this would amount to inflicting upon him an extra dose of training, obviously with a very dubious chance of success and in all probability even against his definite desire.

3. by the destruction of the excessive share of the overprivileged party in the way suggested by the proverbial Solomonic justice. An equalization of mental differences would in this case have to consist in withholding from the overprivileged party a normal education or in other appropriate measures of stultification, certainly again of very problematical effectiveness, quite apart from more serious objections.

Mechanical equalization is, then, in a good many cases a physical impossibility. There remains, however, even in such cases the possibility of achieving at least an equivalence of benefits. And such an equalization of benefits in goods of equal significance may again be obtained by two different procedures:

1. by giving the underprivileged party benefits which would make his status equivalent to that of the overprivileged. It is by no means certain that this is always possible. In what sense physical enjoyments could, for instance, make up for inaccessible intellectual benefits is quite a problem, not to say a moot question.

2. by taking equivalent benefits away from the overprivileged. Even here we should have to consider that certain mental advantages simply cannot be taken away from its owners without destroying his entire personality. And how are we to determine such equivalences?

Which one of these five possible methods of equalization are we to choose, supposing that all or several of them are applicable to the case in question? The principle of equalization or redress in itself cannot help us to decide this. For such a decision we need an additional standard. The one which would

recommend itself best appears to be that of the common well-being of all those fellow beings involved in the fate of inequality.

This principle would rule out from the very start any kind of Solomonic justice. For any destruction of values would impoverish the community as a whole and thus reduce the common well-being. The only exception to this rule would be the case where the existence of inequalities promotes a spirit of caste snobbery and segregation destructive of the solidarity of the fellows-in-fate. In such situations the destruction of individuality may be preferable to the preservation of inequality, however valuable for other reasons. Also it should be considered that the destruction of native advantages may easily constitute a cruel injustice against the better equipped individual. To keep him down and prevent him from developing his special gifts would penalize him for a fate which was, after all, his too through no fault of his own. To choose this destructive way of equalization would simply mean to give way to the forces of envy and blind resentment.

For the same reason it will be, as a rule, undesirable to choose the method of equalization by transfer, unless the implied deprivation of the overprivileged works at the same time for the general, including his own, good. What seems most important is that the underprivileged person receive an improvement of his lot. In this it should however be carefully considered whether such a compensation is likely to work out for his own good. It is very doubtful whether this can be achieved by an equalization in kind, considering how different the meaning of equal goods may be for unequal persons. All that can safely be stated is that the underprivileged should be granted such equivalents for his handicaps as will provide him with the means for that type of well-being for which he is best fitted. It would by no means be a suitable compensation to give the mentally handicapped more means for physical pleasures if these would only endanger his well-being and would be used in a way injurious to the community. All that he can expect is, for instance, more facilities for his physical development, for healthful recreation and enjoyment, and similar compensations for the handicap of not being able to share the more exacting enjoyments accessible to the mentally privileged. It would be definitely against the common interest to waste a useless amount of goods and education on the handicapped. It may well be that such limitations make it permanently impossible for us ever to achieve a full and satisfactory compensation. Regrettable though this may be, it does not constitute a good reason for taking to destructive equalization against the overprivileged party. It is after all in the equal interest of all that his gifts be not wasted. Equality thus does, for instance, not stand in the way of a qualitative democracy which would offer an individualizing education adjusted to the individual needs, inclinations, and capacities, of its members. If such treatment should involve special privileges for the superior members of society, it only demands that they be accepted in the spirit of favors which entail special obligations.

It appears, then, that equal consideration of their cases, regardless of the chance inequalities of birth, is the only absolutely equal claim shared by all. This consideration implies that, with respect to the fundamental boons of human existence, everyone should have equal opportunities; or, if unable to utilize them, access to equivalent resources of a life worth living, *i.e.*, to those sources of "happiness" which are suited to his individual nature. In considering individual cases we should, therefore, not disregard the relevant inequalities of the persons involved. What we *should* disregard is that the person we have to deal with is either friend Tom or Mr. Jones, whose nose we happen to dislike.

It is this claim to equal respect of men's ultimate selfhood, based on their equal existential plight, which seems to me to be at the root of what we mean by the phrase "equal human dignity". Certainly, with regard to their actual achievements and conditions in life, men seem to have very different degrees of dignity and may, for that reason, be worthy of more or less respect. Still, no one who is born into this world can claim any special birthright over anyone else; for in a moral sense all start equally, without initial merit or demerit. To this extent no one has ever more and ever less than an equal claim to impartial consideration of his case in all of its relevant aspects. This basic claim to equal respect of his selfhood gives man a certain ultimate dignity. Such dignity does by no means grant to man anything like absolute perfection worthy of veneration or worship, as an exaggerated humanism *à la* Comte seems to imply. Dignity in the sense here upheld means nothing but a fundamental claim implied by human nature. In this sense, but only in this sense, is it true that "each one is to count for one and no one for more than one", as Bentham postulated so justly but, in view of his predominant interest in sheer maximization of happiness, so inconsistently.

How far can the use of a category like moral chance be reconciled with a religious interpretation of human existence? Is it not a flat denial of "Divine Providence" to speak about the human situation as a matter of chance?

Such an objection would be a serious misunderstanding of what I have in mind. "Moral chance" denies divine providence as little as it denies strict mechanistic determination. In fact, the Christian interpretation of human existence supplies most valuable confirmation of the considerations suggested above. Thus the Christian idea of Grace implicitly acknowledges the ethical unaccountability of the inequalities of our initial fates. Because of this unaccountability it stresses the special obligations implied in our privileges, which are not, and even cannot be, morally deserved. It is only the speculation about a migration of the souls, as represented in ancient mysticism or in Indian thought, which, by explaining our earthly fates from merit or guilt incurred in a previous existence, flatly contradicts the idea of such moral chance of birth. But not only is the hypothesis of preexistence gratuitous. It is certainly not without significance that Plato, in order to free the Deity of any suspicion of injustice, felt the need of justifying the inequalities of our births and fates by a prenatal choice of our lots, a choice in which, as he is anxious to show, the odds were even for every participant.

Related Arguments

It may be worth pointing out that it is not only justice in the form of the demand for the redress of undeserved discriminations which supports the equalitarian demand. It is, for instance, but the minimum of *charity* to fulfil the demands of justice. Already justice expects that we should give equal consideration to all those who are initially unequal. How much more does charity enjoin that we should not let others be at the undeserved disadvantage to which the "accident of birth" exposes them.

Moreover, on quite a different level, it is precisely Nietzsche's ideal of *nobleminded-ness* which, if thought through to its full consequences, would lead to the demand of equal treatment as a duty of the privileged, if not as a right of the underprivileged. Nietzsche himself seems to be dangerously close to such an unaristocratic conclusion when he gives expression to his love for "this one who is ashamed when the die has fallen in his favor and asks: Have I, then, been cheating?" Certainly it would be unworthy of anybody who shares this lofty attitude to accept unearned privileges over his fellow-beings such as the ones granted by the "accident of birth".

And even from the recent cult of heroic selfreliance, which would like to owe everything to its own efforts, it is not a far cry to the acknowledgment of the demand for an equal start.

But these alternative arguments are hardly conclusive to anyone who does not accept the ideals of charity, or noblemindedness, or self-reliance, as binding. It is largely for this reason that the argument based on the demands of justice seems to me to carry much more weight. Besides, all other arguments have to use the additional premise of the "moral chance" of our inequalities of birth.

Conclusion

To restate, then the central idea of my principal vindication of human equality: The postulate of equality, as far as it is valid, has its ultimate basis in the demands of a fundamental human justice which requires equal consideration even of unequals who equally owe their factual inequalities to the "chance of birth". It is thus not equality of factual being but equality of ethical status, as indicated by the equal initial ethical score of each individual, which constitutes the foundation for the postulate of human equality. The paradox of the ideal of equality in the face of all the factual inequalities among men disappears once one discovers its basis in the need of redress for the unwarranted privileges and handicaps of our unequal stations at birth.

NOTE

1. In a correspondence about this point Dr. Arnold Brecht of the New School for Social Research raised the objection that the argument above proved too much. For it would not only apply to human beings but would have to be extended to animals as well, from the anthropoids down to the smallest microbes, since ostensibly they also are what they are without any previous desert, merit, or demerit. This objection overlooks the question of what it involves "to be born into" any kind of existential station. Obviously there must be a being of its own which, in such a case, would have to be *born into* whatever station or plight. Unless one should plead for some kind of speculative panpsychism, it does not make any sense to say that something is born into being, for instance, a particular plant or stone.

   Now this situation may be somewhat different in the case of higher animals. To be sure, it seems highly improbable that they are capable of any behavior involving ethical merit or demerit. And that in itself would make the correlative term "moral chance" inapplicable. I should, however, not hesitate to admit that, if the selves of animals were really as human as children's stories and animal fables would have it, our attitude toward them would have to change fundamentally. Meanwhile it seems noteworthy to me that even our actual behavior toward them does vary, apparently according to the closeness of their mental structure to our own. We do not treat anthropoids, horses, dogs, and cats, whether domestic or not, on the same level with insects or even with cattle. Does perhaps the greater similarity of their expressions and of their other behavior to our own suggest to us subconsciously that, after all, we might as well have been in their places?

   It appears, then, that as far as the moral chance of birth is concerned, we have to consider the basic difference between human and animal selves (if any). Human selves simply would not fit into the mould of an animal and vice versa. By this I do not mean to say that a human self requires exactly the kind of equipment which we empirically find in men, *i.e.*, the actual human body and its peculiar mental outfit, with its special type of sensation, perception, memory, speech, and the like. But this human self must be one with at least the possibility of reflective consciousness of his selfhood. Under such circumstances, then, it seems reasonable that we do not grant animals an equal status with ourselves, even if they should have

selves who are born into their existential station by the mere "chance of birth".

It may be added that basically the same consideration would apply to the problem of our attitude toward imbeciles and lunatics, only in an increased degree. What is it that forbids us to dispose of these "unfortunate" fellow beings in the way in which totalitarian eugenics is reported to do? Is it not again the consciousness that it is through no merit of our own that we have been spared their fate and that it is through no fault of theirs that they do not share our better lot?

18. A Theory of Justice

JOHN RAWLS

John Rawls has enjoyed a long and distinguished career at Harvard University, where he is Professor Emeritus in Philosophy. A Theory of Justice, which Rawls published in 1971, is the most influential work of ethics to appear in the second half of the twentieth century. His most recent book is Political Liberalism (1993).

A central element of Rawls's theory of justice is "the difference principle." According to it, inequalities of wealth, status, and other goods are just only if the institutional arrangements that permit those inequalities lead also and necessarily to maximum improvements in the lives of the worst off. In practice, the difference principle would require the most advantaged members of society to sacrifice perhaps a great deal of the benefits they might otherwise enjoy so that the lives of the least advantaged could be maximally improved. Thus, while Rawls's theory does not require strict equality of resources, the difference principle would have an equalizing effect on society.

In this selection, Rawls considers versions of the objection that the difference principle ignores desert. One version is that the well off deserve to keep the goods they have; they worked for them, inherited them, or are entitled to them by the rules. Another version rests on the fact that application of the difference principle would have no tendency to reward the morally virtuous with the happiness they deserve or to punish the wicked with the unhappiness they deserve. On either objection, the difference principle ignores desert and therefore is thought to fail as a principle of justice.

Rawls's replies involve several claims, two of which have been especially influential: (i) The effort one is willing to make and one's moral character are largely determined by factors, such as genetic endowment and social position, that are "arbitrary from a moral point of view." Therefore, effort and moral worth are unsuitable grounds for determining the justice or injustice of a distribution; (ii) Desert in the sense of "legitimate expectation" can be defined as entitlement according to Rawlsian principles of justice, and desert in the sense of "moral worth" can be defined as the possession of an effective desire to comply with those same principles. Either way, the assumption (implicit in the desert-inspired objections) that institutions ought to be arranged so that people get what they deserve is analogous to the absurd claim that property ought to be invented so that thieves can be punished!

The Tendency to Equality

I wish to conclude this discussion of the two principles by explaining the sense in which they express an egalitarian conception of justice. Also I should like to forestall the objection to the principle of fair opportunity that it leads to a callous meritocratic society. In or-

Reprinted from *A Theory of Justice* (Cambridge, Mass.: Harvard University Press, 1971), by permission.

der to prepare the way for doing this, I note several aspects of the conception of justice that I have set out.

First we may observe that the difference principle gives some weight to the considerations singled out by the principle of redress. This is the principle that undeserved inequalities call for redress; and since inequalities of birth and natural endowment are undeserved, these inequalities are to be somehow compensated for.[1] Thus the principle holds that in order to treat all persons equally, to provide genuine equality of opportunity, society must give more attention to those with fewer native assets and to those born into the less favorable social positions. The idea is to redress the bias of contingencies in the direction of equality. In pursuit of this principle greater resources might be spent on the education of the less rather than the more intelligent, at least over a certain time of life, say the earlier years of school.

Now the principle of redress has not to my knowledge been proposed as the sole criterion of justice, as the single aim of the social order. It is plausible as most such principles are only as a prima facie principle, one that is to be weighed in the balance with others. For example, we are to weigh it against the principle to improve the average standard of life, or to advance the common good. But whatever other principles we hold, the claims of redress are to be taken into account. It is thought to represent one of the elements in our conception of justice. Now the difference principle is not of course the principle of redress. It does not require society to try to even out handicaps as if all were expected to compete on a fair basis in the same race. But the difference principle would allocate resources in education, say, so as to improve the longterm expectation of the least favored. If this end is attained by giving more attention to the better endowed, it is permissible; otherwise not. And in making this decision, the value of education should not be assessed solely in terms of economic efficiency and social welfare. Equally if not more important is the role of education in enabling a person to enjoy the culture of his society and to take part in its af-

fairs, and in this way to provide for each individual a secure sense of his own worth.

Thus although the difference principle is not the same as that of redress, it does achieve some of the intent of the latter principle. It transforms the aims of the basic structure so that the total scheme of institutions no longer emphasizes social efficiency and technocratic values. We see then that the difference principle represents, in effect, an agreement to regard the distribution of natural talents as a common asset and to share in the benefits of this distribution whatever it turns out to be. Those who have been favored by nature, whoever they are, may gain from their good fortune only on terms that improve the situation of those who have lost out. The naturally advantaged are not to gain merely because they are more gifted, but only to cover the costs of training and education and for using their endowments in ways that help the less fortunate as well. No one deserves his greater natural capacity nor merits a more favorable starting place in society. But it does not follow that one should eliminate these distinctions. There is another way to deal with them. The basic structure can be arranged so that these contingencies work for the good of the least fortunate. Thus we are led to the difference principle if we wish to set up the social system so that no one gains or loses from his arbitrary place in the distribution of natural assets or his initial position in society without giving or receiving compensating advantages in return.

In view of these remarks we may reject the contention that the ordering of institutions is always defective because the distribution of natural talents and the contingencies of social circumstance are unjust, and this injustice must inevitably carry over to human arrangements. Occasionally this reflection is offered as an excuse for ignoring injustice, as if the refusal to acquiesce in injustice is on a par with being unable to accept death. The natural distribution is neither just nor unjust; nor is it unjust that persons are born into society at some particular position. These are simply natural facts. What is just and unjust is the way that institutions deal with these facts.

Aristocratic and caste societies are unjust because they make these contingencies the ascriptive basis for belonging to more or less enclosed and privileged social classes. The basic structure of these societies incorporates the arbitrariness found in nature. But there is no necessity for men to resign themselves to these contingencies. The social system is not an unchangeable order beyond human control but a pattern of human action. In justice as fairness men agree to share one another's fate. In designing institutions they undertake to avail themselves of the accidents of nature and social circumstance only when doing so is for the common benefit. The two principles are a fair way of meeting the arbitrariness of fortune; and while no doubt imperfect in other ways, the institutions which satisfy these principles are just.

A further point is that the difference principle expresses a conception of reciprocity. It is a principle of mutual benefit. We have seen that, at least when chain connection holds, each representative man can accept the basic structure as designed to advance his interests. The social order can be justified to everyone, and in particular to those who are least favored; and in this sense it is egalitarian. But it seems necessary to consider in an intuitive way how the condition of mutual benefit is satisfied. Consider any two representative men A and B, and let B be the one who is less favored. Actually, since we are most interested in the comparison with the least favored man, let us assume that B is this individual. Now B can accept A's being better off since A's advantages have been gained in ways that improve B's prospects. If A were not allowed his better position, B would be even worse off than he is. The difficulty is to show that A has no grounds for complaints. Perhaps he is required to have less than he might since his having more would result in some loss to B. Now what can be said to the more favored man? To begin with, it is clear that the well-being of each depends on a scheme of social cooperation without which no one could have a satisfactory life. Secondly, we can ask for the willing cooperation of everyone only if the terms of the scheme are reasonable. The

difference principle, then, seems to be a fair basis on which those better endowed, or more fortunate in their social circumstances, could expect others to collaborate with them when some workable arrangement is a necessary condition of the good of all.

There is a natural inclination to object that those better situated deserve their greater advantages whether or not they are to the benefit of others. At this point it is necessary to be clear about the notion of desert. It is perfectly true that given a just system of cooperation as a scheme of public rules and the expectations set up by it, those who, with the prospect of improving their condition, have done what the system announces that it will reward are entitled to their advantages. In this sense the more fortunate have a claim to their better situation; their claims are legitimate expectations established by social institutions, and the community is obligated to meet them. But this sense of desert presupposes the existence of the cooperative scheme; it is irrelevant to the question whether in the first place the scheme is to be designed in accordance with the difference principle or some other criterion.

Perhaps some will think that the person with greater natural endowments deserves those assets and the superior character that made their development possible. Because he is more worthy in this sense, he deserves the greater advantages that he could achieve with them. This view, however, is surely incorrect. It seems to be one of the fixed points of our considered judgments that no one deserves his place in the distribution of native endowments, any more than one deserves one's initial starting place in society. The assertion that a man deserves the superior character that enables him to make the effort to cultivate his abilities is equally problematic; for his character depends in large part upon fortunate family and social circumstances for which he can claim no credit. The notion of desert seems not to apply to these cases. Thus the more advantaged representative man cannot say that he deserves and therefore has a right to a scheme of cooperation in which he is permitted to acquire benefits in ways that do not contribute to the welfare of others. There is no basis for his making this claim. From the standpoint of common sense, then, the difference principle appears to be acceptable both to the more advantaged and to the less advantaged individual. Of course, none of this is strictly speaking an argument for the principle, since in a contract theory arguments are made from the point of view of the original position. But these intuitive considerations help to clarify the nature of the principle and the sense in which it is egalitarian.

. . . A society should try to avoid the region where the marginal contributions of those better off to the well-being of the less favored are negative. It should operate only on the upward rising part of the contribution curve (including of course the maximum). One reason for this, we can now see, is that on this segment of the curve the criterion of mutual benefit is always fulfilled. Moreover, there is a natural sense in which the harmony of social interests is achieved; representative men do not gain at one another's expense since only reciprocal advantages are allowed. To be sure, the shape and slope of the contribution curve is determined in part at least by the natural lottery in native assets, and as such it is neither just nor unjust. But suppose we think of the forty-five degree line as representing the ideal level of a perfect harmony of interests; it is the contribution curve (a straight line in this case) along which everyone gains equally. Then it seems that the consistent realization of the two principles of justice tends to raise the curve closer to the ideal of a perfect harmony of interests. Once a society goes beyond the maximum it operates along the downward sloping part of the curve and a harmony of interests no longer exists. As the more favored gain the less advantaged lose, and vice versa. The situation is analogous to being on an efficiency frontier. This is far from desirable when the justice of the basic structure is involved. Thus it is to realize the ideal of the harmony of interests on terms that nature has given us, and to meet the criterion of mutual benefit, that we should stay in the region of positive contributions.

A further merit of the difference principle is that it provides an interpretation of the principle of fraternity. In comparison with liberty and equality, the idea of fraternity has had a lesser place in democratic theory. It is thought to be less specifically a political concept, not in itself defining any of the democratic rights but conveying instead certain attitudes of mind and forms of conduct without which we would lose sight of the values expressed by these rights. Or closely related to this, fraternity is held to represent a certain equality of social esteem manifest in various public conventions and in the absence of manners of deference and servility. No doubt fraternity does imply these things, as well as a sense of civic friendship and social solidarity, but so understood it expresses no definite requirement. We have yet to find a principle of justice that matches the underlying idea. The difference principle, however, does seem to correspond to a natural meaning of fraternity: namely, to the idea of not wanting to have greater advantages unless this is to the benefit of others who are less well off. The family, in its ideal conception and often in practice, is one place where the principle of maximizing the sum of advantages is rejected. Members of a family commonly do not wish to gain unless they can do so in ways that further the interests of the rest. Now wanting to act on the difference principle has precisely this consequence. Those better circumstanced are willing to have their greater advantages only under a scheme in which this works out for the benefit of the less fortunate.

The ideal of fraternity is sometimes thought to involve ties of sentiment and feeling which it is unrealistic to expect between members of the wider society. And this is surely a further reason for its relative neglect in democratic theory. Many have felt that it has no proper place in political affairs. But if it is interpreted as incorporating the requirements of the difference principle, it is not an impracticable conception. It does seem that the institutions and policies which we most confidently think to be just satisfy its demands, at least in the sense that the inequalities permitted by them contribute to the well-being of the less favored. . . . On this interpretation, then, the principle of fraternity is a perfectly feasible standard. Once we accept it we can associate the traditional ideas of liberty, equality, and fraternity with the democratic interpretation of the two principles of justice as follows: liberty corresponds to the first principle, equality to the idea of equality in the first principle together with equality of fair opportunity, and fraternity to the difference principle. In this way we have found a place for the conception of fraternity in the democratic interpretation of the two principles, and we see that it imposes a definite requirement on the basic structure of society. The other aspects of fraternity should not be forgotten, but the difference principle expresses its fundamental meaning from the standpoint of social justice.

Now it seems evident in the light of these observations that the democratic interpretation of the two principles will not lead to a meritocratic society. This form of social order follows the principle of careers open to talents and uses equality of opportunity as a way of releasing men's energies in the pursuit of economic prosperity and political dominion. There exists a marked disparity between the upper and lower classes in both means of life and the rights and privileges of organizational authority. The culture of the poorer strata is impoverished while that of the governing and technocratic elite is securely based on the service of the national ends of power and wealth. Equality of opportunity means an equal chance to leave the less fortunate behind in the personal quest for influence and social position. Thus a meritocratic society is a danger for the other interpretations of the principles of justice but not for the democratic conception. For, as we have just seen, the difference principle transforms the aims of society in fundamental respects. This consequence is even more obvious once we note that we must when necessary take into account the essential primary good of self-respect and the fact that a well-ordered society is a social union of social unions. It follows that the confident sense of their own worth should be sought for the least favored and this limits the forms of hierarchy and the degrees of inequality that justice permits. Thus, for example, resources for education are not to be allotted solely or necessarily mainly according to their return as estimated in productive trained abilities, but also according to their worth in enriching the personal and social life of citizens, including here the less favored. As a society progresses the latter consideration becomes increasingly more important. . . .

Legitimate Expectations and Moral Desert

There is a tendency for common sense to suppose that income and wealth, and the good things in life generally, should be distributed according to moral desert. Justice is happiness according to virtue. While it is recognized that this ideal can never be fully carried out, it is the appropriate conception of distributive justice, at least as a prime facie principle, and society should try to realize it as circumstances permit. Now justice as fairness rejects this conception. Such a principle would not be chosen in the original position. There seems to be no way of defining the requisite criterion in that situation. Moreover, the notion of distribution according to virtue fails to distinguish between moral desert and legitimate expectations. Thus it is true that as persons and groups take part in just arrangements, they acquire claims on one another defined by the publicly recognized rules. Having done various things encouraged by the existing arrangements, they now have certain rights, and just distributive shares honor these claims. A just scheme, then, answers to what men are entitled to; it satisfies their legitimate expectations as founded upon social institutions. But what they are entitled to is not proportional to nor dependent upon their intrinsic worth. The principles of justice that regulate the basic structure and specify the duties and obligations of individuals do not mention moral desert, and there is no tendency for distributive shares to correspond to it.

This contention is borne out by . . . common sense precepts and their role in pure procedural justice. For example, in determining wages a competitive economy gives weight to the precept of contribution. But as we have seen, the extent of one's contribution (estimated by one's marginal productivity) depends upon supply and demand. Surely a person's moral worth does not vary according to how many offer similar skills, or happen to want what he can produce. No one supposes that when someone's abilities are less in demand or have deteriorated (as in the case of singers) his moral deservingness undergoes a similar shift. All of this is perfectly obvious and has long been agreed to. It simply reflects the fact . . . that it is one of the fixed points of our moral judgments that no one deserves his place in the distribution of natural assets any more than he deserves his initial starting place in society.

Moreover, none of the precepts of justice aims at rewarding virtue. The premiums earned by scarce natural talents, for example, are to cover the costs of training and to encourage the efforts of learning, as well as to direct ability to where it best furthers the common interest. The distributive shares that result do not correlate with moral worth, since the initial endowment of natural assets and the contingencies of their growth and nurture in early life are arbitrary from a moral point of view. The precept which seems intuitively to come closest to rewarding moral desert is that of distribution according to effort, or perhaps better, conscientious effort. Once again, however, it seems clear that the effort a person is willing to make is influenced by his natural abilities and skills and the alternatives open to him. The better endowed are more likely, other things equal, to strive conscientiously, and there seems to be no way to discount for their greater good fortune. The idea of rewarding desert is impracticable. And certainly to the extent that the precept of need is emphasized, moral worth is ignored. Nor does the basic structure tend to balance the precepts of justice so as to achieve the requisite correspondence behind the scenes. It is regulated by the two principles of justice which define other aims entirely.

The same conclusion may be reached in another way. In the preceding remarks the notion of moral worth as distinct from a person's claims based upon his legitimate expectations has not been explained. Suppose, then, that we define this notion and show that it has no correlation with distributive shares. We have only to consider a well-ordered society, that is, a society in which institutions are just and this fact is publicly recognized. Its members also have a strong sense of justice, an effective desire to comply with the existing rules and to give one another that to which they are entitled. In this case we may assume that everyone is of equal moral worth. We have now defined this notion in terms of the sense of justice, the desire to act in accordance with the principles that would be chosen in the original position. But it is evident that understood in this way, the equal moral worth of persons does not entail that distributive shares are equal. Each is to receive what the principles of justice say he is entitled to, and these do not require equality.

The essential point is that the concept of moral worth does not provide a first principle of distributive justice. This is because it cannot be introduced until after the principles of justice and of natural duty and obligation have been acknowledged. Once these principles are on hand, moral worth can be defined as having a sense of justice; and . . . the virtues can be characterized as desires or tendencies to act upon the corresponding principles. Thus the concept of moral worth is secondary to those of right and justice, and it plays no role in the substantive definition of distributive shares. The case is analogous to the relation between the substantive rules of property and the law of robbery and theft. These offenses and the demerits they entail presuppose the institution of property which is established for prior and independent social ends. For a society to organize itself with the aim of rewarding moral desert as a first principle would be like having the institution of property in order to punish thieves. The criterion to each according to his virtue would not, then, be chosen in the original position. Since the parties desire to advance their conceptions of the good, they have no reason for arranging their institutions so that distributive shares are determined by moral desert, even if they could find an antecedent standard for its definition.

In a well-ordered society individuals acquire claims to a share of the social product by doing certain things encouraged by the existing arrangements. The legitimate expectations that arise are the other side, so to speak, of the principle of fairness and the natural duty of justice. For in the way that one has a duty to uphold just arrangements, and an obligation to do one's part when one has accepted a position in them, so a person who has complied with the scheme and done his share has a right to be treated accordingly by others. They are bound to meet his legitimate expectations. Thus when just economic arrangements exist, the claims of individuals are properly settled by reference to the rules and precepts (with their respective weights) which these practices take as relevant. As we have seen, it is incorrect to say that just distributive shares reward individuals according to their moral worth. But what we can say is that, in the traditional phrase, a just scheme gives each person his due: that is, it allots to each what he is entitled to as defined by the scheme itself. The principles of justice for institutions and individuals establish that doing this is fair.

Now it should be noted that even though a person's claims are regulated by the existing rules, we can still make a distinction between being entitled to something and deserving it in a familiar although nonmoral sense. To illustrate, after a game one often says that the losing side deserved to win. Here one does not mean that the victors are not entitled to claim the championship, or whatever spoils go to the winner. One means instead that the losing team displayed to a higher degree the skills and qualities that the game calls forth, and the exercise of which gives the sport its appeal. Therefore the losers truly deserved to win but lost out as a result of bad luck, or from other contingencies that caused the contest to miscarry. Similarly even the best economic arrangements will not always lead to the more preferred outcomes. The claims that individuals actually acquire inevitably deviate more or less widely from those that the scheme is designed to allow for. Some persons in favored positions, for example, may not have to a higher degree than others the desired qualities and abilities. All this is evident enough. Its bearing here is that although we can indeed distinguish between the claims that existing arrangements require us to honor, given what individuals have done and how things have turned out, and the claims that would have resulted under more ideal circumstances, none of this implies that distributive shares should be in accordance with moral worth. Even when things happen in the best way, there is still no tendency for distribution and virtue to coincide.

No doubt some may still contend that distributive shares should match moral worth at least to the extent that this is feasible. They may believe that unless those who are better off have superior moral character, their having greater advantages is an affront to our sense of justice. Now this opinion may arise from thinking of distributive justice as somehow the opposite of retributive justice. It is true that in a reasonably well-ordered society those who are punished for violating just laws have normally done something wrong. This is because the purpose of the criminal law is to uphold basic natural duties, those which forbid us to injure other persons in their life and limb, or to deprive them of their liberty and property, and punishments are to serve this end. They are not simply a scheme of taxes and burdens designed to put a price on certain forms of conduct and in this way to guide men's conduct for mutual advantage. It would be far better if the acts prescribed by penal statutes were never done. Thus a propensity to commit such acts is a mark of bad character, and in a just society legal punishments will only fall upon those who display these faults.

It is clear that the distribution of economic and social advantages is entirely different. These arrangements are not the converse, so to speak, of the criminal law, so that just as the one punishes certain offenses, the other rewards moral worth. The function of unequal distributive shares is to cover the costs of training and education, to attract individuals to places and associations where they are most needed from a social point of view, and so on. Assuming that everyone accepts the propriety of self- or group-interested motivation duly regulated by a sense of justice, each decides to do those things that best accord with his aims. Variations in wages and income and the perquisites of position are simply to influence these choices so that the end result accords with efficiency and justice. In a well-ordered society there would be no need for the penal law except insofar as the assurance problem made it necessary. The question of criminal justice belongs for the most part to partial compliance theory, whereas the account of distributive shares belongs to strict compliance theory and so to the consideration of the ideal scheme. To think of distributive and retributive justice as converses of one another is completely misleading and suggests a different justification for distributive shares than the one they in fact have.

NOTE

1. See Herbert Spiegelberg, "A Defense of Human Equality," *Philosophical Review,* vol. 53 (1944), pp. 101, 113–123; and D. D. Raphael, "Justice and Liberty," *Proceedings of the Aristotelian Society,* vol. 51 (1950–1951), pp. 187f.

19. Anarchy, State, and Utopia

ROBERT NOZICK

Robert Nozick is Professor of Philosophy at Harvard University. His many works include *Anarchy, State, and Utopia* (1974), *Philosophical Explanations* (1981), and *The Nature of Rationality* (1994).

Perhaps the most fundamental assumption of John Rawls's theory of justice is that distribution of benefits and burdens (across society and within individual lives) should not be determined by factors that are "arbitrary from a moral point of view." It is mainly this assumption that leads Rawls to reject desert as irrelevant to justice.

In this selection, Nozick investigates the meaning and merit of Rawls's assumption. Nozick makes several important claims: (i) Rawls's anti-desert position seems to imply that human beings are incapable of being responsible agents. This "unexalted picture of human beings" is inconsistent with Rawls's own desire to "buttress the dignity and self-respect of autonomous beings"; (ii) Any distribution, including those permitted by Rawlsian principles, "will have some morally arbitrary facts as part of the explanation of how it arises"; (iii) Rather than rejecting desert, Rawls's arguments sometimes seem to presuppose it; (iv) Rawls implies that the conditions for desert must themselves be deserved, but it is not obvious that "the foundations underlying desert are themselves deserved, *all the way down*." Perhaps some conditions for desert, such as natural talent, need not be deserved.

Natural Assets and Arbitrariness

Rawls comes closest to considering the entitlement system in his discussion of what he terms the system of natural liberty:

> The system of natural liberty selects an efficient distribution roughly as follows. Let us suppose that we know from economic theory that under the standard assumptions defining a competitive market economy, income and wealth will be distributed in an efficient way, and that the particular efficient distribution which results in any period of time is determined by the initial distribution of assets, that is, by the initial distribution of income and wealth, and of natural talents and abilities. With each initial distribution, a definite efficient outcome is arrived at. Thus it turns out that if we are to accept the outcome as just, and not merely as efficient, we must accept the basis upon which over time the initial distribution of assets is determined.
>
> In the system of natural liberty the initial distribution is regulated by the arrangements implicit in the conception of careers open to talents. These arrangements presuppose a

background of equal liberty (as specified by the first principle) and a free market economy. They require a formal equality of opportunity in that all have at least the same legal rights of access to all advantaged social positions. But since there is no effort to preserve an equality or similarity, of social conditions, except insofar as this is necessary to preserve the requisite background institutions, the initial distribution of assets for any period of time is strongly influenced by natural and social contingencies. The existing distribution of income and wealth, say, is the cumulative effect of prior distributions of natural assets—that is, natural talents and abilities—as these have been developed or left unrealized, and their use favored or disfavored over time by social circumstances and such chance contingencies as accident and good fortune. Intuitively, the most obvious injustice of the system of natural liberty is that it permits distributive shares to be improperly influenced by these factors so arbitrary from a moral point of view.

Here we have *Rawls'* reason for rejecting a system of natural liberty: it "permits" distributive shares to be improperly influenced by factors that are so arbitrary from a moral point of view. These factors are: "prior distribution . . . of natural talents and abilities as these have been developed over time by social circumstances and such chance contingencies as accident and good fortune." Notice that there is no mention *at all* of how persons have chosen to develop their own natural assets. Why is that simply left out? Perhaps because such choices also are viewed as being the products of factors outside the person's control, and hence as "arbitrary from a moral point of view." "The assertion that a man deserves the superior character that enables him to make the effort to cultivate his abilities is equally problematic; for his character depends in large part upon fortunate family and social circumstances for which he can claim no credit." (What view is presupposed here of character and its relation to action?) "The initial endowment of natural assets and the contingen-

cies of their growth and nurture in early life are arbitrary from a moral point of view . . . the effort a person is willing to make is influenced by his natural abilities and skills and the alternatives open to him. The better endowed are more likely, other things equal, to strive conscientiously. . . ." This line of argument can succeed in blocking the introduction of a person's autonomous choices and actions (and their results) only by attributing *everything* noteworthy about the person completely to certain sorts of "external" factors. So denigrating a person's autonomy and prime responsibility for his actions is a risky line to take for a theory that otherwise wishes to buttress the dignity and self-respect of autonomous beings; especially for a theory that founds so much (including a theory of the good) upon persons' choices. One doubts that the unexalted picture of human beings Rawls' theory presupposes and rests upon can be made to fit together with the view of human dignity it is designed to lead to and embody.

Before we investigate Rawls' reasons for rejecting the system of natural liberty, we should note the situation of those in the original position. The system of natural liberty is *one* interpretation of a principle that (according to Rawls) they *do* accept: social and economic inequalities are to be arranged so that they both are reasonably expected to be to everyone's advantage, and are attached to positions and offices open to all. It is left unclear whether the persons in the original position explicitly consider and choose among *all* the various interpretations of this principle, though this would seem to be the most reasonable construal. Certainly they explicitly consider one interpretation, the difference principle. Rawls does not state why persons in the original position who considered the system of natural liberty would reject it. Their reason cannot be that it makes the resulting distribution depend upon a *morally* arbitrary distribution of natural assets. What we must suppose, as we have seen before, is that the self-interested calculation of persons in the original position does not (and cannot) lead them to adopt the entitlement principle. We, however, and Rawls, base our evaluations on different considerations.

Rawls has explicitly *designed* the original position and its choice situation so as to embody and realize his negative reflective evaluation of allowing shares in holdings to be affected by natural assets: "Once we decide to look for a conception of justice that nullifies the accidents of natural endowment and the contingencies of social circumstance. . . ." (Rawls makes many scattered references to this theme of nullifying the accidents of natural endowment and the contingencies of social circumstance.) This quest crucially shapes Rawls' theory, and it underlies his delineation of the original position. It is not that persons who *did* deserve their natural endowments would choose differently if placed in Rawls' original position, but rather that, presumably, for such persons, Rawls would not hold that the principles of justice to govern *their* mutual relations were fixed by what they would choose in the original position. It is useful to remember how much of Rawls' construction rests upon this foundation. For example, Rawls argues that certain egalitarian demands are not motivated by envy but rather, because they are in accord with his two principles of justice, by resentment of injustice. This argument can be undercut, as Rawls realizes, if the very considerations which underlie the original position (yielding Rawls' two principles of justice) themselves embody or are based upon envy. So in addition to wanting to understand Rawls' rejection of alternative conceptions and to assess how powerful a criticism he makes of the entitlement conception, reasons internal to his theory provide motivation to explore the basis of the requirement that a conception of justice be geared to nullify differences in social circumstances and in natural assets (and any differences in social circumstances they result in).

Why shouldn't holdings partially depend upon natural endowments? (They will also depend on how these are developed and on the uses to which they are put.) Rawls' reply is that these natural endowments and assets, being undeserved, are "arbitrary from a moral point of view." There are two ways to understand the relevance of this reply: It might be part of an argument to establish that the distributive effects of natural differences ought to be nullified, which I shall call the positive argument; or it might be part of an argument to rebut a possible counterargument holding that the distributive effects of natural differences oughtn't to be nullified, which I shall call the negative argument. Whereas the positive argument attempts to establish that the distributive effects of natural differences ought to be nullified, the negative one, by merely rebutting *one* argument that the differences oughtn't to be nullified, leaves open the possibility that (for other reasons) the differences oughtn't to be nullified. (The negative argument also leaves it possibly a matter of moral *indifference* whether the distributive effects of natural differences are to be nullified; note the difference between saying that something ought to be the case and saying that it's not that it oughtn't to be the case.)

The Positive Argument

We shall begin with the positive argument. How might the point that differences in natural endowments are arbitrary from a moral point of view function in an argument meant to establish that differences in holdings stemming from differences in natural assets ought to be nullified? We shall consider four possible arguments; the first, the following argument A:

1. Any person should morally deserve the holdings he has; it shouldn't be that persons have holdings they don't deserve.
2. People do not morally deserve their natural assets.
3. If a person's X partially determines his Y, and his X is undeserved then so is his Y.

Therefore,

4. People's holdings shouldn't be partially determined by their natural assets.

This argument will serve as a surrogate for other similar, more complicated ones. But Rawls explicitly and emphatically *rejects* distribution according to moral desert.

> There is a tendency for common sense to suppose that income and wealth, and the good things in life generally, should be distributed according to moral desert. Justice is happiness according to virtue. While it is recognized that this ideal can never be fully carried out, it is the appropriate conception [according to common sense] of distributive justice, at least as a *prima facie* principle, and society should try to realize it as circumstances permit. Now justice as fairness rejects this conception. Such a principle would not be chosen in the original position.

Rawls could not, therefore, accept any premiss like the first premiss in argument A, and so no variant of this argument underlies his rejection of differences in distributive shares stemming from undeserved differences in natural assets. Not only does Rawls reject premiss 1, his theory is not coextensive with it. He favors giving incentives to persons if this most improves the lot of the least well off, and it often will be because of their natural assets that these persons will receive incentives and have larger shares. We noted earlier that the entitlement conception of justice in holdings, not being a patterned conception of justice, does not accept distribution in accordance with moral desert either. Any person may give to anyone else any holding he is entitled to, independently of whether the recipient morally deserves to be the recipient. To each according to the legitimate entitlements that legitimately have been transferred to him, is not a patterned principle.

If argument A and its first premiss are rejected, it is not obvious how to construct the positive argument. Consider next argument B:

1. Holdings ought to be distributed according to some pattern that is not arbitrary from a moral point of view.

2. That persons have different natural assets *is* arbitrary from a moral point of view.

Therefore,

3. Holdings ought not to be distributed according to natural assets.

But differences in natural assets might be *correlated* with other differences that are not arbitrary from a moral point of view and that are clearly of some possible moral relevance to distributional questions. For example, Hayek argued that under capitalism distribution generally is in accordance with perceived service to others. Since differences in natural assets will produce differences in ability to serve others, there will be some correlation of differences in distribution with differences in natural assets. The principle of the system is *not* distribution in accordance with natural assets; but differences in natural assets will lead to differences in holdings under a system whose principle is distribution according to perceived service to others. If conclusion 3 above is to be interpreted in extension so as to exclude this, it should be made explicit. But to add the premiss that any pattern that has some roughly coextensive description that is arbitrary from a moral point of view is itself arbitrary from a moral point of view would be far too strong, because it would yield the result that *every* pattern is arbitrary from a moral point of view. Perhaps the crucial thing to be avoided is not mere coextensiveness, but rather some morally arbitrary feature's *giving rise to* differences in distributive shares. Thus consider argument C:

1. Holdings ought to be distributed according to some pattern that is not arbitrary from a moral point of view.
2. That persons have different natural assets is arbitrary from a moral point of view.
3. If part of the explanation of why a pattern contains differences in holdings is that other differences in persons give rise to these differences in holdings, and if these other differences are arbitrary from a moral point of view, then the pattern also is arbitrary from a moral point of view.

Therefore,

4. Differences in natural assets should not give rise to differences in holdings among persons.

Premiss 3 of this argument holds that any moral arbitrariness that underlies a pattern infects the pattern and makes it too morally arbitrary. But any pattern will have some morally arbitrary facts as part of the explanation of how it arises, including the pattern proposed by Rawls. The difference principle operates to give some persons larger distributive shares than others; which persons receive these larger shares will depend, at least partially, on differences between these persons and others, differences that are arbitrary from a moral point of view, for some persons with special natural assets will be offered larger shares as an incentive to use these assets in certain ways. Perhaps some premiss similar to 3 can be formulated so as to exclude what Rawls wishes to exclude while not excluding his *own* view. Still, the resulting argument would *assume* that the set of holdings should realize some pattern.

Why should the set of holdings be patterned? Patterning is *not* intrinsic to a theory of justice, as we have seen in our presentation of the entitlement theory: a theory that focuses upon the underlying principles that generate sets of holdings rather than upon the pattern a set of holdings realizes. If it be denied that the theory of these underlying principles *is* a separate theory of distributive justice, rather than merely a collection of diverse considerations from other areas, then the question becomes one of whether there *is* any separate subject of distributive justice which requires a separate theory.

On the manna-from-heaven model given earlier, there might be a more compelling reason to search for a pattern. But since things come into being already held (or with agreements already made about how they are to be held), there is no need to search for some pattern for unheld holdings to fit; and since the process whereby holdings actually come into

being or are shaped, itself needn't realize any particular pattern, there is no reason to expect any pattern to result. The situation is not an appropriate one for wondering, "After all, what is to become of these things; what are we to do with them." In the non-manna-from-heaven world in which things have to be made or produced or transformed by people, there is no separate process of distribution for a theory of distribution to be a theory of. The reader will recall our earlier argument that (roughly) any set of holdings realizing a particular pattern may be transformed by the voluntary exchanges, gifts, and so forth, of the persons having the holdings under the pattern into *another* set of holdings that does not fit the pattern. The view that holdings *must* be patterned perhaps will seem less plausible when it is seen to have the consequence that people may not choose to do acts that upset the patterning, even with things they legitimately hold.

There is another route to a patterned conception of justice that, perhaps, should be mentioned. Suppose that each morally legitimate fact has a "unified" explanation that shows it is morally legitimate, and that *conjunctions* fall into the domain of facts to be explained as morally legitimate. If *p*, and *q* are each morally legitimate facts, with their respective explanations as morally legitimate being *P*, and *Q*, then if *p* Λ*q* is also to be explained as morally legitimate, and if *P*Λ*Q* does not constitute a "unified" explanation (but is a mere conjunction of different explanations), then some further explanation will be needed. Applying this to holdings, suppose there are separate entitlement explanations showing the legitimacy of my having my holdings, and of your having yours, and the following question is asked: "Why is it legitimate that I hold what I do *and* you hold what you do; why is that joint fact *and all the relations contained within it* legitimate?" If the conjunction of the two separate explanations will not be held to explain in a unified manner the legitimacy of the joint fact (whose legitimacy is not viewed as being constituted by the legitimacy of its constituent parts), then some patterned principles of distribution would appear to be necessary to show its legitimacy, and to legitimate any nonunit set of holdings.

With scientific explanation of particular facts, the usual practice is to consider some conjunctions of explained facts as not requiring separate explanation, but as being explained by the conjunctions of the explanations of the conjuncts. (If E_1 explains e_1 and E_2 explains e_2 then $E_1 \wedge E_2$ explains $e_1 \wedge e_2$.) If we required that any two conjuncts and any n-place conjunction had to be explained in some unified fashion, and not merely by the conjunction of separate and disparate explanations, then we would be driven to reject most of the usual explanations, and to search for an underlying pattern to explain what appear to be separate facts. (Scientists, of course, often do offer a unified explanation of apparently separate facts.) It would be well worth exploring the interesting consequences of refusing to treat, even in the first instance, any two facts as legitimately separable, as having separate explanations whose conjunction is all there is to the explanation of them. What would our theories of the world look like if we required unified explanations of *all* conjunctions? Perhaps an extrapolation of how the world looks to paranoid persons. Or, to put it undisparagingly, the way it appears to persons having certain sorts of dope experiences. (For example, the way it sometimes appears to me after smoking marijuana.) Such a vision of the world differs fundamentally from the way we normally look at it; it is surprising at first that a simple condition on the adequacy of explanations of conjunctions leads to it, until we realize that such a condition of adequacy must lead to a view of the world as deeply and wholly patterned.

A similar condition of adequacy on explanations of the moral legitimacy of conjunctions of separate morally legitimate facts would lead to a view that requires sets of holdings to exhibit an overall patterning. It seems unlikely that there will be compelling arguments for imposing such a principle of adequacy. Some may find such a unified vision plausible for only one realm; for example, in the moral realm concerning sets of holdings, but not in the realm of ordinary nonmoral explanation, or vice versa. For the case of explaining nonmoral facts, the challenge would be to produce such a unified theory. Were one produced that introduced novel considerations and explained no *new* facts (other than conjunctions of old ones) the decision as to its acceptability might be a difficult one and would depend largely on how explanatorily satisfying was the new way we saw the old facts. In the case of moral explanations and accounts which show the moral legitimacy of various facts, the situation is somewhat different. First, there is even less reason (I believe) to suppose a unified explanation appropriate and necessary. There is less need for a *greater* degree of explanatory unity than that provided when the same underlying principles for generating holdings appear in different explanations. (Rawls' theory, which contains elements of what he calls pure procedural justice, does not satisfy a strong condition of adequacy for explaining conjunctions and entails that such a condition cannot be satisfied.) Secondly, there is more danger than in the scientific case that the demand for a unified explanation will shape the "moral facts" to be explained. ("It can't be that both of those *are* facts for there's no unified patterned explanation that would yield them both.") Hence success in finding a unified explanation of such seriously primed facts will leave it unclear how well supported the explanatory theory is.

I turn now to our final positive argument which purports to derive the conclusion that distributive shares shouldn't depend upon natural assets from the statement that the distribution of natural assets is morally arbitrary. This argument focuses on the notion of equality. Since a large part of Rawls' argument serves to justify or show acceptable a particular deviation from equal shares (some may have more if this serves to improve the position of those worst off), perhaps a reconstruction of his underlying argument that places equality at its center will be illuminating. Differences between persons (the argument runs) are arbitrary from a moral point of view if there is no moral argument for the conclusion that there ought to be the differences. Not all such differences will be morally objectionable. That there is no such moral argument will seem important only in the case of those differences we believe oughtn't to obtain unless there is a moral reason establishing that they ought to obtain. There is, so to speak, a presumption against certain differences that can be overridden (can it merely be neutralized?) by moral reasons; in the absence of any such moral reasons of sufficient weight, there ought to be equality. Thus we have argument D:

1. Holdings ought to be equal, unless there is a (weighty) moral reason why they ought to be unequal.
2. People do not deserve the ways in which they differ from other persons in natural assets; there is no moral reason why people ought to differ in natural assets.
3. If there is no moral reason why people differ in certain traits, then their actually differing in these traits does not provide, and cannot give rise to, a moral reason why they should differ in other traits (for example, in holdings).

Therefore,

4. People's differing in natural assets is not a reason why holdings ought to be unequal.
5. People's holdings ought to be equal unless there is some other moral reason (such as, for example, raising the position of those worst off) why their holdings ought to be unequal.

Statements similar to the third premiss will occupy us shortly. Here let us focus on the first premiss, the equality premiss. Why ought people's holdings to be equal, in the absence of special moral reason to deviate from equality? (Why think there *ought* to be *any* particular pattern in holdings?) Why is equality the rest (or rectilinear motion) position of the system, deviation from which may be caused only by moral forces? Many "arguments" for equality merely *assert* that differences between persons are arbitrary and must be jus-

tified. Often writers state a presumption in favor of equality in a form such as the following: "Differences in treatment of persons need to be justified." The most favored situation for this sort of assumption is one in which there is one person (or group) treating everyone, a person (or group) having *no* right or entitlement to bestow the particular treatment as they wish or even whim. But if I go to one movie theater rather than to another adjacent to it, need I justify my different treatment of the two theater owners? Isn't it enough that I felt like going to one of them? That differences in treatment need to be justified *does* fit contemporary *governments*. Here there is a centralized process treating all, with no entitlement to bestow treatment according to whim. The major portion of distribution in a free society does not, however, come through the actions of the government, nor does failure to overturn the results of the localized individual exchanges constitute "state action." When there is no *one* doing the treating, and all are entitled to bestow their holdings as they wish, it is not clear why the maxim that differences in treatment must be justified should be thought to have extensive application. Why must differences between persons be justified? Why think that we must change, or remedy, or compensate for any inequality which can be changed, remedied, or compensated for? Perhaps here is where social cooperation enters in: though there is no presumption of equality (in, say, primary goods, or things people care about) among all persons, perhaps there is one among persons cooperating together. But it is difficult to see an argument for this; surely not all persons who cooperate together explicitly agree to this presumption as one of the terms of their mutual cooperation. And its acceptance would provide an unfortunate incentive for well-off persons to refuse to cooperate with, or to allow any of their number to cooperate with, some distant people who are less well off than any among them. For entering into such social cooperation, beneficial to those less well off, would seriously worsen the position of the well-off group by creating relations of presumptive equality between themselves and the worse-off group. . . . Here we need only note that the connection argument D forges between not deserving natural assets and some conclusion about distributive shares *assumes* equality as a norm (that can be deviated from with, and only with, moral reason); and hence argument D itself cannot be used to establish any such conclusion about equality.

The Negative Argument

Unsuccessful in our quest for a convincing positive argument to connect the claim that people don't deserve their natural assets with the conclusion that differences in holdings ought not to be based upon differences in natural assets, we now turn to what we called the negative argument: the use of the claim that people don't deserve their natural assets to rebut a possible counterargument to Rawls' view. (If the equality argument D were acceptable, the negative task of rebutting possible counterconsiderations would form part of the positive task of showing that a presumption for equality holds unoverridden in a particular case.) Consider the following possible counterargument E to Rawls:

1. People deserve their natural assets.
2. If people deserve X, they deserve any Y that flows from X.
3. People's holdings flow from their natural assets.

Therefore,

4. People deserve their holdings.
5. If people deserve something, then they ought to have it (and this overrides any presumption of equality there may be about that thing).

Rawls would rebut this counterargument to his position by denying its first premiss. And so we see *some* connection between the claim that the distribution of natural assets is arbitrary and the statement that distributive shares should not depend upon natural assets. However, no great weight can be placed upon *this*

connection. For there are other counterarguments, in a similar vein; for example the argument F that begins:

1. If people have X, and their having X (whether or not they deserve to have it) does *not* violate anyone else's (Lockean) right or entitlement to X, and Y flows from (arises out of, and so on) X by a process that does not itself violate anyone's (Lockean) rights or entitlements,[1] then the person is entitled to Y.
2. People's having the natural assets they do does not violate anyone else's (Lockean) entitlements or rights.

and goes on to argue that people are entitled to what they make, to the products of their labor, to what others give them or exchange. It is not true, for example, that a person earns Y (a right to keep a painting he's made, praise for writing *A Theory of Justice*, and so on) only if he's earned (or otherwise *deserves*) whatever he used (including natural assets) in the process of earning Y. Some of the things he uses he just may *have*, not illegitimately. It needn't be that the foundations underlying desert are themselves deserved, *all the way down*.

At the very least, we can parallel these statements about desert with ones about entitlements. And if, correctly, we describe people as entitled to their natural assets even if it's not the case that they can be said to deserve them, then the argument parallel to E above, with "are entitled to" replacing "deserve" throughout, *will go* through. This gives us the acceptable argument G:

1. People are entitled to their natural assets.
2. If people are entitled to something, they are entitled to whatever flows from it (via specified types of processes).
3. People's holdings flow from their natural assets.

Therefore,

4. People are entitled to their holdings.
5. If people are entitled to something, then they ought to have it (and this overrides any pre-

sumption of equality there may be about holdings).

Whether or not people's natural assets are arbitrary from a moral point of view, they are entitled to them, and to what flows from them.[2]

A recognition of people's entitlements to their natural assets (the first premiss of argument G) might be necessary to avoid the stringent application of the difference principle which would lead, we already have seen, to even stronger property rights in other persons than redistributive theories usually yield. Rawls feels that he avoids this because people in his original position rank the principle of liberty as lexicographically prior to the difference principle, applied not only to economic well-being but to health, length of life, and so on. . . .

We have found no cogent argument to (help) establish that differences in holdings arising from differences in natural assets should be eliminated or minimized. Can the theme that people's natural assets are arbitrary from a moral point of view be used differently, for example, to justify a certain *shaping* of the original position? Clearly if the shaping is designed to nullify differences in holdings due to differences in natural assets, we need an argument for this goal, and we are back to our unsuccessful quest for the route to the conclusion that such differences in holdings ought to be nullified. Instead, the shaping might take place by excluding the participants in the original position from knowing of their own natural endowments. In this way the fact that natural endowments are arbitrary from a moral point of view would help to impose and to justify the veil of ignorance. But how does it do this; why should knowledge of natural endowments be excluded from the original position? Presumably the underlying principle would be that if any particular features are arbitrary from a moral point of view, then persons in the original position should not know they possess them. But this would exclude their knowing *anything* about themselves, for each of their features (including rationality, the ability to

make choices, having a life span of more than three days, having a memory, being able to communicate with other organisms like themselves) will be based upon the fact that the sperm and ovum which produced them contained particular genetic material. The physical fact that those particular gametes contained particular organized chemicals (the genes for people rather than for muskrats or trees) is arbitrary *from a moral point of view;* it is, from a moral point of view, an accident. Yet the persons in the original position are to know some of their attributes.

Perhaps we are too quick when we suggest excluding knowledge of rationality, and so forth, merely because these features *arise from* morally arbitrary facts. For these features also have moral significance; that is, moral facts depend upon or arise from them. Here we see an ambiguity in saying that a fact is arbitrary from a moral point of view. It might mean that there is no moral reason why the fact ought to be that way, or it might mean that the fact's being that way is of no moral significance and has no moral consequences. Rationality, the ability to make choices, and so on, are not morally arbitrary in this second sense. But if they escape exclusion on this ground, now the problem is that the natural assets, knowledge of which Rawls wishes to exclude from the original position, are not morally arbitrary in this sense either. At any rate, the entitlement theory's claim that moral entitlements may arise from or be partially based upon such facts is what is now at issue. Thus, in the absence of an argument to the effect that differences in holdings due to differences in natural assets ought to be nullified, it is not clear how anything about the original position can be based upon the (ambiguous) claim that differences in natural assets are arbitrary from a moral point of view.

Collective Assets

Rawls' view seems to be that everyone has some entitlement or claim on the totality of natural assets (viewed as a pool), with no one having differential claims. The distribution of natural abilities is viewed as a "collective asset."

> We see then that the difference principle represents, in effect, an agreement to regard the distribution of natural talents as a common asset and to share in the benefits of this distribution whatever it turns out to be. Those who have been favored by nature, whoever they are, may gain from their good fortune only on terms that improve the situation of those who have lost out. . . . No one deserves his greater natural capacity nor merits a more favorable starting place in society. But it does not follow that one should eliminate these distinctions. There is another way to deal with them. The basic structure can be arranged so that these contingencies work for the good of the least fortunate.

People will differ in how they view regarding natural talents as a common asset. Some will complain, echoing Rawls against utilitarianism, that this "does not take seriously the distinction between persons"; and they will wonder whether any reconstruction of Kant that treats people's abilities and talents as resources for others can be adequate. "The two principles of justice . . . rule out even the tendency to regard men as means to one another's welfare." Only if one presses very hard on the distinction between men and their talents, assets, abilities, and special traits. Whether any coherent conception of a person remains when the distinction is so pressed is an open question. Why we, thick with particular traits, should be cheered that (only) the thus purified men within us are not regarded as means is also unclear.

People's talents and abilities *are* an asset to a free community; others in the community benefit from their presence and are better off because they are there rather than elsewhere or nowhere. (Otherwise they wouldn't choose to deal with them.) Life, over time, is not a constant-sum game, wherein if greater ability or effort leads to some getting more, that means that others must lose. In a free society, people's talents do benefit others, and not only themselves. Is it the extraction of even more benefit to others that is supposed to justify treating people's natural assets as a collective resource? What justifies this extraction?

> No one deserves his greater natural capacity nor merits a more favorable starting place in society. But it does not follow that one should eliminate these distinctions. There is another way to deal with them. The basic structure can be arranged so that these contingencies work for the good of the least fortunate.

And if there weren't "another way to deal with them"? Would it then follow that one should eliminate these distinctions? What exactly would be contemplated in the case of natural assets? If people's assets and talents *couldn't* be harnessed to serve others, would something be done to remove these exceptional assets and talents, or to forbid them from being exercised for the person's own benefit or that of someone else he chose, even though this limitation wouldn't improve the absolute position of those somehow unable to harness the talents and abilities of others for their own benefit? Is it so implausible to claim that envy underlies this conception of justice, forming part of its root notion?[3]

We have used our entitlement conception of justice in holdings to probe Rawls' theory, sharpening our understanding of what the entitlement conception involves by bringing it to bear upon an alternative conception of distributive justice, one that is deep and elegant. Also, I believe, we have probed deep-lying inadequacies in Rawls' theory. I am mindful of Rawls' reiterated point that a theory cannot be evaluated by focusing upon a single feature or part of it; instead the whole theory must be assessed (the reader will not know how whole a theory can be until he has read all of Rawls' book), and a perfect theory is not to be expected. However we have examined an important part of Rawls' theory, and its crucial underlying assumptions. I am as well aware as anyone of how sketchy my discussion of the entitlement conception of justice in holdings has been. But I no more believe we need to have formulated a complete alternative theory in order to reject Rawls' undeniably great advance over utilitarianism, than Rawls needed a complete alternative theory before he could reject utilitarianism. What more does one need or can one have, in order to begin progressing toward a better theory, than a sketch of a plausible alternative view, which from its very different perspective highlights the inadequacies of the best existing well-worked-out theory? Here, as in so many things, we learn from Rawls.

We begin this chapter's investigation of distributive justice in order to consider the claim that a state more extensive than the minimal state could be justified on the grounds that it was necessary, or the most appropriate instrument, to achieve distributive justice. According to the entitlement conception of justice in holdings that we have presented, there is no argument based upon the first two principles of distributive justice, the principles of acquisition and of transfer, for such a more extensive state. If the set of holdings is properly generated, there is no argument for a more extensive state based upon distributive justice. (Nor, we have claimed, will the Lockean proviso actually provide occasion for a more extensive state.) If, however, these principles are violated, the principle of rectification comes into play. Perhaps it is best to view some patterned principles of distributive justice as rough rules of thumb meant to approximate the general results of applying the principle of rectification of injustice. For example, lacking much historical information, and assuming (i) that victims of injustice generally do worse than they otherwise would and (2) that those from the least well-off group in the society have the highest probabilities of being the (descendants of) victims of the most serious injustice who are owed compensation by those who benefited from the injustices (assumed to be those better off, though sometimes the perpetrators will be others in the worst-off group), then a *rough* rule of thumb for rectifying injustices might seem to be the following: organize society so as to maximize the position of whatever group ends up least well-off in the society. This particular example may well be implausible, but an important question for each society will be the following: given *its* particular history, what operable rule of thumb best approximates the results of a detailed application in that society of the principle of rectification? These issues are very complex and are best left to a full treatment of the principle of rectification. In the absence of such a treatment applied to a particular society, one *cannot* use the analysis and theory presented here to condemn any particular scheme of transfer payments, unless it is clear that no considerations of rectification of injustice could apply to justify it. Although to introduce socialism as the punishment for our sins would be to go too far, past injustices might be so great as to make necessary in the short run a more extensive state in order to rectify them.

NOTES

1. A process, we might strengthen the antecedent by adding, of the sort that would create an entitlement to *Y* if the person were entitled to *X*. I use "Lockean" rights and entitlements to refer to those (discussed in Part I) against force, fraud, and so on, which are to be recognized in the minimal state. Since I believe these are the only rights and entitlements people possess (apart from those they specially acquire), I needn't have included the specification to Lockean rights. One who believes some have a right to the fruits of others' labor will deny the truth of the first premise as stated. If the Lockean specification were not included, he might grant the truth of 1, while denying that of 2 or of later steps.

2. If nothing of moral significance could flow from what was arbitrary, then no particular person's existence could be of moral significance, since which of the many sperm cells succeeds in fertilizing the egg cell is (so far as we know) arbitrary from a moral point of view. This suggests another, more vague, remark directed to the spirit of Rawls' position rather than to its letter. Each existing person is the product of a process wherein the one sperm cell which succeeds is no more deserving than the millions that fail. Should we wish that process had been "fairer" as judged by Rawls' standards, that all "inequities" in it had been rectified? We should be apprehensive about any principle that would condemn morally the very sort of process that

brought us to be, a principle that therefore would undercut the legitimacy of our very existing.

3. Will the lexicographic priority that Rawls claims for liberty in the original position prevent the difference principle from requiring a head tax on assets and abilities? The legitimacy of a head tax is *suggested* by Rawls' speaking of "collective assets" and "common assets." Those underutilizing their assets and abilities are misusing a public asset. (Squandering public property?) Rawls may intend no such strong inferences from his terminology, but we need to hear more about why those in the original position wouldn't accept the strong interpretation. The notion of liberty needs elaboration which is to exclude a head tax and yet allow the other taxation schemes. Assets and abilities can be harnessed without a head tax; and "harnessing" is an appropriate term—as it would be for a horse harnessed to a wagon which doesn't *have* to move ever, but if it does, it must draw the wagon along.

With regard to envy, the difference principle, applied to the choice between either *A* having ten and *B* having five or A having eight and B having five, would favor the latter. Thus, despite Rawls' view, the difference principle is inefficient in that it sometimes will favor a status quo against a Pareto-better but more unequal distribution. The inefficiency could be removed by shifting from the simple difference principle to a staggered difference principle, which recommends the maximization of the position of the least well-off group, and *subject to that constraint* the maximization of the position of the next least well-off group, and this point also is made by A. K. Sen (*Collective Choice and Social Welfare*, p. 138, note) and is acknowledged by Rawls. But such a staggered principle does not embody a presumption in favor of equality of the sort used by Rawls. How then could Rawls justify an inequality *special* to the staggered principle to someone in the least well-off group? Perhaps these issues underlie the unclarity as to whether Rawls accepts the staggered principle.

20. Liberalism and the Limits of Justice

MICHAEL SANDEL

Michael Sandel is Professor of Government at Harvard University. He is the author of *Liberalism and the Limits of Justice* (1982) and *Democracy's Discontents* (1996).

In this influential critique, Sandel argues that Rawls's anti-desert position requires a (perhaps implausible) conception of the self according to which it has no essential attributes and no intrinsic value. Sandel also argues that Rawls allows for the preinstitutionality of moral desert in retributive justice (criminal punishment), but not in distributive justice. It is not clear (to Sandel) how Rawls's conception of the self is consistent with this.

The Basis of Desert

The notion of possession leads naturally to claims of desert and entitlement. The argument over what people possess, and on what terms, has a direct bearing on the question of what people deserve or are entitled to as a matter of justice. It is to the issues of desert and entitlement that we now turn, to consider the second strand of Nozick's critique of justice as fairness. Rawls rejects the principles of natural liberty and liberal equality on the grounds that they reward assets and attributes which, being arbitrary from a moral point of view, people cannot properly be said to deserve, and adopts the difference principle on the grounds that it nullifies this arbitrariness. Nozick attacks this line of reasoning by arguing first that arbitrariness does not undermine desert, and second that, even if it did, a version of natural liberty and not the difference principle would emerge as the preferred result.

Stated in terms of possession, Rawls' objection to natural liberty and liberal equality is that under these principles, persons are allowed unfairly to benefit (or suffer) from natural and social endowments that do not properly *belong* to them, at least not in the strong, constitutive sense of belonging. To be sure, the various natural assets with which I am born may be said to 'belong' to me in the weak, contingent sense that they reside accidentally within me; but this sense of ownership or possession cannot establish that I have any special rights with respect to these assets or any privileged claim to the fruits of their exercise. In this attenuated sense of possession, I am not really the owner but merely the guardian or repository of the assorted assets and attributes located 'here'. By failing to acknowledge the arbitrariness of fortune, the principles of natural liberty and liberal equality go wrong in assuming that 'my' assets belong to me in the strong, constitutive sense,

Reprinted from *Liberalism and the Limits of Justice* (Cambridge: Cambridge University Press, 1982), by permission.

and so allowing distributive shares to depend on them.

Expressed in terms of desert, Rawls' objection to the principles of natural liberty and liberal equality is that they reward assets and attributes that people cannot properly be said to deserve. Though some may think the fortunate deserve the things that lead to their greater advantage, 'this view is surely incorrect'.

> It seems to be one of the fixed points of our considered judgments that no one deserves his place in the distribution of native endowments, any more than one deserves one's initial starting place in society. The assertion that a man deserves the superior character that enables him to make the effort to cultivate his abilities is equally problematic; for his character depends in large part upon fortunate family and social circumstances for which he can claim no credit. The notion of desert seems not to apply to these cases.

Because no one deserves his good luck in the genetic lottery, or his favored starting place in society, or for that matter the superior character that motivates him to cultivate his abilities conscientiously, no one can be said to deserve the benefits these assets produce. It is this deduction that Nozick disputes. 'It is not true,' he argues, 'that a person earns Y (a right to keep a painting he's made, praise for writing *A Theory of Justice*, and so on) only if he's earned (or otherwise *deserves*) whatever he used (including natural assets) in the process of earning Y. Some of the things he uses he just may *have*, not illegitimately. It needn't be that the foundations underlying desert are themselves deserved, *all the way down*'.

Now what are we to make of this claim? If I do not necessarily have to *deserve* everything I use in producing a thing in order to deserve the thing, what *does* my desert depend on? Nozick says that some of the things I use I 'just may *have*, not illegitimately' (and, presumably, possibly arbitrarily). Once again, the notion of possession enters the scene. To

see whether my having a thing, not illegitimately, can enable me to deserve what it helps me produce, we must explore in greater detail the relation between possession and desert, and sort out once more the sense of possession being appealed to.

For this purpose, it may be helpful to consider a recent discussion of justice and personal desert by Joel Feinberg, who analyzes the bases of desert with an admirable clarity in terms suggestive for the arguments before us. Feinberg begins with the observation that no one can deserve anything unless there is some basis for the desert. 'Desert without a basis is simply not desert'. But the question immediately arises what *kind* of basis is necessary. As Feinberg writes, 'Not any old basis will do'. Once again, the notion of possession provides the key. 'If a person is deserving of some sort of treatment, he must, necessarily, be so in virtue of some *possessed characteristic* or prior activity' [emphasis added].

> A characteristic of mine cannot be a basis for a desert of yours unless it somehow reveals or reflects some characteristic of yours. In general, the facts which constitute the basis of a subject's desert must be facts about that subject. If a student deserves a high grade in a course, for example, his desert must be in virtue of some fact about *him*—his earlier performances, say, or his present abilities. . . . It is necessary that a person's desert have a basis and that the basis consist in some fact about himself.

Feinberg's analysis, tying a person's desert to some fact about the person, would appear to support Nozick's claim that 'the foundations underlying desert needn't themselves be deserved, *all the way down*'. In fact, the reliance of desert on some possessed characteristic of the person suggests a thesis even stronger than Nozick's: that the foundations underlying desert *cannot* themselves be deserved, *all the way down*, any more than the foundations underlying possession can themselves be possessed, *all the way down*. We have already seen how the notion of possession requires that somewhere, 'down there', there must be a subject of possession that is not *itself* possessed (for this would deny its agency), a subject 'doing the possessing', so to speak. The analogy for desert must be a *basis* of desert ultimately prior to desert. For consider: if desert presupposes some possessed characteristic, and if possessed characteristics presuppose some subject of possession which is not itself possessed, then desert must presuppose some subject of possession which is not itself possessed, and therefore some basis of desert which is not itself deserved. Just as there must be some subject of possession prior to possession, so there must be some basis of desert prior to desert. This is why the question whether someone deserves (to have) his sterling character, for example, is notoriously difficult (for it is unclear who or what is left to judge once his character has been removed), and why, beyond a certain point, asking just wholesale whether someone deserves to be the (kind of) person he is becomes incoherent altogether. Somewhere, 'down there', there must be a basis of desert that is not itself deserved. The foundations underlying desert cannot themselves be deserved, all the way down.

This result would seem amply to confirm Nozick's claim against Rawls that I do not necessarily have to *deserve* everything I use in producing a thing in order to deserve the thing, that some of what I use I 'just may *have*, not illegitimately'. And if this claim can be established, then it would appear that Rawls' argument from arbitrariness fails to undermine desert after all. To say, as Rawls does, that I do not deserve the superior character that led me to realize my abilities is no longer enough. To deny my desert, he must show that I do not *have* the requisite character, or alternatively, that I *have it*, but not in the requisite sense.

But this is precisely the argument Rawls' theory of the person allows him to make. For given his sharp distinction between the self, taken as the pure subject of possession, and the aims and attributes it possesses, the self is left bare of any substantive feature or charac-

teristic that could qualify as a desert base. Given the distancing aspect of possession, the self *itself* is dispossessed. On Rawls' theory of the person, the self, strictly speaking, *has nothing*, nothing at least in the strong, constitutive sense necessary to desert. In a move similar to the one invoked to show that the difference principle does not use a *person* as a means, only a person's *attributes*, Rawls can accept that some undeserved desert base is necessary to desert, only to claim that, on an adequate understanding of the person, this condition could never in principle be met! On Rawls' conception, the characteristics I possess do not *attach* to the self but are only *related* to the self, standing always at a certain distance. This is what makes them attributes rather than constituents of my person; they are *mine* rather than *me*, things I *have* rather than *am*.

We can see in this light how Rawls' argument from arbitrariness undermines desert not directly, by claiming I cannot *deserve* what is arbitrarily given, but indirectly, by showing I cannot *possess* what is arbitrarily given, that is, that 'I', *qua* subject of possession, cannot possess it in the undistanced, constitutive sense necessary to provide a desert base. An arbitrarily-given asset cannot be an essential constituent but only an accidental attribute of my person, for otherwise my identity would hang on a mere contingency, its continuity constantly vulnerable to transformation by experience, my status as a sovereign agent dependent on the conditions of my existence rather than epistemologically guaranteed. On Rawls' conception, no one can properly be said to deserve anything because no one can properly be said to possess anything, at least not in the strong, constitutive sense of possession necessary to the notion of desert.

A theory of justice without desert would seem a dramatic departure from traditional conceptions, but Rawls is at pains to show that it is not. In his opening pages, Rawls acknowledges that his approach 'may not seem to tally with tradition', but seeks to reassure that in fact it does.

The more specific sense that Aristotle gives to justice, and from which the most familiar formulations derive, is that of refraining from *pleonexia*, that is, from gaining some advantage for oneself by seizing *what belongs to another*, his property, his reward, his office, and the like, or by denying a person that which is due to him. . . . *Aristotle's definition clearly presupposes, however, an account of what properly belongs to a person, and of what is due to him. Now such entitlements are, I believe, very often derived from social institutions and the legitimate expectations to which they give rise.* There is no reason to think that Aristotle would disagree with this, and certainly he has a conception of social justice to account for these claims. . . . There is no conflict with the traditional notion [emphasis added].

In comparing justice as fairness with traditional conceptions, Rawls confirms its novelty rather than denies it. What he presents as an incidental qualification to justice as classically conceived turns out on inspection to signal a striking departure. As Rawls suggests, traditional notions freely refer to 'what properly belongs to a person', institutions, presumably, aside; they presuppose thickly-constituted persons with a fixity of character, certain features of which are taken to be essential, 'all the way down'. On Rawls' conception, however, none of these concepts is available. In so far as a theory of justice 'presupposes an account of what properly belongs to a person' (in the strong sense of 'belongs'), Rawls effectively acknowledges that he has none. Nor, he seems to imply, given the precedence of plurality, the priority of right, and the theory of the person they require, is it reasonable to think that such a theory of justice could be true. We are not essentially thick enough selves to bear rights and deserts antecedent to the institutions that define them. Given these constraints, the only alternative is to opt for a theory of justice based on entitlements to legitimate expectations, ruling out desert altogether. Rawls hedges this claim at first, saying only that 'such entitlements are, I believe, *very*

often derived from social institutions and the legitimate expectations to which they give rise' [emphasis added]. But as the full consequences of Rawls' view emerge, 'very often' becomes 'always', for it becomes clear that 'such entitlements' can arise in no other way. While Aristotle might not disagree that entitlements can arise in this way, it seems far from his view that they can arise in no other way. In denying that justice has to do with giving people what they deserve, justice as fairness departs decisively from the traditional notion after all.

Rawls' apparent view that no one can properly be said to deserve anything, and the connection of this view with the notion of the self as 'essentially unencumbered', emerges more fully in his discussion of legitimate expectations and moral desert. He begins by acknowledging that justice as fairness, in rejecting desert, runs counter to common sense.

> There is a tendency for common sense to suppose that income and wealth, and the good things in life generally, should be distributed according to moral desert. Justice is happiness according to virtue. While it is recognized that this ideal can never be fully carried out, it is the appropriate conception of distributive justice, at least as a prima facie principle, and society should try to realize it as circumstances permit. Now justice as fairness rejects this conception. Such a principle would not be chosen in the original position. There seems to be no way of defining the requisite criterion in that situation.

There seems to be no way of defining the requisite criterion of a person's virtue or moral worth in the original position because no substantive theory of the person antecedent to social institutions exists. For moral desert to provide an independent criterion of justice, there must be some substantive theory of the person, or of the worth of persons, to get it going. But for Rawls, the worth of persons is subsequent to institutions, not independent of them. And so a person's moral claims must await their arrival.

This leads to the distinction between moral desert and legitimate expectations. Once a person does the various things established institutions encourage him to do, he acquires certain rights, but not before. He is entitled that institutions honor the claims they announce they will reward, but he is not entitled that they undertake to reward any particular kind of claim in the first place.

> A just scheme, then, answers to what men are entitled to; it satisfies their legitimate expectations as founded upon social institutions. But what they are entitled to is not proportional to nor dependent upon their intrinsic worth. The principles of justice that regulate the basic structure and specify the duties and obligations of individuals do not mention moral desert, and there is no tendency for distributive shares to correspond to it.

The principles of justice do not mention moral desert because, strictly speaking, no one can be said to deserve anything. Similarly, the reason people's entitlements are not proportional to nor dependent upon their intrinsic worth is that, on Rawls' view, *people have no intrinsic worth*, no worth that is intrinsic in the sense that it is theirs prior to or independent of or apart from what just institutions attribute to them.

> The essential point is that the concept of moral worth does not provide a first principle of distributive justice. This is because it cannot be introduced until after the principles of justice and of natural duty and obligations have been acknowledged. . . . [T]he concept of moral worth is secondary to those of right and justice, and it plays no role in the substantive definition of distributive shares.

Rawls could agree with Feinberg that 'desert is a *moral* concept in the sense that it is logically prior to and independent of public institutions and their rules', but would deny that there is any 'antecedent standard for its definition', and so disagree with Feinberg that 'one of the aims of [a system of public bestowals] is to give people what they deserve'. For Rawls, the principles of justice aim neither at rewarding virtue nor at giving people what they deserve, but instead at calling forth the resources and talents necessary to serve the common interest.

> None of the precepts of justice aims at rewarding virtue. The premiums earned by scarce natural talents, for example, are to cover the costs of training and to encourage the efforts of learning, as well as to direct ability to where it best furthers the common interest. The distributive shares that result do not correlate with moral worth.

To illustrate the priority of just institutions with respect to virtue and moral worth, Rawls suggests an analogy to the relation between the rules of property and the law of robbery and theft.

> These offenses and the demerits they entail presuppose the institution of property which is established for prior and independent social ends. For a society to organize itself with the aim of rewarding moral desert as a first principle would be like having the institution of property in order to punish thieves. The criterion to each according to his virtue would not, then, be chosen in the original position.

The analogy is intriguing, but one wonders whether it works entirely to Rawls' advantage. While it is apparent that the institution of property has a *certain* priority with respect to its correlative offenses, it is less clear why the dependence must run only in one direction, especially given Rawls' own commitment to the method of reflective equilibrium. For example, is our belief in the validity of the institution of property in no way enhanced by a conviction that robbery and theft are wrong? Would our confidence in the institution of property in no way be diminished if it turned out that those it defined as robbers and thieves were invariably good and virtuous men? And what of more extreme cases? While the norms and rules protecting human life can no doubt be defended on a variety of grounds, such as keeping people alive, avoiding suffering, and so on, is it logically mistaken to think that one justification of prohibitions against murder could be to punish murderers?

Rawls' position here appears especially perplexing in the light of a contrast he draws between distributive justice and retributive justice, suggesting that in the second case, some notion of moral desert may be appropriate after all. The view that distributive shares should match moral worth to the extent possible, writes Rawls, 'may arise from thinking of distributive justice as somehow the opposite of retributive justice'. But the analogy is mistaken. In a reasonably well-ordered society, 'Those who are punished for violating just laws have normally done something wrong. This is because the purpose of the criminal law is to uphold basic natural duties . . . and punishments are to serve this end'.

> They are not simply a scheme of taxes and burdens designed to put a price on certain forms of conduct and in this way to guide men's conduct for mutual advantage. It would be far better if the acts prescribed by penal statutes were never done. *Thus a propensity to commit such acts is a mark of bad character*, and in a just society legal punishments will only fall upon those who display these faults.

> It is clear that the distribution of economic and social advantages is entirely different. These arrangements are not the converse, so to speak, of the criminal law so that just as the one punishes certain offenses, the other rewards moral worth. The function of unequal distributive shares is to cover the costs of training and education, to attract individuals to places and associations where they are most needed from a social point of view, and so on. . . . *To think of distributive and retributive justice as converses of one another is completely misleading and suggests a moral basis of distributive shares where none exists* [emphasis added].

Unlike the benefits that flow from distributive arrangements, the punishments and prohibitions associated with the criminal law are not simply a non-moral system of incentives and deterrents designed to encourage some forms of behavior and discourage others. For Rawls, the pre-institutional moral notions excluded in distributive justice somehow find meaning for retributive purposes, and there is a tendency for punishment to correspond to them.

The immediate puzzle is how this account can possibly fit with the analogy of property and theft. If retributive justice differs from distributive justice precisely in virtue of its prior moral basis, it is difficult to see how the example of property and theft could demonstrate the priority of social institutions with respect to virtue and moral worth, if this priority holds for distributive justice alone. This relatively minor confusion aside, the more basic question is how Rawls can admit desert in retributive justice without contradicting the theory of the self and related assumptions that ruled it out for purposes of distributive justice. If such notions as pre-institutional moral claims and intrinsic moral worth are excluded from a theory of distributive justice in virtue of an essentially unencumbered self too slender to support them, it is difficult to see how retributive justice could differ in any relevant way.[1]

Do not the same arguments from arbitrariness exclude desert as a basis for punishment as for distributive shares? Is the propensity to commit crimes, any less than the propensity to do good, the result of factors arbitrary from a moral point of view? And if not, why would the parties to the original position not agree to share one another's fate for the purpose of criminal liability as well as distributive arrangements? Since under the veil of ignorance, none can know whether he shall have the misfortune to be born into the unfavorable social and family circumstances that lead to a life of crime, why would the parties not adopt a kind of difference principle for punishments as well as distributive shares, and agree, in effect, to regard the distribution of natural and social liabilities as a common burden?

Rawls holds that 'those who are punished for violating just laws have normally done something wrong', and so deserve their punishment. But suppose, by an act of vandalism, I deprive the community of a certain measure of well-being, say by throwing a brick through a window. Is there any reason why I deserve to bear the full costs of my destructiveness any more than the person who produced the window *deserves* to enjoy the full benefits of his productiveness? Rawls may reply that my 'propensity to commit such acts is a mark of bad character'. But if the worker's industriousness in making the window is not a mark of good character (in the moral, pre-institutional sense), why is my maliciousness in breaking the window a mark of bad character (in the moral, pre-institutional sense)? To be sure (following Rawls), given a just system of criminal law, those who have done what the system announces it will punish are properly dealt with accordingly and in this sense are 'deserving' of their penalty. 'But this sense of desert presupposes the existence of the [retributive] scheme; it is irrelevant to the question whether in the first place the scheme is to be designed in accordance with the difference principle or some other criterion'.

Some may think that the criminal deserves his punishment in the strong moral sense because he deserves the low character his criminality reflects. Perhaps this is what Rawls has in mind when he writes that 'propensity to commit such acts is a mark of bad character', and punishments properly fall on those who display these faults. Because the transgressor is less worthy in this sense, he deserves the misfortune that befalls him. But again (following Rawls), this view is surely incorrect. It seems to be one of the fixed points of our considered judgments that no one deserves his place in the distribution of native endowments or liabilities, any more than one deserves one's initial starting place in society. The assertion that a man deserves the inferior character that prevents him from overcoming his liabilities is equally problematic;

for his character depends in large part upon unfortunate family and social circumstances for which he cannot be blamed. The notion of desert seems not to apply to these cases. None of which is to say that, generally speaking, a non-moral theory of distributive justice is incompatible with a moral, or desert-based theory of punishment, only that given Rawls' reasons for rejecting desert-based distributive arrangements, he seems clearly committed to rejecting desert-based retributive ones as well.

The apparent inconsistency between Rawls' retributive and distributive theories need not do serious damage to the theory as a whole. Given the method of reflective equilibrium, 'justification is a matter of the mutual support of many considerations, of everything fitting together into one coherent view'. From the standpoint of the overall theory, little hangs on Rawls' retributive theory, apart from the measure of plausibility it lends justice as fairness for those committed to a strong, desert-based notion of punishment. If Rawls' distinction succeeds, they need not choose between their retributive intuitions and the difference principle; if it does not, one or the other of those convictions must give way. If, on reflection, a non-moral theory of punishment appears unacceptable, even in the light of the arbitrariness of criminal characteristics and dispositions, then the difference principle—rejecting as it does the notion of desert—would be called into serious question. If, on the other hand, our intuition that criminals deserve punishment proves no more indispensable than our intuition that virtue deserves reward (an intuition of common sense Rawls explicitly rejects), then we may adjust our intuitions in a direction that affirms the difference principle rather than opposes it. Desert would be rejected as the basis for both distributive and retributive arrangements, and so the inconsistency resolved.

But such a resolution returns us to the larger difficulties of a theory of justice without desert and a notion of the self as essentially dispossessed, or barren of constituent traits. Nozick argues against Rawls that the foundations underlying desert need not themselves be deserved, all the way down. But as we have seen, Rawls' denial of desert does not depend on the thesis Nozick refutes, but instead on the notion of the self as a pure, unadulterated, 'essentially unencumbered' subject of possession. Rawls is not committed to the view that a person can only deserve a thing he produces if he deserves everything he used in producing it, but rather to the view that no one possesses anything in the strong, constitutive sense necessary to a desert base. No one can be said to deserve anything (in the strong, pre-institutional sense), because no one can be said to possess anything (in the strong, constitutive sense). This is the philosophical force of the argument from arbitrariness.

That the argument from arbitrariness works in this way can be seen by viewing the moves from natural liberty to fair opportunity to the democratic conception, as traced by Rawls, as stages in the dispossession of the person. With each transition, a substantive self, thick with particular traits, is progressively shorn of characteristics once taken to be essential to its identity; as more of its features are seen to be arbitrarily given, they are relegated from presumed constituents to mere attributes of the self. More becomes *mine*, and less remains *me*, to recall our earlier formulation, until ultimately the self is purged of empirical constituents altogether, and transformed into a condition of agency standing beyond the objects of its possession. The logic of Rawls' argument might be reconstructed as follows:

At the far end of the spectrum, even before natural liberty appears, are aristocratic and caste societies; in such societies, a person's life prospects are tied to a hierarchy into which he is born and from which his person is inseparable. Here, the self is most fully ascribed, merged almost indistinguishably with its condition, embedded in its situation. The system of natural liberty removes fixed status of birth as an assumed constituent of the person, and regards each as free, given his capacities and resources, to compete in the marketplace as best he can, and to reap his reward. By shifting the basis of expectations from status to contract, the system of natural liberty repairs the arbitrariness of hierarchical societies by taking the person more narrowly, so to speak, as distinct and separable from his surroundings. Still, some arbitrariness remains, most notably in the form of social and cultural contingencies. In the regime of natural liberty, a person's life prospects are governed by factors no more ascribable to the person (in the strong, constitutive sense) than his inherited status. Having relieved the person of his hierarchical baggage, the principle of natural liberty still conceives a thickly-constituted self, burdened by the accidents of social and cultural contingency. And so the move to fair opportunity, which strips the self of social and cultural accidents as well as inherited status. In a 'fair meritocracy', the effects of class status and cultural disadvantage are understood to reflect more on the society and less on the person. Those with comparable talents and 'the same willingness to use them, should have the same prospects of success regardless of their initial place in the social system, that is, irrespective of the income class into which they are born'. In this way, the meritocratic conception extends the logic of natural liberty by ascribing less to the self and more to its situation.

But even the principle of fair opportunity, in rewarding individual effort, conceives the province of the self too expansively. For even 'the effort a person is willing to make is influenced by his natural abilities and skills and the alternatives open to him. The better endowed are more likely, other things equal, to strive conscientiously, and there seems to be no way to discount for their greater good fortune'. The self is still over-ascribed. Given its arbitrariness, even the character that determines a person's motivation cannot properly be regarded as an essential constituent of his identity. And so finally the move to the democratic conception, in which the self, short of all contingently-given attributes, assumes a kind of supra-empirical status, essentially unencumbered, bounded in advance and given prior to its ends, a pure subject of agency and possession, ultimately thin. Not only my character but even my values and deepest convictions are relegated to the contingent, as features of my condition rather than as constituents of my person. 'That we have one conception of the good rather than another is not relevant from a moral standpoint. In acquiring it we are influenced by the same sort of contingencies that lead us to rule out a knowledge of our sex and class'. Only in this way is it possible to install the self as invulnerable, to assure its sovereignty once and for all in a world threatening always to engulf it. Only if the fate of the self is thus detached from the fate of its attributes and aims, subject as they are to the vagaries of circumstance, can its priority be preserved and its agency guaranteed.

This is the vision of the person that Nozick and Bell, as defenders of natural liberty and meritocracy, respectively, emphatically reject, even if they do not spell out in any detail the conception of the self they rely on instead. Both object that the argument from arbitrariness, consistently applied, leads ineluctably to the dissolution of the person, and the abnegation of individual responsibility and moral choice. 'This line of argument can succeed in blocking the introduction of a person's autonomous choices and activities (and their results) only by attributing *everything* noteworthy about the person completely to certain sorts of "external" factors', writes Nozick. Echoing his argument against the notion of common assets, Nozick questions whether, on Rawls' account, any coherent conception of the person remains, and if so, whether it is any longer the kind of person worth the moral fuss deontological liberalism makes on its behalf.

So denigrating a person's autonomy and prime responsibility for his actions is a risky line to take for a theory that otherwise wishes to buttress the dignity and self-respect of autonomous beings; especially for a theory that founds so much (including a theory of the good) upon a person's choices. One doubts that the unexalted picture of human beings Rawl's theory presupposes and rests upon can be made to fit together with the view of human dignity it is designed to lead to and embody.

Bell summarizes the objection in an epigram: 'The person has disappeared. Only attributes remain'. Where Rawls seeks to assure the autonomy of the self by disengaging it from the world, his critics say he ends by dissolving the self in order to preserve it.

To recapitulate our reconstructed version of the argument between Rawls and Nozick on the issue of desert: Nozick first argues that the arbitrariness of assets does not undermine desert, because desert may depend not only on things I deserve, but also on things I just *have*, not illegitimately. Rawls' response is to invoke the distinction between the self and its possessions in the strongest version of that distinction, and so to claim that, strictly speaking, there *is* nothing that 'I', *qua* pure subject of possession, *have*—nothing that is attached, rather than related, to *me*—nothing at least in the strong, constitutive sense of possession necessary to a desert base. Nozick's rejoinder is that this defense cannot succeed for long, for it has the consequence of leaving us with a subject *so* shorn of empirically-identifiable characteristics as to resemble once more the Kantian transcendent or disembodied subject Rawls resolved to avoid. It makes the individual inviolable only by making him invisible, and calls into question the dignity and autonomy this liberalism seeks above all to secure.

NOTE

1. In a footnote, Rawls cites Feinberg in apparent support of this claim, but Feinberg allows a role for desert in both distributive and retributive justice. Feinberg's point is that retributive justice involves what he calls polar desert (where one either deserves good or deserves ill), whereas distributive justice involves nonpolar desert (where, as with a prize, some deserve and others do not). But both cases involve desert in the moral, preinstitutional sense.

21. Desert and Institutions

OWEN MCLEOD

Owen McLeod, the coeditor of this anthology, is Lecturer in Philosophy at Yale University. He has published papers in ethics and in the history of philosophy. His doctoral dissertation is titled *On Being Deserving* (1995).

In this paper, McLeod advances a compromise between a preinstitutional conception of desert, on the one hand, and a purely institutional conception on the other. His suggestion is that entitlement, which is purely institutional, is a basis for desert; yet, other bases for desert, such as being a person, are not purely institutional. On his view, which is meant to capture what is plausible in both the institutional and the preinstitutional conceptions, some desert is institutional and some is not. He tries to prepare the way for this compromise by questioning the recent retreat from preinstitutional desert and by indicating the difficulties that face a purely institutional conception.

I. Introduction

In 1963, in his seminal paper "Justice and Personal Desert," Joel Feinberg claimed that desert is "logically prior to and independent of public institutions and their rules."[1] What Feinberg meant, I believe, is that desert cannot be explained in terms of institutional rules and that desert can arise in the absence of such rules. This can be called a "preinstitutional" conception of desert.

Much of the subsequent literature has not favored a preinstitutional conception.[2] The tendency, at least among some of the most influential contemporary moral and political theorists, has rather been toward understanding desert in terms of the rules or purposes of institutions, in such a way that desert could arise only within such institutions.[3] Samuel Scheffler has recently called attention to this tendency, writing that "none of the major strands in contemporary liberal philosophy assigns a

significant role to desert at the level of fundamental principle."[4] Instead, Scheffler writes, the tendency has been to understand desert "as an institutional artifact rather than as one of the normative bases of institutional design."[5]

Thus, there seems to be a serious conflict of views. This is regrettable, since each view is plausible. To see this, consider the preinstitutional conception of desert. There are at least two considerations in favor of it.

(i) Suppose it were suggested that the institution of criminal law (for example) was erected so that people who violated its rules would *thereby* come to deserve punishment— as if, in the absence of those rules, no one could deserve punishment for, say, murder or rape. This should strike one as odd. Even in the absence of those laws (even in the total absence of social institutions, one might say), people would deserve punishment for committing such wrongs. If so, then there is preinstitutional desert ("p-desert").

This article was written for this anthology and appears in print here for the first time.

(ii) Institutional rules are sometimes criticized on the grounds that they permit *undeserved* distributions. (Think again of our institution of criminal law.) What is the institutionalist to make of this sort of criticism? Perhaps he will say that it amounts to the claim that some set of institutional rules is inconsistent (one rule permitting a distribution that another rule forbids). But this seems wrong. When rules are criticized for permitting undeserved distributions, this seems to be more than a merely logical claim. It is a charge of moral deficiency: The rules do not "match up" with what people p-deserve.

Nonetheless, one might be led to an institutional conception of desert in the following way. Consider some typical *objects* of desert, or things that can be deserved: grades, monetary awards, championships, promotions, and so on. Each of these seems to be an artifact of some social institution. Next, consider some typical *bases* for desert, or grounds for deserving good or ill: excelling on a physics exam, winning the Boston Marathon, closing the big deal with Microsoft, engaging in Medicare fraud or insider trading, and so on. None of these could exist without social institutions. Reflection on these facts might lead one to the conclusion that all desert is institutional desert (or "i-desert").

Thus, the preinstitutional and the institutional conceptions of desert are plausible. But both cannot be correct. What is to be done?

The central claim of this paper is that there is a middle way between an institutional and a preinstitutional conception of desert. According to it, the rules of social institutions generate entitlements, and entitlement, though distinct from desert, is nonetheless a basis for it. If so, then at least one basis for desert is institutional, since entitlement (as understood here) is purely institutional. Other bases for desert, however, are not institutional. (Some of these bases are discussed later on.) In this way, it is possible to capture what is plausible both in institutional and preinstitutional views of desert.[6]

The major obstacle in the way of this compromise is the institutional conception of desert. Because of its current preeminence, any talk of a compromise between it and the preinstitutional conception may seem premature. So, before turning (in Sections V and VI) to the compromise, it is important to do two things. First, it should be asked why the preinstitutional conception has been so widely rejected (Section II). Second, it should be determined whether the alternative, institutional conception really is defensible (Sections III and IV).

II. Why Reject the Preinstitutional Conception?

Why do many contemporary philosophers reject p-desert? Scheffler, in the aforementioned paper, attempts to answer this question. He offers a "diagnosis" of the flight of recent political philosophy from p-desert. Scheffler's diagnosis is found in the following passage:

> The widespread reluctance among political philosophers to defend a robust notion of preinstitutional desert is due in part to the power in contemporary philosophy of the idea that human thought and action may be wholly subsumable within a broadly naturalistic view of the world. The reticence of these philosophers—their disinclination to draw on any preinstitutional notion of desert—testifies in part to the prevalence of the often unstated conviction that a thoroughgoing naturalism leaves no room for a conception of agency substantial enough to sustain such a notion. This problem, the problem of the relation between naturalism and individual agency, is of course a descendant of the problem of determinism and free will. . . . Thus my suggestion is that the reluctance of many contemporary philosophers to rely on a preinstitutional notion of desert results in part from a widespread though often implicit skepticism about individual agency, a form of skepticism that is the contemporary descendant of skepticism about freedom of the will.[7]

Scheffler's diagnosis seems to be this. Contemporary political philosophers accept, perhaps tacitly, naturalism.[8] Naturalism is inconsistent with the view that individuals have free will. The denial of free will, finally, is (thought to be) incompatible with a preinstitutional conception of desert. Hence, contemporary theorists tend to reject such a conception. As Scheffler puts it, these philosophers reject p-desert "out of the sense that, given our best current understanding of the way the world works, [the] preinstitutional notion can no longer be taken seriously."⁹

Scheffler's diagnosis may seem plausible. At any rate, he is not the first to suppose that skepticism about free will is tantamount to skepticism about desert. Daniel Dennett, for example, has made remarks suggesting a line of thought similar to Scheffler's:

> It could be . . . that the concept of personal responsibility enshrined in traditional (Western) morality is subtly incoherent, and that we ought to revise or even jettison that concept and the family of ideas surrounding it: guilt, desert, moral praise, punishment, to mention the most important.¹⁰

However, Scheffler's diagnosis is not really plausible. There are many reasons for this. First, there is no direct textual evidence in the writings of the political theorists Scheffler has in mind—Rawls and Nozick, most notably—that would suggest their rejection of free will. On the contrary, Rawls and Nozick depend heavily on such notions as liberty, freedom, and autonomy. So even if those theorists do embrace "naturalism," they seem to view it as compatible with human freedom.

Second, let us suppose with Scheffler that contemporary political theorists accept a conception of the world that is incompatible with human freedom. Then why would they reject desert only and not also the "family of ideas" that seems to surround it: guilt, praise, punishment, and so on? Rawls and Nozick, at least, do not reject this family of notions. Thus, if such notions are, along with desert, inconsistent with naturalism, then Scheffler's diagnosis implies the following: Contemporary theorists have internalized naturalism, accepted that it is incompatible with desert, but failed to grasp its incompatibility

with a host of related notions. This seems unlikely.¹¹

Third, there are other contemporary philosophers who are, I presume, no less susceptible to the "power" of naturalism but who nevertheless make a place in their theories for p-desert.¹² Scheffler's diagnosis implies that these theorists are even less capable than their anti-desert colleagues of seeing the supposed significance of naturalism. In the face of these implausible implications, I conclude that Scheffler's diagnosis is incorrect.

However, even if Scheffler's diagnosis is incorrect, it suggests an *argument* for rejecting p-desert. The argument suggested is this. Given "our best current understanding of the way the world works," there is reason to doubt the existence of free will. If so, then there is reason to avoid any theory that relies on concepts whose application presupposes that agents are free. P-desert is one such concept. Thus, there is reason to avoid a theory that treats desert as anything more than purely institutional.

The central flaw in this imagined argument is the assumption that p-desert is a concept whose application presupposes the existence of free will. If taken as a completely general claim, this assumption is false.¹³ There are cases of desert that do not presuppose responsibility. So, for example, consider desert of compensation. In typical cases, this is deserved for suffering a harm or loss that is not one's fault or responsibility. Of course, in some such cases, there is someone who is responsible—say, for the injury that you have suffered. But not all cases are like this. Consider respect. Simply in virtue of being people, we deserve some modicum of it, even though no one is responsible for the fact that anyone else is a person. Or consider medical treatment. One might deserve it in virtue of suffering from some disease for which no one can be held responsible. Consider, finally, objects that altogether lack free will: the Olympic Peninsula, or the Theory of Special Relativity. The first might deserve preservation, and the second serious study. These cases show, I think, that desert does not necessarily presuppose free will or responsibility.

The institutionalist might reply by agreeing that desert does not necessarily presuppose free will, provided that the desert in question is i-desert. But p-desert, the reply continues, necessarily presupposes free will or responsibility. And since no one is ultimately responsible for anything, there can be no p-desert.[14]

It is important to see that this reply involves not rejection but rather *acceptance* of a concept of p-desert. The concept is not dismissed as incoherent. Otherwise, it could not be argued that p-desert implies responsibility. Rather, what is rejected is the *substantive* thesis that this condition of responsibility is sometimes satisfied.

Once this is seen, it becomes clear that the imagined argument suffers from two weaknesses. First, the conceptual claim that p-desert necessarily presupposes responsibility has not been defended. Second, even if this conceptual claim could be defended, it has not been shown, nor is it plausible, that no one is responsible for anything.

It appears, then, that the preinstitutionalist is in a strong position. He can deny the conceptual claim that p-desert necessarily implies responsibility; or he can accept this but deny the substantive claim that no one is ultimately responsible for anything. (I take it that these are clearly plausible alternatives and so leave this much discussed matter here.)

The upshot is that even though the current trend is away from p-desert and toward i-desert (if any), neither the explanation nor the justification of this trend is obvious.

Still, the fact remains: Many recent philosophers seem attracted to an institutional conception of desert. And so far, nothing has been said directly against it. Let us now turn to that project.

III. Some Crude Institutional Theories

It might be useful to begin by considering some crude institutional theories. By noting their defects, we can get a clearer view of the nature of institutional theories and the difficulties to which they are liable. Let us begin with this:

T1 S deserves x in virtue of F iff there is some social institution, I; a rule of I is that those who participate in I and have F shall receive x; the rules of I apply to S; S has F.

T1 can be illustrated as follows. Consider the social institution of *inheritance*: that is, the complex of legal rules that governs the passage of an estate from testator to beneficiary. A central rule of this institution is that if a testator, in a legally binding will, names a certain person as the beneficiary of the estate, then that person shall receive the estate. Now suppose that a rich old uncle has named his nephew the sole beneficiary of his vast estate. Suppose further that the uncle dies. The nephew now deserves the estate, according to **T1**: There is the institution of inheritance; a rule of that institution is that those who are named beneficiaries to estates shall receive those estates; the rules apply to the nephew; and the nephew is thus named.

Right away, **T1** faces a problem. Intuitively, it seems that it is still possible for the nephew to fail to deserve his inheritance: He is a sloth and a rogue who never did anything to make him worthy of the fortune that is now his. Surely the wicked do not deserve to prosper. This nephew is wicked. Thus, he does not deserve the estate. Since **T1** implies that he does, **T1** is false. (If anyone deserves the estate, it is the uncle's virtuous daughter, who always looked after him and who took care of him as he died.)

This example reveals at least one problem with **T1**: It conflates desert and entitlement. For in the story just told, the natural thing to say is that the roguish nephew is *entitled* to the inheritance but does not *deserve* it and that the loving daughter deserves the inheritance but, unfortunately, is not entitled to it. If **T1** were true, this natural assessment would border on nonsense.

The distinction between entitlement and desert has been acknowledged in the literature. It is nothing new.[15] What is of interest is that this distinction has been acknowledged even by some who accept an institutional theory of desert. According to these theorists, an institutional conception of desert need not conflate desert and entitlement. How is this possible?

Their idea is to explain desert not in terms of institutional rules but rather in terms of institutional *purposes*. (Institutional rules are supposed to express or promote institutional purposes, and are thus distinct from them.) David Cummiskey is one philosopher who is attracted to this idea. He illustrates it as follows:

> A race [for example] is a social institution which is usually constructed for some specific purpose. We cannot conclude that someone deserves to win the race without . . . appealing to the purpose of the race. When we say that the most skilled deserves to win then we are assuming that the point of the race is to reward skill. Since rewarding skill is the point of the institution it is also the appropriate basis for desert.[16]

In this way, Cummiskey claims, "desert bases are determined by the point of the institutions." If so, then "desert is an institution-dependent concept."[17]

At this point, it is fair to raise questions about the notion of an "institutional purpose." What exactly is an institutional purpose? Is it determined by the members of the institution? By those who created the institution? Is the purpose determined by all the members or creators or by only a select few? Who *are* the members? If an institution has more than one purpose, which purpose or purposes are supposed to be relevant to desert? These questions must be answered by anyone interested in developing a full-blown theory of desert in terms of institutional purposes. It is not clear (to me) what the answers would be.[18]

Let us put those questions aside. I presume that an account of desert in terms of institutional purposes would resemble the following:

T2 S deserves x in virtue of F iff there is some social institution, I; a purpose of I is that those who have F shall receive x; S participates in I; S has F.

T2 does in fact preserve a distinction between desert and entitlement. To see this, suppose (with Cummiskey) that the purpose of the institution of racing is to honor the most skilled runner. Then, according to **T2**, the most skilled runner deserves to be honored. Now suppose the most skilled runner does not win the race. (Suppose she is unintentionally tripped near the finish line and winds up placing fifth.) It is possible that the rules of racing will not entitle her to any honors. But she does deserve them: She has fulfilled the "purpose" of racing. Thus, **T2** does not conflate desert and entitlement.

However, the really serious defect with **T1** and **T2** is obvious: Each implies morally repugnant conclusions. This is not hard to see. Suppose, for example, that there is a social institution with the rule or purpose that those who are black shall be denied the front seats of buses, or stools at the counters of soda fountains, or admission to universities, movie theaters, and shops. Suppose, in other words, that there is a social institution with rules or purposes that demand racial oppression and discrimination. If either **T1** or **T2** were true, then black people who fall under those rules would *deserve* to be discriminated against. But this clearly is wrong. No one deserves to be oppressed in those ways.

This is just one example. Any number of similarly repugnant results could be generated, simply by imagining institutions with morally unacceptable rules or purposes. As I see it, this is a serious objection to **T1** and **T2**: They fail to correspond to our firm convictions about what people can deserve.

IV. More Sophisticated Institutional Theories

The fundamental problem with **T1** and **T2**, then, is that neither places any moral constraint on the rules or purposes of supposedly desert-generating institutions. Without some such constraint, the door is left open to morally repugnant results. This suggests that a plausible institutional theory of desert must include some such constraint. What will it be?

One thing is clear: The constraint cannot be that the rules or purposes of social institutions must produce *deserved* outcomes. For *this* desert is either p-desert or i-desert. If it is p-desert, then the institutional theory ultimately depends on a preinstitutional theory of desert. If it is i-desert, then the problem of moral repugnance simply reemerges at a higher level.

Another possible constraint is justice: The rules or purposes of supposedly desert-conferring institutions must be *just*. However, for reasons just described, this option is unavailable to those who accept that justice is at least partly explicable in terms of *desert*. The rather startling result is that an institutional theorist who wishes to use justice as a moral constraint on the rules or purposes of institutions is actually forced to reject the ancient idea that justice has at least something to do with desert.

Of course, this will not worry those who do reject the idea that justice is at least partly explicable in terms of desert. Such a theorist can accept, without circularity, the following account of desert:

T3 S deserves x in virtue of F iff there is some social institution, I; a rule or purpose, P, of I is that those who have F shall receive x; P is just; S participates in I; S has F.

My view is that even without knowing anything about the particular concept of justice involved, **T3** is defective. The defect can be brought out as follows. **T3** implies that for every true desert-claim (a claim of the form 'S deserves x in virtue of F'), there is a corresponding institutional rule or purpose that covers it. So, for example, if a man deserves condemnation for racial hatred against another man, then there is some institutional rule or purpose that covers this or makes it so.

Even if there actually is some such rule or purpose, things might have been different. Indeed, there was a time (not long ago) when things *were* different. Still, it would clearly be incorrect to suppose that back then, no one could deserve condemnation for acts of racial hatred. However, if **T3** were true, that *would* be correct, because **T3** implies that, in the absence of a social institution with the rule or purpose that acts of racial hatred will be condemned, no one would deserve condemnation for such acts. As I see it, this shows that **T3** is false.

This forces the institutionalist to introduce another modification. The modification is based on the idea that, even if in this world there are no rules or purposes to cover clear cases of desert, in a *morally perfect world* there would be. In other words:

T4 S deserves x in virtue of F in the actual world iff there is some world, w, and some social institution, I, in w; a rule or purpose, P, of I is that those who have F shall receive x; w is morally perfect; S has F in the actual world.

I believe that **T4** is tantamount to abandoning the institutional conception of desert. According to that conception, as I understood it, desert arises only within the context of social institutions; desert is "parasitic" on institutions. **T4** diminishes desert's alleged dependence on social institutions to the point where people in a world with *no* social institutions could deserve various things.

If this is possible, then perhaps the explanation is that desert is not purely institutional. In other words, there now seems to be room for an alternative conception of desert, one that is not purely institutional. In the next two sections, I explain and defend such a conception.

V. The Compromise

There is something attractive about institutional theories of desert. As I suggested at the outset, this might be explained by the fact that many objects of desert, and many bases for desert, could not exist without the existence of social institutions. Reflection on this fact might lead to the idea that all desert is dependent on social institutions and that desert itself is to be explained in terms of their rules or purposes.

For reasons discussed in Sections III and IV, I think this idea is mistaken, at least if taken as a general theory of desert. My view is that the apparent institutionality of desert can be explained by the hypothesis that entitlement is a basis (one of many) for desert and that entitlement is purely institutional. By way of explaining this hypothesis, let me begin by explaining my understanding of entitlement.[19]

Suppose a person is named in a legally binding will as the beneficiary of the testator's estate. Then that person is *entitled* by a rule of law to the estate. Consider next the runner who first crosses the finish line in the Olympic 200-meter race. This runner is *entitled* by an Olympic rule to the gold medal. Consider the host of a dinner party. He is *entitled* by a rule of etiquette to an expression of thanks from his guests. Consider, finally, a man convicted of a crime for which the legal sentence is five years in prison. He is "entitled" by a rule of law to five years in prison. These cases suggest the following view of entitlement:

E   S is entitled to x in virtue of F iff there is some social institution, I; a rule of I is that those who participate in I and have F shall receive x; S participates in I; S has F.

E should look familiar: it is just like **T1**, except that 'deserves' as it appears in **T1** has been replaced by 'is entitled to'. Indeed, my view is that **T1** is best understood as an account not of desert but rather of entitlement.

I believe that entitlement is a basis for desert. So, for example, if Jones is entitled to the estate by a rule of law, then this is a basis for his deserving it. If Smith is entitled to the gold medal by a rule of sports, then this is a basis for his deserving it. If Ralston is entitled to a show of thanks from his dinner guests, this is a basis for his deserving it. If Spike is "entitled" to five years in prison, then this is a basis for his deserving it. In this way, institutions generate desert—perhaps quite a lot of it.

But not all. This is because entitlement is not the only basis for desert, and some of these other bases are preinstitutional. Consider the property of *being deliberately cruel to others.* For having this property, one might deserve condemnation. Consider next the property of *having innocently suffered.* In virtue of having this property, one might deserve sympathy or compensation. Consider next the property of *having exerted effort.* In virtue of acquiring this property (say, by clearing and cultivating a small patch of land in an institutionless "state of nature"), one might deserve the fruits of one's efforts. Or consider the property of *being a person.* In virtue of this property, one might deserve respect. Yet, in all of these cases, it seems (to me) that the existence of social institutions is not necessary for having the relevant property, nor is the property plausibly explained in terms of the rules or purposes of social institutions.[20]

My suggestion, then, is this. There are many desert bases. At least one basis for desert (namely, entitlement as expressed in **E**) is purely institutional: It is explicable in terms of the rules or purposes of social institutions and cannot arise in their absence. But there are other bases for desert (being cruel, innocent suffering, performing hard work, being a person, and perhaps others) that are not institutional; they are not necessarily explicable in terms of the rules or purposes of institutions, and they can arise in their absence. If this is correct, then it might be said that some desert is institutional, and some desert is preinstitutional.

I have been claiming that entitlement is a basis for desert. But why should anyone accept this claim? Let me offer three (admittedly sketchy and inconclusive) arguments.

(i) The institutional concept of desert is (apparently) quite plausible. This requires an explanation. A possible explanation is that the institutional conception is true. I think this is a poor explanation, since, as I have argued, there is room for doubting the institutional conception. A better explanation, I believe, is the hypothesis that entitlement (which is purely institutional) is capable of generating desert. If so, then there is some reason to accept that entitlement is a desert base.

(ii) This argument is grounded in an example and a view about the nature of justice.[21] Suppose you are entitled to something—say, a piece of land—and I am not. Suppose further that there is no difference between us with respect to other desert bases: hard work, being a person, innocent suffering, moral worth, and so on. We are the same in those respects. Suppose, finally, that you inherit and enjoy the piece of land, and I do not. As I see it, there is no injustice here. (Think of a person who wins a large sum in the lottery. This person is entitled to the money. Other things being equal, there is no injustice in her receiving it.)

If this sort of example is combined with a certain view about the nature of justice, it follows that entitlement is a basis for desert. The view of justice I have in mind is the ancient one that justice obtains only to the extent that people get what they deserve. And the argument is that since, as it seems, there is no injustice in your receiving and enjoying the land, and since your being entitled to it seems to be the only relevant difference between us, it follows that entitlement is a desert base. More simply, entitlement affects justice; justice is the getting of what's deserved; thus, entitlement affects desert.

(iii) Suppose Jones is legally entitled to receive a sum of money from Smith. As I see it, Smith is now *prima facie* morally obligated to see to it that Jones gets this money. This is because entitlements are akin to promises, and promises generate *prima facie* moral obligations. So, in general, if S is entitled to receive x from S′, then S′ is *prima facie* morally obligated to see to it that S gets x. Furthermore, it seems that if S′ is *prima facie* morally obligated to see to it that S gets x, then S *prima facie* deserves x. This is because moral obligations are bases for *prima facie* desert: If it is *prima facie* morally obligatory for you to treat me in a certain way, then, in virtue of that fact, I *prima facie* deserve to be treated in that way. So, for example, if you *prima facie* morally ought to refrain from lying to me, then I *prima facie* deserve that you not lie to me. Therefore, if entitlements generate *prima facie* moral obligations, and if *prima facie* moral obligations are bases for desert, then entitlement is a basis for *prima facie* desert.

VI. Objections and Replies

I presume that those attracted to an institutional conception of desert will not quarrel with the suggestion that entitlement is a desert base. But it might be that a staunch preinstitutional theorist *would* object to this. So, by way of conclusion, let me consider two objections to the view that entitlement is a basis for desert.

The first objection is similar to one that I earlier raised against institutional theories of desert. The objection is that if entitlement were a basis for desert, then the door would be left open to morally repugnant results. So, for example, suppose a Nazi law entitles SS officers to property that was seized from Jews.[22] My view that entitlement is a basis for desert seems to imply that the SS officers therefore *deserve* that property!

This objection rests on a misunderstanding of my view. To see why, consider a relatively uncontroversial basis for desert: hard work. If we know anything about desert, we know that those who diligently struggle to achieve some end deserve success. Furthermore, I doubt that anyone would be shaken from believing this by being reminded that some people strive to achieve *evil* ends; the claim that hard work is a basis for desert is meant to be a claim of *prima facie* desert. It is the claim that, other things equal, those who work hard deserve success. If other things are not "equal"—for example, if the hard work is directed toward an evil end—then the *prima facie* desert generated by the hard work is outweighed. Put another way, hard work is not sufficient for "all things considered" desert; it is sufficient only for *prima facie* desert.

Likewise for the claim that entitlement is a basis for desert. Other things equal, people deserve that to which they are entitled. If other things are not equal—for example, if the relevant rules are morally unacceptable—then the desert generated by the entitlement is outweighed. Put another way, entitlement is not *sufficient* for all-things-considered desert. It is sufficient only for *prima facie* desert.

So the first objection fails. My view does not imply that the Nazi officers, in virtue of being entitled to property seized from Jews, deserve (all-things-considered) the property. Their entitlement-generated desert is clearly outweighed by the moral unacceptability of the relevant law.

A second objection is based on the idea that desert, unlike entitlement, is bound to responsibility. So, for example, suppose your rich uncle dies. For no apparent reason, this uncle leaves you a fortune. You did nothing to earn it. You are in no way responsible for being named the beneficiary. However, in virtue of being thus named, you are entitled to the fortune. If entitlement were a basis for desert, it would therefore be possible for you to deserve something for which you are not at all responsible. But this is not possible. You cannot come to deserve something in virtue of that for which you are not responsible. Thus, entitlement is not a basis for desert.

The problem with this objection is the assumption that one cannot deserve something on the basis of that for which one is not responsible. I have already pointed out that this assumption is false. People often come to deserve things in virtue of facts for which they are not responsible. Thus, for this objection to work, some relevant difference between these cases and the case of entitlement must be pointed out. I doubt that this could be done, so I doubt that this second objection succeeds.

There are other objections and replies that could be discussed, but let me conclude. In this paper, I have noted a rift in our thinking about desert. The rift is between an institutional conception of desert and a preinstitutional conception. The currently dominant tendency, at least among political philosophers, is toward an institutional conception. I have argued that there is room for doubting the institutional conception. I have suggested that there is nevertheless a way to capture

what is plausible about the institutional conception (namely, that social institutions can generate desert) without actually embracing that conception. This can be done by treating entitlement, which is purely institutional, as one basis for desert and by recognizing other bases for desert as preinstitutional.

NOTES

➤ This paper has benefited from the comments of several friends and colleagues, especially Fred Feldman and Shelly Kagan. I owe a special debt of gratitude to Feldman for extensive discussions on this and other desert-related topics.

1. In Feinberg's *Doing and Deserving* (Princeton University Press, 1970), pp. 55–94.
2. This is not to say that the preinstitutional conception has no adherents other than Feinberg. William Galston, for example, writes: "Desert does not arise out of existing public institutions and rules. It is prior to and independent of them and may in certain circumstances be used as a criterion for judging them." *Justice and the Human Good* (University of Chicago Press, 1980), p. 170.
3. John Rawls is sometimes seen as the impetus of this tendency, due to some remarks that he makes in *A Theory of Justice* (Harvard University Press, 1971). But I take no position here as to whether these remarks really do commit Rawls to an institutional theory of desert or even as to whether they signal a rejection of preinstitutional desert. The issue is complicated due to Rawls's apparent acceptance of preinstitutional desert in the case of retributive (or criminal) justice. For discussion of this wrinkle in Rawls's work, see Michael Sandel, *Liberalism and the Limits of Justice* (Cambridge University Press, 1982), pp. 89–92.
4. "Responsibility, Reactive Attitudes, and Liberalism in Philosophy and Politics," *Philosophy and Public Affairs* 21 (Fall 1992), pp. 299–323. The cited remark is found on p. 301.
5. Ibid., p. 305.
6. I am not the first to propose that desert has institutional and preinstitutional elements. In *Desert* (Princeton University Press, 1987), George Sher adopts "the working hypothesis that [desert] involves both natural and conventional elements, and that any adequate account must illuminate the connections between them" (p. 17).
7. Scheffler, "Responsibility, Reactive Attitudes, and Liberalism in Philosophy and Politics," pp. 309–310.

8. Scheffler does not say exactly what he means by "naturalism"; neither will I. Nothing hinges on it.

9. Ibid., p. 311.

10. *Elbow Room: The Varieties of Free Will Worth Wanting* (MIT Press, 1984), p. 156.

11. Scheffler ("Responsibility, Reactive Attitudes, and Liberalism in Philosophy and Politics," p. 310) tries to anticipate this objection as follows:

    [O]f all moral notions, the notions of desert and responsibility are the ones that depend most obviously and immediately on an understanding of what human agency involves. Thus if the internalization of a broadly naturalistic outlook were to produce skepticism about any single aspect of morality, this would surely be the one.

    Notice how, in the first sentence, Scheffler blurs desert and responsibility. Scheffler might be right that skepticism about *responsibility* would result from an acceptance of "naturalism," but he has not shown, nor would he be right to claim, that acceptance of "naturalism" would (or should) result in skepticism about *desert*.

12. These theorists include not only Feinberg and Galston but also Fred Feldman, "Adjusting Utility for Justice: A Consequentialist Reply to the Objection from Justice," *Philosophy and Phenomenological Research* (1995); J. L. Lucas, *On Justice* (Oxford University Press, 1980); David Miller, *Social Justice* (Oxford University Press, 1976); Wojceich Sadurski, *Giving Desert its Due* (D. Reidel, 1985); George Sher, *Desert*; Michael Slote, "Desert, Consent, and Justice," *Philosophy and Public Affairs* 2 (Summer 1973), pp. 323–347.

13. As has been amply demonstrated in recent literature: see Fred Feldman, "Desert: Reconsideration of Some Received Wisdom," *Mind* 104 (1995), pp. 63–77; Geoffrey Cupit, "Desert and Responsibility," *Canadian Journal of Philosophy* 26 (March 1996), pp. 83–100.

14. John Rawls, of course, is sometimes interpreted as arguing in this way in *A Theory of Justice*, pp. 103–104, 310–312. See, for example, Robert Nozick, *Anarchy, State, and Utopia* (Basic Books, 1974), p. 225; Alan Zaitchik, "On Deserving to Deserve," *Philosophy and Public Affairs* 6 (1977), pp. 37–388; George Sher, *Desert*, pp. 22–36.

15. John Kleinig makes the distinction in "The Concept of Desert," *American Philosophical Quarterly* 8 (January 1971), p. 74. So does David Miller, *Social Justice*, p. 91. The distinction is now standard fare in the literature on desert.

16. "Desert and Entitlement: A Rawlsian Consequentialist Account," *Analysis* 47 (1987), pp. 15–19; the passage cited is from p. 18. A similar idea can be found in Julian Lamont, "The Concept of Desert in Distributive Justice," *Philosophical Quarterly* 44 (1994), pp. 45–64:

    This practice [of grading students] normally has behind it some purpose, or at least some defining value, which plays an essential role in the setting of the desert-basis. . . . What is important to notice is that *the desert basis is determined by other values or purposes*, rather than by something internal to the notion of desert itself. (p. 51)

17. "Desert and Entitlement: A Rawlsian Consequentialist Account," p. 18 and p. 19, respectively.

18. In "Why Profits are Deserved," *Ethics* 97 (January 1987), pp. 387–402, N. Scott Arnold tries to shed some light on the notion of institutional purpose. He writes:

    [F]or any social institution in which desert claims can be made, there is a goal or set of goals that are [*sic*] essential in that the institution would of necessity cease to exist if it lacked those goals. A World Series [for example] could exist even if it made no money. It could not exist if it was not intended to discover the best team in U.S. professional baseball. It is these essential goals that determine basal reasons for desert claims. (pp. 390–391)

    But is it really true that the World Series could not exist if its purpose were not to discover the best team in U.S. professional baseball? I doubt it. Besides, even if the notion of "essential goal" were clear, *why* should an institution's "essential goal" be the one that determines a desert base?

19. It should be clear that I am introducing a technical notion. It may or may not bear any resemblance to other notions of entitlement.

20. These claims obviously require more defense—especially the claim that being a person is not explicable in terms of social institutions. For one might plausibly claim that in the absence of such institutions, there are no genuine people. At best there would be creatures.

21. I am indebted to Fred Feldman for this argument.

22. A natural-law theorist might object to this example on the grounds that such an obviously unjust "law" is, in fact, no law at all. I do not accept natural-law theory.

22. Responsibility, Reactive Attitudes, and Liberalism in Philosophy and Politics

SAMUEL SCHEFFLER

Samuel Scheffler is Professor of Philosophy at Berkeley, where he specializes in ethics. His books include *The Rejection of Consequentialism* (1982) and *Human Morality* (1992).

Scheffler chronicles and attempts to diagnose the recent flight from preinstitutional desert by the contemporary "liberal" political philosophy. His view is that this flight is due to widespread but tacit acceptance of "naturalism" and, with it, a reluctance to employ concepts that depend too heavily on the idea of human freedom. Since preinstitutional desert is one such concept, liberal political philosophers have abandoned it. Scheffler goes on to argue that since preinstitutional desert is nevertheless a fixture of commonsense morality and is deeply entrenched in some of our most basic moral attitudes, liberals in both politics and philosophy ignore it at some peril.

History will record that, during the 1980s, liberalism came under sustained and politically devastating attack in the United States. The bearing of this attack, if any, on contemporary liberal philosophical theories, such as those advanced by John Rawls and others, is not obvious. In part, this is because the relation between American political liberalism and contemporary philosophical liberalism is not a simple one.[1] On the one hand, nobody would wish seriously to suggest that the United States, during the period that began when Franklin Roosevelt became president and ended when Ronald Reagan did, was a well-ordered Rawlsian society, or that the social welfare programs implemented during that period gave full expression to the difference principle. Yet, at the same time, Rawls's work is naturally understood as providing a theoretical justification for many of the sorts of programs advocated by political liberals, and it would surely be a mistake to think of liberalism in the philosophical context as entirely unrelated to the liberal politics of the day. Thus it is reasonable to wonder about the philosophical relevance of the political repudiation of liberalism represented by the "Reagan revolution."

The conservatives who came to power during the 1980s are standardly interpreted as having tapped into two different sources of dissatisfaction with political liberalism. The first was primarily economic, and focused on liberal taxation and social welfare policies. The second was primarily social, and focused on liberal policies with respect to issues like abortion, pornography, and the role of religion in society. To the extent that social con-

Reprinted from *Philosophy and Public Affairs* 21:4 (Fall 1992). Notes edited.

servatives emphasized traditional values of family and community, their concerns had something in common with the opposition by communitarian philosophers to the purportedly excessive individualism of liberalism. At the same time, however, much of the dissatisfaction with political liberalism in the 1980s was due not to the belief that it was excessively individualistic but rather to the belief that it was, in an important respect, not individualistic enough. In saying this, I do not mean merely that liberalism was perceived as insufficiently individualistic in economic terms. It is certainly true, as everyone agrees and as I have said, that the overwhelming success of the political right was due to its capacity to appeal both to social conservatives and to economic conservatives. It is also true, and it has been widely noted, that the alliance between these two groups was sometimes an uneasy one, precisely because of the tension between the libertarian spirit of laissez-faire capitalism and the broadly communitarian tendency of much social conservatism. But when I say that liberalism came under attack partly because it was perceived as insufficiently individualistic, I am not just alluding to the conservative criticism of liberal economic policies. Rather, I mean that a more general conception of individual responsibility, a conception whose appeal cuts across political lines, was perceived as under threat both from liberal programs of economic redistribution and from liberal policies on certain social issues. Both types of liberal position were perceived, in effect, as resting on a reduced conception of individual agency and responsibility. And so resistance to this diminished conception of responsibility helped to fuel opposition to both parts of the liberal agenda.

Of course, many liberals would vigorously deny that the programs and policies they favor rely on a reduced conception of responsibility, as opposed to a proper understanding of the standard conception. These liberals might expect that support for their position could be found in contemporary liberal philosophical theories. I will argue in this article, however, that the reason various liberal pro-

grams may appear incompatible with ordinary thinking about responsibility is that they assign important benefits and burdens on the basis of considerations other than individual desert. And, I will argue, it is noteworthy that none of the most prominent contemporary versions of philosophical liberalism assigns a significant role to desert at the level of fundamental principle. Moreover, contemporary philosophical defenses of liberalism appear to underestimate the importance of the human attitudes and emotions that find expression through our practices with respect to desert. If these claims are correct, then contemporary philosophical liberalism may provide little support for the view that liberal policies can be reconciled with ordinary notions of responsibility. Indeed, if these claims are correct, then there are deeply entrenched ideas about responsibility that have contributed to the political repudiation of liberalism, and that leading contemporary versions of philosophical liberalism simply do not accept. This suggests that, far from helping political liberals to rebut the charge of incompatibility with ordinary notions of responsibility, contemporary philosophical liberalism may itself be vulnerable to such a charge.

I

There are a variety of liberal political positions that have been perceived as incompatible with ordinary beliefs about the responsibility of an individual agent for his or her actions. For example, liberals have long been accused of responding to crime by advocating policies that emphasize the social causes of criminal behavior while neglecting the responsibility of the individual who engages in such behavior. In the area of criminal justice in particular, this emphasis is said to have manifested itself in interpretations of the insanity defense and related pleas that treat an excessively broad range of conditions and circumstances as nullifying an individual's responsibility for his or her criminal conduct. Liberalism has also been blamed, relatedly, for the growing tendency in our culture to reinterpret what were previously viewed as vices—excessive drinking or gambling, for example—as diseases or addictions, thus relocating them outside the ambit of personal responsibility. Liberal social welfare programs, meanwhile, have been accused of undermining individual responsibility by making society bear the cost of meeting its poorest members' most urgent needs. This is said to provide the poor with strong incentives to avoid making efforts to support themselves, thus producing a permanent class of dependent citizens who view social welfare programs as "entitlements," and who see no need to take responsibility for improving their own material position. Finally, liberal affirmative action programs have been perceived as implying a reduced conception of individual responsibility insofar as they award social positions and opportunities on the basis of membership in targeted social groups rather than on the basis of individual effort, merit, or achievement. Thus, on some of the most important and intensely controversial social issues of the day, the liberal position has met with resistance at least in part because of a perception that it rests on an attenuated conception of personal responsibility.

To avoid misunderstanding, let me emphasize that I am not endorsing the criticisms of liberalism that I have mentioned. I am merely calling attention to the range of liberal positions and policies that have been subject to political attack on the grounds of their supposed incompatibility with ordinary principles of personal responsibility. In so doing, I am trying to focus attention on an important question that arises for liberals about the form that their response to such criticisms should take. Should liberals dispute the charge that the policies they advocate are incompatible with the standard conception of personal responsibility, or should they instead concede that the alleged incompatibility is genuine, but argue that this reveals a flaw in the standard conception rather than in liberalism?

As a matter of political strategy, liberals may well be reluctant to present their position as resting on a reduced conception of responsibility. For any such conception would appear to run counter to the dominant ethos of American society. The extraordinary litigiousness of modern-day America has been widely commented upon. In combination with other features of the prevailing cultural climate, it has led some observers to conclude that Americans no longer believe in simple bad luck, but think instead that any misfortune that befalls a person must be somebody's fault. Offhand, this would not seem to be a promising climate in which to argue the virtues of a reduced conception of responsibility. Admittedly, it may be argued that much of the litigiousness of American society has been made possible by developments in tort law that have themselves been taken to illustrate the erosion of traditional standards of responsibility. Yet the erosion of those standards cannot plausibly be said to explain the prevalence of the underlying litigious impulse, still less the wider impulse to blame and find fault. It is true, as earlier noted, that there has been a growing tendency in our society to extend the concept of *disease* to certain patterns of behavior that were previously regarded as vices, thus narrowing the scope of individual responsibility in some areas. Yet, at the same time, countervailing tendencies have also developed, including, interestingly enough, a sharply increased level of moralizing about personal health itself: with the individual's habits of diet and exercise, for example, treated increasingly as appropriate objects of moral approval or disapproval. Thus, in short, although the perceived boundaries of individual responsibility are to some extent in flux, and although, as the political controversies we are discussing indicate, there is a widespread sense that traditional notions of responsibility are under attack and that their influence is eroding, there is no evidence that the impulse to employ the concepts and categories of responsibility is disappearing or even diminishing significantly in strength.

In view of these considerations, it would seem that the more promising political strategy for liberals would be to present the policies they advocate as compatible with traditional notions of responsibility. This would presumably mean arguing that any appearance of incompatibility is due to a failure properly to interpret the implications of those notions. The question, however, is whether this argument can be successfully made. In the case of each of the liberal policies I have mentioned, the appearance of incompatibility arises, as I have said, from the fact that the policy in question assigns important benefits or burdens on the basis of considerations other than those of individual desert. In order to reconcile these policies with ordinary notions of responsibility, what liberals would need to argue is not that we should, in general, be skeptics about desert, but rather that ordinary principles of desert, properly understood, do not have the policy implications in these cases that critics of liberalism suppose them to have. Many liberals would undoubtedly say that they are fully prepared to offer such arguments. As I shall attempt to show, however, it is a striking fact that, according to the dominant philosophical defenses of liberalism that are current today, desert has no role whatsoever to play in the fundamental normative principles that apply to the basic social, political, and economic institutions of society. This suggests that political liberals can expect to receive little assistance from contemporary liberal philosophers as they attempt to demonstrate the compatibility of their agenda with ordinary notions of desert and responsibility. And this cannot but raise the question of whether there is any theoretically defensible interpretation of liberalism that would support such a demonstration.

Of course, philosophical defenses of liberalism continue to be offered, as they always have been, from a variety of importantly different perspectives. My claim, however, is that none of the major strands in contemporary liberal philosophy assigns a significant role to desert at the level of fundamental principle. This is most obvious in the case of the utilitarian strand. Although Rawlsian liberalism explicitly defines itself in opposition to utilitarianism, there is of course an important tradition of utilitarian support for liberal institutions that extends from Mill to the present day. Yet there is no form of utilitarianism that treats desert as a basic moral concept. In-

deed, utilitarianism as it is most naturally interpreted presents a radical challenge to ordinary notions of responsibility. On the one hand, utilitarianism greatly widens the scope of individual responsibility, insofar as it treats the outcomes that one fails to prevent as no less important in determining the rightness or wrongness of one's actions than the outcomes that one directly brings about. On the other hand, the responsibility whose scope is thus widened is also quite shallow, on the utilitarian view, for assignments of responsibility carry no direct implications of blame or desert, and amount to little more in themselves than judgments about the optimality of acts. The shallowness of utilitarian responsibility is reflected in J. J. C. Smart's well-known comment that "the notion of *the* responsibility [for an outcome] is a piece of metaphysical nonsense." This does not mean that utilitarians are incapable of recognizing that, in order to function efficiently, a social institution or cooperative scheme may need to assign distinct functions and roles to different individuals, thus producing a clear division of responsibility among the participants in that institution or scheme. Nor need utilitarians deny that there are often sound reasons for social institutions to distribute benefits and burdens of certain types in accordance with publicly acknowledged standards of individual merit or demerit, or that when they do so, individuals who meet the relevant criteria or standards may be said to deserve the benefit or burden in question. But here desert is understood as an institutional artifact rather than as one of the normative bases of institutional design.

For the purposes of my argument, it is an important fact that the most influential contemporary proponent of a purely institutional view of desert is not a utilitarian at all, but is rather Rawls himself. As is well known, Rawls maintains in *A Theory of Justice* that it is "one of the fixed points of our considered judgments that no one deserves his place in the distribution of native endowments any more than one deserves one's initial starting point in society." He takes this uncontroversial judgment to imply that the better endowed also do not deserve the greater economic advantages that their endowments might enable them to amass under certain possible institutional arrangements. According to Rawls, the "principles of justice that regulate the basic structure [of society] and specify the duties and obligations of individuals do not mention moral desert," or desert of any other kind for that matter. Nevertheless, he says:

> It is perfectly true that given a just system of cooperation as a scheme of public rules and the expectations set up by it, those who, with the prospect of improving their condition, have done what the system announces that it will reward are entitled to their advantages. In this sense the more fortunate have a claim to their better situation; their claims are legitimate expectations established by social institutions, and the community is obligated to meet them. But this sense of desert presupposes the existence of the cooperative scheme; it is irrelevant to the question . . . [of how] in the first place the scheme is to be designed.[2]

On this way of understanding desert, the idea that social institutions should be designed in such a way as to ensure that people get what they deserve makes about as much sense as the idea that universities were created so that professors would have somewhere to turn in their grades, or that baseball was invented in order to ensure that batters with three strikes would always be out.

The fact that Rawlsian and utilitarian liberals agree about the derivative status of desert suffices to establish this view as the prevailing liberal orthodoxy in philosophy. This does not mean, however, that it has attracted no opposition. The best-known criticism of Rawls's position on desert is the one developed by Robert Nozick in *Anarchy, State, and Utopia*. Nozick is especially critical of the way Rawls moves from the premise that people do not deserve their "natural assets" to the conclusion that they do not deserve the advantages that those assets may enable them to amass. "It needn't be," Nozick writes, "that the foundations underlying desert are themselves deserved, *all the way*

down." Yet when Nozick develops his own conception of distributive justice, the concept of desert once again plays no role. Instead, he argues that individuals are "entitled" to their natural assets whether or not they can be said to deserve them, and that they are also entitled, within limits, to the "holdings" that those assets enable them to acquire.

Although Nozick's libertarian conception of justice is not a liberal position in the sense we are discussing, it does of course belong to the older tradition of Lockean liberalism, to which the version of liberalism that we are considering stands in a complex relationship both historically and conceptually. And if there is any position capable of laying claim to the term *liberal* that might be expected to assign an important role to the concept of desert, it is surely this type of Lockean libertarianism. It is therefore a remarkable fact that the most conspicuous contemporary proponent of such a position makes no more use of the notion of desert in elaborating his own view of distributive justice than do the Rawlsian and utilitarian positions he so severely criticizes. It is even more remarkable when one considers that these three positions—Nozick's, Rawls's, and the utilitarian's—represent three of the four viewpoints that, taken together, have dominated American political philosophy for the last twenty years.

Nor do things look very different when we consider the fourth position, communitarianism. Readers of Michael Sandel's influential book *Liberalism and the Limits of Justice* might be tempted to think otherwise. In that book, Sandel provides an extended critique of Rawlsian liberalism from a communitarian perspective, and he devotes considerable attention both to Rawls's treatment of desert and to Nozick's criticism of that treatment. The main thrust of Sandel's argument is that Rawls's treatment of desert is an outgrowth of his reliance on an unsatisfactory conception of the self: a conception that leaves the self "too thin to be capable of desert." In Sandel's view, the Rawlsian self is a "pure subject of possession," whose identity is fixed independently of the aims, attributes, and attachments that it happens to have. Conceived of in this way, the self is said to lack any features by virtue of which it could be thought to deserve anything; it is a mere "condition of agency standing beyond the objects of its possession." "Claims of desert," by contrast, "presuppose thickly-constituted selves," whose very identity is in part determined by their particular aims, attachments, and loyalties.

Since Sandel thinks that we "cannot coherently regard ourselves" in the way that he believes Rawls requires us to do, but must instead regard ourselves as "thickly-constituted," one might expect that he would then go on to assign a more important role to desert than Rawls does. Yet that is just what he does not do. In the course of a discussion of affirmative action, he considers the "meritocratic" position "that the individual possesses his attributes in some unproblematic sense and therefore deserves the benefits that flow from them, and that part of what it means for an institution or distributive scheme to be just is that it rewards individuals antecedently worthy of reward." Rather than endorsing these propositions, Sandel says that "Rawls and Dworkin present powerful arguments against these assumptions which defenders of meritocracy would be hard-pressed to meet." And although Sandel reiterates his claim that the liberal vision provided by philosophers like Rawls and Dworkin nevertheless depends on unsatisfactory notions of community and the self, nowhere does he actually argue that a proper understanding of community and self would vindicate the conception of desert that Rawls and Dworkin reject.

Not only, then, do the main lines of contemporary philosophical liberalism agree in avoiding any appeal to a preinstitutional conception of desert—any appeal, that is, to an independent standard of desert by reference to which the justice of institutional arrangements is to be measured—but, moreover, some of the most prominent critics of contemporary liberalism also shy away from such appeals. And they do so even when, like Sandel, they see the liberal rejection of preinstitutional desert as associated with an unsatisfactory conception of the self, and even

when, like Nozick, they are clearly sympathetic to the idea of preinstitutional desert. How is this surprising degree of convergence to be explained? Doubtless there are a number of factors at work, no single one of which will suffice to explain the thinking of each and every philosopher. However, I believe that there is one factor that any adequate explanation of the general phenomenon will need to cite, and that is the influence of naturalism. The widespread reluctance among political philosophers to defend a robust notion of preinstitutional desert is due in part to the power in contemporary philosophy of the idea that human thought and action may be wholly subsumable within a broadly naturalistic view of the world. The reticence of these philosophers—their disinclination to draw on any preinstitutional notion of desert in their theorizing about justice—testifies in part to the prevalence of the often unstated conviction that a thoroughgoing naturalism leaves no room for a conception of individual agency substantial enough to sustain such a notion. This problem, the problem of the relation between naturalism and individual agency, is of course a descendant of the problem of determinism and free will. Or, more accurately perhaps, it is the variant of that problem that seems most urgent from a contemporary standpoint. Thus my suggestion is that the reluctance of many contemporary political philosophers to rely on a preinstitutional notion of desert results in part from a widespread though often implicit skepticism about individual agency, a form of skepticism that is the contemporary descendant of skepticism about freedom of the will.

It might be thought an objection to this diagnosis that the same contemporary philosophers who avoid any reliance on desert nevertheless make heavy use of other moral notions, including notions of rights, justice, equality, and the like. As in the case of free will and determinism, however, the moral notions that seem most directly threatened by modern naturalistic outlooks are the notions of desert and responsibility. That is because the threat to morality posed by such outlooks proceeds via their threat to individual agency, and of all moral notions, the notions of desert and responsibility are the ones that depend most obviously and immediately on an understanding of what human agency involves. Thus if the internalization of a broadly naturalistic outlook were going to produce skepticism about any single aspect of morality, this would surely be the one. Of course, it might be argued that, in the end, naturalism supports skepticism about desert only if it also supports skepticism about moral thought more generally, so that it is ultimately inconsistent to forswear any reliance on desert while continuing to use other moral notions as before. Even if this is correct, however, it does not impugn the diagnosis I have offered. For, as I have said, desert and responsibility are the moral notions that are most conspicuously threatened by a thoroughgoing naturalism. So whether or not their position is ultimately consistent, it is not implausible that political philosophers whose justificatory ambitions give them every reason to resist skepticism about morality in general, but who have also absorbed a broadly naturalistic view of the place of human beings in the world, should register their uneasiness about the implications of naturalism through a reluctance to rely on any preinstitutional notion of desert.

II

If the diagnosis just offered is correct, then the project of reconciling the policies advocated by political liberals with traditional ideas about individual responsibility is one that contemporary philosophical liberals are poorly equipped to undertake. For they reject the preinstitutional notion of desert on which the traditional ideas rely, and, if I am right, they do so, at least in part, out of a sense that, given our best current understanding of how the world works, that preinstitutional notion can no longer be taken seriously. The defense of political liberalism would therefore appear to require either a liberal theory unlike those that dominate contemporary political philosophy or a frank repudiation of traditional ideas about responsibility, at least insofar as those

ideas rely on a preinstitutional notion of desert. I have already argued that such a repudiation is unlikely to be popular politically. However, this invites a further question. If indeed the repudiation of traditional ideas about responsibility would be politically unpopular, is that owing to contingent features of the present political climate, or do those ideas have a deeper and more securely entrenched hold on our thought?

There is at least some reason to think that the latter may be the case. This can be seen most readily by considering the relation between the conception of desert advocated by contemporary philosophical liberals and some of the attitudes recommended by a familiar form of "compatibilism" about free will and determinism. As against those who believe that the truth of determinism would leave no room for traditional notions of desert and responsibility, and would, therefore, undermine our existing practices of moral praise and blame, one standard version of compatibilism holds that even if determinism were true, such practices would continue to be justified by virtue of their social efficacy or utility. As P. F. Strawson has noted, however, far from reassuring those "pessimists" who see determinism as posing a threat to our practices of praise and blame, this compatibilist argument seems to them not to provide "a sufficient basis, . . . or even the right *sort* of basis, for these practices as we understand them." For the argument represents the practices in question "as instruments of policy, as methods of individual treatment and social control." And, Strawson says, pessimists react to this representation with both conceptual and emotional shock: conceptual shock, because the compatibilist construal omits an important feature of our actual concepts of praise and blame, and emotional shock, because this omission suggests that compatibilism, if accepted, would require a drastic change in human attitudes and personal relations. What the compatibilist construal leaves out is any acknowledgment of the fact that our actual practices of moral praise and blame, in addition to having social utility, serve to express a variety of feelings and attitudes, such as gratitude, resentment, and indignation, liability to which is essential to participation in most of the types of human relationship that we value most deeply. Strawson refers to these emotions as "reactive attitudes," because, he says, they are reactions to the attitudes and intentions of others, either toward ourselves or toward third parties. When we do not regard an individual as capable of participating in ordinary human relationships, because, for example, of some extreme psychological abnormality, then the reactive attitudes tend to be inhibited and replaced by an "objective attitude" in which the person is viewed, in a clinical spirit, as someone to be managed or treated or controlled. The compatibilist construal of our practices of moral praise and blame is unnerving because the exclusively instrumental role that it assigns to those practices would be appropriate only in a relationship in which the reactive attitudes were absent and a thoroughgoing objectivity of attitude prevailed. Thus the effect of that construal is to convince pessimists that determinism may threaten not only our existing practices of praise and blame but also the wide range of ordinary human relationships that could not exist if, as this version of compatibilism appears to require, the reactive attitudes were systematically suspended.

Strawson himself believes that, in the end, such pessimism is unwarranted, for the reactive attitudes as a whole neither need nor admit of any justification, and so no thesis of determinism could possibly give us a reason to suspend them, still less "require" us to do so. If certain influential compatibilist formulations treat our practices of praise and blame in isolation from their connections to the reactive attitudes, that is just a defect in those formulations. It does not testify to any genuine incompatibility between determinism and the attitudes themselves.

Much as I admire Strawson's article, I find myself more persuaded by his diagnosis of what troubles pessimists about the form of compatibilism he discusses than by his conclusion that pessimism is in the end unwarranted. My aim here, however, is not to argue against that conclusion. It is rather to call attention to the way in which the issues Strawson raises are relevant to debates about liberalism. What makes them relevant is the close connection between the compatibilist construal of praise and blame to which Strawson objects and the purely institutional conception of desert favored by liberal philosophers. Strawson's compatibilist seeks to justify the practices whereby we hold people responsible or accountable for their actions by reference to the social utility of such practices. Liberal philosophers, meanwhile, regard the defensibility of the practices whereby we treat individuals who behave in certain ways as deserving certain rewards or penalties as entirely dependent on the prior defensibility of the social institutions that are said to give rise to those practices. In each case, the assignment of benefits and burdens in accordance with a conception of merit or desert is seen as requiring justification by reference to something putatively more fundamental: either to the utility of such assignments or to their placement within a larger institutional framework that is thought of as independently justifiable. In neither case is a conception of merit or desert treated as morally fundamental nor as an independent normative constraint on the design of social institutions.

It is true that liberal philosophers, or at least those liberal philosophers whose orientation is not utilitarian, need not conceive of our practices with respect to merit and desert in the narrowly instrumental way that is characteristic of what Strawson calls "the objective attitude." In this respect, their position differs from the type of compatibilist position that Strawson criticizes. Yet it resembles that position in the ways that I have described, and this is sufficient to raise the question of whether it too is insufficiently sensitive to the role of the relevant practices in giving expression to our reactive attitudes. Admittedly, some liberal philosophers who reject the idea of preinstitutional desert in favor of the notion of legitimate institutional expectations would nevertheless agree that punishment, at least, has an important "expressive function." Yet these philosophers need to show that the reactive attitudes whose expression through the institution of punishment they acknowledge do not rest on just the sorts of assumptions about preinstitutional desert that they reject. Offhand, it would seem that if the punishment of a murderer or a rapist, say, serves to express the community's outrage and indignation, it does so by answering to the thought that the perpetrator *deserves* a severe penalty, where this does not mean merely that he has reason to expect one. Furthermore, the liberal philosophers I am discussing do not treat desert-based judgments about the assignment of social and economic benefits as serving to express significant interpersonal reactions at all. Yet it is clear that judgments to the effect that certain individuals do or do not deserve certain benefits have an important expressive function in many contexts. This might not present a problem for liberals if the reactive attitudes were sufficiently plastic that they were capable of finding full expression via whatever system of institutional expectations and entitlements happened to be in place. To the extent that those attitudes are less than fully flexible, however, any purely institutional conception of desert runs the risk of conflicting with them, and hence of presenting itself as incompatible with a web of fundamental interpersonal responses. Thus, if liberalism proposes to replace our ordinary notion of desert with the idea of legitimate institutional expectations, and if that proposal meets with political resistance, the possibility cannot be excluded that such resistance is responsive in part to an underlying tension between liberalism and the reactive attitudes, rather than stemming exclusively from contingent features of the prevailing political climate.

The upshot of the discussion to this point may be summarized as follows. Political liberalism has come under heavy attack in this country owing in part to a perception that many of the programs and policies advocated by liberals rest on a reduced conception of individual responsibility. Although some liberals might wish to reject this perception as erroneous, it is a striking fact that the dominant contemporary philosophical defenses of liberalism, by virtue of their reliance on a purely institutional notion of desert, do indeed advocate a reduced conception of responsibility. And in so doing, they may to some extent be underestimating the significance of the human attitudes and emotions that find expression through our practices with respect to desert and responsibility. If so, then two conclusions seem to follow. The first is that contemporary philosophical liberalism may be vulnerable to a criticism not unlike the one that has been directed at contemporary political liberalism. The second is that the prospects of political liberalism might best be served, not by additional arguments in favor of a purely institutional conception of desert, but rather by a demonstration that liberal programs and policies do not in fact require such a conception.

As I have indicated, these conclusions could perhaps be avoided, at least in the case of liberal principles of distributive justice, if it could be shown that the reactive attitudes were sufficiently plastic as to render them fully compatible with an institutional system of economic expectations that was insensitive to any independent considerations of desert. It is unclear whether a convincing argument to this effect is available. To the best of my knowledge, the closest thing to such an argument that one finds in contemporary liberal theory is Rawls's argument for the stability of his conception of justice. That argument turns on the claim that citizens in a well-ordered society regulated by Rawlsian principles would acquire a more effective sense of justice than would citizens in societies ordered by other conceptions of justice, most notably utilitarianism. In order to establish this claim, Rawls sketches an account of the development of the moral sentiments with the aim of demonstrating that an effective sense of justice would be the normal outcome of the processes of moral development in a Rawlsian society. Rawls's account emphasizes the intimate relation between the sense of justice and reactive attitudes like shame, guilt, and resentment, and he takes pains to argue that these attitudes would tend to develop in a well-ordered society in such a way that, in their mature form, they would naturally come to be regimented by the Rawlsian principles of justice. That is, people would feel guilty if they violated those principles, they would feel resentful of violations committed by others, and so on. Rawls takes the psychological plausibility of his account to depend on the idea that his principles of justice embody an ideal of reciprocity or mutuality, and it is therefore natural that he should contrast his account primarily with the moral psychology of utilitarianism. For the ideas of reciprocity and mutuality have no fundamental ethical significance for utilitarianism, and as a result utilitarian moral psychology seems forced to make implausibly heavy demands on the human capacity for sympathetic identification. In so doing, utilitarianism seems to underestimate the psychological constraints on the design of stable social and political institutions, and Rawls's account has great force by comparison. Yet Rawls never explicitly addresses the question whether his own repudiation of preinstitutional desert may not itself involve such an underestimation, albeit one of a less extreme sort. In other words, he never explicitly considers, and thus never convincingly rules out, the possibility, first, that our judgments about the proper distribution of benefits and burdens in society may, in addition to regimenting our reactive attitudes, serve as a vehicle for expressing those attitudes; and, second, that the attitudes in question may rest on an assumption that individuals are responsible agents in a sense that implies that their distributive shares ought to be influenced in certain ways by their behavior.[3] Here it seems relevant to note that, whereas Strawson says that resentment and other reactive attitudes are "essentially reactions to the quality of others' wills toward us," resentment in political contexts—whether it arises on the left or on the right—is more often a reaction to (what are perceived as) the *undeserved advantages* of others, and not to the quality of their wills at all.

III

There is some irony in the fact that the difficulty to which I have been calling attention arises for nonutilitarian versions of contemporary liberal theory. For such theories tend to appeal to people who regard utilitarianism's aggregative character as rendering it incapable of providing a tolerably secure foundation for individual rights, and who regard its instrumental, goal-oriented structure as rendering it incapable of attaching sufficient weight, or the right kind of weight, to those features of human life and personal relations about which we care most. Many such people would view the failure of familiar forms of compatibilism to appreciate either the role of our practices of praise and blame in giving expression to our reactive attitudes or the role of the reactive attitudes in human interpersonal relations as an unsurprising consequence of the instrumental, utilitarian character of those compatibilist formulations. In this way, they would see the failings of such formulations as serving to illustrate the very sorts of considerations that make nonutilitarian versions of liberal theory look attractive. Hence the irony in the fact that those versions of liberalism may themselves be insufficiently sensitive to the significance of the reactive attitudes in relation to our notions of desert and responsibility.

Even if this is granted, of course, it may be thought to reveal nothing more important than the existence of an internal tension in the views of a certain group of people. However, I believe that the tension between philosophical liberalism and ordinary notions of desert and responsibility has wider significance, for three main reasons. The first reason, which I have already emphasized, is that the prospects of political liberalism may depend in part on how this tension is resolved. This will be so, at any rate, at least insofar as it is contemporary philosophical liberalism, with its disavowal of preinstitutional desert, that is seen as providing the theoretical foundation for the positions and policies advocated by political liberals.

The second reason is that an appreciation of the tension between liberalism and desert helps to illuminate the intense philosophical controversy surrounding liberalism's alleged "neutrality" among competing "conceptions of the good." Liberalism's claims to neutrality have always struck critics of varying persuasions as involving a certain degree of bad faith. There are a number of reasons for this, but one of the most important is that liberalism seems to many of its critics to presuppose a conception of human life and an understanding of the place of human beings in the world that is itself in conflict with many conceptions of the good. To these critics, the difficulty is not that liberalism directly endorses some particular conception of the good or directly condemns some other conception. The fundamental problem arises much earlier, at the stage at which liberalism defines the "individuals" among whose conceptions of the good it purports to be neutral. To its critics, the liberal framework itself seems to incorporate an understanding of what it is to be a human individual that is highly contentious, and that leads inevitably to the design of institutions and the creation of conditions that are far more hospitable to some ways of life than to others. The argument I have been developing in this article reveals one of the bases for this criticism. For, as I have said, the unwillingness of liberal philosophers to rely on any preinstitutional conception of desert is due in part to their internalization of a broadly naturalistic outlook, and to their skeptical understanding of how robust a notion of individual agency is compatible with such an outlook. Yet a purely naturalistic understanding of human life *is* contentious. The modern world is deeply divided in its attempt to come to terms with the power of naturalism, and one of the defining features of modern life is a deep uneasiness about what place there may be for our selves and our values in the world that science is in the process of discovering. It is clear, moreover, that different conceptions of the good respond to this uneasiness in very different ways. Thus if liberalism does presuppose a naturalistically based skepticism about individual agency, it is hardly surprising that its claims to neutrality among diverse conceptions of the good should seem suspect. Moreover, although the political prospects of liberalism might be improved if liberal policies could be defended by appeal to a more robust conception of agency and responsibility, there would be no gain in neutrality if liberalism were seen to rest upon such a conception. For as long as a purely naturalistic understanding of human life remains controversial—as long as the place of human beings in the world of science is subject to debate—*no* conception of agency and responsibility can claim to be neutral among conceptions of the good. This may seem to imply that, in order to preserve its neutrality, liberalism should refrain from endorsing any conception of individual agency or responsibility. However, even if such abstinence were a conceptual possibility, as it almost certainly is not, it would have the peculiar effect of reducing liberalism to silence on the very subject that was supposed to be its specialty, namely, the nature and moral importance of the individual human agent.

The third reason why the tension between philosophical liberalism and ordinary notions of desert and responsibility is significant is that it raises a philosophically and politically important question about the moral psychology of liberalism. I have already argued that the question of the plasticity of the reactive attitudes assumes great importance for liberal philosophers in view of their reliance on a purely institutional conception of desert. However, this is really but an instance of a more general challenge facing liberalism. The more general challenge is to allay the suspicion that the interpersonal attitudes that liberals value in the private sphere may be psychologically continuous with social and political attitudes whose implications are uncongenial to liberalism. The suggestion that our reactive attitudes may presuppose a preinstitutional notion of desert that is incompatible with liberal principles of justice represents one way in which this suspicion can arise. Another way in which it can arise is via the suggestion that the very same psychological proclivities that lead people to develop personal loyalties and attachments may also lead them to develop forms of group identification and allegiance that liberalism cannot easily accommodate. The suggestion, in other words, is that the psychology of friendship and close personal relations is also the psychology of communal solidarity and partiality. This suggestion receives support from communitarianism in the domain of theory, and from the rise of nationalism and multiculturalism in the domain of political practice. Indeed, it is at this point that the communitarian criticism of liberalism and the desert-based criticism begin to converge. For each sees liberalism as demanding, at the level of political interaction, an individual psychology of bland impartiality: a psychology that is thoroughly unrealistic, and that would be incapable, even if it *were* realistic, of sustaining the rich interpersonal relations that liberals are prepared to celebrate in the realm of private life.

IV

I should emphasize that my aim in this article has not been to defend the preinstitutional notion of desert that is embedded in traditional conceptions of responsibility. Indeed, liberals (among whom I number myself) may well be right to be skeptical of this notion, and, hence, of the traditional conceptions that rely on it. My aim has merely been to call attention to the extent of such skepticism among liberals, and to its significance. Before concluding, however, let me address two objections to my argument that will long since have occurred to the reader. The first objection is that my characterization of contemporary liberal philosophy as having internalized a naturalistically based skepticism about individual agency and responsibility cannot possibly be correct, at least as applied to the liberalism of Rawls. For, especially in those writings that postdate *A Theory of Justice*, Rawls takes pains to emphasize the Kantian roots of his theory, and to highlight the role played in that theory by a conception of citizens as "free and equal moral persons." Moreover, he says it is a feature of that conception that citizens "are regarded as taking responsibility for their ends and [that] this affects how their various claims are assessed." Thus it may seem clearly inaccurate to represent Rawls as relying on

an attenuated conception of agency and responsibility.

In response, however, I would make two points. First, the doctrine of "responsibility for ends," as Rawls presents it, does not involve any preinstitutional conception of desert, nor is it intended as an independent constraint on the design of just institutions. Instead, it simply amounts to the claim that

> given just background institutions and the provision for all of a fair index of primary goods (as required by the principles of justice), citizens are capable of adjusting their aims and ambitions in the light of what they can reasonably expect and of restricting their claims in matters of justice to certain kinds of things. They recognize that the weight of their claims is not given by the strength or intensity of their wants and desires, even when they are rational.

Rawls's argument in this passage is that people have the capacity to adjust their aims and aspirations in light of their institutional expectations, provided that the institutions in question are just. The purpose of this argument is to explain why a reliance on primary goods as an index of well-being is not inappropriate, despite the fact that someone with unusually expensive tastes and preferences may derive less satisfaction from a given bundle of those goods than someone with more modest tastes and preferences. Rawls's claim is that just institutions need make no special provision for expensive preferences, not because individuals are responsible in some preinstitutional sense for their own preferences, but rather because people living in a just society have the capacity to adjust their preferences in light of the resources they can expect to have at their command. To be sure, this capacity may itself be preinstitutional in some sense. However, there is an important difference between the claim that people possess preinstitutional capacities that would enable them to adapt to a certain institutional assignment of responsibility and the claim that the assignment of responsibility is itself preinstitutional. Thus, whatever one thinks of

Rawls's argument, there is, as far as I can see, nothing in it that has any tendency to vindicate traditional notions of responsibility or desert.

A similar conclusion applies, incidentally, to Ronald Dworkin's treatment of expensive tastes. Dworkin appears at one point to express sympathy for the position that people do not *deserve* compensation for expensive tastes, or at least for those expensive tastes that they have deliberately cultivated. However, it quickly emerges that, for Dworkin, the claim that some individual does not deserve compensation for his expensive tastes may be legitimate only insofar as it is based on a judgment that the individual in question has already received what has independently been identified as his fair share of social resources. For Dworkin, in other words, there is no prior standard of desert that determines what counts as a fair share or as a just institutional arrangement. Thus Dworkin does not appeal to a preinstitutional conception of desert any more than do the other liberal theorists we have discussed.

Returning to Rawls, the other point I want to make is simply that, although his broadly Kantian conception of the person may well be incompatible with the attenuated notion of individual agency to which I have referred, explicit endorsement of the former is compatible with tacit reliance on the latter. Insofar as Rawls's unwillingness to accept preinstitutional desert gives rise to a reduced conception of individual responsibility, any tension between such a conception and Rawls's Kantian ideal of the person must be viewed as a tension internal to his theory. Moreover, a tension of this sort seems likely to afflict any form of liberalism that defers at crucial points to the authority of a naturalistic outlook, while seeking simultaneously to situate itself within the philosophical tradition of Kant.[4]

The second objection that I wish very briefly to address may be put as follows. If, as I have argued, there is a surprising degree of agreement among contemporary philosophical liberals and their critics about the advisability of avoiding any appeal to prein-

stitutional desert, then why should it be a special problem for political liberalism if it too avoids any such appeal? The answer is that although liberalism's most prominent philosophical critics may be reluctant to appeal to preinstitutional desert, its most prominent political critics certainly are not. On the contrary, conservative politicians do not hesitate to invoke traditional notions of desert and responsibility in attacking liberal positions. Thus if political liberalism does require the rejection of preinstitutional desert, then although it will be in tune with the prevailing philosophical consensus, that may not suffice to prevent its political isolation. Indeed, if one takes the view that our reactive attitudes require a preinstitutional conception of desert that is incompatible with a broadly naturalistic outlook, then, to the extent that political liberalism reflects the prevailing philosophical consensus, pessimism about the philosophical implications of naturalism may translate into pessimism about the political prospects of liberalism.

NOTES

1. In recent work Rawls has distinguished between "political liberalism," which is said not to depend on any "comprehensive moral doctrine," and "comprehensive liberalism," which does so depend. See "Justice as Fairness: Political Not Metaphysical," *Philosophy & Public Affairs* 14, no. 3 (Summer 1985): 223–51, and "The Idea of an Overlapping Consensus," *Oxford Journal of Legal Studies* 7 (1987): 1–25. His own view is said to be an instance of the former, while those of Kant and Mill are cited as examples of the latter. The distinction I am drawing is, as should be evident, a different one. I am concerned with the relations between liberalism as a position in American political life and liberalism as a view in contemporary political philosophy. In this sense, Rawls's view is an example of philosophical liberalism.

2. Ibid., p. 103. Curiously, Rawls appears to suggest (on pp. 314–15) that reliance on a preinstitutional conception of desert *is* appropriate in the case of retributive justice, despite the fact that it is inappropriate in the case of distributive justice. As Michael Sandel argues (in *Liberalism and the Limits of Justice* [Cambridge: Cambridge University Press, 1982], pp. 89–92), it is very difficult to see what basis Rawls has for making this distinction,

since the considerations that lead him to reject pre-institutional desert in the case of distributive justice seem to apply with equal force to the case of retributive justice. And, as T. M. Scanlon observes, "Rawls' theory of distributive justice" employs "a general philosophical strategy" that is equally available in the retributive case:

> In approaching the problems of justifying both penal and economic institutions we begin with strong pretheoretical intuitions about the significance of choice: voluntary and intentional commission of a criminal act is a necessary condition of just punishment, and voluntary economic contribution can make an economic reward just and its denial unjust. One way to account for these intuitions is by appeal to a preinstitutional notion of desert: certain acts deserve punishment, certain contributions merit rewards, and institutions are just if they distribute benefits and burdens in accord with these forms of desert.
>
> The strategy I am describing makes a point of avoiding any such appeal. The only notions of desert which it recognizes are internal to institutions and dependent upon a prior notion of justice: if institutions are just then people deserve the rewards and punishments which these institutions assign them. In the justification of institutions, the notion of desert is replaced by an independent notion of justice; in the justification of specific actions and outcomes it is replaced by the idea of legitimate (institutional) expectations. ("The Significance of Choice," in *The Tanner Lectures on Human Values VIII*, ed. Sterling McMurrin [Salt Lake City: University of Utah Press, 1988], p. 188)

Scanlon himself is generally sympathetic to the strategy he describes, and his own account of the "significance of choice" also avoids any reliance on a preinstitutional notion of desert. Because Rawls's view of retributive justice is not developed at any length and plays virtually no role in the overall argument of his book, and because it is dubiously consistent with his account of distributive justice, I will not devote any further attention to it. I regard it as a small and insufficiently motivated departure from the general attitude toward desert that dominates his work and the work of the other liberal theorists with whom I am concerned.

3. In an unpublished manuscript ("Justice as Fairness: A Restatement" [Cambridge, Mass., 1990], pp. 58–64), Rawls says that he does not reject preinstitutional desert altogether; he merely denies that it can play any role in a "political" conception of justice designed for a modern, pluralistic democracy, and believes that it must be replaced for the purposes of such a conception by the idea of legitimate expectations. This seems to me to represent a significant departure from the views expressed in *A Theory of Justice*, at (for example) pp. 312–13. And, in any case, it leaves the question I have raised in the text unanswered.

4. Rawls's recent assertion (see note 3) that he does not *reject* preinstitutional desert, but merely believes that it is too controversial to play any role in a political conception of justice designed for a modern pluralistic democracy, may seem to provide another reason for thinking that my claim about the influence of naturalism cannot be correct. As I indicated in note 3, however, I believe that Rawls's recent discussion understates the extent of the skepticism about preinstitutional desert that is expressed in *A Theory of Justice*. Nor is there any hint in *A Theory of Justice* that Rawls's reason for avoiding preinstitutional desert is that he believes the notion to be too controversial to play a role in a political conception of justice. In any event, my claim about the influence of naturalism is not a claim about the explicit premises of liberal arguments, nor does it purport to be an exhaustive statement of the factors responsible for the liberal aversion to preinstitutional desert.

D. THE ROLE AND SIGNIFICANCE OF DESERT

23. Desert, Consent and Justice

MICHAEL A. SLOTE

Michael Slote is Professor of Philosophy and Chair of the Philosophy Department at the University of Maryland, College Park. A member of the Royal Irish Academy, he is the author of several books on ethics, including, most recently, *From Morality to Virtue*. Another book, *Three Methods of Ethics: A Debate*, written with Marcia Baron and Philip Pettit, is forthcoming.

In this essay Slote inquiries whether an ideally just society should reward people according to their actual success or their conscientious effort. He offers the thought experiment of two women searching for their friend's lost book. Does the woman who finds the book deserve more gratitude than the one who tried equally hard to find it? Slote uses this case as a paradigm of distributive justice and argues that the difference between capitalist and socialist views about the ideally just way for society to distribute goods can be reduced to the two different ways of answering this question. However, Slote adds a proviso, namely, that whatever people freely consent to is just. Finally, Slote rebuts views, like Rawls's, that are incompatible with the notion of desert as a basis for justice.

In this essay, I intend to deal with an important problem about the nature of just societies. I shall not endeavor to solve the problem, but hope, rather, to indicate its centrality to the whole question of the nature of social justice and to show why it is so difficult to resolve it in any satisfactory way. The issue I wish to discuss is whether an ideally just society whose members were to some appropriate degree willing to work for the general good and not merely for their own selfish interests would reward people (workers) in accordance with their actual *success* in contributing to society or in accordance with their (conscientious) *efforts* to contribute to society.

Reprinted from *Philosophy and Public Affairs* 2 (Summer 1973), by permission. Notes edited.

For convenience, but also because there is more than a grain of truth to it, we can consider this to be, in effect, the question whether society is more justly organized according to a democratic capitalist scheme or according to a (utopian) socialist scheme. For although there have been many other arguments for the superiority of capitalism to socialism, and even other arguments for the superior justice of capitalism, one very important argument for capitalism over (certain forms of utopian) socialism has been that those who through ability or "luck" contribute more to society in all justice and fairness deserve more from society than those who, despite their greatest efforts, make less of a contribution to society. Similarly, though there have been many kinds of socialism and many kinds of argument for socialism, one thing that seems often to have had great force in persuading people to be socialist is the view that it is only just to reward people for their conscientious efforts, and that it is unfair for someone to reap more of the rewards society has to distribute simply because he happens, through greater innate talents or other "lucky breaks," to (be able to) do more for society.

It may be asked at this point why I speak of socialism, rather than of Marxism or Communism. My reason is not that I conceive Marxism to be one kind of socialism and thus automatically or naturally included when I talk about socialism. It is, rather, that I think there is no good reason to think that the main issue between capitalism and Marxism is over the nature of the just society or over the justness of capitalist society, in particular. Despite long-standing misconceptions on this point, it has recently been very convincingly argued by Robert Tucker and (especially) Allen Wood that Marx had no great interest in decrying the injustice of capitalist society and, even, that Marx thought that capitalist society as he knew it was not basically unjust.

The problem whether a just society rewards its members in accordance with their efforts to contribute, or in accordance with their success in contributing, is an important issue that divides capitalist theorists and socialist theorists, but does not, in general, divide capitalist theorists and orthodox Marxists. Moreover, this issue, however important it may be, does not even divide capitalist theorists from non-Marxian socialists in any clean-cut way. Many socialists have held that workers should receive the full product of their labor (which they are presumed not to receive under capitalism); and this seems to entail what I have called the democratic capitalist view that one should be rewarded according to his actual contribution to society rather than according to his conscientious efforts in behalf of society. Be this as it may, there is another view about the compensation of labor that I think is more typical of socialism. This view is often expressed in the motto or adage: "from each according to his ability, to each according to his needs." It is this view, it seems to me, that brings out the most important differences between socialism and capitalism and that is (part of) the best expression of socialism as an "ideal type." So when I speak of the differences between socialism and capitalism, I am not talking about all socialism, but only about a certain ideal type of socialism that stands opposed to a certain ideal type of capitalism. I say "ideal type of capitalism" because it is not even clear that all capitalist theorists want, or should want, to claim that distribution according to actual (successful) contribution is ideally just. A capitalistic theorist might well want to claim that such distribution is somewhat unjust, but nonetheless socially justifiable on the grounds of its efficiency or benefits, or the unworkability of alternative distributive schemes. But as a rule one who defends capitalism will feel that rewarding according to contribution, rather than effort, is fair and just; and it is such a form of capitalistic theorizing that I mean to discuss here.

I

The kind of socialism I refer to is, I have said, exemplified by the view: "from each according to his ability, to each according to his needs." But even among people who in some sense adhere to this adage there is dispute as to how, or how strictly, it is to be interpreted. For example, are aesthetic needs to count equally with "basic" needs, and what, indeed, are to be considered (basic) human needs? If, in particular, it is necessary to reduce everyone to a bare subsistence level in order, say, to keep certain people with rare diseases alive and functioning, does the adage tell us that we must (in all fairness) do so? It appears that different socialists would respond differently to these questions. What can be said, roughly, to characterize socialism generally or as an ideal type, however, is that according to its conception of social justice, goods, benefits or rewards for work should be in accordance with conscientious effort in behalf of society, assuming certain basic similarities or equalities in people's needs, and, in any case, should not be distributed in accordance with actual success in benefiting society. And such a view, vague though it my be, does stand in sharp contrast with what I have been claiming to be the typical capitalist conception of what is necessary to a just society.

Now Tucker has claimed that the motto "from each according to his ability . . ." (which we can henceforth, for brevity, refer to as the socialist motto) expresses a social ideal, but not an ideal of social justice. And there is some support for this in the fact that Marx, who believed that capitalism was not unjust, presents himself as an adherent of the socialist motto in *A Critique of the Gotha Program*. But whatever Marx's, or Tucker's, views about justice, or about the socialist motto, it is quite clear that many writers on political theory have felt that this motto expresses an ideal, often their ideal, of social justice. The impressive list of such writers includes: Babeuf,[1] J. S. Mill,[2] O. D. Skelton,[3] F. H. Knight,[4] John Strachey,[5] C. Frankel,[6] and John Rawls.[7] Furthermore, it seems obvious to me that the socialist motto can very naturally and easily, even if mistakenly, be thought to express an ideal of social justice, and perhaps the only support this assumption requires at this point can be supplied by the reader's own intuitions on the matter. If, furthermore, Tucker thinks that the socialist motto does not express an ideal of justice, that is perhaps because it expresses an ideal

of social justice that he thoroughly disagrees with; for Tucker says that the socialist motto does not express an ideal of social justice because a person's needs may be in inverse proportion to his ability and to his contribution to society. Tucker, then, seems to be espousing what I have called a capitalist conception of social justice. And there are numerous other places where one can find a capitalist conception of justice expressed.[8]

In this essay, I hope to clarify the nature and sources of the disagreement between democratic capitalists and non-Marxian socialists concerning the relative importance of effort as against successful contribution in determining an ideally just distribution of goods in society. Following J. S. Mill, in "Utilitarianism," I shall argue that this disagreement stems from a disagreement about whether effort or success (i.e., actual contribution) is more important in determining what one *deserves* to receive from society. That is because, like Mill, I think that the notion of desert is crucially involved in the notion of justice. (However, an attempt will be made here to show that Mill is significantly mistaken about the *kind* of desert that is analytically involved in the concept of justice.) I shall first attempt to show why disagreement about the relative importance of effort and success in determining what one deserves from society very naturally arises and remains impossible to resolve in a way that will satisfy everyone. Then it will be argued that an appropriate notion of desert is centrally involved in the concept of justice, despite John Rawls's notable recent attempts to discredit such an idea. If all this can be accomplished, then perhaps we will have cast some light on the sources of the disagreement between capitalists and socialists about the nature of social justice, and on the immense difficulty, if not the actual impossibility, of resolving that disagreement in any philosophically satisfying way.

II

I think it will be easier to see how the question of the importance of effort as against success in determining what one deserves from society (or what one's just reward or recompense from society is) arises so naturally and remains so difficult to resolve definitively, if we consider a parallel, but non-political question. Imagine, then, that a certain woman has lost a book and two friends of hers come by and volunteer to help her find it. The friends make equally conscientious, energetic, and intelligent efforts to find the book, and one of them succeeds in finding it and returning it to the woman who lost it. One might well wonder about such a case whether the woman who actually found the book deserves more (by way of gratitude or reward) from the friend who lost the book than does the woman who tried equally hard but failed to find the book. And this is a difficult question. On the one hand, it is possible to feel that since the friends made equal efforts, etc., in behalf of the woman who lost the book, she is equally in their debt and should reward them equally. It may seem that neither deserves more than the other at her hands. We are, after all, imagining that the person who does not find the book fails through no intellectual, emotional or moral defect of her own and that her failure to find the book can be attributed to "bad luck" or "accident." And can greater desert, or a greater debt of gratitude, arise through mere luck or accident?

But there is another side to the question. For surely there is in general a human tendency to be more grateful to someone who tries to help and succeeds than to someone who tries equally hard and fails. And one may feel that such a tendency is at least some evidence of an ethical distinction, that it reflects our recognition that those who (somehow) do more for us also deserve more from us, other things being equal. Furthermore, even if the two friends who search for the book demonstrate equally good character, or equal moral worth, by their efforts, the notion of desert at someone's hands, or desert from someone, is different and may not apply in the same cases. For one thing, a given person may do things for certain people and thereby come to deserve things from those people; and yet another person, equally morally worthy, may

never enter into any relations with those people on the basis of which he could come to deserve gratitude or rewards from them. Of course, it could be claimed that even if desert at someone's hands is not equivalent to moral worth or goodness in general, desert at a person's hands is equivalent to the moral goodness of one's (past) behavior towards, or activity concerning, that person. But this is by no means obviously correct, even if only because in the above example of the lost book, it is much clearer that the two helping friends are equally good from a moral point of view in their behavior towards the loser of the book than that they deserve equal gratitude or reward from her.

On the other hand, there are reasons for doubting whether our natural inclination to feel greater gratitude towards those who succeed in benefiting us than towards those who only try (conscientiously) to benefit us really indicates that we should feel greater gratitude towards those who benefit us, or that such people are more deserving of our gratitude or of rewards from us. Perhaps such feelings are irrational; perhaps they have some evolutionary survival value, but are (in some appropriate sense) morally neutral. It is hard to know what to say. At this point, it might, therefore, be useful to examine some other case where problems of desert and gratitude arise, and to use our intuitions about that case to help us decide the issue of desert in the lost book case. Imagine, then, a circumstance in which someone accidentally falls against my heart-lung machine and turns it on. Imagine further that if the man in question had not turned the machine on, I would have died, since the machine had accidentally been turned off (by someone else) without anyone's knowledge. Do I owe the person who has accidentally turned on my heart-lung machine any special debt of gratitude? Does he deserve anything from me that some other man in the room does not? If I feel more gratitude to the man who has turned my machine on, is this merely a natural human response? Is it like the case where a person feels grateful when a tree blocks a bullet aimed at him, but does not or should not feel that the tree deserves anything from him? Or does desert arise from the mere fact that the man was involved in doing or causing me some good? If the latter is the case, then it can be argued that since the fact of causing someone good can make a difference to what is deserved in a case, like the heart-lung machine case, where no conscientious effort occurs, it can make a difference to what is deserved in a situation where equal conscientious effort takes place. One will conclude that in the lost book case the woman who actually finds the book deserves more from her friend who lost the book. But unfortunately, the question of desert in the heart-lung machine case seems every bit as difficult as the question of desert in the lost book case, so I doubt whether the former can help us to decide about the latter. If anything, I think the heart-lung machine case serves further to emphasize the great difficulty of deciding whether actual (success in) doing good or making a contribution can make any difference to what one deserves. What I would like now to argue is that the difficulty of deciding between capitalist and socialist views about the ideally just way for a society to distribute goods in some sense reduces to, and can be understood in terms of, the difficulty of deciding the question of desert that arises in the non-political case of the lost book (or in the non-political case of the heart-lung machine). To do this I shall first show that in the area of the distribution of goods in society, a parallel, indeed virtually the same, question about desert arises as does in the lost book case (or the heart-lung machine case). More will then be said about the assumption that the notion of desert is central to the notion of social justice, and some arguments and views—among them those of Rawls—that seem incompatible with this contention will be rebutted.

III

A just society is often thought of as being something like a large corporation that fairly recompenses those who work for it. Society is conceived as a kind of agent that people benefit or try to benefit, that people can de-serve more or less from according to their contributions or efforts, and that rewards and punishes. If so, then a situation in which people are doing socially useful work together in society will be parallel to that of the lost and found book. If people are to some appropriate degree working for the good of society, attempting to do work that is socially useful, even if also very concerned about their own private interests, then the difference between those who make great contributions to society through their work and those who work just as hard but fail to make such contributions is much like the difference between the friend who tries to find the book and succeeds and the friend who tries to find the book and fails through no fault of her own. And the question whether the friend who finds the book deserves more from the woman who lost it is like the question whether those who actually contribute a great deal to society deserve more from society than those who try and fail to do so.[9]

Now one objection to our claim of parallelism might be that in the book case differences of ability between the two friends were ruled out, or said to be irrelevant, but that this does not seem possible in talking about different people's differing contributions to society, since differences in abilities are a (the?) major cause of differing contributions to society. But as long as we assume that differences in abilities do not in and of themselves make a difference to what one deserves from society, but (at most) affect what one deserves from society only as they affect one's contribution to society, the cases are, I think, close enough for our purposes. And I think both capitalist and socialist theorists would agree with such an assumption. That socialists would agree with it is obvious enough, without argument. But even democratic capitalists do not seem to hold that those with greater ability prima facie deserve more from society, independently of their relative contributions to society. Surely, to take an extreme case, a talented social parasite is not thought by them to deserve more from society than an untalented one, even if other things are equal. But even in more usual cases it is not ability taken alone that typically is stressed by democratic capitalist theorists as a source of individual desert from society, but rather ability as a means to, and sign of, greater individual contribution to society. Such thinkers, I believe, usually stress the propriety of rewarding people according to their talents or abilities because they assume that with great talents or abilities go greater contributions to society, greater productivity and greater benefits conferred. It is greater contributions that capitalists really have in mind as the source of greater deserts. According to such theorists, if two men (say, entrepreneurs) of equal talent expend equal amounts of energy to produce something that people need or want and one of them, through "good breaks" or "luck" or what have you, is more successful in doing so, then that person deserves the greater rewards or benefits he reaps through his success. So far I see nothing to mar the parallelism I have been suggesting between the problem of the lost book and the problem whether those who do more for society deserve more from it.

Another objection to this parallelism might be that it assumes an unrealistic amount of willingness on the part of people to work in behalf of society. The two women who look for the book want to help their friend to a degree that people working in society do not in general desire to contribute to society. All this may be so, but it does not, I think, constitute a serious objection. We have raised a question about desert in a certain kind of slightly idealized (and, presumably, desirable) situation where men are willing to work together for the benefit of society. And it is at least one major issue between socialist theory and capitalist theory whether in *such* a case effort or success (actual contribution) is the source of desert, or justly derived benefits, from society. It is not entirely to the point to claim that in actual fact men are not this benevolent or unselfish, at least if one is willing to grant that such people are psychologically possible. Furthermore, if someone assumes that such devotion is beyond all human possibilities, he will, I think, still be able to acknowledge a parallelism between the case

of the heart-lung machine and that of the distribution of goods in society, since in the heart-lung machine case there is only an accidental and unintentional contribution to the sick person's welfare and, presumably, everyone is willing to grant that selfish people who are not devoted to their society can and do make accidental or unintentional contributions to society.

IV

We know that people differ over whether effort or (democratically regulated) success is what a just society rewards. We can explain this if we assume that the notion of desert is appropriately built into the notion of justice. For then the question whether social justice entails that people be recompensed according to effort or actual contribution (success) will be tantamount to the question whether effort or actual contribution is paramount in determining what people deserve from society. And we can see why *this* question is so hard to resolve because of the parallel we have drawn between it and a non-political question whose difficulty can, I think, readily be appreciated. So the assumption that the notion of desert plays a role in the notion of justice may to some degree be justified in terms of its explanatory power. It is, of course, also not a particularly implausible idea. And it is an old idea that can be found, for example, in Mill's "Utilitarianism" and Henry Sidgwick's *Methods of Ethics*. Indeed, both these philosophers seem to have thought that social justice consisted simply in the distribution of goods in society according to desert. I do not doubt that some notion of desert has a role to play in the concept of justice, but in no case do I think that that notion exhausts the idea of justice. There is I believe, an important further element in the notion of justice, the notion of free consent.

One way in which we could assure ourselves of a perfectly just society (or basic social structure) would be, I believe, by creating a society where all the equalities and inequalities provided for by the society—and not, say, by chance, individual differences, or certain failures to live up to the norms and rules of the society—were deserved, by which I mean a situation where everyone received from society just what he deserved from society. But this is not, it seems to me, a *necessary* condition of ideal social justice. If certain equalities or inequalities are freely consented to, then the society that creates these equalities or inequalities can be perfectly just, no matter whether those equalities or inequalities are deserved or not. To give one very simple example, if there really were differences of desert among members of society, but those who deserved more from society all agreed to everyone's receiving equally, then the equalities that resulted would not, presumably, be deserved, but no injustice would arise from their existence either. Similarly, if everyone in society *x* deserves equally from *x*, but the members of *x* agree to let certain popular or well-liked people have certain privileges, and do so out of sheer affection for those people, then *x* may still be perfectly just.

I have spoken of *freely* consented to equalities and inequalities for a reason. It seems to me that an injustice may be done if people are, e.g., literally brainwashed into being people who will consent to certain inequalities. One might say that in such a case they are not even consenting to the inequalities, but then consent is tantamount to free consent, and it will still be the case that not everything that appears to be free consent is free consent. At worst, adding the word "free" is redundant. Conditions I have in mind as eliminating free consent include: brainwashing, inability to understand certain issues, certain sorts of ignorance, the presence of threats or dangers, economic duress, certain moods, etc. I do not think I should include freedom of the will in any traditional sense as a necessary condition of free consent. By "free consent" I mean more a politically desirable kind of consent than a metaphysically desirable kind. I am inclined to assume that there is a sense of "free" that does not entail free will. Otherwise, assuming that equalities and inequalities are unjust unless deserved or (in some sense) freely consented to, we get the undesirable result that intelligent and sensitive beings who lack metaphysical free will—and thus quite possibly we ourselves—cannot, e.g., justly (or fairly) institute a situation of non-deserved equality for all by their common consent. And this conclusion is surely counter-intuitive. Sidgwick has maintained that if there is no freedom of the will, there are no such things as deserts or justice. But this simply seems wrong and wrong-headed to me; and I shall assume that political theory can be made independent of the free will question in something like the way I have been suggesting.

In addition to problems about the nature of free consent, there are also problems about whether or when one consents to certain consequences of what one directly consents to. This is where the so-called paradox of democracy arises, for example. Such problems may, indeed, arise from vagueness in the notion of consent, but even if this is so, that will not necessarily constitute a problem for attempts to define justice in terms of consent, since justice itself may have vague edges corresponding to the vagueness in the notion of consent.

The concepts of desert and consent both seem to play a role in the concept of (ideal) justice. Indeed, I think we can say that it is true by definition that a society is ideally or perfectly just if and only if all the equalities and inequalities it provides for are deserved "at its hands" (i.e., from it) or freely consented to by all its members. If such a definition is substantially correct, we can explain why disagreement arises between socialists and democratic capitalists over the question whether ideal justice requires distribution of the benefits or rewards of work in accordance with conscientious effort for society or in accordance with actual contribution to society. And that is because of the difficulty of deciding whether effort or success is more important in determining what one deserves from someone or something.

There are, however, objections to our definition of justice that I would like to consider. Some of these derive from the work of John Rawls, and since Rawls's work on the subject of justice is so important, and so focal for current discussions of justice, I shall try to relate what I am doing here to Rawls's work and to the criticisms he makes of ideas similar to those I have been defending.

V

In his major work, *A Theory of Justice*, Rawls criticizes the view that social justice involves goods' being distributed in proportion to moral desert, and so seems to oppose a definition of justice of the sort here proposed. But in fact what Rawls is objecting to is a view slightly different from the one I have been espousing. When Rawls speaks of moral desert, he uses that expression interchangeably with "moral worth." But earlier I distinguished between moral worth (or goodness of character) and what a man deserves from some other person or from society. It is not my view that a just society will reward people in accordance with their general moral worth or desert, but rather that it will (other things, like consent, being equal) reward them in accordance with what they deserve *from it*, and as we have seen, this is conceptually different. Thus we have left it (conceptually) open that two men should make different contributions to society and therefore deserve different rewards from society (here talk of *morally* deserving different rewards from society seems out of place), but still be of equal moral worth. If a certain kind of capitalist view is correct, then this often happens, and in no case, in my opinion, is such a thing ruled out by the very meaning of "desert" and "deserve." If it were, how could we explain how capitalist thinkers could so easily speak in a self-contradictory manner?

Presumably, Rawls directs his criticisms of views that equate justice with distribution according to moral worth or moral desert at such historical figures as Mill, Sidgwick, and Ross. But like those figures, he does not distinguish, or at least he does not explicitly distinguish, desert as moral worth from desert as desert from a particular person or society for actions involving that person or society. We

have defined ideal justice in terms of this latter kind of desert, rather than moral desert or worth. But our definition might still be open to Rawlsian criticisms. At one point, for example, Rawls says that the idea of rewarding desert is impracticable. Though he seems to have in mind here the rewarding of moral worth or character, Rawls might want to say the same thing about rewarding desert of the kind we have been talking about. It might be argued that it is hopelessly difficult to determine what men deserve from society, so that the idea of rewarding men in accordance with what they deserve from society is hopelessly impracticable and other means or standards of establishing how people should be recompensed for their work ought to be used. Now I am perfectly willing to admit the impracticality or difficulty of using my definition of justice in terms of desert in making social decisions about how to reward people for their labor. Indeed, in arguing that one very basic question about deserts for work seems unresolvable, I have made it plain that I can offer no practical scheme for justly distributing goods in society. But I think this simply shows that it is difficult to decide what is just and recompense people accordingly. It may, therefore, be a good idea to deemphasize justice in attempting to set up or govern a good society. The fact that it is difficult to make practical use of the notion of justice as I have defined it would count against the *accuracy* of my definition only if we had antecedent reason to think that the dictates of justice are bound to be, or likely to be, capable of practical implementation. And in fact I think we have antecedent reason to believe the contrary. In the first place, there is the very fact of the existence and seeming insolubility of the issue between capitalists and socialists as to whether it is just to reward people according to their efforts or according to their actual contributions. For if it is difficult to know what is just, it is surely difficult to implement the dictates of justice. In the second place, there are our attitudes towards divine or cosmic justice. We feel that if God or the world is just, then people are rewarded according to their merits or worth, but that a man's merit or worth is enormously difficult for anyone (except perhaps God) to determine. But if it is difficult to know the dictates of cosmic or divine justice, why should this not be (at least to some degree) true of the dictates of social justice. And if it is reasonable to assume that it is difficult to know the dictates of social justice, then surely we can reasonably assume that the dictates of social justice are difficult to implement. I am inclined, therefore, to think that the lack of utility of our definition of justice for social planning does not count against, and may even count in favor of, its accuracy.

Rawls distinguishes between the concept of justice and various conceptions of justice. To state what the concept of justice is is to state an analytic definition of justice, whereas Rawls himself seeks to provide a conception of ideal justice that is not an analysis of the meaning of "just" but embodies a substantive moral theory or point of view about what justice requires. For Rawls, definitions of (the concept of) justice are relatively trivial and specify what is common to different conceptions of justice. Thus to define justice as the situation that exists when no arbitrary distinctions are made between individuals in the assigning of basic rights and duties and when rules determine a proper balance between competing claims to goods is, for Rawls, to say what the concept of justice is, but it is to say nothing interesting about justice because it is to say nothing substantive about what societies are not arbitrary in assigning basic rights and duties and what societies have a proper balance between competing claims to goods.

The analysis of justice offered here is not quite so trivial as all this, however, even if only because of its emphasis on free consent. That free consent plays such a role in the notion of justice that it can render any situation just is a substantive, or at least (it seems to me) an interesting, idea that is nonetheless also analytic of the notion of justice. (It is also an idea that some will find implausible; and I shall be defending it against important criticisms, below). If I am right about this, then an analysis of ideal justice need not be

as trivial as the kind of analysis Rawls and others have proposed. The definition of justice I have suggested seems, intuitively, to be somewhere between Rawls's definition of the concept of justice and his statement of his conception of justice in its specificity or substantiveness. I think, then, that the concept of justice can be analyzed more substantively and less trivially than Rawls and others have supposed, even though I do agree with Rawls that the concept of justice must be something common to different conceptions of justice. After all, in defining justice as I have, I have specified a concept that is neutral between what I have called capitalist and socialist conceptions of justice and that can even be made use of in explaining how capitalists and socialists can easily have such different conceptions of justice.

This latter is not the kind of thing Rawls is trying to do. He is chiefly offering his own conception of justice, not trying to explain differences among conceptions of justice. But what of Rawls's conception of justice? How does it relate to the socialist and capitalist conceptions or ideas of justice that I have been talking about? Is it not, perhaps, superior to them, and if not, what is wrong with it as a conception of justice? Does our definition of justice give us any grounds for criticizing Rawls's conception of justice, or is not the reverse, perhaps, the case?

VI

Rawls is not very sympathetic to the socialist motto. He grants to it a certain common-sense plausibility, but thinks that it is ultimately unsatisfactory as compared to (the principles embodied in) his own conception of justice. That is not, however, to say that Rawls rules out socialism, if by that one means a state-planned economy; it is only to say that a just state-planned economy must, for Rawls, comply with his two principles of justice; and need not (or cannot) comply with the socialist motto of the Gotha program. It seems somewhat strange to me, however, that this should be so. For Rawls places great emphasis on political equality in society and thinks that a situation where such equality is bargained away as a means to everyone's greater happiness will be (to some degree) unjust. For Rawls, efficiency and benefits for all cannot justify removing certain political (or economic) liberties or opportunities, at least from the standpoint of justice. Rawls also thinks that the distribution of natural assets among people is arbitrary and that this arbitrariness is a reason for establishing rules of justice that mitigate the arbitrary effects of the "natural lottery." But he does not advocate equality of recompense for those who cooperate equally conscientiously in society. He finds unequal recompense for work and unequal inheritance of wealth unobjectionable from the standpoint of justice so long as they satisfy his "difference principle," so that, roughly, those who are worst off benefit from those inequalities. And so if Rawls is correct, efficiency and utility have a weight in the distribution of rewards or material goods for work that they lack in the area of political liberties and political and economic opportunities. And such a view seems a bit arbitrary, at least to me, though it need not on that account be mistaken. Why should the two areas be treated so differently; if the arbitrary effects of the natural lottery must, in all justice, be mitigated to the extent of letting society be governed by the difference principle, why not go further and say that the natural lottery (and the effects of luck in determining success) must, in all justice, be mitigated by rewarding people in accordance with their conscientious efforts in behalf of society? Why treat equal liberties and opportunities as axiomatic to justice, but not equal recompense (for equal effort, let us say, to make things more plausible)? In other words, if in the sphere of liberties and opportunities one should be equal with everyone else unless one is a criminal, why should one not be equal with everyone else in the area of economic reward unless one is "criminally" or immorally lazy or unconscientious in one's work (or supererogatorily industrious or conscientious in one's work)? In effect, it seems on the face of it somewhat arbitrary or odd for someone like

Rawls to insist on equal political and economic liberties and yet also deny that justice requires the distribution of goods according to conscientious effort and reject the socialist motto.

Apparently Rawls wants to argue that one would not consent to the socialist motto as a means of regulating society, if one were in his "original position," so that that motto or principle is not constitutive of (ideal) justice. But this seems to beg too many questions. If we wish to know whether the original position is that in which just principles are chosen, we must see what principles would be chosen in that position and whether those principles yield decisions about particular cases that fit in well with our prior views or intuitions about those cases, as Rawls himself points out. Rawls believes that his views and principles about justice coincide more with those intuitive views, better account for those views and introduce more order into them, than other views and principles about justice that have been offered. So it is really not open to Rawls to dismiss a conception of justice simply because it embodies principles that would not be arrived at in his original position. If the socialist conception of justice as embodied (approximately) in the socialist motto formulates our intuitions and commonsense views better than Rawls's principles of justice, that may (tend to) show that the original position defines not justice, but at best only some other social norm or ideal. On the other hand, if Rawls's principles approximately coincide with our common views or intuitions about justice, then so much the worse for socialism as a view of justice, since Rawls's principles pretty clearly conflict with the socialist motto in particular cases.

For example, Rawls's principles of justice permit the existence of great differences of wealth and income if such differences serve to improve the lot of those who are worst off in society and even if everyone makes equally conscientious efforts in behalf of society. But such a situation conflicts with the socialist motto and with the socialist conception of ideal justice. And since Rawls is clearly attempting to put forward a conception of ideal or perfect justice, Rawls's views are in sharp conflict with those of socialist theorists.

At this juncture, Rawls might point out that in the situation just described the worst off are better off than they would be if the socialist motto were in force and, if they are rational and not envious, should prefer their situation to that which would exist if everyone were rewarded equally. In what way, Rawls might then ask, is such a situation less than just? But I am inclined to think that little is proved by such an argument. Unless one already assumes that Rawls's original position is one in which ideally just principles would be chosen, he may be inclined to say that this merely shows that people faced with (the possibility of) a hard lot in life are willing to tolerate certain injustices in order to achieve certain benefits. And if one thinks that what people deserve from society simply depends on their conscientious efforts in behalf of society, he might well think that the situation we are discussing is unjust because goods are not distributed in accordance with deserts, even though people (in the original position) might be willing to accept that situation for reasons of self-interest.

Of course, Rawls might want to deny that the notion of desert (even as something other than moral worth) plays a major role in the concept of justice in the way I have specified or in the way that some socialists assume. If this were correct, it would certainly block what seem to be the main socialist arguments for the less than ideal justice of the situation described above and, in general, for the inadequacy of Rawls's conception of ideal justice. But people do speak as if questions of desert were immediately relevant to questions of justice. And, furthermore, it is hard to believe that desert plays no large role in the notion of social justice, since it so clearly plays a large role in the notion of cosmic or divine justice. Even if the notion of divine or cosmic justice is somewhat metaphorical, it would seem reasonable to assume that there is at least *some* major element common to both social justice and cosmic or divine justice, and is not the notion of desert the appropriate common element? (Nonetheless, there are problems here because of the ambiguities, or at least the different strands, that we have pointed out within the usage of "desert.")

On the other hand, Rawls might be willing to grant the place of the notion of desert from society in the concept of ideal social justice, but insist on the correctness of the capitalist view that actual contribution to society makes a difference to what one deserves from society. He might, perhaps, then go on to claim that any situation permitted by his principles in which there were great differences of wealth or recompense for work would be one in which people got what they deserved from society, and thus (considerations of consent aside) perfectly just. For in such a situation people who get more from society make the worst off better off than they would be if everyone received equally and so, one might think, make more of an actual contribution to society than other people do. In any case, we will have doubts about the adequacy of Rawls's conception at least to the extent that we believe that the notion of justice involves that of desert and have doubts (of a socialist kind) about the capitalist view of the relation between desert and actual contribution.

Whatever the strengths or weaknesses of Rawls's views on the relation between desert and justice, I think Rawls clearly underestimates the role actual free consent has as an element in ideal justice. Rawls seems to think that certain sorts of hypothetical free consent suffice for justice, so that if people would have consented to a certain social arrangement in an original position of equality, then such an arrangement is just even when people have not actually consented to it. But the difference between actual and hypothetical (free) consent is very important in matters of justice. To give one example of this (that Rawls would, presumably, be able to agree with, consistent with his principles), consider a situation where certain people somehow manage to call off an election whose eventual winner, the incumbent, everyone knew would win in advance, and then simply arrange for the incumbent to remain in office. Clearly an injustice has been done here by denying people their right to give or withhold their *actual* consent to the incumbent's remaining in office.

Rawls seems to think that, independently of whether goods are or are not distributed according to desert in societies governed by the difference principle (and his other principles), such societies are (ideally) just because they (or the principles that govern them) would have been chosen in the original position. And I believe that this is mistaken. Where inequalities of reward and the like are undeserved, only actual consent to their existence seems to me to be capable of rendering those inequalities, and the society in which they exist, completely just. It does not, intuitively, seem enough that people would have consented to the undeserved inequalities had they been asked. For even when one knows that this is so, one may feel resentment and feel unfairly treated because one *wasn't* asked. Rawls's emphasis on merely hypothetical consent seems to me to be out of line with our actual concept of justice. And there is not enough emphasis in his work on the importance of actual consent in rendering situations just. There seem to be situations involving actual consent that contravene Rawls's difference principle and yet are perfectly fair and just. Consider, for example, the situation mentioned earlier in which everyone in society *x* deserves equally from *x*, but the members of *x* freely agree or consent to let certain popular or well-liked people have certain privileges, and do so out of sheer affection for those people. There would surely be nothing unjust about such a society even if the privileges of the well-liked individuals in no way improved the lot of anyone else, and so even if the society offended against Rawls's difference principle. Of course, I am relying on intuition here, and perhaps the intuitions of Rawls and others will differ with mine about the two cases we have just been describing. But if what I have said about these cases is correct, then Rawls's conception of ideal justice is inadequate. (However, for our earlier definition of justice to be correct, what I have said about the situations just described must follow from the *very notion* of justice. And I am inclined to believe that this is so.)

Although Rawls attempts to correct the failures of Utilitarianism, and in large measure puts justice ahead of efficiency or utility, I think our arguments here tend to show that Rawls nonetheless overemphasizes the role of utilitarian considerations in the notion of ideal justice, or at least allows such considerations too much of a role in his own conception of ideal justice. I do not think that Rawls has succeeded in specifying, via his principles and his general ideal contractualism, an ideal of social justice. He has instead, I think, defined or specified a social ideal that is in some sense a compromise between justice and utility (or efficiency). Those who might protest the lack of ideal justice in a society meeting Rawls's principles still cannot complain too loudly, since things are effectively run for their benefit; and those who think things are not run efficiently enough can be told that efficiency is not everything and that a society should be just at least to the extent of making the worst off better off than they otherwise would be. Rawls's views may not embody an adequate conception of ideal social justice, but, in the end, they may embody something even more important, an adequate conception of the society that is best at combining and compromising justice and utility, an adequate conception of the ideal practicable society. Moreover, Rawlsian societies may deserve to count as just *simpliciter*, even if they are not (all) ideally just. Perhaps what I should be thought of as doing here, then, is not criticizing Rawls's enterprise in his book, but rather criticizing his way of interpreting the force and significance of his enterprise. And perhaps we should not be too surprised if it turns out that Rawls's principles are best thought of as specifying a conception of the (an?) ideal practicable society rather than a conception of the (an?) ideally or perfectly just society. For those principles are generated with reference to Rawls's original position, and it is by no means clear that people in that position would unanimously choose an ideally just society, rather than simply an ideal or ideally good society, in which justice played an important, but not necessarily an all-important, role.

It might be said, however, that even if Rawls confuses justice with certain broader or more inclusive social ideals and even if he underestimates the importance of actual consent in rendering situations just, our definition of justice sins in the opposite direction by assuming that universal free consent can make anything just. Given that definition, for example, it is in no way unjust for all the members of a society freely to consent to an equal, but unnecessary, limitation on their freedom. But Rawls's first principle of justice says that "each person is to have an equal right to the most extensive total system of equal basic liberties compatible with a similar system of liberty for all." And I assume that this is incompatible with what our definition commits us to counting as just. I think, however, that the condition of the greatest possible equal liberty is not a condition on justice, but on rational social planning. Universal free consent to equal, but unnecessarily limited, freedom for all is not unfair or unjust, but irrational or arbitrary or bad for some other reason. Rawls's first principle of justice involves an extension of the notion of justice, or a confusion of justice in the ordinary sense with other social or personal ideals; or so, at least, it seems to me.

The same sort of extension or confusion seems also to be involved in the criticism that our definition has the implausible consequence that it would be perfectly just for a man freely to consent to being stoned or shot by the other members of his society and for such stoning or shooting to occur. Assuming that such free consent really is possible, it will, I presume, be wrong or inhuman for the other members of the man's society to stone him; but it seems to me to involve an extension of usage (or a real confusion) to say that it is unfair or unjust for people to stone a man who freely consents to being stoned. However, it might be claimed, finally, that if a man freely consents to work for the welfare of people who do not deserve his help and who take advantage of his good nature, there will exist an unjust but freely consented-to situation. If such a situation *is* possible, our definition of social justice is inadequate, but

I have myself never been able to imagine such a situation in enough detail so that it is clear that *both* free consent and injustice exist within it. In describing a situation in which a man helps undeserving people, the closer one comes to seeing an injustice in the situation, the closer one seems to come to depriving the helpful man of *free* consent by imagining him as ignorant, under duress, etc. So it is by no means clear to me that any examples from this quarter can undermine our earlier definition of ideal social justice.

If people speak and think about justice in the ways that I have suggested, then there is reason to accept the definition of ideal social justice given above and Rawls's putative conception of justice is perhaps more profitably thought of as a conception of a certain kind of ideally good society. But the most important result of this paper seems to me to be the fact that our definition enables us to understand better why socialists and democratic capitalists disagree so persistently and so hopelessly about social justice. Rawls neither attempts nor, I think, is able to explain the particular nature of this disagreement within his contractarian enterprise. And, or course, this disagreement is one of enormous political and social significance in the world today. Ideally, we would like to be able to resolve the issue here between capitalism and socialism; but failing that, we have at least attempted to make the important first step of understanding how and why that issue is so difficult to resolve in any definitive and universally acceptable way.

NOTES

1. *La Doctrine des Egaux*, ed. Thomas (Paris, 1906).
2. "Utilitarianism," in *The English Philosophers from Bacon to Mill*, Modern Library ed. (New York, 1939), p. 942.
3. *Socialism: A Critical Analysis* (Boston, 1911), pp. 200ff.
4. *The Ethics of Competition* (New York, 1935), p. 56.
5. *The Theory and Practice of Socialism* (New York, 1936), pp. 120f.
6. "*Justice and Rationality*" in S. Morgenbesser, P.

Suppes, and M. White, eds., *Philosophy, Science, and Method* (New York, 1969), p. 409.

7. *A Theory of Justice* (Cambridge, Mass., 1971), pp. 304f.

8. E.g., in *Mill, loc. cit.*, Frankel, *loc. cit.*, and Rawls, *op. cit.*, pp. 304–311.

9. Perhaps our talk about what one deserves from society and about society's rewarding or punishing people only makes sense with respect to societies where the distribution of goods for work is highly centralized. If so, then the question we should be asking here is whether in a society with centralized mechanisms for rewarding labor, those who actually contribute a great deal to society deserve more from society than those who try and fail to do so. On the other hand, perhaps the sense that people deserve (different) things from society *justifies* the creation of a centralized mechanism for recompensing work according to desert, instead of *presupposing* such a mechanism.

24. Merit and Meritocracy
NORMAN DANIELS

Norman Daniels is Professor of Philosophy at Tufts University in Massachusetts and the author of numerous works in Ethics and Social Philosophy.

In this article he considers a core type of meritocracy in which efficiency or productivity is the underlying goal (rather than effort or moral goodness). He is concerned with the question of hiring the most qualified person for the job. Daniels argues that meritocrats typically focus on very limited aspects of merit—whether the best qualified person gets the job—whereas, if efficiency is truly our goal, we ought to see overall productivity as the relevant criterion of job placement. Daniels calls the individualistic type of merit *microproductivity* considerations and the overall, corporate type of merit *macroproductivity* considerations. Daniels advocates a macroproductivity version of meritocracy and applies his theory to affirmative action.

I

Sometimes a person has abilities and interests which enable him or her to fill a given job, position, or office—hereafter, I shall use only "job"—better than other available persons. In what sense do such abilities and interests constitute a basis for claiming the more capable person merits the job? Does the fact that someone possesses special abilities and interests which are needed for the superior performance of a job of considerable social importance and prestige allow that person a legitimate claim to greater rewards for the job? I shall explore some of the issues associated with these questions by analyzing the notion of a meritocracy, a social order built around a particular notion of merit. I hope that examination of such a hypothetical social order will allow me to assess the broader implications of this particular notion of merit for a theory of distributive justice.

I am not concerned with certain classical meritocracies, that is, with certain views of aristocracy according to which social class was thought to imply differences in merit or ability with positions and rewards conferred accordingly. Rather, I take as my model variants of the type of meritocracy portrayed by Michael Young who, in his now classic satire or fantasy, *The Rise of the Meritocracy*, anticipated many features of a social ideal adopted by more recent writers. Young imagines a world-wide society in the twenty-first century in which all assignments of jobs and rewards are based on merit. The system (a pervasive extension of the British Civil Service, he remarks) is feasible because great advances in testing for intelligence and ability allow accurate predictions of performance and permit appropriate educational tracking. All social barriers to the development of such abilities—social class, family background (but not the family), race, and religion—are

Reprinted from *Philosophy and Public Affairs* 7:3 (1978), by permission of Princeton University Press. Notes edited.

prevented from influencing decisions on education or career. Basic wages for different jobs are equal in order to avoid tiresome debates about the basis for inequalities in compensation. Nevertheless, vast inequalities of benefits and other rewards accompany jobs. These rewards are justified because they either provide incentives or insure efficient working conditions. Overall, rewards are proportional to merit. Merit is construed as *ability plus effort*.

Though Young's meritocracy can be viewed as the inspirational model behind my remarks, I shall not discuss the details of his construction, except for his notion of merit. Instead, I would like to sketch a theory of meritocracy—or, rather, of meritocracies, since there are many variants—which generalizes some of Young's ideas. We will see that a number of social theories share what might be called a "meritocratic core," though they differ on other critical features of distributive justice. My analysis of the principles underlying this core reveals, I believe, that claims of merit, in the restricted sense of that term relevant to meritocracies, are derived from considerations of efficiency or productivity and will not support stronger notions of desert.

II

I take a meritocracy to be a society whose basic institutions are governed by a partial theory of distributive justice consisting of principles of the following types:

1. A principle of job placement that awards jobs to individuals on the basis of merit;
2. A principle specifying the conditions of opportunity under which the job placement principle is applied;
3. A principle specifying reward schedules for jobs.

It is obvious that such principles constitute only a partial theory of distributive justice: they say nothing, for example, about liberty or its distribution, or about many other questions. But I shall concentrate on just this much here since most meritocrats do. There is, I shall argue, a preferred principle for job placement and one for opportunity to which most meritocrats would agree. But meritocrats will still vary widely on reward principles. My schema allows us to separate problems common to what meritocrats generally share from problems that arise from reward schedules.

Most meritocrats share certain empirical assumptions which give rise to a principle of job placement. First, they assume that different jobs require different sets of human abilities and different personality traits, including motivation, if they are to be performed with maximum competence. Certain motor skills or mental skills are more critical for some jobs than others. Second, meritocrats assume that people differ in the constellation of abilities and personality traits they possess. Some people possess more developed motor skills, some more developed mental skills, than others. Usually, this second assumption is not couched solely in terms of actual skills possessed. Rather, it is assumed people differ in their natively determined capacity to develop a given level of a certain skill. Often the ambiguous word "ability" does double duty here, hedging bets between claims about inequalities of skills and claims about inequalities of capacity. In any case, most meritocrats believe it is obvious that people differ in levels of skill and it is at least probable that they differ in the capacity to acquire levels of skills.[1]

From these two assumptions meritocrats infer that some arrays of assignments of individuals to jobs will be more productive than others. That is, if we take care to match people with the jobs they are best able to perform, then we will have produced a relatively productive array of job assignments. Actually, we are unlikely to find just one particular array of job assignments that is more productive than any other. But it seems likely, given these empirical assumptions, that there is an equivalence class of maximally productive arrays of job assignments for any fixed set of jobs and individuals.

A warning is needed about the notion of productivity. It must be accepted as an intuitively applicable notion for a wide range of jobs, positions, or offices for which no standard measurement of productivity exists. For such jobs, economists often take market-determined wage levels to indicate average productivity. But such a device is not satisfactory for many reasons. So I shall assume we can talk meaningfully about the productivity of doctors, teachers, lawyers, hairdressers, and so on, even though no single quantitative measure seems acceptable. Meritocrats and non-meritocrats alike operate with intuitively acceptable, if imprecise, notions of competent or productive job performance.

The principle I believe would be preferred for job placement makes use of the equivalence class of maximally productive arrays of job assignments. This Productive Job Assignment Principle (PJAP) says that job assignments should be made by selecting a member from this equivalence class; if no assignment of available applicants to open jobs is a member of the maximal equivalence class (because, say, some jobs are already held), select an assignment from the next most productive equivalence class, and so on. Such a principle seems desirable because, in the absence of arguments showing that justice or other considerations of right demand some array other than a maximally productive one, there is good reason to seek productivity in social arrangements. I want to leave it an open question how a meritocrat would respond to a claim that justice demanded—as compensation for past services or past injuries—that someone not selected by the PJAP nevertheless be given a particular job. Some such claims would seem to be weighty enough to justify overriding the presumption in favor of productivity considerations that underlies selecting the PJAP in the first place. But more on this point shortly.

If the PJAP is adopted, then the notion of individual merit can be applied in the following restricted way. An individual may claim to merit one job more than another job, or to merit one job more than another person does, if and only if his occupying that job is an assignment that is part of an array of assignments selected by the PJAP. The claim of

merit or relative merit is dependent for its basis on the rationale for the PJAP. Merit does not derive from having the abilities themselves, but only from the fact that abilities can play a certain social role. We focus on the relevant abilities because of their utility, not because there is something intrinsically meritorious about having them. Clearly the particular notion of merit I am concerned with here should not be confused with the more general concept of desert; it should also not be confused with certain ordinary uses of "merit" which are similar to the broader notion of desert. I am concerned with merit as it plays a role in the types of meritocracies I am analyzing.

To see why the PJAP is the preferred principle, consider the following case. Jack and Jill both want jobs A and B and each much prefers A to B. Jill can do either A or B better than Jack. But the situation S in which Jill performs B and Jack A is more productive than Jack doing B and Jill A (S'), even when we include the effects on productivity of Jill's lesser satisfaction. The PJAP selects S, not S', because it is attuned to macroproductivity, not microproductivity, considerations. It says, "Select people for jobs so that *overall* job performance is maximized."

It might be felt that the "real" meritocrat would balk at such a macroprinciple. The "real" meritocrat, it might be argued, is one who thinks a person should get a job if he or she is the best available person for *that* job. We might formulate such a view as the microproductivity principle that, for any job J, we should select the applicant who can most productively perform J from among those desiring J more than any other job. The microprinciple would select S' not S.

Given the rationale for treating job-related abilities as the basis for merit claims in the first place, namely that it is socially desirable to enhance productivity where possible, I think that the macroprinciple seems preferable. There is something anomalous about basing a merit claim, given our restricted notion of merit, on claims about microproductivity considerations while at the same time ignoring macroproductivity considerations.

We seem to need an explanation why the latter considerations would not overrule the former ones. Alternatively, we might try to divorce the merit claim from all productivity considerations, but this approach makes it completely mysterious why job related abilities are made the basis of merit in the first place.

I suppose one reason some may think the micromerit principle is preferable to the PJAP is that it seems *unfair* to Jill that she gets the job she wants less even though she can do the job Jack gets better than he can. But what is the sense of unfairness here based on? After all, under this arrangement, Jack has the job he prefers and overall productivity is enhanced. If Jill had her way, Jack would not have his, and macroproductivity would suffer as well. It is also important to note that *B* is a job Jill wants, though not as much as she wants *A*. The PJAP does not force people into jobs they do not want at all.

I believe the sense of unfairness here derives from particular, inessential features of our economic system. In many hiring or job placement situations in our society, we make no effort to calculate macroproductivity from job assignments. We assume that macroproductivity is always directly proportional to microproductivity as calculated by relative ability to do a given job considered in isolation. So in most hiring that is done on a merit basis (and of course much is not), we tend to use the microprinciple. From the microproductivity point of view conditioned by such a habitual practice, it does look as though the macro-PJAP makes Jill pay a price we ordinarily might not make her pay.

But if this explanation does *account for* the sense of unfairness some feel, it does not justify it in a relevant way. Our task is not just to describe the intuitions we have, influenced as they are by existing economic arrangements. Rather, where we have some reason to think the intuitions are just a by-product of existing institutions, where our task is to find principles to establish institutions we think more just than existing ones, then we may be forced to modify or abandon some of our habitual intuitions. If the PJAP

appears on theoretical grounds to be a more plausible principle governing the institution of job placement, then our attachment to microproductivity considerations may seem unjustifiable. Moreover, if an individual's sense of fairness were molded by institutions which took macroproductivity into account, not just microproductivity, then our data on unfairness might disappear. If Jill (and others) knew the PJAP and not the microprinciple were determining job placement, no legitimate expectations of hers (or ours) would be unsatisfied if she were selected for *B* rather than *A*.

I have been trying to show that it is appropriate to use the macro-PJAP rather than the alternative microproductivity principle, since the rationale for worrying about job-related abilities at all is their overall connection to productivity. For purposes of my exposition, however, I do not have to rule out some version of the microprinciple wherever it is construed as a rough, practical guide to the application of the macroprinciple. That is, given societies (like ours) in which there is no provision for a more scientific method of calculating maximally productive job arrays, in which most hiring or placement for positions is done on a decentralized, job-by-job basis, then the microprinciple may be the best rule of thumb. Such a compromise in practice is not, however, a compromise with the rationale behind the PJAP. It is important to note, however, that the PJAP seems to presuppose a more sophisticated theory of productivity measurement and may also commit us to more elaborate, centralized hiring than the microprinciple. Since my task here is to analyze where a particular notion of merit leads us, I need not evaluate these last considerations to determine the ultimate desirability of the PJAP or the microprinciple.

In any case, keeping in mind the compromise just proposed, I will assume that meritocrats can agree on the macro-PJAP. But it must be clear what this assumption implies: an individual merits a job if his or her placement in that job is part of an array of maximally productive job assignments. Such a merit claim does not presuppose that any kind of desert claim is present other than what can be derived from productivity considerations. Our obligation to honor a merit claim so derived is only as strong as the prima facie obligation to encourage productivity.

Some may feel that the truncated notion of merit emerging from my analysis must be an incorrect one because it omits any appeal to a stronger notion of desert. They are inclined to assert that if Jill has the greater ability, then Jill *deserves* the job. But the force of my argument is to leave us wondering whether there is a plausible basis for such a desert claim at all, given that our selection of certain abilities as relevant for job placement was based on their connection to productivity. One possible basis is the view that such desert claims derive from a purported "right to self-fulfillment": Jill has a right to be maximally self-fulfilled, and exercising her best abilities in a suitable job is necessary for such self-fulfillment. It is worth noting, however, the lack of any uniform connection between a person's sense of fulfillment and the exercise of his (objectively) best abilities. I may be more fulfilled not doing what I am best at, even more fulfilled than someone who is better at doing the same job. And it would not do at all to say that my right to self-fulfillment should provide a basis for desert only when I would be exercising my objectively best (most productive) abilities. But this would be the only way to grant Jill and deny Jack a desert claim to job *A*, assuming that (subjectively) each would judge *A* more self-fulfilling. I conclude that ability-based merit claims of the type I have picked out do not support claims to "deserve" particular placements.

Before considering the two remaining types of principles regulating meritocracies, I would like to comment briefly on the relevance of merit claims as I have described them to the contemporary issue of affirmative action and preferential hiring. Opponents of the preferential hiring of competent minority members or women sometimes argue that not choosing the most competent job applicant, as measured by some relevant test score or by standard professional criteria, is a violation of the presumed rights of the most competent applicant. Of course, this argument is only one of many and I do not think it is the most powerful, but I am concerned here only with it.

Suppose I am right that the proper way to analyze a merit claim for a job based on possession of certain abilities is to derive the claim from a macroproductivity principle such as the PJAP. Then several difficulties face the opponent of preferential hiring who appeals to a merit claim. For one thing, it becomes much harder to argue that a higher test score or higher standing on relevant professional criteria automatically gives one a stronger claim to a job or position than someone else who can perform it competently but not quite as well. Even assuming valid criteria, such scores would automatically establish a merit claim only on a microprinciple, such as the one we thought less desirable. If we adopt a macroproductivity principle, such as the PJAP, then the strength of my claim to a particular job is not determined by my "pretested" competency for that job. Other macroproductivity factors count. Indeed, if we consider some of the macroproductivity considerations that might result from a better mix of races and sexes in certain positions, it becomes plausible that microproductivity considerations alone would be misleading. A better mix of race and sex in such professions as the law, teaching, and medicine might well pay dividends in terms of services rendered to those who would not otherwise get them, inspiration to long-suppressed motivation, the overcoming of racial and sexual stereotypes which are unproductive in other ways, and so on. But the proponent of affirmative action should beware that the appeal to the PJAP does not backfire. Suppose, for example, productivity is reduced because of sexist or racist opposition to what otherwise would be a meritocratic placement. Then the PJAP might play a conservative role, capitulating to existing biases. (We might have to appeal to considerations of justice to block such applications of the PJAP.)

I think there is an even more important effect of accepting the analysis of merit I have proposed. Whether my claim to merit a particular job more than another depends on the

PJAP or on a microprinciple, it nevertheless depends for its justification only on efficiency or productivity. If considerations of right or justice demand that we override such efficiency considerations—for example, to satisfy a concern for equality in the distribution of certain social goods or to compensate for past injustice or to reward for past service—then we are not faced with a case of pitting claims of right against other claims of right. Rather, we pit considerations of productivity against considerations of justice. Many will feel less concerned about such compromises of productivity than they would if a claim to merit a job was really a claim of right, a claim of justice. If a claim to merit a job is a real desert claim supporting a right claim, if it is derived from considerations other than productivity alone, then it might seem far more problematic why such a claim is given less weight than the other principle of justice appealed to in overriding it. At least, a more clearcut argument would seem to be needed to establish priorities among such claims of justice than would be needed to temper productivity considerations by appeal to principles of justice. I am not implying that we should never temper demands of justice by appeal to efficiency considerations. Rather, I am pointing out the apparent shift in the weight of the objection to preferential hiring when one moves from the assertion, "An appeal to just deserts backs my claim to have a right to that job," to the assertion, "An appeal to productivity supports my claim to have that job."

Of course, my argument here does not take into account the role of expectations in actual situations. One could argue that people who claim a right to a given job on the basis of their better qualifications are doing so because they have been led to form specific expectations about how society distributes social goods, such as desirable positions. When institutions are presumed to and do lead people to form certain expectations, and then society "changes the rules of the game," some sort of compact or contract may be violated. But such an argument from expectations can become woefully conservative if it turns out

that the principles governing those institutions and the expectations they generate are not acceptable principles of justice.

A further objection is that a productivity consideration such as that underlying the PJAP *can* become the basis for a claim of right or an entitlement claim if, for example, the PJAP would be adopted as a principle of justice. Suppose, for example, that Rawlsian contractors in an original position would agree to adopt meritocratic job placement principles and conditions of opportunity as part of a preferred conception of justice. (I think this choice is in fact made by Rawls' contractors.) Then the PJAP, although supported by arguments based on productivity considerations, would give rise to entitlements. I have no quarrel with this objection if it is appropriately qualified. My argument above can provide the appropriate qualifications. Such contractors should not choose the PJAP without first choosing relevant compensatory and retributive principles which take priority over entitlements derived from the PJAP. I need not argue that merit claims can never be construed as entitlements; I need only show that they are entitlements only if they are not superseded by stronger ones.

One last objection is worth noting. It may well be argued that for certain jobs, productivity considerations alone may give rise to claims of right by those most competent to perform them. Suppose it could be shown that recipients of certain services or products—perhaps, for example, patients or students—have a right to the highest quality service or product possible. Then it might be argued that those most capable of providing the service or product have a right to the relevant jobs. At least it might be shown that there is a duty to give such persons the jobs. If the details of such an argument could be satisfactorily provided, it might force an important qualification of the PJAP; it might force us to use the microprinciple for assignments to certain jobs. Alternatively, such cases might be handled simply by giving extra weight to the satisfaction of student or patient interests and rights in the calculation of macroproductivity. The difficulty of deciding which way to handle these cases derives from the unfortunate imprecision of the broad notion of productivity (macroproductivity) I have appealed to; nor can I remedy the imprecision in any simple way here.

III

I would like to return now to discuss the remaining types of principles meritocrats share. Although there may be some exceptions, I believe that most meritocrats would view fair, rather than just formal, equality of opportunity as the appropriate precondition for application of the PJAP. Formal equality of opportunity obtains when there are no legal or quasibarriers to people having equal access (based on merit) to positions and offices or to the means (education and training) needed to qualify one for access to such jobs. Fair equality of opportunity requires not only that negative legal or quasilegal constraints on equality of opportunity be eliminated, but also that positive steps must be taken to provide equality of access—and the means to achieve such equality of access—to those with inferior initial competitive positions resulting from family background or other biological or social accidents.

If we make the empirical assumption that conditions of fair opportunity maximize the availability of human talents which would otherwise be wasted under conditions of merely formal opportunity, then considerations of productivity alone carry us some way toward the preference for fair opportunity. Fair, not formal, opportunity is likely to yield the optimal equivalence class of maximally productive job assignment arrays. Of course efficiency considerations alone may *not* always point to fair rather than formal opportunity. If a tremendous superfluity of available abilities resulted from formal opportunity alone, then in order to produce increases in the maximally productive class of job assignments more might have to be invested in fair opportunity than is justified by the size of those increases. Similarly, if early, arbitrary selection of some individuals for special training for certain jobs was maximally efficient, other nonutilitarian arguments might be

needed before fair opportunity would be preferred. Rawls, for example, does not rest his argument for fair opportunity on grounds of efficiency alone. Rather, he argues that people will feel they do not have fair access to the centrally important social good of self-realization if formal, rather than fair, opportunity is instituted. In any case, I will assume that meritocrats generally treat fair, not formal, opportunity as the precondition for applying the PJAP. Little in my argument hangs on this assumption.

Thus far I have said nothing about the rewards and burdens that accompany different jobs. The PJAP, as I have presented it, is defined without reference to any particular schedule of rewards and burdens. So far, although an individual may claim to merit a job when his having it satisfies the PJAP, there is no sense given to his meriting any particular set of rewards or burdens. I have deliberately dissociated the meritocratic basis for job assignment from the process of determining the schedule of benefits and burdens associated with different jobs or positions.[2]

I think it is possible for meritocrats to differ on the reward schedules they join to the system structured by the PJAP and fair equality of opportunity. Consider the following six meritocracies which differ only in their reward schedules:

1. Unbridled meritocracy. The reward schedule allows whatever rewards those who attain positions of power and prestige can acquire for themselves.
2. Desert meritocracy. The reward schedule allows rewards proportional to the contribution of the jobs (but not constrained by efficiency considerations as in meritocracy 3); alternatively, the desert basis might have nothing to do with productivity—it might be moral worthiness, for example.
3. Utilitarian meritocracy. The reward schedule allows inequalities that act to maximize average or total utility.
4. Maximin meritocracy. The reward schedule allows inequalities that act to maximize the index of primary social goods of those who are worst off.
5. Strict egalitarian meritocracy. No inequalities in reward are allowed.

6. Socialist meritocracy. The reward schedule allows no inequalities in the satisfaction of (basic?) needs.

My list allows for meritocracies which no one may explicitly have supported. And, for the sake of brevity, it does not include all possible favorites. But the main point should be clear, namely, I do not consider it an essential feature of a meritocracy that efficiency is the sole principle governing selection of reward schedules, but I do believe that an appeal to productivity in job assignment is always involved in meritocracy through the PJAP.

A number of qualifying remarks are in order. First, unless certain empirical conditions obtain, meritocracy may prove to be a theory which greatly underdetermines social structure on just the points it was intended to determine. If application of the PJAP is to determine job placement effectively, then the equivalence class of maximally productive jobs would have to be fairly small. I am inclined to believe, however, that the equivalence class of maximally efficient arrays of job assignments will be quite large under real conditions of fair equality of opportunity. With adequate education and training, most people might competently perform almost any job, or at least a very large range of jobs. At the least, relevant abilities will turn out to be far less scarce a resource than most meritocrats think. If I am right, then the claims that individuals can make vis-à-vis one another—for example, that one merits a job more than another—would be substantially weakened. We would lack principles sufficient to justify claims to be placed in a given job since our candidate for a necessary and sufficient condition turns out to be far from sufficient under these empirical conditions.

Second, other empirical difficulties face application of the PJAP. This principle presupposes that we have very good ways of predicting which constellation of abilities and personality traits will lead to successful—that is, productive—performance of a given job. But many of our current efforts in those directions are woefully inadequate. Much is often made, for example, of the fact that IQ scores correlate fairly with job status; the average doctor has a higher IQ score than the average carpenter, and so on. But what is not so often noted is that IQ scores correlate miserably with level of success at a given job. So the argument that knowledge of IQ gives us a good estimate of how well someone will do at a given job is unfounded. All this point means is that we are far from having available to us the measuring and predicting instruments needed to operate a thoroughly meritocratic society such as the one Young describes, since we cannot meet the conditions necessary for applying the PJAP.

Third, my analysis of meritocracy seems to allow too many types of theories in under that name. For example, Rawls explicitly argues that his Second Principle does not lead to the type of meritocracy advocated by Young because natural abilities are viewed as social, not just individual assets and inequalities act to help the worst-off members of the society. But if Rawls, or at least someone much like him who subscribes to type (4) meritocracy, is stuck with the label "meritocrat" on my schema, still, he is not thereby committed to any of the undesirable features of the meritocracies attacked in *A Theory of Justice*. At the same time, the label captures the fact that he shares with other meritocrats certain common principles.

A final, most important qualification. My analysis might seem to imply that we know how to apply the PJAP independently of fixing a reward schedule. But such independence is unlikely. Different reward schedules would presumably affect the motivations of individuals who contemplate entering certain jobs. Just this point is at the heart of Rawls' view that material incentives will be necessary if we are to procure the greatest talent possible for certain burdensome jobs. So it seems we cannot fix on an equivalence class of maximally productive job assignments, which we need for application of the PJAP until we know something of the reward structure. But this fact does not alter my main point: we can distinguish the PJAP from the reward principles, and what all meritocrats share is appeal to the PJAP and fair equality of opportunity, however else they may differ in their use of reward schedules.

If we keep our attention on the shared features of meritocracy, we can see why many varied theorists have found something attractive in it. Indeed, insisting that job placement be meritocratic under conditions of fair equality of opportunity leads to serious criticism of existing institutions. However, these shared principles always operate against a background determined by the reward schedule. And in our society, the reward schedule is rarely itself the target of challenge by meritocrats. Meritocracy becomes controversial when we begin to see the consequences of meritocratic job placement operating in a context of certain reward schedules.

The meritocracies I listed earlier include three types of reward schedules. Inegalitarian meritocracies (unbridled, desert according to contribution, and utilitarian) allow significant inequalities in rewards with no special constraints to protect those with the worst jobs. Egalitarian meritocracies either allow no significant inequalities or allow inequalities not based on the social functions of the jobs but rather on the needs or other deserts of the job holder. The maximin meritocracy allows inequalities but constrains them in ways that act to benefit those whose abilities tend to lead to low reward jobs. Inegalitarian meritocracies may be open to a criticism that egalitarian or maximin meritocracies avoid.

Suppose that the abilities and traits that qualify a person for high reward jobs are primarily the result of natural and social contingencies over which he has little control. We might suppose that even the agent's choices about which abilities he wants to develop are made within a range heavily determined by factors beyond his control. Then it seems one's qualifications for meritocratic job placement are largely the result of happy or unhappy accident, and one has done little to *deserve* them. It is just this fact which made it so hard to establish a desert claim, which connects abilities to jobs, stronger than the weak merit claim I derived from productivity considerations. So it seems that the meritocrat is committed, given his concern for productiv-

ity, to distributing at least some social goods, the jobs themselves, in accordance with a morally arbitrary distribution of abilities and traits.

Suppose further, however, that a reward schedule allows significant inequalities of reward to be associated with different jobs. Then, the fortuitous possession of certain natural abilities and traits makes one the beneficiary of significant social rewards as well. Such a double reward for undeserved abilities and traits seems to ramify morally arbitrary facts into ones of great social significance. This objection, of course, is the basis for Rawls' attack on non-maximin meritocracies. Egalitarian meritocracies avoid the criticism. And maximin meritocracies dodge its main force since they moderate the effects of fortuitous distributions of talents. For anyone who feels the power of this argument against moral arbitrariness (and not everyone does, notably Nozick), the price the meritocrat must pay is the adoption of egalitarian—or fairly egalitarian (maximin)—reward schedules.

Unfortunately, many proponents of meritocracy have been so concerned with combating the lesser evil of non-meritocratic job placement that they have left unchallenged the greater evil of highly inegalitarian reward schedules. One even suspects that an elitist infatuation for such inegalitarian reward schedules lurks behind their ardor for meritocratic job placement. In any case, they often ignore the distinction between principles governing placement and those governing reward and the fact that quite different rationales are involved in justifying two such different types of principles.

NOTES

1. Some meritocrats assume (see Richard Herrnstein, *IQ in the Meritocracy,* Boston: Atlantic, Little Brown, 1973) that there is some one scale of capacity differences, usually taken to be IQ, which suffices to rank-order people for job eligibility across the whole spectrum of jobs. I do not think such a uniquely hierarchical view is presupposed by the meritocratic core principles I describe. For critical discussion of IQ as a basis for such scale,

see my "IQ, Heritability, and Human Nature," in *PSA 1974*, ed. R. S. Cohen et al., in *Boston Studies in the Philosophy of Science,* XXXII (Dordrecht: Reidel, 1976), pp. 143–180; J. Cronin, N. Daniels et al., "Race, Class & Intelligence," *International Journal of Mental Health* 2, no. 4 (1975): 46–132; N. J. Block and G. Dworkin, *The IQ Controversy* (New York: Pantheon, 1976), Part IV; and S. Bowles and H. Gintis, *Schooling in Capitalist America* (New York: Basic Books, 1976), chap. 4.

2. Thomas Nagel makes a related point when he says, "Certain abilities may be relevant to filling a job from the point of view of efficiency, but they are not relevant from the point of view of justice, because they provide no indication that one deserves the rewards that go with holding that job. The qualities, experience, and attainments that make success in a certain position likely do not in themselves merit the rewards that happen to attach to occupancy of that position in a competitive economy." See "Equal Treatment and Compensatory Discrimination," *Philosophy & Public Affairs* 2, no. 4 (Summer 1973): 352.

25. Negating Positive Desert Claims

ROBERT GOODIN

Robert Goodin, who taught for many years at the University of Essex, is presently Professor of Philosophy at the Research School of Social Sciences, Australian National University, Canberra. He is the author of several works in social and political philosophy, including *The Politics of the Rational Man* (1976) and *Political Theory and Public Policy* (1982), as well as the joint editor of *A Companion to Contemporary Political Philosophy* (1993) and associate editor of the journal *Ethics*.

In this article Goodin argues that positive desert does not play a significant role in social policy making but that negative desert does play an important role. Generally, he argues, we can reduce desert claims to what people would receive in the normal course of events "in the absence of certain untoward interventions." When evil happens to people unexpectedly or undeservedly, things ought to be made right again to what they would have been in the absence of the "untoward" event. Not only do negative desert claims make up the moralized core of desert, but positive desert claims are generally either (1) reducible to positive entitlements to probabilistic outcomes (e.g., if you are one of 1,000 players of a given lottery, you deserve an expected payoff of 1/1000 of the prize) or (2) simply trumped by other considerations, such as need. An example of this is the following: Suppose two men have been in an accident of which A is the cause through reckless driving and in which B is the innocent victim. They are brought into the Emergency Room with identical and serious injuries with identical prognoses. According to Goodin, it would be morally outrageous to choose to give the innocent man preferential treatment. Need trumps desert. Goodin's strategy is to knock the props out from under those who oppose economic redistribution.

J. L. Austins's famous paper on "Ifs and Cans" opens with the immortal question, "Are *cans* constitutionally iffy?" By that, he means to query whether every statement about what someone can do must, analytically, contain implicitly within it certain "if" clauses ("if one wants to," "if one really tries," "if the gods are willing," etc.). If so, then a large part of what we really mean by saying that some-one can do something lies in unpacking these suppressed "if" clauses.

Here I want to raise an analogous question about the notion of personal deserts. To embody my thesis in a similarly catchy maxim, I shall be claiming that deserts are constitutionally wouldy. Or, to unpack that phrase, when we say "x *deserves* y" we are really saying "x *would receive* y in the normal

Reprinted from *Political Theory* 13:4 (November 1985). Notes deleted.

course of events." Or, to unpack it further still, "x *would receive* y, in the absence of certain *untoward* interventions z."

The message of this article is that, just as we must excavate the ifs to get at the cans, so too must we focus clearly on the "untoward" intervening factors upsetting the "normal" course of events in order to fix our notion of personal desert. The upshot of my argument will be that that notion is essentially negative in character. The core notion is not that of the "deserved" but rather that of the "undeserved," of those untoward intervening factors upsetting the "normal" course of events. In Austin's phrase, "undeserved" wears the trousers.

To show that this is so, simply recall that "desert" is an inherently moralized notion: To be a notion of "desert" at all, it must imply that, *ceteris paribus*, people ought morally to get what they deserve. The negative notion of the "undeserved" is crucially moralized in this way; the positive notion of the "deserved" is not. Either it is a residual notion lacking moral force or it is a derivative one borrowing whatever moral force it possesses from other nondesert considerations. Usually it is the former. Any notion of what is positively deserved is usually merely residual, what is normally left over after certain confounding features have been factored out. No moral force necessarily attaches to that residual: Removing all that is undeserved leaves us not with something that is necessarily deserved, but perhaps merely with something that is neither deserved nor undeserved. When, as occasionally happens, there are properly moral arguments for ascribing positive deserts (e.g., to prizes or commendations), those arguments look outside the notion of desert for their moral force. It is those nondesert considerations, rather than considerations of desert per se, which give us reasons for believing that people ought—rather than just reasonably (and, in that restricted sense, legitimately) expect—to receive what they would ordinarily receive in the normal course of events.

When talking of "positive desert claims," I mean primarily to refer to "positive asser-

tions"—claims that something or another is deserved. My central argument is that positive claims of that sort do not constitute the core of desert claims at all; rather, the core consists of negative claims about what is not deserved. I shall also be talking primarily about "positive desert claims" in the sense in which the outcomes in view are "positive" (i.e., valued from the point of view of the recipient) rather than "negative" (i.e., disvalued). The latter—deserved punishments—have provided the focus for most discussions of the concept of desert. Perhaps there it is more legitimate to make positive assertions about deserved outcomes. But if so, and if my arguments here are correct, that only goes to show that punishment is a special case, importantly different from social welfare policy, for example. It cannot, therefore, be taken to constitute the paradigm case for all applications of the concept of desert.

The overall aim of this article is to deny notions of positive desert any important role in social policymaking. I shall launch three separate attacks. One is essentially conceptual: The negative notion of the undeserved, rather than the positive notion of the deserved, constitutes the moralized core of the notion of desert. Two others are largely practical. One is that we can make only limited claims, if any at all, about positive entitlements to probabilistic outcomes. Another is that there are certain circumstances in which considerations of desert should be put into abeyance. These three arguments are independent of one another, in the sense that the success of any one is nowise contingent upon the success of any other. But they all converge toward the same conclusion: that notions of positive desert ought not play any important role in social policymaking.

Knocking the props out from under the notion of positive desert doubly undercuts opponents of economic redistribution. Without some such notion they can no longer claim that the poor deserve their plight, and hence ought not to be assisted; nor can they claim that the rich deserve their wealth, and hence ought not have it taken from them by the tax collector. Both those propositions play on the positive sense of personal desert that is here called into question. The negative sense that remains—the notion of the undeserved—is of course what is crucial in arguing for the sort of remedial redistributions that characterize welfare state activities.

Deserts Are Wouldy

Notice the language we employ in describing someone's deserts. We say that "he has it coming." Or we say that "it is due him." Those are forms of words we characteristically employ in making predictions. When we say the train "is coming" or "is due," we mean to say that it will soon arrive—or at least that it should soon arrive, absent the untoward interventions of terrorists, frozen points, failing signals, and so on.

Moving beyond the form of words to the substance of our ordinary judgments about personal deserts, their wouldy nature remains. We typically say that the fastest runner or the one that has trained the hardest deserves to win the race. What more is that than the prediction that, ceteris paribus, the fastest or best trained will win the race? Certainly, he or she would ordinarily be expected to do so in the normal course of events, unless he or she is tripped or tricked. Likewise, we say that the best-qualified applicant deserves the job. And what more is that than the mere prediction that, ceteris paribus, the best qualified will get the job? Certainly he or she would ordinarily be expected to do so in the normal course of events, unless the selection committee were engaging in nepotism, racial or sexual discrimination, or the like.

The same pattern reemerges with the subclass of institutionalized or rule-based desert statements. We say that an elderly person deserves (is entitled to) a pension, provided he or she meets all the conditions laid down in the relevant law. What more is that than merely to say that social security administrators would, in the normal course of events, follow the rules and give him or her one? We say a thief deserves (is negatively entitled to) punishment. What more is that than merely to say that courts would, in the normal course of affairs, mete out such punishments as are laid down in the law?

Of course, not all predictions entail desert claims. Not all things that we would predict happening in the normal course of events to person P are things we would necessarily say P deserves to have happen to him or her. We predict that P will die if his or her lungs cease functioning, but we would hardly say that P deserves to die—unless, perhaps, his or her lung failure stems from cigarette smoking. The prediction "P would normally receive q" can entail "P deserves q" only where that prediction is predicated on some facts about P's character or personal history. We may want to go further, saving the term "deserves" to describe cases in which the facts in view concern actions or character traits that P has voluntarily chosen. Or we may want to go further still, saying that P deserves q only if P has voluntarily acted (or voluntarily chosen character traits that lead him or her to act) with the intention of producing q. Whichever way we choose to mark off the subset of desert predictions, it is nonetheless clear that some way is needed: Not every prediction can be an ascription of desert. The converse proposition is what interests me. Are ascriptions of desert anything more than just predictions, albeit of some special sort?

"Undeserved" Wears the Trousers

There is one ready answer to such questions that is consonant with the more standard analysis of deserts as positive claims. That is to say that what normally happens does normally happen because people deserve to have that happen. Then "normal" would become just another way of saying "deserves," and old-fashioned positive-style desert claims would be vindicated.

Certainly, it is true that the "normal" or "expected course of events," as the phrase functions in moral discourse, characteristically evokes something other than just a statistical, frequentist notion of "normality" or "expectation." When some harm has been done, either accidentally or intentionally, we ordinarily assign responsibility to those who have deviated from the "normal" course of conduct, often defined in a highly moralized way. Similarly, when we are trying to decide whether some proposal constitutes a morally obnoxious threat or a morally honorable offer, we look at how it compares with what would happen in the "normal or natural or expected course of events." If A's proposed action would make B better off than B would be in the normal course of events, we would say that A has made B an offer; if worse, a threat. Here again, the term 'expected' is meant to shift between or straddle 'predicted' and 'morally required'; and usually the "normal" turns out to be an amalgam of the two. Refraining from physical assaults on another's person or property is both morally required and statistically expected.

Much the same is true of those courses of events that are considered as normal for purposes of assessing personal deserts. There, too, the normal course of events is not just the most frequent or most common course that events would ordinarily take, although it is that in part. In deciding what is normal in such contexts, we need to factor out the influence of certain (possibly quite common) "untoward interventions." (That is why the analysis of deserts must be cast in the subjunctive—in terms of what would happen, had nothing untoward occurred, rather than what will happen.) And notice that the notion of the "untoward" (as a sort of inverse of Nozick's "expected") straddles "unlucky" and "improper." In this sense at least, the notion of normality that enters into judgments of personal deserts is a moralized notion.

But if that is the only sense in which it is a moralized notion, then the moralism embodied in the notion of normality would underwrite moral judgments only of a negative sort. It would allow us to say that some outcomes—those proceeding from "untoward interventions"—were morally improper. It would not allow us to make any positive moral judgments about the moral propriety of the particular outcomes that would otherwise have occurred. To say that untoward interventions are morally improper is not necessarily to say that the ordinary course of events is morally proper. That is just not the part of the notion of normality that carries any moral charge, at least according to everything that has been said so far. The distinctively moral component of the notion of normality comes in factoring out immoral untoward interventions. What is left—what would be normal in an idealized world absent such interventions—is normal just in the straight statistical sense.

A tripartite division is crucially at work here. Alongside the more familiar categories of the deserved and the undeserved is a notion of that which is neither deserved nor undeserved. Cancelling out the effects of untoward interventions merely moves us from the moralized category of the undeserved to that morally neutral intermediate category. Some further argument is required to move us from there to any properly moralized notion of what is positively deserved. Clearly, everything that is not undeserved it not itself deserved.

On my analysis, then, what people deserve is what they would receive (or would have received) absent the intervention of certain untoward (statistically unusual/morally improper) circumstances. What the notion of desert essentially does, I argue, is to point the finger at illicit interventions that are undeserved and that preclude people from getting what, in the ordinary course of affairs, they would receive.

Even some ostensibly positive judgments and injunctions actually carry such a fundamentally negative message. Notice, for example, that a "good conscience" consists primarily in the absence of guilt feelings. Or, again, notice that much of what a judge is doing when instructing a jury positively to "decide the case on its merits" is to instruct the jurors to ignore certain things (such as the defendant's color, class, sex, and so on) that should not be taken into consideration in their deliberations.

Or, yet again, notice how that which is deserved is often described as that which is "appropriate," "fitting and proper," "suitable." That form of words seems to point to a positive correspondence of some sort between the characteristics of the person and the characteristics of the things he or she is said to deserve. But in social contexts, just as surely as in sartorial ones, what constitutes a good fit is enormously variable, being largely a matter of taste and style. Any number of things might correspond adequately to characteristics of the person or situation to be deemed "fitting" or "appropriate." The primary use of the notion of "appropriateness" is once again negative. When the sign on the door of a restaurant makes "appropriate attire" a condition of entry, it is not really specifying in any positive way what diners should wear. (If the owners wanted jackets and ties, they would have had to say so explicitly.) The basic function is instead to remind customers of what not to wear (standardly, in Australia, singlets and bare feet). The negative—the concept of the "inappropriate"—here again seems to form the core of the concept.

Positive Deserts Are Derivative, Not Foundational

My wouldy account of desert is basically designed to undermine the notion of positive deserts. I maintain that people are usually said to deserve things merely because that is what they would ordinarily or normally be expected to receive. There may or may not be other moral reasons for their receiving what they ordinarily would. But if there are, these are not reasons of desert per se. This, then, is my second conceptual point: Positive desert claims are parasitic upon some larger scheme, whether natural or social, that gives rise to such expectations about what the "ordinary" or "normal" outcome would be.

We say that winners deserved to win, just so long as no morally groundless intervention interfered with the ordinary scheme of things. If we insist upon running footraces, then truly the lame do not deserve to win; if we insist upon running an apartheid system, then truly blacks do not deserve the same treatment as whites. What we are really interested in, however, is the external rather than just the inter-

nal evaluation of such schemes. If the proposition that P deserves q is to have any real moral force, it must imply more than merely that under existing arrangements P would ordinarily get q. It must also imply that the existing arrangements are themselves morally justifiable. Unless some kind of independent argument can be given for the outcomes that the normal course of events would ordinarily throw up, it constitutes no kind of claim at all merely to insist that, "Well, P normally would get q."

Insofar as desert claims are predicated on the normal operations of the natural (i.e., nonsocial) world, no independent argument can be given. Saying that something would normally come your way naturally amounts to nothing more than making a straightforward statistical prediction. You do not deserve, in a positive sense that is in any way morally charged, that particular outcome.

Insofar as desert claims are predicated on normal operations of the social world there may (or may not) be moral as well as statistical reasons for things to happen as they normally would. We have reasons—moral reasons, among others—for setting up our social institutions to operate as they do. And as there might be moral rather than merely statistical grounds for expecting that P would normally receive q from some social institution S, that might seem to suggest that there may be some moral grounds for claiming that P positively deserves q. That, in turn, threatens to reduce at least this part of my analysis back to the standard one once again: People might deserve what they deserve by virtue of their merits or demerits. All I have done, on this analysis, is to add an intervening variable: People deserve what they deserve by virtue of expectations about the ordinary course of events, which, in turn, are governed by people's merits and demerits.

That, however, would be a mistaken analysis. Although we certainly do have reasons (maybe even moral reasons) for setting up social institutions as we do, these are not reasons of desert or merit. Indeed, to some extent what counts as merits or demerits may depend on the sort of institution we set up.

Physical prowess is a merit when we set people the task of running a race, mental agility when designing a bridge; honesty is a merit when testifying in court, cunning a merit when conducting a military campaign. Insofar as merit is institution-specific, that notion cannot provide any independent basis for choosing between alternative institutions.

In any case, it is evident that the notion of "desert" itself has no place in morally underwriting the scheme of things on whose ordinary operations desert claims are grounded. We may say that the winner of a footrace deserves the medal. But we would never say that anyone deserves to have bits of precious metal allocated according to the outcomes of footraces. We might be able to give all sorts of reasons for running footraces—but desert would never be among them.

My argument, then, is that there can be positive desert claims arising under a set of social rules but not to that set of social rules. Positive desert claims cannot provide the moral foundations for the rules themselves. Those must instead be derivative from some other moral values. So, too, consequently, must any positive desert claims derivative from those rules themselves be ultimately derivative from some other moral values unconnected with personal desert.

When (as occasionally we do) we use the language of deserts in connection with claims to a set of rules, we do so in an extended sense of one sort or another. Usually positive desert claims to rules are just desert claims under metarules that are actually operative in the society. When we say that he or she deserves to have the rules pertaining to treatment of prisoners of war applied to him or her, we are merely saying that there is some metarule (the Geneva Convention) that dictates that he or she receive better treatment. Similarly, we might say that anyone who can climb that rock deserves $50. That, too, is probably just a reference to the fact that we have an implicit metarule in our society: Given that we offer $50 for climbing similar rocks (or for performing feats of similar difficulty), we would ordinarily expect, under that metarule, a similar reward to be offered

for this one. Insofar as arguments of consistency or comparability underlie positive desert claims, they all seem to be rule-based in similar ways. Thus, desert claims—even claims to have certain rules applied—can arise under a metarule. But that metarule itself is not grounded in consideration of desert.

There is another way in which an extended sense of desert is used to lodge claims to have different sorts of rules applied. We sometimes say "there ought to be a mechanism for rewarding behavior like this" or "there ought to be a mechanism for compensating harm like this," without invoking any analogy to how we treat other cases or in any other way invoking any implicit or explicit metarule. In such cases, we truly are saying that this should be the rule, not just that it is (in some extended sense) the rule.

What is going on here might be similar to what we are doing when invoking concepts of "natural rights." To say that P has a right to x is to say that P has that right under existing law; to say that P has a natural right to x may just mean that it is what the law should be. "Desert" might be used in both intrasystemic and extrasystemic senses, although there is no clear marker (akin to "natural" in the case of rights) to warn when we shift from one sense to another. What is crucial is that the extended, extrasystemic senses of both these notions can (and in the case of "desert" I argue does) refer to the form that the entitlements should take, rather than the grounds upon which these expansions are justified. On this interpretation, natural rights are not extralegal rights, but merely claims that should be recognized by the legal system in the form of rights. So too with extrasystemic deserts: Calling them "deserts" merely suggests that they should be recognized by the system as deserts, rather than that they actually are deserts even if the system does not recognize them as such.

To summarize: positive desert claims must be justified in terms of the way the existing scheme of things ordinarily works; and the justification for that, in turn, must be sought outside the notion of desert. The effect of that argument is to put positive desert claims firmly in their place. It proves, in yet another way, that desert claims cannot trump all others. The moral force of positive desert claims derives from other sorts of moral arguments, and the selfsame arguments that justify the systems in terms of which desert claims can be lodged might also justify sacrificing claims of desert to some other sorts of claims altogether.

Chance Undercuts Deserts

So far I have been talking in terms of certainties, of outcomes that would without doubt have obtained in the normal course of affairs. But certainty itself is far from normal. Typically, all we can say is that it is more or less likely that some particular outcome would obtain in the absence of untoward interventions.

In previous sections, we were concerned with the case in which P would get q in the normal course of events. I translated that into a desert statement by substituting "deserves" for the phrase "would (certainly) get in the normal course of events." Here we are concerned with the case in which P would probably get q in the normal course of events. But that cannot be translated into a desert statement by substituting "probably deserves" for the phrase "probably would get in the normal course of events." Surely it is wrong to say that someone who has purchased a lottery ticket probably deserves the prize; and more still that someone who has bought 10 tickets is 10 times more likely to deserve the prize than the person who has bought only 1.

When introducing probabilities into the proposition "P deserves q," the probability does not attach to "deserves." It attaches instead to q. The person who has purchased 1 lottery ticket deserves a chance (i.e., some probability) of winning the prize. The person who has bought 10 deserves 10 times as many chances, or a probability 10 times greater. But we would not (at least until after the drawing) want to say that either of them either absolutely or even probably deserves the prize.

The probability of getting q, which P deserves, is to be analyzed in terms of the probability that would obtain (or would have obtained) in the absence of untoward interventions, analyzed here just as before. If P bought 1 of 1000 lottery tickets, he or she deserves a probability of $P = 1/1000$ of winning the prize. The reason is simply that that is the probability that would obtain absent untoward interventions, such as the organizers removing his or her ticket from the box before the drawing.

The proposition that P deserves the probability p of q might be boiled down still further using the notion of a statistical expectation. That is to say, what P deserves is the product of p times q. If he or she bought 1 out of 1000 tickets for a lottery, the only prize in which is $1000, his or her statistical expection is a payoff of $1. That is what he or she deserves—and that is all he or she deserves. In practice, of course, he or she will inevitably get either a little less or a lot more, either nothing or the whole $1000. And that, in turn, suggests that the outcomes of lotteries (and, indeed, of a broad class of analogous lumpy, probabilistic events) are inherently, to some greater or lesser extent, undeserved: The losers always deserve more (sometimes much more) than they get; the winners never deserve as much (sometimes not nearly as much) as they receive.

That my analysis yields this result is, I think, one of the larger points in its favor. It is in this respect clearly superior to many of the more standard analyses of personal deserts. Some analysts tend to assume that you deserve whatever you get, in the absence of contraindications (what I have called untoward interventions), just so long as there is something in your character or history to ground the desert claim. Other analysts tend to assume that you do not deserve anything, in the absence of strong evidence in your character or history that you deserve it fully.

Both presumptions are untenable. The person who buys a $1 lottery ticket surely has done something to deserve the $1000 prize. But surely the little thing he or she did—buy a $1 ticket—was far too little to ground the claim that he or she deserves the full $1000 prize. Setting the presumption one way leaves him or her deserving too much. Setting it the other way, too little. What he or she really purchased, and what he or she therefore deserves, is no more and no less than a chance of 1 in 1000 of winning $1000. Or, in statistical terms, what he or she bought—and what he or she deserves—is the expected payoff of $1.

Consider, again, someone who takes risks with his or her health—driving without fastening the seat belt, for example. He or she has done something silly, and in some sense deserves to suffer the consequences of such silliness. But being thrown through the windshield is surely far more punishment than he or she could be said to deserve. He or she was, after all, running only a 1 in 10,000 chance of crashing. His or her deserts, calculated as in the lottery example above, would be only 1/10,000th of the pain he or she suffers going through the windshield.

This has enormous practical implications for social policy. Where people are unlucky and risks turn into disasters, they might deserve to suffer somewhat because they have taken the risks. But they do not deserve to suffer that much. We should therefore take steps to alleviate their suffering. Maybe not all their suffering. After all, they deserve some pain; it would be wrong, therefore, to do so much for them that they are left as well off as they would have been had they not taken any risks at all. But more often than not nature takes care of that for us. People will typically have suffered some losses that we can do nothing to set right, so some of their suffering (whether or not it is exactly the right quantum, morally) will remain whatever we do.

Putting Deserts in Deep Freeze

The bulk of this article has been devoted to asking what it means to say that someone does—or, as I have argued is more nearly the paradigm case, does not—deserve something. But what "desert" means is one thing, and how far its influence should extend over so-cial policy is another. Even if we can say that P clearly deserves q, and even if we are using the notion of positive desert in a truly moralized sense (as my previous arguments suggest we usually are not), that would not necessarily entail that P ought morally to receive q.

One reason may be that desert is only one consideration among many others carrying at least as much of a moral charge, and in any particular case those other considerations may outweigh deserts. But another reason that is more interesting and upon which I shall therefore concentrate here is that in certain sorts of circumstances questions of personal deserts are simply out of place.

Needs Trump Deserts

Imagine an automobile accident. The drivers of both cars are brought into the hospital emergency room with identical injuries and identical prognoses. One of them was clearly to blame for the accident: His negligence caused the crash, and the policemen bringing the injured drivers in make sure that the doctors know that fact. The other driver was merely his innocent victim, and the policemen make sure the doctors know that too.

Now, the innocent victim is clearly less deserving of her fate than the reckless driver is of his. In the normal course of events—that is, absent the untoward intervention of reckless drivers—she would never have suffered these injuries. Does that, however, mean that emergency room medics should devote substantially greater efforts to treating the innocent victim than the guilty driver, even though their injuries and prognoses are identical? I think not. And I would stick by that judgment even where resources are desperately scarce, and we have enough to treat only one: Flipping a coin rather than examining driving records is the right way to make that sort of tragic medical choice.

Part of the reason is no doubt that the guilty, although he may deserve some sort of punishment for his recklessness, does not deserve to suffer nearly as much pain in punishment as the accident has in fact inflicted upon him. Let us suppose he took a 1 in 10 chance of crashing: Then he deserves only one-tenth of the pain he is now experiencing; the rest we would put down to pure bad luck, which is totally undeserved.

But that cannot be the whole story. If it were, we would reckon the medics right to devote ten per cent less time and effort to treating the guilty driver than the innocent; or we would think them right in treating the innocent victim first, even though she is less severely injured, just so long as her injuries are at least 90% as bad as those of the guilty driver. Both standard intuitions and the conventions of medical ethics join in rejecting that sort of conclusion.

The real reason, I suggest, is that there are circumstances in which considerations of desert are simply out of place, and this is one of them. A perfectly general characterization of such circumstances remains elusive. But what is going on in this particular case is clear enough. Needs are trumping deserts. They do so not just in the sense of overriding deserts, but of actually cancelling them.

That certainly happens when life is at stake. But I think it also pretty clearly happens when the stakes are substantially lower. Suppose neither of the drivers in my earlier example had sustained life-threatening injuries. I think we would still balk at saying that doctors should treat the innocent driver first, even though the guilty driver was in 9.99% more pain.

Similarly, I think we can all agree that it would be wrong (except, perhaps, as a deterrent to others) for social security administrators to deny public housing or unemployment benefits to people who have recklessly vacated one apartment or job without first having arranged for another. In some sense, homelessness or unemployment is something that such people might "have coming" in the ordinary course of events and, hence, in my terms, to be "deserved" by them. That is the point that those who oppose welfare payments to the "undeserving poor" want to make. But there are various reasons to resist the policy implications of their analysis.

Some have to do with what the "undeserving" poor really deserve or do not deserve. Although the undeserving poor might not positively deserve assistance, neither do they positively deserve in any sense (moral or otherwise) their plight absent assistance. Usually their only sin is recklessness or fecklessness. The most they can be said to deserve, even in purely statistical terms, is therefore some probability of suffering a bad outcome—the statistical expectation, say, of a rather worse job or house. (They might not deserve even that, if their recklessness or fecklessness were itself covered by some further excusing condition.) Complete homelessness or complete joblessness is far worse than the merely reckless or feckless have done anything to deserve.

Another reason is this: The reckless or feckless may deserve bad outcomes in some statistical sense of that being what the consequences of their recklessness or fecklessness would ordinarily be. But such statements about positive deserts are without any moral warrant. All such statements tell us is the way the world ordinarily works. Whether it should work that way is an open question. That is in itself quite enough to defeat any suggestion that bad outcomes are positively deserved in any moral sense. At the very least, we must say that those bad outcomes are neither deserved nor undeserved, morally speaking. And insofar as there is a moral case for making the world work some other way—insofar as there is a moral case for the welfare state—we can go further still. Then the (morally) normal course of affairs should and hence would be one in which welfare officers stepped in to assist the reckless and the feckless. Those people thus deserve assistance. Failure to render it to them would constitute a morally important "untoward" intervention in what is morally the normal course of affairs; any suffering that followed from that failure would itself then be seen as undeserved.

Beyond all that, however, is the further question of whether it would be right to let social unfortunates suffer, even if they deserve to suffer and even if the deserts in questions were genuinely moral deserts. The argument here has been to suggest that it is not, at least where their suffering would be great. Needs trump deserts. Those who are in what might properly be described as "desperate" circumstances should be given assistance, whether they deserve it or not.

Confused Causation Yields "No Fault"

There is another class of cases in which we might be inclined to put considerations of deserts, fault, credit, and blame into abeyance. The paradigm cases, perhaps, arise within the realm of the law of accidents. There "no-fault" principles are coming to enjoy increasing prominence, first (in common law jurisdictions, anyway) with the 1897 British Workmen's Compensation Act, then with various schemes of no-fault automobile insurance, and now with the far broader New Zealand Compensation Act of 1972.

No doubt the no-fault impulse is largely motivated by economic considerations quite unconnected with any notions of moral deserts. And insofar as there is a moral component, it may well derive largely from considerations of proportionality: Whatever fault there may have been on whomsoever's part, the harm suffered is usually wildly out of proportion to the fault. But another important source of this no-fault impulse in accident law—and one that serves to define this as a separate class of exceptions to desert/fault principles—is that there is typically just too much fault on the part of too many agents to make any nonarbitrary allocation of liability or blame. That was clearly what prompted the no-fault principle in Workmen's Compensation legislation: The injured worker was ordinarily partially at fault, but so were his coworkers, his supervisors, and his employers. Likewise in automobile accidents, fault is ordinarily shared between drivers, auto manufacturers, state highway departments, and others. So, too, New Zealanders have come to appreciate with most accidents: The background conditions that society at large has created are often inextricably intertwined with

personal negligence on the part of both the injurer and the injured. As the Royal Commission giving rise to this legislation observed,

> People have begun to recognize that the accidents regularly befalling large numbers of their fellow citizens are due not so much to human error as to the complicated and uneasy environment which everybody tolerates for apparent advantages. The risks are the risks of social progress, and if there are instinctive feelings at work today in this general area they are not concerned with the greater or lesser faults of individuals, but with the wider responsibility of the whole community. It is for these reasons that compulsory insurance for highway and industrial accidents is generally acceptable.
>
> Since we all persist in following community activities, which year by year exact a predictable and inevitable price in bodily injury, so should we all share in sustaining those who become the random but statistically necessary victims. The inherent cost of these community purposes should be borne on the basis of equality by the community [as a whole, through general taxation].

The basic principle seems to be this: Notions of personal fault are appropriate only where there is a small set of actors making discrete (separate or easily separable) and readily identifiable causal contributions to the outcome. Where many causal factors are deeply intertwined, any apportionment of fault between them would be arbitrary; and principles of blame, fault, or desert should therefore not apply.

Because the paradigm cases all come from accident law, the discussion here is invariably cast in terms of fault and liability for disagreeable outcomes. But the same sort of principle can surely apply, *mutatis mutandis*, to questions of how to apportion credit for agreeable outcomes. There, too, desert statements only make sense where there are only a few actors who make discrete and readily identifiable causal contributions to the outcome. Where many causal factors are deeply intertwined, any apportionment of credit between them would be arbitrary; and principles of positive entitlement (the converse of fault) should therefore not apply.

This, again, obviously has enormous implications for social policy. Cluttered causal histories characterize almost all outcomes of consequence in complex modern societies. There are very few things indeed that people can, therefore, be said unequivocally to deserve or not to deserve. There are many possible responses to such a finding, perhaps the most common being to introduce a presumption that will do all the work that proper analysis cannot. But the only legitimate response, I would argue, is to put notions of desert (credit, blame, fault, etc.) into abeyance in such situations. When considering whether or not to provide social assistance to some social unfortunate, in circumstances of radically confused causal relations, the appropriate question is not "do they deserve to suffer" or "do they deserve assistance" but merely "is some social interest served by assisting them?" Similarly, when considering whether or not to tax away some of rich people's fortunes, in circumstances of radical confusion about the causal relations that led to their being rich, the appropriate question is not "do

they deserve their riches" or "do they deserve to have them taken away" but merely "is some social interest served by reallocating these resources?"

Conclusion

The practical question addressed by this article concerns the proper role of considerations of personal desert in social policymaking. Here I have offered three independent reasons for supposing that they should have only a very limited role, if any at all. The first has to do with the concept itself: Usually desert considerations will provide at most a negative moral warrant for remedying the effects of wrongful interventions in the normal course of events; they will only rarely, and even then only derivatively, provide any positive moral warrant for producing one particular outcome rather than another. The second reason has to do with the relationship between probabilities and deserts: Luck largely mitigates deserts. The third has to do with the context in which desert judgments are employed: Where causal relationships are complex or considerations of needs are in play, considerations of deserts are simply out of place.

26. Egalitarianism and the Modest Significance of Desert

ROBERT YOUNG

Robert Young teaches ethics, political philosophy, and metaphysics at La Trobe University in Melbourne, Australia. He is the author of *Freedom, Responsibility and God* and *Personal Autonomy: Beyond Negative and Positive Liberty*, in addition to various papers in professional journals and collections. He was until recently the editor of the *Australasian Journal of Philosophy* and is a Fellow of the Australian Academy of Humanities.

Young argues that an egalitarian need not adopt the extreme view that personal desert can play no role in determining which distributions of benefits and burdens are just. To the extent that we can take credit for our achievements, it is appropriate to regard ourselves as deserving to have thus succeeded. From this it does not follow, however, that we deserve the sort of rewards successful people often obtain. Moreover, if those who lack natural talents are unable to make up for their deficiencies through the expenditure of greater effort, heavy reliance on personal desert as a basis for the distribution of benefits and burdens is, Young argues, apt to prove unfair. He argues his case by way of a consideration of the claims of Sher and others who hold that we can place heavy reliance on desert as a fair distributive base and who oppose egalitarian claims to the contrary. In the final part of the paper he sets out some considerations relevant to giving desert a qualified place in an egalitarian distributive scheme.

I

To the extent that what people deserve is unequal, any distribution of benefits and burdens in accordance with individual deserts is apt to work against equality in that distribution. Not surprisingly, therefore, those who emphasize the place of desert in the determination of fair or just distributions see it as discrediting any thoroughgoing egalitarianism. Egalitarians have responded in various ways to the attempts of desert theorists to discredit egalitarianism, but two in particular have been prominent. Some have argued that desert should at best have a relatively insignificant place in the determination of fair distributions; others, more extremely, that desert should have no place at all in such determinations. In this article I shall defend the former sort of response against objections and then go on to outline how the response can be made applicable to some fundamental distributional questions (or, at least, as applicable as a philosophical theory is likely to be).

Reprinted from *Ethics* 102 (January 1992), by permission. Notes deleted.

Proper consideration of these issues obviously requires being clear about the nature of desert. A comprehensive discussion is not feasible here so I shall simply restate those points which seem agreed as a result of the careful considerations of the concept of desert by, among others, Joel Feinberg (1970), John Kleinig (1971), and George Sher (1979, 1987).

First, to deserve to be given some specified form of treatment a person, nonhuman animal, institution, or object must possess some characteristic or, objects excepted, have done, or refrained from doing, some action which justifies the treatment. Feinberg refers to such characteristics and actions as *desert bases*. Something is an appropriate basis on which a claim of desert may be founded when it makes the claimant *worthy* of the relevant mode of treatment. I have already said that nonpersons can be deserving subjects. In this article, however, I will be concerned only with the deserts of persons, or *personal deserts*. Even then I will be concerned with just a particular subset of personal deserts, namely, those having to do with the desert basis or bases for income and wealth.

Suppose for the sake of argument, that there are some justifiable claims of personal desert. A second point to be noted about desert claims is the bewildering variety of things which are said to serve as personal desert bases. People are said, for example, to deserve the award of prizes and grades for their athletic, recreational, and intellectual achievements, to deserve rewards and punishments for their actions, to deserve compensation for losses they have suffered because of the wrongful actions of others or, indeed, because they have unmet needs even though that is the fault of no one in particular, and so on and so forth. The range seems to cover virtually anything considered desirable (or undesirable) provided only that this attaches to some condition of worthiness such as the having of a certain characteristic or the doing of a certain action. This bewildering diversity makes it improbable that a generic set of necessary and sufficient conditions can be provided for determining the justifiability of claims by persons to deserve something. What is needed is more careful specification on a kind by kind basis (if not a case by case one). Thus, whether someone deserves to win the World Chess Championship will be determined by utterly different considerations from those that are relevant to whether someone deserves to be given life imprisonment, and utterly different again from whether someone deserves to be awarded compensatory damages for injuries sustained as a consequence of medical negligence. Where the personal deserts are incomes and wealth, and any suggestion of the deserts being properly seen as compensation can be ruled out, various qualities of worthiness have been proposed. Three in particular have found prominence: moral merit, value of contribution, and effort. I shall proceed for the greater part of this article without making any attempt to decide as between these claimants or considering complications such as the place of individual motivations and preferences. When I refer to the views of authors with definite convictions about the superiority of one or other proposed basis, I shall ignore the claimed superiority. In the final section I will attempt to adjudicate the matter.

Third, that a person deserves to be treated in a particular way is *a* reason for so treating her or him, but not a conclusive reason since desert claims are true defeasibly (or pro tanto as some would say), rather than true all things considered. They may, for example, clash with claims of entitlement which, though sometimes confused with desert claims, are of quite a different character. That is not to say that one or the other sort has precedence despite the fact that many writers do seem to accord precedence to the claims of right or entitlement (which are thought to 'trump' those of desert). George Sher (1987, pp. 199–202) has plausibly suggested that desert claims are often thought to be weaker just because questions about what individuals are obligated to do (by the legitimate claims of others against them) are more numerous than those about what it would be appropriate for individuals to have, but that this does not establish precedence, only that there are different answers to different questions.

Fourth, we need to note that whereas desert claims have to satisfy 'conditions of worthiness', claims of entitlement require only the satisfaction of whatever rules have been established (or have won recognition) for the purpose. Desert claims thus are founded on axiological or value considerations. What constitutes the conditions of worthiness for any particular case is apt, as a result, to be a matter of dispute (and this partially explains the controversies that have long surrounded talk of desert). With claims of entitlement a claim is justified provided only that people have acted in accordance with the rules established to decide such claims. John Rawls (1971) points out that desert is often confused with legitimate expectations because people are due a certain return when, having been encouraged to act in accordance with just institutions established for determining such returns, they do just that. Their due is to be expressed in terms of expectations to particular distributive shares rather than deserts because considerations of desert cannot properly frame the institutions. Thus, even though the moral value of the rules which establish entitlements is, strictly, irrelevant, that is not the case with Rawlsian legitimate expectations (cf. Arnold, 1987). As will emerge later when I focus specifically on distributional questions to do with income and wealth, the irrelevancy of value to claims of entitlement has been a source of concern to egalitarians who accept the justifiability of some desert claims but who reject the appropriateness of benefits whose scale is not a function of desert at all but, instead, of prior agreement. In such instances the person who receives the benefit is deserving of *a* benefit but not of the actual benefit, since this latter is out of all proportion to the value established by the desert base. A deserving winner of, for example, a professional sports tournament may, therefore, be rewarded entirely in accord with her entitlements (or even legitimate expectations) but far beyond her deserts.

II

In this section I will outline and criticize the extreme view that desert can have no place at all in the determination of fair distributions. In the following three sections I will outline and criticize the best defenses of desert theory known to me. To the extent that my criticisms of these polar opposites are sound, desert can have only a relatively insignificant place in the determination of fair distributions. In the final section I shall endeavor to give some idea of the operational significance of such a position within an egalitarian account of fair distributions.

I noted in my introductory remarks that on one extreme view desert has no place at all in the determination of fair distributions. This is a view that John Rawls (1971, p. 104) has been taken to advocate:

> Perhaps some will think that the person with greater natural endowments deserves those assets and the superior character that makes their development possible. Because he is more worthy in this sense, he deserves the greater advantages that he could achieve with them. This view, however, is surely incorrect. It seems to be one of the fixed points of our considered judgments that no one deserves his place in the distribution of native endowments, any more than one deserves one's initial starting place in society. The assertion that a man deserves the superior character that enables him to make the effort to cultivate his abilities is equally problematic; for his character depends in large part upon fortunate family and social circumstances for which he can claim no credit. The notion of desert seems not to apply to these cases.

Rawls has been widely interpreted (on the basis of this and the surrounding material in sec. 17 and what he says in sec. 48) as drawing the conclusion that no one deserves the greater advantages he or she could achieve with his or her natural endowments and in so doing to have furnished the locus classicus for across-the-board skepticism by egalitarians about personal desert in distributive contexts. To see if this is so, a bit of backtracking will be necessary.

Recall that, according to Rawls, the problem of determining fair distributions arises for those engaged in mutually beneficial cooperative efforts. Justice as fairness requires that social institutions, the public system of rules which defines the rights and obligations of members of the cooperative group, be arranged so as to maximize the expectations of the worst-off. A framework of just institutions arranged to achieve this goal will not provide for differential rewards based on natural advantages because it is arbitrary just who has these advantages. (If no one, e.g., can sing like Sutherland or Pavarotti without training, it is also clear, I take it, that no one can sing like them just as a result of training and so that it is utterly contingent that *they* have the vocal capacities that they do. Though this is a particularly stark instance, the point is generalizable, according to Rawls). Even those who agree that natural talents are arbitrary need not, of course, accept the 'collectivization' of talents which Rawls takes to be implied by his argument.

Robert Nozick, who is famously identified with the view that because of rights of 'self-ownership' entitlements have moral priority over deserts, scathingly criticizes Rawls's theory as one that purports to exalt personal autonomy but denies that those who exercise it may take any credit for what they thereby produce (1974, p. 214). If what Rawls says about desert is looked at in its entirety it is unlikely that Nozick's ad hominem succeeds (Sher 1987, pp. 23 ff.). In the passage previously cited, Rawls claims only that our characters (which are relevant to whether we make the effort to cultivate our native endowments) depend "*in large part* upon fortunate family and social circumstances." And in a later passage dealing explicitly with desert for effort, he remarks that "the effort a person is willing to make is influenced by his natural abilities and skills and the alternatives open to him. The better endowed are more likely, other things equal, to strive conscientiously, and there

seems to be no way to discount for their greater good fortune. The idea of rewarding desert is impracticable'' (1971, p. 312).

It is clear that Rawls is not arguing that people do not deserve a greater return for putting in a greater effort but rather that there is no way, in practice, of determining what part is played by the greater good fortune of those who, in being able to strive conscientiously, put forth a greater effort (cf. Cohen 1989). So when Rawls rejects claims of personal desert he surely intends to say that whereas a person's natural endowments were brought into existence by events independent of anything he or she has done, what the individual makes of those endowments does require the exercise of autonomy. It is his contention that to sort out the relevant contributions is impracticable. That he does think autonomy is required seems to be presupposed when, in discussing moral merit as a basis for desert, he claims (1971, p. 311) that premium income payments, though not deserved, are "earned by scarce talents" and are to be used to "cover the costs of training and to encourage the efforts of learning, as well as to direct ability to where it best furthers the common interest." For incentives to be effective, those offered them must be capable of responding to their availability.

Suppose that Nozick's criticism is thus able to be evaded. There remains the troubling point that, even if Rawls does not endorse 'hard determinism', with its denial of human freedom, his position in practice is going to be indistinguishable from the extreme thesis about personal desert. For some (e.g., Zaitchik 1977) the very fact that desert claims are commonplace in everyday thought and talk is sufficient ground for rejecting either the extreme view or Rawls's claims. Zaitchik contends that, along with milder egalitarians who permit only a qualified place to personal desert, Rawls presumes that to deserve something a person must deserve the desert basis for that thing; that is, one who deserves something has to be in control "all the way down" on pain of being caught in a vicious regress. As Zaitchik (1977, p. 373) puts it: in order to deserve *Z*, a person must deserve *Z*'s desert-basis *Y*; in order to deserve *Y*, he or she must deserve *Y*'s desert-basis *X*; and so on. But, the argument continues, when we make personal desert claims in everyday affairs we don't investigate whether the claimants are in control all the way down, indeed we standardly don't bother ourselves beyond inquiring into whether they have produced the relevant item, done the relevant action, or expended the required effort. Egalitarian critics of desert who insist that people's lack of control all the way down precludes their being deserving are thus at odds with the common conviction that people sometimes are personally deserving. It will be instructive to consider why this argument is unsound.

Zaitchik begs the question in suggesting that just because there is a pretheoretical conviction that personal desert claims are justified, egalitarians who reject certain desert claims must be mistaken (cf. Sher 1987, p. 25). It is a mistake to suggest that egalitarian opponents of everyday desert claims are committed to holding that to deserve something one must not only have the desert-basis but deserve it, and so on ad infinitum. But no egalitarian need deny that there are some appropriate desert claims. Consider Steffi Graf's achievement in winning the Grand Slam of women's tennis in 1989. If we say that, having won the required four titles, Graf deserved to do so, it is implied that her tennis prowess was in an appropriate sense, albeit a sense that is difficult to specify, something she can take credit for or have imputed to her. So, provided she can be said to take credit for her achievement, the claim that she deserves her success stands. Though this anticipates some of what I shall say in the next section, anyone who rejects a hard determinist outlook and who thinks it is not entirely impracticable to measure how much of someone like Graf's success is to be attributed to her conscientious striving to make the most of her natural talents, should acknowledge that it *is* justifiable for her to take credit for her achievements. In maintaining this position I not only distance myself from Rawls's version of egalitarianism but also from that of Ronald Dworkin (1981*a*, 1981*b*, 1983). Contrary to what I have maintained, Dworkin eschews the idea of an egalitarian providing scope for claims that people deserve what they can earn from their talents because he thinks the requirements of equality work against sensitivity to endowments. His chief reason for thinking this appears to be that "the idea of equality depends upon, and so cannot furnish, instructions about where precisely to draw the line between the person and his circumstances" (1983, p. 39; cf. Narveson 1983, pp. 15 ff.) Clearly I am committed to defending our capacity on occasion correctly to draw the line by identifying those matters for which individuals can take credit.

Suppose I am right about Graf's deserving her success. This is by no means to say that she deserves to have her tennis prowess. (In this regard I am at one with other egalitarians like Rawls and Dworkin.) More important still, from an egalitarian viewpoint, even if Graf deserves her tennis success it certainly does not follow that she deserves the high income and great wealth that success at tennis brings her. As we have already seen, desert is often conflated with entitlement. Given that a promoter contracts with the players to provide a certain amount of prize money for a tournament, Graf is entitled to whatever is the agreed level of prize money. Those, at best, are her "legitimate expectations," not her deserts. Indeed it is worth saying that most of the incomes which egalitarians find obscene are contractual or based on negotiated agreements and so are strictly issues of entitlement. So, despite the rhetoric of corporate executives, agents for sports stars, entertainers, and the like, it is not true that such people or their clients *deserve* the rewards of "executive share plan" arrangements or lucrative returns from endorsements (which frequently far outstrip official salaries). Under present arrangements they may be entitled to these things, but to say that they deserve their high incomes presupposes that the relativities are in accord with the appropriate desert-basis (e.g., vastly greater effort, marginal product etc.). That the presupposition is false I shall show in Section VI below.

Those who wish to allow desert only a limited place within the framework of distributive justice thus can resist the suggestion that to deserve something one must deserve the desert-basis and so on ad infinitum. All that has to be insisted on is that at some appropriate level there is a desert-basis over which the claimant has control or which is properly attributable to the claimant. In the matter of native endowments none of us can lay claim to those endowments as a desert-basis. But that does not, pace Rawls, preclude our making out a case for justifiable personal desert claims where individuals display the appropriate control over other putative desert-bases such as effort or contribution. To show that such justifiable claims should only have a relatively insignificant place in the determination of fair distributions of income and wealth, it is necessary not only to defeat the challenge of those more skeptical about desert but also that of those who are convinced it should have a central role. In the next two sections I shall, therefore, offer a critical response to two impressive recent defenses of desert. The way will then be clear to outline just how much store should be put in personal desert claims within a satisfactory account of distributive justice.

III

George Sher (1979, 1987) has argued that if there is to be a resolution of the dispute between egalitarians—he has in mind moderate egalitarians like Rawls—and those more sympathetic to personal desert claims, egalitarians must argue their case from noncontroversial premises. If we assume something like Rawls's claim that our native endowments are undeserved because they are not the result of anything we can take credit for, Sher thinks such a claim can pass muster. But this is not so for a further premise on which Rawls relies when he refers to the possession of a superior character which enables some to make the effort to cultivate their natural endowments, namely, that if S does not deserve X, and X makes Y possible, then S does not deserve Y.

The reason is that it rules out too much. It would allow the rejection of personal desert claims for Y in any circumstance where an undeserved necessary condition for Y exists. Since none of us, for example, deserves to live in a lifesustaining environment, yet it is a necessary condition for anything we may be said to deserve, no one is unfairly advantaged over anyone else as regards particular personal deserts just because such an (undeserved) necessary condition is satisfied. The difficulty can be avoided by shifting from a statement of the conditions necessary for a person's deserving Y simpliciter, to a statement of the conditions necessary for his or her deserving to have Y while someone else does not. This has the effect of making desert claims straightforwardly assessable when the abilities people have are not the result of anything they have done and are near enough equivalent. Where, however, people's abilities are not the result of anything they have done and are unequally distributed, an egalitarian challenge like Rawls's to the significance of judgments of personal desert will remain.

Since Sher develops his own case for the recognition of desert claims in the distribution of income and wealth by way of a critique of Rawls's arguments, it will be necessary to consider his contention (1987, pp. 28 ff.) that his representative egalitarian uncritically assumes that people differ in effort-making abilities and that the differences are best explained environmentally. But it will need to be borne in mind that no egalitarian need be committed even to a view on deserved incomes as strong as the one Rawls accepts.

As Sher sees it, when confronted by persons who exert different amounts of effort, especially when the difference in their efforts is pronounced, systematic, and to the obvious disadvantage of the less industrious, we should, according to Rawls, regard this as being best explained by their unequal powers to make the effort. Sher thinks that Rawls is not entitled to his assumption that people differ in effort-making capacities and that the explanation Rawls offers is not the most powerful available. Here is Sher's defense of the contrary view that people's effort-making capacities are equal: "Anyone who accepts the equal-ability thesis will of course wish to maintain that when some person *N* fails to exert efforts that are plainly in his own long-range interest, he is either momentarily inattentive to those interests or else momentarily unconcerned to further them. And when the equal-ability thesis is supplemented by these premises, the resulting explanation of *N*'s lack of effort is every bit as plausible as its alternative" (1987, pp. 29–30).

Sher advances an additional argument in the endeavor to refute a possible reply by Rawls. Suppose, notwithstanding the previous argument, that Rawls is right to hold that people do differ in effort-making abilities. It will still be true that people deserve the benefits of their superior efforts, says Sher, provided only that those with lesser effort-making abilities take steps to help them match the superior efforts of others (e.g., by maintaining a special vigilance against those factors they know to be personally distracting or enervating and so increasing their chances of getting maximum return). Should it be claimed that these steps, as well as the efforts themselves, are blocked by lesser effort-making capacities, this would implausibly depend on denying that people can do any of the many things that help enhance such capacities. So even genuine differences in effort-making ability, should they exist, seem unlikely to have the moral significance attributed to them by Rawls (and, perhaps, other egalitarians).

Neither of these arguments of Sher's is persuasive. Consider the first of them. It is certainly true that people are sometimes neglectful of their long-term interests and show this by not exerting themselves when those interests require them to expend a significant amount of effort. Were Sher's aim only to show that the extreme claim, that desert has no place in our thinking about the fairness of distributions, is mistaken, this might be a sufficient reply. But quite apart from the fact that this is not strictly what Rawls claims, nor something an egalitarian need be committed to, Sher surely has to show more than that in some instances the extreme claim is mistaken, given that he wishes to champion the plausi-

bility of the credentials of an alternative explanation (the equal-ability thesis coupled with supplementary premises). The alternative explanation has a remarkable structural similarity with Plato's view that no one who is knowledgeable and free can pursue any but the good. But just as that view is implausible so, too, there seem to be clear instances of individuals who are attentive to, and desire to further, their interests but are incapable of producing the effort needed to manage this. Of course, Sher might deny this and insist instead that a persistent failure to make the required effort shows a lack of serious concern for those interests rather than an inability to make the effort needed to secure them. I agree that in some cases the sheer persistency of the failure will incline us to this alternative explanation. But I do not concede that all cases can be handled this way (any more than they can be with weakness of will). The sort of cases I have in mind are those where victims of continuing oppression suffer such losses of self-esteem that they fall into an extreme lassitude about their future. If these are clear enough counterinstances to Sher's contention, the most that follows from his first argument is that an extreme thesis about people's effort-making abilities, which no egalitarian need endorse, is subject to counterexamples and so cannot command our assent.

This concession to Sher may be thought to pose a problem. It might seem that, in claiming there are those who lack the appropriate effort-making abilities, I am implicitly agreeing that there are those who have the effort-making abilities. If the latter exist, the disposition to expend effort cannot be undercut as a desert-basis for everyone. It can only be undercut for those who suffer from the inability to make an effort. However, since my stance is not an antidesert one, but one critical of desert being given a major role in the determination of fair distributions, the concession made above creates no problem. Moreover, whether or not it is within an individual's capacity to exert a certain effort, the natural assets he or she has certainly will affect the benefits likely to be obtained through the exertion of that effort.

Suppose that I am right about what follows from Sher's first argument. The issue still remains whether the differences in people's effort-making abilities can be overcome. It is to this issue that Sher's second argument is directed. If that second argument were to succeed, then when we observe, as is everywhere agreed, that there are pronounced and systematic differences in the efforts people expend and that many of those who do not make much of an effort suffer as a result, Sher could properly claim that there is a host of things such people might do to help improve their effort-making capacities. Should we then agree that there *is* a host of things that might be done (as I think we must) the issue will not, however, have been resolved in Sher's favor. The reason is simple: unless among the host of things that in general might be done, there are relevant options accessible to particular individuals, the truth to which Sher points will be of no particular importance. What is empirically dubious, according to those of us who deny that there are only a few cases of genuine and irremediable inequality in effort-making capacities, is the availability to particular individuals of the specific help they need from among the no doubt many and various helps that are available.

It might be thought that Sher and other desert theorists could accept that this is so but contend that all it shows is that we must improve access by individuals to the sort of help they need. In the event that in practice this turns out to be impossible, desert theorists need not yield ground if they can show that reliance on desert still offers greater hope of generating more just outcomes (fewer unjust outcomes) than any alternative that might be proposed by egalitarians. This would be the case, for instance, if allowing people to enjoy the rewards generated by their achievements came closest to giving everyone what he or she deserved despite at the same time giving rise to some undeserved inqualities (Sher 1987, p. 33; Goldman 1987). Interesting as this defense of desert theory is, it seems to me to ignore the following important considerations. Given a background of massive in-

equality in natural talent, if there is reason to think that many people cannot or will not overcome their lack of natural talent through vigorous effort, nor gain access to help that would enhance their effort-making capacities, then there is reason to doubt the claims of desert theory to furnish the most adequate basis for distributive justice. Some egalitarians who would disagree with my judgment that there is a background of massive inequality in natural talent see the present differentials in achievement as the result of barriers such as inequality of opportunity for the similarly talented to achieve similar results. The empirical disagreement between them and me as to how unequally placed people are as regards natural talents cannot be resolved here, but its resolution would obviously make a lot of difference to how much of a role desert should be given. Supposing the resolution of that question to go as I have claimed, it will, of course, be necessary for egalitarians like me to elaborate a more adequate basis for distributive justice than that given by desert theorists, but that is a task for another occasion.

IV

Reflections on desert like those that I have been making have been criticized on a yet further ground. According to Sher (1987, pp. 34 ff.; cf. Nozick 1974, pp. 235–36), critics of desert falsely presuppose all questions of desert to arise in competitive contexts. To the extent that Rawls's own argument focuses on the idea that some have unfair advantages over others, there is some initial plausibility in his claim. Certainly there are noncompetitive contexts in which talk of desert is quite appropriate, for example, those where compensation is deserved. With deserved compensations comparisons may be involved without there being competition. But why should Rawls (or any other egalitarian critic of desert theory) have to deny this? Desert as compensation is one of the defensible forms which desert-based income differences can take and hence is something which egalitarians should support. Nonetheless, despite the validity of such a rejoinder there is no doubt that many do see questions of economic desert in terms of a competition for shares of national wealth. So, no matter how restricted the purposes of Rawls and other egalitarian critics of desert may be, something still needs to be said to show the aptness of talk of unfair advantages in the competition for income and wealth.

Notice, first of all, that private enterprise economies are often characterized as reliant on competition, indeed often trumpeted as being more successful than socialist economies precisely because they are competitive. The recent history of Eastern Europe bears eloquent testimony to the point. Suppose, for the sake of argument, that desert theory favors rewards in terms of individual contribution as measured by marginal product. Under perfect competition the equilibrium position will be one where prices exactly match the costs of employing the various factors of production. But there is overwhelming evidence that the so-called comparative advantage enjoyed by the 'winners' within private enterprise economies is often the result of unfair competition. Private enterprise under perfectly competitive economic conditions would produce deserved outcomes, but to the very great extent that perfect competition does not hold sway there can be little comfort for supporters of desert-based distributions that in the theoretical model it does (cf. Christman 1988).

Second, it does seem true that for situations involving scarcity of resources, opportunities, and so on that there is a competitive aspect to societies like ours. Indeed the very intensity of the competition (e.g., among school-leavers) is frequently remarked. It is somewhat surprising then that even in these sorts of circumstances Sher wishes to reject understandings of desert which appear to presuppose a competitive context. He says, "The best qualified claimant's desert may arise, not through any victory over his rivals, but directly from the comparative closeness of the 'fit' between his qualifications and the requirements of the job or opportunity to be awarded'' (1979, pp. 374–75; cf. 1987, pp.

119–28). But the relative closeness of the fit between one person's qualifications and, say, the requirements of a job is surely a function of the closeness of the fit that others present. Moreover, for all that Sher says, nothing follows about whether the individual whose qualifications best fit him or her for some position has obtained any unfair advantage to make him or her so well fitted. Suppose, as political libertarians find especially troubling (Nozick 1974, pp. 178–82; Steiner 1981), that someone's acquisition of a scarce, nonrenewable resource at a particular time diminishes the access others can subsequently have. Though individuals from future generations would have been more fitted to use the resource, its exhaustion prior to their birth may not only disadvantage them but do so in an unfair way (Railton 1985). Moreover, it surely is self-evident that for the more prized educational and work opportunities (and to a lesser extent cultural opportunities) the competition that exists is not fully fair competition. If supporting evidence be needed it requires only to draw attention to the way in which initiatives have been demanded in the form of affirmative action, reverse discrimination, quotas, head-start programs, and the like to help achieve a more competitive equality of opportunity.

Third, it is worth noting that some who would agree that it is a mistake to think of the distribution of income and wealth in terms of a competition do not draw the conclusion that we should instead think in terms of personal desert. Feinberg (1970, pp. 88–94), for instance, argues that it is improper to think of economic income as a prize and unhelpful to think of it in terms of reward. He contends that it is only the element of compensation involved in the income some receive that may appropriately be a matter of desert. Though I shall later argue that this goes too far, he is surely right that the deprivations occasioned by unpleasant, onerous, hazardous, or lonely circumstances of work deserve to be compensated for, at least up to a point which puts the deprived individual back on a par with his or her fellows. Because of his exclusivity claim he urges that "to say that income ideally ought to be distributed only according to desert is to say that, in respect to all social benefits, all men should ideally be equal" (1970, p. 94).

So even if there is some inappropriateness about thinking of economic distributions in terms of a competition it is not at all clear that this should force us to a greater reliance on personal desert in economic affairs. The onus is on advocates of personal desert in economic affairs to make out the case. Sher, at least, has attempted to do so. He believes that anyone with sympathy for the idea will wish to hold that "people may . . . come to deserve things in a variety of . . . ways: by working especially hard, by possessing special moral characteristics, or simply by exercising their own creative capacities in building houses, painting pictures, or otherwise producing or improving objects of value" (1979, p. 374).

But a moment's inspection of these categories will show that with the exception of the first (which relates to effort-making capacities) they all turn on the possession of certain native endowments or dispositions (what we often call 'gifts') or on the possession of these things plus appropriate effort-making capacities. Granted there are significant inequalities in native endowments, those who start at a disadvantage as regards such gifts must be able to make up for their disadvantage through the exertion of extra effort, or if this is out of the question it must still be fairer to rely on a desert-based distribution with all its inequalities rather than on any alternative. We have come full circle. . . .

VI

I have argued that though the extreme view that there is no role for personal desert in fair distributions of income and wealth is implausible, the position of many that it instead has a quite strategic role has not been plausibly made out even in the strongest defenses of that position. So desert cannot just be ignored, or ignored because it is too hard to determine the rate at which it should be discounted. Nor

(following Feinberg) can desert be limited to compensation. Finally, given unequal innate endowments, the truth cannot be that whatever people achieve through their own efforts or contributions should deservedly bring a reward through higher incomes than are available to others who make comparable efforts but lesser contributions. But these conclusions leave us well short of any useful idea of how desert should be factored in to a fair incomes policy. I shall endeavor in this concluding section to give some substance to my hitherto rather abstract claim.

Many supporters of desert have argued that to fail to accord people their deserts is to fail to treat them as autonomous beings, as beings who can actively and purposefully intervene in the world. This contention is a good place from which to commence my account of the role to be accorded desert in a fair incomes policy. Some (e.g., Miller 1989, pp. 157 ff.) who have stressed that the relevant desert base is the value of the contribution an individual makes have urged that, when agents autonomously put their energies into the achievement of a goal, they deserve in return the value of what they have contributed. Sometimes desert as contribution has been cited to justify rights to ownership and use of property (e.g., Becker 1977; Munzer 1990, chap. 10). When the goal is the furtherance of someone else's purposes, such as an employer's, it is held that the worker still deserves a return in accordance with contribution because the worker's goals have been subordinated to those of the employer.

Just how, though, is the value of the individual's contribution to be measured? Does the person, for example, have to succeed in creating something of 'real value'? Does the person have to succeed in creating something of value to others? How is the value of the person's contribution affected by what others contribute? And what of the part played by the element of good fortune in determining the value of a person's contribution? These traditional questions about the contribution thesis demand answers if the value of someone's contribution is to be made the measure of their deserved income.

Given that the thesis is underpinned by a view about the exercise of individual autonomy a connection needs to be established between desert for contribution and the choices and efforts made by an individual in contributing value. Miller (1989) argues that because of this connection value is best determined via a market mechanism since such a mechanism enables an individual to relate his or her choices and efforts to what others are prepared to give by way of return. This ensures that resources are efficiently allocated. (Market prices need not, however, be relied upon to determine the distribution of incomes since that is subject to political determination via the mechanism of taxation.) There are some obvious difficulties with relating desert to contribution in this way. Miller acknowledges several, but the following seem to me to remain as difficulties. First, marketing a particular contribution (e.g., for inventions) may be very difficult. Second, where risk-taking is involved, individuals may be uncertain whether their talents will be attractive in the market (as with singers, sportspersons, creative artists, designers, and others who need time to develop their talents) or may suffer because of intermittent opportunities once the talents are developed, or their talents may no longer be marketable by the time they are developed. Third, since markets in the world as we know it are neither perfect nor stable, some individuals who direct their energies to making a particular contribution may face a market which is subject to manipulation or artificial restriction by other players—this is a problem that particularly affects small scale primary producers and manufacturers but bears as well on problems of relativities. Consider, for instance, how the salaries that have to be offered to judges are affected by what barristers can earn. Fourth, for an egalitarian there can be no getting away from the fact that massive inequalities in resource holdings, including, but not only, personal talents, influence market assessments of the value of contributions to such an extent as to make those assessments dubiously reliable. Last, but not least, we have already had occasion to observe how markets in our world can be,

and are, undermined as means to the measurement of marginal product through agreements which are struck without reference to desert. The price that is agreed on then impedes the market's operation and relativities are distorted.

Perhaps it is open to a contribution theorist to hold that, for all that they give rise to anomalies concerning relativities and have various other deficiencies, market mechanisms are out best hope and so rather than rejecting them what is needed is to regulate them so that they approximate as nearly as possible their textbook counterparts. There is obviously much to be said for such a response since few egalitarians these days are likely to want to put all their store in a 'command economy' approach. Nonetheless, even with that fact recognized, the contribution thesis certainly cannot be the whole of the story if only because there are instances where personal desert claims seem justifiable without any valuable contribution having been made. Indeed, many of these instances seem to show that contribution cannot even be the primary base for personal deserts. Consider the case where someone's well thought out contribution comes to nought because others, too, have done the selfsame planning, expended similar efforts and so forth with the result that the value of the contribution each ends up making is significantly diminished. Or, again, consider what happens when what Dworkin (1981*b*) calls *brute luck* intrudes on an individual's well-planned activities and these suddenly decline in market value (e.g., where a naturally occurring substance is displaced by a manufactured product, or when a researcher who has worked systematically on the discovery of the cause and cure of a disease is "pipped at the post" [overtaken at the winning post in a race] by another who, while not actively engaged in the search, flukes their discovery). The individual's efforts, though rendered unproductive in market terms, clearly do justify some claim to reward for desert since the thwarting of the contribution does not gainsay the fact of the autonomous, goal-directed effort that was expended. This is especially the case where the worker has subordinated his or her purposes to those of an employer (Sher 1987, p. 103). Though effort seems often to be primary in the determination of desert, on its own it is not normally sufficient. If it were sufficient then no matter how socially useless someone's intense efforts they would have to be rewarded. Picking the wings off flies is not, ceteris paribus, an activity deserving of an income.

Even effort that leads to a valuable product is not the whole story. The motivations of agents seem, as well, to bear on whether they can rightly be thought of as deserving. Certainly where the benefits obtained are merely accidental fall-out from an agent's self-interested pursuits, there is doubt about the agent's deserving our gratitude for the benefits he or she has generated (Feinberg 1970, p. 90). But it would give too great a place to intentions to conclude that no economic return is deserved. A worker whose only motivation was the financial return given for the work could not then deserve that return.

It might be thought that it is implausible to consider effort in isolation from the preferences of individuals. Thus given two persons with similar natural talents and effort-making capacities, but different preferences as between work and leisure, isn't the one who prefers to work deserving of greater returns? Insofar as our concern is simply with effort-making capacities this criticism has force. But once the efforts our two people actually expend are taken into account (granted these are going to be functionally related to their preferences) there is no need to give separate attention to those preferences.

The probability that some well-intentioned individual will succeed in benefiting others if he or she should expend the effort to do so seems also to have a bearing on whether a reward is deserved (cf. Ake 1975). The reason is not hard to find, namely, that to the extent that individuals with comparable natural talents and effort-making capacities expend similar amounts of energy, have similar motivations, and are each pursuing some worthwhile goal, it is the individual with the greater control over whether the goal is achieved who has the higher probability of success. Here

we find echoes of a point made earlier: the merely fortuitous achievement of the goal by some individual gives rise to no justifiable claim of desert. But in the case where an individual succeeds against all odds just because he or she is highly motivated to achieve some worthwhile goal, the case for his or her deserving to be rewarded based on that effort seems stronger than that against, where that is based on improbability of success. While probability of success thus has some bearing on desert, it can be overridden by other factors, perhaps most especially, motivational ones.

This analysis suggests that it is important to avoid simplistic accounts of the basis of personal deserts in any consideration of a fair incomes policy. What has emerged is that the bases will range from those relevant to compensation such as danger, unpleasantness, inconvenience, and remoteness of location with its attendant loss of facilities, through reward for efforts which produce valuable products, to reward for risk-taking which is aimed at producing something valuable, and on even to efforts which do not result in the production of value but warrant a return simply because the effort was well motivated and had a reasonable probability of success. In this latter sort of circumstance there may not even be the difference we earlier found between the self-employed person and the employee. Consider the case of detectives who don't solve a particular crime. Though employed detectives might be entitled to a paycheck we also want to say that their diligent efforts made them deserving of one. Their freelance counterparts, by contrast, have no entitlements (though they would have, had they been successful), yet they may be equally deserving.

What, then, is the egalitarian to say about the place of personal deserts in an incomes policy? My contention has been that an egalitarian should recognize various desert bases as appropriately underpinning differentials in income. However, I have also drawn attention to reasons why egalitarians should insist that the role of desert in the determination of fair economic distributions must be kept in proportion in a world where labor markets are unreformed and unregulated. Let me recap the main points and then mention in passing one further relevant consideration which it has not been possible to discuss in this article.

I argued that it is only where agents in circumstances of fair equality of opportunity can take credit for what they do, that any of the various desert bases can ground justifiable claims of desert. Given that there exists no fair equality of opportunity to acquire in relation to natural endowments, personal desert claims have to be circumscribed. Second, I argued that because market-based assessments of the value of an individual's contribution are, as things stand, dubiously reliable, there is a reason to think that accurate desert-based differentials would not be anything like those that are presently justified by reference to desert. Moreover, an egalitarian can point out that reliance even on a reformed and regulated market with support from a progressive taxation system is apt to result in the emphasis being entirely on monetary differentials. What economists term *psychic income* (non-monetary differentials stemming from greater job satisfaction, the challenge of a position, the opportunity to be involved in democratic workplace structures, and so on) is left out of the equation, to say nothing of the place of public recognition for an individual's valued efforts. Finally, while I have said nothing in this article about them, there are important fair distributional bases other than desert and entitlement which should influence an incomes policy. Any complete account of distributional fairness will, for instance, have to accommodate the principle of need (Scanlon 1975; Wiggins 1985; Braybrooke 1987). For all these reasons, then, personal deserts ought not dominate the determination of incomes or income differentials, and certainly ought not be allowed to lead to the serious inequalities in power relations that egalitarians oppose.

It is a different story altogether with entitlements. In present circumstances it is entitlements based on contracts devised under distorted market conditions which are the greatest source of inequalities in income. The problem with entitlements is not that they are in themselves unfair but that where the social arrangements under which they arise are unfair, they exacerbate the unfairness. For egalitarians it is entitlements, then, not deserts that are 'public enemy number one'. Of course, to say this is only to declare the battle not to enter it. Antiegalitarians will counter that only a system which permits of the sorts of incentives that entitlements (and perhaps deserts) make possible can hope to be efficient enough to sustain an economy that produces benefits at an acceptable level for all. That claim must be the subject of discussion on another occasion.

References

Ake, Christopher. 1975. Justice as Equality. *Philosophy and Public Affairs* 4:68–89.

Arnold, Scott. 1987. Why Profits Are Deserved. *Ethics* 97:387–402.

Becker, Lawrence. 1977. *Property Rights*. London: Routledge & Kegan Paul.

Braybrooke, David. 1987. *Meeting Needs*. Princeton, N.J.: Princeton University Press.

Christman, John. 1988. Entrepreneurs, Profits and Deserving Market Shares. *Social Philosophy and Policy* 6:1–16.

Cohen, Gerald. 1986a. Self-Ownership, World Ownership and Equality. In *Justice and Equality Here and Now*, ed. Frank Lucash, pp. 108–35. Ithaca, N.Y.: Cornell University Press.

Cohen, Gerald. 1986b. Self-Ownership, World Ownership and Equality: Part II. *Social Philosophy and Policy* 3:77–96.

Cohen, Gerald. 1989. On the Currency of Egalitarian Justice. *Ethics* 99:906–44.

Dick, James. 1975. How to Justify a Distribution of Earnings. *Philosophy and Public Affairs* 4:248–72.

Dworkin, Ronald. 1981a. What Is Equality? I. Equality of Welfare. *Philosophy and Public Affairs* 10:185–246.

Dworkin, Ronald. 1981b. What Is Equality? II. Equality of Resources. *Philosophy and Public Affairs* 10:283–345.

Dworkin, Ronald. 1983. Comment on Narveson: In Defense of Equality. *Social Philosophy and Policy* 1:24–40.

Feinberg, Joel. 1970. Justice and Personal Desert.

In *Doing and Deserving*, ed. Joel Feinberg, pp. 55–94. Princeton, N.J.: Princeton University Press.

Goldman, Alan. 1987. Real People: Natural Differences and the Scope of Justice. *Canadian Journal of Philosophy* 17:377–93.

Green, S. J. D. 1989. Competitive Equality of Opportunity: A Defense. *Ethics* 100:5–32.

Haslett, D. W. 1986. Is Inheritance Justified? *Philosophy and Public Affairs* 15:122–55.

Kleinig, John. 1971. The Concept of Desert. *American Philosophical Quarterly* 8:71–78.

Miller, David. 1989. *Market, State, and Community*. Oxford: Clarendon.

Munzer, Stephen R. 1990. *A Theory of Property*. Cambridge: Cambridge University Press.

Nagel, Thomas. 1973. Equal Treatment and Compensatory Discrimination. *Philosophy and Public Affairs* 2:348–63.

Narveson, Jan. 1983. On Dworkinian Equality. *Social Philosophy and Policy* 1:1–23.

Nell, Edward. 1987. Deserving Profits. *Ethics* 97:403–13.

Nielsen, Kai. 1985. *Equality and Liberty: A Defense of Radical Egalitarianism*. Totowa, N.J.: Rowman & Allanheld.

Nozick, Robert. 1974. *Anarchy, State, and Utopia*. New York: Basic.

Rachels, James. 1978. What People Deserve. In *Justice and Economic Distribution*, ed. John Arthur and William H. Shaw, pp. 150–63. Englewood Cliffs, N.J.: Prentice Hall.

Railton, Peter. 1985. Locke, Stock and Peril: Natural Property Rights, Pollution and Risk. In *To Breathe Freely: Risk, Consent and Air*, ed. Mary Gibson, pp. 87–123. Totowa, N.J.: Rowman & Allanheld.

Rawls, John. 1971. *A Theory of Justice*. Cambridge, Mass.: Harvard University Press.

Rosenberg, Alexander. 1987. The Political Philosophy of Biological Endowments: Some Considerations. *Social Philosophy and Policy* 5:1–31.

Sandel, Michael. 1982. *Liberalism and the Limits of Justice*. Cambridge: Cambridge University Press.

Scanlon, Thomas. 1975. Preference and Urgency. *Journal of Philosophy* 72:655–69.

Sher, George. 1979. Effort, Ability and Personal Desert. *Philosophy and Public Affairs* 8:361–76.

Sher, George. 1987. *Desert*. Princeton, N.J.: Princeton University Press.

Steiner, Hillel. 1981. Liberty and Equality. *Political Studies* 29:555–69.

Walzer, Michael. 1983. *Spheres of Justice: A Defense of Pluralism and Equality*. New York: Basic.

Wasserstrom, Richard. 1976. The University and the Case for Preferential Treatment. *American Philosophical Quarterly* 13:165–70.

Wiggins, David. 1985. Claims of Need. In *Morality and Objectivity: A Tribute to J. L. Mackie*, ed. Ted Honderich, pp. 149–202. London: Routledge & Kegan Paul.

Zaitchik, Alan. 1977. On Deserving to Deserve. *Philosophy and Public Affairs* 6:370–88.

27. Adjusting Utility for Justice: A Consequentialist Reply to the Objections from Justice

FRED FELDMAN

A bio-sketch of Fred Feldman appears in Chapter 24.

Traditional forms of consequentialism are open to objections based on considerations of justice. Classic cases such as the Southern Town, the Organ Harvest, and the Coliseum show that such forms of consequentialism, focusing exclusively on the total value of available outcomes, are insensitive to questions about the manner in which that value is distributed among the various recipients in the outcome. As a result, such theories sometimes permit serious injustices. In this paper Feldman formulates an axiology that is sensitive to justice, and combines it with a consequentialist normative theory. The central novelty of the proposed approach is that the values of goods and evils are adjusted to reflect the extent to which their recipients deserve them. He tries to show that the resulting view generates correct results in cases involving justice.

1. Introduction

In a famous passage near the beginning of Λ *Theory of Justice*, John Rawls discusses utilitarianism's notorious difficulties with justice. According to classic forms of utilitarianism, a certain course of action is morally right if it produces the greatest sum of satisfactions. And, as Rawls points out, the perplexing implication is ". . . that it does not matter, except indirectly, how this sum of satisfac-

tions is distributed among individuals any more than it matters, except indirectly, how one man distributes his satisfactions over time." He concludes the passage by saying that "[u]tilitarianism does not take seriously the distinction between persons."

As I understand him, Rawls is here alluding to a very well known problem. It has been illustrated by appeal to a host of remarkably striking and ingenious examples. Among these are the Organ Harvest,[1] the Small South-

---

Reprinted from *Philosophy and Phenomenological Research* 60:3 (September 1995), by permission of the author and the Editor of *Philosophy and Phenomenological Research*. Some notes have been deleted and others renumbered.

ern Town,[2] and the Colosseum.[3] One of the most straightforwardly relevant examples is given by Ross in *The Right and the Good.* Ross sketches a case in which someone has the choice of either (a) giving 1000 units of value to a very good man, or else (b) giving 1001 units of value to a very bad man.[4] Ross points out that utilitarianism implies (given the standard set of provisoes) that it is morally obligatory that the value be given to the bad man, since the total value then enjoyed would be slightly greater. Ross believes that the implications of utilitarianism are mistaken.

Reflection on this case may clarify what Rawls must have had in mind when he said that "utilitarianism does not take seriously the distinction between persons." In Ross's example, some benefits must be distributed. One way of distributing the benefits would be on balance best, but that distribution gives all the benefits to the less deserving man. Utilitarianism pays no attention to facts about past behavior and meritorious character. It requires that the benefit be given in whatever way will be best, regardless of the history and character of the recipients. In this way, it may be said to fail to take seriously the distinction between people.

Certain traditional forms of consequentialism are refuted by this sort of objection. However, I am convinced that the objection does not reveal any defect in the basic consequentialist insight—that we ought behave in such a way as to make the world as good as we can make it. As I see it, what the objection reveals is that there are defects in the axiologies traditionally associated with consequentialism. I want to show that it is possible to construct an axiology that is sensitive to matters of justice. If we combine consequentialism with such an axiology, we can maintain the core insight of consequentialism while rebutting the objection from justice.

In this paper, I first present a fairly typical form of consequentialism and I show in somewhat greater detail how it goes wrong with respect to justice. I then sketch a novel value theory that takes explicit account of justice. I attempt to show that when we combine con-

sequentialism with the new value theory, we get more palatable results in the problem cases. In a final section, I discuss some objections.

2. Consequentialism: A Preliminary Statement

Typical forms of consequentialism are based on the idea that on each occasion of moral choice, there are several possible acts available to the agent. These are his "alternatives" on that occasion. For each alternative, there is a "total consequence." This is the combination of all the things that would happen as a result if the alternative were performed.

In order to state the bare bones of a typical consequentialist theory, we need a ranking of total consequences in terms of intrinsic value.[5] Let us assume for a moment that this has been given: for each possible total consequence, there is a number indicating the total intrinsic value of that consequence. Let the numbers be assigned in the standard way with higher numbers representing better outcomes, and say that an act "maximizes intrinsic value" if and only if no alternative has a total consequence with greater intrinsic value.

We can now formulate the central principle of this form of consequentialism:

C: An act is morally right if and only if it maximizes intrinsic value.

In order to give real substance to the theory, we must add an axiology, or theory of value. This will specify what it is about a total consequence that gives it its intrinsic value.

In virtue of its simplicity and familiarity, let us provisionally make use of a traditional form of hedonism.

According to this view, the fundamental bearers of intrinsic value are episodes of pleasure and pain, where an episode is an event that consists in someone's feeling some amount of pleasure (or pain) for some stretch of time. Let us also assume that for each episode of pleasure or pain there is a number indicating the amount of pleasure or pain contained in the episode. We assign the numbers in the standard way, so that we can evaluate any episode of pleasure or pain in terms of its "hedonic level"—a measure of the amount of pleasure or pain in that episode.

According to this simple form of hedonism, the intrinsic value of an episode of pleasure or pain is a function of its hedonic level. We can display the function in a simple graph. The North-South axis of the graph indicates amounts of intrinsic value, with positive numbers representing intrinsic goodness, and negative numbers indicating intrinsic evil. The East-West axis indicates hedonic level, with amounts of pleasure (increasing to the East) and pain (increasing to the West). The import of the graph is this: the intrinsic value of an episode of pleasure or pain is equal to the hedonic level of that episode.

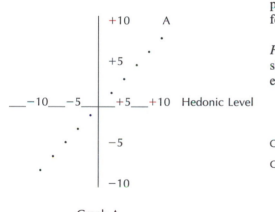

Graph A

Now we can state a principle concerning the intrinsic value of a whole consequence. According to this view, the intrinsic value of a consequence is the sum of the intrinsic values of the episodes of pleasure and pain that occur in that consequence. Let us call this axiology 'H' (for 'hedonism'). When we combine H with principle C we get perhaps the most familiar form of consequentialism—hedonic act utilitarianism.

3. Three Clean Cases

Some of the examples discussed in the literature involve puzzling and controversial combinations of extraneous moral issues, and so their impact is not entirely clear. For purposes of illustration it would be better to have "cleaner," less complicated cases. Let us attempt to construct some simple cases of this sort.

Suppose I am required to give away a ticket that will entitle its bearer to a free lunch. Suppose I can give this ticket either to A or to B. Each of them would enjoy a free lunch, getting (let us say) ten units of pleasure from the experience. Suppose, furthermore, that B would be slightly disappointed if A were to get the ticket. A, on the other hand, would be somewhat more disappointed if B were to get the ticket. Suppose that A and B are in all relevant respects quite similar, except that A has already enjoyed hundreds of free lunches, whereas B has never gotten even one. Suppose, finally, that no third party would be affected by my choice of A or B.

In this case, which we may call the *First Free Lunch*, C + H implies that the ticket should go to A. Here is a chart that helps to explain why:

Actions	Value for A	Value for B	Total value
Give ticket to A	+10	−1	+9
Give ticket to B	−2	+10	+8

Chart One

Provided that A would be slightly more disappointed than B by failure to receive the ticket, and A and B would be equally pleased to receive the ticket, and no one else would be affected by the distribution of the ticket, total intrinsic value is maximized by giving the ticket to A, even though he has already enjoyed far more free lunches than B. C + H then yields the result that it is my moral obligation to give the ticket to A. But this result is counterintuitive. Surely it would be more just to let B enjoy at least one free lunch—after all, B is in all relevant respects just like A except that he has so far had no free lunches, and A has had hundreds of them. Utilitarianism seems to ignore an important difference between people.

The *Second Free Lunch* is very similar to the first. Again I am required to give out a lunch ticket. Again I have my choice of giving it to A or giving it to B. Again each would enjoy the lunch, and each would be disappointed to fail to get the lunch—A a bit more than B. Let us imagine this time that A and B are alike with respect to past receipt of tickets for free lunches. However, in this case let us imagine that A has stolen and destroyed hundreds of lunches. Hundreds of decent people have gone hungry as a result of A's malicious thievery. B on the other hand is a decent fellow who has never stolen anyone's lunch.

We may assume that the numbers in Chart One apply again in this case. Again, C + H implies that it is my moral obligation to give the ticket to A. And again the implications of the theory conflict with my moral intuitions. In light of A's miserable past behavior, it seems to me that the ticket should go to B in spite of the fact that utility would not thereby be maximized. There is a "distributional impropriety" in giving the free lunch to A when he has so wantonly destroyed the lunches of others. Therefore, as I see it, the *Second Free Lunch* reveals another way in which C + H fails to take account of differences between people.

Let us now imagine a third example. Suppose this time that B is the legal owner of a ticket for a free lunch. Now A comes along and steals the ticket. He justifies his theft by appeal to a set of facts much like those illustrated in Chart One. Since he (A) would be more disappointed by failure to get the free lunch, utility is maximized by his getting it. Thus, he claims, when he stole the ticket he was doing the right thing.

Given the expected set of background assumptions, C + H implies in the *Third Free Lunch* that it was morally right for A to steal the ticket and that it would be right for him to get the lunch. And again it seems perfectly

clear to me that the implications are false. If such a case were to occur, it would be unjust for the ticket and the free lunch to go to A. This injustice is sufficient, it seems to me, to make it morally wrong for A to steal the ticket. In this case the relevant difference between A and B is that B owns the ticket. C + H seems to ignore this fact.

I mentioned a number of examples at the outset. These include the Small Southern Town, the Colosseum, and the Organ Harvest. Although these cases are vastly more complex, each of them is in certain ways similar to the cases I have described. In every case, harms and benefits must be distributed in one of several ways. One distribution is stipulated to maximize utility. Unfortunately, that distribution also seems to involve substantial injustice. If the injustice is great enough, C + H yields the wrong moral judgment.

4. A New Proposal

Reflection on such examples leads some philosophers to say that consequentialism is false. As they see it, the examples reveal that sometimes, because of its injustice, the best outcome is not the one we ought to produce. But there is another way to interpret these cases. Following Brentano and others, we might take them to show that there is something wrong with the axiologies traditionally associated with consequentialism. A different axiology—one sensitive to justice and injustice—might imply that the acts that seem to be morally right in these examples have consequences that are in fact better than the consequences that would have been produced by their alternatives. And the greater value might arise, on the new axiology, from the amount of justice in the consequence.

In an attempt to develop these intuitions about the place of justice in axiology, I want to formulate an axiology that starts with hedonism, but incorporates the idea that the value of a pleasure or pain may be increased or decreased depending upon whether it is justly or unjustly experienced. When we combine the new axiology with C, we will get a consequentialist normative theory that deals more successfully with the problems about justice.

My conception of justice is based on the ancient and plausible idea that justice is done when people receive goods and evils according to *desert*. The closer the fit between desert and receipt, the more just the outcome. Other things being equal, the more just outcome is the better. Before turning to the formulation of the axiology, I should say a few words about desert.

I will not be able to provide any analysis of the concept of desert. It functions here as a conceptual primitive. However, the idea should be familiar. We often hear people say that a particularly vicious criminal "deserves to have the book thrown at him"; or that a sick child "does not deserve to suffer in this way," or that those who have labored in the background "deserve their day in the sun." Roughly, to say that a person deserves some good is to say that it would be "distributionally appropriate" for him to get it. I assume that desert is a matter of degree, so that it makes sense to say that a certain person deserves a certain pleasure or pain *to a certain extent*. I will represent the various extents with numbers, in the usual way.

It is important to note that desert is not defined here in terms of moral obligation. The statement that a person deserves some good is not equivalent to the statement that she ought to get it, or to the statement that someone else ought to provide it. In some cases, although someone deserves some good, no one is in position to provide it; in other cases, for various reasons, some other considerations override the demands of justice. So the statement that someone deserves something does not entail the statement that she morally ought to get it. Equally, the statement that someone ought to get a certain good does not entail that she deserves it. If the results would be good enough, there could be a case in which someone morally ought to give a certain good to a certain recipient, even though the recipient does not deserve it.

Many different factors influence the extent to which a given person deserves a certain pleasure or pain. One of these is *excessive or deficient past receipt*. Excessive past receipt lowers your desert level for a good; deficient past receipt increases it. To see how this works, imagine a case in which there are two possible recipients for some good. Suppose the potential recipients are alike in all relevant respects except that one of them has already received far more of that good than the other. Then, since other things are equal, the one who has so far been short-changed has greater desert. His desert level for the good is greater than the desert level of others who have already received more.

A recipient's *moral worthiness* may have an impact on his desert level, too. Suppose two potential recipients of good are alike in all other relevant respects, except that one of them has been good, whereas the other has been bad. Then the one who has been good has greater desert. If no other factors complicate the case, it would be more just for the good to be given to him.

A third factor is based on rights and claims. Other things being equal, someone with a *legitimate claim* on some good has greater desert relative to that good than does someone with less claim on it. Thus, if two recipients are in other respects similar, but one legally owns the means to a certain pleasure and the other does not, then the owner deserves more to have the pleasures arising from ownership of that object.

There are undoubtedly other factors that may influence the extent to which a person deserves some pleasure or pain, and in a full exposition of the theory of desert, each of them would be described in detail. Furthermore, in real-life cases several of the factors may be jointly operative. The ways in which the factors clash and harmonize so as to yield an overall desert-level must also be investigated. However, since my aim here is primarily to show that it is possible to formulate an axiology that takes account of justice, and to show how such a theory can be combined with consequentialism to rebut the objection from justice, I shall not pursue these lines of inquiry here.

According to the axiology I want to defend, the intrinsic value of an episode of pleasure or pain is a function of two variables: (i) the amount of pleasure or pain the recipient *receives* in that episode, and (ii) the amount of pleasure or pain the recipient *deserves* in that episode. Roughly, the theory maintains that pleasure is generally intrinsically good; but it is better if it is fully deserved, and it is less good if it is not deserved. In extreme cases, if it is undeserved, it may be worth much less—indeed, it may be worthless or even bad. Pain, on the other hand, is generally intrinsically bad. However, it is even worse when the person who suffers it does not deserve it. It is less bad—and may even be good—if the person who suffers it fully deserves it.

Part of the content of the axiology may be expressed by some principles about desert and receipt. Each principle governs a class of cases involving a range of receipt and desert levels. One principle governs cases in which a person experiences some pleasure when she deserves it. It seems to me that it is especially good if someone who has "positive desert" gets to experience precisely the pleasure she deserves. Following Chisholm and Moore, I use the term "enhancement" to indicate this axiological phenomenon. This is the first principle of "just deserts":

P1:   Positive desert enhances the intrinsic goodness of pleasure.

Part of the import of P1 is illustrated in Graph B. In Graph B, we focus on the case of someone who deserves exactly 10 units of pleasure. The graph displays the outputs of intrinsic value generated by the function for various inputs of pleasure. However, this graph applies only to the case of a person who deserves to be getting 10 units of pleasure and so gives only a suggestion about cases involving people with other desert levels.

Point A on the graph indicates that when a person deserves 10 units of pleasure and gets 10 units of pleasure, then the episode as a whole has an intrinsic value of +20. Since justice is done when the deserving get what

they deserve, intrinsic value is enhanced. Notice that the curve begins to flatten out as it moves northeast. This shows that as a person begins to receive more than she deserves, additional increments of pleasure have decreasing marginal intrinsic value. Again, this is a matter of justice. Point B is of interest, too. It indicates that it is intrinsically bad for a person who deserves 10 units of pleasure to get nothing instead.

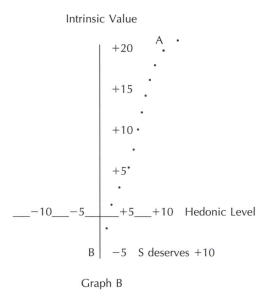

Graph B

The second principle concerns what happens when someone who deserves pain gets pleasure instead. If a person with negative desert enjoys pleasure, justice is not done, and the value of that pleasure is diminished, or "mitigated." The general principle here is:

P2:   Negative desert mitigates the intrinsic goodness of pleasure.

Graph C illustrates one possible view about how negative desert might mitigate the value of pleasure. Again, we consider only one class of cases: the cases in which the recipient deserves exactly 10 units of pain. The graph shows outputs of intrinsic value for various inputs of pleasure:

Intrinsic Value

```
        |
___-10__-5___|___+5__+10   Hedonic Level
        |  · · · · · ·
        |
        | -5
        |
S deserves -10 | -10
```

Graph C

The significance of the graph is this: when a person has negative desert, positive receipt is worthless. In such cases, pleasures—of any intensity—have no intrinsic value.

According to a somewhat more extreme view, when a person on the whole deserves pain, but receives pleasure instead, then the injustice of the situation is so great as to make it intrinsically bad. If we accept this view, we will want to go beyond saying merely that negative desert *mitigates* the intrinsic goodness of pleasure. We will want to say that in some cases, negative desert "transvaluates" the goodness of pleasure. By this I mean to indicate that if a person's desert level is negative enough, positive receipt becomes intrinsically bad. We can illustrate one version of this view as follows:

Intrinsic Value

```
            |
___-10__-5__|__+5__+10   Hedonic Level
       ·    |
            |
       ·    |
       B    | -2.5
            |  ·
            |       ·
S deserves -10 | -5    · · · A · ·
```

Graph C′

We have so far considered two sorts of cases: those in which a person with positive desert receives pleasure, and those in which a person with negative desert receives pleasure. What about the case in which a person has "neutral" desert—he neither deserves pleasure nor deserves pain? In such cases the value

of the pleasure is neither enhanced nor mitigated. Hence, the intrinsic value of an episode of pleasure of this sort is directly proportional to the amount of pleasure it contains. The principle here is:

P3: Neutral desert neither enhances nor mitigates the intrinsic goodness of pleasure.

The fourth principle concerns the case in which someone deserves pleasure, but gets pain instead. As I see it, pain is bad enough; but when someone who deserves pleasure gets pain instead, the evil of that pain is made even worse, or (to use another Chisholmian term) "aggravated," by its injustice:

P4: Positive desert aggravates the intrinsic badness of pain.

P4 is the principle that stands behind the axiological intuition that it is worse for bad things to happen to good people than it is for bad things to happen to bad people. Graph D illustrates one view about how positive desert might aggravate the evil of pain.

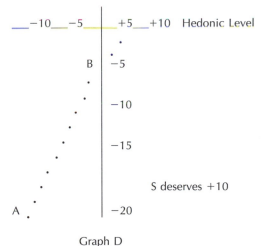

Intrinsic Value

Graph D

Graph D applies only to cases in which someone deserves 10 units of pleasure. It illustrates a view about how this positive desert makes it especially bad for such a deserving person to get pain. Note, for example, Point A. This indicates that when a person deserves +10, but gets −10 instead, the whole episode is so unfair that it has an intrinsic value of −20.

The fifth principle concerns the case in which someone who deserves pain gets pain. Pain is generally bad; but it is not so bad for it to be experienced by someone who deserves it. In this case, since justice is done, the badness of the episode has been mitigated.

P5: Negative desert mitigates the intrinsic badness of pain.

A graph illustrating one possible interpretation of P5:

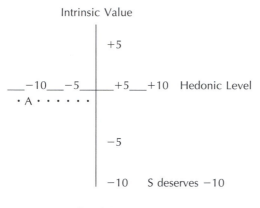

Graph E

Point A indicates what happens when ten units of pain are received by a person who deserves exactly ten units of pain. Since in this case the person gets exactly what he deserves, justice is done. The evil of the pain is mitigated by the negative desert of the recipient. Although he suffers some pain, the world is not made worse. The intrinsic value of the episode is zero.

Some philosophers seem to believe that the world is made *better* when the guilty suffer precisely the harm they deserve.[6] This phenomenon may be called the "transvaluation of the evil of pain by negative desert." One interpretation of this view is illustrated in Graph E'.

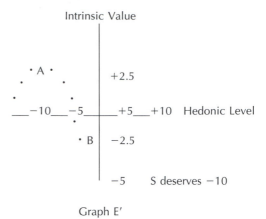

Graph E'

Point A on Graph E' serves to illustrate the idea that it is slightly good (+2.5) for a person to receive ten units of pain when this is precisely what he deserves. This expresses the retributivist axiological intuition that sometimes it is good for bad people to be punished. The curve slopes downward in both directions from Point A in order to illustrate the idea that it is not so good for a person who deserves pain to get either more or less pain than he deserves. This corresponds to the intuition that punishment must be proportional to the crime.

The views expressed in Graphs E and E' are reminiscent of views endorsed by Meinong, Brentano, Chisholm, and Moore. Brentano, for example, discussed the case in which someone takes sorrow in someone else's sorrow. Since sorrow is precisely the right reaction in such a case, Brentano declared the whole state of affairs to be good. Moore's views about hatred of evil and ugliness are again similar. In my view, each of these cases illustrates the same general thesis: the evil of pain is mitigated (and in some cases perhaps transvaluated) by negative desert.

The final principle concerns the case in which a person with neutral desert receives pain. As I see it, the intrinsic value of any such episode of pain is directly proportional to the amount of pain it contains. Thus the principle is:

P6: Neutral desert neither enhances nor mitigates the evil of pain.

According to "justice adjusted hedonism" (or "JH"), the fundamental bearers of intrinsic value are episodes of pleasure and pain. In each case, the intrinsic value of the episode of pleasure or pain is not a simple function of hedonic level. Desert plays an essential role, too. As a result, some pleasures are not good (as shown in Graph C) and some pains are not bad (as shown in Graph E). In every case, the justice-adjusted intrinsic value of the whole episode is a function of the receipt level and the desert level of the recipient. The intrinsic value of a whole consequence is the sum of the justice-adjusted intrinsic values of the episodes of pleasure and pain that occur in that consequence.

If we combine C with our new axiology, the resulting normative theory ("C + JH") is sensitive to matters of justice. It takes account of the enhancing, aggravating, mitigating, and perhaps transvaluating factor of desert. My claim is that the resulting theory generates correct results in the problem cases.

5. Reevaluation of Puzzle Cases

In Section 3 I presented three cases in which C + H generated incorrect normative judgments. In order to apply C + JH to these cases, we have to recalculate the intrinsic values of the relevant consequences according to JH.

In the *First Free Lunch*, there were two potential recipients of a ticket for a free lunch. One recipient, A, had already received hundreds of such tickets. The other, B, had received none. But it was stipulated that A would suffer slightly greater disappointment if he failed to get the ticket. C + H implied that it was my obligation to give the ticket to A, and this seemed mistaken. Now let us consider what C + JH implies for the *First Free Lunch*.

Chart Two contains some numbers illustrating the application of the new axiology to the example:

Actions	Value for A	Value for B	Total value
Give ticket to A	+8	−2	+6
Give ticket to B	−2	+20	+18

Chart Two

If A gets the ticket, he will experience ten units of pleasure. But in virtue of his excessive past receipt of tickets, his desert level is low—perhaps even negative. He doesn't deserve the pleasures derivable from more free lunches. As a result, the intrinsic value of his pleasure is mitigated. This is the import of principle P2. I have accordingly reduced the value of A's pleasure from +10 to +8.

If the ticket goes to A, then B will be disappointed again. He will suffer one unit of pain. But B does not deserve this pain. In virtue of his deficient past receipt, he deserves the pleasures of a free lunch. In accordance with Principle P4, it follows that the evil of B's pain is aggravated by his positive desert. I have therefore represented the value of B's pain as −2 rather than as −1. The justice-adjusted intrinsic value of giving the ticket to A is +6 (rather than +9 as before).

Now let's consider the results of giving the ticket to B. If B gets the ticket, A will suffer 2 units of pain. The happiness of B, if he gets the ticket, is fully deserved. After all, he has had far less than his fair share of free lunches, and has suffered far more than his fair share of disappointment. According to Principle P1, the value of his happiness is enhanced by his positive desert. Following the suggestion of Graph B, I have assigned it a value of +20.

So the act that intuitively seems to be morally right—giving the ticket to B—also has better results according to JH. Thus, an example that refuted C + H does not refute C + JH.

The treatment of the *Second Free Lunch* and the *Third Free Lunch* according to JH is similar. In each of these cases JH implies that the best outcome is the one in which the ticket goes to the more deserving B. In the *Second Free Lunch*, this follows from the stipulated fact that A has behaved miserably, and has thereby lowered his desert level. In the *Third*, it follows from the fact that B is the legitimate owner of the ticket: he deserves the pleasures arising from ticket ownership; A does not.

I noted earlier that Rawls claimed that "utilitarianism does not take seriously the distinction between persons." As I understand it, the point of this remark is that utilitarianism advocates the distribution of goods and evils in whatever way will maximize total utility—with no regard for the character or the past behavior of the various recipients. Recipients of good and evil function merely as "vessels" into which value may be poured. The theory implies that the value should be poured out in whatever way will yield the greatest total. It should be clear, however, that this charge cannot be leveled against the axiology proposed here. The value of a given distribution of goods and evils depends crucially on the extent to which each recipient deserves his or her share. Past receipt and character play central roles in the determination of desert. Hence, the theory recognizes and pays careful heed to the morally relevant differences between persons.

Although I will not attempt to show it here, I believe that the other puzzle cases mentioned at the outset pose no special threat to C + JH. In each of those cases, C + H implied that some grave injustice should be committed. In some of those cases C + JH delivers normative results different from, and more palatable than those delivered by C + H. In such cases, once we adjust utility for justice, it will turn out that the best consequence is the one in which no injustice is committed. Thus, as I see it, C + JH does not have the defect that Rawls had in mind in the passage cited.

It is important to keep in mind that the actual implications of the theory in these cases would depend upon details about the receipt levels and desert levels of the participants in all the outcomes. In some cases C + JH will imply that a serious injustice is required in order to assure the best outcome, and so (sadly) ought to be committed. The theory does not imply that justice must always be maximized; it implies that justice-adjusted intrinsic value must always be maximized.

6. Some Objections

A critic might object to C + JH, claiming that it is covertly circular. The circularity, it might be alleged, arises in this way: first we purport to explain the normative concept of *moral obligation* by appeal to the value-theoretic concept of *intrinsic betterness*. Then when it comes time to give substance to the concept of intrinsic betterness, we appeal to the concept of *justice*. Justice is explicated in terms of *desert*. And desert, finally, is explained by saying that a person deserves some pleasure or pain precisely when he *ought* to get it—and thus the circle is completed. We have made covert use of the concept of moral obligation in our attempt to explain moral obligation.

This objection turns on a misunderstanding of the proposal. The objection goes wrong at the final step, where it is alleged that we explain desert by appeal to moral obligation. I endorse no such explanation. The concept of desert is not defined by appeal to the concept of moral obligation. Indeed, it is not defined in any way here. It functions as a conceptual primitive for purposes of the present theory.

In my discussion of desert, I have made liberal use of evaluative terminology. Thus, I have spoken of "fair shares," "worthiness of receipt," "moral rights," and "fittingness." However I have tried to avoid use of the concepts of moral rightness, wrongness, or obligatoriness. The statement that a person *deserves* some pleasure must not be confused with the statement that *it would be morally right* for him to get that pleasure. In order for the theory as a whole to avoid circularity, it is important that the concept of desert is not explicated by appeal to the concepts of right and wrong. For, as I see it, desert plays a role in the determination of justice, and justice plays a role in the determination of the intrinsic value of outcomes, and the intrinsic value of outcomes plays a central role in the determination of right and wrong.

My approach involves a somewhat unorthodox view about the place of the theory of justice in moral philosophy. Traditionally, the theory of justice has been thought to belong in normative ethics. I have always been puzzled about its implications for action. Suppose the theory of justice firmly establishes that some sort of behavior is unjust. Is it supposed to follow that we should not engage in that sort of behavior? If so, the theory of justice seems to have invaded the turf of ordinary normative ethics. If not, the import of the theory of justice is obscure.

My approach firmly locates the theory of justice in axiology. Our axiology determines the value of each outcome, in part, by the justice or injustice of the distribution of pleasures and pains within that outcome. Justice and injustice, in turn, are understood to be determined by reflections on the quality of the fit between pleasures and pains received and pleasures and pains deserved in each outcome. Thus, as I see it, a full-blown axiological theory would have to include an account of justice. Normative ethics then takes the information provided by axiology, and generates prescriptions for right action. In my view, the prescription is very simple: behave in such a way as to make the world as good as you can.

I turn now to a second objection. It might be claimed that even if the theory presented here is acceptable, it cannot possibly figure in a defense of *consequentialism*—for the theory is not a form of *consequentialism*. The problem, according to the objection, is that my proposed axiology ascribes intrinsic value to complex states of affairs. The values of these states of affairs turn on normative features, such as desert and justice. No consequentialist theory, it might be claimed, makes use of normative features in this way.

In reply to this objection, I would first want to insist that C + JH is as much a form of consequentialism as the hedonistic utilitarianism of Mill and the pluralistic "ideal" utilitarianisms of Brentano and Moore. In each of these cases, the axiology is complex. In the case of Mill, the axiology is based on "higher" and "lower" pleasures, which allegedly have higher and lower intrinsic values. In the cases of Moore and Brentano, the axiology is based on such complex states of affairs as "the love of good" and "the hatred of evil." For Moore and Brentano, the value of a state of affairs turns crucially on normative features internal to that state of affairs. If Mill and Moore and Brentano are consequentialists, then so am I.

I can go beyond this merely historical point. I think the definition of "consequentialism" is a matter of great controversy. The literature is filled with incompatible (and sometimes idiosyncratic) definitions. It would be hard to find any characterization that would meet with universal approval. Perhaps it would be interesting to consider a typical, and obviously relevant characterization. In *The Theory of Justice*, Rawls gives his own account. He says:

> The structure of an ethical theory is, then, largely determined by how it defines and connects these two basic notions [the right and the good]. Now it seems that the simplest way of relating them is taken by teleological theories; the good is defined independently from the right, and then the right is defined as that which maximizes the good.

Inspection will reveal that C + JH conforms to this characterization of teleological theories. I admit, of course, that in my "definition" of the good, I have made numerous references to matters involving justice. But, as I have already emphasized, my account of justice does not appeal to the central normative concepts of *right* and *wrong*. So far as I can tell, my characterization of the good is independent of my characterization of the right.

NOTES

1. The Organ Harvest is discussed in Judith Thompson's "Killing, Letting Die, and the Trolley Problem," *The Monist* 59 (1976): 204–17. Philippa Foot discusses essentially the same case in her "Abortion and the Doctrine of the Double Effect," *Oxford Review* 5 (1967).

2. Most of the elements of the case of the Small Southern Town can be found in E. F. Carritt's *Ethical and Political Thinking* (Oxford: Oxford University Press, 1947), in a passage that is cited in John Rawls, "Two Concepts of Rules," *The Philosophical Review*, 64 (1955): 3–32. Rawls' own "telishment" case is again quite similar. Kai Nielsen's case of the Magistrate and the Threatening Mob, described in his "Against Moral Conservatism" *Ethics* 82 (1972): 113–124, makes the same point. Nielsen's essay is reprinted in Louis Pojman, *Ethical Theory* (Wadsworth: Belmont,

California, 1998) Third Edition: 218–226. The example appears on p. 220.

3. The case of the Christians in the Colosseum is briefly sketched by Amartya Sen in "Rights and Agency," *Philosophy and Public Affairs*, 11, **1** (Winter, 1982); reprinted in Samuel Scheffler, *Consequentialism and its Critics* (Oxford: Oxford University Press, 1988): 191.

4. *The Right and the Good* (Oxford: Oxford University Press, 1930); reprinted in Pojman, op. cit., p. 320.

5. I am not proposing an account of the "essence of consequentialism." Very many normative theories that I would classify as consequentialist do not make use of rankings of total consequences in terms of intrinsic value. For example, consider the form of utilitarianism that says we ought to maximize preference satisfaction. One could maintain this view and insist that nothing has intrinsic value. Another case is supplied by egoism. A typical form of egoism tells me to maximize my own welfare—it says nothing about intrinsic value. Finally, expected utility utilitarianism tells us that our moral obligation is to maximize expected utility, not intrinsic value.

6. In *The Metaphysical Elements of Justice*, Kant describes a case in which some isolated society is about to disband. One murderer is still in prison, yet to be executed. Kant seems to want to say that even though in a case like this there is no utilitarian justification for carrying out the sentence, still the criminal ought to be executed. If we approach the case from the perspective of the principle of the transvaluation of the evil of pain by negative desert, we might claim that the world is made better by the infliction of deserved pain on the murderer. Thus, though traditional forms of utilitarianism might not be able to explain it, a version of C + JH might be able to explain why retributive punishment is justified.

28. Desert and Wages

OWEN MCLEOD

For biographical information on McLeod, see Chapter 21.

In this paper, McLeod explains and evaluates some of the main theories for deserving wages. He argues that each view suffers from its own defects but that there is a defect they all share: Each assumes that for each form of deservable treatment, there is a desert base or set of desert bases unique to it. He argues that reflection on the main theories of desert of wages suggests that this standard (Feinberg-ian) view of desert is incorrect. He goes on to offer an alternative way of thinking about desert, according to which there is a single set of desert bases, and one's desert of any form of deservable treatment can be influenced by one's possession of any or all of those bases.

Introduction

Women tend to earn less than their male colleagues. Furthermore, women tend to earn less than men who hold jobs that are nominally different but relevantly similar to their own. Advocates of 'comparable worth' protest these facts. Their protest sometimes takes this form: Those differences in pay between men and women are *undeserved*.[1] The argument for this claim is simple. Some facts are relevant to the wage one deserves for performing a given job; some aren't. In the vast majority of cases, the argument continues, gender is not relevant to the wage one deserves; relevant are, say, the skill, responsibility, and working conditions required by the job. When jobs are comparable with respect to these facts, those who work in them deserve equal pay. Therefore, women and men who work the very same jobs deserve equal pay; likewise for women and men whose jobs are nominally different but relevantly similar.

This argument clearly presupposes an account of what is and what is not a basis for deserving a wage, or a theory of desert of wages.[2] Such a theory interests not only advocates of comparable worth. It also interests those (like me) who believe that justice obtains to the extent that people get what they deserve. For us, the question of what wage a person deserves is an important question of justice.

Theories of desert of wages have been proposed. In the first few sections of this paper, I consider the most prominent among them. Each (I claim) suffers from unique difficulties, but they share a fundamental defect. As I see it, this defect is symptomatic of a common but misguided way of thinking about desert in general. In the penultimate section, I describe this way of thinking and suggest an alternative. I conclude by applying this alternative way of thinking about desert in general to desert of wages in particular, and by sketching some of its implications for the comparable worth debate.

Before proceeding, some terminological points are in order. Let a wage be whatever payment is given to a person in return for his

Reprinted from *Utilitas* 8:2 (July 1996), by permission.

or her contracted work.[3] The wage may be cash or some other benefit such as food, lodging, vacation time, and so on. Work is the attempted provision of some service, such as lawn-mowing or lawyering. Thus, a necessary condition on deserving a wage is doing some contracted work. Contracted work is, of course, work that has been contracted. But as I understand them, contracts can be formal or informal, explicit or implied. There need not be a signed document. There need be only some sort of agreement among the relevant parties that the service will be provided in return for some sort of payment. In some circumstances, this agreement need not even be actual.[4]

The Effort Theory

With those points made, let's begin by considering the effort theory of desert of wages. Joel Feinberg describes a version of it:

> the principle of effort . . . would distribute economic products not in proportion to successful achievement but according to the degree of effort exerted. According to the principle of effort, justice decrees that hard-working executives and [equally] hard-working laborers receive precisely the same remuneration. . . .[5]

Feinberg's statement captures the basic idea behind the effort theory: The more effort one exerts on the job, the higher the wage one deserves. This idea can be put as follows:

ET Worker A deserves a higher wage than worker B if A exerts more effort than B; A and B deserve the same wage if A exerts the same amount of effort as B.

At least one philosopher has recently accepted something like ET. This is Wojceich Sadurski, who maintains that 'effort is the only legitimate basis and measure of desert'.[6]

The leading argument for ET appears to be this.[7] Wages are deserved either for our efforts or for their success. Our efforts are within our control; their success is not. The success of one's efforts is a matter of luck or accident. Desert, however, cannot arise through mere luck or accident. Thus, wages are deserved not for the success of our efforts, but rather for our efforts alone.

This is a bad argument. First, there is no reason to believe that effort and success exhaust the possible bases for deserving a wage. At the very least, substantial argument is needed to support such a claim. Second, it's not true that desert cannot arise through mere luck or accident. If it were true, then bad luck and horrible accidents could not make one deserving of, say, compensation. Finally, it's highly implausible that the success of one's efforts is always a matter of luck or accident—unless this means merely that there is some chance that one's efforts will not succeed. *That* is certainly true, but there's a difference between the chance of one's efforts failing, on the one hand, and their success being 'lucky' or 'accidental' on the other. For example, your efforts to read this paper may fail; but if they succeed, this probably will not be a matter of luck or accident.

Besides, the effort theory generates implausible results. Compare two garbage collectors. One finds it very easy to lift heavy bags of garbage all day, and can do it quickly. Another finds the task difficult, and must exert three times the effort to achieve the same results. If ET were true, the second garbage collector would deserve a higher wage than the first. This seems incorrect. Surely it's more plausible that they deserve the same wage—or even that the first collector, who performs his job more efficiently, deserves a wage higher than the second.

Or compare two corporate executives. Each works as hard as the other, and each works tirelessly. ET entails that each deserves a generous wage. But one does excellent work. Her diligent efforts lead to dramatic profits for the company. For this, she deserves a raise. Meanwhile, the other's efforts constantly backfire. His efforts, though conscientious, result in substantial losses to the firm. For this, he may deserve demotion to a lower-paying position. Certainly he doesn't deserve a raise.

The advocate of ET cannot reply to these examples by saying that 'other things being equal' workers who exert more effort deserve more pay. For this is to admit that factors other than effort can affect one's desert of a wage. This is precisely what an advocate of ET must deny.

In rejecting ET, I'm not rejecting the idea that effort is a basis for deserving a wage. On the contrary, I think it is. I'm arguing that effort is not the *only* basis for deserving a wage. Later I'll discuss some of those other bases. In the meantime, let's consider a different theory.

Market Value Theories

The literature on desert of wages can often seem like a debate between those who think that a worker's *effort* is the appropriate basis for deserving a wage, and those who think the worker's actual *contribution*, regardless of effort, is the appropriate basis.[8] Typical statements of this latter view, often called the 'contribution theory', include:

> A man's reward should depend on the value of the contribution which he makes to social welfare in his work activity.[9]

> Justice, according to this principle [of contribution], requires that each worker get back exactly that proportion of the national wealth that he has himself created.[10]

> According to the contribution theory, the wage you deserve is a function of the amount of contribution you have made.[11]

Common to these remarks is the idea that the wage a worker deserves is somehow proportional to the 'value' of his or her contribution. In principle, this 'value' could be identified with at least one of many things—say, its utility, intrinsic value, beauty, or whatever. Thus, in principle, there are many versions of the contribution theory of desert of wages.[12] But the most prominent version identifies the value of a worker's contribution with its *market* value. In this section, I restrict

my attention to this version of the contribution theory. I call it the 'market value theory' of desert of wages.

According to the market value theory, the wage one deserves for providing a service is equal to the free market value of that service. In *Spheres of Justice*, Michael Walzer describes such a theory:

> the market, if it is free, gives to each person exactly what he deserves. . . . The goods and services we provide are valued by potential customers in such-and-such a way, and these values are aggregated by the market, which determines what price we receive. And that price is our desert, for it expresses the only worth our goods and services can have, the worth they actually have for other people.[13]

A market value theory of desert of wages seems to be based partly on the plausible intuition that unless one's work is valuable to others, then one cannot deserve a wage for it. The theory simply identifies this value with market value. Also, this identification makes for a relatively 'objective' theory. This is because the market value of a thing—in contrast to its utility, intrinsic value, or some other form of value—is in principle empirically determinable. As David Miller writes:

> if we want desert to form the basis of a social practice—rather than being an idea that is used merely to form a series of idiosyncratic judgements—we need a non-arbitrary public standard to measure it. In this light, the attraction of a market-based criterion is very considerable.[14]

However attractive a market value theory of desert of wages may be, it cannot be properly evaluated without stating it more precisely.[15] This will require attention to the notion of a 'free market'.

The United States is often said to have a 'free market' economy. Presumably, this is because a significant portion of the means of production is in private hands, and there is much less governmental interference in the workings of the U.S. economy than in the economies of, say, France or Cuba. If this is the sort of 'free market' that advocates of the market value theory have in mind, then they must accept that all wages currently received in the U.S. are deserved.

Accepting this would trivialize the comparable worth debate. Advocates of comparable worth maintain that women tend to earn less than they deserve, given that their male colleagues, or men who work in similar jobs, tend to earn more. If, however, it's necessarily true that the wage one *receives* in a U.S.-style 'free market' is precisely the wage one *deserves*, then advocates of comparable worth are contradicting themselves. They would be maintaining (in effect) that women in the U.S. manage to earn less-than-deserved wages while earning precisely what they deserve! Surely advocates of comparable worth are not guilty of this.

Thus, what advocates of the market value theory may have in mind is not a U.S.-style free market, but rather an 'ideal' or 'perfectly free' market. This is what Robert Young, for example, seems to have in mind when he writes: 'Private enterprise under perfectly competitive economic conditions would produce deserved outcomes. . .'.[16] In neoclassical economics, a perfectly free market is a hypothetical market with the following features. There is supply and demand for goods and services. The means of production are entirely privately owned. There is no state interference in the market's operations. Firms and consumers in this market are psychological egoists; that is, they always seek to maximize their own welfare. What's more, they operate under certainty: They know the outcomes of their alternative actions. As a consequence of certainty, firms and consumers in a perfectly free market have, in the words of economists Richard Wolff and Stephen Resnick, 'perfect information about price and wage movements'.[17]

This conception of a free market may be used to formulate a version of the market value theory of desert of wages:

MVT   S deserves wage W at t for providing some service R in market M at t if (i) S provides R in M

at t; and (ii) if M were free at t, then W would be the market price of R at t.

To find out the wage someone deserves for providing a wage in the actual market, MVT directs us to consider the closest possible free market in which that service is provided. The price of that service in that market is the wage one deserves for providing it in the actual market.

I believe that MVT is not the correct theory of desert of wages. It entails that people who intuitively deserve wages deserve no wages at all. To see this, consider the case of Mr. Porkbelly. He is a commodities trader in the actual market. Mr. Porkbelly excels at his job. He assiduously researches the market, works long hours, and almost always turns a profit for his clients. Intuitively, Mr. Porkbelly deserves a decent wage for his work.

MVT entails that Mr. Porkbelly deserves nothing. As noted above, consumers in a perfectly free market possess perfect information about price movements. They don't have to speculate. But commodities trading *is* speculation about the price movements of commodities. Thus, consumers in a perfectly free market of the sort described would not demand the services of commodities traders. The price of that service would therefore be zero. It follows that Mr. Porkbelly deserves no wage at all for the work he does. Indeed, if MVT is true, then legions of Wall Street workers deserve nothing. (Perhaps some readers will not find this result at all rebarbative!)

This difficulty can be avoided by adjusting the idea of a free market. Let this free market be similar to the one described above, except that firms and consumers do not operate under certainty. Call the theory that incorporates this conception of a free market 'MVT*'. MVT* avoids the conclusion that Wall Street workers deserve nothing. In that market, people must speculate about price movements.

However, MVT* falls to the following case. Consider Ivan, who works in a Soviet-style controlled economy. His job is to set the price of corn. This job requires a high level of mathematical and organizational skills. It also involves extensive training and considerable responsibility. Moreover, the working conditions are abysmal: Ivan's cramped office is cold and windowless. Despite this, Ivan works hard and does his job well. Intuitively, Ivan deserves a decent wage.

MVT* entails that Ivan deserves nothing. If the market in which Ivan works were of the sort just described, there would be no such job as 'setting the price of corn'. The price of corn would be 'set' entirely by market forces. Put another way, if we go to the possible free market (of the kind described) closest to Ivan, we find that his service of setting the price of corn has no market price whatsoever. Since that price would be Ivan's deserved wage, it follows that Ivan—in the actual market—deserves nothing for doing his job.

An advocate of MVT* might reply that Ivan has marketable skills, e.g., mathematical and organizational, and their exercise would have a price in a free market. That price is what Ivan actually deserves for doing his job. In other words, Ivan's job should not be thought of as 'setting the price of corn', since that would indeed be a worthless service in a perfectly free market, but rather as 'exercising such-and-such degree of mathematical and organizational skills', which would have a positive market value and which does deserve a wage. A similar reply might be made by advocates of MVT on behalf of Mr. Porkbelly and his pinstriped colleagues.

This reply assumes that exercising mathematical and organizational skills 'in the abstract' counts as a service. This is implausible. As I see it, the exercise of a skill counts as a service only if directed toward some task. In Ivan's case, the task is setting the price of corn. That task has no positive value in a free market. Of course Ivan could apply his skills to a different project, but the question is not whether Ivan *would* deserve a wage for providing some service, but rather whether he deserves a wage for the service he *actually* provides. MVT* entails that Ivan deserves nothing.

Besides, there are displays of skill that have no market value, but they may nevertheless deserve a wage. Suppose, for example, you are a wealthy but slightly eccentric person who lives a near a sandy beach. One day a derelict man knocks on your door asking for work. You pity him, but have no meaningful work for him to do. So you make the following arrangement. If only he will count grains of sand at the beach, you will pay him some sort of wage. The man agrees to this. So every day he counts thousands of grains of sand. This requires tremendous patience, steady hands, and a relatively high degree of mathematical skill. It also involves eye and back strain, not to mention sunburn. For doing this, you pay him a wage. He deserves it. However, this is not because his particular display of skill has market value; it doesn't.

This is not to say that the market value of the service one provides, or the skill that one exhibits in providing it, are irrelevant to the wage one deserves. It's to say that there is more to deserving a wage. Thus, we must look elsewhere if we wish to find the correct theory of desert of wages.

Compensation Theories

Work can be drudgery, an imposition on one's time, or a danger to one's health. This has suggested to some philosophers that if wages are deserved, they are deserved as compensation. James Dick, for example, writes that the notion of compensation 'proves the most powerful and important ground in justifying differences in incomes'.[18] Feinberg agrees: 'economic income cannot be plausibly construed as prizes or rewards, and can be spoken of as "deserved" only insofar as it is compensation'.[19] Feinberg continues:

> Not only unpleasant and hazardous work but also terribly responsible positions and functions requiring extensive preliminary training deserve compensation. Here is the real basis for the claim that the executive and physician deserve higher incomes: not that their superior abilities deserve rewards, but rather that their heavier loads of responsibility and worry and (for doctors) their longer periods of impoverished apprenticeship deserve compensation.[20]

Feinberg's idea seems to be that wages are deserved as compensation for at least three factors: length of training, working conditions, and responsibility. The more training and responsibility, and the worse the conditions, the higher the wage one deserves. Let's formulate Feinberg's compensation theory thus:

CT   S deserves wage W for doing job J if (i) S does J; and (ii) W is adequate compensation for the training, responsibility, and working conditions that J involves for S.

For purposes of evaluating CT, it's important to be clear about the notion of compensation. Feinberg claims that 'persons deserve compensation for harm wrongly inflicted by others'. In another place, he says that compensation is deserved for 'losses which are no one's fault'.[21] In each case, the idea is the same: The basis for deserving compensation is some sort of harm or loss. This seems right. At any rate, it more or less captures the ordinary understanding of 'compensation'.

However, if this is how compensation is understood, then CT implies that wages are deserved only on the basis of harm or loss. If taken as a general view about deserving wages, this is clearly false. Consider the medical student who enjoys the rigors of medical school, later thrives as an impoverished intern, and still later takes tremendous pleasure in practicing medicine. Or consider the happy graduate student who finds no pleasure greater than hours of intense study and writing, who later savors the demands and responsibilities of teaching. Indeed, consider anyone who is deeply satisfied with his or her job, and who enjoyed qualifying for it. In no such case will it be plausible to say that this person has suffered a 'harm' or 'loss'. But it would be absurd to say, as CT implies, that these people therefore deserve no wages. Thus, CT is false.

Perhaps George Sher's compensation theory will fare better than CT. Sher's view is that 'a wage is deserved when a worker's receiving it would rectify the subordination of his purposes to others'.[22] Sher's argument is this:

when a person works for another, his unremunerated labor violates a standard that requires that no one's purposes be subordinated to the purposes of others. This situation is clearly rectified by the restoration of equality between what the worker has done for others and what those others have done for him. . . . A wage, which the employee can convert to goods or services of his own choosing, is singularly well suited to serve this function. And this, I suggest, is the basic reason the wage is deserved.[23]

Sher's idea is that working involves subordinating one's own interests to the interests of one's employer, and that this sort of subordination makes one deserving of compensation or 'rectification' in the form of a wage. The deserved wage, in other words, compensates for having one's interests thus subordinated; or:

CT*   S deserves wage W for doing job J if (i) S does J; and (ii) W is adequate compensation for the subordination of interests that S must undergo to do J.

CT* hinges on the assumption that work involves a subordination of one's purposes to another's. As Sher writes, 'our account presupposes that labor is not among workers' primary goals'.[24] This may be true in some or even many cases. But if taken as a claim about all wage-deserving workers, Sher's presupposition is clearly false. There are those whose work involves no subordination to the goals of others—for example, those whose goals don't conflict with (or are the same as) their employer's goals. In all such cases, the question of 'subordination' doesn't arise. If CT* is true, then if these willing workers deserve any pay at all, they deserve less pay than unwilling workers whose interests *are* being 'subordinated.

Sher realizes that this poses a problem for CT*: 'the stronger intuition appears to be that willing workers deserve as much pay as others'.[25]

Thus, to defend our account, we must somehow disarm that intuition. This is . . . not difficult to do. It is a commonplace that the most committed and willing workers are generally also the best. Thus, although these workers come closer than others to pursuing their own purposes, they also generally do more to advance the purposes of others. In part, the intuition that they deserve to be paid as much as others may reflect a belief that these two factors cancel.[26]

As I read it, Sher's argument now appears to be that there are two factors determining the wage a person deserves. These are (i) the extent to which her work requires the subordination of her goals to others' goals; and (ii) the extent to which her work promotes the interests of others, or how much good her work does for others. If her work requires very little subordination, she deserves a correspondingly lower wage—unless her work does a lot of good for others, in which case 'these two factors cancel'.

Apart from abandoning CT[*], Sher now assumes that the most committed workers are 'generally also the best'. This seems plausible, but irrelevant. It's possible for there to be committed workers whose work is no better, or better for others, than [that of] those who are not as committed and willing. Sher's new account implies that these workers deserve less pay than workers whose work is of equal quality but who are not as committed and willing. This seems wrong. Other things being equal, these workers deserve equal pay.

A related difficulty arises with respect to discontented workers. Sher's new account implies that they deserve more pay than their less discontented colleagues. But, Sher asks, 'isn't it highly counterintuitive to say that a worker with negative attitudes deserves a higher wage than his more constructive colleagues?'.[27] Sher's response:

> Just as a very willing worker is apt to perform well, a very unwilling worker is apt to perform badly. The dissatisfied worker's labor is likely to be relatively unproductive. This means that he is apt to be less deserving than others by one measure even if more deserving by another.

It's a plausible empirical assumption that workers who are dissatisfied with their jobs often fail to be as productive as those who are satisfied. But this is irrelevant. A worker who dislikes his job may perform as well (or better) than a worker who likes his job. Sher's new account implies that the unhappy worker deserves more pay than his happy colleague. This seems wrong, as Sher himself admitted.

I believe these arguments reveal a basic flaw of compensation theories: People can deserve wages even when there is nothing to 'compensate' them for. They haven't suffered any harm or loss, nor have their interests been subordinated. This is not to say that harm, loss, and interest-subordination are irrelevant to the wage one deserves. But it's oversimple to construe all deserved wages as compensation.

A Different Approach

I believe that an acceptable theory of desert of wages will be more complicated than any of those considered thus far. This is mainly because the range of bases for deserving a wage is much broader than those theories allow. My own view is that those bases include not only the effort one makes, the value of one's services, and one's working conditions, but also the wage to which one is entitled by contract or custom, the fact that one is a person, certain needs one may have, one's moral worth, one's past receipt of goods and evils, and perhaps others. I believe that a theory of desert of wages must allow that the wage one deserves may involve any of these factors.[28]

Rather than develop this suggestion in detail, I will instead defend it against two objections. This may shed a bit more light on my view of desert of wages.

The first objection is this. It seems that my view of desert of wages contradicts a presupposition behind a standard way of thinking about desert. This presupposition can be brought out as follows. There are various forms of treatment that people can deserve: punishment, reward, apology, compensation, prizes, gratitude, and so on. The presupposition is that for each sort of deservable treatment, there is a desert base or set of desert bases unique to it. Thus, for example, it is said that punishment is deserved for committing some wrong (but not for anything else); reward is deserved for good deeds (but not for anything else); apology is deserved for being insulted (again, not for anything else); compensation is deserved for being wrongly harmed; grades are deserved for academic performance. And wages, depending on the theory, are deserved for effort; or for providing a marketable service; or for the harm or loss one suffers on the job. My suggestion that wages can be deserved for any number of bases—bases that are also clearly relevant to the desert of other forms of deservable treatment—flies directly in the face of this presupposition.

This presupposition of the standard view of desert is at the very core of Feinberg's influential paper, 'Justice and Personal Desert'.[29] In that paper, Feinberg attempts to 'analyze' the concept of desert. His analysis proceeds in the following way. First he draws up a list of the sorts of treatment that people can deserve:

1. Awards of prizes
2. Assignments of grades
3. Rewards and punishments
4. Praise, blame, and other informal responses
5. Reparation, liability, and other modes of compensation.[30]

Then Feinberg attempts to specify the bases for deserving each form of treatment. In each case, the purported desert bases are unique to the form of treatment. This is why Feinberg says 'the bases for desert vary with the mode of deserved treatment'.[31] And since for Feinberg wages are deserved as compensation, the bases for deserving a wage are just those that are bases for deserving compensation. Thus, bases for deserving a wage are not to be confused with bases for deserving prizes, rewards, grades, or any other sort of deservable treatment.

Other writers accept Feinberg's assumption that for each form of deservable treatment, the basis (or set of bases) for deserving it is unique to it. David Miller, for one, claims:

> the basis for desert—the characteristics in virtue of which people are said to deserve this or that—appears to change according to the kind of benefit in question.[32]

Robert Young, to take another example, writes:

> whether someone deserves to win the World Chess Championship will be determined by utterly different considerations from those that are relevant to whether someone deserves to be given life imprisonment, and utterly different again from whether someone deserves to be awarded compensatory damages for injuries sustained as a result of medical negligence.[33]

I believe that this way of thinking about desert in general, and hence about desert of wages in particular, is fundamentally misguided. I therefore believe that it's no objection to my view of desert of wages that it contradicts this standard way of thinking about desert. To see why I think the standard view is false, let's begin by considering something other than wages.

Consider prizes in athletic contests. An important condition for deserving prizes in such contests is, I believe, showing up and performing well. But this need not be the only basis. Suppose one of the athletes ('Nancy') is attacked just weeks before the contest by a thug hired for this purpose by one of the athlete's rivals ('Tonya'). Suppose further that in spite of the attack, Nancy manages to show up and perform quite well. Suppose finally that Tonya, the one responsible for the attack, performs just as well. Nonetheless, it's natural to feel that Nancy, in virtue of having innocently suffered the attack, deserves the prize more than Tonya, who committed a moral and criminal wrong. Thus, it appears that innocent suffering, and moral and criminal wrongdoing, can affect one's desert of prizes in athletic contests.

Next, consider grades. An important basis for deserving a good grade is (in many cases) performing well on tests and assignments. But this need not be the only basis. Suppose there is a student with a slight learning disability, and a physical disability that makes getting to class difficult. This student may not perform as well as others. But if he performs at all well, then it is natural to feel that he deserves a higher grade than 'unchallenged' students whose work is no better. Here, in addition to performance, effort and (medical) needs seem relevant to what grade he deserves. Or suppose a gifted freshman takes a senior seminar. Her work may not be up to the seniors' level. But if it's rather good, she may deserve a higher grade than those seniors whose work is no better. Here, age and skill seem relevant. Or suppose a teacher announces at the beginning of the semester that anyone with perfect attendance will receive at least a 'C'. Now imagine a student with a perfect attendance record, but not much else. This student may nevertheless deserve a 'C' in virtue of the teacher's promise. Here, something akin to entitlement is relevant.

Next, consider apologies. A condition on deserving an apology is being insulted. But this is not the only relevant fact. Another is the insulted party's moral worth. If he is a scoundrel, then perhaps he deserves only the slightest apology. Since he is a person, however, he may deserve some sort of apology no matter how morally despicable he might otherwise be. Also relevant, I believe, is the fact that he is entitled by the rules of etiquette to an apology.

Next, consider medical care. Need is a basis for deserving it. But so is moral worth, and being a person. For imagine that Smith, a morally despicable person, and Jones, a morally outstanding person, need a heart. Only one heart is available. Each deserves it insofar as each needs it, but Jones may deserve it more in virtue of his superior character. Suppose further that Jones is entitled by a living will to the heart, but Smith isn't. That too would be relevant to whether he deserved it more than Smith. Suppose also that Smith has already had an (unsuccessful) heart transplant, and that Jones has had none. Then past receipt seems relevant to deserving the heart. Also relevant, I think, are the efforts that Smith and Jones have made to stay relatively healthy.

Next, consider punishment. It can be deserved for committing some wrong. But other factors can affect the offender's desert. The harm caused by the crime is usually treated as relevant. Also relevant, I believe, are the offender's background, his motive, any special medical needs he may have, the fact that he is a person, his moral character, and the penalty to which offenders of that crime are usually 'entitled'.

I suggest that what is true of prizes, grades, apologies, medical care, and punishment—namely, that each can be deserved for an indeterminate number of non-exclusive bases—is also true of wages. We've already seen that something is plausible in each of the theories of desert of wages considered in previous sections. Effort, the value of one's contribution, the harm or loss one's work involves: All are relevant to the wage one deserves. But even these do not exhaust the bases for deserving a wage. Consider, for example, a terrifically successful but morally wicked corporate executive. Surely the wicked do not deserve to prosper. Thus, her wickedness makes her less deserving of the handsome salary she takes home. So, *moral character* should be included in the list of bases for deserving a wage. Consider next a shoe shiner who, through no fault of his own, is especially financially needy. As I see it, his need makes him deserve a somewhat higher tip than the shoe shiner of equal skill who isn't as financially needy. So, *need* should be added to the list of bases for deserving a wage. Consider next the employee who has signed a contract that entitles her to a certain wage. Other things being equal, the fact that she has entered into this agreement is a basis for deserving the wage to which she is now entitled. So, *entitlement* should be added to the list. Consider next the man who performs a menial and economically valueless job. He is nevertheless a person, and this fact affects his desert of a wage. The fact that he is a person provides a 'floor' below which his wage cannot, without injustice, fall. So, *being a person* should be added to the list.

It begins to appear, then, that not only is there a large number of factors relevant to the wage one deserves, but also that these factors are by no means unique to desert of wages.

At this point it may be objected that I haven't provided any principled reason for deeming something a desert base. I rely on unsupported 'intuitions'. To this second objection I reply as follows: The other theories of desert of wages are no better off in this respect than mine. Effort theorists, market value theorists, compensation theorists: All rely on intuitions about what is (and, just as significantly, what isn't) a basis for deserving a wage. True, my theory posits more desert bases than the others. But as far as appeals to intuition go, my theory and the others are partners in the supposed crime.

Comparable Worth

I conclude by briefly noting some implications that the foregoing has for the comparable worth debate. The first can be brought out as follows. Advocates of comparable worth may be tempted by at least two of the three theories of desert that I criticized—namely, the effort theory and the compensation theory. This is because neither theory counts gender as a basis for desert. So, if either theory were true, it would follow that differences in pay that correspond to differences in gender are almost certainly undeserved. However, if my arguments against those theories are sound, then advocates of comparable worth cannot use either theory to support their case.

As it happens, many advocates of comparable worth *don't* rely on the effort or compensation theories described in this paper. Rather, what they tend to assume is that three or four factors—typically, skill, responsibility, training, and working conditions—determine the deserved wage. But if my own suggestions about desert of wages are correct, then there are even more bases than these. These other bases have so far gone unmen-

tioned by advocates of comparable worth. Perhaps they should start mentioning them.

A third and related point is that, if my suggestions about desert of wages are correct, then there are inherent limitations to certain 'job evaluation schemes'. The schemes I have in mind attempt to specify, in effect, the bases for the wage a job deserves.[34] But people, not jobs, deserve wages. And the wage a person deserves depends (I have argued) not only on facts about the person's job, but also on facts about the person. Unfortunately, there is no way to know all these facts—no way to know, for example, each person's moral character, need, or the amount of good and evil she has already received. Therefore, there is no practical way to include these factors in job evaluation schemes.

The upshot is that job evaluation schemes, at least as we know them, cannot be used in the way that some advocates of comparable worth use them: namely, to support the claim that women and men who work in either the same jobs or jobs that are 'relevantly similar' deserve equal pay. This is because many of the relevant features—that is, many of the desert bases—are not and cannot be feasibly included in those schemes. Thus, if my view of desert of wages is correct, then all that current job evaluation schemes support is the claim that *other desert bases being equal*, women generally earn less-than-deserved wages. For the just cause of securing better wages for women, perhaps this is sufficient. But for philosophical purposes, it isn't. This is because it's unlikely that those other desert bases are equal. If so, then for all that advocates of comparable worth have said thus far, it's still possible that a woman who is paid less (or *more*) than a man who works in the same or in a similar job is getting precisely what she deserves.

NOTES

Thanks to Fred Feldman for his extensive comments on this paper, and for discussion on this and other desert-related topics. Thanks also to Jack Hanson and David Waller.
1. For a book-length version of this argument, see

K. E. Soltan, *The Casual Theory of Justice*, Berkeley, 1987. For more discussion, see also Paula England, *Comparable Worth: Theories and Evidence*, New York, 1992; and Michael Gold, *A Dialogue on Comparable Worth*, Ithaca, 1983.

2. A full-blown theory of desert of wages would include more than a list of bases for desert. I suspect that it would have to contain some principles about how to rank those bases in different circumstances, how to combine them in such a way as to represent a worker's 'desert-level', and how to map that level to a more or less specific wage. Whether this can actually be done is not something I address in this paper.

3. Why say that wages are deserved for *contracted* work? Consider the following case. While you are away on vacation, I take it upon myself, without your ever having asked me, to tend to your lawn and garden. On your return, I present myself at your doorstep and ask for payment. You might choose to reward me for what I've done, but to say that this reward is a *wage* is counter-intuitive. The reason, I suggest, is that the work I have done was not done under contract. Note also that on my understanding of wages, the money that self-employed people pay themselves isn't a wage. This is because people cannot, I presume, make contracts with themselves. (I don't insist on this, and the point doesn't affect the paper's arguments.)

4. I have in mind the following sort of case. Suppose I'm hit by a speeding car. I am knocked unconscious. My injuries will kill me unless I receive immediate emergency surgery. Fortunately, a surgeon witnesses the accident and performs the requisite surgery. The operation succeeds, and I survive. A week later, I receive a bill from the surgeon for services rendered. The surgeon's argument is that there was an 'implicit' or 'quasi-contract': If I had been able to consent to the surgery, I would have. If so, then any payment I make to the surgeon should count as a wage. For a case involving precisely these facts, see *Cotnam v. Wisdom*, Supreme Court of Arkansas, July 15 1907. My thanks to Thomas Kearns for this and other helpful references.

5. Joel Feinberg, *Social Philosophy*, Englewood Cliffs, 1973, p. 117. Useful discussions of the effort theory can be found also in David Miller, *Social Justice*, Oxford, 1976, pp. 103 and 109–110; and in James Dick, 'How to Justify a Distribution of Earnings', *Philosophy and Public Affairs* 4 (1975), pp. 259–260.

6. Wojceich Sadurski, *Giving Desert its Due*, Dordrecht, 1985, p. 116.

7. Miller, p. 109, offers (but doesn't endorse) a version of this argument for the effort theory:

   The argument in its favor is usually expressed as follows: a man can deserve reward only for what it is within his power to do. If two men try equally hard, and work for an equally long time, they deserve equal renumeration even if one of them, by virtue of superior ability, manages to produce more goods, or goods of a better quality.

   Another version of this argument is suggested by Michael Slote, 'Desert, Consent, and Justice', *Philosophy and Public Affairs* 2 (1973), pp. 327–329.

8. See, for example, Julian Lamont's 'The Concept of Desert in Distributive Justice', *Philosophical Quarterly* 44 (1994).

9. Miller, p. 103.

10. Feinberg, p. 114.

11. Soltan, p. 147.

12. It's worth noting that William Galston, *Justice and the Human Good*, Chicago, 1980, p. 201, advocates what he calls a 'contribution' theory of desert of wages, but he understands the notion of contribution very broadly. On Galston's view, 'Contribution to production has five major components: sacrifice, duration, effort, productivity, and quality'. But Galston's inclusion of 'effort' and 'sacrifice' makes his theory a hybrid of effort, compensation, and contribution theories. Thus, I think he misleads by calling it a 'contribution' theory.

13. Michael Walzer, *Spheres of Justice*, Oxford, 1983, p. 108.

14. David Miller, *Market, State, and Community*, Oxford, 1989, pp. 161–162.

15. Several authors seem to accept some version of the market value theory. See, for example, Louis Kelso and Mortimer J. Adler, *The Capitalist Manifesto*, New York, 1958, pp. 52–86; David Miller, *Market, State, and Community*, pp. 151–174 (note that Miller places an important 'socialist' spin on the theory); Robert Young, 'Egalitarianism and Personal Desert', *Ethics* 102 (1992), p. 330. In *Economics: Marxian versus Neoclassical*, Baltimore, 1987, p. 246, the economists R. D. Wolff and Stephen Resnick claim that neoclassical economic theory is committed to the idea that in a free market 'each gets his or her just deserts'. For an old but impressive criticism of the market value theory of desert of wages, see Henry Sidgwick, *The Methods of Ethics*, 7th ed., Indianapolis, 1981, pp. 287–290. For further reflections on the morality of a free market, see David Gauthier, *Morals by Agreement*, Oxford, 1986, pp. 83–112.

16. Young, p. 330. In fairness to Young, he finishes this sentence with: 'but to the very great extent that perfect competition does not hold sway there can be very little comfort for supporters of desert-based distributions that in the theoretical model it does'.

17. Wolff and Resnick, p. 123. As is well-known, neoclassical economists use these assumptions to derive theoretically interesting results—for example, that such a market will be Pareto optimal.

18. Dick, p. 264.
19. See Feinberg's appendix to 'Justice and Personal Desert', reprinted in his *Doing and Deserving*, Princeton, 1970, p. 94.
20. Feinberg, ibid., pp. 92–93.
21. Feinberg, ibid., pp. 74 and 75.
22. George Sher, *Desert*, Princeton, 1987, p. 102.
23. Sher, p. 106.
24. Sher, p. 107.
25. Ibid.
26. Ibid.
27. Sher, p. 108.
28. Two important caveats. First, I don't view possession of any of these bases as *sufficient* for deserving a wage—or anything else. I view them as base for *prima facie* desert. Second, I accept what many authors have noted: namely, that need and entitlement are distinct from desert. What I don't accept is that need and entitlement are therefore not *bases* for desert. For a detailed discussion of these and many other desert-related topics, see my *On Being Deserving*, Ph.D. dissertation, University of Massachusetts, Amherst, 1995.
29. See note 19.
30. Note that Feinberg, 'Justice and Personal Desert', p. 62, does not claim 'taxonomic precision or completeness' for this list.
31. Ibid., p. 61.
32. Miller, *Market, State, and Community*, p. 157.
33. Young, p. 319.
34. A survey of different sorts of job evaluation schemes can be found in England, pp. 189–224.

29. Does Equality Trump Desert?

LOUIS P. POJMAN

Louis Pojman, the coeditor of this anthology, is Professor of Philosophy at the United Military Academy. He received his D.Phil. from Oxford University and has taught at the University of Notre Dame, the University of Texas/Dallas, and the University of Mississippi. He is the author of several articles and books in ethics, epistemology, and philosophy of religion.

In this article Pojman considers the contemporary egalitarian thesis that equality trumps desert. He examines each concept, distinguishing among desert, merit, and entitlement, and argues that egalitarians are mistaken. Equality does not trump desert, but the reverse is true. From a moral point of view, desert trumps equality. What we object to is not inequalities, but undeserved inequalities. He attempts to provide an explanation why we do value merit and desert so highly.

> Justice is a constant and perpetual will to give every man his due. The principles of law are these: to live virtuously, not to harm others, to give his due to everyone. Jurisprudence is the knowledge of divine and human things, the science of the just and the unjust.
>
> Law is the art of goodness and justice. By virtue of this [lawyers] may be called priests, for we cherish justice and profess knowledge or goodness and equity, separating right from wrong and legal from the illegal. (Ulpian in the *Digest* of the Roman book of law, *Corpus Juris*, ca. A.D. 200)

I. The Contemporary Attack on Desert/Merit

Merit has been demerited and desert declared undeserving of a serious place in contemporary political theory. The leading political philosophers of our time, John Rawls, Ronald Dworkin, Thomas Nagel, Brian Barry, Norman Daniels, Robert Goodin, John Schaar, Kai Nielsen, Samuel Scheffler, Amy Gutmann, Michael Young, Iris Young, and Richard Wasserstrom[1]—to name a few—reject or undermine the idea of justice as rewarding desert or merit as inegalitarian and/or based on false consciousness. It is inegalitarian in that meritocracy is inherently hierarchical, holding that some people are better than others. It is based on false consciousness, since the view of human nature these philosophers accept tends to be skeptical about the individual free will and responsibility that underlies the notion of desert. Brian Barry writes,

This paper is based on Louis P. Pojman's "Equality and Desert," *Philosophy* vol. 72 Oct. 1997. Used by permission.

In examining the concept of desert we are examining a concept which is already in decline and may eventually disappear. 'Desert' flourishes in a liberal society where people are regarded as rational independent atoms held together in a society by a 'social contract' from which all must benefit. Each person's worth (desert) can be precisely ascertained—it is his net marginal product and under certain postulated conditions . . . market prices give each factor of production its net marginal product. Life is an obstacle race with no special provision for the law but if one competitor trips up another, the state takes cognizance of this fact; thus compensation is given only when there is negligence on one side but not on the other.[2]

Barry seems to be criticizing the notion of rewarding according to desert from a socialist or communitarian perspective. Desert-based distribution presupposes both an atomistic view of personality and the epistemic credentials to be able to determine desert quotients.

Rawls's theory of "justice as fairness," perhaps the most influential in its rejection of desert as a basis of distribution, attacks desert as a fundamentally incoherent notion:

It seems to be one of the fixed points of our considered judgments that no one deserves his place in the distribution of native endowments, any more than one deserves one's initial starting place in society. The assertion that a man deserves the superior character that enables him to make the effort to cultivate his abilities is equally problematic; for his character depends in large part upon fortunate family and social circumstances for which he can claim no credit.[3]

Even the willingness to make an *effort*, to try, and so to be deserving in the ordinary sense is itself dependent in practice upon happy family and social circumstances.[4]

Our talents and abilities are products of the Natural Lottery (heredity, family, and environment). We don't deserve our talents, including the talent to be moral or make an effort to learn and work. So, the argument proceeds, we don't deserve what our talents

produce. Moral and intellectual excellence and superior ability to perform important tasks are from a moral point of view arbitrary and must not be used as bases for differential distribution of primary goods, including economic goods, social status, or respect. The notion of natural or *preinstitutional* desert evaporates. Justice as the tendency toward equal distribution of primary goods replaces the classical notion of justice as giving each person his or her desert. The criterion of desert is replaced largely by that of rights and entitlements, the language of the Law Court. Rawls writes, "It is incorrect to say that just distributive shares reward individuals according to their moral worth. But what we can say is that . . . a just scheme gives each person his due: that is, it allots to each what he is entitled to as defined by the scheme itself" (313). As Dworkin puts it, *rights are trump* cards that beat everything else. Even though philosophers like Rawls and Dworkin would disassociate themselves from some of the aberrations of rights rhetoric, their work has lent support to the proliferation of entitlement talk. In our time, whenever an interest group desires special recognition, it claims a right: civil rights, women's rights, prisoners' rights, children's rights, gay rights, the rights of the handicapped, animal rights, the rights of nature, the rights to paid holidays and to medical coverage. Some parents have even claimed the right to retire from parenting small children.[5] Rights are institutional constructions or programs that flow out of the principles chosen by rational agents in the original position. The two principles that Rawls says would be chosen behind the "veil of ignorance" are the right to maximal equal liberty and the difference principle—which mandates that no one is to be allowed to achieve a higher social or economic position unless it is raises up the worst-off members of society.[6] Other political philosophers, belonging to the new Post-Rawlsian Liberalism, have similar strategies, all agreeing that rights must replace natural desert, yielding institutionally created desert. The Liberal ideal, which has largely replaced merit in the minds of many persons, holds that not the individual but the society at large owns individual talents.[7] Essentially, preinstitutional desert is an incoherent concept.[8]

Many egalitarians, including Kai Nielsen, Tom Nagel, and Robert Goodin, have replaced the notion of desert with that of need, reflecting Marx's dictum "From each according to his ability, to each according to his need." Tom Nagel offers the illustration of a family that has the choice of moving to the city where the handicapped child will receive important therapy or to a suburban neighborhood where the elder son and the rest of the family are likely to prosper but where the handicapped child will not get the treatment he needs. Nagel argues that the morally right act is to move to the city for the sake of the handicapped child, thus promoting equality rather than overall flourishing. Robert Goodin illustrates the principle of overriding desert for need this way. Suppose two men have been in an automobile accident and have the same serious injury, but one is guilty of gross recklessness, which caused the accident, while the other is an innocent victim. Who should get priority treatment in the emergency room? Goodin asserts that even if everyone involved has clear knowledge of the facts, it would be morally outrageous to give preferential treatment to the innocent victim. If both cannot be saved, the Emergency Team must flip a coin to determine who shall be saved. The right to equal treatment trumps desert.[9]

Affirmative action programs are to a large extent based on one of three antimeritocratic moves—either the denial of the coherence of merit altogether (replacing the idea with a more therapeutic ideal of enabling everyone to be autonomous), the justified overriding of merit because of considerations of need or utility, or the denial that we can really know who deserves what.[10]

Equality

Egalitarians typically promote the coercive redistribution of goods from the well-off to the worse-off. They hold to what Derek Parfit has labeled the Priority of the Worse-Off Principle: Whenever feasible, transfer goods from the better off to the worse off, even if it reduces overall utility.[11] Many egalitarians view equality as an intrinsic good, good for its own sake as well as an instrumental good. Egalitarians typically base their policies on the thesis that human beings are all of equal and positive moral worth. We have equal rights to life prospects, resources, happiness, or welfare. Elsewhere I have argued that no secular argument for equal human worth succeeds.[12] Given any property deemed to constitute the criterion for such worth, be it reason, freedom, conscientiousness, or the ability to deliberate, people have differential amounts of this property. I have also argued that attempts to work out threshold states is arbitrary and does not give us anything like the normative force that egalitarians need to justify their policies. Where a case for human equality can be made, viz., within rich metaphysical traditions such as religions, equality is only seen as a starting point, not an overriding principle by which to govern society. The best moral arguments reduce to equal opportunity, but these are offset by considerations of freedom. The *free enterprise system* of economics, with its practice of free exchange based on supply and demand, and the *family*, with its practice of giving special benefits to its children (e.g., I don't aim at causing it to be the case that my neighbor's children are as capable as mine; I educate and train mine to be superior), are both inegalitarian institutions. They are not desert-based, either, but are based on the values of freedom (we want to be left alone to do what we want) and welfare (allowing these institutions to flourish promotes over all utility). In this paper I do not deal with the importance of freedom. I allow the possibility that some version of egalitarianism, say the Primacy of the Worse-Off Principle, has some *prima facie* validity. What I argue is that even if the Principle of Merit is a weightier principle, what we object to in unequal distributions is not their inequality but their undeservingness. In general, desert trumps equality.

Merit and Desert

Allow me to clarify how I am using the terms *desert* and *merit*. Although ordinary language uses them in multifaceted and overlapping ways, I want to identify several meanings.[13] Merit is a broader concept, the *genus* of which desert is the *species*. Merit, corresponding to the Greek word *axia*, is any feature or quality that is the basis for distributing positive (or, in the case of demerit, negative) attribution or appraisal, such as praise, rewards, prizes (or, negatively, condemnation, penalties, and punishments). It is a broad normative term, roughly equivalent to *value*. Nondeserved merit can be features that the Natural Lottery has distributed, such as basic intelligence, personality type, skin color, good looks, and physical endowments. The most beautiful dog in the canine beauty contest merits the first prize; the tallest person in the city merits the prize for being the tallest person in the city; a black actor merits the part of playing Othello over equally good white actors because race is a relevant characteristic for that part, even though he did nothing to deserve his blackness. In these situations beauty, tallness and blackness become meritorious traits, whereas ugliness, shortness, and whiteness are demerits. We even speak of arguments and ideas having merit and beautiful objects meriting admiration. Joel Feinberg (see his Chapter 9) calls such meritorious qualities as intelligence, native athletic ability, and good upbringing "the bases of desert," meaning that, while we may not deserve these traits, they can generate desert claims. According to my classification, we should call these "bases of merit." The formula for merit is:

S merits M in virtue of some characteristic
(or quality) Q that S has

where S is the subject, M is the thing S ought to receive, and Q is the merit base, the good (or bad) quality possessed by S.

Desert, on the other hand, is typically or paradigmatically connected with action, since it rests on what we *voluntarily* do or produce.

It is connected with intention or effort. As George Sher writes:

> Of all the bases of desert, perhaps the most familiar and compelling is diligent, sustained effort. Whatever else we think, most of us agree that persons deserve things for sheer hard work. We believe that conscientious students deserve to get good grades, that athletes who practice regularly deserve to do well, and that businessmen who work long hours deserve to make money. Moreover, we warm to the success of immigrants and underprivileged who have overcome obstacles of displacement and poverty. Such persons, we feel, richly deserve any success they may obtain.[14]

I deserve to win the race because I have trained harder than anyone else. You deserve praise for your kind act because it was a product of a morally good will. The man or woman who works hard at a socially useful job deserves more in terms of salary than the person who loafs or works halfheartedly. Two soldiers who try equally hard to do their duty in battle are equally deserving of praise and honor, even though one fails and the other succeeds. The Good Samaritan deserved gratitude for helping the helpless, wounded Jew, but he would have deserved praise even if his efforts had failed. A prize for being the youngest person in the room is merited but not deserved, since there's nothing the person did to deserve it. Similarly, a black actor's claim on the part of playing Othello has merit although the actor did nothing to deserve his skin color. We may say that kind of desert— let us call it *active* desert—entails responsibility. A necessary condition for actively deserving anything is that one is responsible for some act for which some treatment is fitting.

The formula for desert is:

S deserves D in virtue of doing
(or attempting to do) A

where S is a subject, D is the property, thing, or treatment deserved, and A is the act, the desert base for D.[15] I assume that a necessary condition for action is that one is responsible for what one has done.

While I speak of merit as the genus term, I also contrast desert as the type of merit involving effort with the type of *specific* merit involving no effort at all. Although specific meritorious traits are not deserved, one may deserve what one gains by use of those traits through mixing one's labor with them, that is, by acting in order to achieve the appropriate goals.

I said that desert was *typically or paradigmatically* connected with what we do or intend to do, with what we are responsible for, but a secondary *negative* or *passive* use concerns what happens to us. We say that the innocent infant or child didn't deserve to get cancer and that the woman killed by a stray bullet deserved to have been spared. In these cases we posit a base line of innocence and reason that the innocent deserves an opportunity to develop, which in this case is thwarted by natural catastrophe. The infant is innocent *tout court*, and the woman is innocent with regard to the behavior of the bullet. Perhaps we can designate such instances *compensatory* or *passive desert*, signifying that people should ideally be compensated for evils that were in no way their fault, evils that were either brute bad luck or brought on by other agents' behavior.

The formula for *compensatory desert* is:

S deserves C in virtue of X's
happening to S

where C is the compensation due to S on account of some harm that has happened, is happening, or will likely happen to S. We contrast this *passive* property with *active* desert, that which has to do with our actions. So the concept of desert involves the disjunctive features of what agents do or have done to them. People should *prima facie* receive according to their overall endeavor, so that what happens to them by place them above or below that equilibrium level.[16]

We must also contrast moral and nonmoral desert. All active desert involves intentionality, but not all desert bases are moral. We may agree that the person who strives hard to be a painter or climb a mountain deserves to succeed without attaching any moral significance to the endeavor. However, the central kind of desert I am interested in is moral desert, having a good will, striving to do your duty or become a morally good person. I call this *active moral desert*. Two people, Jack and Jill, may try equally hard to become altruists, but, due to a defect of nature, to paraphrase Kant, Jack fails to achieve good results in his actions. According to my Kantian interpretation of desert, they are equally deserving of moral approbation.

Desert, then, is closely connected to effort and intention, whereas merit signifies positive qualities that call forth positive response. While God, knowing our inner motivations, rewards purely on the basis of desert, we fallible beings, being far less certain as to how to measure effort and intentionality, tend to reward merit, the actual contribution or positive results produced. You and I may both get the same *merit* pay bonus for producing 100 more widgets than the average worker, but I may deserve them more than you do, since your superior native ability enabled you to produce them effortlessly, whereas I had to strain every ounce of strength to get the same result.

An interesting example of the conflict between desert and merit occurred during the Olympic Games in Atlanta, Georgia, on August 3, 1996. Carl Lewis, one of the leading U.S. athletes, having won his ninth gold medal in the long jump, requested that he be added to the United States men's 400-meter relay team. He argued that, because of his superior ability, he merited it. Many athletes and fans agreed with him and requested that the coach substitute Lewis for one of the other runners. Some of the other spectators and runners, including those who feared being displaced by Lewis, were outraged at his audacity. They argued that Lewis shouldn't be put on the team because he didn't deserve to be on it in spite of his great talent, for he had turned down the opportunity to enter the tryouts for the team. Those who made the team played by the rules, won their places in fair competition, and could legitimately expect to run. Here is a case where merit and desert seem to conflict and where desert, it seems to me, wins out over merit. It wins out because we have a legitimate institution (the process of competing for a position on a team) in which those who play by the rules deserve to be rewarded with the positions they fairly won.[17]

Finally, we may distinguish desert and merit from *entitlement*, positive rights. Even though I am a lazy bum who is undeserving of any wealth, I am entitled to the inheritance that my rich uncle bequeaths to me because of institutional arrangements. For Rawls, all desert claims reduce to entitlements, and justified entitlements are those obtaining in a society governed by the principles of justice-as-fairness. In the Olympic relay case, discussed in the preceding paragraph, Carl Lewis was not entitled to a place on the relay team, since he had failed to fulfil the steps necessary for team membership. Sometimes desert and entitlement coincide.

There are other normative concepts (e.g., need and contribution) that need to be assessed in relation to desert and its relatives. All of these concepts entail presumptive normative force. In the words of W. D. Ross, whom I follow in much of the spirit of my analysis, desert or merit claims create *prima facie* obligations on others to enable the subject to receive the things deserved or merited or to which the subject is entitled.

As I mentioned earlier, *merit* seems to be the genus type and *desert* a species of it (dealing in its main use with effort), but we also speak of *specific merit* as focusing on the actual outcome or contribution of actions. I am concerned in this essay with the importance of both conscientious effort and contributory aspects. My general thesis, which may be called "Justice as Merit," is that considerations regarding these concepts provide strong *prima facie* grounds for distributing benefits and burdens, including coveted positions and occupations. In other words, I offer in broad outline a defense of meritocracy. In section II I outline my main arguments for the meritocratic thesis that desert claims constitute a strong prima facie ground for the distribution

of appropriate goods. In section III I argue that desert trumps equality.

I. A Defense of Meritocracy

Why should we value desert? Why should we reward and punish people according to their merit? Why not reward them according to their needs? or according to a utilitarian calculus? or according to their entitlements, which flow from institutional arrangements and expectations?

Utility and Merit

The answer to these puzzling questions leads us to the deepest regions of human experience. No doubt, one can give a partial explanation of our belief in the propriety of rewarding and punishing people according to the nature of their acts by utilitarian considerations. Rewarding good works encourages further good works, and punishment deters bad actions. By recognizing and rewarding merit, we promote efficiency and welfare. We want the very best surgeons to perform vital surgery, the very best judges to decide hard legal cases, the very best business persons to lead corporations in which we have investments, the very best soldiers to defend our country from the enemy, the very best engineers to design our bridges, nuclear power plants, airplanes, and automobiles. Even the most ardent advocate of affirmative action on university campuses refrains from advocating that positions on the football, basketball, or track team be awarded on any other criterion than merit. In other words, utilitarians justify merit-based distributions on the basis of efficiency. But it is efficiency as *macroproductivity*, the overall efficiency of the operation, not *microproductivity*, the efficiency of the individual person. Norman Daniels gives the following example:

> Jack and Jill both want jobs A and B and each much prefers A to B. Jill can do either A or B better than Jack. But the situation **S**

in which Jill performs B and Jack A is more productive than Jack doing B and Jill A (**S′**), even when we include the effects on productivity of Jill's lesser satisfaction. [Meritocracy] selects **S**, not **S′**, because it is attuned to macroproductivity, not microproductivity. . . . It says, "Select people for jobs so that *overall* job performance is maximized. ("Merit and Meritocracy," reprinted in this volume)

Macroproductivity is an important consideration, but a nonutilitarian meritocrat might object to giving it too much importance. It could be used to justify slavery if it turned out that that institution was more attuned to macroproductivity. Or it might be used to justify single-sex colleges, military academies, because, as many have argued, coeducational institutions can distract people and complicate the learning process. Suppose that we determined that confining women to household chores and family raising actually provided macroproductivity. Suppose we could convince women to accept these traditional roles. Wouldn't still be unjust to restrict them in this way? If so, merit would trump utility. Utility and merit are both valid principles of distribution. But they are *prima facie* principles able to override each other in different situations.

Utilitarian considerations would also enjoin us to punish the innocent in order to deter crime. Suppose a sheriff has weighty evidence that if he frames and hangs a vagrant for a crime he didn't commit, the crime rate in his town will be greatly reduced and the well-being of the town greatly enhanced. Why not frame and hang the vagrant? The answer is, "Because he is innocent. He does not *deserve* to be punished. So it would be unjust to inflict harm on him." Even deeply committed utilitarians tend to shy away from applying punishment on the basis of utility alone (what Rawls calls "telishment"). A necessary condition for just punishment is guilt. The criminal must have done something that deserves harm. That is, a retributive theory of justice underlies the practice of punishment. We believe that not only should only the guilty be

punished but, absent mitigating circumstances, all the guilty should be punished and punished in proportion to the severity of the crime. "Let the punishment fit the crime." As Emile Durkheim noted, "There is no society where the rule does not exist that the punishment must be proportioned to the offense."[18]

Justice as Merit as a Deontological Principle

It is interesting to observe how deeply the notion of justice as desert or merit is embedded in human history. It seems a prereflective, basic idea of primordial or Ur-justice. One finds it grounded in every known culture and religion. The ancient Greek poet Simonides defined justice as "rendering each person his due."[19] Ancient Roman law, as indicated by the quotation from the Roman jurist Ulpian at the beginning of this chapter, similarly defined justice as giving people what they merited, their due. The eminent sociologist George Caspar Homans observed, "Men are alike in holding the notion of proportionality between investment and profit that lies at the heart of distributive justice," and further noted, "Fair exchange, or distributive justice in the relations among men, is realized when the profit, or reward less cost, of each man is directly proportional to his investment."[20]

The idea is explicit in the Hindu and Buddhist idea of karma, where in succeeding reincarnations each person is rewarded in exact proportion to his or her desert. In Islam the Koran is filled with similar passages. One of the least known is the dictum "A ruler who appoints any man to an office, when there is in his dominion another man better qualified for it, sins against God and against the State."

In my historical introduction at the beginning of this book I documented the long history of the idea of *justice as desert*, beginning in our religious tradition and proceeding to such unlikely bedfellows as Locke, Mill, and Marx. The reason there is so little analysis of the thesis is that it was uncontested, which is to say it was a basic assumption, not needing elaborate defense. Leibniz thought that the principle of desert, of rewards and punishment, was founded on the *principle of the fitness of things*, "which has seen to it that affairs were so ordered that the evil action must bring upon itself chastisement."[21] And Marx's Labor Theory of Value linked reward with microproductivity: The entrepreneur ought to pay the worker according to his labor value; otherwise, he steals from the worker.

I think we get another hint of this *fittingness* or symmetry in the practice of gratitude. We normally and spontaneously feel grateful for services rendered. Someone treats us to dinner, gives us a present, teaches us a skill, rescues us from a potential disaster, or simply gives us directions. We normally feel spontaneous gratitude to our benefactor. We want to reciprocate and benefit the bestower of blessing. On the other hand, if someone intentionally and cruelly hurts us, deceives us, betrays our trust, we automatically feel resentment. We want to reciprocate and harm that person. Adam Smith and Henry Sidgwick (see their respective chapters) argued that these basic emotions were in fact the grounds for our notion of desert: Punishment was resentment universalized, and rewards—a sort of positive punishment—gratitude universalized.[22] Whether such a reduction of desert to resentment and gratitude completely explains our notion of desert may be questioned, but I for one do feel a universalized sense of resentful outrage when I hear of criminals raping and murdering, and I feel something analogous to gratitude—call it "vicarious gratitude"—when I hear of works of charity, such as those of Mother Teresa. These reactive feelings may well be the natural origins of our sense of justice. They have a normative core: Those whom I resent "ought" to suffer, and those toward whom I feel gratitude "ought" to prosper. Of course, my sentiments and judgments are not infallible and may not even be valid. But if we can link them with the nature of morality itself, with promoting or detracting from human flourishing, we can moralize the reactive attitudes.

This primordial desert-based idea of justice has two parts. Every action in the universe has a fitting response in terms of creating a duty to punish or reward, and that response must be *appropriate* in measure to the original action. It follows that evil deeds must be followed by evil outcomes and good deeds by good outcomes, exactly equal or in proportion to the vice or virtue in question. That is the basis of a primordial meritocracy, recognized in all cultures and religions but denied or undermined by much of contemporary political philosophy.

I cannot prove this principle to you. It is a basic principle, more certain to me than any of the proofs that would support it. I can only ask you to reflect on the nature of desert and determine whether you see it the same way. If you agree that people deserve the results of their voluntary deeds, then do we not have an obligation to enable them to receive their deserts? Consider the following story based on a factual situation: Jane is a devoted wife who puts her husband Jack through medical school, working long hours and sacrificing her education for him. Jack is fully caught up in his medical studies, so he fails to be grateful to Jane for all she is doing. Upon graduating with his M.D., with a lucrative practice in hand, Jack announces to Jane that he has found a younger woman and will be divorcing her. Doesn't Jane deserve an ample alimony, and doesn't Jack deserve not only our censure but to have some of his earnings transferred to Jane? Doesn't Jane have a moral claim on Jack that society in general should help enforce? Or consider again the classical biblical story of the Good Samaritan. He finds a Jew, lying wounded and bleeding on the side of the road, a victim of assault and robbery. He takes the victim to an inn, heals his wounds, restores him to health, and does it all at his own expense. Does he not deserve gratitude from the Jew? But note, on a Rawlsian, preinstitutional interpretation of desert, he deserves nothing from the Jew—for they didn't belong to the same political community. There was no preestablished institution granting the Samaritan any entitlement to any reward. And where there is no institutional entitlement, the doctrine goes, there is no obligation, no desert. But suppose that the Jew was wealthy and the Samaritan poor, needing money to pay for his daughter's leukemia treatment. Would it not be fitting for the Jew to contribute to the Samaritan's needs? Would the Samaritan not deserve it in these circumstances—even without any formal institutional ties?

The same notion of desert-as-creating-obligations underlies our revulsion against prejudicial discrimination. We object to racist and sexist practices because they treat people unfairly—they make irrelevant features, such as race and gender, rather than desert or merit, the criteria for social goods. We have a duty not to harm people unjustly (i.e., not to inflict undeserved harm on them), but we treat them positively according to their moral dignity. Similarly, children who have been afflicted with life-threatening diseases deserve to be compensated by society so that their undeserved suffering is mitigated.

I might point out that the adherence to meritocratic principles is not unique to humans. They are seen in animal behavior as well. The chimpanzee who is groomed by another chimpanzee will come to the aid of his benefactor. Wolves will kill unreliable members of their pack who threaten their well-being. Rather than detracting from justice, these primordial reactions may be the grounds of justice, an Ur-justice. Consider the example of bird grooming. Because they lack limbs that would enable them to pick harmful, even lethal, parasites off their backs and heads, birds must rely on the ritual of mutual grooming. It turns out that nature has evolved two basic types of birds in this regard: those who are disposed to groom anyone and those who refuse to groom anyone but present themselves for grooming like every other bird. Richard Dawkins calls the former "Suckers" and the latter "Cheaters." We might call them pure Altruists and pure Egoists.

Given homogeneous populations, a flock of birds with all Suckers will survive and flourish better than one with all Cheaters. But in a Sucker population with mutant Cheaters, the Cheaters will do better than the Suckers, having more time to hunt for food and reproduce. As the Suckers are exploited, they will gradually die out (if too many die off, the

Cheaters will be condemned to a hell of other birds just like them). Occasionally, nature produces a third variety of bird. These groom all and only those who reciprocate in grooming them. They groom each other and Suckers, but not Cheaters. In fact, once caught, a Cheater is marked for life as a pariah. There's no forgiveness, and Cheaters, who flourished in a population of Suckers, now find themselves outcast. We might call this third kind of bird "Recipocators," or those who live by the principle of "justice as desert," for they return good for good and evil for evil. A society of Reciprocators seems fair. If no selfish Cheaters threatened our existence, perhaps a world of altruist Suckers would be wonderful. But Cheaters do exist, so a world governed by the principles of justice as desert, the principles of the Reciprocators, seems the best we can hope for. Of course, this is a utilitarian justification for reciprocity and meritocracy. The birds themselves do not self-consciously act according to the Categorical Imperative.

One would like to have a nonutilitarian, deontological argument to ground our intuitions that regarding any good and useful function X, the good (at X) should prosper and the bad (at X) should experience appropriate consequences *vis-à-vis* X. I'm not sure any is available. It may be that the belief that the morally good should prosper and that the bad should suffer is a foundational or metamoral thesis which is self-evident upon reflection. W. D. Ross (see his chapter in this volume) offers a thought experiment to support this position. After identifying two intrinsically good things, pleasure and virtue, Ross asks us to consider a third:

> If we compare two imaginary states of the universe, alike in the total amounts of virtue and vice and of pleasure and pain present in the two, but in one of which the virtuous were all happy and the vicious miserable, while in the other the virtuous were miserable and the vicious happy, very few people would hesitate to say that the first was a much better state of the universe than the second. It would seem then that, besides

virtue and pleasure, we must recognize, as a third independent good, the apportionment of pleasure and pain to the virtuous and the vicious respectively. And it is on the recognition of this as a separate good that the recognition of the duty of justice, in distinction from fidelity to promise on the one hand and from beneficence on the other, rests.[25]

Surely Ross is correct. It is intuitively obvious that the appropriate distribution of happiness and unhappiness should be according to virtue and vice. This sort of thought experiment seems to be what underlies the universal commitment to meritocracy mentioned earlier. It seems to be exactly the intuition that motivated Kant's principle of *equality*, a sort of symmetry between input and output in any endeavor. This finds expression in *Groundwork for the Metaphysics of Morals*, where Kant writes that conscientiousness or good will, being the single desert base, is the only moral basis for happiness: "An impartial spectator can never feel approval in contemplating the uninterrupted prosperity of a being graced by no touch of a pure and good will, and that consequently a good will seems to constitute the indispensable condition of our very worthiness to be happy."[26]

III. Desert Trumps Equality

It seems, then, on reflection, that desert has significant normative force. The morally good should prosper over the wicked; those who labor should prosper over the lazy; whatsoever a man sows, that shall he reap. When we see someone working twelve hours a day six or seven days a week in order to build a successful business or career, such as many immigrants in the United States have done, from the Jews to the Koreans and Vietnamese boat people, our sense of justice is satisfied when we see him or her succeed, whereas we feel that justice has not been done when someone who has failed to work hard succeeds over such industrious persons.

Consider a four-person society consisting of David, Samuel, Isaac, and Nabal. David and Samuel are two highly talented men, whereas Isaac and Nabal are low-talented men. David dedicates himself to becoming a successful businessman (or lawyer), and sacrifices time and money in attaining his goals, whereas Samuel spends his time surfing in the Mediterranean Sea, taking harmful drugs when he is not surfing, ending up a failure. Isaac, although he has limited intelligence and education, works diligently, takes whatever work he can find, and does a good job at whatever he does. Nabal, true to his name (the word means "fool") has little talent, squanders his time and money, and ends up a failure. It seems obvious to most of us that David, because of his supreme effort, eminently deserves to be more successful than Samuel and Nabal and merits more success than Isaac (though he may not deserve it) and that Isaac deserves to prosper more than Samuel or Nabal. Suppose that Isaac, through no fault of his own, is laid off from a job and applies for unemployment benefits. Samuel and Nabal also apply. If there is only enough money for one person, we would say that Isaac deserves to receive it over the other two. We might even say that, of the three, only Isaac deserves the benefits from people's tax dollars. We might choose to help Samuel and Nabal, but from a moral point of view that help should be tied to their intention to reform. If no inclination to reform is manifest, no obligation rests on the shoulders of society to provide them with a livelihood. Their demise, especially Samuel's, is tantamount to a self-imposed suicide. We judge Samuel more harshly than Nabal because he had more talents with which to improve his lot. We think that David and Isaac are equally deserving of success, though David, due to his superior talents, merits success in a more complex or highly developed enterprise.

Effort, industry, commitment, good will, conscientiousness—these are the qualities that make up desert; talent, skill, contribution, native ability, and intelligence—these are the qualities that make up merit. Society values merit as the bottom line and the desired result of social endeavors, but it recognizes desert as that which casts moral value on the individual, causing him to shine like a jewel in his own light. At the highly hierarchical U.S. Military Academy, where I teach, cadets often complain about the undeserved status and authority of some of those chosen to be regimental commanders and company officers. When I ask them whether they object to the inequality of authority or the undeserved inequality of authority and status, they invariably answer that it is the undeserved inequality. I think this is the case with most differences in social status and respect and, to a lesser degree, with differences in wealth. We are quite willing to acknowledge that Einstein deserves and merits support for his research program over a mediocre scientist and that the Korean immigrants who, at great costs to themselves, keep their grocery shops open twenty-four hours a day deserve to succeed over those who are content to live on welfare.

Furthermore, there is good reason to reject Goodin's notion that need trumps desert. The innocent victim of a car accident deserves to be restored to wholeness, whereas the reckless driver does not. Even though, *pace* Goodin, the reckless driver does not deserve to die, he deserves some punishment and is, surely, less deserving in this context than his victim. He owes her something, and so do other moral agents. In situations like the accident case, resources come in wholes and can't be split. You can't save three-fourth of the innocent victim's life and one-fourth of the reckless driver's life, so proximate justice requires that we choose the more deserving over the less deserving.

Egalitarians hold that all people are equally worthy. Ironically, this doctrine is subject to the same criticism that Rawls levels at utilitarians—it "does not take seriously the distinction between persons" (TJ 27). The reckless driver and the innocent victim have different moral status, as do David, Samuel, Isaac, and Nabal. While we may have difficulty assessing that status at times, morality itself requires that we do our best to judge impartially and generously, taking our fallibility into account. The idea that all people of equal intrinsic worth itself is one of the uncontested dogmas of modern political liberalism. Frankena and Vlastos speak of all human beings having "infinite value" of being "sacred," and Rawls speaks of equal respect for all human beings as an "inviolable" right. But is this so?[27]

Suppose a Martian visitor asks the egalitarian why he uses such language of mere animals. He invites Vlastos or Rawls to consider Smith, a man of low morals and lower intelligence, who abuses his wife and children, who hates exercising or work, for whom novels are dull and art a waste of time, and whose joy it is to spend his days as a couch potato, drinking beer, while watching mud wrestling, violent sports, and soap operas on TV. He is an avid voyeur, devoted to child pornography. He is devoid of intellectual curiosity, eschews science, politics, and religion, and eats and drinks in a manner more befitting a pig than a person. Smith lacks wit, grace, humor, technical skill, ambition, courage, self-control, and wisdom. He is antisocial, morose, lazy, a free-loader who feels no guilt about living on welfare when he is perfectly able to work, has no social conscience, and barely avoids getting caught for his petty thievery. He has no talents, makes no social contribution, lacks a moral sense, and, from the perspective of the good of society, would be better off dead. But Smith is proud of one thing: that he is "sacred," of "infinite worth," of intrinsic value equal to that of Abraham Lincoln, Mother Teresa, Albert Schweitzer, the Dalai Lama, Jesus Christ, Gandhi, and Einstein. He is inviolable—and proud of it—in spite of any deficiency of merit. From the egalitarian perspective, in spite of appearances to the contrary, Smith is of intrinsic worth equal to that of the best citizen in his community. If he is the worst off, others are not entitled to advance themselves unless they improve Smith's position. We could excuse the Martian if he exhibited amazement at this incredible doctrine.

We already considered Ross's two worlds with equal utility (A) in which the virtuous prosper and the vicious suffer in close equivalence to their virtue or vice and (B) in which the virtuous suffer and the vicious prosper in equivalence to their virtue and vice, seeing that A was to be preferred to B. Let us now compare two worlds C and D, which, like A and B, are equal in utility. In C, however, the virtuous prosper in accordance with their virtue and the vicious suffer in a manner fitting their viciousness, whereas, in D, the good and bad alike are equally but mediocrely happy. I think we would choose C over the egalitarian D.

Recently Dick Arneson has argued for the intrinsic value of equality. He concedes that desert sometimes trumps equality but holds that equality has some intrinsic value.[28] He asks us to consider two worlds, which we may designate E and F, in which the utility is equal and that have the same number of virtuous and vicious people. In E the resources or happiness is distributed randomly, whereas in F everyone has an equal amount, regardless of virtue. Arneson thinks we would choose F, indicating that equality has some intrinsic force. I don't think that it is clear that we would choose the equal world. What I suspect may incline us to F is the epistemic opacity in knowing how to decide in just who is virtuous and who is vicious. When we are uncertain, we may incline towards equal distribution. Perhaps this is what happens in our world. As Barry notes in the quotation at the beginning of this chapter, we cannot know for sure just who is virtuous and to what extent people deserve their holdings, so we incline to a rough egalitarianism. Equality, then, becomes a default position.

I don't think that Barry's criticism or Arneson's thought experiment undermine my version of meritocracy. We do have a sufficient grasp of the concepts of desert and merit to apply them to distribution schemes. In general, we ought to award coveted positions to the best qualified, wages to those who earn for them, rewards to those who achieve excellence in various institutional endeavors, punishments to those who violate just laws in proportion to their gravity. Welfare schemes

should distinguish between the unfortunate who, through no fault of their own, lose out in life and the drones who choose not to do socially useful work.

In this view of distribution, as Harry Frankfurt has suggested, the craving for equality should be replaced by a notion of *sufficiency*.[29] A society like ours, wealthy enough to satisfy basic human biological needs but not resourceful enough to guarantee everyone equal happiness, should aim at providing basic human needs, but after this other considerations should direct our policies. Frankfurt argues that the principle of sufficiency requires that society provide a floor under which no one is allowed to fall except where he is clearly at fault. He shows how this policy would take care of Nagel's handicapped child without mandating equal welfare. The reason the family with the handicapped child should move to the city where he can receive basic care is to bring him to a place not where he has equal life-prospects with his siblings but where his basic needs are met so that he can live a good life. The pure egalitarian would opt to bring him to a place where he would have prospects equal to those of his more able siblings, but that doesn't seem necessary, especially when it would require severe sacrifices on their part, perhaps bringing everyone to a level below sufficiency. Frankfurt offers the following thought experiment against thoroughgoing equality. Suppose we have ten people who each need five units of nourishment in order to survive. We have only forty units. How should we distribute these? The thoroughgoing egalitarian would urge us to give four units to each even though that would result in the death of all. A utilitarian very likely would advise us to draw lots so that eight people would receive the requisite five units and two people would die. The meritocrat, agreeing that eight should live and two die, would advise us to use a criterion of desert or merit (including perhaps likelihood of future contributions, e.g., the ability to allocate scarce in a manner necessary for the future well-being of their society) in dividing up the resources.

Conclusion

Does Equality trump Desert? No, not generally. I have argued that merit, interpreted broadly as conscientious effort and social contribution, has both intrinsic and instrumental value. It trumps equality. I think it also generally trumps utility. We reward people for their work or achievements in order to give them what they deserve or have merited. We punish in order to give criminals what they deserve. If, in the process, we can deter crime as well, so much the better, but the underlying justification of rewards and punishment is desert (or merit). I have not argued that desert is a moral absolute that can never be overridden by other considerations such as utility. In fact, I believe that utility can sometimes override merit, but the presumption is always on the side of merit/desert. Finally, I have urged that, where need is involved, the principle of sufficiency, not strong equality, should be the operative companion of merit-based justice. If further work sustains my conclusions, our notion of justice must be radically transformed, returning to an earlier tradition, which egalitarians have largely disowned and discounted.

NOTES

A previous version of this paper was read to the Philosophy Department at SUNY Geneseo, March 28, 1996, and to the Philosophy Department at Ben Gurion University, Beer-Sheva, Israel December 2, 1996. To the members of these departments and to Robert Audi, John Kekes, Michael Levin, Owen McLeod, Tziporah Kasachkoff, and Wallace Matson, who commented on earlier versions of this paper, I am grateful.

1. John Rawls, *A Theory of Justice* (Harvard University Press, 1971); Ronald Dworkin, "Why Bakke Has No Case," *New York Review of Books*, Nov. 10, 1977; Thomas Nagel, *Mortal Questions* (Cambridge University Press, 1979); Brian Barry, *Political Argument* (Routledge & Kegan Paul, 1965); Norman Daniels, "Merit and Meritocracy," *Philosophy and Public Affairs* 7:3 (1978). Robert Goodin states that it is morally repugnant to make distinction between deserving and unde-

serving people when allocating scarce resources: "Negating Positive Desert Claims" *Political Theory* 13:4 (1985); John Schaar, "Equality of Opportunity, and Beyond," in J. R. Pennock and J. Chapman, eds., *Equality: Nomos IX* (Atherton Press, 1967); Richard Wasserstrom, "Racism and Sexism," in Richard A. Wasserstrom, eds., *Today's Moral Problems* (Macmillan, 1985); Kai Nielsen states he has "reservations about the whole category of desert" and holds that "Everyone should be treated equally as persons and, in spite of what will often be rather different moral conduct, everyone should be viewed as having equal moral worth": *Equality and Liberty: A Defense of Radical Egalitarianism* (Rowman and Littlefield, 1985), pp. 56, 53; David Miller argues that each person must be treated with equal respect and is entitled to self-respect irrespective of desert: "Democracy and Social Justice," *British Journal of Political Science* 8 (1977) [Miller has subsequently altered his position in favor of merit; see his "Two Cheers for Meritocracy," *Journal of Political Philosophy* 4:4 (1996)]; Amy Gutmann, *Liberal Equality* (Cambridge University Press, 1980); Iris Young, *Justice and the Politics of Difference* (Princeton University Press, 1990); and Michael Young, *The Rise of Meritocracy: 1870–2033* (Penguin Books, 1958). John Kleinig, in his "The Concept of Desert" (APQ 1971), one of the earliest analyses of desert, notes that in contemporary philosophy it seems "by and large to have been consigned to the philosophical scrap heap." This anthology contains the selections by Rawls, Goodin, Scheffler, Daniels, Miller, Kleinig, and Robert Young.

2. Brian Barry, *Political Argument* (London: Routledge & Kegan Paul, 1965), p. 112f.

3. John Rawls, *Theory of Justice*, p. 104.

4. Rawls, op. cit., p. 74. The attack on moral desert is perhaps the most radical move that egalitarians like Rawls and company have made against meritocracy, and the ramifications of their attack are far-reaching. For example, since I do not deserve my two good eyes and two good kidneys, the social engineers may take one of each from me to give to persons who need an eye or a kidney, even if their organs became damaged through their own voluntary actions. Since no one deserves anything, we do not deserve pay for our labors or praise for a job well done or first prize in a race we win. The notion of moral responsibility vanishes in a system of leveling. So does the notion of *self-respect*, deemed the basic primary good, for if we are simply products of the Natural Lottery, how can the self deserve anything at all, including respect?

5. A couple in Montclair, New Jersey, Warren and Patricia Simpson, have recently declared that they're not very good at child rearing and don't

much like it, so they're exercising their right to retire from it. "Between the crying and the fighting and asking for toys, it was getting to be very discouraging," Mrs. Simpson said. "We're both still young, and we have a lot of other interests." They've put their three small children up for adoption, and, after seven years of parenting, they "are moving on." See "Retirement Fever," by Michael Rubiner, *New York Times*, February 1996. This may be an extreme example of the abuse of the philosophy of entitlements, but it is indicative of a trend.

6. Note that Rawls allows incentive but not desert to justify rewarding people. If so, then we might imagine two workers, Dennis and Ivan. Dennis works hard out of a commitment to his job, produces 50 percent more than the average worker, stays overtime to help out, is an inspiration to others, and never misses a day's work. Ivan bargains with his boss for every advantage he can get, produces exactly what his contract calls for (even less if he can get away with it), but would produce more if he had incentive to do so. He takes off every time he can get away with it. Suppose Dennis and Ivan are making the same pay. On Rawls's model, we are morally justified to raise Ivan's pay as an incentive to produce more, so that we can help the least best off, but we are not permitted to reward Dennis with more, since he doesn't need an incentive. He works from the spontaneous goodness of his heart. There seems something grotesque about this arrangement.

7. Rawls says, "The difference principle represents . . . an agreement to regard the distribution of natural talents as a common asset . . . those who have been favored by nature . . . may gain from their good fortune only in terms that improve the situation of those who have lost out" (TJ 101f).

8. See George Sher, *Desert* (Princeton University Press, 1987), for a defense against some of these charges. My work has been profoundly influenced by this seminal work. But a lot of work needs to be done on behalf of meritocracy, which, as my introduction indicates, has taken a serious beating in our time.

9. Robert Goodin, "Negating Positive Desert Claims," *Political Theory* 13:4 (November 1985), pp. 575–598.

10. Merit—in terms of accomplishments or present ability to carry out the traditional roles of workers—should not be the only thing that counts. Role modeling (in terms of race and gender) and the goal of breaking social stereotypes themselves come to constitute a new type of merit, merit for attaining social goals that have no direct connection to the subject at hand (e.g., black or white skin is irrelevant to flying an air plane, but it might be relevant to inculcating a message about how we are to evaluate people of different races).

Preferential treatment, race norming, reverse discrimination, goals, and time tables—different euphemisms for affirmative action—all flow from the undermining of the traditional meritocratic notion of justice—rendering to each his or her due.

11. Derek Parfit, unpublished manuscript, "On Giving Priority to the Worse-Off" (1989). I do not have access to this manuscript but have heard it referred to by others.

12. Louis P. Pojman, "On Equal Human Worth: A Critique of Contemporary Egalitarianism," in Louis P. Pojman and Robert Westmoreland, eds., *Equality: Selected Readings* (Oxford University Press, 1996).

13. See my Introductory Essay to the historical section of this book, "Desert: An Historical Introduction."

14. George Sher, *Desert*, p. 53.

15. This is not a full characterization, since temporal indexicals need to be included. The reader can easily apply these. I leave them out in order to keep the discussion focused on the essential differences.

16. See Fred Feldman, "Desert: Reconsideration of Some Received Wisdom" *Mind* 104 (January 1995), reprinted in this book, for an acute discussion of this point. See also Spiegelberg's and Rawls' articles, also in this volume, which use this idea to justify an egalitarian project. The irony, which no one has heretofore pointed out, is that Rawls actually makes use of natural *compensatory* desert in order to defeat an *active* desert-based system. Some may contend that I have two separate concepts of desert (*active* and *passive*), rather than one disjunctive concept, centering on two relevant aspects of agency. But nothing hangs on this division. I would be willing to call them *desert 1* and *desert 2* or even to confine desert to what we are responsible for and call compensatory desert a type of merit. Sometimes it is argued (or asserted) that being a person entails deserving some types of treatment. I would prefer to say that personhood *merits* certain kinds of treatment, since we are not responsible for being persons.

17. One may even say that they have a right to the spot. In this case the language of rights (or entitlements) and desert seem to coalesce. The other runner had a right to be on the relay team because of the nature of the rules he followed, but he also deserved to be on it by his action of winning that place in fair competition. The controversy over Lewis's participation was exacerbated by the fact that in the end Canada unexpectedly beat the United States to win a gold medal. Could Lewis's participation have prevented that? Should it have mattered?

18. Emile Durkheim, *The Rules of Sociological Method* (Oxford University Press, 1952).

19. Quoted in Plato's *Republic* 331. Although Socrates argues against Polemarchus's interpretation of this view, he holds a version of it himself.

20. George Caspar Homans, *Social Behavior: Its Elementary Forms* (Routledge & Kegan Paul, 1961), pp. 246 and 264.

21. Leibniz, *Theodicy*, trans. E. M. Huggard, 1698.

22. Henry Sidgwick, *The Methods of Ethics* (Indianapolis: Hackett), Book III, chap. 5.

25. W. D. Ross, *The Right and the Good* (Oxford University Press, 1930), p. 138.

26. Immanuel Kant, *Groundwork of the Metaphysic of Morals*, trans. H. J. Paton (Hutchinson University Library, 1948), p. 59.

27. See Gregory Vlastos "Justice and Equality" reprinted in Pojman and Westmoreland, *Equality. Cited in no. 12.*

28. Richard Arneson, "Justice and Responsibility," paper delivered to the Philosophy Department at New York University, November 15, 1996.

29. Harry Frankfurt, "Equality as a Moral Ideal" *Ethics* 98:1 (October 1987).

30. Equality and Desert

SHELLY KAGAN

Shelly Kagan is Henry R. Luce Professor of Social Thought and Ethics at Yale University. He received his Ph.D. from Princeton University and has taught at the University of Illinois at Chicago and at the University of Pittsburgh. He is the author of several works on moral philosophy, including *The Limits of Morality* (1989). He is currently writing a book on desert.

Many people believe that *equality* has intrinsic moral significance, so that an outcome is better—in and of itself—if it leads to greater equality. In fact, however, many of the cases that might be thought to support this belief are compatible with an alternative explanation: that what actually has intrinsic value is giving people what they deserve (for when people are equally deserving, they will deserve to be equally well off). So should we believe in both equality and desert, or just one of the two? Kagan argues, first, that the value of equality is at best conditional, since most of us don't think that inequality is bad if it is truly deserved. Of course, even if that's right, it still might be that equality does matter in its own right in those cases where the inequality is not deserved. Constructing the relevant case to test this sort of "restricted" egalitarianism proves to be surprisingly difficult. Ultimately, however, Kagan concludes that equality has no intrinsic moral significance at all. We should, instead, believe in desert alone.

1

Pluralists in ethics believe in the intrinsic moral significance of more than one basic value. The pluralism might be at the level of the theory of the right (as with those who think that several factors are relevant to determining the moral status of an act), or it might be at the level of the theory of the good, the theory that tells us how good a given outcome is (perhaps as compared to alternatives). In this paper, I am concerned solely with pluralism at the level of a theory of the good.

Such pluralism is perfectly familiar. Many people, for example, believe in the moral significance of both well-being *and* equality.

That is, they believe that the overall goodness of an outcome is a function not only of the amount of well-being but also the amount of inequality (if any). Of course, even someone who rejects the thought that equality has intrinsic moral significance might think that it matters for various practical reasons; for example, increasing equality might maximize well-being. But I am interested only in claims about which factors have *intrinsic* moral significance. The *egalitarian* believes that equality makes an outcome intrinsically better, above and beyond whatever impact this might have on levels of well-being.

Obviously, one might accept various other values as well. For example, one might think

---

an outcome better if people are getting what they (morally) *deserve*. Or one might think an outcome intrinsically better if people are more *virtuous*. I am sympathetic to a number of these values, but here I want to focus on just two: equality and desert. Although equality is widely thought to have intrinsic moral significance, many moral philosophers have their doubts about desert. Interestingly, I think this gets things backwards. Or so I will argue.[1]

2

But first we need some background. Equality is a surprisingly complex notion, as we discover when we try to measure the *degree* of inequality. This emerges especially clearly for cases involving more than two people, and more than two levels of well-being. Luckily, I think we can put this particular problem aside.[2] I also think we can put aside the "equality of what?" debate. I am going to assume that what matters is equality of well-being, but I believe that what I have to say would carry over for other views as well (for example, equality of resources or equality of opportunity).

However, one important and sometimes overlooked fact about equality should be faced: If we have a simple situation of inequality, with A at a lower level of well-being than B, we can improve the situation in terms of equality either by raising A *or* by lowering B. As far as *strict equality* is concerned, either change is an improvement.

Many people, when they face this fact, decide that they may not believe in strict equality after all. They sometimes urge that what they liked about equality was its concern for the plight of the "have-nots"; now that they see that equality per se has no concern for have-nots per se, they find that strict equality doesn't really capture what they cared about. One proposal as to what it is that these disillusioned egalitarians really care about is this: giving priority to those who are worse off. The thought here is that increasing someone's well-being by a fixed amount makes a *greater* contribution, the lower the person's absolute

level of well-being. We can call this view *weighted beneficence*.[3]

Note that in our simple situation of inequality, assuming that we can help one or the other but not both and that we can help either by the same fixed amount, weighted beneficence favors helping A, since the welfare gain counts for more going to A than it would going to B, given that A is at a lower level absolutely than B. In contrast, *lowering* B is no improvement at all, as far as weighted beneficence is concerned.

Note, as well, that weighted beneficence is essentially noncomparative. Increases in well-being count for more (or less), depending on the absolute level of the recipient. To know what kind of a "boost" there is, we don't need to know anything at all about how a person fares relative to another. Of course, it will fall out from weighted beneficence that it is always better to help the worse off (some fixed amount) rather than the better off—but that is just a matter of comparing what is essentially noncomparative information.

In contrast, strict equality is essentially comparative. To know whether a situation will be improved by altering someone, we need to know how that person fares relative to others.

Some would argue that whatever the merits of weighted beneficence, it is certainly not an *egalitarian* value. Others would argue that weighted beneficence is simply the noncomparative egalitarian value, just as what I have been calling strict equality is the comparative egalitarian value—and that both deserve to be called egalitarian values. (Presumably, one might think this whether or not one accepts both of these values.) I won't try to settle this debate, though I suppose the possibility of this last view explains why I am going to consider weighted beneficence in a paper called simply "*equality* and desert."

As I have noted, some find that they don't believe in strict equality at all and that they believe simply in weighted beneficence. Others, I presume, believe in both. And, no doubt, still others believe simply in strict equality. Because of this, I want to examine desert in connection with *both* types of egalitarian values, that is, both weighted beneficence and strict equality.

Luckily, for most of the points that will concern us, the differences between weighted beneficence and strict equality won't be important. Both agree that when A is worse off than B and we can only help one (by the same amount), the outcome is made better if we help A rather than B. For our purposes, I believe, this point of agreement will normally suffice. Accordingly, we can, for the most part, disregard the differences between weighted beneficence and strict equality and simply talk (indifferently) about the value of *equality*. Obviously, however, whenever it is useful to do so, we can still distinguish between the specific egalitarian values.[4]

One final point: in situations where equality favors helping someone, we can talk of that person's *claim* to be helped.[5] But this should not be misunderstood as bringing in notions of rights. The idea is just that we can improve the outcome a greater or lesser amount by helping the person in question—the greater the amount, the greater the claim.

3

Desert is also a complex notion, even if we restrict our attention (as I intend to) to moral desert—the notion of one person being more or less morally deserving than another. I need to put aside many important questions here, for example, what is the relevant desert base? That is, what is it that makes one person more or less morally deserving?

I am going to assume, without argument, a number of things about desert. One is that more deserving people deserve to be doing better in terms of some relevant magnitude. Again, for simplicity, I am going to assume that the relevant magnitude is well-being. So I am assuming that more deserving people deserve to be doing better than less deserving people.

I am also going to assume that for each person there is an absolute level that the person deserves to be at. This is what the person deserves absolutely. If people have what they

deserve, this is good from the point of view of desert. If people have less than they deserve, then this is less good, or perhaps even bad, from the point of view of desert. More controversially, I also believe that if someone has *more* than they deserve, this is less good, or perhaps even bad, from the point of view of desert. This pair of beliefs explains why I refer to the absolute desert level for a given person as his *peak*—for it is the level of well-being at which the person has exactly what he absolutely deserves, and so things are most fitting or best from the point of view of desert. Too little or too much well-being, and things are less good as far as desert is concerned. Thus the contribution to goodness of outcomes made by desert (that is, the goodness accruing to an outcome by virtue of someone getting or not getting what they deserve) is at a "peak" when someone is exactly at the level they absolutely deserve.

These ideas can be helpfully portrayed graphically. Let the X axis represent the level of well-being that the person is at, and the Y axis the level of goodness from the point of view of desert. (More precisely, the Y axis represents the contribution to the goodness of the outcome made by the person's getting or not getting what she deserves.) Then the "desert graph" for a normal person looks like a mountain, with a peak at the point the person absolutely deserves:[6]

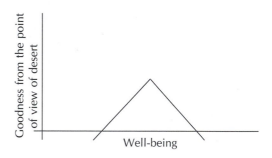

If someone has less than she absolutely deserves, she is "below" her peak (that is, on the western slope of the mountain), and anyone who believes in the intrinsic moral significance of desert for goodness of outcomes will believe that raising the person will make the outcome better—provided that you don't raise her too much. If she ends up having more than she absolutely deserves, she is beyond her peak (on the eastern slope of the mountain), and now making her even better off makes things worse, not better (as far as desert is concerned).

Note that this view is essentially noncomparative. For any given person, I first find out how deserving he is, absolutely speaking. This tells me where his peak is. (That is, it tells me the location of his peak on the X axis, how much well-being he *deserves*.) I then find out where he actually is in terms of well-being (his actual location on the X axis). This tells me whether I will improve things from the point of view of desert (moving up the Y axis) by making him better off, or by lowering him. (Of course, if he is at the peak, I should leave him alone.)

All of this information has nothing to do with anyone else. Of course, by comparing this information with the noncomparative information about someone else, I may find that I can do more good by helping someone else—but this is basically a matter of compounding noncomparative information. (Similarly, weighted beneficence compounds noncomparative information to tell me to help the worse off in situations of simple inequality.)

Two possible complications must be noted. First, should we assume that the drop-off rate (loss of value for having too much or too little) is the same for all people, regardless of how deserving they are? I am inclined to think that it is worse, say, if a very good person has a certain amount less than she deserves than if a very bad person has that same amount less than he deserves. That is to say, the slope on the western side should be steeper for better people. Similar considerations lead me to think that the slope on the *eastern* side should be *milder* for better people (that is, having too much is less bad the better you are). If we accept both of these thoughts, then the mountain actually swings like a bell (if we think of the peak as fixed): to the left as you have less deserving people, to the right as you have more deserving people. I call this *bell-motion*. Not everyone believes in it, but I find it plausible.

Second, should we assume that the drop-off rate is *linear*? That is the way I drew my picture, where the slopes are straight. If, for example, you have less than you deserve, then each extra unit of well-being you have less than you deserve makes the same incremental decrease in value. Perhaps, however, and this does seem plausible, the *further* you are from your peak, the *greater* the significance of each additional unit change in well-being. Then the slopes would not be straight, but curved, getting steeper and steeper, the further from the peak. Not everyone believes this either, but I find it plausible, too. Call this *curved desert*. Those who reject it believe in *straight desert*.

Bell-motion won't be important for what follows, except as a nagging complication. Curved desert will be rather important.

4

Also important for our purposes will be the notion that not all desert considerations are essentially noncomparative. There is also, I think, essentially comparative desert. Again, I must skip over many details, but the basic idea is this: It matters—from the point of view of comparative desert—how I am doing compared to you, in light of how (absolutely) deserving we are. If I am as absolutely deserving as you, I should be doing as well as you. If I am more deserving than you, I should be doing better than you. These are essentially comparative judgments, for they say not how well we should be doing in absolute terms, but only how well we should be doing relative to each other; they are based not solely on what I deserve absolutely but more essentially on how what I deserve absolutely compares to what you deserve absolutely.

Comparative desert is not the same thing as noncomparative desert, even though it is based on it, in the way I have just sketched. Suppose A and B are equally deserving (they have the same peak), but A is at the peak, while B is beyond it. Suppose we cannot move B but could push A up to the same level of well-being as B. Should we?

Noncomparative desert says no: Doing so merely gives A more than he deserves; from the point of view of noncomparative desert, this is making things worse. The fact that B is beyond the peak is bad, but moving A beyond doesn't help.

But comparative desert says yes. Since A is just as (absolutely, noncomparatively) deserving as B, A should be doing just as well as B. Improving A to B's position is an *improvement* from the point of view of comparative desert.

Note that you can believe in comparative desert while still thinking noncomparative desert considerations are *more* significant. (I can't pursue here the question of the relative weights of comparative desert and noncomparative desert.) Of course, not everyone believes in the existence of comparative desert. The reasons vary, but one important reason is the fact that (like strict equality) comparative desert can favor lowering those who are better off, even though this does nothing for those who are worse off, and even if the person being lowered has less than he absolutely deserves. For example, suppose A and B are equally deserving, and both are below their shared peak, though A is even lower than B. And suppose that we cannot move A but could lower B. Comparative desert says there is some reason to do this (since it is bad if A, who is just as deserving as B, does less well than B). Of course, there is also a *noncomparative* reason *not* to do this, since it moves B further from her peak. But still, comparative desert says there is at least *some* reason to lower B. And so some people (especially those who reject strict equality) may reject comparative desert. But many people do accept comparative desert, and in fact I find it rather attractive.

Some people find comparative desert attractive but deny that it has anything to do with *desert*. (Perhaps, instead, it is a matter of *fairness*.) They would restrict desert to the noncomparative theory. I am unclear what turns on the label—what really matters is that the value has moral significance. But I am inclined to think that just as equality might have

its comparative aspect (strict equality) and its noncomparative aspect (weighted beneficence), so desert has its noncomparative aspect (as captured by the desert graph) and its comparative aspect (comparative desert). Anyway, so I will assume.

Even if we accept the reality of comparative desert, it is not clear what the relevant metric is. If your peak is X, and mine is Y, and you are at some point—Z—other than X, where should I be to satisfy comparative desert? I won't enter this debate here either, but hopefully it won't much influence what follows.

One final piece of vocabulary. Whether we make a bigger improvement from the point of view of noncomparative desert by improving A or B cannot be settled merely by knowing who has a higher peak. For even if B has a higher peak and so deserves more *absolutely*, she might be closer to her peak, while A is quite far below his—and so helping A a fixed amount might do more good (in terms of desert) than would helping B (curved desert, for example, might yield this). Thus, in this specific case, we do more good—as far as desert is concerned—to help A. We can say that A is more *specifically* deserving, even though less absolutely deserving. Note, finally, that if one accepts comparative desert, then this might influence specific desert too (though whether one could be more specifically deserving in terms of noncomparative desert, and yet not be more specifically deserving in terms of comparative desert, is a question I won't pursue).

5

On the face of it, I suppose, one might think that both equality *and* desert matter. Or one might accept one but not the other. (As I noted, many people initially accept equality, and they are at least less certain about desert, though I shall argue that this gets things backwards.) Alternatively, one might think that neither of these matter at all. I won't be defending the claim that *either* of these is a plausible value, though I do think that, on the face of it, *both* are.

The question I really want to pursue is this: Given that one is attracted to a pluralism that includes (at least initially) equality, and (perhaps) desert, how exactly should this be worked out? As I have already suggested, I suspect that at the end of the day we should have some uncertainty about equality and be more confident about desert.

But my *central* goal is to argue that it is at least far from clear what view we should take about this and far more difficult to test distinct views here than meets the eye.

6

Suppose we start with equality. We have—or at least many of us have—the intuition that if A is worse off than B, and we can help one but not both by some fixed amount, then it is better to help A. Helping A makes a greater improvement in terms of the overall goodness of the outcome than does helping B; we can say, in this light, that A has a greater claim than B. Of course, the improvement in terms of the *amount* of well-being would be the same regardless of whom we help (this is stipulated). But that is the very reason that it seems we should accept the value of equality, since it supports the intuition that it is better to help A: From the point of view of equality, since A is worse off than B, an increase in A's well-being makes a greater contribution to the good than does a similar increase in B's well-being (recall that both weighted beneficence and strict equality agree about this). There is, in effect, a "boost"—because of the importance of equality—to A's claim to being helped as compared to B's claim. (Strictly, weighted beneficence gives a boost to *both* A and B, though a stronger one to A, while strict equality gives a boost to A alone; either way, however, we can talk of the "equality boost" given to A's claim as compared to B's.)

For our purposes, the trouble with this argument is this: Equality offers *one* way to explain the intuition that we should help A rather than B; but it is not the only way. What about considerations of desert?

We might try to block this rival explanation by making A and B equally deserving. Suppose they have the same peak—and suppose that both are below this peak, so desert favors helping both. And suppose further that slopes are linear (that is, straight desert). Then each unit of extra well-being makes the same contribution, regardless of which person we help. So desert is indifferent between helping A and helping B. And so, if we do think it better to help A, this must be due to something other than desert. (It might not be equality, of course, but at least that appears to be a live possibility.)

But this is all too quick. For even given that A and B have the same peak, one might accept views in the theory of desert that would entail that A is in fact more *specifically* deserving. First of all, we might accept comparative desert. Note that A is further from the shared peak than B. Since they are equally deserving, comparative desert considers it bad that A has less than B—which is to say that it would be an improvement as far as comparative desert is concerned if we help A rather than B (helping B rather than A makes things *worse*).

Second, we might prefer *curved* desert. For straight desert, of course, distance from the peak makes no difference to the slope, and so the fact that A is further from the peak than B makes no difference in terms of the noncomparative claim that each can make: helping either a fixed amount makes the same improvement. But if we accept curved desert, then each extra unit of well-being we fall further and further below the peak makes for a greater and greater *incremental* drop in terms of desert. So curved desert says that it is better to help A than B, since A is further from the shared peak.

In short, both comparative desert and curved desert advocate helping A—just as equality does. And this leaves it at least somewhat unclear whether we should believe in equality alone, or both equality and desert (in the guise of comparative desert and curved desert)—or perhaps just desert alone.

7

What about the possibility of *lowering* B? Suppose, as before, that A is worse off than B, and that both are below their shared peak, but assume now that we cannot help A. We can, however, lower B somewhat (while still leaving her no worse off than A). Is this an improvement?

As we have seen, egalitarians differ over this point. From the standpoint of weighted beneficence, of course, there is nothing to be said in favor of lowering B (since doing so hurts B without helping A). On the other hand, those who accept strict equality hold that, in at least one respect, this is indeed an improvement—for lowering B reduces the level of (strict) inequality. Of course, it may not be an improvement *overall*; lowering B obviously involves a loss in well-being as well, and this may outweigh the gain in equality. But still, according to strict equality, there is at least *something* to be said in favor of lowering B.

So if we, too, think that there is at least something to be said in favor of lowering B, does this show that we, too, should accept strict equality? Do we have here a potential egalitarian intuition that cannot be accommodated by desert?

Not necessarily. Admittedly, noncomparative desert (including curved desert) gives us no reason to lower B (since we are assuming that both A and B are below their shared peak). But *comparative* desert is like strict equality in holding that there is *some* reason to lower B. After all, A and B are assumed to be equally deserving, and so comparative desert considers it a bad thing if B is doing better than A. According to comparative desert, then, this gives us some reason to lower B.

Of course, as I noted in section 4, some people are inclined to reject comparative desert for this very reason. But, obviously enough, no one who accepts strict equality is

going to argue for rejecting comparative desert on this basis. So even if we *do* believe that there is some reason to lower B, this leaves it open as to whether we should accept both equality (including, in particular, strict equality) *and* desert (including, in particular, comparative desert) or only one of the two.

Suppose, on the other hand, that we believe that there is *no* reason to lower B. Obviously, we will now have reason to reject both strict equality *and* comparative desert (since both hold that there is indeed some reason to lower B). But doing so still leaves open the possibility of accepting either weighted beneficence or noncomparative desert (including curved desert), or both. And so we are no further along in trying to choose between equality and desert.

So what should we accept? Equality *and* desert? Or only one, and if so, which one? Ultimately, it seems, we will need to find some other test case to help us with all of this.

8

Various cases are relevant, but here is an important one. Call this case *Twin Peaks*.[7] We might think of this situation in these terms: A is a sinner, who is doing better than his peak, better than he absolutely deserves to be doing. B is a saint and is doing less well than she deserves to be doing; she is below her peak. We can help either A or B by some fixed amount of well-being. Who should we help?

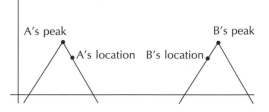

Equality says to help A, since A is at a lower level than B. Both strict equality and weighted beneficence agree about this.

But *desert* says to help B, since she is below her peak, while A is above his, and so helping B is an improvement, whereas helping A makes things worse off. Both noncomparative desert and comparative desert agree about this. (Note that this is a case—unlike the one discussed in the preceding section—where comparative desert differs from strict equality. Since A is far less deserving than B, yet is doing better than he deserves to be, while B is doing worse than she deserves to be, comparative desert—unlike strict equality—favors helping B rather than A, even though A is worse off than B.)

Now I think it quite clear, intuitively, that we should help B. I imagine that virtually everyone will agree. After all, B is a saint who is getting less than she deserves, while A is a sinner who is doing better than he deserves. Surely, say I, it is better to help B. For simplicity, I will assume that you agree, too.

At a minimum, then, this supports the thought that desert is a genuine value. But this is still compatible with two further rival claims. The first holds that desert is a genuine value, but equality is not. The alternative is that equality is a genuine value as well (although here it is outweighed by desert). According to the second claim, there is at least a *respect* in which it would be better to help A than B (even though it is outweighed); there is at least *some* reason to favor A over B.

I suppose intuitions may be less forceful on this second question, but when I ask whether there is any respect at all in which it would be better to help A rather than B, I am inclined to think the answer is no. Intuitively speaking, it seems to me that there is *no* reason to favor A over B in this case. (This should not be confused with the claim that there is nothing at all to be said in favor of helping A. There is certainly some reason to help A, since helping A increases the total amount of well-being. But since B's benefit would be just as big, well-being won't favor helping A *rather* than B.)

Does this show, then, that equality is not a genuine factor at all? It seems to. But appearances may be deceptive.

9

Perhaps we should *weaken* equality so that it says something like this: Equality matters, but only for equally deserving people.

The thought here, of course, is that there are different ways to be a pluralist, even with the very same values. So far we have been assuming a kind of *strong* pluralism, which holds that equality is always relevant, always weighing in (even though it can be outweighed). But a more *modest* pluralism might hold that equality has weight only under certain conditions, and, in particular, only if the people concerned are equally deserving. Since the Twin Peaks case involves someone far more deserving than A, namely B, there is no equality boost to A's claim.

Speaking more generally (and somewhat roughly), there are at least the following possibilities for pluralists that recognize two real factors, X and Y: (1) X always matters (though it can be outweighed), and Y always matters (though it can be outweighed); (2) X always matters, but Y matters only when it is supported by X (or vice versa); (3) X and Y both matter, but only when supported by the other. The first is what I have just called strong pluralism—the moral factors are independent of one another. The second is a kind of "interactive" pluralism, since, in effect, one factor, X, is a condition of the relevance of the other, Y, but it is an asymmetric dependence (since X matters even in the absence of Y). In the third case, the dependence relation is symmetric, which means, in effect, that there is really just a "single" complex factor (X&Y).

Twin Peaks seems to show that strong pluralism is the wrong model for thinking about equality and desert. According to strong pluralism, equality should weigh in on behalf of helping A (rather than B), regardless of considerations of desert. But I am assuming that equality doesn't weigh in on behalf of helping A in Twin Peaks, so, at the very least, equality is not strongly independent of desert.

It could be that equality doesn't matter at all. But the other two pluralistic models remain open as well. It might be, as I have noted, that equality comes into play only among equally deserving people. This would be pluralism of the second kind. Equality would depend on considerations of desert, but when it did come into play, it would add an *extra* (or extra-strong) boost to the claim of the person at the lower level (beyond whatever effect desert might have). So this would be a genuine pluralism. According to this second model, however, the situation would be asymmetric: Desert could come into play, regardless of equality.

What about the third pluralistic possibility? Could it be that the dependence is symmetric, that desert is conditionally dependent on equality? This doesn't seem likely, since it would presumably mean something like this: that desert matters only when it is a matter of helping the worse off of two individuals. But, in the Twin Peaks case, considerations of desert seem relevant, and they seem to point in favor of helping the better-off person.

So the two remaining possibilities are these: Equality doesn't matter at all, or it does matter, but only for equally deserving people, where it adds an extra boost. In comparison to egalitarianism as we originally understood it, where equality was an independent value, this would be a *restricted* version of egalitarianism, with a corresponding value of *restricted equality*. Restricted equality would agree with our intuitive verdict in Twin Peaks: Given that A is less deserving than B, restricted equality doesn't even come into play, and thus there is no extra boost for A. So should we accept *restricted* equality, or should we reject equality altogether?

10

To test between these two alternatives, we need to find a case involving "equally deserving people" at different levels—to be sure to bring the restricted equality effect into play. What we want to do, obviously, is to see in such a case if the worse-off person gets an extra boost that cannot be explained in terms of desert. Of course, even if there is an extra boost, there might be some explanation other

than restricted equality, but if there is no boost, then that pretty much should rule out restricted equality.

But first we need to get clear about the restriction we have added. What exactly is the condition that restricted equality requires before giving a differential boost to the worse-off person? I've talked loosely about it needing to be the case that people are "equally deserving" before getting the restricted equality boost, and it is clear that this condition—whatever exactly it comes to—is not supposed to be met in the Twin Peaks case. But what, exactly, does it come to?

First, I assume that we don't really mean to require that, if there are two parties, they must both be equally deserving. If the worse-off individual is *more* deserving than the better off individual, I presume that restricted equality can still come into play and give the worse-off individual an extra boost. Surely, all we mean to rule out is restricted equality's weighing in on behalf of someone who is *less* deserving than another party we could help. That is, restricted equality has no boost when considerations of desert *oppose* helping the person who would otherwise be boosted by restricted equality. Provided that the lower person is *as* deserving as the other person we could help (which is compatible with his being *more* deserving), this will suffice.[8]

Second, when we insist that restricted equality give a boost only to someone who is as deserving, do we mean "absolutely" deserving or "specifically" deserving? These can come apart. Someone's peak might be lower; hence, he is less deserving, absolutely speaking. But he might, say, be further from his peak, and so (given curved desert or comparative desert) it might be that more good would be done by helping him a fixed amount, which is to say he is more deserving in this specific situation—more *specifically* deserving. So what do we want before restricted equality can provide a boost? Must the person be at least as deserving in terms of (1) absolute desert, (2) specific desert, (3) either, or (4) both?

I am inclined to think that specific desert alone is the relevant condition for a plausible version of restricted equality. Consider a case in which A is only very slightly less absolutely deserving than B—that is, his peak is slightly lower—but A is considerably farther *away* from his peak, so that he is far more specifically deserving. I am inclined to think that if restricted equality does indeed ever provide a boost, it will do so in such a case as well. (After all, this is *almost* like a case in which someone is far worse off and doesn't deserve *any* of the inequality—a paradigm case for restricted equality. It is just that in this case a very *small* amount of the difference between A and B can be justified in terms of desert, and it is hard to believe that his deprives restricted equality of any purchase at all.) So, it seems that being as specifically deserving should suffice for restricted equality, even in the absence of being as absolutely deserving. (Note that if there is comparative desert, then this can enter into specific desert, too, and I presume that this too can be relevant for restricted equality. But if not, then it could still be that restricted equality responds to non-comparative specific desert.)

What about the reverse? Could absolute desert suffice in the absence of specific desert? As far as I can see, the kind of case we would need to think about can't arise. We would need to imagine A worse off than B (to get restricted equality into play), but A would have to be as absolutely deserving as B. But together these mean that A is farther from his peak than B, and so—given curved desert and comparative desert—A is more specifically deserving as well. That is, specific desert can favor the worse off, whether or not he is more absolutely deserving, and that seems enough for restricted equality. But the worse off cannot be absolutely more deserving without also being more specifically deserving. So it seems that the worse-off person's being as specifically deserving is both necessary and sufficient for the restricted equality boost. (Might the restricted equality boost be even bigger when A both specifically and absolutely deserves it, rather than merely specifically? I will put this possibility aside.)

One way of summarizing all of this would be to say that according to restricted equality, the claims of the worse off get a boost compared to the claims of the better off—unless considerations of specific desert oppose this (perhaps because someone is more specifically deserving), in which case there is no such boost.[9]

11

We can now return to the question of choosing between accepting restricted equality (suitably interpreted) and denying that equality has any relevance at all. What kind of case could we use to test between these alternatives?

The easiest case to start with might be this: Imagine that A and B have the same peak, but A is worse off. Since A is as deserving as B, restricted equality can give a boost to A's claim to be helped rather than B. So all we have to do is decide whether or not this is so. If there is such a boost, then restricted equality might be true; if there isn't, it can't be.

Unfortunately, it is hard to tell whether there is such a boost, since, of course, desert favors helping A too. (Straight desert wouldn't do this, but curved desert and comparative desert would.) When we feel that it is better to help A, are we merely responding to the fact that A is more specifically deserving, or are we also responding in part to the effect of restricted equality?

In principle, I suppose, if we had a well-developed theory of desert, we might be in a position to determine how great A's claim should be on the basis of desert. If we then decided that A's claim was even greater than this, that would support the thought that restricted equality was at work, and not just desert. But we obviously have nothing like this, and so we will need some other way to tell whether restricted equality has any effect.[10]

In general terms, then, the situation is this. To detect whether restricted equality has any genuine effect, it seems we need to compare the claims of people at different levels of well-being. Since restricted equality gives a (greater) boost to the claims of the worse off, this should make the lower person's claim (to be helped a fixed amount) greater. But, as we know, if considerations of desert oppose helping the lower person, then restricted equality won't come into play at all. So desert must either favor helping the lower person or be neutral. But, as we have just seen, if desert *favors* helping the worse-off person, then it will be difficult or impossible to be sure that there is any *further* effect at work beyond desert.

So it seems we must find a case where desert is neutral as to helping the better-off or the worse-off person. If we could find such a case, and then found that intuitively it still seemed as if the worse-off person had a stronger claim, this would support the thought that something more than desert was at work—perhaps restricted equality.[11]

12

The sort of case we need seems to be this. A must be lower than B. Now if A and B have the same peak (and assuming, for simplicity, that both are below it), then A is further from his peak than B is, and so curved desert favors helping A. But we are trying to avoid having a case where desert favors helping A. So A must have a lower peak than B. Of course, if A's peak is so far down that A is in fact beyond it (as in the Twin Peaks case), desert will oppose helping A, and we don't want that either. So A must be below his lower peak. Indeed, A must be the same distance below his peak as B is below her higher peak. This will keep curved desert indifferent between helping A and helping B. (And, given plausible views concerning comparative desert, this will be indifferent too.) The situation will look like this:

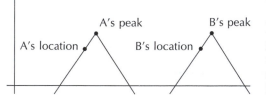

Call this case *Revised Twin Peaks*; it seems to be the case we were looking for. Desert is indifferent between helping A and helping B, so restricted equality can come into play, giving an extra boost to A's claim over B's. So, if restricted equality is a genuine value, A should have a stronger claim to being helped than B does.

Now I can hardly pretend that our intuitions are likely to be firm here, or that everyone will agree. But, for myself, I don't find myself at all inclined to think that A's claim is *stronger* than B's. Rather, I find myself inclined to think that B's claim is every bit as strong as A's. And this certainly seems to speak against restricted equality.

Actually, however, I often find myself inclined to think that A's claim is *weaker* than B's. This is the result, usually, of my thinking that A might well be a sinner, and B a saint. If they are equal distance from their peaks, I find myself thinking, it is more important to help the saint, B.

But this brings to mind one of the complications I noted in section 3, the possibility of bell-motion. For those who accept bell-motion, the more absolutely deserving you are, the steeper the slope on the western side of the peak. This means that an equal distance from the peak is worse, the more deserving you are. And so, if we stipulate that A is the same distance from his low peak as B is from her high peak, then in fact desert will favor helping B—which, of course, is the very intuition I have. But this is something we were trying to avoid, for if desert actually favors helping B, then A is not at least as specifically deserving, and so restricted equality will not give A the boost we were trying to detect.

Accordingly, anyone who accepts bell-motion should actually make B slightly *closer* to her peak than A is to his, to correct for this effect and keep desert indifferent.

But now the problem is obviously this: How *much* closer should we make B to her peak? If we had a general theory of desert, we might know how much closer (if any) we need to make B, to exactly correct for the bell-motion, so as to keep desert indifferent.

But we lack such a theory. Sadly, this leaves the test rather limited in its usefulness. If we correct too little, then the advocate of restricted equality can properly insist that the fact that we favor helping B proves nothing about restricted equality. But if we correct too much—bringing B too close to her peak—then A will now be more specifically deserving, and even if we agree that we should favor A rather than B, we won't be able to tell whether this is because of a restricted equality boost rather than being due to desert alone.[12]

By this time, I suspect, most people will be unwilling to put all that much weight upon their intuitions about this case. I certainly don't find my own intuitions all that strong. But this is not to say that I have no intuitions whatsoever. As I said, I find myself inclined to think that B's claim is at least as strong as A's (perhaps even stronger, when distance from the peak is kept constant). At the very least, it is worth emphasizing the fact that these intuitions provide no support for restricted equality.

13

Of course, one might well have a general methodological qualm about thinking about cases as "thinly" described as the ones I have been giving. Perhaps such cases are too abstract for us to generate intuitions about them, or perhaps we shouldn't trust those intuitions that we do have.

Unfortunately, I can't take the space here to give a full response to this worry. I certainly do think there is a limit to how much justificatory weight we should give to our case-specific intuitions. But I think this about more concrete cases, too; I am not especially inclined to dismiss our intuitions about our abstract cases merely because they are so abstractly described. Obviously, this is not to deny that our intuitions about some of these abstract cases will be more forceful than for others. And I have, in fact, just pointed out that in what seems to be the key relevant case

for deciding whether or not restricted equality is a factor along with desert, our intuitions may be rather weak. But I think we would overgeneralize to think that thin and abstract cases never generate intuitions at all.

Furthermore, I suspect that we don't have all that much practice thinking directly about issues of desert and equality; so it might be that with further dialectical exercise, the relevant intuitions would become clearer. Alternatively, it might be that the intuitions would become firmer if we were to put some flesh on these cases, instead of reflecting upon the mere structural bones. I won't try to do that here, though I do think something of value would still have been accomplished if we simply got clearer about what underlying structure the relevant test cases would have to have. And, if nothing else, thinking about these abstract cases, and seeing that the intuitions are less straightforward than we might have hoped, may demonstrate that our own beliefs about equality and desert are less clear than we might have otherwise taken them to be.

For the most part, then, I am content if I succeed in showing what some of the issues are in thinking about equality and desert, and what sorts of cases are relevant for distinguishing between rival views. But there is no point in my pretending that I have no intuitions about these cases, and so I will continue to report my tentative conclusions as well.

14

Here is a slightly different sort of case (a variant on the one described in section 12) that it may be helpful to think about as well. Really, what I want to consider is a *range* of cases, in which all the basic facts about A and B are kept fixed, except that we vary the location of B's peak. We can call this range of cases *Moving Peaks*.

Suppose, then, that A is rather far below his peak and is considerably worse off than B. (For simplicity, we can imagine that B is doing better than A's peak.) I want to keep all of this fixed in what follows; all that varies is the location of B's peak. We can begin by imagining that B's peak is even lower than A's. In this case, obviously, since B is less absolutely deserving than A, and A is below his peak, while B is beyond hers, A is far more specifically deserving than B. And since this trivially means that A is at least *as* specifically deserving as B, it should also mean that A's claim gets a further boost from restricted equality.

Now consider what happens as we slowly increase B's peak, imagining B as more and more absolutely deserving. Slowly but surely, B's specific desert claim grows stronger—although, no doubt, for a good long time B's specific desert claim remains weaker than A's. At some point B's peak will actually be higher than A's, and so A will be more deserving absolutely than B, but, even when this happens, at least initially, B will still be beyond her peak, while A will remain below his, and so it will remain the case that A is more specifically deserving than B. Eventually B's peak will increase sufficiently so that B is just immediately below it. But, even at this point, A will be more specifically deserving, since A will be *so* much further below his peak than B is below hers.

At a later point still, B's peak will be sufficiently high, and B will be sufficiently far below her peak, so that B will now be just as specifically deserving as A. Desert will now be indifferent between helping A and helping B. This is, of course, the Revised Twin Peaks case, described in section 12. As we saw there, it is difficult to be sure where exactly B's peak needs to be to have such a case (it depends on whether there is bell-motion or not, and, if so, how much), but nothing called into question the claim that there must be such a point. Call this the "indifference point."

Now make B even more deserving absolutely. As B's peak moves beyond the indifference point, it is now the case that B is *so* far below her (now extremely high) peak that she is *more* specifically deserving than A. And the higher the peak, of course, the greater is her specific desert claim compared to A's.

Consider what happens to *A's* claim during all of this. As far as A's noncomparative desert claim goes, nothing ever changes: He remains a fixed distance below his unchanging peak. But initially A has a comparative desert claim as well (since A is initially below his peak, while B is beyond hers). Of course, as we increase B's peak, A's comparative desert claim grows progressively weaker, eventually vanishing, and, after that, comparative desert favors helping B more and more. Thus, if we look at A's *overall* specific desert claim, it grows steadily smaller and smaller.

Now think about A's claim in terms of restricted equality. Initially, as we saw, A was more specifically deserving, and so A's claim got the restricted equality boost. Even when B's peak has reached the indifference point, A remains *as* specifically deserving as B, and so the restricted equality boost remains in place. But the very moment that B's peak moves beyond the indifference point, B becomes *more* specifically deserving than A, and so, according to restricted equality, A no longer receives the boost.

According to restricted equality, therefore, A's claim should show a marked discontinuity: As B's peak increases, A's overall claim—desert plus restricted equality boost—should grow steadily and smoothly smaller, since A's desert claim grows continuously smaller. But just beyond the indifference point, A's restricted equality boost disappears completely in a single step—and so the overall strength of A's claim should drop discontinuously. Indeed, given that A is considerably worse off than B, the boost from restricted equality (when it's there) should be rather significant; when that boost disappears, the discontinuous drop in A's claim should itself be a significant one.

But, when I think about this range of cases, I find *no* intuitive discontinuity at all. When I think about how the strength of A's claim varies, it gets smaller, but smoothly, not discontinuously. I certainly don't find myself inclined to think that at some point there is a sharp and significant discontinuous drop.

The same intuitive judgment remains when I think about this question in terms of comparing how A's claim compares to B's during all of this. According to restricted equality, it not only should get progressively smaller compared to B's—initially it is larger, but eventually it is smaller—but should do so discontinuously. But I don't find myself at all tempted to ascribe such a discontinuity. It seems to me that A's claim does grow smaller compared to B's, but smoothly, without discontinuity.

I conclude, therefore, that restricted equality is not in fact a genuine value. Perhaps others will have different intuitions than mine when thinking about Moving Peaks, or perhaps none at all. But I find that I am not at all tempted to ascribe the discontinuity that restricted equality needs. And so, however tentatively, I reject restricted equality.

But the original Twin Peaks case (from section 8) seemed to show that egalitarianism itself was implausible unless understood in keeping with *restricted* equality. And so I tentatively conclude that egalitarianism should not be accepted after all.

15

We saw in sections 6 and 7 that various aspects of desert—in particular, curved desert and comparative desert—could explain some of the cases that might otherwise be thought to support equality. But we wondered, nonetheless, whether there might still be some further boost due to equality alone. I have now argued that this is not the case. Beyond considerations of desert itself, there is no *further* reason to eliminate inequality (not even when that inequality is undeserved). Once we accept *desert*, there is no reason to accept equality as well.

Some would object, however, that even if my arguments are sound, I have not actually shown the irrelevance of equality. Rather, they would claim, I have simply incorporated egalitarian considerations directly into my theory of desert. Obviously, if anything like this is correct, it is hardly surprising that equality has no *further* significance—beyond that already implicitly recognized by the (equality-influenced) account of desert.

For example, one might think that there is no real choice to be made between curved desert and equality. After all (it might be argued), *curving* the graph, which is what curved desert does (as opposed to straight desert, which keeps the slope linear) is simply a way of *incorporating* the thought behind weighted beneficence that the lower down someone is, the more reason there is to help her. That is (it might be suggested), all that "pure" desert by itself supports is straight desert; if we then add weighted beneficence, the joint result is curved desert. So curved desert already admits the relevance of weighted beneficence.

But this claim is mistaken. According to weighted beneficence, what's relevant (for determining the strength of the boost to someone's claim) is the person's absolute level of well-being. According to curved desert, in contrast, what matters is the *distance* from the person's *peak*. In and of itself, the absolute level of well-being is irrelevant.

So the motivations behind the two views are rather different, and we can easily see this by noting that they can come apart. Compare the strength of A's claim to be helped, when he is at a certain level of well-being, and a certain distance below his peak, with his claim when he is at a *higher* level of well-being, but is now even *further* from his (now even higher) peak. Weighted beneficence says that the claim gets weaker, since A is now better off. But curved desert says that the claim gets stronger, since A is now further from his peak. For myself, I think that A's claim does get stronger, though I suppose that some might disagree. But in any event, this simple case does at least show that weighted beneficence and curved desert have different intuitions lying behind them. Appeal to curved desert does not simply smuggle in an unrecognized concern with equality.[13]

In a similar vein, some might argue that talk of comparative desert just *is* a way of accepting the importance of strict equality—that it is the very same concern, incorporated into the theory of desert.

It is not quite as easy to dismiss this new suggestion, for both strict equality and comparative desert are sensitive to relative standings, and restricted strict equality in particular seems quite similar to comparative desert: Both hold that when one person is worse off than another but just as deserving, there is more reason to help the worse-off person than the better-off, and there is some reason to lower the better-off.

Nonetheless it seems to me rather misleading to say that comparative desert is fundamentally egalitarian in its concern, in the way that restricted strict equality obviously is. It is, of course, true that when we are dealing with two people who are equally deserving, then comparative desert favors equality. But this is just a particular case. It gives us no good reason to think of comparative desert as being especially egalitarian. After all, it is just as true that in all other cases, where the two people are *not* equally deserving, comparative desert favors *inequality*. So there is no more reason to think of comparative desert as being fundamentally egalitarian than the opposite. (Furthermore, since I presume that in realistic cases differences in desert will be rather common, there is also no reason to say that, from a *practical* point of view, comparative desert will tend to be egalitarian.) Comparative desert, like strict equality, is concerned with relative standings—but the nature of the concern is really rather different.

16

Let me mention one final suggestion that might be made on behalf of the egalitarian. In this essay I have tried to avoid taking a detailed stand concerning the question of what it is that makes one person more morally deserving than another. I have assumed, of course, that one person's peak can indeed be higher or lower than that of another, but beyond some vague talk about good and bad people, and saints and sinners, I've said nothing about how it is that a given person's peak is fixed.

One possible view on this issue holds that everyone "starts off" equally deserving. That is, according to this view, there is a certain level of well-being that *everyone* deserves, at least initially (perhaps simply by virtue of being a person). Presumably, of course, our moral track record can alter this level, leaving us more or less deserving, with higher or lower peaks. But such individual variation should be seen as just that—a departure from the initial shared baseline. If a view like this is correct, then equality still plays an important role in our moral theory, for the initial desert baseline is presumed to be the same for everyone; it is, in effect, an *egalitarian* baseline.

Although this is not the only possible view concerning these matters, this is, undeniably, a plausible and attractive possibility. So let me concede that if something like this view is correct, then there is indeed a sense in which equality remains a genuine value.

But it is important not to exaggerate or misunderstand this sense. Equality would be important simply as a *part* of the theory of desert. If this is the only genuine role for equality, then it cannot be claimed that equality has a content that can be understood independent of considerations of desert, making a contribution to the goodness of outcomes (at least, under the right circumstances) that goes beyond that made by considerations of desert itself. Nor could it be accurately claimed that the theory of desert avoids giving at least a partially independent role to equality by the somewhat illicit subterfuge of *incorporating* egalitarian notions that would otherwise be extraneous to a more "pure" theory of desert. On the contrary, equality would not be a value that could be appropriately *contrasted* with desert at all; it would simply be that in *some* ways (though not in others) people are equally *deserving*.

17

I suspect that if you were to take a poll among moral philosophers, the result would show that many or most believe in equality, while far fewer are confident about whether desert has any intrinsic moral significance. For reasons that I have been trying to bring out, however, I think that this may get things rather backwards. It seems to me that the intuitive support for desert is strong and clear. What is rather less clear is whether there is any reason to believe that equality matters, too. Even if it does, it seems to me quite unlikely to be a strongly independent value. At best, it seems to be asymmetrically dependent upon considerations of desert. But, as we have now seen, there is in fact some reason to suspect that equality may not have even this much significance. It may simply be that in some ways people are equally deserving, while in others they are not.

Perhaps, then, we should not believe in equality at all, but only desert.

NOTES

1. In what follows I draw from a considerably larger work in progress, *The Geometry of Desert*.
2. See Larry Temkin, *Inequality* (Oxford, 1993), for a wonderful discussion of these issues.
3. Following Derek Parfit, who defends it in *Equality or Priority* (University of Kansas, 1995). The idea is also discussed by Temkin, in *Inequality*, under the label "extended humanitarianism."
4. Perhaps I should mention another possible egalitarian view. Like strict equality, it is essentially comparative—it comes into play only when someone is worse off than another. But unlike strict equality, which in such a situation thinks it is an improvement to either raise the worse off, or lower the better off, this new view would only consider it an improvement if the worse off were raised.

    Such a view would lead to intransitive judgments. Consider three worlds. In W_1, A is below B. In W_2, A is at B's high level. In W_3, B is at A's low level. Obviously, this new view will say that W_2 is better than W_1. How do W_2 and W_3 compare? Both have perfect equality, so, as far as this new view is concerned, W_3 is no worse than W_2. But if W_3 is no worse than W_2 which is better than W_1, then by transitivity we have W_3 is better than W_1. Yet this new view does *not* consider W_3 better than W_1 (since inequality is improved, says this view, only when we help the worse off).

    Since this view violates intransitivity, I put it aside (though anyone attracted to it should note that perhaps we are too quick to assume transitivity of "better than." See Larry Temkin, "Intransitivity and the Mere Addition Paradox," *Philosophy & Public Affairs* 16 [1987]: 138–187).
5. Following Temkin, in *Inequality*.

6. For simplicity, I am neglecting details and complications that I explore more fully in *The Geometry of Desert*.
7. Note that, for simplicity, I continue to draw the desert graphs with straight lines. But those who—like me—accept curved desert, rather than straight desert, should imagine the lines slightly curved (that is, with the mountains puffed out on both sides).
8. I take it, however, that even if there is just *one* person in a world, the restriction we are imagining is satisfied, provided that considerations of desert don't oppose helping him. Of course, if there is indeed only one person, then considerations of *strict* equality cannot come into play at all (this being an essentially comparative notion), so no matter how deserving the person is, restricted strict equality won't be relevant. But *weighted beneficence* gives everyone a boost of some sort, even isolated individuals (the lower the person, the greater the boost). Thus, restricted weighted beneficence provides a boost even to an *isolated* individual, provided that considerations of desert don't oppose this.
9. Note, in passing, that restricted equality is an essentially comparative notion (even when it takes the form of restricted weighted beneficence). We can't tell whether restricted equality gives a boost to A's claim merely by looking at facts about A; we must also make sure that no one else is more deserving.
10. Of course, if we *could* do this, then those who believe in restricted weighted beneficence could appeal to an even simpler test case. We would simply imagine a world with a single individual below his peak. (See note 8, on the possibility of doing this.) Given our general theory of desert, we would see how strong his claim should be, and then we would see whether his claim is in fact stronger. If it is, this would support the thought that restricted weighted beneficence was providing the extra boost. Of course, such a test won't work for restricted strict equality, since that comes into play only for situations involving more than one person. But, in any event, we have no such general theory of desert, so these "simple" tests are inadequate.
11. Note that, for restricted weighted beneficence (but not for restricted strict equality; again, see note 8), there appear to be two different ways we might set up a test like this. We might imagine a single world with two individuals (one lower than the other, but equally specifically deserving). Or we might imagine two different worlds with one isolated individual each (one lower than the other, but equally specifically deserving). Either way, we would compare the strength of the claim of the worse off to that of the better off and see if it was stronger.

    There are, perhaps, some mild advantages to the second approach. Since each individual is imagined to be the only person in the world, it is slightly easier to guarantee that considerations of desert don't oppose helping the person. Some of this would follow trivially: Since there is no one else, no one else in that world can have a greater desert claim. And since there is no one else, comparative desert will be silent as well. (Of course, we will still have to be sure that each person is below her peak.)

Despite these slight differences, however, I think it somewhat easier to think about the more familiar cases with two people in a single world. Most important, I don't think we get different intuitive responses when we run the tests one way rather than another (though I may be wrong about this). At any rate, for simplicity, I'll stick to cases of the familiar kind; this also allows us to continue examining restricted weighted beneficence and restricted strict equality at the same time.

12. Might this be a place where it would be helpful to compare the claims of two isolated individuals, rather than two people in a single world (see note 11)? Suppose the case is otherwise as we originally described: A is lower than B and is the same distance from his low peak as B is from her higher one. Even if there is bell-motion, if A and B are not in the same world, there won't be anyone in A's world who is more deserving than A,

so it seems that restricted weighted beneficence could still come into play, giving a stronger boost to A than to B (who is, after all, better off). We also don't have to worry about finding the exact amount to move B closer to her peak, to correct for bell-motion. (Of course, if there is bell-motion, then B is more deserving than A—but it might still be that A's restricted equality boost is great enough to outweigh this.)

Here, too, however, I find no inclination to think that A's claim is greater. And so the example provides no support for restricted weighted beneficence in my own mind. At this point, of course, the advocate of restricted weighted beneficence could claim that the restricted equality boost is outweighed by the fact that B is more deserving. But, to test this, we would have to make desert indifferent, and so we would need to correct for bell-motion after all. And this means we still need to determine how *much* to correct. In short, there seems to be no real advantage to altering the example.

13. What curved desert and weighted beneficence do have in common, of course, is that both give *priority* to the claims of those who fall most short in terms of some favored value (well-being for weighted beneficence; getting what you deserve for curved desert).

Bibliography

Adkins, A. W. H. *Merit and Responsibility: A Study of Greek Values*. Chicago: University of Chicago Press, 1960.

Adler, Jonathan. "Luckless Desert is Different Desert," *Mind* 96 (April 1997), pp. 247–249.

Annis, David B., and Cecil E. Bohanon. "Desert and Property Rights," *Journal of Value Inquiry* 26 (October 1992), pp. 537–546.

Arnold, N. Scott. "Why Profits are Deserved," *Ethics* 97 (January 1987), pp. 387–402.

Atkinson, Max. "Justified and Deserved Punishments," *Mind* 78 (1969), pp. 354–374.

Barry, Brian. *Political Argument*. London: Routledge and Kegan Paul, 1965.

———. *Liberty and Justice: Essays in Political Theory* 2. Oxford: Clarendon Press, 1991.

Becker, Lawrence C. *Property Rights: Philosophic Foundations*. London: Routledge and Kegan Paul, 1977.

Benn, S. I., and R. S. Peters. *The Principles of Political Thought*, New York, NY: The Free Press, 1959.

Campbell, Tom. *Justice*. Atlantic Highlands, N.J.: Humanities Press International, 1988.

Card, Claudia. "On Mercy," *Philosophical Review* 81 (1972), pp. 182–207.

Cummiskey, David. "Desert and Entitlement: A Rawlsian Consequentialist Account," *Analysis* 47 (1987), pp. 15–19.

Cupit, Geoffrey. "Desert and Responsibility," *Canadian Journal of Philosophy* 26 (March 1996), pp. 83–100.

———. *Justice as Fittingness*. Oxford: Clarendon Press, 1996.

Davis, Michael. "How to Make the Punishment Fit the Crime," in *Criminal Justice: Nomos XXVII*, ed. Roland J. Pennock and John W. Chapman. New York: New York University Press, 1985, pp. 119–155.

Dennett, Daniel. *Elbow Room*. Cambridge: Massachusetts Institute of Technology Press, 1984.

Dick, James. "How to Justify a Distribution of Earnings," *Philosophy and Public Affairs* 4 (Spring 1975), pp. 248–272.

Duncan-Jones, Austin. *Butler's Moral Philosophy*. Harmondsworth: Penguin Books, 1952.

England, Paula. *Comparable Worth: Theories and Evidence*. New York: Aldine de Gruyter, 1992.

Ezorsky, Gertrude (ed.). *Philosophical Perspectives on Punishment*, Albany: New York University Press, 1972.

Feinberg, Joel. *Doing and Deserving*. Princeton: Princeton University Press, 1970.

———. *Social Philosophy*. Englewood Cliffs, N.J.: Prentice-Hall, 1973.

Feldman, Fred. *Confrontations With the Reaper*. Oxford: Oxford University Press, 1992.

———. "Justice, Desert, and the Repugnant Conclusion," *Utilitas* 7 (November 1995), pp. 189–206.

———. *Utilitarianism, Hedonism, and Desert*. Cambridge: Cambridge University Press, forthcoming, 1997.

Fields, Lloyd. "Parfit on Personal Identity and Desert," *Philosophical Quarterly* 37 (1987), pp. 432–440.

Galston, William. *Justice and the Human Good*, Chicago: University of Chicago Press, 1992.

Garcia, J. L. A. "A Problem about the Basis of Desert," *Journal of Social Philosophy* (1988), pp. 11–19.

Gaus, Gerald F. *Value and Justification: The Foundations of Liberal Theory*. Cambridge: Cambridge University Press, 1990.

Gold, Michael Evan. A Dialogue on Comparable Worth, Ithaca, N.Y.: ILR Press, 1983.

Goldman, Alan. "Real People (Natural Differences and the Scope of Justice)," Canadian Journal of Philosophy 17 (June 1987), pp. 377–394.

Goodwin, Barbara. *Justice by Lottery*. Chicago: University of Chicago Press, 1992.

Griffin, James. *Well-Being: Its Meaning, Measurement, and Moral Importance*. Oxford: Clarendon Press, 1986.

Hayek, Fredrich A. *The Constitution of Liberty*. Chicago: University of Chicago Press, 1960.

———. *Law, Legislation, and Liberty*, vol. 2. London: Routledge and Kegan Paul, 1976.

Hestevold, H. Scott. "Disjunctive Desert," *American Philosophical Quarterly* 20 (July 1983), pp. 357–363.

Hill, Christopher. "Desert and the Moral Arbitrariness of the Natural Lottery," *Philosophical Forum* 16 (Spring 1985), pp. 207–222.

Holborow, Les. "Desert, Equality, and Injustice," *Philosophy* 50 (1975), pp. 157–168.

Holmgren, Margaret. "Justifying Desert Claims: Desert and Opportunity," *Journal of Value Inquiry* 20 (1986), pp. 265–278.

Husak, Douglas. "Why Punish the Deserving?" *Nous* 26 (1992), pp. 447–464.

Jackson, Michael W. *Matters of Justice*. Wolfeboro, N.H.: Croom Helm, 1986.

Kekes, John. *Against Liberalism*. Ithaca, N.Y.: Cornell University Press, 1997.

Kernohan, Andrew. "Desert and Self-Ownership," *Journal of Value Inquiry* 27 (1993), pp. 197–202.

Kleinig, John. *Punishment and Desert*. The Hague: Martinus Nijhoff, 1973.

Lucas, J. R. *On Justice*. Oxford: Clarendon Press, 1980.

———. *Responsibility*. Oxford: Clarendon Press, 1993.

Matson, Wallace. "On the Irrelevance of Free-will to Moral Responsibility, and the Vacuity of the Latter," *Mind* 65 (1956), pp. 489–497.

———. "What Rawls Calls Justice," *Occasional Review* (Autumn 1978), pp. 45–55.

McLeod, Owen. *On Being Deserving*, Ph.D. diss., University of Massachusetts, Amherst, 1995.

Miller, David. *Market, State, and Community*. Oxford: Clarendon Press, 1989.

———. "Deserving Jobs," *Philosophical Quarterly* 42 (1992), pp. 161–181.

———. "Distributive Justice: What the People Think," *Ethics* 102 (1992), pp. 555–593.

———. "Two Cheers for Meritocracy," *Journal of Political Philosophy* 4 (1996), pp. 277–301.

New, Christopher. "Time and Punishment," *Analysis* 52 (January 1992), pp. 35–40.

Nielsen, Kai. *Equality and Liberty*. Totowa, N.J.: Rowman and Allenheld, 1985.

Perleman, C. *Justice, Law and Argument*. Dordrecht: D. Reidel, 1980.

Persson, Ingmar. "Feldman's Justicized Act Utilitarianism," *Ratio* 9 (April 1996), pp. 39–46.

Pojman, Louis. "The Moral Status of Affirmative Action," *Public Affairs Quarterly* (1991), pp. 181–206.

————. "Merit: Why Do We Value It?" *Journal of Social Philosophy* (forthcoming, 1998).

Primoratz, Igor. *Justifying Legal Punishment*. Atlantic Highlands, N.J.: Humanities Press International, 1989.

Rachels, James. "What People Deserve," in *Justice and Economic Distribution*, ed. John Arthur and William Shaw. Englewood Cliffs, N.J.: Prentice-Hall, 1978, pp. 167–196.

Raphael, D. D. "Justice and Liberty," *Proceedings of the Aristotelian Society* 51 (1950–51).

Rashdall, Hastings. *The Theory of Good and Evil*. London: Muston, 1907.

Rescher, Nicholas. *Distributive Justice*. Indianapolis: Bobbs-Merrill, 1966.

Richards, Norvin. "Luck and Desert," *Mind* 95 (April 1986), pp. 198–209.

Ripstein, Arthur. "Equality, Luck, and Responsibility," *Philosophy and Public Affairs* 23 (Winter 1994), pp. 3–23.

Ross, W. D. *The Right and the Good*. Oxford: Oxford University Press, 1930.

Ryan, John. *Distributive Justice*. New York: Macmillan, 1942.

Sadurski, Wojceich. *Giving Desert its Due*. Dordrecht: D. Reidel Publishing, 1985.

Scanlon, Thomas. "The Significance of Choice," in *The Tanner Lectures on Human Values* 8, ed. Sterling McMurrin. Salt Lake City: University of Utah Press, 1988, pp. 149–216.

Sher, George. *Desert*. Princeton: Princeton University Press, 1987.

Simon, Robert. "An Indirect Defense of the Merit Principle," *Philosophical Forum* 10 (1978–79), pp. 224–241.

Sterba, James. "Justice as Desert," *Social Theory and Practice* (Spring 1974), pp. 101–116.

————. "Justice and the Concept of Desert," *Personalist* 57 (Spring 1976), pp. 188–197.

Sverdlik, Steven. "The Logic of Desert," *Journal of Value Inquiry* 17 (1983), pp. 317–324.

————. "The Nature of Desert," *Southern Journal of Philosophy* 21 (1983), pp. 585–594.

Temkin, Larry. "Weighing Goods: Some Questions and Comments," *Philosophy and Public Affairs* 23 (Fall 1994).

Vallentyne, Peter. "Taking Justice Too Seriously," *Utilitas* 7 (November 1995), pp. 207–216.

Waller, Bruce. "Just and Nonjust Deserts," *Southern Journal of Philosophy* 25 (Summer 1987), pp. 229–238.

————. "Uneven Starts and Just Deserts," Analysis 49 (October 1989), pp. 209–213.

Walzer, Michael. *Spheres of Justice*. New York: Basic Books, 1983.

Weinreb, Lloyd L. *Natural Law and Justice*. Cambridge, Mass.: Harvard University Press, 1987.

Wicclair, Mark. "Preferential Treatment and Desert," *Social Theory and Practice* 12 (Fall 1963), pp. 287–308.

Wolf, Susan. *Freedom Within Reason*. Oxford: Oxford University Press, 1990.

Young, Iris. *Justice and the Politics of Difference*. Princeton: Princeton University Press, 1990.

Young, Michael. *The Rise of the Meritocracy*. London: Thames on Hudson, 1958; CITY: Transaction Press, 1994.

Zaitchik, Alan. "On Deserving to Deserve," *Philosophy and Public Affairs* 6 (1977), pp. 370–388.